A

[signature: Philip E. Lilienthal]

B O O K

The Philip E. Lilienthal imprint
honors special books
in commemoration of a man whose work
at University of California Press from 1954 to 1979
was marked by dedication to young authors
and to high standards in the field of Asian Studies.
Friends, family, authors, and foundations have together
endowed the Lilienthal Fund, which enables UC Press
to publish under this imprint selected books
in a way that reflects the taste and judgment
of a great and beloved editor.

The publisher and the University of California Press Foundation gratefully acknowledge the generous support of the Philip E. Lilienthal Imprint in Asian Studies, established by a major gift from Sally Lilienthal.

In Search of Our Frontier

ASIA PACIFIC MODERN
Takashi Fujitani, Series Editor

In Search of Our Frontier

*Japanese America and Settler Colonialism
in the Construction of Japan's
Borderless Empire*

———

Eiichiro Azuma

UNIVERSITY OF CALIFORNIA PRESS

University of California Press
Oakland, California

Library of Congress Cataloging-in-Publication Data

Names: Azuma, Eiichiro, author.
Title: In search of our frontier : Japanese America and settler colonialism in
    the construction of Japan's borderless empire / Eiichiro Azuma.
Description: Oakland, California : University of California Press, [2019] |
    Series: Asia Pacific Modern; 17 | Includes bibliographical references and
    index. |
Identifiers: LCCN 2019002016 (print) | LCCN 2019005124 (ebook) |
    ISBN 9780520973077 (ebook) | ISBN 9780520304383 (cloth : alk. paper)
Subjects: LCSH: Japan—Colonies—History. | Japanese—North America—
    History. | Imperialism. | Transnationalism.
Classification: LCC DS885.48 (ebook) | LCC DS885.48 .A98 2019 (print) |
    DDC 970.004/956—dc23
LC record available at https://lccn.loc.gov/2019002016

Manufactured in the United States of America

28   27   26   25   24   23   22   21   20
10   9   8   7   6   5   4   3   2

CONTENTS

ILLUSTRATIONS

MAPS

FIGURES

TABLES

This book has been nearly twenty years in the making. My first monograph, *Between Two Empires* (Oxford University Press, 2005), examined the entanglements of Japanese America and imperial Japan through the experiences of Japanese immigrants and their US-born children in the American West. As I conducted research for that book, I constantly stumbled upon primary sources pertaining to first-generation Japanese Americans who had given up on white-dominated America and returned to their own racial empire. Whereas *Between Two Empires* focused on those who stayed in the United States, I have always wanted to write about those remigrants who swapped their lives and identities as minoritized immigrants for those of colonial masters as the result of crossing back over the Pacific—from Japanese America to imperial Japan. But this book had to wait until I had established my career as a historian in academia, where the spatially organized manner of research keeps Asian history and Asian American history separate and usually incongruent. Fortunately my first book on prewar Japanese America, albeit framed in a transnational context, earned me recognition as a historian of Asian America and US immigration history—and hence tenure at my home institution. Now, without as much pressure to act like a "proper" Americanist (or an Asianist), I have put together this book in such a way as to defy conventional dichotomized ideas about Japanese colonial history and Japanese American history in terms of the geographic spaces and historical agents I look at and narrate.

During my years of research, I came to realize that the existing theoretical formulations and analytical frameworks often did not work, and I have decided to let the research findings dictate my narrative in this monograph. While tracing the footsteps of Japanese American settler-colonists across the Pacific, I myself ended up becoming a migrant of sorts, too, traveling internationally between and across the archives and primary source collections, which are fundamentally nation based and set up separately for Asianists and Asian Americanists. As my long journey of intellectual border crossing has come to an end, I am hoping that this book can do justice to those transmigrants whose lives and experiences had been chopped up and presented simply as Japanese American (or sometimes only as imperial Japanese) in existing scholarship and public memory. Although my narratives are generally critical of and negative about their colonial actions and racist thinking, these historical agents still deserve to be treated with complexity and nuance. And such narratives, as readers will see in the ensuing pages, can also divulge the intimate relations of the US and Japanese empires and their settler colonialisms and racisms, which these transmigrants helped link up and fuse. If this book manages to confuse and disrupt readers' sense of distinctions between imperial Japanese and Japanese Americans, and between Japanese history and US history, I will consider my endeavor to be successful and meaningful.

This book would not have been possible without the support of many institutions and individuals. University of Pennsylvania has provided me with occasional research subventions as well as an endowed term chair named after my esteemed (former) colleague. I would like to extend special thanks to George Herbert Walker IV, the donor/sponsor of that endowed chair, which allowed me to take frequent research trips to various locations in the United States and Asia over the past ten years. In 2008–2009 I served as Donald D. Harrington Visiting Faculty Fellow at the University of Texas, Austin, where I was fortunate to be able to dedicate myself to full-time research and writing. During the summer and fall of 2018 I was also blessed with a Taiwan fellowship from the Foreign Ministry of the Republic of China and a short-term research fellowship from the Japan Foundation. The National Taiwan University's History Department and the Institute of Taiwan History at Academia Sinica sponsored my four-month research stay in Taipei.

The following institutions invited me to share portions of my research with diverse groups of scholars across disciplinary and national borders: Japanese History Workshop, Monash University (Australia); History Workshop, University of Zürich (Switzerland); Hoover Institution, Stanford University; Davis Center and American Studies Workshop, Princeton University; Graduate School of Global Studies, Sophia University (Japan); Research and Development Bureau, Saitama University (Japan); Center for Japanese Studies, UCLA; Asia Institute, University of Toronto; German Historical Institute-West, University of California at Berkeley; New York University at Abu Dhabi (UAE); Pacific Empires Work Group, Georgetown University; Centers for Japanese Studies and the Study of the Pacific

Northwest, University of Washington; Advanced Training Program, Harvard-Yenching Institute; Global Asia Research Center, Waseda University (Japan); Trans-Imperial Studies International Workshop, Dōshisha University (Japan); Hamilton Library and Center for Japanese Studies, University of Hawai'i; History Department Lecture Series, University of California at San Diego; and Penn Humanities Forum, Modern Japan History Workshop, and History Department Annenberg Seminar, University of Pennsylvania.

I cannot possibly name all of the people who have rendered assistance in the long process of research and writing. Given the limited space, I will only mention those who read draft chapters, provided feedback on them personally or at conferences and workshops, and/or offered me other forms of critical support for this book project, but I would like to emphasize that they represent only a small portion of the much longer list that I cannot include in its entirety here. Many thanks to, in Asian American history and US history, Katherine Benton-Cohen, Sucheng Chan, Gordon Chang, Donna Gabaccia, Andrea Geiger, Sayuri Guthrie-Shimizu, Lane Hirabayashi, Stacey Hirose, Madeline Hsu, Evelyn Hu-DeHart, the late Yuji Ichioka, Michael Jin, David Johnson, Moon-Ho Jung, Monica Kim, Richard Kim, Ben Kobashigawa, Paul Kramer, Lon Kurashige, Scott Kurashige, Erika Lee, Beth Lew-Williams, Mary Lui, Simeon Man, Valerie Matsumoto, the late Don Nakanishi, Mae Ngai, Brian Niiya, Franklin Odo, Michael Omi, Gary Okihiro, Naoko Shibusawa, Susan Wladaver-Morgan, Mari Yoshihara, David Yoo, and Henry Yu, and in Japanese studies and global history, Jeremy Adelman, Emily Anderson, Tokiko Bazzell, Adam Clulow, Prasenjit Duara, Martin Dusinberre, Takashi Fujitani, Sheldon Garon, Anne Giblin Gedacht, Kenneth George, Andrew Gordon, Katsuya Hirano, Reto Hofmann, Akira Iriye, Seth Jacobowitz, Mire Koikari, David Ludden, Ted Mack, William Marotti, Mark Metzler, Jennifer Munger, Fred Notehelfer, Lucy Riall, Kenneth Ruoff, Jordan Sand, the late Miriam Silverberg, Naoko Shimazu, John Stephan, Yuma Totani, Beatrice Trefalt, Jun Uchida, Barbara Weinstein, Duncan Williams, Sandra Wilson, and Lisa Yoneyama; my colleagues and former students at Penn, Kathleen Brown, Linda Chance, Fred Dickinson, David Eng, James English, Siyen Fei, Ann Farnsworth-Alvear, Antonio Feros, Steve Hahn, Robert Hegwood, Peter Holquist, the late Michael Katz, Alan Charles Kors, Walter Licht, Sidney Xu Lu, Grace Kao, Firoozeh Kashani-Sabet, Fariha Khan, Josephine Park, Kathy Peiss, Daniel Richter, Leander Seah, Thomas Sugrue, Eve Troutt Powell, and Beth Wenger, in Taiwan, Lung-chih Chang, Han-shu Chen, Shu-ming Chung, Ming-Ju Hsieh, Tiwei Hsu, Tingyu Kuo, Shichi Mike Lan, Shaun-Lin Lee, Yu-Ju Lin, Akira Tomita, Chin-Fang Wu, and Hsin-Ju Yen; and in Japan, Shinzō Araragi, Toyomi Asano, Mariko Iijima, Satoshi Mizutani, Hiromi Monobe, Tomoko Ozawa, Tōru Shinoda, Yasuko Takezawa, Shōhei Yao, Tarō Tsurumi, Ken'ichi Yasuoka, and Ryō Yoshida.

Emily Anderson read the entire first draft of the book manuscript and provided invaluable editorial support and astute advice for revisions. Along with Takashi

Fujitani, Emily is one of the few historians familiar with the historiographies of modern Japanese history and Japanese American history. Her interventions were indispensable before I became confident enough to send off the book manuscript for press consideration.

At the University of California Press, it was a great pleasure to work with Takashi Fujitani, editor of the Asia-Pacific Modern book series, and Reed Malcolm, press executive editor. When I had difficulty finding an academic press that did not reify the divide between Asian history and Asian American history, Tak encouraged me to consider submitting the manuscript for his book series. Reed also remained interested in and supportive of my idiosyncratic project in a professional manner throughout the review process. Their selection of anonymous readers was superb, because I benefited greatly from their comments and suggestions, for which I am very grateful. Archna Patel, Reed's editorial assistant, was always responsive to my questions—even trivial ones. Jessica Moll, production editor, made sure the publication process was smooth and timely, while Jon Dertien of BookComp stayed on the top of every step between copyediting and proofing. Bill Nelson prepared the maps for this book, and Sharon Langworthy took care of copyediting and formatting in the final phase of manuscript preparation. Sharon's perceptive eyes and meticulous editing saved me from many embarrassing errors and ambiguities; without her help, this book would not have been even remotely as readable. Tom Sullivan, associate marketing director, made it possible to get the word out about this book as widely as possible. I consider it fortunate to work with such a dedicated group of professionals at the University of California Press. Thank you all.

Chapters 3 and 7 contain portions of previously published journal articles. Reprinted with permission are parts of "Japanese Immigrant Settler Colonialism in the U.S.-Mexican Borderlands and the U.S. Racial-Imperialist Politics of the Hemispheric 'Yellow Peril,'" *Pacific Historical Review* 83, no. 2 (May 2014): 255–276; and "'Pioneers of Overseas Japanese Development': Japanese American History and the Making of Expansionist Orthodoxy in Imperial Japan," *Journal of Asian Studies* 67, no. 4 (November 2008): 1187–1226. I thank these journals for permission to reprint, and their editors and anonymous readers for valuable comments. The Saga Prefectural Library and the Manuscript Division, Center for Modern Japanese Legal and Political Documents, University of Tokyo, generously allowed me to use images from their collections for this book.

Finally, my family has always been a big help from across the Pacific, and Hiromi has given me the moral support I often needed. I regret to note that my father passed away in January 2018 without seeing the completion of my second monograph. I dedicate this book to his memory, and to my mother, who cannot read English but who I hope will appreciate the fruits of my long endeavor in this material form.

Eiichiro Azuma
April 1, 2019

Introduction

Transpacific Japanese Migration, White American Racism, and Japan's Adaptive Settler Colonialism

At the site of the first Japanese immigrant village on Taiwan's eastern "frontier," a stone-made memorial still stands, bearing the following epitaph that celebrates the "joint endeavor" by Japanese settlers and local Taiwanese to build modern settlements, agricultural industry, and a new civilization. Erected in 1940, the memorial reads:

> In the Hualian region that is isolated by high mountains and a rough sea, early efforts at land reclamation and cultivation . . . failed due to obstructions by [indigenous] attacks and tropical diseases. . . . Master farmer Mr. Ōtsuki Kōnosuke was invited [to Hualien in 1910] to take charge of colonial development by facilitating the transplantation of Japanese settlers and steering local indigenous peoples benevolently toward agricultural development.[1]

In other parts of the empire, similar memorials were also erected to mark the ascendancy of Japanese settler colonialism, although almost all of them are gone now, along with any trace of local Japanese presence. In the outskirts of Harbin, for example, there used to be a massive monument called a "cenotaph of patriots," which commemorated the heroic deeds of Yokokawa Shōzō and his associate, who were executed as Japanese military agents by Russians on the eve of the Russo-Japanese War of 1904–1905. Yokokawa's contributions to Japan's victory and its subsequent settlement making in that part of Manchuria were so widely recognized before 1945 that additional monuments and memorial parks were built in his honor in central Tokyo and his home prefecture of Iwate.[2]

In Search of Our Frontier explores the complex transnational history of Japanese immigrant settler colonialism, which linked together Japanese America and Japan's colonial empire through the exchanges of migrant bodies, expansionist ideas, colonial expertise, and capital in the Asia-Pacific basin before World War II. The likes of Ōtsuki and Yokokawa and the migration circuits and interchanges that underpinned borderless settler colonialism across the vast Pacific Ocean constitute that neglected history. Currently, few people, including historians of Japanese colonialism, know about these individuals, whom the empire glorified as pioneer leaders of Japanese settlements in Taiwan and Manchuria. Even more critically, these colonial heroes shared a history of immigration to North America before eventually joining in Japan's imperial endeavors in East Asia. Indeed, during the last decade of the nineteenth century the two transpacific migrants were self-proclaimed frontiersmen and early founders of Japanese Hawai'i and Japanese California, respectively. What may at first glance appear to be an odd coincidence is in fact a key part of their imperial trajectories that have been buried into oblivion, and hence it forms a central contribution of this historical study.

Japan was a latecomer in the imperialist scramble for new territories and settlements in the Asia-Pacific basin. After the restoration of imperial rule (known as the Meiji Restoration) in 1868, the new nation-state self-consciously sought to build a modern monarchy patterned after western models, especially Prussia and Britain. From the outset, not only were Japan's new leaders concerned with establishing the structures and policies that would signal to the West that Japan was not a candidate for colonization, but they also actively set out to engage in imperialistic practices. In this sense, to be a modern nation-state was to be a modern empire. And in Japan's case, this imperialism and its modernity were inextricably tied to mass migration and agricultural colonization, which the government initially experimented with in its northern hinterlands of Hokkaido in the 1870s before shifting its developmentalist gaze to the exterior of the home archipelago. Thus, agrarian settler colonialism was always integral to modern Japanese imperialism, and it constituted one of the many ways in which state officials and social leaders adopted policies and initiated reforms that were intended to both defend the nation against being colonized by western powers and demonstrate that they were worthy imperialists as well in the Eurocentric international order of the time.

Japan's imperial aspirations were finally realized when it gained Taiwan as part of China's war indemnity following the first Sino-Japanese War of 1894–1895. Faced with the challenge of administering and developing a new colony, Japanese officials again looked to agrarian settler colonialism for a solution. Around the turn of the twentieth century, Taiwan's eastern frontier emerged as the first site of attempts at "private" immigrant settlement making, albeit with the full support of the colonial regime and its military forces.[3] After migrating from Hawai'i to Hualien, Ōtsuki played a central role, as the 1940 memorial attests, in "facilitating the transplantation of Japanese settlers" there. Yokokawa also moved across the Pacific, to Manchuria on the eve of the Russo-Japanese War, with the intent to help Japan's imperial army take over the land and claim it as the empire's new frontier. These individuals carried the idea of borderless settler colonialism with them and practiced it to wherever they thought was an ideal frontier at a given time. And as the memorialization of Ōtsuki and Yokokawa reveals, their migration-led expansionism most often buoyed Japan's efforts at empire making, or so it was understood.

In Search of Our Frontier excavates the buried history of these transmigrants who crisscrossed the Pacific, carrying the banner of Japanese "overseas development (or progress)" (*kaigai hatten*). Since they traversed and inhabited the colonial spaces of the Japanese and American empires, their idiosyncratic backgrounds and experiences call into question the entire premise of research and interpretation in the studies of imperial Japan and Japanese America. Ōtsuki and Yokokawa, like many others featured in this book, held dual identities as trailblazers of Japan's colonial development and early "pioneers" of the Japanese ethnic community in Hawai'i and the continental United States—the first notable hub of overseas migrant residents, whose history traces to the mid-1880s. Indeed, years before his celebrated role as the pioneer of agricultural settlement making in eastern Taiwan, Ōtsuki had already enjoyed a similar accolade as the first Japanese in the mid-Pacific Islands to grow sugarcane and coffee on his own, and he operated a sugar mill in the early 1890s near Hilo while striving to establish an autonomous "all-Japanese village."[4] By the same token, Yokokawa was among the first batch of Japanese immigrants to enter California's Sacramento region with an eye to settling down as a frontier farmer in the mid-1890s, long before he found himself in Manchuria.[5]

The ideas and trajectories of Ōtsuki and Yokokawa exemplified a national structure of thought and practice that characterized Japanese settler colonialism, one that not only functioned to shore up the backbone of Japan's empire building but also promoted the borderless quest of Japanese overseas development in accordance with the western precedent of frontier conquest and civilization building. Like these founders of Japanese America, many early immigrants moved across the Pacific to North America because they were inspired by the success of Anglo-Saxon colonialism and economic development in its settler societies, especially the United States. Back home in Japan, ideologues and aspiring agents of national expansion shared a popular notion of frontier conquest with the American West as a key prototype. The first group of self-styled Japanese "frontiersmen" thus congregated in California and Hawai'i between the mid-1880s and the 1910s, boasting that their own agrarian colonization and settlement in the New World frontier constituted an integral part of Japan's overseas expansion. Nonetheless, white settler racism and exclusion propelled many Japanese, including Ōtsuki and Yokokawa, to leave North America in search of their own frontiers to conquer as colonial masters, instead of living as minoritized immigrants under the thumb of another race. *In Search of Our Frontier* teases out the complex mobility, motivations, and actions of those transpacific remigrants, who refashioned themselves into facilitators of Japanese colonial settlement and agriculture inside and outside imperial Japan across the Asia-Pacific with the backing of their home compatriots.

The ambiguity of the identities that these transmigrants held stemmed from ideas and practices that fused and confused the act of moving among imperial Japan's territories with immigrating to extraterritorial foreign lands, especially the frontier of the American West. Scholars have deemed these matters almost completely separate and different, with the history of Japanese colonizers forming a domain of Japan's national history and that of Japanese immigrants being an integral part of the US multiethnic experience. In their minds and behavior, however, Ōtsuki and Yokokawa never distinguished these matters when they traveled across the transpacific; even before moving to Japanese-controlled Taiwan and Manchuria, they had fully intended to lay the foundation of a "new Japan" in the frontier lands of Hawai'i and California. And just as these transmigrants found no conflict in their pursuit of settler colonialism on both sides of the Pacific, imperial Japanese and their empire could view these early pioneers of Japanese America as their own heroes. Who were these people then? Should we see Ōtsuki and Yokokawa as Japanese Americans or imperial Japanese? These seemingly simple questions actually call for more profound inquiry into the nature of Japanese colonialism, the meaning of migration and settlement, and the accepted ways in which the histories of Japanese America and imperial Japan have been narrated in both academic and public discourse.

JAPANESE MIGRATION AND SETTLER COLONIALISM IN THE COMPARTMENTALIZED IMPERIAL PACIFIC

Addressing such questions empirically and theoretically, this book narrates a transnational history of what I call "adaptive settler colonialism" among pre–World War II Japanese, who viewed both the inside and outside of Japan's colonial empire as their frontiers to conquer and where they would build "new Japans." This settler colonialism also enabled Ōtsuki, Yokokawa, and many other self-styled "frontiersmen" of borderless Japanese expansion to reconcile and coalesce their idiosyncratic thoughts, seemingly variant practices, and conflicting identities. As I flesh out in the ensuing pages, the concept of adaptive settler colonialism emphasizes its contingency vis-à-vis an array of factors and forces. That concept also takes into account settler colonialism's specificity as a historical process in terms of where and how Japanese migrant settlements were established, who moved there, when and why settlers migrated and often remigrated, how they related not only to the colonial metropole but also to the local political economy they entered at different points in history, and the variety of ways in which Japanese settlers constituted interracial/ethnic relations with "natives" and other immigrants at different locations.

This study offers a particularly new approach to the study of settler colonialism because it addresses the Japanese example within a dynamic, multifaceted context of multiple settler colonialisms. In general, settler colonialism has been treated solely within the context of each empire, with little regard for the ways that different empires—and their subjects—overlapped and interacted. Typically, encapsulated in a vacuum of stand-alone imperial rule, settler colonialism is understood and characterized as a combination of immigrant land control; agricultural development; and various forms of indigenous oppression, such as displacement and removal, mass killing and wholesale confinement, and forced assimilation, rooted in what Australian scholar Patrick Wolfe calls the "logic of elimination."[6] The history of Japanese settler colonialism shares aspects with that conventional Anglophone model. Yet insofar as it was actually entangled with, or often imagined against, rival settler colonialisms of other empires, the aforementioned characterization does not suffice to explain the degree to which Japanese settler colonialism was situationally adaptive, historically variable, modally diverse, and fundamentally transpacific, spanning multiple imperial spaces through the flexible mobility of (re)migrants, as well as the ideas and practices that they carried across sovereign national boundaries. Because the United States was Japan's chief imperial rival and the location of what its people saw as the most authentic New World frontier, that white settler society—and its Anglo-Saxon brethren of Canada and Australia—was a crucial factor in the transpacific colonial settler history of pre–World War II Japanese and its constitutive story of first-generation Japanese Americans, who also or subsequently acted as vanguards and exemplars of migration-led expansionism for the home empire.

The intertwined trajectories of Japanese America and the Japanese empire reflected the conflation of Japanese thinking relative to the acts of "migrating" overseas (*imin*) for temporary work and of "colonizing" overseas territories (*shokumin*) as settlers, which culminated in a peculiar expansionist concept and practice of *ishokumin*.[7] More than a simple combination of the two Japanese terms, this coinage accounted for a nativized idea of settler colonialism in prewar Japan. In tandem with the related notion of "overseas development"—another common expression in the lexicon of Japanese settler colonialism—the convenient and yet elusive concept facilitated the (con)fusion of formal colonial territories and extraterritorial migrant settlements as well as their respective constituents, their diverse experiences, and their contrasting subject positions. Devoting serious attention to this nativized idea, this book examines settler colonialism as an ideology and a practice of moving to a location external to the home archipelago, of engaging in wage labor as a preliminary stage to primitive accumulation (a distinct feature of Japan's case, as explained later), of sinking roots there by way of farming endeavors, and of building a family and consanguineous settlement of other Japanese immigrants. Rendered as historically specific processes of these developments,

Japanese settler colonialism and its consequences inevitably involved the usurpation of land and other fundamental modes of production directly or indirectly from local "native" residents, the development of commercial agricultural economy, and the rise of a transplanted "national"/"racial" community—one that settlers often referred to as a "new Japan" or a "second Japan." In essence, the idea of *ishokumin* mirrored a particular understanding of nation that transcended physical territorial boundaries and politico-legal jurisdictions—that is, an idea of borderless empire bound by racial ties and national consciousness, even more than an actual nation-state or a formal empire.

The Japanese idea of *ishokumin* complicates the theoretical distinctions that scholars of Anglophone settler colonialism have made between "colonialism" and "settler colonialism." Patrick Wolfe and Lorenzo Veracini argue that the monopolized control of land is absolutely central to (Anglophone) settler colonialism, and hence they identify it as a relationship marked by the dispossession and replacement of natives with settlers' bodies, cultures, and political economies. On the other hand, they explain that the domination and exploitation of native labor and resources are prominent features of conventional colonialism, in which other agendas, such as industrial development, trade and military control, and administrative minority governance, prevailed over the goal of land seizure and settler community building based on native "elimination."[8] According to the Japanese concept of *ishokumin*, however, these separate developments and constructs were packaged as an indivisible pair. That is to say, Japanese settler colonialism looked at its migrant laborers and settler-colonists in a similar vein within the context of their encounter and competition with indigenous residents and other "foreign" groups, immigrants and settlers included. The formative process of constructing a new Japan was inseparable from the triangular relationship that encompassed not only land-grabbing settlers and dispensable indigenes but also preexisting non-Japanese residents and other competing immigrant-settler groups. In the multi-group context of Japanese settler colonialism, the polarized relations of power and the outright elimination of indigenes/natives were neither easily imaginable nor readily practicable, except perhaps in Hokkaido, southern Sakhalin, central-eastern Taiwan, and parts of Micronesia.[9] Outside these locations, Japanese settler colonialism differed from Euro-American examples in terms of its definitive emphasis on coexistence and assimilation—in rhetoric at least—more than exclusion or annihilation.

The anomaly of Japanese settler colonialism has to do with the timing of Japan's entry into the global scramble for new territories in the late nineteenth century. When Japanese people started to migrate in search of frontiers, the Asia-Pacific basin—far more densely populated than the "New World" in the first place—had already been partitioned by European powers, with their settlers, industries and moneyed interests, and administrative states. Three notable features emerged from this geopolitical situation. First, Japan's late adoption of settler colonialism meant that ordinary Japanese "settlers" often found themselves being employed by non-Japanese enterprises rather than working as independent landowning farmers or self-supporting colonial entrepreneurs. Thus, the wage labor of immigrant settlers was always an essential component of Japanese colony making, especially at the initial stage. Furthermore, under the triangular social relationship, the cheapness of labor—whether Japanese immigrants' or natives'—sustained the competitiveness of Japanese settler business endeavors, which were usually exposed to severe competition with enterprises owned by other (non-Japanese) settler groups. The exploitation of coethnic and native labor could not be divorced from the exploitative land grabs and primitive accumulation in the overall scheme of overseas Japanese development.

Second, because of the lateness of Japan's involvement in colony making, the landmasses that the settlers envisioned as their frontiers, including the US West or Brazil, were harder to consider "untouched" than in the earlier peak years of European settler colonialism. Outside of their homeland, Japanese migrants found many extraterritorial frontiers already being placed under the grip of white colonial regimes and their exclusionary race politics. Inside Japan's formal colonies, land was available for legally sanctioned usurpation, but local resident populations were too large to be eliminated, replaced, or shoved out of the settler space. Indeed, Japanese settler-farmers in Taiwan and Korea never exceeded 7 percent and 4 percent of the total populations, respectively, before World War II.[10] This dilemma is another reason that colonialism's practice of native exploitation rather than elimination remained a prevalent feature of Japanese settler colonialism regardless of location. Asymmetrical group relations took more diverse forms in Japanese settler colonization than scholars of western settler colonialism have theorized.

Third, the concept of borderless settler colonialism is inseparable from the problem of Japan's late entry into imperial competitions. Although the logic and operation of every imperialism was inherently borderless, that aspect of Japanese settler colonialism revealed particularly powerful valence in comparison with other imperial projects. This point is tied to the politics of immigration exclusion among other settler societies and colonies in the Pacific basin. Because white settler colonies and nation-states endeavored to seal off the expanding regions of the Asia-Pacific to create bordered spaces for their own development, Japanese were compelled to valorize the borderless (or sometimes transborder) aspect of migration-led national expansion and settler colonization to seek opportunities outside the (seemingly) contracted sphere of sovereign influence and control. Therefore, as I narrate throughout this book, "extraterritorial" and "private" forms of settler colonialism were as important as state-sponsored military conquests and the establishment of legally claimed land territories within and around Japan's formal empire. Furthermore, illuminating Japan's response to race-based immigration exclusion, its borderless settler colonialism also tended to privilege the (purportedly) immutable ties of blood over other bonds, such as culture and citizenship, in its imaginaries of global imperial diaspora and empire building.

This book represents the first serious attempt to write this idiosyncratic settler colonialism into the interconnected histories of prewar Japanese Americans and imperial Japanese.[11] Despite an increase in settler colonial/indigenous studies in the Anglophone world, the paradigm has rarely entered scholarly discourse in the existing literature on the Japanese empire or the non-Anglophone Asia-Pacific.[12] In pursuit of the domestic political imperative of minority civil rights and racial justice, Asian Americanists have generally presented Japanese immigrants as yet another group of racialized Americans who have been wrongly discriminated against under white supremacy. Critics of "Asian settler colonialism" do scrutinize the position and behavior of Japanese and other Asian immigrants relative to Native Hawaiians in terms of the former's complicity in the oppression of the latter. Yet their critique still stays firmly within the domestic civil rights/racial justice paradigm, without paying attention to imperial Japan as the main source and reference point of a different kind of immigrant settler colonialism—a more transnational one.[13] Likewise, in Japan studies, migration and settler colonialism has largely escaped attention from historians, although the recent works of Jun Uchida, Emer O'Dwyer, Emily Anderson, Sidney Xu Lu, and Katsuya Hirano take the subject seriously.[14] Still, there is a void in our historical knowledge about the intersecting and overlapping histories of Japanese migration and settlements inside or outside national borders, let alone substantive scholarly deliberations on the relevance of the Japanese experience in North America to Japan's endeavors to build a settler empire in East Asia, and vice versa.[15]

Dichotomized scholarship on Japanese America and imperial Japan, and on transpacific migration and state-backed colonialism, has resulted from the conventional, spatially organized way of learning and research. It has perpetuated the prevailing cartographic practice in North American academia in which the northern Pacific basin is divided into the domain of Asian American studies, which is locked onto the eastern half of the vast ocean and its rim, and that of Asian studies, which focuses on the western half. (The southern part of the Pacific is entirely missing.) The most important reason for this spatial, epistemological, and disciplinary compartmentalization is the institutional split between US domestic "ethnic studies" and foreign "area studies"—the artificial rift that mirrors contemporary politics within academia rather than actual historical circumstances. In the existing literature, thus, the study of the transpacific migration experience traditionally takes place within Japanese American history and U.S. *im*migration history, usually classified as subfields of US national history.[16] Neither the reverse mobility out of the "nation of immigrants" nor the lives of migrants before their arrival in America constitutes a matter of concern for researchers. On the other hand, the study of colonial mobility and settlement in the northwestern Pacific forms a research agenda for modern Japan specialists. Asian area studies have reified these separate realms of research by disowning transpacific migrants as well as returnees from Japanese America, since they once left the physical boundaries of the "area" the field is supposed to study.

Consequently, the intertwined circuits and fluidity of Japanese migration between the eastern and western halves of the Pacific have generally escaped serious scholarly gaze, and they have been narrated as ostensibly unrelated streams of human mobility and experience within the enclosed spaces of the US and Japanese empires.[17] Due to their flexible movement, crisscrossing two national/area histories, Japanese remigrants from the American West and Hawai'i to the home empire have been stuck in a historical terra nullius—one that remains invisible between the well-studied world of the colonial master in modern Japanese history and that of a racialized minority in US national history. This book aims to uncover the entire trajectories of some of these transpacific migrants without chopping up their experiences according to the arbitrarily determined boundaries of disciplinary distinctions. A serious examination of the activities of US-originated Japanese colonial migrants and settlers in toto will make it possible to explore the blind spots that have existed between the hitherto nationalized/regionalized historiographies and narratives.

Traversing the uncharted territories of Japanese American studies and Japan studies, this book presents a new way to understand the complexities of Japanese migration and settler colonialism. It specifically looks into the consciousness, practices, and experiences of US Japanese immigrants and their integral and complicit role in the deployment of Japan's settler colonialism and its racism as well as the making of a borderless and formal empire. As this book narrates empirically, Japanese America and imperial Japan were in fact deeply connected through human mobility and the various forms of adaptation and interchange that they facilitated between and across the bounded national spaces. Nonetheless, the revisioning of transpacific migration and settlement as an essential part of Japan's colonial history, and vice versa, requires a new interpretive paradigm and analytical scheme, more than the simple critique of disconnected scholarship.

NARRATING TRANSPACIFIC MIGRATION AND SETTLER COLONIALISM FROM AN INTER-IMPERIAL PERSPECTIVE

In order to deterritorialize studies of migration and settlement beyond the prescribed spatial framing of Japanese and American colonial histories, I employ what can be termed an inter-imperial perspective.[18] Such a frame of analysis is useful when thinking about the mutually entangled relations between national colonialisms and about the complex subjectivity that transmigrants shaped across the intertwined worlds of the two Pacific powers. The inter-imperial relations or intimacies between Japan and the United States comprised what Ann Laura Stoler calls "compounded colonialisms" in global history. As she explains, every national colonialism possessed some "modular qualities" by which to allow different colonial regimes to "build projects with blocks of one earlier model and then another."[19] In accordance with this view, there are emergent scholarship and vibrant collaborations that examine the formation of compounded colonialisms between and among Euro-American/western powers.[20] Yet to date, Japanese colonialism, let alone its settler colonialism and racism, has been a missing piece of the puzzle. Implicitly and explicitly, this book seeks to put the cross-fertilization of colonial projects between imperial Japan and Japanese America (as its colonial diaspora and a part of the rival US empire simultaneously) in conversation with this emergent scholarship.

The inter-imperial framework makes it possible to interject the study of Japanese settler colonialism into the global history of compounded colonialism—with serious attention paid to intimacies and interchanges of the US and Japanese empires. My approach resonates with Robert Thomas Tierney's characterization of Japanese colonialism as "mimetic." Predicated on Homi Bhabha's formulation, Tierney stresses "Japanese agency," that is, the capacity to appropriate and nativize ideas, precedents, and practices of other imperialisms to suit Japan's own goals, which also requires the recognition of "Japanese responsibility for its colonization" instead of problematizing deviations from the western models.[21] Seen from this comparative standpoint, imperial mimicry was not unique to Japan, for the chain of mutual learning and historical referencing involved all imperialisms, including other latecomers such as Germany, Russia, Italy, and the United States. As fellow "latecomers to the colonial division of the globe," for instance, some leaders of nationalist Italy expressed an admiration for "the example of Japan," which "had chosen to expand [its] empire through . . . emigration policy . . . [as] one of [its] strongest weapons." Indeed, Mark I. Choate contends that the history of Italy's emigration-led colonialism resembled Japan's borderless empire building more than any other case.[22]

Notwithstanding such mutual referencing and parallels, however, Japan's colonialism was burdened with something different from its western counterparts: its ambivalent position as a "colored empire," to borrow Tierney's term.[23] This is the very context in which Japanese settler colonialism negotiated with its US counterpart; former and current residents of Japanese America generated convoluted identities and made politico-ideological moves, and they were able to influence public discourse, national debate, and state policy making in Japan. For example, as much as Japanese practitioners of migration and agricultural colonization were keen students of America's past frontier development, they were also victims of its race politics, and they developed a peculiar sensitivity and an aversion to the problem of white settler discrimination. Yet once back in their home empire or under its influence, they could and did victimize other "colored" people as colonizing settlers by referencing the practice of the US racial empire.[24] Crisscrossing the vast Pacific basin from one imperial sphere to another, and sometimes back, border crossers of Japanese America were a key link in the compounded colonialisms and racisms between the United States and imperial Japan.

By tracing the footsteps of these colonial settlers across multiple seas and ocean rims, *In Search of Our Frontier* unravels the enigma of their identities and subject positions, which took shape variously in relation to the particular lands and political economies that they viewed as their frontiers to master. The notion of a colored empire and its settler colonialism complicates the biocultural binaries of the categories of historical agents that colonial and postcolonial theories generally presuppose. In European/American imperial examples, colonizers were usually deemed western and white and their victims nonwestern and colored. The case of Japanese transmigrants and (re)settlers, especially those like Ōtsuki and Yokokawa who went back and forth between white America and imperial Japan, defies such a Manichean binarism and the conventional definitions of the colonized or colonizers.[25] Depending on where they were situated, prewar Japanese had varied life experiences that ranged from being the colonial master to being a racialized minority. When they resided in the United States or other white settler societies, they were subject to race-based discrimination and treated no differently from those whom they looked down upon as inferior, such as Chinese or Koreans. But even then they were still entitled to the protection of imperial Japan, not to mention they had the option of moving back physically to their home empire to live the life of unmolested and oppressing colonizers. Thus, members of and transmigrants from Japanese America inhabited an interstitial terrain that differed qualitatively from the world of the subaltern stuck in western colonies or white settler societies. Their in-betweenness resembled, albeit with some critical distinctions, the duality of the "colonized colonizer" in Eve Troutt Powell's study of the Khedivate of Egypt or the shifting positionality of African American settler-colonists who moved from the US South to the black republic of Liberia to serve as purveyors of a "civilized" American lifestyle in West Africa.[26]

Migration and the contingent race/ethnic relations that it produced between settlers and locals in a given space were absolutely crucial in a context where all sorts of ambiguity took shape. Transpacific migration allowed Japanese frontier trotters to pursue drastically different life chances, identities, and roles in the liminal space of inter-imperial interchange between Japan's colored empire and America's white supremacist republic. In order to elucidate the contingency of subject positions in multiple imperial spheres and racial conditions, this book presents many stories of individual (male) migrants from Japanese America, despite the risk of reinforcing the masculine and celebratory nature of orthodox colonial narratives. Detailed biographies help illuminate diverse (albeit sharing certain common trends) personal choices and trajectories; the stories allow readers to recognize that the self-styled pioneers of Japanese expansion held a significant degree of agency—and hence responsibility—for their decisions and actions. These Japanese Americans did what they did not simply because they were victimized by white racism or driven by Japanese expansionist ideology. Whereas some, like Ōtsuki and Yokokawa, opted to migrate from Hawai'i or California to the frontiers of Japan's formal empire, many others did not leave North America, despite living under common circumstances and being moved by similar enchanting ideas and forces. By offering diverse accounts of personal motivations and experiences of (re)migration, this book intends to delve into the nuances, complexities, and above all randomness of human agency that social science theories cannot predict or generalize.

My analysis of transpacific Japanese border crossing exceeds the problem of migrant/settler identities and subjectivity. It entails serious inquiry into the mobility and circulation of colonialist ideas, agricultural expertise, science and technology, labor management methods, and investment monies between Japanese America and imperial Japan. Bridging imperialisms and colonial capitalisms of the United States and Japan, versatile transmigrants traveled with hard-to-get knowledge in large-scale scientific farming and settlement making. Even when they did not physically move out of Japanese America, many immigrants also lent financial and various logistical support to Japan's pursuit of frontier conquest as colonial investors and absentee landowners. The visions and experiences of settler colonialism that these first-generation Japanese Americans had nurtured on the world's best-regarded New World frontier carried a lot of weight and reverberated throughout the Japanese empire before the Pacific War (1941–1945). This narrative dovetails with the theoretical observation made by some scholars of empire in recent years that forces at work in a colonial periphery often dictated the formation of the imperial metropole's ideologies and practices as much as, if not more than, the latter influenced the former.[27] Nevertheless, its peripheral standing within Japan's borderless empire alone does not explain the preponderance of Japanese America's role. This particular community of overseas Japanese had a decisive impact on the imperial formation of prewar Japan because of its integral position in the borderlands of the two competing settler-racial empires. Not only was this community's impact especially notable in the areas of Japan's migration-led expansionism and settler racism, but it was also heavily colored by the examples of US colonial ideas and practices experienced and referenced by these first-generation Japanese Americans.

Given the US residents' precarious but crucial positionality, the state-migrant nexus is another important theme of this book's narrative, which traces both complementary and contradictory relations between the two parties. On the basis of their lived experiences across the Pacific, transmigrants had specific expectations and desires about how the home state should act with regard to the question of national expansion; conversely, the state treated its overseas compatriots according to its own idea of what imperial subjects should do for the promotion of national interests. Negotiations between state power and migrant agency were always complex and contingent. The contingency derived from a situation in which a wide array of challenges and obstacles was presented constantly by the United States and other competing imperial powers, hostile native/local populations, and the diverse political economies and their power structures. These variables differently affected Japanese migrant settlements and their ties to the homeland/colonial metropole. This also means that the state was unable to keep a firm grip on the action and thinking of its overseas compatriots—including colonists of Japan's formal territories—as Jun Uchida shows in her study of Japanese settlers in Korea.[28] As for members of Japanese America who lived outside the realm of Japan's coercive state control, it was up to them to push for, act in conjunction with, or respond to state mandates and policy guidelines. The best the state could do and often did was to invoke the persuasive power of the shared belief in "overseas development" to get them involved of their own volition as self-induced participants in state-backed agricultural colonization, wherein they could see the possibility of reaping personal profits.

Tenuous state-migrant relations became even more convoluted at times for another reason: neither side had a consistent or unified vision. The question of national migration policy, for example, created multiple points of contention among state officials, political ideologues, and social elites at home, as well as overseas residents, including those in Japanese America. A constant tug of war between state and migrant, and internal frictions within each side, provided a crucial context in which Japanese settler colonialism obscured the boundaries between state colonial projects and private migrant enterprises and those of sovereign colonies and foreign ethnic communities. In constructing a settler colonial empire, the Japanese state relied especially on transpacific migrant initiative and service, but it could never master them insofar as the transmigrants were motivated and influenced by their own sense of necessity grounded in their US experiences. Their settler colonialism could not be divorced from its constitutive American context, and despite the contentious relationship with Japanese America, it was that brand of agricultural development and settlement making that Japan's colonial state wished to appropriate for its own frontiers.

AMERICAN FRONTIER MYTH, RACIAL EXCLUSION, AND THE ADAPTABILITY OF JAPANESE SETTLER COLONIALISM

Mediated by the lived experiences of self-styled Japanese frontiersmen in the US West and Hawai'i, "American-style" settler colonialism served as a guiding principle of modernization projects and civilization building in new colonies of Japan and beyond throughout the pre–World War II era. In the context of compounded colonialisms, prewar Japan came to bear imprints of diverse imperial references. Whereas British imperialism, for example, often had a greater impact than other powers in the area of Japan's endeavor to set up colonial administrative structures and governance, the US model left its most visible mark with regard to migration, colonial settlement, and agriculture-based development.[29] In other words, when imperial Japanese expounded on the best form for their settler colonialism, it was likely that they would first consult the historical example and modality of American frontier conquest. In the global context, such a fascination with New World mythology was not restricted to Japanese settler colonialism. Early twentieth-century Italy, for example, likened colonial Libya to a new frontier "awaiting Italian cultivation," characterizing it as "the new America, ripe for emigrant settlement."[30] Given the "similar environmental constraints to the development of [scientific] agriculture," Russian settler-farmers in the steppes also eagerly "learn[ed] from the American experience in the prairies and Great Plains" after the late nineteenth century.[31] Indeed, as historian David Wrobel reveals, the US West was "very often viewed in the nineteenth century as a global West, as one developing frontier, one colonial enterprise, among many around the globe" despite, or perhaps because of, the contrary discourse on "a mythic, exceptional, and quintessentially American frontier West." The "globally contextualized discussions and representations of the [US] West" as a reference were as prevalent in Japan as in Europe and the United States.[32]

The American frontier myth, and the teleological narrative of national expansion, progress, and racial ascendancy that it extolled, had begun to take hold in modern Japanese consciousness rather seamlessly from the late 1860s through the system of new knowledge appropriated from the West. Intended to inspire feudal Japanese to commit to the project of national modernization, one of the earliest intellectual sources was a five-volume compilation of world geography and history. In 1869, Fukuzawa Yukichi, the father of Japan's "western studies," put together this compendium based on his reading and translation of various imported Dutch and Anglophone treatises, including US publications. Entitled *Sekai kuni zukushi* (All the countries of the world), the book made the idea of "frontier" (*shinkaichi* or *shintenchi*) and its "development" (*kaitaku* or *hatten*) readily available to educated imperial subjects, who were eager to learn and figure out the preferred course of action for them and their nation in the era of intensifying imperialist competition. Fukuzawa particularly lauded the prosperity, progress, and prowess of the United States—which had supposedly rivaled Great Britain and already outstripped France—by ascribing its strength to the vast western frontier and to Americans' national character, which their experience of conquest had purportedly molded.[33] "Their land produce[d] an abundance of grains, animals, cotton, tobacco, grapes, fruits, sugar cane, gold, silver, copper, lead, iron, coal," marveled Fukuzawa, who went on to declare, "nothing necessary in daily life [wa]s lacking" in the United States.[34] Progress seemed to be limitless there, he continued, because "yearly multiplying millions" of American settlers "ke[pt] on opening up the frontier land and stretching its boundaries east and west, and north and south" for further development of the nation and its economy.[35]

The American imprint made its first appearance in Japan's domestic settler colonialism during the 1870s in Hokkaido, the scarcely populated northernmost prefecture. Exemplified in Fukuzawa's extolment, the popular discourse on US frontier conquest and progress inspired Tokyo officials to invite white American agricultural experts to participate as special advisers in the colonization of the northern domestic territory when the new imperial regime adopted that project as a top priority in the making of a modern nation-state and economy. In 1871, only three years after the Meiji Restoration, the Japanese government hired Horace Capron, who subsequently resigned as the commissioner of the US Department of Agriculture and went to Hokkaido with his colleagues. Capron's party transplanted American-style agricultural methods (later called "plow farming") using mechanized farming implements; brought new seeds for western fruits, vegetables, and other crops; and introduced livestock for ranching.[36] This imported form of large-scale agriculture served to mesh the Japanese understanding of US frontier development with the notions of modern science and advanced technology. Thereafter, tens of thousands of jobless ex-samurai and other Japanese migrated into Japan's first settler colony—which was being constructed under American guidance—as armed farm settlers, who endeavored to erect a modern civilization there while fending off the threat of Russian invasion. In sum, as Katsuya Hirano explains, "Japanese settler colonization of Hokkaido was . . . outlined and facilitated by the joint forces of the Japanese state and U.S. experts and technology."[37] This American-inspired frontier conquest established the historical precedent for many enterprises of mass migration and agricultural colonization within and without the Japanese empire.

While Tokyo officialdom envisioned the Hokkaido frontier as part of what Wrobel calls the "global West" and embraced American-style settler colonialism as a model for national development and empowerment, US-based immigrants helped shape the general mind-set of home compatriots accordingly through transpacific print media and involvement in Japan's domestic politics. Even though Fukuzawa played a predominant role in associating the term "frontier" with "America" in the public discourse of early Meiji Japan, that invention was far from a foregone conclusion until later, because the popular belief in the authenticity and centrality of the US frontier went through a process of being reified and solidified by the writings and actions of residents of Japanese America, returnees therefrom, and their allies in Japan. From the late 1880s, these individuals acted as transmitters and promoters of key concepts of American settler colonialism in a transpacific discursive space. The idea of historically mandated national expansion, the extolling of civilizational developmentalism, and the theory of "racial statism" (the supremacy of a nation-state consisting of a master race) all contributed to the rise of a Japanese-style "manifest destiny" and the search for frontiers where Japanese could be the colonial overlords as the modern and civilized power. Whereas Anders Stephanson describes these concepts as the ideological bases of US Anglo-Saxonist Manifest Destiny during the latter half of the nineteenth century, this book shows that imperial Japanese adopted and adapted them to forge their own identity as an expansive Asian nation and race.[38] As the most trusted interpreters of those concepts, first-generation Japanese Americans often brokered this process.

Immigrants based in the United States also took the lead on the nativization of the American frontier thesis, contributing to the systematization of what can be called a "discourse on overseas development" (*kaigai hattenron*). Popularized after the 1880s, it formed the ideological underpinning of Japanese settler colonialism and state-sponsored colony-making projects. Often accompanied by pseudoscientific theories that stressed the overseas origins of the ancient Japanese, this discourse posited the inherently expansive traits of the present-day Japanese people, which presumably prevailed in their shared blood and lineage. It also extolled the maritime destiny of the island empire and its people, not only as a colonizing power but also as a nation "racially endowed" for expanding to frontiers all over the world with a superior civilization.[39] Still, the ill-defined concept of overseas development was open to a broad range of interpretations, discursive manipulations, and arbitrary spins by pundits who might hold different agendas and conflicting goals. Ironically, for this reason a large number of Japanese could embrace the concept, albeit defined in multiple ways, which made it possible for the discourse to function as a powerful popular/social ideology in pre–World War II Japan. Japanese America stood constantly as a foremost source of authoritative "frontier" knowledge and reference points in that discourse.

The pursuit of overseas development frequently came with an advocacy of "peaceful expansion(ism)"—an associated ideology that enabled Japanese settler colonialism to present itself as something different from state-led military aggression.[40] This national expansionist claim to being peaceful (and benevolent) was not unique in the context of global imperial history, for not only the United States but also others, such czarist Russia, held a similar conceit that their project of settlement and colonization was a kinder, gentler, nonracist, and even altruistic sort. Indeed, in their important study of comparative settler colonialism, Caroline Elkins and Susan Pedersen contend that early European settlers on New World frontiers, including the American West, commonly envisioned the control of land properties and the suppression of natives through more diverse methods than outright military aggression, thereby maintaining the pretense of the master race's benevolence.[41] Japanese settler colonialism's conceit about its peacefulness was not a coincidence at all, because it was US frontier discourse that directly inspired members of Japanese America and their homeland allies to follow suit in what they regarded as the shared civilizationist enterprise intended for universal good. And just like the myth of America's frontier conquest, the Japanese ideology of peaceful expansion obfuscated the aggression and coercive nature of settler migration and colonization in the teleological language of civilization's triumph. Not surprisingly, then, the ostensible opposites of violence (military invasion) and nonviolence (settler colonialism) actually formed inseparable twins in the history of Japanese imperialism.

Settler/migrant racism constituted another site of inter-imperial accommodation through the agency of members of Japanese America. The capacity and propensity of Japanese settler colonialism to adapt to American frontier mythology and its race politics revealed its fundamental character and modus operandi. Although Anglo-Saxonism, embedded in US frontier discourse, helped give rise to the racist Japanese belief in their own expansive and superior traits, white American racism against Japanese immigrants complicated the public rendition of settler colonialism in imperial Japan. Because the discourse on overseas development (con)fused different forms of migration and most often deemed external migrant settlements interlinked and indivisible, the problem of anti-Japanese racism in the United States and other Anglo-Saxonist settler societies held tremendous sway over the shaping of the minds and behaviors of *all* Japanese who were interested in the cause of migration-based national expansion, regardless of where they were situated or intended to move.

In Search of Our Frontier examines the processes of Japanese adaptation to US racism, its consequences in the articulations of their settler colonialism, and the multifaceted roles played by US-based immigrants and transpacific/transimperial returnees. First, adaptive Japanese settler colonialism generated the complex migration circuits of ordinary imperial subjects in response to American racism. The first public expression of "Yellow Peril" demagoguery in California convinced early proponents of national expansion to put together a well-greased machine to disperse ordinary working-class migrants in pursuit of alternative frontiers throughout the Asia-Pacific region, especially the Pacific Islands and Mexico. Between 1894 and 1907 proprietors of these "emigration companies" largely comprised returnees from the US West Coast and their moneyed allies in Japan. After the United States engineered the 1907–1908 Gentlemen's Agreement with Japan to stop the arrival of the laboring masses, the Japanese migration flow suddenly shifted from Anglophone North America to "racially friendly" Latin America and Japanese-controlled Korea. Similarly, the US exclusion of all Japanese immigrants in 1924 greatly amplified the volume of mass migration to Brazil's frontier land, since Japan adopted the South American country as a top target of state-sponsored colonization enterprises. These key moments of US settler racism also caused a reorientation of the vectors of

Japanese migrant mobility toward the occupied regions and colonies of imperial Japan that were obviously devoid of anti-Japanese exclusionism (see map 1). In particular, the post-1924 colonial diaspora included enlarged streams of transpacific return migration from Japanese America. Immigration exclusion by the United States and the denial of agricultural land rights in its western states propelled many Japanese residents, especially the farming class, to move back to the bosom of their home empire.[42] These resettlers were often integral to instances of formal state colonization projects in the sovereign frontiers of imperial Japan, especially Manchuria and Taiwan. Insofar as the usefulness of their US-bred expertise and settler experience was dependent on the particular conditions and environments of Japanese colonial territories to which they moved, their remigration and adaptive settler colonialism unfolded in a specifically trans*local* context, such as one connecting the similar "tropical" political economies of US-controlled Hawai'i and Japanese-ruled Taiwan. The translocal lens occupies a significant place in this book's narrative on inter-imperial migration circuits and entanglements.

Second, the US politics of immigration exclusion figured prominently in the contestation of competing factions in Japanese settler colonialism and imperialism, helping to shape trichotomized outward flows of the migrant mobility from the home archipelago. Tied to different groups of Japan's officialdom, academia, and business sectors, three expansionist factions advocated "eastward/transpacific expansion" (*tōshinron*), "southward expansion" (*nanshinron*), and "continental/ northward expansion" (*tairiku shinshutsuron* or *hokushinron*).[43] The first expansionist school looked toward the Americas; the latter two laid their colonial gaze on significant portions of Japan's formal empire and its surrounding regions, namely Taiwan, Micronesia, and the greater Nan'yō (South Seas) on the one hand, and Korea, Manchuria, and Mongolia on the other. Pundits and practitioners of all three expansionist schools included former US residents, such as Ōtsuki and Yokokawa, who had originally taken part in the first stripe of settler colonialism but later switched their allegiance to the others. White settler racism compelled these two pioneers of Japanese America to take up new identities, one as a trailblazer of Japanese settlement in Taiwan (hence that of southward expansionism) and the other as a flag bearer of Japanese penetration into Manchuria (hence that of continental expansionism). The same consideration—whether or not similar rival settler racism existed—was often at work in the decision-making processes of individual (re)migrants in Japanese America and Japan about where they would like to pursue a life of settler colonialism. In public discourse, too, the problem of racial exclusion often dictated the course of debate among the three schools of expansionism with regard to where to find an ideal frontier—one that increasingly denoted a location without US-style anti-Japanese politics.

In this book race serves as a central interpretive frame by which to analyze Japanese migrant thinking and actions vis-à-vis competing white settlers as well as East

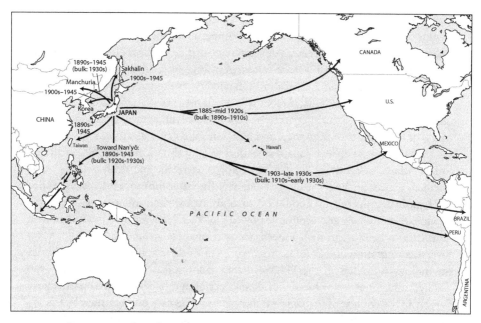

MAP 1. Outmigration flows from Japan, 1880s–1940s. Map by Bill Nelson.

Asian and other colored residents, including Mexicans, Brazilians, Pacific Islanders, and Taiwanese aborigines. The race-based interpretive frame also provides insight into the process of Japan's policy making pertaining to the mandate of national expansion, one purportedly meant for the Japanese as a master race in accordance with a Spenserian view of group hierarchies and struggles. In the historiography of Japanese colonial history, the discussion of settler-native relations does not generally entail as much an analysis of a "race" factor as that of its ethnocultural counterparts. Put differently, race—as an analytics intertwined but distinct from ethnicity or culture—is not among the most notable features of historical inquiry, for Japan's formal empire comprised mostly the colonial territories inhabited by other "Mongolian" or "Asiatic" subgroups, who were supposed to have ethnic and cultural differences, not (pseudo)biological racial ones, from a theoretical standpoint.[44] This book interjects into the study of Japanese colonialism the variable of "blood-will-tell" racial *thinking* on the part of settlers and migrants even when I look at their inter-"ethnic" relationship to other Asians, sociologically speaking. In the *historical* context of this study, a Japanese rendition of interethnic and intercultural relations was "racialized" more often than not, as far as their settler colonialism was concerned.[45]

This is not to say that race (as opposed to ethnicity or culture) was always central to the operation of Japanese colonialism. Far from privileging race over the

other analytics, it is my contention that a racialized definition of inter-ethnic or
-cultural relations mattered, or shall I say, imperial Japanese felt it mattered, *when*
they engaged in acts of overseas development and tackled problems with respect
to that national (or "racial") cause. When prewar Japanese moved to a "new Japan"
abroad, their settler colonialism almost inevitably resulted in clashes of some form
with non-Japanese residents, thereby leading to the rise of an essentialized idea of
group difference and the otherization of the original inhabitants or competing settlers. In the context of migration and agricultural colonization, thus, asymmetric
"ethnic" relations between Japanese settlers and local natives/residents, including
other Asians, were often "racially" imagined, narrated, and dealt with as if the
former perpetually held the upper hand over the latter for more intrinsic/pseudo-
biological reasons (e.g., "bloodlines" or body types) than differences in culture,
language, or military and economic power. This racial lens worked in tandem with
ethnicity and culture in such a way as to stain Japanese visions of and outlooks on
overseas migration and colonization. And just as their appropriation of frontier
mythology unfolded in the US West, their adoption of that racial lens—even
though other sources of racist worldviews certainly existed—figured particularly
largely in the context of the Japanese awareness of US race politics, thereby tracing
its roots to a pivotal group experience that originally transpired in the frontier
land of North America. There, early founders of Japanese America were engulfed
in race-based discrimination and white exclusionist agitation—the reason that the
likes of Ōtsuki and Yokokawa decided to search for an alternative frontier in the
first place. It was also in the US West that resident Japanese were compelled to
"racially" distinguish themselves from Chinese immigrants, who had suffered
legalized ostracism as an undesirable race under the 1882 Chinese Exclusion Act.[46]
After that, the problem of race—especially the idea of racial struggle—never
ceased to occupy a significant place in Japanese settler colonialism.

Indeed, narrated by former and current residents of Japanese America, the stories of white settler racism particularly influenced Japanese attitudes and practices
with regard to the "civilized" management of colonial social relations. Often at the
behest of US residents, imperial Japanese reciprocated against outright oppression
with the advocacy of pan-Asianism or assimilationism toward natives in a "new
Japan."[47] This is where the racial experience of members of early Japanese America
came to matter most to the home empire, which underwent its own colonial race/
ethnic problems in the form of "native" revolts and nationalist/independence
movements after the turn of the twentieth century. Imperial Japanese grappled
with the difficult question of what to do with these "ungrateful" colonial wards
who obstructed their work as purveyors of advanced civilization. Due to their
firsthand experience of race-based persecution in the United States, transpacific
immigrants could speak authoritatively about the wicked precedent of white
American racism. They could offer useful advice on how to best behave as racially

superior settlers by stressing the importance of the paternalistic effort at assimilation over exclusion. Their interpositions helped reconfigure Japanese thinking
about what it meant to be the colonial master race—in terms of egregious "mistakes" made by white American settlers. Commonly, returnees from Japanese
America told their home compatriots that exclusionist racism mirrored unjust and
hence inferior aspects of Anglo-Saxon settler colonialism. This contention dovetailed with, if not directly influenced, the views of Japanese officials and ideologues
that valorized assimilation policy in order to demonstrate the superiority of their
"peaceful" brand of settler colonialism and colonial governance.[48]

While US race politics often had an effect on Japan's racial attitudes through the
words and deeds of Japanese immigrants in America and returnees therefrom, it is
also important to note that America's anti-Japanese measures simultaneously constituted a part of global white supremacy, which produced the interlinked politics
of immigration exclusion in Anglophone settler colonies and later in Brazil and
Peru under US influence.[49] Adaptive Japanese settler colonialism addressed these
geopolitical challenges posed by the United States and its racial allies, most notably Australia and Canada, in their attempt to construct a "white Pacific." Inspired
by American Anglo-Saxonist discourse and its racist legal practice, white residents
of other settler societies implemented their own versions of race-based exclusion
against Japanese immigrants. Transnational Yellow Peril scaremongering resulted
from this development, in which domestic race politics linked up with geopolitical
endeavors to organize the white racial (and economic) blocs by "drawing the global colour line."[50] This racial geopolitics vilified Japanese migrants and settlers,
portraying them simply as transplanted front-line soldiers of imperial Japan who
allegedly conspired to invade and usurp white men's frontiers, such as Hawai'i,
California, British Columbia, and Queensland, as well as America's backyard,
Mexico. The persistent, albeit not always consistent, responses of Japan's settler
colonialism to global exclusionist agitation paved the way for the specific migration and settlement patterns of Japanese people in the Pacific basin. Again, Japanese America always figured prominently in these complex historical unfoldings.

One notable result of global white supremacy and the Japanese response to it
was the racial partitioning of the imperial Pacific, since Japanese became equally
intent on putting together their own sphere of influence without being obstructed
by white men. Their adaptive settler colonialism sought to build a counteractive
"Japanese Pacific" through the networks of agrarian migrant communities inside
and outside the formal empire, including North America's ethnic enclaves. Because
imperial Japanese rationalized their pursuit of overseas development in equally
racial terms, the networks of their migrant settlements were meant to reterritorial-
ize segments of the Asia-Pacific region as zones of Japanese domination in contestation with white racial blocs. In the context of this reciprocal spatial partitioning,
external "ethnic" communities of Japanese immigrants were fused with internal

"colonial" territories of imperial Japan to form cohesive units of its global empire and colonial capitalism after the mid-1920s. This grandiose vision of a borderless colonial empire, as this book teases out, drew as much from the aspirations of self-styled frontiersmen in Japanese America as from the well-studied contrivances of Japan's militarists, elite statesmen, monopoly capitalists, and ultranationalists.

VARIED FACES AND PHASES OF JAPANESE SETTLER COLONIALISM

Organized both chronologically and thematically, this book consists of eight chapters, split into four separate clusters. In part I, the first two chapters trace the complex origins and trajectories of Japanese settler colonialism, with a focus on the immigrant pioneers who laid the foundation of ethnic communities in California and Hawai'i between the mid-1880s and the beginning of the 1900s. An early form of "discourse on overseas Japanese development," which derived largely from their work, was intertwined with the rise of a nationalist-populist movement in 1880s Japan. Connected to Tokyo's major political parties and societies of the late nineteenth century, especially the Seikyōsha and Liberal Party, founders of early Japanese America contended that modern Japan should act as a full-fledged imperialist power, like its Euro-American rivals, by extending its influence through various means, including but not limited to migration and overseas settlement. While supporting the idea of state-led military conquest of foreign lands, especially Korea and China, these immigrants viewed American-style agrarian colonization in the New World frontier as an integral part of Japan's peaceful expansion, which they believed they were spearheading individually. In cooperation with their supporters and like-minded expansionists in Japan, they forged transpacific networks of advocacy for mass migration and settler colonialism. Chapter 1 explores their thinking and practice roughly between 1884 and 1893.

In the early 1890s these wide-eyed leaders of Japanese America bore the first brunt of white settler racism and organized anti-Japanese agitation in California, which conflated them with the already-excluded Chinese. Simultaneously, resident white (*haole*) elites of Hawai'i began to severely discriminate against Japanese residents there after they took over political sovereignty and land from the native monarchy in collaboration with the US Marines. In the eyes of many immigrant expansionists, these events registered as the loss of California and Hawai'i to white American rivals, thereby propelling them to look for their own frontiers elsewhere throughout the greater Asia-Pacific basin after 1893. Chapter 2 explains that this incipient surge of transpacific remigration paved the way for the establishment of Japan's first national expansionist society dedicated to the promotion of overseas settler colonialism and a proactive state role in it, including the use of military means. In the Colonization Society of Japan, returnees from the United States led the process of knowledge production and public debate on how and where Japan should seek its expansionist destiny through mass emigration and colonization. Out of the national debate emerged three schools of national expansionism, each pushing for a diverging vector of popular mobility, especially after Japan's victory over China in 1895. These different brands of settler colonialism coexisted with and influenced each other in the activities of the Colonization Society and its members. Former US residents provided the society with a common frame of discussion with reference to their lived experiences as the first group of Japanese colonists and victims of rival settler racism.

As the home empire began to stretch its physical boundaries by military conquest, some of these first-generation Japanese Americans carried out their own colonization ventures and were often involved in Japan's state imperialism after their return. The transmigrants applied their firsthand expertise to private endeavors to erect a "new Japan" in such locations as Thailand, British North Borneo, northern Australia, southern Manchuria, central-western China, and Korea. Others collaborated with US-based immigrant expansionists and homeland supporters in the operation of emigration companies, which shipped off thousands of ordinary Japanese to new sites of overseas development. Focusing on the roles of these returnees in the formative years of Japanese imperialism between 1893 and 1908, the second chapter looks into their work as pivotal ideologues and agents of settler colonialism within and without Japan's emergent borderless empire and its "peaceful expansion" after its victories against China and Russia.

Part II disentangles the multilayered processes in which private and state endeavors of Japanese settler colonialism, often spearheaded by transmigrants, intersected and eventually converged during the decades between 1908 and 1928. The initial catalyst of these processes was the US-Japanese Gentlemen's Agreement of 1907–1908. Not only did it terminate new labor immigration from Japan to the United States, but it also ignited a fierce national debate on Japan's future as a colonial-imperial power following the exclusion of working-class Japanese from North America and the acquisition of new territories, such as Korea, the Kwantung Leased Territory, and southern Sakhalin, in the aftermath of the Russo-Japanese War (1904–1905). While the three schools of national expansionism collided and colluded in terms of whether Japan should stretch its colonial diaspora eastward, northward, or southward, the empire and its public started to build up the necessary infrastructure for the promotion of multidirectional settler colonialism. The new infrastructure encompassed the domestic print media and private educational institutions dedicated to the cause of overseas development, as well as an academic discipline known as "colonial (policy) studies" at imperial universities. Moreover, state agencies, including the home and foreign ministries and later the newly established colonial ministry, took on the task of promoting mass emigration and agricultural colonization in various locations of the greater Pacific. The problem of US settler racism and its imperialist diplomacy against Japanese mobility was an indispensable component of these developments.

During the 1910s a parallel development of settler colonialism in colonial Korea, Brazil, and the US-Mexican borderlands entailed the blurring of boundaries between the state and the private sector as well as the active participation of Japan's monopoly capital in settler colonialism. In the first half of the following decade, the escalation of white American exclusionism augmented the state's formal role as the chief agent of mass migration to and agricultural colonization in Brazil and other potential sites of overseas development that had not yet experienced the menacing effect of race-based immigration exclusion. As chapters 3 and 4 detail, both Japanese immigrant society in the United States and returnees therefrom were deeply involved in these instances of state-sponsored enterprises in the Americas, East Asia, and elsewhere. In the meantime, their search for alternative "racism-free" frontiers propelled the United States to extend its exclusionist politics and the imperialist diplomacy of the Monroe Doctrine south of the border in order to check what was perceived as the specter of hemispheric Japanese "invasion."

The passage of the US Immigration Act in 1924 and its resonance with the chauvinistic attitudes of Canada and Mexico served to shield North America entirely from Japanese settler colonialism and rendered residents of Japanese America thoroughly minoritized and subordinated. While the quintessential New World frontiers slammed the doors on practically all new migrants from Japan, institutionalized racial discrimination caused Japanese America to throw its windows wide open for the remigration of the dejected "pioneers" back into the bosom of the home empire. This generated many more points of intersection between Japan's state endeavors to colonize new territories and the activities of former US residents as teachers and investors in frontier agricultural development. Part III narrates the stories of reverse transpacific migration that elevated the status of first-generation Japanese Americans in the settler colonialism of Japan's formal empire. As the imperial regime aspired to populate its colonial outskirts with ordinary farmers from rural Japan, remigrants and entrepreneurs from the United States lent critical support to Japan's official projects of settlement colony making in East Asia and the Nan'yō. Their lived experiences and monopoly on expertise in American-style scientific agriculture were highly regarded by Japan's colonial technocrats and capitalists. Chapters 5 and 6 shed light on examples of translocal interchanges that tied the US West and Hawai'i to Japanese-controlled territories of Manchuria, Taiwan, and the Northern Mariana and Western Caroline Islands (Micronesia) from the mid-1920s through the 1930s. Mechanized rice farming, plantation-style pineapple cultivation and canning, and tropical coffee growing were among the "gifts" that some of these transpacific resettlers and immigrant investors brought from the US empire at the behest of the developmentalist colonial regime in the home empire.

Part IV delves into the varied politico-ideological efforts that imperial Japan made to construct a borderless settler empire after its military takeover of Manchuria in 1931. In these state efforts, the immigrant and US-born generations of Japanese Americans performed a crucial role as actual and metaphorical symbols of Japan's expansionist past, present, and future—the symbols that aimed to rationalize its global hegemony. Forged in partnership with Japanese America, albeit for different goals, the expansionist orthodoxy of imperial Japan appropriated the chronicle of the ethnic Japanese experience in the United States, which Japanese immigrant intellectuals had compiled since the mid-1920s. Imperial Japan's orthodoxy rendered Japanese America's ethnic experience a foundational element in the contrived state-certified history of Japanese as an expansive race and the country's emergent global empire through the 1930s and the early 1940s. Not only did it define Japanese American history as a chief reference point for Japan's present and future settler colonialism, but that orthodoxy also made up a major component of its imperialist ideology of the time. The state-sponsored Conference of Overseas Japanese in 1940 emerged from this ideology, which aspired to create a centralized network of all ethnic Japanese communities with the home empire as the nucleus. In the public representation and actual government policy, the settlements of minoritized immigrants and their foreign-born children, including those from Japanese America, became linked up and conflated with those of colonizing settlers under the protection of the national flag. What can be termed a "diasporic Yamato race" took hold of the imaginations of imperial Japanese and their overseas compatriots, according to a belief in the immutability of blood ties. This development effectively shored up Japan's concurrent ideologies and policies of *hakkō ichiu* (spreading imperial influence to the eight corners of the world) and the Greater East Asian Co-Prosperity Sphere (an extension of pan-Asianism). Chapter 7 unravels the social, cultural, and political developments that gave birth to the making of Japan's monolithic expansionist history and pan-Pacific empire, as well as the central role that Japanese America unwittingly played in that endeavor.

The last chapter examines the so-called second-generation problem, which appeared to be a major challenge to the future of the rapidly expanding borderless empire. During the 1930s Japanese America and imperial Japan collaboratively tackled the question of how to keep children of settler-colonists sufficiently "Japanese" so that those foreignized souls could still carry the torch of national/racial expansion after the passing of the pioneer generation. The partnership between the immigrants and the home state helped produce expansionist pedagogy in the Japanese empire and a new system of nationalist education exclusively for children of Japanese migrant residents abroad. Given the chronological order of Japan's modern emigration history, US-born Japanese (Nisei) were deemed the first cohort of the new generation of overseas-born compatriots, whose number was expected to increase exponentially with the ongoing colonization of Manchuria.

Regardless of citizenship status or cultural upbringing, there was a common belief in Japan that these overseas-born racial brethren were destined to serve as a locally bred vanguard of Japanese development throughout the Asia-Pacific basin. Hence, the heritage education of second-generation Japanese Americans in the ancestral home formed an important site of pedagogical experimentation and ideologization, while the Japanese empire worked hard at building settler colonial societies in the Asian continent and other spheres of influence before the Pacific War. Chapter 8 also sketches out the struggle that Japanese American pupils engaged in desperately against imperialization in order to safeguard their bicultural and international identities as the self-proclaimed "bridge of the Pacific"—the bridge that did not stand a chance of holding out in a destructive all-out war.

The memories of Ōtsuki, Yokokawa, and countless other transpacific frontier trotters, as well as the deep and intricate bonds that Japanese America held with prewar Japan's borderless empire, are nowhere to be found in the existing literature or historical narrative. If anything, the pioneers of Japanese communities in the New World frontiers are simply remembered as the first generation of ethnicized "Americans," "Canadians," "Brazilians," and so forth in the respective national histories. This book salvages the buried memories, lost narratives, and complex identities of these Japanese transmigrants—along with the records of all their complacencies and complicities with imperial Japan's settler colonialism and associated oppressions.

PART ONE

Imagining a Japanese Pacific, 1884–1907

1

Immigrant Frontiersmen in America and the Origins of Japanese Settler Colonialism

The United States is the emergent center of world civilization, a land of new development with an untouched landmass that awaits the coming of the adventurous and strong-willed. Come thy ways, our brothers and sisters of 3,700,000 [in Japan]! Why must you cling onto the tiny ancestral home? But when you come to the United States, you must have the determination to create the second, new Japan there.[1]

Entitled "Come Japanese!," an 1887 treatise celebrated the popular act of international border crossing and overseas settlement making with America's frontier land as the focal point from the dual standpoint of Japanese "compatibility with white" settler-civilization builders and the "national honor and interest of Japan."[2] As this first "guide" to overseas settler colonialism, authored by a resident of San Francisco, articulated so poignantly, the modernizationist visions of "progress" and "civilization" catalyzed the rise of Japanese interest in emigration and colonization in the mid-1880s. Simultaneously, in much the same way that the "New World" had aroused the "expansive" minds of Europeans to desire colonial conquest and pursue new markets in earlier centuries, the imported concept of the "frontier" drew the attention of the early Japanese colonialist imagination toward the American West and the Hawaiian Islands—the most authentic frontier of all New World frontiers. More than a decade after US-inspired agro-industrial development had taken hold in the domestic wilderness of Hokkaido, North America appeared increasingly attractive as the ideal overseas site to build a "new Japan" in the eyes of the exponents of national expansion and borderless settler colonialism during the mid-1880s.[3]

Before Japan attained the world's recognition as an imperial newcomer following its victory over China in 1895, certain Japanese intellectuals and political factions had already begun to look favorably on emigration-led national expansion during the decade between 1884 and 1894. The mainstay of early Japanese settler colonialism featured what later would be referred to as "eastward expansionism" (*tōshinron*), in which transpacific migration from Japan was deemed the best means to further Japan's destiny as a global colonial empire. A competing discourse promoting "continental (northward) expansionism" (*tairiku shinshutsuron* or *hokushinron*) initially did not garner much support—except within a small segment of military strategists and political hawks—before the Sino-Japanese War of 1894–1895. Nor did the idea of "southward (maritime) expansion" (*nanshinron*) present itself as an equally notable discourse until around the 1890s.[4]

The critical decade 1884–1894 witnessed the Japanese encounter with the Western Hemisphere and the Pacific Islands, the initial colonial "promised lands" that would be gradually overshadowed by newer frontiers of northeast Asia and the Nan'yō (South Seas) after the 1910s. This shift in the Japanese expansionist gaze accompanied two significant factors in the history of settler colonialism in pre–World War II Japan. The first has been well studied in the cases of Korea and Manchuria, where settler colonialism was supported and augmented by the increasing scale of state intervention, including the use of imperial armed forces, the displacement and subordination of local residents by Japanese colonizers, and the politics of cultural assimilation directed at "natives."[5] The second, almost completely neglected by historians, is concerned with the role of the United States—and its Anglo-Saxonist racism, which took the lead in "white world supremacy"—as a major stumbling block to Japan's attempt to expand freely in various directions. The existing literature on Japanese colonialism generally concentrates on the Asian continent and surrounding maritime areas only, defining the first Sino-Japanese War as the official beginning of Japan's empire making in this contained region.[6] Nevertheless, transpacific migration and settler colonialism in the Western Hemisphere, especially in the US West, played a crucial role in informing and even helping shape Japanese imperialism on the Asian continent and in the Nan'yō. Thus, salvaging the role of the United States and the neglected theme of "race" is not only necessary, but it should also require the reconsideration of what historians have presumptuously taken for granted as Japan's colonial "space" in the story of imperialism. Unbound by the physical limits of the empire's sovereign power, the borderless dimensions of Japan's expansionism, especially overseas migration and settlement making, are discernible when we factor in the impacts of US racism and immigration exclusion on the complex unfolding of Japanese settler colonialism.

With a focus on the decade 1884–1894, this chapter sets out to shed light on interrelated historical developments, in which state-sponsored imperialism over China and Korea took shape in response to Japanese immigrant entanglement with white American racism. What happened to early Japanese immigrants in California and Hawai'i influenced Japanese discourse on national expansion and global racial struggle, and for that reason it illuminates the extent to which eastward expansionism came to dictate the basic terms of public debates and policy formulation in Meiji Japan before the turn of the twentieth century. As the chief advocates and practitioners of transpacific migration and agricultural colonization, immigrant intellectuals in San Francisco were instrumental in presenting a prototypical definition of a "frontier" for the modern Japanese and their emergent empire to conquer. The nascent phase of Japanese settler colonialism, which would subsequently figure largely in the state-led colonization of Korea, Manchuria, and other parts of the formal empire, entailed a close collaborative endeavor between early Japanese America and imperial Japan.

FUKUZAWA YUKICHI AND THE NATIVIZING OF SETTLER COLONIALISM IN 1880S JAPAN

Japanese fascination with the New World frontier resembled white Americans' enchantment with the mythical image of China as a new market for expanding US industrial capitalism and Christian evangelism. As the popular ideology of Manifest Destiny advocated, many Americans found it imperative to extend US commercial and moral power westward to China and other parts of the Asia-Pacific "frontier" beyond the US shores in the latter half of the nineteenth century. Though subsumed under a logic of altruistic uplift, the pursuit of material gain and racial supremacy served as a driving force for the making of America's Pacific empire, which eventually engulfed Hawai'i, Guam, and the Philippines as way stations to the China market and Asia in general during and after the Spanish-American War of 1898.[7]

Looking in the opposite direction across the Pacific, contemporary Japanese discussions about the North American frontier bore many similarities, albeit without conspicuous Christian undertones, insofar as pundits viewed the area with a mixture of romanticism and adventure, a sense of entitlement as modern men, and utilitarian economic and geopolitical calculations. And just as white Americans looked on Chinese (and other "Orientals") as the uncivilized masses who should be assimilated into or subjugated by Americans' superior way of life and sociopolitical system, early expansionists of Japan believed that they had a "sacred" role to play in bringing civilization and modernity to undeveloped lands and uncultured peoples around them and in the New World. As a modern nation and a civilized race, the Japanese reasoned, they must join the historic project of global conquest and development that had been carried out by European settler-colonists since the seventeenth century. Viewed from their embrace of the universalist progressivism that western modernity purportedly promised, the Japanese initially did not question whether or not they were sufficiently qualified in terms of their racial and cultural background to partake in the teleological project hitherto spearheaded and monopolized by white Euro-Americans. Not until after 1892 did many Japanese begin to realize that the purported universalism of western modernity entailed racially prescribed boundaries and Eurocentric exclusivity in accordance with Orientalism and social Darwinism.

In Japan, the mid-1880s saw the first notable articulation of this type of "innocent" expansionism, which defined transpacific emigration and colonization as a duty of modern Japanese in the global community of civilized nations. Advocates came from a circle of early westernizers and their nationalist-minded students: the "new generation in Meiji Japan."[8] These pundits were by no means politically homogeneous and were not simply moved by their embrace of western modernity or reactive love for Japan. A diverse group that included Meiji oligarchs, government bureaucrats, party politicians, journalists, scholars, businessmen, and impecunious young students (*shosei*), early expansionists produced specific discourses for specific audiences in accordance with their divergent agendas and goals. The heterogeneity of the ideological terrain, as well as the diversity of the ideologues, characterized the formative process of early Japanese expansionism.[9] Yet there also emerged a set of common visions and preferences that would characterize Japanese-style settler colonialism, one that emphasized the importance of migration and overseas community making in the form of agricultural colonization and commercial development. In this discursive process, the landmass of North America and the historical precedent of the Anglo-Saxon conquest of the US frontier served as inspirations and a crucial reference point.

Fukuzawa Yukichi was the most influential ideologue in the initial phase of the formation of this expansionistic discourse, because he had hundreds of dedicated disciples who took his words to heart and often acted on them. Japan's foremost scholar in "western studies," Fukuzawa founded the prestigious Keiō Academy, started the *Jiji Shinpō* newspaper, and published myriad books and articles that helped the transition of the Japanese nation from feudalism to modernity.[10] In this context, he first propagated new ideas associated with overseas migration and colonization around 1884 and 1885. Although scholarship on this important Meiji intellectual generally fails to acknowledge his contribution, it was Fukuzawa who forged the central underpinnings of emigration-based national expansionism, which would subsequently become systematized as a coherent discourse on "overseas development" (*kaigai hatten*) by the turn of the twentieth century. Fukuzawa's core assertions included mercantilist expansion, racial superiority, and agricultural settler colonialism.

An admirer of British imperial success, Fukuzawa first put forth a vision of Japanese emigrant mercantilism modeled after the global ascendancy of English commerce. Rather than seeking the outright takeover of foreign lands by military force, this position envisioned the peaceful establishment of overseas trade hubs, exemplified by the ubiquitous presence of British merchant posts all over the world. Japanese traders, Fukuzawa elaborated, similarly should emigrate abroad in large numbers, creating new markets for Japanese products in the land of their new residence.[11] The growth of exports through the medium of emigrant merchants would promote Japan's domestic industrial expansion, he anticipated. The origin of Fukuzawa's interest in entrepreneurial expansionism (albeit not a British example) was his trip to California in 1860 as a member of the first Tokugawa Shogunate mission to the United States. In San Francisco's Chinatown, the then lower-ranking samurai bureaucrat witnessed the impressive commercial "success" of Chinese immigrants and fantasized about "the future migration of Japanese people to California" to experience the same result. Fukuzawa thought to himself then that "those with resources should conduct trade and commerce, and those without them work in gold mines" to create capital.[12] Despite the passage of the US Chinese Exclusion Act of 1882, Fukuzawa's naïve faith in the universalist virtue of modern civilization blinded him to the problem of race, making Japan's foremost scholar continuously optimistic about his people's ability to emulate not just Chinese but also Anglo-Saxon accomplishments.

Although he might have discussed these ideas in his classroom at an earlier date, Fukuzawa expounded publicly for the first time in 1884 on the need for promoting popular emigration to build up the mercantilist foundation of imperial Japan. His newspaper became the main vehicle for disseminating such ideas, especially among the emergent urban bourgeoisie of Japan. By that time seventeen years had passed since the Meiji Restoration, and Fukuzawa's school had produced hundreds of business-minded youth equipped with a capitalistic mind-set and strong national consciousness. Directed primarily at an educated readership, *Jiji Shinpō* printed a series of commentaries and editorials to expound on the centrality of emigration relative to the national motto of the time: "Enrich the nation, strengthen the military (*fukoku kyōhei*)."[13] In Fukuzawa's view, *fukoku kyōhei* had to be followed in the order stated; amassing national wealth would precede building up military power. With a weak industrial base and a small domestic market, Japan in the mid-1880s badly needed to increase its exports to earn foreign currency. For Fukuzawa, trade was the best way to enrich the country to ensure its independence, much less its expansion.[14] This argument in and of itself was nothing unique, but he was the first intellectual of prominence to link commercial development to the question of emigration in the context of contemplating national security and empowerment, the number one priority in Japanese diplomacy and statecraft at the time.

Fukuzawa emphasized that emigration was not simply a pursuit of individual happiness and profit, but rather a patriotic deed that had serious implications for the future of modern Japan. He envisioned that emigrant traders would serve as a "commercial linkage between their homeland and their new country of residence."[15] Fukuzawa likened such traders to loyal soldiers who would sacrifice their lives to defend their homeland. Comparing the past expansion of the British Empire with the future rise of imperial Japan, one of his *Jiji Shinpō* editorials in 1884 urged readers to "leave your homeland at once":

> In considering the long-term interest of the country, the wealth that [English traders abroad] have garnered individually has become part of England's national assets. The land they developed has turned into regional centers of English trade, if not its formal colonial territories. This is how Great Britain has become what it is today. In a similar vein, [a Japanese emigrant] shall be regarded as a loyal subject. For while sacrificing himself at the time of national crisis is a direct way of showing loyalty, engaging in various enterprises abroad is an indirect way of demonstrating patriotism.[16]

In particular, Fukuzawa recommended North America as offering abundant opportunities for entrepreneurial-minded emigrants.[17]

The second theme in Fukuzawa's expansionist thought stemmed from his belief in the competitiveness of Japanese immigrants once they settled in the United States. His idea of Japanese racial superiority, however, was neither monolithic nor categorical. It valorized the moral character of upper-class individuals rather than the biological traits that comprised the entire nation. According to Fukuzawa, not everyone was capable of competing as an immigrant entrepreneur and demonstrating innate superiority. He was very specific about who should emigrate, for he felt that "the enrichment of Japan" was contingent upon whether an emigrant possessed certain traits that would enable him to act as a "loyal subject" of the modern nation-state. Fukuzawa's thinking specifically mirrored the Meiji intellectuals' class bias toward *shizoku*, or people of samurai background, as well as their prevailing distrust of the Japanese peasantry's capacity to be self-conscious "nationals."[18] Sharing the same social origin, Fukuzawa believed that *shizoku* youth should be given an opportunity to leave for North America for trade and business ventures. "[These] Japanese do not compare unfavorably to various European nationals [in the United States] at all," he proudly argued, "because they, too, are a superior race."[19] With tens of thousands of immigrants in North America, Fukuzawa forecasted, "new Americans of Japanese birth might even exert tremendous political influence" after achieving commercial success "to produce the president of the United States or control the Congress." This was how these *shizoku* should "erect dozens of new Japans all over the world."[20] Not only did the notion of Japanese racial compatibility with Europeans (especially Anglo-Saxons) shore up Fukuzawa's optimism about their entrepreneurial ascent abroad, but it also led him to see relations between the Japanese and other nonwhites (including Asians) hierarchically.

In his proemigration editorials, Fukuzawa specifically advanced a theory of racial difference between Japanese and Chinese. Recalling the prosperity of Chi-

nese immigrants he had witnessed in California a quarter century before, Fuku-
zawa predicted the historical inevitability of an even better result for the superior
Japanese: "Some say that those Chinamen with pigtails engage in slave work in the
United States, thereby allowing Americans to treat them like domestic animals.
But aren't those so-called animals making tons of money before going home to
China? Compare that with the lack of motivation that our compatriots have shown
through their reluctance to emigrate. . . . Are [the Japanese] inferior to those with
pigtails?"[21] The answer of course must be in the negative, but that would require
action to refute Fukuzawa's rhetorical question. Inasmuch as Japanese superiority
to the "uncivilized" Chinese was indisputable according to his rendition of global
race relations, an actual practice of emigration would mandate boundless progress
and prosperity for individual migrants and their homeland.

It is important to note that these burgeoning ideas of transpacific settler colonialism took hold in Japan's public discourse just as Fukuzawa was becoming
involved in one of its first imperialist ventures in Korea. In the mid-1880s, despite
disparaging Japan's East Asian neighbors with condescension, the foremost westernizer of Meiji Japan still held a pan-Asian view, in which he advocated helping
Korea (and through it China) modernize under Japanese guidance. Fukuzawa
even attempted to directly influence reform efforts in Korea. He took in Korean
students sympathetic to the Gaehwapa, or Enlightenment Party, in order to shape
how they would direct reform efforts upon their return to Korea. He also dispatched some of his most trusted Japanese disciples to Seoul as agents in modernization and sent one of them, Inoue Kakugorō, as a diplomatic adviser to Pak
Yonghyo, a reformist leader in the Korean court. Fukuzawa's attempt was doomed,
however, due to the complex political dynamics in Korea. When modernization-
influenced reformers tried to push through their changes, they were rebuffed by
conservatives surrounding the Korean court, who were backed by the Qing army.
This then led to the Gapsin coup in 1884, which failed miserably, and Fukuzawa's
disciples, Korean students, and other reformers sought refuge in Japan.[22] Subsequently, his optimistic outlook for Korean modernization and pan–East Asian
cooperation quickly gave way to the notion that there was an unbridgeable rift
between the Japanese and other Asians in terms of their capacity for becoming
modern. Published in March 1885, a *Jiji Shinpō* editorial entitled "On Abandoning
Asia (*Datsu-a ron*)" encompassed Fukuzawa's blatant racism toward Japan's East
Asian neighbors, his vision of Japanese-white compatibility, and a new spatially
prescribed idea of Japanese expansion. While he proposed to treat the "undesirable neighbors" just as Europeans and Americans had done, Fukuzawa came to see
the Asian continent being closed off to Japanese advancement, whether in the
form of emigration or commercial activities.[23]

Combined with his sense of kinship with the white race, the closure of East Asia
induced Fukuzawa to actively advocate for transpacific migration in the form of

agrarian settler colonialism reminiscent of the Puritan colonization in North America. In 1887 Fukuzawa recruited Inoue Kakugorō to take on a new project of establishing an agricultural colony—a "new Japan"—in rural California by leading a group of ordinary Japanese farmers across the Pacific.[24] From Korea to California, and from political intrigue to conquering the wilderness, Inoue's shifting colonialist endeavors crystallized the imperialist imagination of Fukuzawa and other Meiji intellectuals, which saw no qualitative difference between Northeast Asia and North America as an object of national expansion.[25] Moreover, the 1887 California venture set an important precedent in Japan's borderless colonialism. Indeed, the systematic transplantation of emigrant rural masses to a permanent settlement would become a common method of imperial Japan's colony making.

In June 1887 a group of some thirty men and women under Inoue's leadership departed Japan for a new settlement in rural California. In order for them to acquire an initial twenty acres in Valley Springs, Calaveras County, thirty-five miles west of Stockton, Fukuzawa provided the group with $10,000. Kai Orie, a Keiō alumnus who had opened the first Japanese immigrant business in San Francisco in response to Fukuzawa's earlier urging, acted as an intermediary for all business transactions relating to this colonization scheme on behalf of his mentor.[26] In line with his entrepreneurial expansionism, Fukuzawa expected the modest farm settlement to serve as a cornerstone of greater national expansion in North America, facilitating further migration and exports from Japan.[27] Inoue's agricultural colony was also expected to form a vital economic circuit with Kai's commercial enterprise for Japanese development on the American frontier. When sending his disciple off on this transpacific journey, Fukuzawa emphasized the advantages of establishing control over land to eke out an independent living rather than working here and there in competition with white and other workers. Yet Fukuzawa and Inoue also felt that those of *shizoku* origin would be too "noble" and hence inexperienced for the type of manual labor required for turning barren fields into agricultural land. They made sure that although the settlers included a few Keiō graduates, the majority were of farming background. While the main contingent worked on the farm, Inoue had some recruits engage in railroad work to earn extra income. In January 1888 Inoue returned to Japan to secure more funds and additional emigrant settlers for the expansion of the colony. Confident that this venture enjoyed favorable prospects, Fukuzawa pledged an additional $20,000, but the project unexpectedly came to a halt. Inoue was prevented from leaving Japan when the police took him into custody for his past political activities in Korea. Unable to sustain the operation of the farm without additional funds and their leader, the remaining settlers eventually abandoned the colony and dispersed to join the ranks of the founders of early Japanese America.[28]

This first example of organized settler colonialism, although it was short-lived, presaged what would become a preferred method of "overseas development" in

the history of pre–World War II Japan. Revealing a notable change from his earlier classism, Fukuzawa exhibited openness to the inclusion of rural commoners—the "ignorant masses" he used to disparage—in the 1887 venture. But it is equally important that these ordinary emigrants were placed under the "guidance" of Inoue and a few other "enlightened" leaders. The division of labor between the two cohorts of Japanese was key to this setup. Whereas classic mercantilism only posited the involvement of educated traders and entrepreneurs, the building of an agricultural settlement required primitive manpower over and above capital and enlightened leadership. This version of entrepreneurial expansionism therefore depended on rural commoners as a source of labor while select elites managed the entire colonialist venture, with an eye to benefiting the greater interests of not only all members but also the homeland. Moreover, enlightened leaders were supposed to steer laboring masses toward anchoring themselves in a new Japan without moving around. Thereafter, most advocates of overseas development would stress mass labor migration, permanent settlement, and the presence of "enlightened leadership"—which could refer to themselves, the state, or both—as prerequisites for colonial success on the frontier, wherever that might be.

A TRANSPACIFIC EXPANSIONIST NETWORK, AND THE US WEST AND HAWAI'I AS A JAPANESE FRONTIER

Between 1884 and 1887 Fukuzawa laid down the basic groundwork for public discourse on expansionistic overseas development. A curious mixture of mercantilism, racism, and settler colonialism would manifest itself again and again, albeit with many variations and gradations, in the ensuing decades. Even though Fukuzawa was fundamentally an armchair ideologue who left the actual task of expansion to his Keiō disciples and readers of his newspaper, those who followed him often played the dual role of theorist and practitioner in implementing their brand of settler colonialism. From around 1888 through 1894, a group of these activist-ideologues appeared in the transpacific space that linked Tokyo and San Francisco. Originating from the first generation of young Japanese educated under the modern school system, they fused popular nationalism (*kokumin shugi*) with a social Darwinist notion of racial struggle, loudly criticizing Tokyo's lack of commitment to emigration and colonialism. This was a pivotal moment in Japanese history, in which the question of "overseas development" became a locus of domestic political contestation for the first time.

Two loosely organized factions undertook the politicization of a national expansion agenda, especially the matter of transpacific migration. The first was known as Seikyōsha, a nationalistic assemblage of young urban intellectuals that called for state intervention in promoting mass emigration as well as a proactive imperialist policy.[29] Established in 1888, Seikyōsha took the lead in a nationwide debate over the course of foreign policy when Japan was about to present itself as a full-fledged constitutional monarchy. A legacy of US-initiated gunboat diplomacy during the final years of the Tokugawa Shogunate, the unequal treaties that the Meiji government maintained with western powers accorded the privilege of extraterritoriality to American and European residents and placed Japanese tariffs under international control. The revision of these treaties remained a top priority for Japanese diplomacy until 1911, when these sections were eliminated. In 1886 Japan's foreign minister began to negotiate with western powers for the abolition of extraterritoriality. His proposal, which contained the provision that Tokyo would accept a mixed court system over which foreign judges would preside, drew a storm of criticism from a wide array of the educated populace for its abrogation of full Japanese authority. Among the most vocal critics were the members of Seikyōsha, who represented an emerging faction of "Japanists" (*Nihon shugisha*), nationalistically inclined activists who looked back critically at the wholesale westernization of the 1870s and the government's knee-jerk response to western impositions of power.[30]

Seikyōsha consisted of two contingents of Japanist intellectuals. The first included scholars of "eastern philosophy" associated with a private academy called Tetsugaku-kan, the predecessor of Tōyō University. Many were graduates of Tokyo Imperial University. The second had its base at the Tokyo English School. Some key members of this group had graduated from Sapporo Agricultural College, the predecessor to Hokkaido Imperial University, which had produced Meiji Japan's prime internationalists, such as Nitobe Inazō and Uchimura Kanzō. One generation younger than those westernized intellectuals, they struggled to recuperate Japan's national "essence" while carrying on with the building of a modern empire. The union of these factions thus did not signify the disavowal of things western; rather, their eclecticism indicated a desperate attempt to reclaim an indigenous national identity in the making of adapted modernity that was Euro-American in origin. Inasmuch as the notion of being a "Japanese" imperial subject was a recent construct after the Meiji Restoration, the curious manifestation of nationalist assertions did not contradict the seemingly antonymous desire for western-style colonial aggression and extraterritorial "frontier conquest" that Japanists simultaneously professed.[31]

Often allied with other dissident nationalists and jingoists, Seikyōsha's members formed a fluid movement of bellicose "hard-liners" (*taigaikō*) and remained a powerful advocate of state-sponsored imperialist endeavors on the eve of the Sino-Japanese War. After the successful campaign against the official efforts at half-baked treaty revision, Seikyōsha's members and associates turned their attention to what they considered another betrayal of the "national mandate" by the Japanese government: its utter failure to take charge of national expansion. One poignant example was the nation's restrictive emigration policy, which had allowed for the departure of contract laborers to Hawaiian sugar plantations since 1885 but not settler-colonists to other "frontiers." Seikyōsha's criticism of the Tokyo authorities often invoked the notion of the Japanese as an "expansive nation/race" and presented it as a historical imperative—one that the government had supposedly neglected.[32] To these advocates of Japan's imperial destiny, the main question was not whether or not to expand, but in which direction and by what means. Whereas some demanded an aggressive solution—including military action—to the political roadblock in Korea under the yoke of Qing interventionism, a good majority of Seikyōsha pundits preferred transpacific eastward expansion when it came to the question of emigration and settler colonialism.[33]

Another group of expansionists shared an almost identical outlook with their Seikyōsha counterparts, but they were associated with a radical wing of the now-defunct Liberal Party (Jiyū-tō). Founded in 1881, Japan's first major political party had spearheaded the Freedom and Popular Rights movement after Tokyo had announced its plan to set up a parliamentary system. Liberal Party members were subsequently involved in rural uprisings and protests after Tokyo's shift to a deflationary policy devastated Japan's rural economy and hence the livelihood of land-owning farmers, its primary support base. Government crackdowns and arrests followed, and the Liberal Party formally declared it was disbanding in 1884.[34] When the problem of treaty revisions precipitated the revival of dissident activities among Japanist hard-liners, remnants of the former Liberal Party frequently joined forces with them, hoisting the common banner of overseas development. Between 1888 and 1893 various voices calling for open emigration, national expansion, and state imperialism arose from the overlapping circles of Seikyōsha and Liberal Party activists.

Importantly, their expansionistic voices were also transpacific. During the latter half of the 1880s both groups had dozens of members living in the United States, around San Francisco. While they published their own bulletins in California, these immigrant activists frequently sent commentaries to Japanese political journals sponsored by Seikyōsha and Liberal Party groups. A significant volume of ideas and information went back and forth between Tokyo and San Francisco despite the distance. Those who resided in the United States had an upper hand in this transpacific discursive formation, not only because they were free from the threat of legal persecution and censorship in Japan, but also because they could claim a firsthand "frontier" experience when discussing matters relating to migration and overseas development. Their opinions, supported by real examples and anecdotes, carried more weight than the ideas cranked out by armchair ideologues back home. Of the aggregate six hundred Japanese in the city of San Francisco in 1889, some two hundred were most likely such wide-eyed young expansionists. With the kind of patriotic sentiments and a sense of collective mission that Fukuzawa idealized, these self-styled pioneers of national development clearly distinguished themselves from other Japanese immigrants of rural farming origin—those they despised as "lowly laborers, ruffians and prostitutes"—in the American West. Indeed, orthodox narratives of Japanese American history portray them as founders and pillars of early ethnic society.[35]

Established in 1888 and 1890, respectively, the Japanese Patriotic League of San Francisco (Sōkō Nihonjin Aikoku Dōmei) and the Expedition Society (Enseisha) played the most pivotal role in formulating a reality-based theory of overseas development for the benefit of armchair homeland expansionists. On the one hand, the core membership of the Patriotic League consisted of some thirty political activists from the former Liberal Party. Their Tokyo supporters collaborated with them in the transpacific oppositional politics against the Meiji government through fund-raising and distribution of the weekly bulletin within Japan.[36] Once the Liberal Party was revived following the inception of Japan's Imperial Diet in 1890, its party organ frequently carried reports and commentaries from the San Francisco comrades. In Tokyo, key supporters of California-based expansionists, along with a few returnees from San Francisco, formed the New Japan League (Shin Nihon Dōmei) as the Patriotic League's branch in Japan, which was also formally affiliated with the Liberal Party.[37]

On the other hand, many members of the Expedition Society, affiliated with Seikyōsha, were purportedly more concerned with how to devise practical methods of colonial and entrepreneurial development on the American frontier than with political argumentation or polemics. The group's active core membership, numbering more than sixty in 1893, had a forum for disseminating members' voices across the Pacific, mainly through Seikyōsha's Tokyo-based weekly journals.[38] Their differences notwithstanding, the two expansionist political societies had close interactions in San Francisco, for some key members of the Expedition Society were simultaneously associated with the Patriotic League, and vice versa. Whereas most had to eke out a livelihood as indigent workers, just as other Japanese immigrant residents did, these self-proclaimed frontiersmen were still proud nationalists in consciousness and behavior, attempting to buoy imperialist politics back home by inserting their visions into Japan's public discourse through their humble publications.[39] Members of the two expansionist societies also cooperated to form the first unified Society of Great Japan Compatriots (Dai-Nihonjinkai) for the goal of not only augmenting Japan's national influence on this New World frontier but also defending the rights of imperial subjects in racially exclusive California.[40] In this important community organization of early Japanese America, nationalist, imperialist, and ethnic agendas and representations were fused in such a way as to make it difficult to differentiate between overlapping developments of Japanese settler colonialism and American minority politics.

From 1888 through 1893 the Patriotic League put out a succession of weekly mimeographed bulletins with a circulation of more than 250, some of which were distributed in Japan through Liberal Party channels. Every time the bulletin violated Tokyo's political censorship and its domestic circulation was banned, the name changed, from *Jūkyū Seiki* (Nineteenth century) at the beginning to *Aikoku* (Patriotism) in the end. The Expedition Society put together a handwritten biweekly paper with a smaller circulation of 130, named after itself, the *Ensei* (*The Expedition*; see figure 1).[41] In addition to these print venues that discursively linked both sides of the Pacific, the two immigrant groups locally sponsored political lectures and public debates on a variety of topics, including homeland politics and world affairs, the conditions of Japanese residents in America, and migration and colonial expansion.[42] These forums helped San Francisco's Japanese enclave form a pivotal site of expansionist knowledge production relating to settler colonialism. The forums attracted keen attention from the educated class of the ethnic community in San Francisco and its vicinity, for even ordinary Japanese residents were still hungry for news about the homeland and the wider world given the difficulty of reading English news reports. For this reason, the Patriotic League and the Expedition Society exerted considerable ideological influence on less-politicized immigrants, thus shaping the general mind-set of early Japanese America along the lines of their advocacy of multidirectional national expansion.

Settler colonialism, often referred to as an endeavor to erect an "overseas Japanese [farm] village," constituted the backbone of the organizations' vision, which cut across and often fused the different brands of national expansionism, especially continental and eastward schools.[43] In one *Aikoku* editorial, immigrant expansionists expounded on the "three goals of [Japan's] colonial enterprise": to promote commerce, trade, and new industry in foreign places; to establish the control of local lands; and to capture political power there. "While the first is absolutely necessary," this editorial continued, "the latter two goals should prove to be more crucial [in the long run]."[44] Put differently, permanent settlement on farmland was considered the best and ultimate form of overseas Japanese ascendancy. Here one can detect the differing emphasis that existed between British-style mercantilist expansionism and US-style agricultural colonization, although the two forms of settler colonialism were not mutually exclusive or in a fixed relationship. Dedicated specifically to the theme of "[mass] emigration and colonization," the *Ensei* likewise advocated the transplantation of ten million Japanese people—or one-quarter of Japan's entire population—to overseas frontiers, since "the progress of Japan proper, as well as its defense, should need no more than [the work of] thirty million."[45] The steering of surplus human resources toward the development of overseas frontiers, especially agricultural colonization across the Pacific, would "serve a long-range strategy of the empire, for it ensures not only the permanent survival of the national language (culture) and people [inside and outside the Japanese archipelago] but also Japan's rise as a mover and shaker of world [affairs and history]."[46]

FIGURE 1. Title page of the October 1891 issue of *Ensei* (*The Expedition*), showing the New World frontiers to be conquered by self-styled Japanese pioneers. *Source: Ensei* 6 (1 October 1891). Courtesy of the Manuscript Division, Center for Modern Japanese Legal and Political Documents, University of Tokyo, Japan.

As these ideas were transmitted to Japan, where they had the ear of like-minded pundits, it is not surprising that their transpacific collaborations would pave the way to instances of actual experimentation in agricultural colonization in the American West. In 1888 a group of Liberal Party members and associates under the leadership of Seattle residents Itō Yonejirō and Hirota Katsumi migrated to the Lake Washington area to carve out a "new Japan" there. In order to procure capital and additional manpower for the clearing of the land, Hirota sailed back to his home prefecture, Kochi, to meet with Kataoka Kenkichi, a former vice president of the Liberal Party and later the chairman of the Japanese House of Representatives. Recruiting a dozen emigrant colonists, including Kataoka's younger brother, Hirota returned to Seattle for what turned out to be an unsuccessful endeavor at frontier conquest.[47] This effort nonetheless engendered a localized fascination in Kochi Prefecture with the idea of transpacific overseas development and the search for an alternative new Japan, which gave birth to the Kochi Colonization Society in 1893.[48]

The 1888 endeavor also inspired Arai Tatsuya, Itō's friend and another immigrant activist with Liberal Party ties, to acquire 160 acres of untouched land in nearby Snoqualmie, Washington, in 1889. Arai tried to exploit his political connections to marshal support when he returned to Tokyo to arrange a meeting with Mutsu Munemitsu, the former ambassador to Mexico and the then minister of agriculture and commerce. With Mutsu's blessing, Arai took fifty emigrant laborers from Japan to his Pacific Northwest colony, but a shortage of funds forced him to seek additional investment from his political mentor, Hoshi Tōru, a close ally of Mutsu and soon to be mayor of Tokyo and chairman of the House. In 1890 Hoshi dispatched ten more emigrants and $10,000 (20,000 yen) under the care of one of his disciples, Watanabe Kanjūrō, a Patriotic League member who would also become involved in the founding of the Expedition Society in San Francisco. As these examples reveal, the homeland backers frequently marshaled crucial political support and furnished money, manpower, and other resources for endeavors abroad; the US residents offered on-the-spot leadership and guidance based on their experience as bona fide frontiersmen.[49] These transpacific networks of early expansionists, which encompassed key Liberal Party bosses and government officials, such as Kataoka, Hoshi, and Mutsu, and extremely mobile founders of early Japanese America, such as Itō, Arai, and Watanabe, dovetailed with the burgeoning of transpacific settler colonialism. A few years prior to Japan's first imperialist assault on China and Korea, their thinking and actions mirrored and articulated how the symbolism of the North American frontier inspired—and muddled—political support for mass emigration, borderless settler colonialism, and state expansionism altogether throughout the Asia-Pacific basin.[50] Deeply entrenched in the early political history of modern Japan and the ethnic politics of first-generation Japanese Americans, migration and settler colonialism made the home empire and its US-based diaspora inseparable.

All of these settler-colonial schemes in the American West ended in failure due to poor planning, as well as the practitioners' lack of capital and farming experience. As Fukuzawa had already advised Inoue Kakugorō in 1887, it became all too clear that overseas development would require the brute manpower and farming expertise of rural commoners, albeit under the guidance of enlightened leaders. These early endeavors convinced Japanese expansionists on both sides of the Pacific even more of the need for the systematic importation of farming-class migrants to a new Japan. In 1894, when they became united as owners and managers of so-called emigration companies (see chapter 2), the preexisting networks of Japanese America's expansionistic leaders and Japan's political bosses would prove indispensable for the institutionalization of a new mechanism to ship out tens of thousands of emigrants from Japan to new settlements and worksites abroad. Aside from the frustrated efforts at frontier conquest, a major catalyst of this shift was the rise of exclusionary American racism between 1892 and 1894.

WHITE SUPREMACY AND THE LOSS OF JAPANESE FRONTIERS IN CALIFORNIA AND HAWAI'I

When immigrant expansionists initially crossed the vast Pacific Ocean, California and Hawai'i (still an independent monarchy) had already borne the brunt of organized Anglo-Saxonist agitation against "Orientals," which had culminated in formal policy against Chinese immigration in 1882 and 1886, respectively. Replacing their Asian neighbors as a chief source of labor, the Japanese entered those frontier economies. It was not surprising that the white exclusionist gaze shifted quickly to the new "Oriental" hordes from Japan, provoking a resurgence of racist rhetoric and political actions against Japanese newcomers. Through a transnational network of print media and personal communications, stories of racial discrimination subsequently spread to Japan, where the experience of immigrant expansionists meshed with theoretical discussions of global racial hierarchy and struggle formulated by armchair thinkers such as Fukuzawa. The white American conflation of Japanese and Chinese, bitterly reported by their compatriots in San Francisco, came into sharp contrast with the prevailing notion in Japan that the Japanese were superior to their Asian neighbors and on a par with Europeans and Americans on account of their capacity to civilize. Situated on the front lines of this ostensible contradiction, immigrant expansionists took it upon themselves to rectify the situation, which they posited was predicated on simple misunderstandings among white Americans about the real worth of Japanese people. In 1890, for example, one California resident volunteered to bring a lawsuit in San Francisco in cooperation with homeland supporters to seek a formal court ruling that "the Japanese do not belong to the uncivilized Mongolian (Chinese) race, because they are more progressive than the rest of the world's races."[51]

Yet in the spring of 1892 an organized racist press campaign against Japanese in San Francisco drove a decisive wedge between their self-consciousness as racially superior and the contrary reality of being minoritized in white supremacist California. Ten years after the passage of the Chinese Exclusion Act, San Francisco newspapers cranked out one report after another on the new "Oriental" threat, drawing a parallel between the excluded Chinese and the increasing Japanese in the midst of the white republic. Pages of the *Aikoku* and the *Ensei* became filled with warnings and protests against the injustice and peril of American racism, and a series of angry reports and commentaries was soon printed in Seikyōsha's journal and the Liberal Party bulletin in Tokyo.[52] Since they still sustained a firm belief in their collective superiority to the Chinese, self-styled leaders of Japanese America vigorously protested the offensive comparison. They declared in public: "In no way do we, energetic and brilliant Japanese men, stand below (or on par with) those lowly Chinese. . . . The Japanese . . . are progressive and competent."[53] Infuriated by sensationalized accounts of this so-called Japanese menace in white American print media, Patriotic League leaders even met with a local white newspaper editor in protest and tendered a written complaint.[54] Yet the situation soon changed for the worse, for San Francisco's Japanese not only experienced numerous acts of violence but also faced a formal school board resolution for the segregation of Japanese students in the ensuing months of 1892 and 1893.[55]

Under escalating racist assaults, the settlers' optimistic outlook on overseas Japanese development on the New World frontier suffered a rude wake-up call. This firsthand experience of white supremacy, of which immigrant expansionists indignantly and sensationally informed their friends in Japan, complicated the idea of racial compatibility that Fukuzawa and other westernizers had propagated in their rendition of modernity as universal. To many immigrant expansionists in California, it came to look as if being modern, civilized, and expansive did not automatically earn the Japanese fair treatment and acceptance.[56] With this realization, race increasingly became an important matter of consideration in Japanese expansionist discourse, and the view of a particular "frontier" often hinged on the state of race relations—or specifically that of "racial struggle"—in that location. North America appeared to have too many white residents, especially Anglo-Saxonists, who refused to treat Japanese as equal partners in the epic historical project of frontier settlement and development. And this message from the front lines of the interracial clash greatly influenced how their homeland compatriots imagined and debated the course and possibility of national expansion in a world dominated by white men. As a biography of a Patriotic League founder describes, the "disillusionment about the land of the free became all the more prevalent" within and without Japan due to the San Francisco incidents.[57]

A discursive shift in the Expedition Society's official bulletin exemplifies the general trajectory of Japanese expansionist thought, which revolved around the

problem of race rooted in the North American experience. In August 1891, months before the organized racist press campaign, the *Ensei* featured a special column that confidently predicted that Japanese would successfully conquer the California frontier on the basis of the precedent set by "various foreign settlers (Europeans) for the last thirty some years [*sic*]" (since the Gold Rush).[58] After the spring of 1892, however, commentaries in the journal clearly presented a prognosis that California's potential as a new Japan could no longer be divorced from the negative impact of anti-Japanese racism. Thenceforth, the *Ensei* revealed little trace of its earlier optimism, lamenting instead the "prevalence of white domination" that "would not allow other races to prosper" in California.[59] In order to ensure the favorable outcome of Japanese immigration and colonization, the bulletin editorialized, it was imperative to search for "an untouched land with a people and political system that would not dare to shut us out."[60] No longer did the American West embody such a site.

While the North American continent looked increasingly prohibitive due to US settler exclusionism, the years 1892 to 1894 also marked the emergence of new geopolitical conditions in the middle of the Pacific, where the problem of race called into question the status of another desired site of Japanese development. In 1893 Hawai'i drew sudden attention from immigrant expansionists in San Francisco and their like-minded compatriots in Japan, subsequently effecting a major shift in their perspective on the islands. Behind this change lay the overthrow of the native Hawaiian kingdom by US-supported white conspirators in January of that year. The islands had been a main destination of Japanese labor immigrants since 1885, and over the next eight years some twenty-nine thousand people had arrived to work on Hawaiian sugar plantations, constituting the second largest ethnic group after about forty thousand native Hawaiians. Although these laboring masses were not settler-colonists of samurai background, self-styled immigrant frontiersmen in San Francisco viewed their Hawaiian counterparts as a viable part of overseas Japanese development. Contributors to both the *Ensei* and the *Aikoku* frequently expounded on Japanese colonial destiny in Hawai'i by anticipating popular political control through democratic means—the franchise and electoral action—by these plantation workers and their children in the years to come.[61] Nonetheless, the "insurgent revolution" by the white minority, they argued, rendered the future of the islands contingent on the response of the Japanese majority. As one author stressed in May 1893, a well-devised plan would be vital for Hawai'i's Japanese to take power away from "the foreign (white) race," who "had been trampling Hawai'i" as they wished with no regard for "weak" and "doomed" natives.[62]

A member of the Expedition Society and Seikyōsha, Nagasawa Betten (Setsu), offered by far the most systematic blueprint for the peaceful takeover of Hawai'i in the face of a US-backed coup d'état in his 1893 treatise *Yankii* (Yankee).[63] Nagasawa's rendition of national expansion as a consequence of racial struggle

characterized a central conceptual strain in the emergent settler colonialist discourse of imperial Japan. Born as a son of a prominent samurai in 1868, Nagasawa attended an Anglican school, where he studied English language and literature and developed a fascination with Britain's imperial success. After serving as the editor of *Nihonjin*, the Seikyōsha's official bulletin, Nagasawa went to San Francisco in 1891 to attend Stanford University, frequently contributing commentaries to the *Ensei* in San Francisco and the *Nihonjin* in Tokyo. During that period he encountered the menacing power of white supremacy in the United States. This experience, which Nagasawa later described as "a clash between the Mongolian race and the Aryan race," left a profound impression on his mind, convincing the young nationalist once and for all that the two races could not coexist amicably.[64] It is important to note that the rise of such racial thinking corresponded to that of what is called "American racial Anglo-Saxonism," which shored up US imperialism during the Spanish-American War of 1898. In this sense, what Nagasawa described as a racial struggle was but one manifestation of growing imperial conflict between the two Pacific racial empires.[65]

Mired in social Darwinist expressions, Nagasawa's writings on Hawai'i in particular, and on emigration and colonization in general, revealed a dialectical vision of historical progress, in which the conflict between "the Mongolian race and the Aryan race" had purportedly determined the course of world history for the last millennium. He contended that the cultural and military domination of the Mongolian race had once reached much of the Old World under the reign of Genghis Khan. With their progress in "literature, science, and industry" after the fifteenth century, the Aryan race, especially Anglo-Saxons, had struck back and eventually come to dominate every corner of the "Orient" except for mighty Japan and ever-weakening China. Since "the law of nature determines that 'the one who rises will always fall,'" Nagasawa continued, "it is inevitable that these two [master] races will once again clash head-on, leading to a resurgence of the Mongolian race" in the end. Thus, Nagasawa proclaimed that "the subjects of the cherry-blossom land (Japan)," as the current leaders of the Mongolian race, were destined to be at the helm of this progressive history in the coming twentieth century.[66] His teleological history was typical of an intellectual trend of the 1890s. A decade earlier, before completely "abandoning Asia," Fukuzawa had struggled with a seeming contradiction unfolding before him between the Enlightenment framework of the unilinear progress of humankind and the perpetual backwardness and inferiority of "Asia" and "Asians" compared to the West. Japanese intellectuals of the 1890s could evade the problem because the progress they knew was no longer unilinear. Informed by social Darwinism, many now understood that the progress of a nation (or the lack thereof) depended on its ability to adapt to its environment. In this new paradigm, the conflict of two races mirrored the contestation between the different levels of adaptability that they purportedly possessed due to their inherent biological traits.

In Nagasawa's opinion, Hawai'i formed the first notable site for the epic struggle between the Japanese and Anglo-Saxons in modern times. There were tens of thousands of Japanese migrants on the islands, who not only exceeded the population of Anglo-Saxons in number but were also rapidly approaching that of the native Hawaiian majority.[67] Unlike in the United States or Canada, white settler-colonists had not yet established their incontestable sovereign control of Hawai'i as of 1893, even though the small *haole* elite had for some decades dominated its sugar plantation economy. In a sense, the islands constituted a power vacuum, in which the teleology of racial struggle would express itself without the hindrance of institutionalized white supremacy, unlike in California. Neither Japanese nor Anglo-Saxons had managed to pull themselves ahead by relying on the sovereign state apparatuses that favored one race over another in Hawai'i, a situation that would not last long, considering the ongoing *haole* efforts to solidify their political influence through the backing of the United States.

Despite a strong sense of urgency, Nagasawa appeared cautiously optimistic about the outcome of racial struggle in Hawai'i, not only because the Japanese outnumbered whites but also because he firmly believed in the racial superiority of his compatriots. According to the San Francisco–based immigrant, the upper hand that white capitalists had over Hawai'i's sugar industry resulted primarily from the racial and cultural "deficiency" of the native islanders, who would "rather dance the hula than sacrifice their lives for the sake of their nation."[68] With their "superior" qualities, however, once they joined forces to apply their racial talent, the Japanese—even plantation workers—would be able to overwhelm other groups, bring Hawai'i's politics and economy under their control, and consolidate a firm underpinning for a new Japan in the islands. Nagasawa's theory of Japanese ascendancy presented a good example of Japan's adaptive settler colonialism, which borrowed significantly from US frontier discourse even as it served to empower immigrant expansionists to imagine their predominance over white American supremacy in Hawai'i. Just as Anglo-Saxon settlers reduced indigenous people to an object of conquest on the North American frontier, Nagasawa depicted native Hawaiians as an object of inevitable Japanese domination. When he began to ponder the practical means of expediting such a teleological unfolding in Hawai'i, Nagasawa referenced another pivotal assumption of US frontier discourse: the importance of permanent settlement.

Nagasawa, as well as other Japanese expansionists based in California, thought that immigrants should put down roots permanently in a foreign land to undertake a colonial venture of lasting influence. In Hawai'i, the vast majority of Japanese residents had lacked commitment to their new land and its colonial potential, thereby preventing them from moving past the status of subjugated plantation workers. Because they went as *dekasegi* (temporary) workers with the self-centered intention of making quick money before returning to rural Japanese villages, Nagasawa felt that the laboring masses did not possess the kind of mental disposition required of patriotic agents of overseas national expansion. While some pundits stressed the need for preemigration screening to weed out those with deficient patriotic sentiments, Nagasawa presented a concrete postemigration measure to convert *dekasegi* workers into full-fledged settler-colonists with a strong nationalist consciousness. Estimating the total monthly income of all of Hawai'i's Japanese at around $160,000, he recommended that $60,000 be set aside every month to establish a special fund for the systematic promotion of Japanese commerce and farming in the islands. It should be deposited at a new Japanese-run industrial bank, which would play a leading role in housing development and real estate acquisition to create autonomous Japanese settlements all over Hawai'i.[69] Leadership, of course, should come from self-proclaimed frontiersmen, such as Nagasawa and his colleagues.

The conquest of the frontier was not simply a matter of racial competition; it was also about nationalizing an "unclaimed" land. Just as white settlers had annexed the western frontier as a territory of the United States (or Canada), Nagasawa considered it to be crucial to paint Hawai'i's topography in Japan's national colors. As noted previously, mapping the islands with Japanese-controlled institutions and permanent settlements was one way of turning Hawai'i into a "new Japan." Yet the banks and residential districts would be useless if the people who occupied them were devoid of Japanese consciousness and the patriotic behavior that it should induce in them. The national identity of immigrants and their local-born children must be kept undiluted through sustained educational efforts at nationalization. In this vein, Nagasawa insisted that Japanese grammar schools be built all through the Hawaiian islands for the preservation of their primary allegiance to the emperor, since local public education was currently designed to make them "Americans in their ideas and beliefs" under the dictates of white Christian missionaries from the United States. It was necessary to offset the process of "Americanization" by "imperializing" the future generation of Japanese settlers, that is, by a concerted effort at cultural preservation that would in turn ensure the maximum exertion of their racial strength. "If we fail to give the children a [proper] Japanese education," Nagasawa hence declared, "our Hawaiian colonization will not bear any returns" for Japan.[70] Such a failure also meant that another expected role of the local Japanese settlements would no longer be tenable. To Nagasawa, Japanized Hawai'i should also serve as "our [way] station to Mexico, South America, and Oceania."[71]

Nevertheless, race and culture alone would not suffice to put Japanese completely ahead of white residents of Hawai'i—especially sugar planters and missionaries—who had enjoyed privileged control of the local political economy, especially after they foisted the Bayonet Constitution of 1887 onto the Hawaiian monarch.[72] It is for this reason that the issue of suffrage lay at the heart of the colonialist blueprint of Nagasawa—and many other Japanese expansionists. Through his American experiences, Nagasawa came to believe that the franchise was a precondition for successful colonization. During his stay in California, this young immigrant student learned firsthand how powerless he was to fight white exclusionists without the basic political right to vote. While it seemed almost impossible for Japanese to obtain suffrage in the United States due to the white monopoly of the electoral process, the prospect looked much more promising in Hawai'i in 1893. Nagasawa wrote: "If the Japanese acquire the right of suffrage in Hawai'i and elect five or six congressmen or one or two ministers, they would not have to meet the same fate as the Chinese have met (racial exclusion). The dominance of the Japanese will reign over the Sandwich Islands with countless benefits extending to all the spheres of commerce, agriculture, and navigation."[73] Suffrage was crucial not only for Japanese in Hawai'i but also for the future of Japan's national expansion in general, he asserted, because it would enable Japanese to take on white Americans and Europeans in the islands on equal grounds and demonstrate their inherent racial superiority.[74]

The views of Nagasawa and his fellow Seikyōsha/Expedition Society members harmonized almost perfectly with those of the leaders of the San Francisco–based Patriotic League. In 1893 Toyama Yoshifumi published a book titled *Nippon to Hawai* (Japan and Hawai'i), around the same time as Nagasawa's *Yankii*. Echoing the latter's ideas of racial struggle and historical teleology, this Patriotic League leader wrote: "Despite the presence of over 20,000 compatriots of ours, [Hawai'i] is now on the verge of being usurped by Anglo-American powers, and we are faced with the need to counteract once and for all. The world in the twentieth century will be a battleground for a race war. The White and the Yellow races are destined to meet for a decisive battle. . . . Representing the Yellow race are the Japanese, who lay hold of the destiny of not only Asia but also the entire Eastern Hemisphere (including the islands of the Pacific)."[75] On the method to turn Hawai'i into a "little Japan," Toyama's blueprint also converged neatly with Nagasawa's, in that he advocated the control of land, capital consolidation, and industrial development (modeled after the British East India Company) and the retraining of *dekasegi* contract laborers as permanent colonial settlers.[76]

It makes perfect sense that the ideologues of the two immigrant expansionist groups concurrently produced almost identical messages to their friends and allies in Tokyo in 1893. In the first month of that year Hawai'i became engrossed by the successful overthrow of the native kingdom by the small landed white elite in collaboration with the American minister to Hawai'i and US Marines. After January the provisional government moved toward the institutionalization of a US-style racial hierarchy, in which Asians would be denied the franchise and rights to citizenship.[77] When *Yankii* and *Nippon to Hawai* were published in Tokyo, it appeared as though Hawai'i was on the verge of becoming another California, which had already blocked the chance of unrestrained Japanese development under the clutches of white settler Anglo-Saxonism. These books did not simply offer abstract political rhetoric; even before the treatises came off the press in Tokyo, a number of immigrant expansionists had rushed over to Honolulu from San Francisco to "counteract" the white conspiracy supported by US imperialism. Separately from two Expedition Society activists, Nagasawa had gone to the islands alone, armed with a pistol and a book of poetry by Lord Byron. Revering the British poet as his inspiration, this youthful romantic sought to exhibit heroic resistance to the rival of his race and civilization, just as Byron had fought the Ottoman Empire to defend the white race and its Judeo-Christian tradition.[78] To Nagasawa's dismay, there was no battle to be had when he arrived in Honolulu, as forcing the abdication of Queen Lili'uokalani took white conspirators only a few days. Nagasawa left it to others to take back Hawai'i, as that required practical skills of political mobilization. A career writer and more of an ideologue than a mobilizer, Nagasawa was not up to that task and instead went on to author *Yankii* in hopes of creating favorable public opinion for the rescuing of Hawai'i from the hands of Anglo-Saxon rivals and the United States that backed them.

However, many of Patriotic League members were experienced political agitators. In January 1893 Sugawara Tsutau and three other leaders sailed to Honolulu, where they managed to unite forces with a circle of local Japanese immigrant activists.[79] They traveled around the islands propagating their views, hoping to affect the consciousness of common plantation workers and marshal support from them. What these activists advocated did parallel Nagasawa's contentions in many ways. As Sugawara later explained, they focused on the need for Japanese male suffrage in order to create a politically level playing field for unmediated racial competition and to arrest the ascendancy of US imperialism over Hawai'i.[80] "The world of the coming twentieth century," he predicted, "would be a battleground for clashing races"—a prediction that resonates with W. E. B. Du Bois's statement, although Sugawara contrarily saw the new era as one of Japanese ascendancy as a colonial master race rather than white supremacy's reign and minority resistance to it.[81] Thus, he declared that the Japanese were destined to "represent the Yellow race" to win this "survival of the fittest for Asia [and the Pacific]."[82] Yet to achieve that end, immigrant permanent settlement, economic empowerment, and land-ownership would be indispensable to transform Hawai'i into a Japanese "second home."[83] Sugawara made his observations and recommendations widely available through the Liberal Party bulletin, as well as at its political lecture venues, in Tokyo during his brief trip home.[84]

In the triangular transpacific network of Japanese expansionists, San Francisco, Tokyo, and Honolulu/Hilo formed pivotal sites of discursive formation and political activism for racial struggle and Japanese development in the critical years 1893 and 1894. In San Francisco, remaining members of the Patriotic League compiled a special weekly bulletin to report Sugawara's activities in Hawai'i to audiences in California and Japan.[85] In Tokyo, those who had returned from California, including Toyama, strove to "arouse public opinions [in Japan] about the Hawaiian situation and devise a long-range plan."[86] Setting themselves up as the League's Tokyo branch, this auxiliary group worked closely with the leadership of the Liberal Party, which had become the majority party once Japan's parliamentary system came into effect in 1890. Under the initiative of Hoshi Tōru, a close ally and patron of US residents and returnees, the party's board of executive officers adopted the matter of Japanese suffrage in Hawai'i as a major national policy and diplomatic agenda. The special legislative committee, headed by Hoshi, went on to successfully pressure the Meiji government into negotiating with the provisional government of Hawai'i.[87]

In Hawai'i, Sugawara and other Patriotic League activists found a number of sympathetic local Japanese, although few were plantation workers. Established under their influence, the Japanese Alliance (Nihonjin Dōmei) successfully assembled around the cause of Japanese suffrage some five hundred members from the hitherto polarized immigrant intelligentsia of the islands, including Buddhist priests and Christian ministers. Honolulu and Hilo constituted hubs of this political mobilization, with over 300 and 150 members, respectively, concentrated in their locations.[88] Backed by San Francisco activists, subgroups of the Japanese Alliance called themselves "concerned [Hawai'i] residents," including Ōtsuki Kōnosuke, and produced four separate petitions to the Japanese consulate in Honolulu during 1893. All petitions demanded that Tokyo take a proactive role in championing the cause of national expansion and render its full support for their struggle to secure suffrage in Hawai'i.[89]

Illuminating the common colonialist visions in the transpacific network, the petitions unambiguously echoed Nagasawa's central argument. They warned that the triumph of the white conspiracy would relegate disenfranchised Japanese to a permanently subordinate position, thereby jeopardizing Japan's future as a dominant maritime power in the Pacific. If the white elite of Hawai'i managed to monopolize political power as in California, the petitioners warned, it would be not only "a loss of dignity for all imperial subjects" but also a "national humiliation for the Great Japanese Empire." White Americans and Europeans would surely take it as a sign of Japan's weakness, "leading them to think that the Japanese [were] an inferior race that would not deserve the political control of a world (frontier)."[90] One petition went as far as to request that Tokyo "dispatch a few warships," not only to ensure the safety of residents in Hawai'i, but also to protect their political rights.[91] In response to these petitions, as well as the similar "public opinion [that] prevail[ed] in the Imperial Cabinet and the Parliament," Tokyo eventually filed a strongly worded protest against Japanese disenfranchisement with Sanford B. Dole, the president of Hawai'i's provisional government.[92] Yet the *haole* oligarchy took no notice of Japan's formal protest and subsequently wrote racial discrimination into the constitution of the new white republic in 1894. As Nagasawa and others feared, the *haole*'s triumph in racial struggle over Japanese led Dole to declare that Hawai'i was "the western outpost of Anglo-Saxon civilization and a vantage ground for American commerce in the Pacific," paving the way to the eventual annexation of the Islands by the United States four years later.[93]

Thus, despite the concerted efforts by expansionists in San Francisco, Tokyo, and Honolulu/Hilo, Hawai'i was lost for all practical purposes by 1894, following the fate of anti-Japanese California. Thereafter, there was an exodus of many self-styled Japanese frontiersmen from California and Hawai'i, because both frontiers dropped out of their imaginary map of Japanese overseas development. Dejected over the monopoly of the mid-Pacific Islands by white American rivals, Sugawara Tsutau and his associates unceremoniously left Hawai'i. After a brief return to San Francisco to wind up their affairs, they set sail for their home empire, which was rapidly gearing up for its first major imperialist war with China. The Japanese Patriotic League of San Francisco ceased to exist shortly after the departure of its key activist-ideologues. Only two original members chose to remain in the United States to play the role of ethnic community leaders in early Japanese America, the "original" new Japan. The Expedition Society and smaller expansionist groups continued to exist for the next several years, but their membership shrank steadily as more and more immigrants relinquished their enterprise in the American West. A number of Hawai'i's immigrant expansionists also bade farewell to the islands as they found that nothing had come of their 1893 petitions for Japanese suffrage.[94]

Armed with the vision of settler colonialism bred during their US experience, these returnees subsequently searched for alternative outposts of a new Japan elsewhere. Adapted from the American model of frontier conquest, their settler colonialism would spread through Japan's neighboring regions and the Nan'yō, which would eventually make up parts of Japan's formal and bona fide colonial empire in the ensuing decades. In the meantime, the minoritized frontiersmen who opted to remain in the American West started to draw a different kind of map for Japanese development, a map that gravitated toward Mexico and its southern neighbors, devoid of white hegemony.[95] Through their discursive intervention and settler-colonial practices, the Asian continent, Southeast Asia, and briefly Oceania, as well as Latin America, emerged as contending frontiers in the transpacific public discourse on and actual endeavors for overseas Japanese development between 1894 and 1908.

2

Vanguard of an Expansive Japan

Knowledge Producers, Frontier Trotters, and
Settlement Builders from across the Pacific

From 1894 through 1908—especially during the years between Japan's imperialist wars against China (1894–1895) and Russia (1904–1905)—Japanese settler colonialism underwent another round of adjustment, in accordance with the spread of Anglo-Saxonist racism within and without North America as well as Tokyo's efforts to build a settler colonial empire. Building on racist politics against Chinese immigrants, anti-Japanese agitation in the United States employed the language of social Darwinism and civilizational hierarchy after its first articulation in 1892. Initiated by the first organized press campaign against Japanese immigrants in San Francisco (see chapter 1), it became a full-fledged political movement by the turn of the twentieth century, involving organized labor, local political machines, and the intelligentsia, with the growing support of ordinary white citizens in the Pacific Coast states. To many white Americans, the problem of Japanese immigration and settlement had to do with the survival of the white race and republic—an idea that subsequently culminated in various forms of discriminatory statutes being passed by state legislatures and eventually the US Congress by the mid-1920s.[1] Corresponding to the escalation of anti-Japanese exclusionism in US domestic race politics, the Spanish-American War of 1898 and the subsequent Philippine-American War (1899–1902) accounted for the extension of US imperialism and Anglo-Saxonist racism into Northeast Asia and the Pacific Islands. With the acquisition of Guam, Wake Island, and the Philippines (in addition to Hawai'i), the United States drove a dagger into the southern "backyard" of imperial Japan, creating multiple points of racialized conflict between the two Pacific colonial empires. Furthermore, extending beyond the physical boundaries of the continental United States, American Anglo-Saxonism united with its cousins in Oceania and Canada and enrolled them in a common battle against transborder Japanese racial "invasion" and the pursuit of what can be called a "white Pacific."[2]

In response to these tangled developments of domestic and international white supremacy, the Japanese search for a new frontier—if not the outright construction of a "Japanese Pacific"—became more organized and institutionalized after 1893. Two important forms of expansionist apparatus emerged in interwar Japan: the Colonization Society of Japan (Nihon Shokumin Kyōkai) and emigration companies (*imin gaisha*). The former offered a unified forum for national debate regarding an important goal of overseas Japanese development. The institutionalization of expansionist discourse, which valorized mass migration and agrarian settler colonialism, dovetailed with Japan's state endeavors to extend its formal territories through belligerent diplomacy and military action after the first Sino-Japanese War. Emigration companies systematized the migration process for ordinary Japanese workers, especially in terms of their transpacific/eastward mobility and southward mobility. In other words, the business of recruiting and shipping out rural peasants methodized and sustained the large-scale exodus of the brute labor force required for Japanese civilization's conquest of a frontier according to the ideology of overseas development. Thus, while the Colonization Society functioned as the brains of Japan's adaptive settler colonialism, emigration companies acted as the muscle, deemed an integral and indispensable component of national expansion by the early 1890s. Former and current residents of the American West, armed with US-bred visions of frontier conquest, played a central role in the establishment of these two key institutions of borderless colonialism in Meiji Japan. This chapter examines the complex unfolding of Japanese migration and overseas colonial-settlement history during this pivotal interwar decade.

TRANSPACIFIC IMMIGRANT EXPANSIONISTS AND THE COLONIZATION SOCIETY OF JAPAN

After the loss of the American West and Hawai'i as sites of expansion in 1892–1894, the discourse on overseas development entailed a much wider range of educated Japanese, albeit with constant interjections from transpacific immigrants and recent returnees from the United States. Because the three brands of national expansion (eastward/transpacific, northward/continental, and southward) became increasingly distinct in terms of their relationships to state power, sovereign control, and local race relations after 1894, pundits fervently deliberated on where and how to expand, as Tokyo began to steer the national policy toward extending a Japanese sphere of influence in East Asia in the form of territorial acquisition by military means. Established in March 1893, two months after the *haole* coup d'état against the native Hawaiian monarch, the Colonization Society provided hundreds of Japan's political elite, intellectuals, and business leaders with a unified public forum to discuss what the future might hold for the expansive race and empire in the greater Pacific basin. While expansionistic Liberal Party bosses, such as Hoshi Tōru, Inoue Kakugorō, and Kataoka Kenkichi, were among the society's chief founders, Enomoto Takeaki, the former cabinet minister, assumed its presidency, revealing its close ties to segments of the Japanese government, especially the foreign ministry.[3] The society constituted what historian Carol Gluck calls a key "institution of ideological dissemination" in the formative years of Japan's empire making. It allowed a diverse group of expansionists from within and without Tokyo to spell out their visions for alternative Japanese frontiers after what appeared to be the white takeover of Hawai'i and North America.[4] For the first time, a common discursive space took shape in Japan for the three schools of expansionisms through the society's monthly journal, periodic lectures, and public meetings.

The Colonization Society encompassed two major factions of Japan's expansionists when the nation commenced its state-sponsored imperialist ventures in Northeast Asia in the late nineteenth century. One faction had its organizational base in the Oriental Society (Tōhō Kyōkai). Comprising bellicose intellectuals and oligarchic statesmen, it leaned toward continental and southward expansionism while casting its imperialist gaze toward China, Manchuria, Siberia, Korea, and sometimes also the Philippines, Indochina, and Thailand/Malay Peninsula. These expansionists, including core members of Seikyōsha, found it necessary to form a race-based unity in greater Asia under Japanese leadership to fend off western encroachment. To them, mass emigration and colonization, backed by strong state/military power, would be a first step toward that goal. The white control of California and Hawai'i further gave a significant boost to that contention. While taking part in public discourse on imperial Japan's future path, this group formed an ideological and institutional underpinning of the Kokuryūkai (Black Dragon/Amur River Society).[5] As historian Jun Uchida shows, some of these early pan-Asianists, such as Sugiura Shigetake (Jūgō), "brought a vast array of territories within [their] purview" of southward "maritime" expansion as much as they held onto another "basic . . . vector," that is, continental expansionism that focused on China.[6] Some remigrants from Japanese America were connected to this group.

The other leading faction of the Colonization Society embraced settler colonialism in what traditionally had been defined as the "New World," that is, the Americas and/or Oceania. It included not only those who had advocated transpacific migration since the 1880s but also the inner circle of Enomoto, who had many followers in government bureaucracy, especially the ministries of foreign affairs and of agriculture and commerce, over which he had presided at one time. In the Colonization Society, most US-based pundits and recent immigrant returnees aligned themselves closely with this group's renditions of Japan's colonial future, often citing their own real-life frontier experience in the New World. Familiar names, including Sugawara Tsutau, Hinata Terutake, and Watanabe Kanjūrō, appeared on the roster of the society's board members and top officials.[7] Although transpacific expansionism temporarily lost steam during the Sino-Japanese War vis-à-vis the continentalist faction, the national search for a new Japan never excluded the Western (or Southern) Hemisphere because of the continuous intervention of these pundits—one that domestic armchair theorists, like career bureaucrats and intellectuals, could not simply ignore. Entitled *Shokumin Kyōkai hōkoku*, the society's monthly journal subsequently printed dozens of reports, travelogues, and commentaries on Mexico and other non–Anglo Saxon parts of the Americas. These transpacific expansionist writings dwarfed in number and substance their counterparts that covered other parts of the world. Because of Enomoto's close ties to the foreign ministry, a number of diplomats also produced some of these reports in the course of their official duty.[8]

The second half of the 1890s saw actual instances of Japanese settler colonialism that involved members of the Colonization Society on both sides of the Pacific. In this nascent phase of Japan's imperial formation, conscious efforts to colonize foreign soil were still largely unheard of except in North America, even though the migration of Japanese commoners had also taken place in parts of Northeast Asia. Existing studies and an analysis of Japanese passport statistics reveal that those who went to Korea and China before the Russo-Japanese War were mainly itinerant merchants and peddlers; seasonal fishermen; and women in the service sectors, most likely maids, cooks, waitresses, and prostitutes, not wives of male settlers. Although they often originated from similar geographic locations and shared a common rural class background, these early "continental" migrants did not operate within the purview of existing settler colonial discourse or imagination. According to meticulous research on Hiroshima emigrants, the numbers of agriculturalists and farmworkers bound for Korea did not increase until 1907.[9] Indeed, only after Japan's victory over Russia did China, Korea, and Far Eastern Siberia become generally recognized as rivaling the Americas in Japanese expansionist discourse, although some returnees from California and Hawai'i pioneered colonization efforts to create a new Japan in Manchuria and China before the widespread public acknowledgment of the potential for continental expansionism. In the wake of Japan's successful execution of imperialist war against China, the Triple Intervention of 1895—a diplomatic intervention by rival Russia and its German and French allies—effectively, if temporarily, canceled out its hard-earned dominance over Korea and China's Liaodong Peninsula. This turn of events allowed proponents of transpacific migration to remain influential in Meiji Japan's interwar public discourse.

Thus, during the latter half of the 1890s many ideologues of national expansion still cast their gaze on the Western Hemisphere, where they sought to build an outpost of expansive Japan through the transplantation of imperial subjects.

Indeed, the first semi-state-sponsored enterprise of overseas agricultural colonization took place in Mexico under the auspices of Enomoto Takeaki and his supporters in the Colonization Society. This expansionist statesman was something of a maverick, having once defied the imperial government by commanding a Tokugawa Shogunate naval fleet and briefly attempting to found an independent republic in Hokkaido. In the mid-1870s, as a rehabilitated public official, Enomoto advocated the purchase of the Caroline and Mariana Islands from the Spaniards in order to make Japan into a maritime power. Serving as the foreign minister, he then found himself in the middle of discussions on the frontier advantage of Mexico. In 1893, during his inaugural presidential address at the Colonization Society, Enomoto characterized "our eastern neighbor, [particularly] the Pacific seaboard of Mexico" as the most desirable "site of settler migration (colonialism)."[10] Echoing the perspective of transpacific immigrant expansionists such as Nagasawa Betten, he declared that the state of racial struggle was a crucial factor in his selection of Mexico. Contrary to that nation's "friendly" attitude, Enomoto argued, public opinion in the United States called for the "exclusion of other nations (races)," especially Japanese.[11] According to his positive view of Mexico, Enomoto had already ordered the establishment of a Japanese consulate in Mexico City and of the emigration bureau within the foreign ministry in 1892.[12] In his capacity as foreign minister and later through his proxies within the Japanese diplomatic corps, the Meiji statesman also dispatched four separate contingents of investigators—including foreign ministry officials—to assess prospects for mass migration and agricultural colonization in Mexico.[13]

Known as "Colonia Enomoto" or "Colonia Japonesa," Enomoto's project operated under the discursive sway of transpacific Japanese expansionists in California. Their "informed" discussion of colonial methodologies and racial struggle, especially the peril of white exclusionism, carried tremendous weight when members of the Colonization Society deliberated on where to emigrate and how to build a new Japan. Self-proclaimed US-based frontiersmen had already begun to adopt a favorable attitude toward Mexico from the standpoint of race. Not only would that country pose no resistance to "foreign" (nonwhite) settlers because of their innate friendliness, they predicted, but also Mexicans were allegedly "as spineless as Chinese and East (Asian) Indians," whose homelands had already been (semi-)colonized. Hence, they looked "easy to dominate"—so much so that Japanese newcomers would have little trouble rising to the status of a "master" race after "infiltrating Mexican society."[14]

Infected with similar racist biases, Takekawa Tōtarō spearheaded the rise of the new discourse on migration and colonization in Mexico, while Enomoto was probing the possibilities of mass migration and settlement there. Takekawa was a key ideologue in the San Francisco expansionist circle and a well-connected overseas member of the Colonization Society. Published in the California-based *Ensei*,

Takekawa's commentaries articulated his enthusiasm about Mexico, which Enomoto shared and incorporated into the society's central agenda. A typical argument, for example, defined the Latin American country as "a site for a decisive struggle of [racial] survival that ambitious men of the cherry-blossom nation (Japan) must undertake with bravery and grand tact."[15] After encountering white America's determination to monopolize its western frontier, Takekawa and his associates were no longer content with a vacuous discussion of a colonial fantasy— no matter how lofty and romantic it might have sounded—not supported by real action to achieve it. This frustration, backed by a sense of urgency following the racial situation in Hawai'i, led Takekawa to attribute the failure to stop white ascendancy to the complicit attitude of homeland political elites and armchair expansionists. He accused them of indulging in the comfort of a luxurious life while casually spewing ideas they would never take up on their own. "The time has come," Takekawa thus urged, "for our compatriots to leap out of complacency and inaction with determination to put them in the middle of a great battle on the tablelands of Mexico."[16] Enomoto was among those who were moved by this appeal from across the Pacific.

According to Takekawa, the first step was to organize "investigative expeditions" to that country, and California Japanese should assume a primary responsibility in that endeavor. A number of San Francisco–based Expedition Society members and their associates acted on this vision, embarking on extended trips from California to Mexico, as well as other Latin American destinations, such as Guatemala, Nicaragua, Panama, and Peru. Some of their reports were published in the Colonization Society monthly in Tokyo, followed by a 330-page "compendium on Mexican exploration" to "enable the [home] public to appreciate the suitability of colonial settlement and trade [there]."[17] More than thirty immigrant expansionists in San Francisco also organized a Spanish study group to equip them with the command of the language necessary for expeditions and future colonization efforts south of the border.[18]

Enomoto's private "investigative team," which consisted of founders of the Colonization Society, availed themselves of assistance from Takekawa's group during their eight-month "expeditionary mission" to Mexico. After their "investigation," the team met with local Japanese in San Francisco, where they echoed Takekawa's praise of the Mexican frontier, accentuating it with detailed and concrete descriptions of their own observations and experiences during their mission.[19] After their return to Japan, Enomoto's colonial investigators presented a series of lectures at the Liberal Party's assemblies with a formal recommendation for mass migration to and agricultural colonization in Mexico, which the Colonization Society subsequently adopted as its first sponsored project.[20]

Based on the careful assessment of voluminous reports and testimony produced by both his investigators and Takekawa's San Francisco group, Enomoto selected the southern state of Chiapas along the Mexico-Guatemala border.[21] Between 1894 and 1896 Enomoto and his allies in transpacific settler colonialism used the Colonization Society as a platform for fund-raising and logistical support until the formal incorporation of the Japan-Mexico Colonization Company. They also felt that the building of stable migration and economic circuits between the homeland and an overseas settlement would require the control of transport routes by the Japanese capital and state. Enomoto filed with the minister of transportation a formal petition for "shipping lines to Mexico and Australia." At that juncture, the Japanese government considered it a first priority to start a regular steamship service to Southeast Asia and Australia, followed by the European and North American routes, in that order. Enomoto insisted that a shipping and transport service with Mexico was "most urgently needed" because the ports of "Mazatlan, Manzanillo, and Acapulco constitute[d] access points to the most promising sites of settlement colonies and trading posts [for Japanese]."[22] Although regular steamship service to the Mexican Pacific seaboard and other Latin American ports had to wait until 1910, Enomoto's pet project received enthusiastic support from within and without the Colonization Society, including segments of Tokyo's government brass. Once the Japan-Mexico Colonization Company was formed with a capital of 200,000 yen (about $100,000) in the summer of 1895, Inoue Kakugorō, a then national legislator, and Nemoto Shō, a Liberal Party member and onetime student immigrant in San Francisco, joined Enomoto as its board members and major shareholders.[23] In 1896, with the Japanese consul in Mexico City serving as intermediary, Enomoto struck a formal deal with a Mexican official for the purchase of 160,550 acres in Escuintla, Chiapas. As Enomoto often stressed, this agricultural colonization should serve as a precedent for Japan's future policy of concerted settler colonialism.[24]

Established in the spring of 1897, Colonia Enomoto represented the first entry of Japanese settler-colonists into the Latin American country. Designated one of the formal colonization projects commissioned by the Mexican government, the Escuintla Japanese holding welcomed a group of thirty-four newcomers from Japan in May. The composition of this group resembled the immigrant-initiated precedents in California and Washington, in which a handful of "enlightened" leaders deliberately took on the task of guiding and managing common laborers. Six leaders of the thirty-four settlers were indeed highly educated, with specialized knowledge of and skill in agricultural science; the vast majority came from farm villages.[25] With a goal of developing a large-scale plantation, they started coffee cultivation. Yet before the first batches of coffee plants yielded crops, Colonia Enomoto fell apart. Some members found the project mired in a constant shortage of funds; others, especially laborers, were dissatisfied with living conditions and contractual terms. Homesickness, illness, and poverty further depleted community morale in this colony, already divided along class lines. Several fieldworkers fled Colonia Enomoto to seek assistance from the Japanese consul in Mexico City, foreshadowing the quick demise of the first Japanese settler-colonial venture in Latin America.[26] Some remaining settlers nonetheless put down roots in Chiapas, creating the backbone of what would become the Japanese ethnic community there—the celebrated origin of present-day Japanese Mexico.

If Enomoto's project—even in its failure—resulted in a permanent, albeit modest, footing for Japanese settlement in southern Mexico, the contiguous frontier of Guatemala (only fifty miles south of Escuintla) featured another semigovernmental effort of Japanese settler colonialism in the Western Hemisphere with members of early Japanese America as the driving force. In 1894 a group of Seattle immigrant expansionists led by Itō Yonejirō and Arai Tatsuya joined forces to schematize the sustained importation of Japanese masses into Guatemala. The business of large-scale labor transport that they envisaged was supposed to be interwoven into a broader effort to build a new Japan in Central America. At that juncture, because Enomoto's inner circle were too busy drafting their own blueprint for Mexico to provide support for this Guatemalan scheme, the Seattle group looked to their allies in the Liberal Party establishment, especially Hoshi Tōru, the former speaker of the House of Representatives and a board member of the Colonization Society. To investigate the local customs, economy, and "racial" conditions, Itō first set out on an "expedition" to Guatemala. Through the agency of Hoshi and his friend in the Japanese cabinet, the Seattle expansionist successfully arranged a meeting with Guatemalan officials and local plantation owners, which allowed Itō to masquerade as someone in an official capacity negotiating for the Japanese government. Convinced of the country's colonial potential and the profits to be made in a labor-transporting enterprise, Itō and his associates then returned to Japan to seek the formal endorsement of Hoshi and other like-minded statesmen and entrepreneurs connected to the Liberal Party, as well as members of the Colonization Society. Greatly intrigued by Itō's report, Foreign Minister Mutsu Munemitsu pledged his full support and assigned a diplomat to the task of formal research and assessment in Guatemala.[27]

Itō's depiction of Guatemala as a "promised land" paralleled Nagasawa Betten's thesis on racial struggle and the US-style frontier discourse that underpinned it. In order to emphasize the advantage of systematic labor migration and Guatemalan colonization, Itō gave a lecture at the Colonization Society in January 1895 and subsequently published a lengthy two-part report in its monthly journal.[28] The Seattle immigrant particularly stressed agricultural and commercial opportunities, good climate, easy accessibility from Japan, and most important, what he called a "racial advantage" that Guatemala would offer. Referencing his own firsthand experience in the United States and the recent white takeover of the native Hawaiian monarchy, Itō contended that the most crucial step toward successful colonization was to choose a land with residents of a "lower cultural standard." He compared the people of Guatemala with the "Kanakas" of Hawai'i in terms of their "tropical" propensity for "laziness" and "spinelessness" that allegedly made them incapable of defending their own nation, let alone coping with racial competition with civilized settlers. In Guatemala, just as in Hawai'i, Japanese immigrants, including the common laboring class, should be able to "overwhelm" the local "Indians" and "mestizos" and eventually seize economic, if not sovereign, control of Guatemala through peaceful domination and assimilation. As long as mass migration resulted in the settling of that country with a sufficient number of Japanese, Itō reasoned, their higher level of "enlightenment and civilization" would guarantee racial ascendancy.[29] And there was no concern about white Anglo-Saxon settlers posing a challenge or obstruction to Japanese development in that part of the Americas. These "findings" and racial arguments resonated with the similar set of presumptions about Mexicans that Enomoto and Takekawa expressed.

Despite its ideological appeal, however, the time was not ripe for Itō's venture, because no Japanese steamship company had the resources to enable large-scale passenger transportation across the Pacific at that juncture. It was not until 1896 that the first regular transpacific shipping service began between Yokohama and Seattle.[30] Moreover, unfortunately for the Seattle group, 1894 saw the outbreak of the Sino-Japanese War, which not only halted the nonmilitary use of steamships but also kept the government preoccupied with East Asian geopolitics. The ambitious dream of Japanese settlement in Guatemala was quickly buried in oblivion. Yet the collaborative relationships and personal ties between immigrant expansionists and state officials fostered by this abortive project and others proved vital for subsequent developments in the history of borderless Japanese settler colonialism.

TRANSPACIFIC FRONTIERSMEN IN NORTHEAST ASIA AND THE NAN'YŌ

Because US-based expansionists, returnees, and their allies in the Colonization Society dominated the discourse on national expansion, their rendition of settler colonialism generally prevailed in valorizing Latin America, especially Mexico and its vicinity, as settler migrant destinations. Yet although the three divergent schools of expansionism allowed for contingency and flexibility in ongoing national debates concerning which frontier to colonize, Japan's victory over China and its subsequent acquisition of Taiwan in 1895 made the Asian continent, Southeast Asia, and even Oceania look increasingly attractive. Here again, transpacific expansionists helped project—and practice—a US-bred frontier vision on Japan's surrounding regions. Combined with the ascent of American Anglo-Saxonism that compounded the closure of Hawai'i and California, the successful conclusion of the Sino-Japanese War energized and empowered segments of the Colonization Society's membership, as well as government and military officials, who had imagined Japan's colonial destiny on the Asian continent. For a short time during the mid-1890s, Korea and Manchuria came to dwarf other parts of the Asia-Pacific basin in the Japanese expansionist imagination. The Triple Intervention of Russia, Germany, and France resulted in Japan's retrocession of the Liaotung Peninsula to China and its political retreat from Korea, and this unexpected setback provided the background for the subsiding of "continental fever" and the resurgence of the idea of colonizing Mexico, exemplified by Enomoto's 1897 venture.

This shift in the Japanese expansionist gaze toward their Asian neighbors conforms to emigrant passport statistics. Data from 1893, for example, reveal that only 1,676 passports were issued for Korea-bound emigrants, but in 1895 a total of 10,391 were issued, more than a sixfold increase. The percentage of Korea-bound passports compared to that of total passports issued annually almost quadrupled, from about 12 percent to 46 percent between 1893 and 1895. Yet the figure suddenly dropped by more than half, to 4,745, in 1896—only about 17 percent of total passports issued to emigrants. In the 1896–1902 period, the number of passports issued to those bound for Korea hovered between 3,000 and 5,000, with a total of 35,434 emigrants, and the number of China-bound emigrants was 29,052.[31] The United States and Hawai'i, meanwhile, drew 31,231 and 74,705 emigrants, respectively, during those seven years (see table 1). Although most of these emigrants were average people, not self-conscious settlers, the ebb and flow of the statistical figures mirrored the malleability of Japanese expansionist discourses and practices.

In this context, many members of the Colonization Society—especially those connected to the pan-Asianist faction—found it an opportune time in the mid-1890s to extend the Japanese sphere of influence westward toward Korea and China or even southward toward Southeast Asia and Oceania. A number of transpacific expansionists likewise demonstrated their characteristic adaptability, switching their allegiance to a new cause of Japanese development in Northeast Asia in tandem with Japan's military conquest (see map 2). The post-California trajectories of Ishibashi Usaburō, a leading member of San Francisco's Expedition Society, provide a good glimpse of how North America and other frontiers of the Asia-Pacific basin appeared to be mutually compatible and hence interchangeable, depending on the variable balance of power in the local context and international relations. Leaping from transpacific expansionism to continental/southward expansionism, Ishibashi tried his hand at starting an agricultural settlement in Thailand through the transplantation of Japanese settler-farmers between 1894 and 1895. It was the first attempt of its kind in Southeast Asia. Born in 1869, this *shizoku* transmigrant was heavily influenced by the Japanist brand of expansionism, and after studying English in Tokyo, he set sail for California in 1888. Once in San Francisco, Ishibashi was involved in the Expedition Society, frequently making contributions to its official bulletin. His interest in the vast New World, combined with youthful adventurism and bellicosity, led him to join a US naval expedition as a deck worker aboard the

TABLE 1 Numbers of Passports Issued to Emigrants for Selected Destinations, 1894–1912

Year	Hawai'i	USA	Canada[a]	Mexico	Peru	Brazil	Australia	Korea	China	Russia	World Total[d]
1894	4,036	1,497	779	6	2	—	963	6,065	402	1,418	16,726
1895	2,445	1,049	454	3	—	—	169	10,391	1,510	4,721	22,411
1896	9,486	1,764	938	15	—	—	843	4,745	880	7,177	27,565
1897	5,913	1,945	261	21	—	43	351	4,547	4,588	4,899	23,857
1898	12,952	2,936	2,532	—	—	—	1,128	4,987	2,929	3,375	33,297
1899	27,155	6,942	2,853	1	814	—	258	4,701	1,973	4,001	51,057
1900	4,760	10,562	3,247	1	—	—	314	4,327	7,539	5,818	41,339
1901	2,982	1,986	69	152	—	—	427	4,843	5,686	4,903	24,034
1902	11,457	5,096	490	187	—	—	255	3,026	5,457	4,354	32,900
1903	9,091[b]	5,215	455	281[b]	1,303[b]	—	220	4,258	6,005	3,881	34,157
1904	12,621	3,490	341	1,261[b]	—	—	222	5,113	3,302	8[b]	27,377
1905	7,146	3,134	329	374	—	—	60	523	5,256	230	19,466
1906	30,393	8,466	1,098	5,321	1,000	—	36	—[c]	5,191	5,233	58,851
1907	14,758	9,618	3,613	3,945	108	15	48	—[c]	3,808	5,522	43,627
1908	3,619	3,214	730	18	3,026	709	40	—[c]	2,842	5,089	21,344
1909	1,273	2,002	344	13	1,276	16	26	—	2,623	6,503	15,740
1910	1,921	2,900	629	37	492	847	1,053	—	2,478	8,771	21,899
1911	2,950	3,895	865	60	411	9	386	—	2,143	16,216	29,950
1912	5,243	6,021	1,125	74	713	1,125	52	—	2,030	650	20,811

SOURCE: "Kaigai ryoken uketori jin'in," in *Nihon Teikoku tōkei nenkan*, vols. 14–32 (1895–1912).
[a]The source sometimes offers separate figures for "Vancouver" and the rest of Canada. This table shows the combined numbers.
[b]The figures in the source appear to be erroneous and/or typos. Instead, Japanese foreign ministry statistics on "emigrants" are provided here.
[c]Only a negligible number are presented in the source. The vast majority of Japanese began to travel to Korea without passports after 1905.
[d]The numbers in each row do not add up to the totals in the "World Total" column because the figures in miscellaneous/minor locations are not included in this table.

USS *San Francisco* during the Chilean Civil War in 1891. After the ship stopped at Panama, he opted to jump ship in Lima, Peru, to reach Iquique on foot across the Chilean border. He intended to see not only modern military combat but also a Latin American frontier with his own eyes. Though he was also momentarily enchanted by the idea of finding a way from there to Southeast Asia via Polynesia, Ishibashi decided to return to California in early 1892 with a renewed passion for settler colonialism in the Americas.[32]

In San Francisco, however, the first organized exclusionist agitation against the Japanese disillusioned this eccentric young expansionist, inducing Ishibashi to rekindle his interest in Southeast Asia. To Ishibashi, Thailand registered as one of the few "open" frontiers unmolested by white men in the region, but the cession of Laos to France after the Franco-Siamese War of 1893 resulted in his developing an intense feeling of urgency to make a move there. Typical of those with colonial

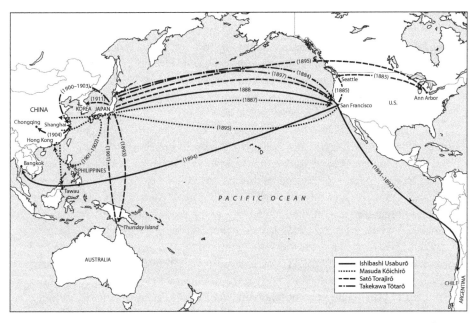

MAP 2. Remigration of self-styled frontiersmen from Japanese America, 1890s–1900s. Map by Bill Nelson.

delusions of grandeur at that time, Ishibashi thought big, imagining that systematic agricultural colonization would pave the way to "the [eventual] infiltration of Japanese residents into the [Thai] government," "the control of railroad rights," and even the "purchase of [parts of] the larger Malay Peninsula."[33] All these developments, according to him, would be necessary for Asia, under Japanese leadership, to fend off the threat of westerners.

Ishibashi's hostility toward white encroachment on Asia formed an ideological bridge to some key advocates of pan-Asianism, the rising political faction in the body politic of Meiji Japan, who specifically sought Japan's colonial destiny in the Asian continent and the Nan'yō. Having grown up in northern Kyushu, the former Expedition Society member had maintained close ties to members of the ultranationalist Genyōsha, the parent body of the Kokuryūkai that would soon play a notable role in consolidating political support for a war against Russia and the seizure of Korea and Manchuria under the banner of "Greater Asianism" (*dai-ajia shugi*).[34] Through a network of ultranationalists, Ishibashi forged a partnership with like-minded capitalists, government officials, and military men whom he could not otherwise have had access to. Part of the operating funds for his Thai agricultural colonization, for example, came from Tsuda Seiichi, a Kumamoto-based expansionist entrepreneur who later attempted (albeit in vain) to build the first sugar plantation in Colonial Taiwan with a few dozen settlers from Japan.[35] In the meantime, a former army officer named Iwamoto Chizuna was acting on his own belief in southward expansionism to negotiate with Thai officials for the lease of agricultural fields outside Bangkok and the importation of Japanese farmers there. Ishibashi decided to collaborate with Iwamoto, volunteering to sink the first Japanese plow into Thai soil and set up the basis of Japanese development there as the representative of the newly established Siamese Colonization Company (Shamu shokumin kaisha). Miyazaki Torazō (Tōten), famous for his pan-Asianist support for Emilio Aguinaldo during the Spanish-American War and for Sun Yat-sen during the Xinhai Revolution in 1911, joined Ishibashi and Iwamoto in transporting separate contingents of thirty-two and twenty agricultural settlers in 1894 and 1895, respectively. Though the settlement collapsed soon afterward, Ishibashi organized a small banking scheme and ran an import/wholesale store in Bangkok—a basis of the growing Japanese presence before World War II.[36]

Connected to the Japanese Patriotic League of San Francisco, Masuda Kōichirō was another former California resident who strove to transplant the torch of Japanese development in Southeast Asia after the rise of white racism on the US frontier (see map 2). After eight years of schooling and labor in Japanese America between 1887 and 1895, this transpacific remigrant directed his colonialist gaze southward, first toward the Philippines and then toward British North Borneo. Despite the difference in approach between Masuda's pragmatism and Ishibashi's grandiosity, both men were moved by a similar sense of anxiety and mission in their respective endeavors of racialized settler colonialism in Southeast Asia. Whereas the rising tide of French colonialism propelled Ishibashi to seek intervention in and around Thailand, the extension of US colonialism to the western Pacific induced Masuda to do the same during the Philippine-American War. After engaging in various business activities in Japan and China to create capital, Masuda joined forces with a relative to set up a coastal trade network between Nagasaki, his home region, and Manila. His ship, loaded with merchandise, was diverted by US authorities, who had already developed a fear of Japanese encroachment—political, economic, and racial.[37] Unable to enter the US-controlled Philippines, another lost frontier, Masuda took refuge in Hong Kong to sell off all the cargo and raise funds for a new venture. At the time he felt there were many "cracks" in the British-controlled regions of Southeast Asia, where a small number of Britons were only interested in setting up administrative colonies without a large-scale influx of their own settlers. North Borneo particularly looked like an open frontier that welcomed foreign newcomers and was eager to offer them land concessions for economic development. In 1902 Masuda assembled a group of like-minded Japanese for his new project of agricultural colonization. When Masuda and a dozen other Japanese traveled to Sandakan, the home of the British North Borneo Company and the regional governor's office, British custom agents and the police chief indeed welcomed the

Government House,

Sandakan 29. 4. 1903.

I am prepared to give Mr. Masuda and his friends if they can find a Capital of about $ 10,000 a land concession in Sebatik Island opposite Tawao on the East Coast of North Borneo,

Say one thosand acres and at the end of five years for every acre of land cultivated a further grant of two acres.

The option of taking of the concession is left open for 8 months-i. e. to the 31st. December 1903.

After it is taken up there must be 200 acres planted up every year.

There will be no rent for 3 years and after that 50 cents per acre per anum.

This concession carries no mineral rights but the concessionaire may work Timber on payment of a royalty of one cent per cubic foot and the usual Export duty.

He may also work Jungle produce on taking out the usual passes and paying the usual duty.

The lease for the land will be for 999 years.

Sd/— E. W. Birch.

Governer B. N. B.

Government House,

Sandakan 29. 4. 1903.

If Mr. Masuda who is the bearer of this note imports Japanese Labors in to British North Borneo. I undertake that they will be given every protection by British Officers and I am prepared to give any undertaking or reply to any questions which the Japanese Gov't may requir or ask.

Japanese Labors to work Coal mines or engager in agriculture will be welcomed in the state.

Sd/— E. W. Birch C. M. G.

Governer of British North Borneo,

and Labuan.

FIGURE 2. Masuda Kōichirō's settler-colonial contracts in British North Borneo, April 29, 1903. *Source:* Masuda Kōichirō, "Boruneo Kigyōkai shuisho," 1909. Courtesy of the Saga Prefectural Library, Japan.

newcomers from Japanese America and Japan.[38] Masuda's party then traveled to the less-developed region of Tawau for "frontier conquest."

Intending to lease the entire British portion of nearby Sebatik Island for 999 years, Masuda's enterprise began with the clearing of tropical forests. In April 1903 his settlement received the formal approval of the governor of British North Borneo in Sandakan, who promised the concession of one thousand acres in return for the clearing of two hundred acres for each of the first five years (see figure 2). Masuda and his partners were also entitled to an additional two acres for every acre of land cultivated. In order to facilitate their work, they were also granted the right to "import Japanese Laborers in to British North Borneo (sic)," with an additional note that the immigrants would be "welcomed in the state."[39] In his published appeal, Masuda told his "friends and others [in Japan] who have small capital to join in opening up this country," where "living is cheap and the laws are equal to any British Colony."[40] In the absence of race-based discrimination, he felt success was guaranteed, since "the enormous quantity of virgin forest affords an unlimited supply of the best woods for every purpose."[41] The export of lumber from his Sebatik colony to Hong Kong and Taiwan went well for several years, until conflicts with other Japanese residents led to its folding.

Named the Asahi Shōkai (Rising Sun Mercantile Company), Masuda's logging business branched out into pearling and farming. His California connections proved to be crucial in the diversification of his economic endeavors in North Borneo. In 1906, for the harvest of natural pearls near Semporna Masuda partnered with Watanabe Kanjūrō, an old friend from his San Francisco days, who recruited Japanese divers in Nagasaki for this enterprise. A contemporary observer expressed optimism about the venture, since there was only small-scale, German-owned competition in North Borneo. Indeed, Masuda's pearling business survived through the 1930s, and he remained a central figure in the industry there.[42]

In early 1909 another transnational collaboration between Masuda and Watanabe kicked off full-scale agricultural colonization on Sebatik Island, near the town of Tawau, where the large tract of cleared land was now ready for planting. Incorporated as the Borneo Enterprise (Boruneo Kigyōkai), the company enlisted the support of prominent statesmen, peers, and military men of Japan, including Koga Renzō, future head of the Cabinet Colonial Bureau, as well as Ozaki Yukio, the mayor of Tokyo. Its statement of purpose stressed the suitability of British North Borneo for Japanese development in terms of its "land, weather, and political conditions" unlike exclusionistic "North America and Canada."[43] What Masuda and Watanabe called a "model colony" would be erected in North Borneo by ordinary Japanese—aged eighteen to fifty—with "healthy bod[ies] and strong will," who would be treated as full members if they invested 250 yen ($125). Although it was a considerable amount of money, it was not out of reach for average emigrants. A decade before, a Hawai'i-bound plantation worker, for example, had to possess at least $50 to be admitted as a lawful immigrant. Indeed, because Masuda's firm was specifically designed to allow ordinary people to partake in the development of Japan's new frontier, it did not take the Borneo Enterprise much time to organize the first contingent of a few dozen emigrants from Japan.[44]

In 1916 Masuda secured financial and logistical backing through a partnership with another San Francisco friend named Inoue Keijirō for a cotton plantation enterprise in North Borneo.[45] While focused on the lumber business, Masuda had marveled at the quick growth of cotton plants, which he felt were not only "remarkably easy and cheap to cultivate . . . [but also] strong enough to take care of themselves."[46] Almost a decade later, he took up this promising native crop for commercial cultivation in cooperation with moneyed *zaibatsu* interests in Tokyo through the good offices of Inoue, a former member of the Japanese Patriotic League of San Francisco and a close associate of Watanabe Kanjūrō and Hoshi Tōru. Since his return from California in the early 1890s, Inoue had taken up various projects to promote settler colonialism and mass migration, which encompassed the operation of an emigration company that shipped thousands of labor emigrants to Hawai'i and Mexico, as well as the establishment of a rubber plantation in British Malaya and a palm oil farm in the Philippines. All these enterprises had attracted investment from Japan's leading financiers and business firms, and so did the cotton venture with Masuda.[47] Organized as the Borneo Shokusan Co. Ltd., the 1916 venture was capitalized at 1 million yen ($500,000) in Tokyo, and Masuda was instrumental in the negotiation of a 999-year lease for ten thousand acres near Sandakan. While Inoue and his business associates did their share of work in Tokyo for capital consolidation, Masuda requested that his local business partner—another former US resident—carry out experimental cotton cultivation on separate land, which the latter obtained on a palm oil farm owned by his brother-in-law.[48] During the first year of the company's operation, the clearing of the ten-thousand-acre estate had barely started, but the experimental farm produced an "extremely favorable result" in the year's cotton harvest, which prompted a Japanese diplomat in Singapore to anticipate a bright future for the enterprise.[49] To the dismay of Masuda and Inoue, however, this optimistic prognostication was not borne out in actual commercial success, making it impossible for them to catalyze a large influx of Japanese immigrant labor. Years later, despite the suspension of farming there, the ten-thousand-acre tract in North Borneo remained in the possession of the same company, because "Japanese navy brass desire[d] the preservation of its control," presumably for military strategic reasons.[50]

Except for modest pearl farming and operating hotels, Masuda's settler colonialism failed to grow into anything notable in the long run. Yet due to his status as a leading pioneer in the Tawau region, he played a central role in facilitating Japanese settlement building there. Fluent in English and well regarded by British administrators, this Stanford-educated resettler held the presidency of the local Japanese association, assisting newcomers and negotiating with the authorities on behalf of his compatriots. Often dubbed the de facto Japanese consul in Tawau, Masuda worked tirelessly to enhance the interests of "respectable" Japanese residents and the cause of national expansion. In order to provide a healthy atmosphere for stable family life in the settlement, he did not yield to corrupt influences from "ruffians" (buraikan) and "women of disgraceful occupation" (shūgyōfu).[51] In the area of economic development, the example of Masuda's cotton firm, which a diplomat praised as a "keystone" in this new hub of Japanese settlers, paved the way for the subsequent entry of Japan's monopoly capital, such as the Mitsubishi and Kubara conglomerates, into large-scale palm oil and rubber production during the economic boom of World War I.[52] In this regard, transmigrants from California, such as Masuda, functioned as the vanguard of Japan's expansive colonial capitalism despite their fiercely independent temperament. And his crusade for community moral reform was in line with the general structure of expansionist thought that sustained Japan's formal effort to build an empire of self-disciplined patriots and settler families—a Japanese America–inspired state policy adopted and carried out from the 1910s, as explained in chapter 3.

PURSUIT OF A RACISM-FREE FRONTIER ACROSS THE PACIFIC, AND THE RISE OF JAPANESE SETTLER ASSIMILATIONISM

Satō Torajirō was another former US resident, whose career as an ideologue and practitioner of migration and agricultural colonization crisscrossed the three schools of national expansionism after 1893 (see map 2). His activities epitomized the important roles that US-bred frontier trotters played in the formation of a full-fledged colonial empire in pre–World War II Japan. First, Satō's trajectory paralleled the phenomenon of multidirectional Japanese migration throughout the Asia-Pacific basin. Second, his endeavors over a span of forty years also exemplified the interconnected spread of agricultural settlement and colonization within and beyond imperial Japan's formal territories. And finally, backed by his firsthand experiences, Satō's work as an ideologue influenced—and reflected—the shaping of prewar Japanese thinking and policy on colonial race/ethnic relations and assimilation. Between the late 1880s and the early 1920s, he specifically helped steer Japanese mobility to and settler colonialism in Oceania and Northeast Asia after returning from the United States, tying together the Japanese "frontiers" of North America, northern Australia, and colonial Korea. Satō's trajectory was punctuated by white settler racism, and his idea of race/ethnic relations in a colonial context, especially his assimilationist gaze toward colonized Koreans, drew on the lessons learned from his bitter encounters with Anglo-Saxonist exclusion from North America and Australia. Those lessons taught him what *not to do* when Japanese sought to carry out their settler colonial endeavors as a master race in the Asia-Pacific region, thereby compelling him to get deeply involved in the politics of cultural assimilation in colonial Korea.

Born to a village headman in Saitama, Satō grew up in the midst of the region's grassroots entrepreneurship, which produced modern Japan's business tycoons such as Shibusawa Eiichi and Hara Zensaburō. With a keen interest in international trade and English literature, Sato first worked under Hara, a leading silk trader in Yokohama. In 1885 Satō went to the United States and subsequently lived the life of a working student in San Francisco and near Seattle.[53] It was during this time that he became acquainted with other immigrant expansionists—the politico-ideological ties he would maintain even after he moved to Ann Arbor to attend the University of Michigan. There, Satō was instrumental in publishing a newspaper called *Dai Nippon* (Great Japan), which was a de facto sister paper of the Japanese Patriotic League weekly in San Francisco. In its first issue, dated February 1889, his unsigned editorial called on emigrants to display strong national consciousness and patriotism as subjects of "Great Japan." His enthusiasm for "extending Japan's national power abroad" was imbued with a deep sense of indignation at being treated as "a Jap" in the United States.[54] Even before the rise of the anti-Japanese campaign in San Francisco, the problem of race had already troubled Satō greatly, because he had grappled with white supremacy outside the comfort zone of West Coast ethnic enclaves. In 1891 he returned to Japan in search of a new racism-free frontier.

Satō's expansionist gaze was locked onto northern Australia—a relatively neglected part of the New World, which had not yet formed strong sovereign control of its own as a white country. In 1893 Foreign Minister Mutsu Munemitsu, who also supported Itō Yonejirō's Guatemalan scheme, requested that Satō tour Oceania to assess the feasibility of Japanese emigrating there and establishing colonial enterprises. On Thursday Island, located within the Torres Straits between New Guinea and Queensland, he observed that although the pearling business was nascent but booming, it also suffered from a shortage of experienced divers. Satō had a perfect solution, one that would also render him a major player in the local pearling industry as well as the business of labor importation from Japan. Because he had married into a prominent merchant family in Wakayama, he had easy access to experienced Japanese divers in that prefecture, known for pearl making. After forging a new migration circuit that linked his home region and Queensland, Satō himself moved to Thursday Island and settled into what he deemed to be Japan's new southern frontier. His pearling business subsequently brought out hundreds of experienced divers and fishermen, contributing to the predominance of Wakayama-born Japanese in the prewar ethnic community of Australia.[55] With several dozen boats and over one thousand immigrants working under him, Satō was known as the "king of Thursday Island" by the late 1890s.[56]

The long reach of Anglo-Saxonism caught up to Sato in due time, however. As the sight of many vessels with Japanese divers and the rising sun flag alarmed more and more local Australians, Satō's competitors took issue with the success of the yellow men in their business. Spearheaded by white pearling ship owners, a growing cry for Japanese exclusion triggered full-fledged Yellow Peril scaremongering in Queensland, which resulted in the enactment by the provincial legislature of a ban on Japanese ownership of pearling boats, denial of their naturalization, and the refusal of new immigration from Japan by 1898.[57] As recent scholarship attests, this development was interlinked with the synchronized formation of white supremacy in California, Hawai'i, and Canada, constituting part and parcel of a transnational attempt to "draw the global colour line."[58] Rekindling his deep-seated indignation at white racism, the series of discriminatory measures by the Queensland legislature led Satō to protest loudly against Australians' quest for Japanese exclusion. Calling Queensland's action a "national insult," his angry manifestos urged the Colonization Society to lobby for diplomatic intervention by the Japanese foreign ministry.[59]

Nevertheless, Satō had no other choice but to grudgingly stand on the sidelines in the end, because the emergent Australian Federation swiftly incorporated Queensland's exclusionist legislation into its general "White Australia" policy by 1901. Since the Japanese population quickly shrank on Thursday Island, Satō gave up on settler colonialism in white-dominated Oceania, selling all his interests to his competitors before returning to Japan.[60] Despite the continuing presence of working-class Japanese in northern Australia's pearling industry and sugar economy, Oceania effectively dropped out of the cartography of Japanese settler colonialism.

As Anglo-Saxonism shut off the far south of the Nan'yō, Korea and China were restored to their pivotal places in the expansionist imagination of late Meiji Japan by the Russo-Japanese War. Despite Russian obstruction, a number of former US residents became torchbearers of continental expansionism during the first decade of the twentieth century. Satō Torajirō was one of them. Even after his twofold "defeats" on white-dominated frontiers, he remained firmly committed to the national mission of overseas development, but his settler-colonist career no longer unfolded outside the realm of Japan's sovereign influence. Indeed, Satō had learned two valuable lessons from his humiliating experiences in the United States and Australia: that Japanese settler colonialism must take place under the "rising sun flag" and that it must seek ethnic/racial harmony with local populations rather than the outright exclusion and domination exemplified by Anglo-Saxon settler colonialism.[61] The first lesson paved the way for Satō's business enterprise of land development and agricultural colonization in colonial Korea, and the second propelled him to spearhead the organization of the most important assimilationist society, the Dōminkai, in Seoul.

As soon as he returned from Thursday Island, Satō began to share the story of his sixteen-year stint as a self-styled pioneer of national expansion. In 1901 he obtained a small commercial newspaper in Yokohama, which he later renamed the *Yokohama Shinpō*, a predecessor of the present-day *Kanagawa Shinbun*. Through this newspaper, as well as books and public lectures, Satō linked his renewed advocacy of settler colonialism with the familiar theme of racial struggle. Private endeavors of colonization must follow in the footsteps of Japan's sovereign power, Satō argued, since "my own experience of the past decade taught me that [doing otherwise] would spoil all the labor and money invested, leaving nothing for Japan's advantage in the end." Outside the presence of the Japanese flag, the "alliance of white men" always jealously strove to stamp out signs of Japanese development. Thus, Satō contended, "raising the rising sun flag takes precedence over individual efforts of colonization as a matter of national policy."[62] State "imperialism and settler colonialism [we]re now inseparable," according to him.[63]

Satō felt that Korea and China should be the first sites to experiment with the fusion of state imperialism and private settler colonialism. This thinking motivated him to run successfully for the Japanese House of Representatives in 1903 before taking part in the Alliance against Russia (Tai-Ro Dōshik member.[64] At that juncture, Satō felt not only that Russia was not si from the standpoint of national security, but also that this imperial first obstacle for Japan when it looked to extend its sovereign politic into Manchuria through Korea. As Anglo-Saxon North America an ceania were sealing off their respective frontiers with exclusionary immigration laws, Satō warned his compatriots that the Japanese would lose their competitive edge as an "expansive race" unless Japan checked Russian encroachment. Otherwise, Japanese might become another example of "anthropological specimens along with Ainu" in a museum operated by a western power.[65] On the eve of the Russo-Japanese War, Satō's earlier racial experiences outside East Asia made him a full-fledged imperialist, who advocated for the militarily-led colonization of Korea and Manchuria with like-minded statesmen and jingoistic ideologues of the time.

Satō also comprised a prominent part of the nascent intellectual current that stressed the need for pan-Asianism—another lesson that this self-styled frontiersman had acquired from his encounter with white settler racism. This particular line of racial thinking resembled what Tokutomi Sohō—a leading political critic—later propagated as an "Asian Monroe Doctrine," which called for the construction of an autonomous racial bloc under Japanese leadership in Northeast Asia.[66] In one of his publications, Satō discussed the imperative of keeping Russia and other western powers out of the region by using his favorite point of comparison: geopolitics and racial exclusionism of the United States.[67] He argued that "while the United States has dared to enforce its invasive Monroe doctrine, we, the Japanese, shall rise up and carry out our Monroe doctrine for self-defense. We shall rise up with our neighboring nations for the future's sake. That is our manifest destiny."[68]

These "neighboring nations" included China and Korea, to which Japanese supposedly owed the duties of guidance and protection—an idea that drew from earlier proponents of what historians Eri Hotta and Jun Uchida described as "Sinic Pan-Asianism."[69] Calling it a "principle of the care and love for Chinese," Satō traced the origin of his ethnoracial and colonial paternalism to what he had seen in California and Thursday Island. The Chinese, according to him, lacked a martial temperament, whereas the Japanese came from the tradition of samurai warriors. Thus, the Chinese had not been able to defend themselves, nor had they been able to stand up for themselves when they had faced racial oppression in America or Australia. Armed with a martial spirit, the Japanese should act as guardians of the Chinese.[70] Satō's condescending views were far more blunt as far as Koreans were concerned. Due to their long history as a tributary nation, he argued, they were prone to kowtow toward the powerful. Thus, it would be necessary to "deem [Koreans] simply an inferior race and assume a stern attitude when dealing with them. . . . It is crucial to impress upon them thoroughly with

[Japanese] dominance and power, and the best policy to govern Korea would be to populate [its land] with as many [Japanese] people as possible to establish our solid (numerical) hegemony there."[71]

The lived experience of being racially persecuted compelled those like Satō to do away with outright exclusion or oppression in their interactions with "natives" and instead to advocate paternalistic assimilation, at least on the level of rhetoric. Yet their disavowal of white supremacist practice did not make them antiracist, just as Satō was quick to find deficiencies in Chinese attitudes and denigrated Koreans as perpetually subordinate—characterizations that resonate with Itō Yonejirō's portrayal of Guatemalans and Mexicans or Nagasawa Betten's criticism of "lazy" hula dancers in Hawai'i. To borrow historian Takashi Fujitani's concept, Satō's "polite racism," and the specific type of paternalistic assimilationism that stemmed from it, articulated his response to the US/Australian practice of racial exclusion, although he described white supremacy as a negative reference point, an example of how *not* to behave as a superior expansive nation and race. Bearing an uncanny resemblance to the US practice of "inclusionary" racism in the colonial Philippines, that reference point represented—and was publicly represented as—Satō's most prized "gift," which no one else could offer in the context of Japan's public discourse on national expansion and colonialism.[72] Armed with their firsthand knowledge of racial struggle on the New World frontiers, former US residents such as Satō stood at the helm of public debate regarding preferred terms of settler-native relations. Generally they acted as vocal advocates of interethnic/racial harmony and imperial national inclusion under Japanese leadership, thus contributing to the formation of Japan's assimilationist thinking along the lines of pan-Asianism. Unlike other pundits, however, Satō would find himself in a unique position, in which he would be able to *directly* influence the actual policy and program of colonial assimilation in Japanese-ruled Korea with US-inspired polite racism.

Soon after Japan's military victory resulted in the removal of Russian influence from the Korean Peninsula, Satō resumed his career as a facilitator of Japanese development by adopting Korea as his third and last frontier. Established in 1912, the Korea Agriculture and Forestry Company (Chōsen Nōrin Kabushiki Kaisha) offered Satō a means to practice his dream of settler colonialism under Japan's sovereign control. Hara Zensaburō, a Yokohama silk magnate and longtime supporter of Satō, sponsored his enterprise, just as he had funded Satō's newspaper operation in Yokohama. The company initially obtained over 120 acres near Seoul to develop rice fields and fruit orchards, but the land under its control expanded quickly to include large residential tracts for Japanese settlers in Seoul and Incheon, as well as forests and mountains for logging in Jeolla and Gyoengsang Provinces. Because Hara left it completely up to Satō to select which properties to acquire, the company's operation mirrored the latter's visions and wishes, that is, "to populate [the land] with as many [Japanese] people as possible" in colonial Korea.[73] In accordance with his desire to Japanize Korea with new immigrant settlers, Satō organized a "study group on the city planning of Seoul" with colonial officials and resident leaders in 1919.[74]

While facilitating migration and the permanent residence of Japanese new-comers, Satō did not neglect another mission of Japanese settler colonialism: the practice of pan-Asianist assimilation. In April 1924 he partnered with a well-connected bureaucrat of the colonial regime and a Korean aristocrat to establish the Dōminkai. This semiofficial assimilationist organization "was the largest in scale and occupied an especially important place in [Japan's] measure against the [Korean] nationalist movement," according to Jun Uchida.[75] As her study shows, the organization aimed to "demonstrate unity of Asiatics to the external world, on the one hand, and harmony of Japanese and Koreans inside Korea, on the other."[76] Following Satō's vision, which dovetailed with Japan's new policy of inclusionary "cultural rule," the Dōminkai's core membership drew from elite circles of "set-tlers" and "natives." Publicity campaigns, social reform efforts, and education con-stituted central elements of its assimilationist program.[77]

As Uchida argues, colonial officialdom and settler leaders wanted the Dōminkai to appease intensifying anti-Japanese sentiment following the wanton killing of several thousand Koreans in Tokyo during the Great Kanto earthquake of 1923.[78] It is nonetheless also important to consider the impact of US racism against Japanese immigrants as a crucial background, especially for Satō's initiative and involve-ment as Dōminkai's vice president. Between 1922 and 1924 anti-Japanese agitation in California culminated in the institutionalization of race-based exclusion at the level of federal policy, denying Japanese naturalization and further immigration. Both Japanese state officials and the public took great offense at these acts of "national humiliation," and the early months of 1924 saw a proliferation of anti-American political rallies and an upsurge in pan-Asianist sentiments in Japan. The Dōminkai's localized articulation of pan-Asianism—a variation of inclusionary colonial racism—was not divorced from this larger development, and it was this racial context that moved sixty-year-old Satō to take the lead in organizing three thousand prominent Koreans and Japanese while canceling his plans to retire, as was customary at that age.[79] Even under the protection of Japan's national sover-eignty, his life was still haunted by the effects of America's exclusionary racism.

Importantly, the impact of US racism not only inspired former leaders of Japa-nese America, like Satō, to adopt what they considered a contrary "civilized" tack, but it also propelled many home compatriots to embrace benevolent assimilation when they dealt with the colonized populations. In 1927, for example, the social wel-fare division of the Kobe municipal government compiled a lengthy report on the "problem" of resident Koreans, in which the writers warned against "socially exclud-ing and oppressing them" on account of their "cultural inferiority." Instead, the report advocated providing "equal opportunities" and fair treatment for colonized

Koreans in their midst, which it described as "a challenge [that had to be overcome by the civilized nation/race] in pursuit of justice." The official report rationalized this argument through repeated references to "unjust" American actions against Japanese immigrants. "The exclusion of Koreans—how can we justify it when we know that our own people have been so blatantly discriminated against by Americans?," the report asked rhetorically, and it continued, "insult, oppression, discrimination, and exclusion by white men (in California) should serve as concrete lessons and handy hints on solving . . . our [own] problem of Korean immigration."[80] Intertwined with the public conceit about the superiority of Japanese settler colonialism, this line of assimilationist thinking came to revolve increasingly around the counterexample of US racial exclusion through the early 1920s. In the context of Japan's efforts to build a multiracial empire, that thinking helped many imperial Japanese naturalize the inherent contradiction between the language of mutually beneficial brotherhood and the reality of brutal ethnic domination.[81]

Indeed, although Satō and other remigrants from Japanese America were prone to valorize assimilation as an antithesis of white settler practice, in actuality their idea harmonized perfectly with its alleged antipole: exclusion or elimination of a competing or inferior group as the "uncivilized" other under the state's regulatory disciplinary power. Satō's advocacy offers a glimpse into an important aspect of inter-imperial intimacy between Japanese and US settler colonialisms, both of which embraced the dual politics of racial inclusion and exclusion. In his insightful analysis of Euro-American settler colonialism, Patrick Wolfe deliberates on what he terms "structural genocide," in which "the concrete empirical relationships between spatial removal, mass killings, and biocultural assimilation" take hold, according to "the logic of elimination" of the native. A settler colonial practice of assimilation "can be (actually) a more effective mode of elimination than the conventional acts of genocidal violence," Wolfe argues, "since it does not involve such a disruptive affront to the [civilized] rule of law that is ideologically central to the cohesion of settler society."[82]

When this observation is applied to the United States of the early twentieth century, its "Progressive" politics of assimilation does not look qualitatively different from the simultaneous examples of legal exclusion, displacement and expulsion, and mass confinement that the white republic applied to its indigenous and minoritized populations, including Japanese Americans. US biological racism and its legal regime made it impossible for colored residents to achieve whiteness—the fundamental definition of being American—and hence equal national belonging, despite any degree of acculturation. In this context, America's liberal assimilationist ideology served as a nefarious accomplice in the overall oppression of racialized natives and minorities, for it offered a false sense of hope for full inclusion, thereby often inducing them to pursue of their own volition untenable sameness to white overlords. Moreover, the symbolic effect of assimilation still strikes as genocidal,

insofar as native's/minority's subjectivity, cultural heritage, and economic auton-
omy are all compromised in the process of their quest for something that is never
fully a possibility in the first place. Viewed from the standpoint of assimilation,
settler colonialism's logic of elimination is thus not about actually killing them; it
is all about the elimination of the native *as native*.

In the Japanese empire, the paternalistic assimilation that Satō and other former
US residents championed paralleled the dualistic expressions of American settler
colonialism and its racism.[83] Their adaptive settler colonialism sought to carry out
their brand of "structural genocide," with an emphasis on humanistic "coexistence
and coprosperity" in order to contrast it with US exclusionist politics. Satō's idea of
assimilation still entailed the elimination of colonized Koreans *as Koreans* before
containing their Japanized (but never fully Japanese) bodies in asymmetrical
social relations under Japanese ascendancy through acculturation and intermar-
riage. His professed benevolence to defeated Chinese and colonized Koreans drew
from Satō's firsthand experience of white racism in the United States and Australia,
where he had led a double life as a partner in frontier conquest with Anglo-Saxon
settlers and as a minority subject persecuted by them. It was that lived experience
that compelled Satō to renounce the practice of exclusion while articulating a
sense of entitlement to colonial domination and exploitation as strong as that of
white men in their settler societies. And it was that experience that led him to
adopt the language of "coexistence and coprosperity" as a Dōminkai leader even
when he turned a blind eye to the bloody suppression of dissident Koreans.

The oppressive nature of Satō's polite racism was never lost on Korean nationalists,
even though he constantly spewed sweet-sounding words such as "co-prosperity" and
self-righteously boasted about contributions to amicable ethnic relations through his
leadership in Japan's formal assimilation program. In 1926 Satō was almost assassi-
nated near the government-general building, and two years later he died of the aftereffects of the stab wounds.[84] But Satō's US-bred visions of Japanese development and
pan-Asianist assimilation survived as integral to imperial Japan's policy in colonial
Korea until 1945.

FROM JAPANESE AMERICA TO CHINESE FRONTIERS

China also occupied a pivotal place in the expansionist imagination of other
returnees from the United States on the eve of the Russo-Japanese War. Takekawa
Tōtarō of California exemplified this group of malleable settler-colonists who
switched their affiliation from transpacific settler colonialism to continental
expansionism, thereby forging new migration circuits between North America
and the Asian continent (see map 2). Having immigrated to San Francisco in 1884,
Takekawa had been a leading ideologue in expansionist circles and a frequent con-
tributor to Seikyōsha's journals back home until he returned to Japan in 1897.

Visionary and yet strongly business minded, he strove to maintain a balance between settler colonialism and realistic entrepreneurship as intertwined aspects of overseas Japanese development. Takekawa thus tried his hand at running a bookstore and boardinghouse in San Jose, also arranging farmwork for student migrants so that they could not only eke out a livelihood but also obtain practical training for their future endeavors on the New World frontier.[85] Like many other immigrant expansionists, he was compelled by the rise of white supremacy to leave the US frontier around 1893, but he changed his mind shortly after becoming involved in the organization of the Colonization Society in Tokyo and sailed back to California with his younger brother. For a few years, as already discussed, Takekawa was a leading voice in the extolment of a Mexican frontier in support of Enomoto's venture. Frustrated by escalating racist agitation, however, Takekawa decided to wrap up his thirteen-year struggle in California in 1897.[86] After returning to Japan, he became the editor of the Colonization Society's monthly journal and took charge of compiling the first comprehensive "library of colonization" for the society. Takekawa's brother, inspired by his enthusiasm for Mexico, chose to remain in California to become the head of a Japanese immigrant bank there. Fulfilling for himself Takekawa's dashed dreams, this brother actually sponsored large-scale agricultural colonization in Sinaloa, Mexico, as discussed in chapter 3.

After his return from San Francisco, Takekawa first directed his colonialist gaze toward Manchuria. In order to accumulate capital for a future venture, this converted continental expansionist started a small tobacco manufacturing business in Tokyo based on the skills he had acquired in California. Enomoto Takeaki assisted him in raising part of the start-up capital for this venture. At the same time, Takekawa strove to make friends with like minded individuals, especially those in the growing pan-Asianist camp. As the Boxer Rebellion of 1900 engulfed China in political turmoil, his groundwork paid off for Takekawa. First, he jumped at the chance of working in Beijing as a special correspondent for Seikyōsha's weekly journal. That stint was short lived due to quick suppression of the rebellion, so Takekawa turned to his new patron, Prince Konoe Atsumaro, who was the chairman of the House of Peers, a heavyweight in pan-Asianist circles, and a board member of the Colonization Society. Konoe helped arrange various business deals for Takekawa, including a procurement contract to service the Japanese expeditionary troops in Tianjin and Beijing, a construction deal to erect a pier in Dalian harbor, and importing coal from Kyushu to Tsingtao in partnership with his close friend from San Francisco days. But the meddling of Russians and Germans wound up ruining these ventures.[87]

Takekawa did not waver in his pursuit of an expansionist destiny on his new frontier. He moved from northern China to Shanghai, setting his gaze along the Yangtze River in Sichuan Province. In his racially conscious eyes, that interior region of Central-Western China registered as still an open frontier without a strong presence of European or American rivals. He was now determined to anchor an outpost of imperial Japan there by using logistically more convenient Shanghai as a gateway, just as California was to Mexico. Takekawa felt it necessary to involve the city's Japanese residents and sojourning migrants in his project, since overseas national development would take more than the hard work of a few committed expansionists. Takekawa believed that in order to turn ordinary "ignorant masses" into self-motivated agents of frontier conquest, educational efforts were indispensable for some two thousand Japanese in Shanghai and a few dozen residents in Sichuan. Local Chinese also had to be positively impressed by the leadership of Japanese as an engine of progress in civilization and industry.[88] Like many of his contemporaries, Takekawa began to express "Sinic Pan-Asianism," that is, Japanese solidarity with Chinese and the pursuit of benevolent assimilation.

Tapping into the repository of his California experience, Takekawa organized a newspaper company with his allies, first in Shanghai and then in Chongqing. Founded in December 1903, the *Shanghai Shinpō* was one of the oldest Japanese-language newspapers in the Chinese city.[89] Penned by Takekawa, its first editorial expounded on the special mission that the Japanese supposedly had to build a "new Japan" on the Asian continent: "Now the attention of every [imperialist] power is directed at Asia, and the problem of Asia focused on China. We are an Asian nation [like China], but in dealing with China's problem (to uplift and modernize Chinese), we . . . [must] conduct our affairs in concert with other (Western) civilized powers. Nay, because of our [unique] historical and geographic ties [to China], we cannot but move ahead of the other powers."[90] Specifically, Japanese of Shanghai were expected to take the lead in building new industries, railroads, and commercial and political outposts inward along the Yangtze River before the arrival of more Europeans and Americans. The region then would be a locus of overseas Japanese development. In many other parts of China, Takekawa lamented that white men had already monopolized colonial benefits without leaving much room for Japanese entry.[91]

An important outpost connected to Shanghai, Chongqing was his new frontier of choice in Sichuan. In early 1904, as the *Shanghai Shinpō* was about to print its third issue, Takekawa traveled up the Yangtze.[92] Because his goal entailed both the remaking of resident Japanese into full-fledged settler-colonists and of local Chinese into their faithful followers, the converted continental expansionist took up education as an important part of his enterprise in Chongqing. Reminiscent of America's rhetoric of uplift in its synchronic colonization of the Philippines, Takekawa's modernizationist project utilized a vernacular Chinese newspaper to enlighten local people about world affairs, especially Japan's purported struggle against western encroachment upon Asia, as well as the importance of breaking away from Qing feudalism. Published under Takekawa's editorship from October 1904, the *Chongqing Ribao* (*Jūkei Nippō*; Chunking daily news)—the first daily newspaper in the city—explicated Japan's position against Russia with detailed accounts of military battles in Manchuria. It also took pains to disseminate Takekawa's assertions that Japanese-style modernization would better serve as a model for Chinese than its western counterpart, from the standpoint of racial and cultural similarities.[93] A few young Chinese reformers, including his close friend and editorial assistant Bian Xiao-wu, collaborated with Takekawa in this venture. Although they worked with Takekawa in the reform movement for their own reasons, these Chinese associates comprised a significant driving force in grassroots local activism against the Qing government.[94]

Intertwined with this colonialist cultural diplomacy was Takekawa's second educational endeavor, to operate an "academy of Japanese studies" for young Chinese in Chongqing. With Takekawa as the principal, the school began instruction in March 1905, offering four different tracks of a multisubject program in Japanese for the duration of two to four years. The graduates were promised the chance to study in Japan after completing the program. Purportedly, this colonial education of sorts attracted more than one hundred Chinese adolescents in the year of its inception. For the purpose of uplifting young Chinese women, courses on Chinese literature and mathematics, arts and domestic skills, and Japanese language were made available at a separate school. Impressed by the apparent promise of Takekawa's enterprise, the Japanese foreign ministry committed financial subventions for the 1906 fiscal year.[95] This scale of close collaboration with the home government was generally untenable in the Americas due to the presence of a conflicting national sovereignty. With Japan's ascent as a major imperialist power, which could undermine Chinese sovereignty through unequal treaties and a threat of military attack, Northeast Asia seemed to present an opportunity for a close and effective partnership between individual agents of settler colonialism and their home state—a tangible benefit of continental expansionism.

Takekawa's third venture aimed at getting a Japanese-controlled industry started in the interior of China before white competitors could do so. Surveying local economic conditions, he started a match factory in Chongqing. Transactions in sulfur and the manufacturing of matches from that material had been placed under the tight control of the Qing government, and Chinese citizens were unable to get into the monopolized business. Takekawa evaded the restrictions because his Japanese nationality put him above Qing sovereign control and its economic policy.[96] This, too, illuminated the benefit and promise of continental expansionism under the national flag—one that was absent in North America or Oceania. In California, Takekawa and other expansionists had had to live as racialized minorities because of their background under the oppressive legal apparatuses that favored white Americans. Indeed, Japanese immigrants there were largely excluded from union-controlled manufacturing work, including none other than match making. In Sichuan Province, Japanese residents could enjoy extraterritoriality and all the other privileges reserved for virtual colonial masters. It thus became evident that race and sovereignty formed central matters of consideration even in individual practices of migration and settler colonialism. The flexible mobility of Japanese settler-colonists was often contingent on how these factors played out at a given historical moment between the specific political economies of the regions and countries in which they moved.

Punctuated by Japan's two imperialist wars in 1894 and 1905, the interwar period was marked by the emergence of a pivotal expansionist apparatus in Tokyo, namely the Colonization Society, which served as a central think tank and public forum for a desirable form of national expansion. While the society helped shape the migration circuits of Japanese settlers that connected North America with the Asian continent and the Nan'yō, the critical decade saw the upsurge of another institutional trailblazer in overseas Japanese development: emigration companies (*imin gaisha*). Primarily former US residents and core members of the Colonization Society spearheaded the business of massive labor emigration in order to incorporate rural Japanese commoners into the national expansionist mandate. They were the "ignorant masses" whom educated elites and self-styled frontiersmen had looked down upon but had viewed as a necessary part of their private settler colonial ventures. Between 1892 and 1908, emigration companies, which also functioned as a major vehicle of capital accumulation for aspiring instigators of settler colonialism, swallowed up the seemingly apathetic peasantry in the well-greased machine of systematic human trafficking by stream-lining the transfer of surplus domestic labor to foreign sites of ethnic community formation.

EMIGRATION COMPANIES AND THE SYSTEMATIZATION OF MASS MOBILITY FROM IMPERIAL JAPAN

In Meiji Japan, the initial attempt to organize an emigration company dates back to the Association of Kindred Minds for Overseas Emigration (Kaigai Ijū Dōshikai)—a corporate entity that Liberal Party heavyweight Hoshi Tōru established in July 1891 in cooperation with his US-based associates, including Watanabe Kanjūrō and Inoue Keijirō. Its expressed goal was to contribute to Japanese settlement and colonization through popular participation, but it was also tied to another goal of "freeing the innumerable poor from present difficulties" inside the Japanese archipelago.[97] Imbued with Malthusian fears of out-of-control population growth that appeared to be swallowing up the small island nation, Hoshi's vision of mass migration mirrored the ongoing politico-economic crisis that had hit rural Japan hard since the early 1880s. By 1885 that crisis had induced a number of antigovernment uprisings among small-scale landowning farmers—a linchpin of rural social

order—who found Tokyo's deflationary policy devastating to their family economies. In response, the Japanese government had implemented a state-sponsored
scheme of contract labor migration under a bilateral treaty with the Hawaiian Kingdom for selected rural individuals, totaling about twenty-nine thousand between
1885 and 1894. Known as government-contract migration (kan'yaku imin), this
state-regulated labor recruitment marked a reversal of Tokyo's standing policy
against international migration of ordinary Japanese, but its purpose was to enable
the economic rehabilitation of small landowning farmers and the enlargement of
Japan's foreign reserves through emigrant remittances. Yet by focusing on the
appeasement of the midlevel farming class, the state still imposed a number of
restrictions on who could leave home for overseas work and where they could go
under the rigidly controlled labor recruitment system. Moreover, permanent settlement in Hawai'i was not condoned, for contract immigrants were required to return
home after three years of sugar plantation work.[98] Proponents of national expansion
deplored these restrictions as a serious hindrance to the construction of a permanent Japanese colony abroad.

As previously discussed, Nagasawa Betten and Itō Yonejirō exemplified the
critical expansionist positions that called for a national proemigration policy without restrictions by making laboring masses integral members of a "new Japan."
They argued that common immigrants, even manual laborers, would be able to
function as contributing elements in settler colonization as long as they were
placed under the guidance of enlightened leaders.[99] The Colonization Society also
adopted this promigration agenda, demanding that the government consider the
meaning of migration from a long-term perspective—a perspective that appreciated not only its economic benefits but also migration's role in extending Japanese
influence externally and moderating the rapid population increase at home.[100]

Indeed, as historian Sidney Xu Lu argues, the problem of population control
had constituted an element that could not be ignored in Japanese migration discourse since the 1880s. The earliest Japanese translation of Thomas Robert
Malthus's An Essay on the Principle of Population came out in 1877, and several
years later Japan's first generation of expansionist ideologues, including Fukuzawa
Yukichi, already entertained the idea of overseas emigration and settler colonialism as a combined solution to anticipated problems of overpopulation and unemployment that seemed always to follow national modernization and technological
advancement.[101] Ever paranoid about overpopulation's anticipated perils, the social
elite of Meiji Japan started to detect the stifling effects of population "explosion" as
the end of the nineteenth century neared. By the outbreak of the Russo-Japanese
War, the fallout of industrial development was rampant in Japanese society in the
form of rigid class stratification and political disorder, catalyzing the subsequent
rise of socialist/anarchist movements against Japan's capitalist system and the
imperial institution itself. It was this domestic turn of events against which more

and more proponents of national expansion—especially armchair theorists and politicians in Japan such as Hoshi Tōru—came to understand the imperative of writing mass labor migration into their definitions of settler colonialism.[102] And in response, operators of emigration companies consciously adopted the Malthusian language of population control and surplus labor dispersal in order to justify their exploitative enterprise of labor migrant trafficking. In their eyes, promoting the emigration of jobless commoners was as much a patriotic act of social engineering as it was a buoy to the expansive colonial empire. Another pivotal goal, ruthless profit making, was conveniently subsumed under these nationalist expressions.

Emigration companies mushroomed in Japan between 1892 and 1907.[103] Although little information is available about the companies that were founded before 1898, researchers have surmised the existence of twenty-five entities between 1891 and 1898, or fifty-two entities between 1894 and 1910.[104] Established only five months after Hoshi's 1891 endeavor, the Nihon Kissa Imin Gōmei Kaisha (Nihon Kissa Emigration Company; later renamed Tōyō Imin Gōshi Kaisha) remained one of the most successful and long-lived firms due to its affiliation with the Nippon Yūsen Kaisha, Japan's top shipping concern.[105] Along with the Nihon Kissa, the Morioka Shōkai (Morioka Company), Kaigai Tokō Kabushiki Kaisha (Overseas Travel Company; hereafter Kaigai Tokō), Kumamoto Imin Gōshi Kaisha (Kumamoto Emigration Company; hereafter Kumamoto Imin), and Tairiku Shokumin Gōshi Kaisha (Continental Colonization Company; hereafter Tairiku Shokumin) ranked as the top five emigration companies in terms of the numbers of the migrants they handled (see table 2).[106] Of these firms, the Kaigai Tokō, Kumamoto Imin, and Tairiku Shokumin operated under the decidedly heavy influence of former US residents, especially those associated with the Japanese Patriotic League of San Francisco and Hoshi's inner circle. That is to say, one-half of the six major emigration companies had a strong and direct imprint of US-bred settler colonialism, while the other three firms also operated more or less under a similar vision that allowed them to rationalize profit making through labor migration in the nationalist language of overseas development.

The state deliberately lent politico-legal support to the production of this new infrastructure that catalyzed mass mobility and popular participation in overseas development. In 1894 and 1896, the basic set of regulations that specified the obligations of emigration companies were enacted in the name of "protecting" emigrant welfare and interest. The new national legislation defined an "emigrant" (*imin*) as "a person and his family who travel to foreign countries for the purpose of *labor*" (emphasis added). However, the laws tacitly encouraged—and legitimated—the manner in which labor migration was woven into the larger goal of Japan's overseas economic expansion and settlement under the activities of emigration companies. The kinds of labor that would qualify someone as an emigrant encompassed "farming, fishing, mining, [and] construction."[107]

TABLE 2 Major Emigration Companies, with Names of US Returnees and Residents in Management, 1894–1908

Company Name and Names of U.S. Returnees and Residents in Corporate Management	Location	Years of Operation	Total Emigrants
Kaigai Tokō Kabushiki Gaisha 海外渡航株式会社 (Hinata Terutake, Sugawara Tsutau, Matsuoka Tatsusaburō, Mitsutome Zensuke)	Hiroshima	1894–1907	13,975
Kumamoto Imin Gōshi Gaisha 熊本移民合資会社 (Inoue Keijirō, Yamaguchi Yuya, Watanabe Kanjūrō)	Kumamoto	1898–1907	12,020
Tairiku Shokumin Gōshi Gaisha 大陸殖民合資会社 (Hinata Terutake, Matsuoka Tatsusaburō, Mitsutome Zensuke, Murakami Taizō, Inoue Heisaburō, Shikitsu Rinketsu)	Tokyo	1903–1908	13,133
Emigration Companies that Merged with the Kaigai Tokō to form the Tairiku Shokumin			
Kōsei Imin Kabushiki Gaisha 厚生移民株式会社 (Shikitsu Rinketsu)	Wakayama	1897–1903	3,746
Tōhoku Imin Gōshi Gaisha (includes Chūgai Shokumin) 東北移民合資会社 (中外殖民合資会社) (Inoue Heisaburō, Shikitsu Rinketsu)	Sendai	1902–1903	1,291
Chūō Imin Gaisha 中央移民会社 (Murakami Taizō, Matsuoka Tatsusaburō)	Tokyo	1902–1903	609
Yokohama Imin Gaisha 横浜移民会社 (高田平兵衛)	Yokohama	1901–1903	856
Taiheiyō Shokumin Gaisha 太平洋殖民会社	Tokyo	1902–1903	405
Tosa Imin Kabushiki Gaisha 土佐移民株式会社	Kochi	1903	302
Other Independently Owned Emigration Companies with Japanese American Ties			
Omi Imin Shōkai 小見移民商会 (小見正孝) (Aoyagi Ikutarō)	Tokyo	1902–1907	1,622
Sendai Imin Gōshi Gaisha 仙台移民合資会社 (Ōtsuki Kōnosuke, Tomikawa Yūzō, Ueno Tōnosuke, Iwanaga Keijirō)	Sendai	1902–1907	1,777
Morioka Shōkai 森岡商会 (森岡真) (No former U.S. resident in management, but the company closely linked to Hinata Terutake)	Tokyo	1894–1921	18,313
No Significant Ties to US Returnees or Residents			
Tōyō Imin Gōshi Gaisha [Originally known as Nihon Kissa Imin Gōshi Gaisha] 東洋移民合資会社 (日本吉佐移民合資会社)	Tokyo	1891–1917	10,641

SOURCE: Adapted from Kodama Masaaki, *Nihon iminshi kenkyū josetsu* (Hiroshima: Keisuisha, 1992), 261; Yokoyama Gennosuke, *Meiji fugōshi* (Tokyo: Shakai Shisōsha, 1989 [reprint]), 168–195; and Kurabe Kiyotaka, *Tōge no bunkashi* (Tokyo: PMC Shuppan, 1989), 85–86.

These types of labor were what Takekawa Tōtarō, Itō Yonejirō, and other US-based expansionists had envisaged as integral to the task of laying the material basis of a new Japan on the frontier land. Neither commerce nor white-collar work was mentioned as eligible "labor" for an emigrant governed by the laws of 1894 and 1896. Although this skewed definition likely promoted class-based prejudice against the *imin* in prewar Japan, it also rendered ordinary "emigrant" and mass "emigration" inseparable from agrarian settler colonialism in the realm of public discourse and representation. Codified in national legislation, a consequence of this conflation was that "enlightened" immigrant leaders generally pressured common *dekasegi* (temporary) laborers to adopt the identity of—and act as—frontier conquerors by molding self-consciousness as members of the expansive race. Furthermore, critical differences between shifting labor immigrants and permanent settlers were often obscured not only in the laws of pre–World War II Japan but also in the minds of many Japanese people, for the same reason.[108]

In their endeavors to ship out common laborers and landless peasants from rural Japan to foreign sites of national development, emigration companies mainly looked south toward the Nan'yō and east toward the Americas. The most frequent targets of their human trafficking ventures were New Caledonia and Fiji, Thursday Island, and Northeast Australia, as well as Hawai'i, the western United States, and Mexico. The early enthusiasm over Oceania and the South Pacific waned quickly. In the early 1890s the first attempts at sending a large number of plantation workers to Polynesian islands proved a disastrous failure due to bad employer treatment and disease. In the French colony of New Caledonia and British-controlled Fiji, Japanese were lumped together with indentured Asian Indians and Chinese "coolies" in the local plantation systems, then deadly tropical epidemics debilitated the workers.[109] Oceania fell victim to exclusionary white racism, as Satō Torajirō's experience revealed. This chain of events marked the closing of the Nan'yō for emigration companies by the late 1890s. With much of Northeast Asia now inaccessible due to Russian dominance after the Triple Intervention, Hawai'i and North America, especially the US-Mexican borderlands, increasingly looked like the only viable destination for mass emigration from Japan.

Backed by the government's supportive legislation, the Kaigai Tokō embodied the emergent expansionist apparatus that tied together California, Hawai'i, and Tokyo/Hiroshima in the shipping of nearly fourteen thousand ordinary Japanese between 1894 and 1907.[110] Situated in Hiroshima, which had produced the largest number of Hawai'i-bound workers, the company enabled Sugawara Tsutau, Hinata Terutake, and a few other leading figures of the Japanese Patriotic League to draw a new transpacific map of commoner-based overseas development. In the spring of 1893, following the overthrow of the native Hawaiian monarchy, which they had tried in vain to stop, Sugawara and Hinata went back one last time to California to conclude an important business deal. Representing the newly established Kaigai

Tokō (then known as Hiroshima Kaigai Tokō), they signed a contract with large US businesses to serve as the exclusive agent to arrange employment for Japanese immigrants with railroads, mines, and farms in the American West, Canada, and Mexico. Sugawara and Hinata then entrusted this labor contracting business to their Patriotic League associates in San Francisco and departed for Honolulu to set up another labor contracting office there. Once they returned to Japan, they stood at the helm of the day-to-day management of the Kaigai Tokō headquarters in Tokyo.[111] Tying the origins of working-class emigrants to the places of their predetermined employment, this network, forged by the transpacific immigrant capital, facilitated mass mobility from rural Japan to Hawai'i, the western United States, and its contiguous southern borderlands.

Having observed the unwavering *haole* resolve to colonize Hawai'i, these men, especially Hinata, foresaw the end of state-monopolized Japanese emigration to the islands under the existing bilateral treaty with the native Hawaiian monarchy. It was inevitable, Hinata believed, that the white takeover of the islands' political sovereignty would lead to the nullification of the immigration convention, thereby creating new opportunities for his company to transport Japanese laborers across the Pacific. Intending to dominate the lucrative business of human trafficking, Hinata's firm partnered with Hoshi Tōru to lobby for the privatization of emigrant recruitment and transportation processes.[112] This political intrigue operated flawlessly, because Hoshi was a close political ally of Foreign Minister Mutsu Munemitsu, who was in charge of emigration-related matters. In the summer of 1894 Hinata's shrewd calculations paid off when the white-controlled Republic of Hawai'i refused the renewal of the bilateral migration agreement with Japan.[113] Tokyo promptly issued the first emigration-related edict to legalize private emigration companies for the recruitment and "protection" of "laborers." Picking up a large share of continuous working-class mobility to Hawai'i's sugar plantations, the Kaigai Tokō, as well as a few other smaller firms run by former US residents in so-called emigration prefectures, dominated and perpetuated an existing pattern of chain migrations—particularly from Hiroshima, Yamaguchi, and Kumamoto—to Hawai'i and North America. In addition to the Kaigai Tokō's 13,975 migrants, other smaller returnee-run emigration companies, such as the Tōhoku, Chūgai, Chūō, and Ōmi, handled from several hundred to over sixteen hundred each (see table 2)[114]

These companies did not just personify the first manifestation of imperial Japan's expansionist apparatus that aimed to promote settler colonialism through mass migration. Other implications and consequences were equally important. Owners and operators of emigration companies raked in enormous profits through systematic human trafficking, thereby using their financial power to interject their expansionist visions into national policy and government practice. Indeed, the successful political careers of former Japanese Patriotic League leaders owed much to their control of major emigration companies. Affiliated with the Rikken Seiyūkai

(Friends of Constitutional Government Party), which absorbed the Liberal Party, Sugawara became a member of the Imperial Diet in 1898, Yamaguchi Yuya in 1898, and Hinata in 1902. Because of their connections to Hoshi, who also controlled Tokyo's municipal politics, other returnees from California, such as Inoue Keijirō, Watanabe Kanjūrō, and Shikitsu Rinketsu, took part in the administration of the Tokyo metropolitan government.[115] Backed by their expertise in the matter of migration and overseas colonization, these political insiders held the upper hand in policy debate and formulation during the interwar years.

What lay behind their impressive political ascent was their virtual monopoly over access to the forced deposits that Japanese workers in Hawai'i had to make at the Keihin Bank under Japanese government mandate. Stipulated by Tokyo's 1894 regulations, the "protection" of emigrants entailed the creation of special funds based on deductions withheld from plantation workers' earnings. In order to cover the cost of unexpected return or emergency medical care, emigration companies were charged with this levying responsibility. Taking advantage of this role, Hinata and other heads of emigration companies allegedly misappropriated the emigrant deposits for their own benefit by establishing a special bank under their joint control in 1898. This conspiracy to usurp portions of emigrants' hard-earned salaries gave birth to the infamous Keihin Bank. Its business thrived, and its coffers swelled exponentially, as it monopolized the handling of emigrant remittances as well as insurance. The bank was said to engage in fraudulent and exploitative practices to maximize its profits. Until its corruption was uncovered in 1905 and provoked a mass immigrant protest in Hawai'i, the unholy alliance between emigration companies and the Keihin Bank afforded enormous wealth to Hinata and other architects of the transpacific human trafficking scheme, as well as their political patrons in the Liberal Party and its successor.[116]

Rivaling the Kaigai Tokō in the number of emigrants shipped, the Kumamoto Imin was another product of the US-bred vision of overseas development that quickly infiltrated the politics and economy of interwar Japan. In 1898 Inoue Keijirō, Yamaguchi Yuya, and Watanabe Kanjūrō joined forces to incorporate this firm after returning from San Francisco. Previously an aspiring agriculturalist in Sacramento, Yokokawa Shōzō acted as the company's representative in Honolulu before setting himself up as a national hero in Japanese Manchuria. Just like Hinata of Kaigai Tokō, these former California residents came from Hoshi's political inner circle. During the crackdown on Liberal Party activists in the mid-1880s, Inoue was a cellmate of Hoshi, and after his exile to San Francisco, he participated in the Japanese Patriotic League.[117] Inoue later collaborated with Masuda Kōichirō in the establishment of a Borneo cotton plantation. Yamaguchi was instrumental in the publication of the Patriotic League's newspaper. He and Sugawara were the first US returnees to win seats in the Japanese Parliament, which Yamaguchi did while serving as the auditor for the corrupt Keihin Bank. Watanabe was a live-in disciple at Hoshi's residence before he took a group of new immigrant settlers to the Pacific Northwest under his mentor's auspices in 1891.

A latecomer to the industry, the Kumamoto Imin turned its attention primarily to Mexico instead of Hawai'i, since the latter, albeit the largest market for emigration business, was already under the firm grip of the Kaigai Tokō. The Kumamoto Imin's strategy paved the way for the sudden rush of working-class Japanese to the US-Mexican borderlands between 1901 and 1907. In addition to market considerations, the company's choice of Mexico drew from the ideological baggage of the corporate owners, especially Inoue. Like many others who had directly experienced white racism, he had developed a propensity for adopting a racial lens when he addressed the question of national expansion. In a 1903 op-ed magazine article, for example, Inoue lamented that it seemed "virtually impossible for Japanese to erect a settlement colony in locations other than Mexico and a South American region."[118] He explained that the turn-of-the-century geopolitics of "new imperialism" and the global "scramble" for new territories had already gobbled up much of the New World, which was now off-limits to Japanese. Contrary to Anglo-Saxon frontier societies, Mexico still kept its vast, untouched land open for unrestricted immigration and investment, coupled with "good weather," "abundant coal (energy)," and "lazy, spineless natives" who would pose no competition. Thus far, however, its geographic proximity had allowed white America to monopolize opportunities for agricultural, mining, and infrastructural development there, which, Inoue feared, anticipated the eventual "absorption of Mexico in a hundred years' time by the United States," just like its former territories of Texas and California.[119] A sense of urgency, mixed with a notion of unhindered opportunities for newcomers from Japan, convinced Inoue to travel personally to Mexico to negotiate with potential employers and government officials for the systematic importation of a Japanese workforce on behalf of the Kumamoto Imin.[120] Inoue's ambitious move bore fruit in 1901, as the company dispatched the first group of eighty-two laborers to a coal mine in Chihuahua. A few thousand more Japanese subsequently entered nearby areas and worked at other mines in Sonora.[121]

Around 1904 Hinata and other Kaigai Tokō executives also began to exhibit a strong desire to break into the Mexican market, which was new but already familiar to them. The timing of their entry was not insignificant. The problem of racial exclusion in the United States again induced a further shift in Japanese perceptions of an ideal frontier—one that reaffirmed Mexico and its northern border region. The first few years of the twentieth century witnessed the resurgence of organized anti-Japanese agitation in California and Hawai'i (now a US territory), creating a serious barrier against continuous Japanese immigration, especially the entry of common laborers. The racist political movement propelled Tokyo to virtually suspend Japanese emigration to the continental United States out of diplomatic concerns from August 1900 to June 1902, a temporary measure that became a de facto policy of banning labor migration to that country.[122] Thus, the number of US-bound Japanese emigrants who were identified as laborers plunged from 7,585 to 32 between 1900 and 1901, and the figures remained as low as 70, 318, and 640 for the next three years, respectively.[123]

Moreover, the US Organic Act of 1900 made it difficult for common Japanese laborers to enter Hawai'i because the law invalidated the conventional form of plantation contract labor and mass migration based on it. Now all admissible Japanese had to be "free immigrants" without prior contractual relationships to or travel subventions from plantation owners. Traveling as "free immigrants," however, required much more money, and even with loans from emigration companies, it was unlikely that many ordinary Japanese villagers could afford transpacific steamship fares and "show money" of $50. Thus, between 1899 and 1901, Hawai'i experienced a sharp drop in Japanese arrivals, from 27,155 to 2,982.[124] Mexico picked up much of the loss, as the country took in more than 11,500 newcomers by 1908 (see table 1).[125] Presumably, a vast majority of these Mexico-bound Japanese were contract laborers, who could not afford to go to Hawai'i and the U.S. mainland as "free immigrants."

Given this background, Hinata and his Kaigai Tokō associates found it a matter of life and death to enter the Mexican market in 1904, but their chances of success were questionable due to the presence of the Kumamoto Imin. In order to better compete with this established rival, Hinata decided to consolidate forces with other emigration companies in a similar predicament, convincing several smaller firms to merge with the Kaigai Tokō to form the Tairiku Shokumin. While maintaining the Kaigai Tokō's Hawai'i/US operations under its original name, Hinata worked with the Tairiku Shokumin's top management and major shareholders, which comprised his old friends from San Francisco. Impressively, within a matter of five years (1904–1908) the Tairiku Shokumin brought almost as many laborers to Mexico as the Kaigai Tokō had done in fourteen years (1894–1907).[126] A former member of the Expedition Society and still a California resident, Murakami Taizō especially played a notable role as the company's representative, crisscrossing the US-Mexican borderlands and rural Mexico in search of business deals with potential employers and places for Japanese settlement. Some of the contracts he secured with US-owned corporate interests involved the importation of several hundred Japanese farmworkers to Vera Cruz and Oaxaca, three thousand railroad workers to Colima, and several hundred miners to Chihuahua and Sonora.[127] Together with his colleagues in Tokyo, Murakami had a reason to predict that "a magnificent Japanese settlement would rise so long as mass migration is possible."[128] Yet the deep-rooted fear of US-engineered racial exclusion became all too real when current and former residents of Japanese America suddenly found their transpacific business engulfed in the flames of the Yellow Peril scaremongering in the United States following Japan's victory over Russia, a white empire.

This new phase of organized agitation against transpacific Japanese immigration (or "racial invasion") overflowed to the greater western United States, inducing the federal government to negotiate a "Gentlemen's Agreement" with Tokyo in 1907–1908. Under this bilateral deal, the US government made it unlawful for Japanese to enter the mainland from Mexico, Hawai'i, or Canada. In turn, Tokyo voluntarily stopped issuing passports to ordinary emigrants without family ties to bona fide residents in the United States after the spring of 1908. Because many Mexico-bound Japanese had crossed the US southern border in search of better wages and job opportunities, Tokyo suspended contract emigration practices to Mexico as well. Major emigration companies were now deprived of all viable markets for their labor trafficking enterprise. Although a few firms continued to operate by sending common laborers to the new destination of Brazil after 1908, none of the emigration companies run by expansionist returnees from the American West and their partners there survived the effects of the Gentlemen's Agreement. Having been victimized again by exclusionary white racism, these former and current leaders of Japanese America came to value the importance of Japan's sovereign protection even more and were compelled to forge a closer partnership with the state in the next phase of their settler-colonial endeavors inside and outside the formal Japanese colonial empire.

PART TWO

Championing Overseas Japanese Development, 1908–1928

3

Transpacific Migrants and the Blurring Boundaries of State and Private Settler Colonialism

In today's world, Anglo-Saxons and Japanese are the two races that embody the best of the best expansive character. But we have been expelled from Australia and rejected by North America. Have the world's best colonizers met the limits of their expansion? Some say the [Japanese] empire has demonstrated its military prowess on the [Asian] continent and it is well on its way to swallow up the Korean peninsula and occupy southern Manchuria. They say we should transplant our people there in the continent. . . . Yet, that represents utterly shallow thinking. . . . I insist on the desirability of South (Latin) America for our compatriots to migrate and settle down.[1]

Published in late 1905, the first academic compendium of "Japanese migration" reiterated the importance of transpacific settler colonialism in response to the counterdiscourse that valorized the desirability of the continental region from which Japan had just removed Russian influence. The compendium also featured a foreword by Nitobe Inazō, the author's mentor and the father of Japan's "colonial policy studies," which began: "History [has] taught me that Expansion is everything." Citing the maxim of Cecil Rhodes, Nitobe declared: "Our nation now stands at the crossroads: moving forward [with the tides of that history] or going against them." He emphasized the equal weight that South America and East Asia should carry in the future course of Japan's expansion. These regions, as Nitobe argued, had common features that called for the coming of Japanese migrants and settlers; that is, Latin America, Manchuria, and Korea were all marked by inferior "civilization" and a lack of "enlightenment." Nitobe contended that despite the "failures" (of settler colonialism) in North America and Australia, the experience they had acquired in those Anglo-Saxon frontiers should give the "expansive" Japanese a valuable lesson for achieving "success" in the peaceful conquest of those "inferior" regions.[2]

These observations anticipated what would soon emerge as a major national debate over new formal colonies and extraterritorial foreign lands in the context of overseas migration and settlement and the state's role in fusing and confusing them through policy making and actions. The timing of the book's publication was crucial; the end of the Russo-Japanese War marked not only Japan's rise as a full-fledged colonial empire in East Asia but also the resurgence of California's organized anti-Japanese movement, which led to the Gentlemen's Agreement of 1907–1908 between the United States and Japan. The historical events on both sides of the Pacific heightened and widened public awareness about the questions of sovereign versus foreign, Anglo-Saxon settler societies versus other New World frontiers, and racial difference and hierarchy. Together, Japan's imperial ascent and white Americans' response heralded a new phase in the history of Japanese migration and settler colonialism.

After the Gentlemen's Agreement, the Japanese government began to assume primary responsibility for the national mandate of overseas expansion. Two important developments took place to promote state involvement in migration and settler colonialism. First, the escalation of exclusionist racism in the United States and the increase in new colonial territories in imperial Japan accounted for the developments that brought about politico-ideological changes that convinced Tokyo officialdom to take charge of mass migration and settler colonialism within and without the formal empire. The process was neither instantaneous nor uncontested, however. This phase of Japan's adaptive settler colonialism entailed many contingencies and unexpected twists and turns. The problem of race—specifically, US Yellow Peril scaremongering—punctuated the complex processes, with definitive chronological benchmarks in 1905–1908 and 1919–1924. These periods experienced upsurges in anti-Japanese political mobilization and the institutionalization of racial exclusion in the United States. It is important to note that Japan's acquisition of new colonial territories—formal or de facto—coincided with these temporal punctuations, as it directly affected the rise of a Yellow Peril exclusionist discourse in the United States. In 1905 imperial Japan stretched its sovereign influence to the former Russian possessions of Manchuria's Kwantung Leased Territory and South Sakhalin, and five years later the emergent empire officially annexed Korea. In 1914 Japan went on to take over German-controlled Micronesia as spoils of World War I, which the League of Nations subsequently recognized as its official mandate in 1919.

Second, the synchronous unfolding of US racial exclusion and Japan's territorial expansion was inseparable from the cycles of international capitalism. Global economic contraction precipitated grassroots white racism in the American West. At the same time, it buoyed Japan's pursuit of territorial expansion and overseas spheres of economic influence, as national leaders strove to cope with domestic unemployment and population pressure—perceived or real—through state and private colonialist ventures. Indeed, on the US side the first wave of organized anti-Japanese agitation peaked during the Panic of 1907, which lasted until America's adoption in

1914 of the Federal Reserve System and the beginning of World War I. This exclusionist wave produced the Gentlemen's Agreement and the 1913 California Alien Land Law, which targeted Japanese labor immigrants and settler-farmers, respectively. The second wave of anti-Japanese agitation arose amid post–World War I recessions in the United States and Japan. It resulted in the total exclusion of Japanese immigrants from the United States, the legal reinforcement of their displacement in many western states, and a ban on their naturalization by the mid-1920s.

In this context, on the Japanese side many expansionists were engrossed in another phase of adaptation and adjustment in their settler colonialism, providing a crucial background for the state's enhanced and proactive leadership in coordinating mass mobility and organizing large-scale ventures of settler colonialism abroad. After the first wave of racist assaults in Anglophone America, Japanese-controlled Korea and racially friendly Latin America, especially Brazil and Mexico, emerged as twin focuses of systematic migration and agricultural colonization in Japanese expansionist thought. Thus, imperial Japan formally incorporated settler colonialism into the national policy-making process and adopted a series of new measures between 1907 and the mid-1920s. Interweaving continental expansionism and transpacific expansionism, these measures served to further confound and gloss over distinctions between "foreign" and "sovereign" territories in terms of policy debate and formulation, as well as in the consciousness and self-identities of "emigrants" (*imin*) and "colonialists" (*shokumin*). Because the ebb and flow of white American racism accentuated the trajectory of Japan's state involvement in migration and settler colonialism, former and current US residents and the public understanding of their racial experience continued to exert considerable influence inside and outside the government structure.

Focusing on the years between the first and second upsurges in US anti-Japanese agitation, this chapter discusses what impacts the problem of white American racism had on the course of Japan's national debate and state policy making relative to colonial development and imperial expansion. The combined effects of popular and scholarly discursive formation gave rise to interconnected enterprises of agrarian settler colonization in Korea, Brazil, and Mexico—the top three objects of the Japanese expansionist gaze—during the 1910s. The bulk of this chapter then delineates the simultaneous unfolding of these de jure and de facto national expansionist projects, which blurred the boundaries of state and private endeavors and of sovereign and foreign frontiers.

THE KOMURA DOCTRINE AND THE NATIONAL
DEBATE OVER JAPAN'S COLONIAL FUTURE

Following Japan's victory over Russia in 1905, the unexpected ascendancy of the tiny "Oriental" nation reverberated among Euro-American imperialist powers, striking a chill into the minds of many white supremacists, especially those in California who were faced with the "invading" hordes of Japanese immigrants. To these racial alarmists, Kaiser Wilhelm II's theory of Yellow Peril looked all too real. No sooner did Japan's victory appear certain than the Asiatic Exclusion League (AEL; initially known as the Japanese Korean Exclusion League) came into being in San Francisco. A chief advocate of Yellow Peril scaremongering against alleged Japanese invasion, the AEL enjoyed an alliance with a Canadian sister organization, one that played a central role in the 1907 race riots in Vancouver.[3] While the AEL agitated at the grassroots level for the termination of immigration from Japan, the San Francisco Board of Education ordered the segregation of Japanese pupils from their white counterparts in the city's public school system in 1906. Japanese immigration to the American West again became a major point of contention in US race politics, yet this time its effects cut across international diplomacy, as well as Japan's domestic discourse and policy formulation regarding national expansion.

A product of Tokyo's direct intervention, the Gentlemen's Agreement marked a major break in Tokyo's attitude toward emigration policy and Japan's public discourse on overseas development. Prior to 1908, the Japanese state generally played no larger role than regulating the business of emigration companies through legislation, except for its leadership in government-sponsored labor emigration to Hawai'i between 1885 and 1894. This relatively hands-off approach became formalized by the end of the nineteenth century. In 1898 a government advisory board for agricultural and industrial policy discussed matters relating to "overseas migration." While stressing the need for the state to safeguard the interests of emigrant workers and residents abroad, the board almost unanimously agreed to oppose the government's "active involvement in and promotion" of any form of emigration. Every member expressed enthusiastic support for a national mandate of overseas development, but the board also argued that the task must be left to private individuals, suggesting that the Colonization Society should act as the primary facilitator of emigration to and colonization of foreign places.[4] This board's recommendation, which only stressed the state's responsibility to deter exploitation by emigration companies, explained Tokyo's reluctance to do anything other than amend existing regulatory laws perfunctorily.

This hands-off approach came to an end when Tokyo was compelled to shut the door on the departure of laboring masses bound for the American West after the San Francisco school segregation controversy. For fear of a diplomatic disaster, the Japanese government exerted principal authority in relation to transpacific migration, signaling its enhanced and sustained commitment thereafter. In February 1909, less than one year after the Gentlemen's Agreement came into effect, Foreign Minister Komura Jutarō made a historic speech at the Imperial Diet. He argued that the victory over Russia had radically changed Japan's standing in international relations. Komura thus declared: "Areas that Japan must manage have expanded so much that our people need to be concentrated there without allowing them to scatter through foreign territories." Japanese-controlled Korea and Manchuria (the Kwantung Leased Territory) should be the main destination of emigrants. In order to deter undesirable emigrant dispersal outside those regions, the foreign minister stressed that the Japanese government was prepared to enforce a restrictive policy regarding all forms of emigration to North America (and South America by extension). Because such a policy was to be in accord with the spirit of the Gentlemen's Agreement, it would eliminate the principal cause of Japanese-American friction, which threatened Japan's foreign trade interests, especially exports, according to Komura.[5] This policy became widely known as the "Komura doctrine for concentrating emigration to Manchuria and Korea."[6]

Existing scholarship has characterized this doctrine as a form of the state's "anti-emigration" mandate, which supposedly prioritized formal continental imperialism over popular transpacific mobility. This view also imagines a neat transition of migrant destinations from North America to Japan's formal and de facto territories.[7] Historian Shumpei Okamoto argues that Komura was concerned with the negative influence of US anti-Japanese agitation on national prestige, overseas trade and commercial development, and ongoing negotiations over the revision of the US-Japanese commercial treaty. Komura regarded emigration outside the formal empire as so insignificant that he "even prohibited a Japanese envoy to Brazil [who was] home on leave from making speeches among rural Japanese encouraging their emigration to that country."[8] As Okamoto's explanation reveals, it is commonly understood that Komura sacrificed transpacific emigration for commercial and diplomatic relations with the United States, on the one hand, and for the uninterrupted colonization of Korea and Manchuria, on the other. Not only were transpacific expansionism and continental expansionism mutually exclusive, as he suggested, the former was overshadowed by the latter as Japan continued to increase its colonial territories.

In light of the shifting public discourse on national expansion, this interpretation should be deemed only *partially* correct. Like Komura, some government officials had a strong propensity for separating Japan's colonial possessions from the Americas and other foreign areas, since their first instinct was to consider the question of sovereign power, its reach, and its executability. In 1910, for example, Cabinet Minister Makino Nobuaki called it "Japan's mission to develop Korea, Taiwan, and Manchuria" with settler colonialism, whereas "overseas migration" was not so desirable because it involved—and would be restricted by—diplomatic negotiations with a receiving country.[9] Nevertheless, it is a mistake to assume that the pronouncements of these selected statesmen mirrored the general sociopolitical thinking of the time. Indeed, both inside and outside government circles, many advocates of emigration-led expansionism took exception to the Komura doctrine. It was accompanied by a lively national debate over the preferred vectors and forms of overseas Japanese development—a debate that resembled what had taken

TABLE 3 Major Expansionist and Proemigration Periodicals Published in Late Meiji Japan

Title	First Year of Publication
Seikō 『成功』 (Success)	1902
Jitsugyō no Sekai: Taiheiyō 『実業之世界　太平洋』 (Entrepreneurial world: The Pacific)	1903
Tobei zasshi 『渡米雑誌』 (Magazine for the America-bound) Title changed to Amerika 『亜米利加』	1905
Fugen annai 『富源案内』 (Guide to golconda)	1906
Fugen no tami 『富源之民』 (People of wealth)	1906
Tobei Shimpō 　『渡米新報』 (News for the America-bound) Title eventually changed to Rikkō Sekai 『力行世界』	1907
Shokumin Sekai 『殖民世界』 (Colonizing world)	1908
Jitsugyōkai 『実業界』 (Business world)	1910
Kaigai no Nihon 『海外之日本』 (Overseas Japan)	1911

Special issues/forums on overseas development published in the same period

"Ō-hakujin no shōtotsu" [Clash of the yellow and white races] 「黄白人の衝突」 Taiyō [The sun] 『太陽』 14, no. 3 (15 February 1908).

"Nihon minzoku no bōchō" [Expansion of the Japanese race/nation] 「日本民族の膨張」 Taiyō [The sun] 『太陽』 16, no. 15 (1 November 1910).

"Nihonjin no shōrai hatten subeki tochi" [Places where Japanese shall seek their future development] 「日本人の将来発展すべき土地」 Chūō kōron [Pivotal public opinion] 『中央公論』 27, no. 5 (May 1912): 57–80.

"Kaigai hatten-saku" [Plans for overseas development] 「海外発展策」 Jitsugyō no Sekai [Entrepreneurial world] 『実業之世界』 10, no. 19 (October 1913).

place among Colonization Society members around 1894. Yet this new debate involved a broader spectrum of Japanese society than before, for participants included not only urban intelligentsia but also an increasing number of aspiring rural youths and laboring students (kugakusei), who dreamed of social mobility through education, entrepreneurship, and self-help in places like America. In accordance with this "ideology of striving and success," several expansionist periodicals came out for the new readership of ambitious, if not naïve, expansionist-minded commoners, particularly after 1905 (see table 3).[10]

In language accessible to those without higher/elite education, all these magazines celebrated emigration, overseas work, and settlement through Horatio Alger–esque, rags-to-riches narratives, including glorified stories of Satō Torajirō, the "King of Thursday Island," and many "self-made" individuals of Japanese America. Around that time, many monthlies printed a special forum or even issued a special edition on "overseas development." An undercurrent of US frontier discourse was also impossible to overlook in this success ideology, since the extolment of rugged individualism neatly dovetailed with a teleological idea of Japanese manifest destiny (see table 3).[11] Contrary to the Komura doctrine, this populist expansionism refused to distinguish continental colonialism and its state-sponsored endeavors from other forms of overseas Japanese development, especially "private" migration and settler colonialism outside Japan's sovereign territories. An earlier thrust of expansionistic populism, albeit with classist condescension, had already been articulated by US-based pundits such as Nagasawa Betten and subsequently practiced by operators of emigration companies. Combined with an ideology of striving and success, that expansionistic populism engrossed large segments of Japanese society—especially youths of humble rural origin—thereby further inducing Japanese masses to pursue a national project of emigration-led, borderless colonialism. A close analysis of expansionist magazines provides a glimpse into growing public support for unregulated and multidirectional mass migration. Published in 1911, *Kaigai no Nippon* (Overseas Japan) offers a good example. Many of the featured essays made a point of criticizing Komura's dismissal of transpacific and southward expansion. In the very first article of the inaugural issue, Ōkuma Shigenobu, former premier and elder statesman, described the Komura doctrine as a "frivolous excuse for failed diplomacy toward the United States," asserting that emigration and settlement should be encouraged in any foreign location.[12] The second issue was more explicit about its multidirectional approach to overseas development. In a forum entitled "Where Is the Best Destination of Emigration?," the majority of commentaries called for a flexible choice, with explicit criticisms of the fixation on Korea and Manchuria.[13] Urging readers not to neglect the Western Hemisphere and the Nan'yō, Hinata Terutake lamented "the negative influence of (the doctrine on) concentrating on Manchuria and Korea"—the very title of his commentary. The former San Francisco resident and proprietor of major emigration companies was "greatly perturbed that some government leaders [seem to be] trying to adopt [the Komura doctrine] as [Japan's] formal emigration policy."[14] In other contemporary expansionist magazines and general periodicals, a similar debate unfolded in favor of an eclectic approach over an exclusive focus on Japanese-ruled territories.[15] The juxtaposition of varied colonial visions, positions, and experiences promoted the public view that there existed different sets of advantages in all three schools of national expansionism—the view that illuminated their complementary and mutually reinforcing relationships instead of their divergences or incongruences.

Even after 1909, despite Komura's valorization of Japan's formal imperialism and its territories, the print media refused to discount the wider world as a potential target of overseas Japanese development and validated it with a new language of "peaceful expansion(ism)."[16] Parallel to US "liberal developmentalism," the emerging populist-expansionist ideology of post-1908 Japan dressed its colonialism in the benevolent cloth of a civilization's spread by "means other than military invasion," especially mass migration and agricultural colonization. Ōkuma argued, for instance, that since its victory over Russia, "Japan has emerged as the beacon of civilization in the Orient, and it is on its way to limitless expansion and progress in the context of the world's new civilization."[17] The conquest of new territories by national military forces and the transplantation of violent colonizers that followed it had become an outdated, "fundamentally wrong" idea, Ōkuma stressed. Seen from the standpoint of encouraging "civilized and progressive" processes of population movements and colonization, Japan's new territories were not exactly ideal. Places like Korea and Taiwan were already inhabited by sizable numbers of native residents, making it difficult to accommodate large contingents of settler migrants from the colonial metropole without causing bloody conflicts and using brute suppression. The New World, according to Ōkuma, still promised "so vast a landmass that it [could] easily take three million or even five million Japanese migrant settlers" without disturbing the peace. Instead of the "dangerous thought (of military invasion)," peaceful expansion should be viewed as a new national mission of Japan, whose "development should reach into every nook and cranny of the world."[18] Like many of his contemporaries, Ōkuma recommended South America, which he presented in preference to Korea, for in the truest sense the former offered an open frontier—only scarcely inhabited by nonthreatening natives or mulattoes with "feeble blood."[19] Juxtaposed against the violent military power of state imperialism, the post-1909 discourse on migration and settler colonialism deemed the foreign frontier a different but still important site of national expansion that should coexist with the empire's formal colonialism. In particular, the concept of "peaceful expansion" served as a powerful counterdiscourse to the Komura doctrine, supporting mass migration and settlement making in the Japanese-friendly New World, especially Brazil.

Paradoxically, as Japan emerged as one of five major powers through the use of state violence and military invasion, the rhetoric of peaceful expansion became increasingly prominent in Japanese settler colonialism.[20] This ironic ideology was blatantly racist, because it presupposed the superiority of Japanese migrant settlers over other groups and nations. According to this thinking, their superior "blood" and "culture" would spare overseas Japanese the need to rely on state military support for frontier conquest and civilization building, as long as host societies refrained from applying exclusionist measures against them as white America had done. On the very premise of this racial teleology, Ukita Kazutami, chief editor of late Meiji Japan's most influential monthly *Taiyō*, echoed Ōkuma's racial argument. This prominent US-educated opinion maker predicted the success of Japanese settlement and agricultural colonization in South America by contrasting the "weakness of the Latin race mixed with [indigenous Indio]" with the domineering and exclusionary power of North American Anglo-Saxons.[21] Here again, one can see the centrality of US race relations and exclusionary politics as a key reference point in the colonial thinking of Japanese intellectuals when they embraced Brazil and other "racism-free" frontiers, including Japan's formal colonial territories.

Similarly, from 1908 through the 1910s, popular print media frequently carried special essays and forums on race and racism in relation to migration, with special attention to America's anti-Japanese agitation. In February 1908, for example, *Taiyō* published a full edition entitled "Clashes of the Yellow and the White" (Ō-Hakujin no shōtotsu). Four months later, its June issue offered a forum on the "Race Problem" (Jinshu mondai).[22] In race-related magazine essays, personalized accounts of Japanese immigrants' struggles in California usually offered poignant examples of the inevitable challenges with which imperial Japanese would have to grapple as an expansive nation/race elsewhere in the Asia-Pacific basin. And in direct contrast to the challenges of the "White Peril" in North America (and Oceania), Brazil looked all the more positive as an alternative emigrant destination. Indeed, the prevailing notions of Brazilians' racial "friendliness" and "weakness" were augmented by that country's immigration policy, which allowed the vector of Japanese labor migration to redirect suddenly to the south from North America after the Gentlemen's Agreement. Unlike Americans, Brazilian authorities had clearly differentiated Japanese from Chinese due mainly to the "weight of world power" that the former carried. In its immigration policy, as historian Jeffery Lesser discusses, the São Paulo state government—and later the Brazilian federal government—thus "reconfigure[d] Japanese as non-Asians," thereby often "plac[ing] Japanese immigrants in a hierarchic position equal to or [even] above Europeans."[23]

In addition to Japan's popular print media, the production and dissemination of new knowledge about peaceful settler-colonial expansion and racial superiority took place in the realm of Japanese academia. Shortly after the public declaration of the Komura doctrine in 1909, Tokyo Imperial University formally established a special chair in colonial policy studies in its agricultural department. Sapporo Agricultural College in Hokkaido had offered courses on colonial studies since 1890, but its goal was always tied to the specific challenges of developing Japan's domestic northern frontier. The institutionalization of colonial *policy* studies at Tokyo Imperial University heralded the growing importance of overseas emigration and settler colonialism in Japan's overall national strategy after the Gentlemen's Agreement.[24] Because leading bureaucrats and statesmen of the central government mostly hailed from that university, graduates of the new program would naturally occupy a pivotal place in policy-making processes based on their academic training in colonial planning.

Nitobe Inazō, a former instructor at Sapporo Agricultural College, assumed the first professorship in colonial policy studies at Tokyo Imperial University. Having been educated at Johns Hopkins University in the United States and Germany's University of Halle-Wittenberg, Nitobe was well-versed in the latest western scholarship on colonial political economies and histories, and as his published lecture notes demonstrate, he tended to keep his discussion at the abstract theoretical level. Yet when he examined western historical precedence with an eye to deliberating on Japan's future course of action, Nitobe celebrated the history of America's frontier conquest and settler colonialism as the most desirable model that would "suggest how to get better prepared when the Japanese of the twentieth century [we]re about to embark collectively on overseas expansion."[25] According to his review of modern world history, there were eight forms of colonialism, but he contended that "the pinnacle of the colonial endeavor" belonged to agrarian settler colonization, that is, the inhabitation of "open land" by individual farmers and their private pursuit of a "frontier life." As exemplified by the experience of white settler societies such as the United States, the permanent control and mastery of physical territory with committed, stable farmers laid the foundation of enduring societal and industrial progress in a nation and empire. The "plantation colony"— another important form of colonialism—represented a viable but inferior one, since settlers were outnumbered by native residents and workers despite the former's politico-economic domination, as in Hawai'i.[26]

In his predictions about colonial success and failure, Nitobe also employed a Spenserian concept of racial difference and hierarchy. "Expansive nations" were destined to have settlement colonies, and "non-expansive nations" were all supposed to fall prey."[27] Although the professor of colonial policy studies generally focused on European and American examples and rarely made a direct reference to Japan and the Japanese in his lectures, there was one occasion when he took up the theme of Japanese racial quality in relation to westerners. European and American colonizers, Nitobe argued, had failed to immigrate in large numbers to tropical and torrid regions of the New World and seldom managed to erect settlement colonies there on account of their inability to adapt to the local climate, hence the absence of mass immigration. A "plantation colony," albeit a good way to generate economic profit, remained unqualified for the label of genuine *settlement* society in global imperial history for that reason. On the other hand, the Japanese had been able to acclimate to tropical and torrid environments because they allegedly outstripped white men in physical adaptability. To make this point, Nitobe specifically cited the cases of Thursday Island pearl divers and Hawai'i's sugar plantation workers. This race-based argument dovetailed neatly with ongoing public discourse on mass emigration and settler colonialism as a form of peaceful national expansion, which could coexist with military-led extension of sovereign territories. While Nitobe preferred the tropics of the Pacific to those of South America due to his past experience as a chief agricultural technocrat in colonial Taiwan, his academic deliberations on Japanese racial suitability for tropical settler colonialism generated a powerful ideological effect, obscuring and confusing the differences between the extraterritorial (foreign) regions and the sovereign (Japanese-ruled) territories in Japanese expansionist thought and policy making of the time.[28]

Backed by biological racism, a similar instance of obfuscation unfolded in the realm of government legislation, giving rise to an integrated approach to the empire's formal colonies and foreign sites of Japanese development despite the

Komura doctrine. In 1907 the Imperial Diet enacted an amended Emigrant Protection Act, which regulated how emigration companies operated and what procedure individual emigrants needed to follow before lawfully leaving Japan. Significantly, the amendment contained a new clause that enabled emigration companies or other corporate entities to sponsor agricultural colonization and industrial ventures in a foreign place—a type of business activity in which they previously could not be involved. As a cabinet representative explained on the floor of the Diet, the 1907 law was designed to "enable people to go abroad freely" (except to North America) and to "extend the sphere of emigrant and settler activities as widely as possible" outside East Asia. The official also added that it was now government policy to encourage an increase in Japanese landownership and family-based migration abroad, instead of conventional bachelor migrant sojourning, in order to "allow emigrants to be their own boss and . . . build a foundation of their [permanent settlement] with their wives, children, and siblings."[29] After the enactment of the law, for-profit emigration companies could and actually did begin to obtain land in Brazil for emigrant settlement and manage agricultural colonies in an integrated manner. The 1907 law paved the way for a rapid increase in mass migration to and settler colonialism in that country through these emigration companies, which shifted their business focus from North America to South America.

Yet obfuscation in rhetoric and law did not mean the complete neglect of the boundaries between the foreign and the sovereign in Japanese settler colonialism. Just as the Komura doctrine could and did coexist with its opponents in the nation's expansionist discourse without merging completely, the policy change was accompanied by nuanced differentiations between state-led colonial development in East Asia and private settler colonialism elsewhere. While Tokyo removed the legal obstacles for emigration companies to engage in organized colonization ventures abroad, it also withheld "China (Qing) and Korea" from the application of the 1907 law. The isolation of these two regions had started under the 1902 amendment to the original 1896 Emigrant Protection Act, enabling imperial subjects to travel to those neighboring regions without a passport due to "their close proximity." In 1907, now with exclusive Japanese control of the Kwantung Leased Territory and the Korean peninsula, the distinction between those territories and foreign emigration destinations became "a matter of political consideration" and vitally important from an administrative and diplomatic standpoint. Interrogated by a Diet member, a cabinet representative explained the need for a discrete policy, but this high-level diplomat also acknowledged ongoing government planning for separate legislation from the 1907 act, because "a large number of Japanese [we]re expected to seek development (settlement making and industrial endeavors)" in Manchuria and Korea under Japan's political control. Yet the official had to concede that the government was not prepared to present any "clear blueprint" at that juncture.[30]

Yet at least the 1907 Emigrant Protection Act made it possible for migration and settler colonialism outside Japan's sovereignty and de facto rule to remain legally compatible with state-sponsored territorial aggrandizement and colonial development—the notion that advocates of peaceful national expansion popularized through the print media and academia. It was not until a year later that Tokyo finally addressed the outstanding question of what to do with Korea and Manchuria in the overall scheme of overseas Japanese development, especially in Brazil, in terms of its policy and actual state program. And some former US returnees were instrumental in bridging simultaneous manifestations of state-sponsored and private settler colonialisms in Northeast Asia and South America, respectively, during the 1910s.

INTERCONNECTIONS OF STATE AND PRIVATE ENDEAVORS IN THE CONQUEST OF THE KOREAN AND BRAZILIAN FRONTIERS

In 1908 the Imperial Diet passed the Oriental Development Company Act (Tōyō takushoku kaisha hō) to set up the legal basis for settler migration to and agricultural colonization in Korea and Manchuria under the aegis of a state-sponsored monopoly business. Combined with the 1907 Emigrant Protection Act, the 1908 law functioned as the interdependent wheels of national expansion inside and outside the territories of the Japanese empire. Capitalized at 10 million yen ($5 million), the Oriental Development Company (ODC) was the brainchild of Prime Minister Katsura Tarō and his cronies.[31]

Pursuant to the newly adopted principle of "immigrant colonization" (*imin takushoku*), the Japanese government promised to subsidize the ODC's operations with 300,000 yen annually for the first eight years. Japan's major banks issued company bonds, underwritten by the state, up to 20 million yen. The ODC's ambitious ten-year plan called for the importation into Korea of 240,000 Japanese, who were expected to cultivate over 610,000 acres, or about 14 percent of Korea's arable land, by 1919. Even before formal annexation, the company had already taken more than 34,000 acres from the Korean government, and the land under its ownership grew to 158,900 acres by 1913, despite price rigging by unscrupulous brokers and Korean resistance to displacement. Working toward the goal of Japanizing Korea through agrarian settler colonialism, the ODC's estates spread from north to south, dotting the entire peninsula with Japanese farm settlements. In reality, however, the number of Japanese settlers turned out to be disappointingly lower than the original blueprint. From 1911 to 1920 only a little over five thousand Japanese households moved to the ODC's estates to work as tenants and hired hands. Despite the statistical letdown, these family farmers still represented the kind of pioneer settlers that the company and the colonial regime envisioned as ideal immigrant settlers from Japan. They originated mostly from "middle-scale agri-culturalists" of rural Japan.[32] In the long run, as the ODC president declared, they were supposed to become self-sufficient "landowners," who would "constitute a cornerstone (pillar)" of Japanese Korea, just as they had shored up the backbone of their home villages in Japan.[33] To this end, the official motto *eijū dochaku* (perma-nent residence to take root in the land) was adopted as a central principle of Japan's policy of systematic colonization in Korea.[34]

Contrasted with the more commonplace practice of *dekasegi* labor migration, the concept of *eijū dochaku* had first been popularized in Japan a few years earlier. Although a similar idea had been propagated by early residents of Japanese America and returnees from the US West such as Nagasawa Betten, California's immigrant leaders of the early twentieth century, especially Abiko Kyūtarō, were responsible for its influence in Japan's public discourse and colonial policy making. Having arrived in San Francisco in 1885, Abiko had embraced the popular US nar-rative on frontier conquest, believing that Japanese immigrants ought to put down roots in the American West as pioneer farmers. Whereas many like-minded immi-grant expansionists returned to Japan after 1894, Abiko clung to the dream of build-ing a new Japan in California despite racial exclusion. While remaining devoted to the cause of Japan's overseas development, this immigrant leader was firmly com-mitted to "assimilating" ordinary Japanese residents into American society through moral reform efforts.[35] In his eclectic activities, Abiko maintained strong partner-ships with diplomats, politicians, and social elites of Japan, including those who drafted and pushed for the enactment of the 1907 Emigrant Protection Act. At the same time, he was involved in the publication of a major vernacular newspaper (*Nichibei Shimbun*) in San Francisco, the operation of a labor contracting firm, and then the building of the Yamato Colony in Livingston, California. Starting in 1906, Abiko's third project followed the example of the standard white American frontier myth to promote his long-standing advocacy of family-based settlement. Purchas-ing thirty-two hundred acres of undeveloped land, the immigrant leader subdi-vided the holdings into forty-acre parcels for Japanese Christian immigrants, who pledged to settle down in Livingston as permanent family farmers à la the white Puritan colonists of New England. To Abiko and his supporters, the Yamato Colony project was designed to help facilitate a radical shift in the social orientation of Japanese immigrant society from sojourning to permanent residence—the shift that they had striven to bring about since around 1900.[36]

While spearheading such social engineering among the laboring immigrant masses in Japanese America, Abiko propagated through his newspaper the virtue of *eijū dochaku*, especially after the rise of Yellow Peril fearmongering in 1905. He described permanent settlement as the best solution for the most serious challenge that Japanese America had encountered at that juncture. Abiko and other immi-grant leaders believed that the making of an "assimilable" ethnic community would hinge on the commitment of individual immigrants to their adopted land and its sustained development. They specifically wanted to turn shiftless working-class immigrants into settler agriculturalists with wives and children—the next generation of Japanese America, or a new Japan in America. For this goal, Abiko's *Nichibei Shimbun* fervently "supported the [picture-bride] practice as the most economical and practical way for single men to get married and summon their brides" to California.[37] That practice, which became popular around the time of the inception of the Yamato Colony, enabled ordinary immigrant bachelors to form their own households in America based on the simple exchange of pictures without having to travel back to their home villages in Japan. In his newspaper, and as a leader of the Japanese Association of America, Abiko also contended that permanent settlement and stable family life would serve as powerful counterevidence to white exclusionist accusations, which stressed Japanese unassimilability and the absence of commitment to American society.[38] At the same time, Abiko did not neglect to expound on the centrality of his pet project from the standpoint of Japan's new imperative of "overseas colonization."[39] Between 1906 and 1908 Abiko's view corroborated the thinking of many other first-generation Japanese Americans and often directly inspired some to try their hands at building "new Japanese villages" (commonly called *Shin Nihon-mura*) in Southern California, north-central Oregon, central-western Washington, southern Texas, and even north of the border in Alberta, Canada.[40]

Combined with the actual cases of family-based permanent settlement making in rural California and other frontier locations, Abiko's assertions reverberated in his homeland when Japan was not only reflecting on the reason for US exclusionist agitation but also pondering where and how to expand in conjunction with the Gentlemen's Agreement. In 1907–1908, when the ODC was about to come into being, Japan's domestic print media hailed Abiko's Yamato Colony as the first model case for overseas development. And when Abiko returned to Japan in search of investors, he was invited to speak at the prestigious Economic Studies Association in Tokyo. Following his talk on the experiment in North America, Viscount Sakatani Yoshirō discussed colonial possibilities in Manchuria and Korea. In front of an audience of over one hundred that included state bureaucrats, policy makers, and academics, the Yamato Colony was thus imagined and portrayed as an exemplar for the colonization of Japan's new continental territories.[41] Indeed, key features of the 1907 Emigrant Protection Act mirrored Abiko's valorization of the *eijū dochaku* concept, insofar as the law gave preference to family migration and permanent settlement over *dekasegi* migrant sojourning. In his justification for the 1907 law, a government official—a top diplomat with whom Abiko had worked closely—repeatedly mentioned those key terms, "*eijū*" (permanent settlement) and "*dochaku*" (taking root in land), when he discussed "the government's desire to promote the migration of husband and wife as the basic unit, much less restricting that of working-class women as before."[42] The ODC soon subscribed to the same principle by making *eijū dochaku* a prerequisite for its program of family-based migration and "*dochaku*"-style colonization in Korea, and later Manchuria.

Thereafter, even though it might not be referenced in a direct manner, Abiko's California precedent seems to have become an archetype and pattern of state-sponsored settler colonialism elsewhere—one that defined the family farm as the most basic unit of community building in overseas Japanese settlements. In 1909–1910, as had been done in Korea, the governor-general of Taiwan commenced its official settler colonial program, in which the first contingent of nine "model immigrant" families was brought to the eastern frontier of Taiwan from Tokushima Prefecture—a region that had produced successful pioneer settlers for the American-style agrarian colonization of Hokkaido. In the process of recruiting a few hundred more immigrant settlers, lackadaisical bachelor "fortune seekers" (*hitohata-gumi*) were deliberately excluded when the regime took the lead in organizing the first "immigrant village" in Hualien.[43]

Thus, firmly embedded in Japan's colonial policy in Korea and beyond after 1908, the US-bred idea of *eijū dochaku* served to cement an ideal image of overseas Japanese as stable family settlers through the ODC's migrant recruitment effort. Family migration made it possible for the expansive nation/race to reproduce on the land where the first-generation farm settlers planted the seeds of a "new Japan." This view defined the frontier land as the basis of both economic production and national/racial reproduction, and it resonated with America's Turneresque discourse on national formation and regeneration in the West. In fact, as Jun Uchida observes in her study of Japanese settler colonialism in Korea, the "metaphor" of the American frontier strongly inspired Japanese newcomers there to "liken their struggles to that of pioneers in the New World," which included their efforts to "defend themselves against the unfriendly natives." After Japan's formal annexation of Korea in 1910, as Uchida notes, Japanese permanent settlement was accompanied with peaceful "acts of plunder" from Korean farmers, first by the ODC in its usurpation of farmland and then by replacing them with immigrant settlers who put down roots in the land as theirs.[44] Couched in the language of *eijū dochaku*, it was this process wherein the immigrant pursuit of self-/family interest was harmonized with the state program of settler colony making in Korea, which necessarily entailed the displacement of minoritized "native" inhabitants. Once again, just as the US frontier narrative continued to imbue imperial Japan and its subjects with an idealized vision of colonial development and domination, the Japanese immigrant experience in California remained a crucial knowledge source and reference point.

The ODC's family-based colonization contributed to the stabilization of "highly mobile" social conditions in Japanese Korea.[45] Post-1910 settler agriculturalists brought a new element to Japan's new colony, which had consisted chiefly of itinerant merchants, seasonal fishermen, and other unstable individuals. In a sense, the influx of ODC recruits made Japanese Korea resemble Japanese America despite the difference in their respective administrative structures and relationships to Japan's sovereign power. Notwithstanding the official designation of them as settler-colonists, the majority of Korea-bound family emigrants derived from a similar socioeconomic stratum of rural Japan and shared overlapping characteristics with *dekasegi* workers who had moved to North America and other foreign destinations. Their differing destinations, whether inside or outside the empire's territories, did not signify a fundamental change in the demography of Japanese emigration or in the overall emigrant mind-set. As Kimura Kenji and Martin Dusinberre point out, ODC recruits from Yamaguchi farm villages actually included a number of former US residents, as well as those who had intended to go to North America before the implementation of the Gentlemen's Agreement. Many local villagers also had numerous relatives and family members living across the Asia-Pacific basin, including Korea, Manchuria, Taiwan, Hawai'i, and California.[46] Ordinary migrants were surprisingly flexible in their selection of destination, as long as public discourse on overseas development glossed over essential incongruities between formal colonial territory and foreign migrant settlement. Their decision making was often contingent on which location would offer the most convenient access—logistically and financially—and what benefits they could enjoy, especially the possibility of possessing their own land, farms, and businesses. After 1910, Korea seemed to offer such an opportunity to many Japanese villagers who aspired to landownership or self-employment.

Mainly from an analysis of statistical data, historians generally characterize the ODC's Korean venture as a "failure" or "disappointment," one that propelled the local colonial regime to take agrarian colonization "off the list of state priorities" by the late 1910s. The company brought five to six thousand farm households from Japan to Korea between 1910 and 1926, but only about four thousand remained on the ODC-distributed land throughout the 1920s and 1930s. According to Hyung Gu Lynn, these Japanese farm families accounted for only one-third of the company's target number of thirteen thousand households.[47] Yet what is important for this study is not why and how the ODC failed to achieve its original blueprint of "immigrant colonialism," but rather how the US frontier fantasy and the California Japanese formulation of *eijū dochaku* constituted a significant undercurrent of the ODC's program. Furthermore, there is another crucial point to consider when evaluating the significance of the ODC's agrarian settler colonialism. The first state-sponsored endeavor in Korea was deeply intertwined with another, much less known instance of migration and agricultural colonization in Brazil, which revealed yet more American imprints and US immigrant connections. The close nexus between the 1908 Oriental Development Company Act and the 1907 Emigrant Protection Act underpinned mutually constitutive relations between state-sponsored continental expansionism and (ostensibly) private transpacific emigration. Known as the Katsura Colony, a project of Japanese agricultural colonization in Iguape, São Paulo, was an unofficial twin sister of the ODC's attempt to Japanize Korea's topography through family migration and permanent settlement.

Established in 1913, the Iguape colony exemplified a semiofficial colonization scheme that involved Prime Minister Katsura Tarō and his inner circle. Having served as the premier three times between 1901 and 1913 and as the minister of army, education, and finance, Katsura is regarded as a central political figure in the history of late Meiji Japan. Less known, however, is his commitment to a national imperative of overseas development. Not only did he assume the governorship of colonial Taiwan, Katsura was also instrumental in organizing the colonization bureau within his cabinet—the precursor of the ministry of colonial affairs—that oversaw all affairs pertaining to the management of Japan's colonial possessions and emigrant settlements in foreign lands (except North America, out of diplomatic concerns). In the same vein, while helping to draft a blueprint for the ODC, Katsura praised the publication of the expansionist magazine *Kaigai no Nippon* as "an opportune response to the demands of the time" and a "contribution to [Japan's] colonial governance."[48] As his biographer noted in 1909, Katsura's colonial gaze extended in all directions: to Korea and Manchuria, to the Nan'yō, to South China, and to "a certain big project" in an unnamed location that went unelaborated.[49] The last item was an ongoing, clandestine endeavor to form the "Tokyo Syndicate," a group of top statesmen and financiers that subsequently arranged the concession of 123,500 acres with the São Paulo state government for permanent Japanese settlement. Like the ODC, the syndicate envisioned the establishment of a family-based agricultural colony that would eventually take in two thousand Japanese households (or six thousand people). All newcomers from Japan would be landowning farmers, while some local recruits (working-class Japanese who were already in Brazil) might start out as share tenants before becoming independent.[50]

The leadership of the Tokyo Syndicate drew from three types of expansionists in Tokyo. First, key cabinet members and architects of the ODC Act, such as Prime Minister Katsura, Minister of Agriculture and Commerce Ōura Kenbu, and Home Minister Hirata Tōsuke, backed up its transpacific settler colonialism. Being in charge of the nation's food supply, Ōura and Katsura were particularly interested in seeking wider sources of rice imports for when Japan suffered from serious grain shortages. Just as the ODC was expected to increase rice production in Korea for the Japanese homeland, the government brass thought that an immigrant agricultural colony in Brazil would contribute to the same goal. This political pragmatism meshed well with their expansionistic megalomania regarding overseas development, which was ironically intensified by anxieties about the closing of Anglo-Saxonist North America and Oceania. A close ally to Japan's political establishment, the second contingent of the Tokyo Syndicate consisted of the moneyed interests. The capitalists came onboard with unabashed calculations of investment opportunities and financial profits, which they wrapped in the grandiose language of Japan's manifest destiny. Many of these syndicate members, including prominent statesmen and monopoly capitalists, simultaneously played an instrumental role in the establishment of the ODC.[51]

The eclectic Tokyo Syndicate could not have functioned without the initiative of the third type of expansionist, Aoyagi Ikutarō, a veteran of frontier settler colonialism, emigrant-trafficking business, and colonial expeditions.[52] A former member of San Francisco's Expedition Society, Aoyagi was a longtime self-styled frontiersman who had traveled all over the New World. When he was in California during the early 1890s, the young immigrant went to Peru to see if the country might offer colonial opportunities for Japanese settlers. A report on his 1893 investigative trip was published in the Colonization Society monthly, since he was the first ever Japanese to enter the region for such a survey. In 1896 Aoyagi left his mark again as the first Japanese frontier "explorer" in the Johor region of the Malay Peninsula during an "expedition" commissioned by the president of the Colonization Society.[53] Between 1902 and 1907 the recent returnee from California then tried his hand at running an emigration company, like his contemporaries. When the Tokyo Syndicate was being formed, Aoyagi emerged as its brain and a central driving force for virtually state-sponsored colonization in Brazil. While the first group offered political backing and the second group financial support, it was his US-bred vision of frontier development and firsthand overseas experience that got the Tokyo Syndicate project moving forward.

In 1908 Aoyagi put together a detailed proposal that enticed both Japan's top statesmen and entrepreneurs. Revealing careful attention to the range of interests of those diverse constituents, his draft proposal presented four reasons for agricultural colonization in Brazil. In essence, his four-point contention mirrored the set of ideas propagated by earlier ideologues of transpacific expansionism. First, a Malthusian fear of uncontrollable population increase was coupled with an alarmist claim that Japan needed to disperse its subjects beyond the limits of its controlled regions through mass migration for not only overseas development but also steady progress of the home empire. South America was still full of unoccupied land and short of dwellers, and it should naturally be a prime target of population movements from such a densely inhabited region as East Asia. Second, Brazil in particular was rich with agricultural products and vital natural resources that would benefit the Japanese economy; in the meantime, Japan could foreseeably export silk and various manufactured goods to the untapped Latin American market. In order to promote the transport of those commodities, mass migration was indispensable, for the combination of cargo and passengers would sustain a permanent steamship service, as in the cases of Hawai'i and North America.[54] The first two reasons justified tangential aspects of mass migration within the overall spread of Japanese influence across the globe.

In the proposal, Aoyagi's third point predicted an important consequence of growing Japanese trade with Brazil—a point that valorized the meaning of permanent settlement there. Japanese immigrants, Aoyagi noted, would always prefer to consume imported merchandise from the homeland, and they would also Japanize the local taste and its consumption patterns in the process of their group settlement and assimilation with Brazilians. To support his contention, Aoyagi referred to the example of Brazil's German immigrants, who had apparently succeeded in building a semiautonomous "new Germany" near São Paulo and exerting enormous influence there despite the absence of their homeland's sovereign protection. Japan, too, should have such permanent outposts of Japanese national influence in South America, Aoyagi contended. Another positive product of permanent immigrant settlement—his fourth point—was that a successful example of agricultural settlement making in Brazil would promote the Japanese appreciation of overseas development. "One real model case [of a viable settler colonialist venture]," Aoyagi argued, "would have a far better effect in rousing people to action than do countless lectures given in a classroom." As Japan was building an empire of its own, it was imperative that all imperial subjects be impressed with the need for national expansion and their destiny as an expansive people.[55] Given the magnitude of its advantages to Japan's national interests, Aoyagi's proposal called for full government backing of this Brazilian enterprise.

Although the proposal captured the hearts of Katsura, Hirata, and Ōura, these government leaders were faced with fierce opposition from Foreign Minister Komura Jutarō within the cabinet. Given Komura's stubborn insistence on "concentrating on Korea and Manchuria," Katsura and Ōura agreed to avoid alienating the foreign minister. Komura had warned about the negative implications of transpacific Japanese emigration for US-Japan relations, and the entry of government-sponsored settlers into South America would never have a desirable impact on Yellow Peril demagoguery among US racial exclusionists. Therefore, Ōura privately advised Aoyagi to give up trying to turn the Brazil venture into an official government-sponsored project on a par with the ODC's Korean colonization. Nevertheless, Ōura and his fellow cabinet ministers were intent on proceeding with Aoyagi's blueprint in a less visible and indirect manner by organizing the "private" Tokyo Syndicate, to which each member made an investment according to his personal financial standing. The current cabinet members, such as Ōura, refrained from investing in their own names, using proxies instead, for the purpose of hiding ties to government insiders. In 1910 the syndicate dispatched Aoyagi for negotiations with Brazilians, and during his eighteen months' sojourn, he traveled throughout São Paulo and the neighboring states to identify the most suitable location for Japanese settlement. In the trained eyes of this veteran frontier trotter, a southern coastal region of São Paulo, known as Iguape, stood out. After ten months of negotiation, the local officials awarded Aoyagi the afore-mentioned concession in March 1912.[56]

Under the aegis of Premier Katsura, the Tokyo Syndicate grew into a full-fledged colonization company in one year. In order to adopt it as a de facto state endeavor, albeit with the appearance of a private business, the core syndicate lead-ers, especially the now home minister Ōura, managed to assemble an impressive array of top-level political insiders and business tycoons at an informal conference in January 1913. In addition to Katsura and Ōura, the minister of agriculture and commerce, two vice ministers and three bureau chiefs from the foreign and agri-cultural ministries, as well as the governor of the Bank of Japan, attended the meeting at the foreign minister's office. The other participants were major figures connected to Japan's conglomerates, including Shibusawa Eiichi. This foremost industrialist and his associates were initially dubious about the endeavor, but Kat-sura and Ōura personally convinced them to come onboard by emphasizing how important the project was for Japan's future as a rising global imperial power.[57]

Once his sense of patriotic duty was invoked, Shibusawa took it upon himself to provide this scheme with as much support as was given to the concurrent ODC work in Korea—in which he had already invested a large sum of money from the standpoint of national interest.[58] In the months after the conference, Japan's lead-ing industrialist spent much of his time conferring with many of Tokyo's business and political elite. Shibusawa's published "commentary" on Brazilian colonization offers a good glimpse into what he must have told his colleagues, which reinforced Aoyagi's original rationale.[59] In March 1913 the six years of tenacious work by Aoy-agi, Katsura, and Ōura, which Shibusawa now embraced, finally culminated in the founding of the Brazil Colonization Company (BCC; Burajiru Takushoku Gaisha). While the cabinet members and other government officials again refrained from putting their own names on the roster of shareholders, the company quickly gar-nered a capital of 1 million yen ($500,000) from a total of 557 investors. The heads of the Mitsubishi, Mitsui, Asano, and Yasuda *zaibatsu* conglomerates comprised the major shareholders.[60]

The Katsura Colony of Iguape was a prototypical example of migration-led set-tler colonialism, which subsequently inspired other private and state-led attempts at dotting the greater São Paulo region with permanent Japanese agricultural com-munities. By the mid-1930s the Iguape vicinity alone was home to three separate immigrant farm settlements totaling 189,830 acres, with over eight hundred house-holds (or 5,096 residents) from Japan. The initial 2,120-acre tract was named in honor of Katsura Tarō after he unexpectedly passed away in October 1913.[61] Per his original wishes, the first group of family settlers concentrated on rice cultivation.[62] In addition to the first Katsura settlement, there emerged another 46,180-acre col-ony in the nearby town of Registro by the end of the 1910s, followed by the third

MAP 3. Locations of Brazil's Japanese settler colonies with ties to Japanese America, 1910s–1930s. Map by Bill Nelson.

settlement in Sete Barras, which was almost two times larger than the second (see map 3).[63] In these contiguous Japanese colonies, landowning settlers lived up to the mythical image of rugged frontiersmen, since they all had to clear vegetation and prepare their properties for farming in the beginning. Impressed by the "prevailing air of a pioneer town spirit," a BCC employee who visited the Katsura settlement in 1914 praised the residents for their "enormous dedication to achieving overseas colonization."[64] During the initial years, Aoyagi was at the helm of Iguape settlement making, thus imbuing this Brazilian venture with many quixotic ideas and practices that the self-styled frontier conqueror brought from the American West.

The example of the Katsura Colony represents a hitherto neglected aspect of imperial Japan's settler colonialism that overflowed the boundaries of its sovereign territories. The concurrent unfolding of the BCC venture and the ODC illuminated a strong correlation between the state's initiative in the agricultural colonization of Korea and the less-pronounced government role in the Brazilian enterprise. Moreover, it also signified the complex entanglement of Korea and Brazil in the contemporary imaginations of Japanese colonialism—despite the ostensive public-private divides. As noted, the enactment of the two laws relating to foreign-bound emigration and sovereign colonization between 1907 and 1908 provided a crucial background for the complex entanglements between the migration-based Japanization of Korea and the pursuit of overseas national development on Brazilian soil during the 1910s. These transborder manifestations of settler colonialisms—albeit with different degrees of connection to the home government—obscured the problem of sovereignty while enhancing it at the same time. That is to say, not only did state agency and private initiative forge a curious form of partnership, but the former also shored up the latter to generate the mutually reinforcing outbursts of national expansionism inside and outside the empire. As exemplified by the simultaneous involvement of Shibusawa in the ODC and BCC, this state-private partnership also revealed the indispensable role of Japan's monopoly capital in the global trajectories of adaptive settler colonialism. During the 1910s, another project of agricultural colonization at the US-Mexican borderlands elucidated the ever-growing appetite of Japan's colonial capital, which found an eager ally in immigrant entrepreneurs in California with the tacit backing of segments of the Japanese government.

COLONIAL CAPITAL AND JAPANESE AMERICA IN THE US-MEXICAN BORDERLANDS AND THE FLEETING DREAM OF AN ALTERNATIVE FRONTIER

In Japanese public discourse in the 1910s, Mexico consistently ranked third (after Korea and Brazil) on the list of preferred destinations for ambitious Japanese frontiersmen. As explained in the preceding chapter, the Gentlemen's Agreement of 1907–1908 made it illegal for Japanese to enter the United States from across its southern border, thereby putting a stop to the operation of emigration companies in the region. Yet this did not completely end Japanese mobility and settlement in the US-Mexican borderlands, especially between Baja California and the Golden State. Nor did it cancel out deep-seated ideological legacies of earlier extolments of Mexico as an alternative frontier to US California—a glamorized image that had been constantly reproduced by former and current residents of Japanese America and their allies in Japan's expansionist circles. Yet in the 1910s Japanese settler colonialism in Mexico was generally overshadowed by its counterparts in Korea and

Brazil, which maintained closer ties to the central government
Mexico has been left off the radar screen of historical studies on e
tion. US immigration exclusion and social disorder in war-torn]
1910s, which kept the government-recorded statistics of ne
"immigrants" to a negligible level, have also discouraged scholars from recogniz-
ing the US-Mexican borderlands as a steady object of Japanese expansionist gaze
and one of the most dynamic sites for Japanese mobility. Indeed, while only a small
number of new immigrants came directly from Japan, hundreds of US residents,
especially California farmers, crossed the border in search of better opportunities
for settler agriculture in nonexclusionist Mexico from the 1910s through the mid-
1920s.[65] In this sense, despite the virtual stoppage of new immigration from Japan,
the US-Mexican borderlands continued to experience a high degree of Japanese
settler colonialist activity and cross-border community formation.

Inspired by a California-originated image of the mythic Mexican frontier, many
notable Japanese figures, including some government officials, found investment
opportunities still wide open for agricultural colonization and permanent immigrant settlement there. Similar to the initial phase of the Katsura Colony scheme
in Brazil, Tokyo's interest in Mexico neither involved a public proclamation by the
government nor accompanied a form of full-fledged state policy. Rather, certain
individuals in the central government clique, in cooperation with prominent business leaders, took it upon themselves to move forward with large-scale land purchase and systematic development of settler colonies in northern Mexico. These
frequently clandestine projects included some prominent US residents as indispensable partners—often as initiators or intermediaries—of the colonization
projects, replacing the earlier pattern of transpacific collaboration between Japan's
emigration companies and US immigrant labor contractors/agents.

One such example involved Abiko Kyūtarō and his partner Noda Otosaburō.
With the former as president and the latter as general manager, the American Land
and Produce Company (ALPC) took charge of the Baja California colonization
scheme, which served as a transborder cousin of Abiko's Yamato Colony project in
Livingston, California. That project is well-documented in Japanese American history, albeit in a rather limited manner. Scholars have only examined how Abiko's
group strove to put down roots in US soil by practicing Christian-based social adaptation and family immigrant permanent settlement.[66] What is missing in this nationalist narrative of becoming American is that the ALPC also operated self-consciously
within a larger Japanese colonialist diaspora—one that viewed all manifestations of
migration and colonization as being linked to national expansion, whether they took
place inside or outside the Asian empire. Like many other educated immigrants,
their aspirations to participate in mainstream American society did not contradict
their identities as front-line practitioners of overseas Japanese development.[67]
Printed in a Tokyo monthly, ALPC's advertisement elucidated its embrace of settler

colonialism: "Now that many Japanese nationals are involved in enterprises of overseas colonization, the rise of the homeland depends on the success of them. In view of ongoing Japanese development [in the wider world], the American Land and Produce Company is prepared to help steady entrepreneurs and hardworking farmers to build an ideal colony in the North American frontier."[68]

In early 1911 this expansionistic perspective found another opportunity, when Abiko and Noda were presented with an offer to acquire control of two thousand acres near Magdalena Bay in Baja California. The US-owned Chartered Company of Lower California proposed to sell the Japanese a 35 to 50 percent interest in its entire landholdings.[69] The white landowners were apparently heavily in debt, and this deal was meant to increase the value of their total assets, which they intended to sell off eventually.[70] In order to assess the prospects for agricultural colonization there, Noda personally traveled to Magdalena Bay. He wasted no time in producing a positive report that praised the area in terms of its fertile soil, good weather, and commercial fishing opportunities. Noda concluded that "the Japanese can easily penetrate into the midst of natives to form the core-class [of the local industry and society] to guide them, exploit natural resources, and attain healthy agricultural and fishing development."[71] Because white Americans were generally preoccupied with speculative mining ventures other than farming in Baja California, Noda insisted, the untouched land of Magdalena Bay awaited the arrival of Japanese settlers with open arms.[72] Abiko and Noda decided to solicit support from "homeland capitalists" in Tokyo to make a go of their Mexican colonization.[73]

These "capitalists" referred to a group of mercantile-minded business elites gathered around Shibusawa Eiichi. Strong advocates of US-Japanese friendship and peaceful national expansion, Shibusawa and his associates had forged a tight partnership with US immigrant leaders, especially Abiko, in the transpacific movement to transform *dekasegi* migrants into morally upright members of American society and agents of Japan's overseas expansion.[74] Before Abiko got involved in the Magdalena Bay land deal, Shibusawa had already been in contact with a syndicate of white landowners, including Harry Chandler—the publisher of the *Los Angeles Times*—in the US-Mexican borderlands; the white businessmen wished to entice the Japanese to lease thousands of acres for cotton production, the most important US commodity export to Japan.[75] Though nothing concrete came of this 1909 episode, Shibusawa's circle kept an eye out for the possibility of creating a West Coast base of cotton importation for the textile industry—a backbone of prewar Japan's capitalist economy—because domestic cotton mills and textile factories had relied on the more cost prohibitive land-and-sea transport from New Orleans via San Francisco, and after 1914, the Panama Canal importation route. Perhaps for this reason, the Colorado River Land Company (CRLC), of which Chandler's concern was a major shareholder, received an offer of $30 million from "certain moneyed interests" of Japan in 1915 when Shibusawa and his associates visited the United States again. CRLC executives took it for a formal "Japanese government" offer, which entailed the purchase of a large tract near the border town of Mexicali for "colonization" by Japanese immigrants.[76]

This offer, along with Abiko's earlier deal on Magdalena Bay, did not materialize because the business plans soon ran into a roadblock compounded by the Yellow Peril scaremongering campaign in the United States. In 1911, when Abiko's white business partner informed the US secretary of state of ongoing negotiations for acquiring land in Magdalena Bay, the official warned: "A transfer [of landownership to Japanese] would be quite certain to be interpreted in some quarters in a manner to cause a great outcry."[77] Indeed, once the news leaked out, the American press was quick to portray the Japanese purchase of the Baja California properties as evidence of Japan's nefarious design to undermine the US monopoly of the Western Hemisphere by "the establishment of a Japanese naval station." A *New York Times* editorial actually warned the American public of Japan's "growing appetite for new territory," conflating the Magdalena Bay plan with the recent annexation of Korea.[78] Magdalena Bay had been a site of inter-imperial contestation between Germany and the United States, where the former had unsuccessfully sought landownership "for naval purposes" and the latter had engaged in naval target practice between 1900 and 1910.[79] Imperial Japan suddenly appeared as another player, and its presumed militarist intrigue was deemed congruent with the dubious intentions of Japanese immigrant border crossers from California. Seen from the vantage point of US hemispheric imperialism, Japanese America's attempt to organize an ethnic farming settlement on the Mexican seaboard was no different from the building of a Japanese military outpost.

A long-term advocate of US imperialism, Senator Henry Cabot Lodge, quickly seized on the occasion to clarify with President William Howard Taft "whether or not such acquisitions of property or concessions, if allowed, encroach upon the Monroe doctrine."[80] Lodge had been a familiar voice of belligerence against Japan's expansionist ambitions as early as 1897, when he helped garner congressional support for the annexation of Hawai'i.[81] Fifteen years later, Lodge's question reinforced the powerful admonition of Homer Lea, who had just prophesied the Japanese takeover of California and a coming war with Japan in *Valor of Ignorance* (1909). Now the undifferentiated threat of Japanese migration and military invasion was allegedly being extended to the Pacific shores of the Western Hemisphere, where the invocation of the Monroe Doctrine was reckoned indispensable for its defense. Lodge's sensationalist spin made Abiko's business transaction look like a major assault on US national security via its back door, reawakening the sense of ownership about its hemispheric "backyard," with a strong racial undertone that had seldom been present in the previous articulations directed at Europeans.

Conflating the transborder mobility and resettlement of California Japanese and Japan's alleged imperialistic designs, the emergent Yellow Peril discourse culminated in the 1912 Lodge corollary to the Monroe Doctrine. The US Senate ratified it promptly to prevent "any foreign power" (Japan) from obtaining a place of strategic interest in the Western Hemisphere.[82] While drawing on Theodore Roosevelt's corollary of 1904, which reserved the US right to exert military force in Latin America, this congressional action took an important and fundamental departure from conventional US hemispheric diplomacy. No longer did the Monroe Doctrine simply intend to keep out the political influence of European powers; it now aimed to purge the Americas of a Japanese presence—political, economic, and racial.[83] The fear of geopolitical backlash quickly led Japan and Mexico to publicly declare that they did not support Abiko's acquisition of the properties in Baja California.[84] In 1915 another proposed land deal by Japanese concerns did not even become a matter of public concern, because the CRLC flatly "declined [it] on advice of (the) State Department" before the story hit the newsstands.[85]

The Lodge corollary did not put an end to the transpacific collaborative effort among Japanese at agricultural community building in the US-Mexican borderlands. As usual, the adaptability of their settler colonialism was in full operation in response to American racism. Indeed, after the Magdalena Bay episode, what kept California Japanese residents and homeland expansionists going in their joint endeavor was the escalation of anti-Japanese agitation in the US West, for that agitation rendered Mexico more attractive as an alternative site of agricultural development from a prevailing racial perspective. And ironically, the renewed Japanese interest in the US-Mexican borderlands catalyzed further articulations in US hemispheric imperialism in terms of constructing a race-based national security regime against transborder Japanese penetration. This chain of developments, which entwined US domestic racism, adaptive Japanese settler colonialism, and reactive US imperialist diplomacy, helped make North America virtually off limits to Japanese immigration and settlement by the mid-1920s. Reaffirmed in the 1911–1912 Magdalena Bay controversy, the Monroe Doctrine proved to be not only the most effective device of new race-based diplomacy of the United States, but its very justification in the context of white America's fight against Japanese settler colonialism. Until the mid-1920s, that fight periodically confounded domestic race politics and imperialist diplomacy, revivifying the Lodge corollary in its relations with Mexico and other hemispheric neighbors.

During the 1910s the alarmist rhetoric that drew a parallel between Japanese land control and imperial Japan's "appetite for territory" became a hallmark of the US Yellow Peril argument, and its effects reverberated throughout the race politics of the American West. The national security implications of Abiko's failed land acquisition dovetailed with a notable shift in California's anti-Japanese agitation, a shift from the problem of labor immigration to that of resident land control. In 1911 the Baja California incident promptly moved white American California to produce an alien land bill—in the same time frame when Abiko had commenced negotiations with Magdalena Bay landowners. Enacted shortly after the Lodge corollary, the 1913 California Alien Land Law directly tackled the problems of Japanese land-ownership (permanent settlement) and agricultural success (settler colonization).[86] Yet the extraterritorial dimension of Japanese colonization, albeit still a mere pos-sibility, remained unresolved if Japanese crossed the US-Mexican border to evade the effects of the California statute. Etched in the consciousness of white America, the Magdalena Bay scare served as a powerful reminder of this sober reality.

Both Japanese immigrants in California and their homeland supporters viewed the situation from a similar perspective, albeit by positively embracing the option of resettling in the contiguous but extraterritorial frontier of Mexico. The local immigrant vernacular press propagated a favorable view of racism-free Mexico, contrasting Latin racial cordiality and Anglo-Saxon exclusionism. In the context of US military interventions following the Mexican Revolution of 1910, many Jap-anese Californians also appreciated the growth of anti-American/Anglo-Saxon sentiment in civil war Mexico, which they thought would make Mexicans sympa-thetic to Japanese victims of US racism.[87] At home in Japan, a similar racial dis-course had already become deeply ingrained in people's minds in relation to settler colonialism in Brazil. Just as California Japanese substituted Mexicans for Brazil-ians when they discussed Latin characteristics, Japanese pundits engaged in the same pattern of rhetorical adaptation. Kamiya Tadao, who was Aoyagi's close asso-ciate in the Katsura Colony enterprise, likened Mexico to Brazil on account of a "lack of racial prejudice" and "friendliness." Despite his role as a facilitator of sem-iofficial settler colonialism in Brazil, Kamiya even declared that "emigration to Mexico seems more promising than that to South America."[88] Because of Califor-nia's legal blocking of Japanese permanent settlement and agricultural coloniza-tion, Mexico ironically drew renewed attention from advocates and practitioners of settler colonialism in both the American West and Japan.

California's Alien Land Law caused two interrelated developments in the trans-border and transpacific contexts. First, locally a growing number of immigrant farmers began to move to or invest in northern Mexico for property acquisition and farm operation. The law's ban on Japanese immigrant landownership and severe restrictions on farm tenancy motivated the moneyed class of Japanese America to cross the southern border for resettlement in or business expansion into the contiguous Mexican frontier. And second, in this context, some for-profit concerns emerged to broker immigrant land purchases and build infrastructure for a transborder Japanese agricultural colony in Mexico's *frontera*. From across the Pacific, transnational Japanese capital, backed by like-minded political inter-ests in Japan, often acted as an eager partner in such localized colonization efforts by California Japanese during the 1910s.

Similar to Abiko's Yamato Colony scheme, the Nichi-Boku Industrial Corporation (NBIC) of Los Angeles exemplified a California-based movement for immigrant remigration and colonization in Mexico's borderlands, which many Japanese at home supported discursively and materially. A younger brother of Takekawa Tōtarō, Takekawa Minetarō played a central role in organizing this transborder land company in 1912. The NBIC published a lucid, twenty-page publicity booklet to entice both Japanese American farmers and Japanese investors that underscored the familiar racial rhetoric and (pseudo)scientific data, embellished with scholarly excerpts and eye-catching pictures and elaborate maps. As his brother had done two decades earlier, the younger Takekawa discussed the availability of unoccupied fertile landmasses on the Pacific side of Mexico, as well as the inferiority, manageability, and cheapness of "native" residents, who would "swarm any site of employment opportunities like mindless ants." At the same time, Minetarō did not neglect to mention the company's plans to bring "immigrants from Japan to Mexico," and according to him, these future partners in frontier conquest would be able to "offer much higher-quality labor" and support for colonization and agricultural development by California Japanese transmigrants south of the border.[89]

In the northern coastal region of Sinaloa, not far from Magdalena Bay, the NBIC acquired 85,000 acres, which it subdivided for aspiring frontier settlers from Japanese America. Published in the company's illustrated booklet, the "colony" map shows the land tracts to be sold to Japanese settler-farmers from Southern California. The descriptions (sales pitches) in the margins say: "The State of Sinaloa is called the 'California' of Mexico. And [our] colony is reputed as the most desirable and fertile land in that state. . . . It is the world's only and most ideal colony for our race's development" (see figure 3).[90] Enticed by these propitious images of the new transborder "California" frontier, a total of 104 Los Angeles immigrants signed purchase agreements for a total of 12,379 acres between 1914 and 1921, and an additional 57 individuals reserved purchase orders for 4,820 acres.[91]

Although most investors were Japanese residents of Los Angeles, moneyed interests and elite classes in Japan also chipped in.[92] The Taiwan Seitō (Sugar Production) Company, the most important corporate machinery of industrial development in Japan's southern colonial frontier, made a large investment in the NBIC and sent its own agricultural specialist to conduct a land survey in Sinaloa.[93] Dignitaries, including Ōkuma Shigenobu (former prime minister) and Sakatani Yoshirō (former finance minister and Shibusawa's son-in-law), publicly endorsed the NBIC's project.[94] The Los Angeles Japanese consul also approved it publicly, giving the impression of government support. While he characterized the Sinaloa colony as "an extremely promising enterprise" for "small-scale [individual] settler agriculture" in a company announcement for potential investors in Japan, the diplomat recommended: "The [foreign] ministry should accord every facility for [NBIC] to create a model Japanese farming colony . . . so that more [similar] Japanese undertakings would follow."[95] In 1920 the ODC's subsidiary (Kaigai Kōgyō Kabushiki Kaisha) also dispatched an agent to investigate the feasibility of sponsoring the NBIC's venture. Despite all these

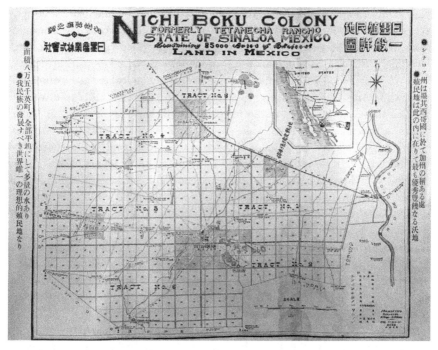

FIGURE 3. Map of Nichi-Boku Colony. *Source:* "Nichi-Boku Colony: Nichiboku shokuminchi" (May 1914), Nichi-Boku Industrial Corporation booklet, author's personal collection.

signs of its promising future, the colony abruptly folded due to a financial scandal in the following year. Yet it allowed a few hundred resettlers from Southern California to dress in the clothes of frontier farmers without facing the constraints of white American racism.[96] A number of first-generation residents in Sinaloa, whom the orthodox narrative of Japanese Mexican history now celebrates as ethnic "pioneers," actually originated from these former California immigrants, who were inspired by a rosy idea of northern Mexico as an integrated frontier.[97]

At the same time, supported by a number of Tokyo government insiders, Asano Sōichirō, Shibusawa's old friend who ran his own industrial conglomerate, was at work to strike a large property acquisition deal with the CRLC along the US-Mexican border region of Baja California. Contrary to the NBIC's localized initiatives, this project represented the "appetite" of transnational Japanese monopoly capital for "new territory," specifically a Japanese-controlled hub of raw cotton production for the benefit of Japan's textile industry. In the expansionist imaginations of many Japanese capitalists, that hub was the Mexicali region, just south of California's Imperial Valley, where hundreds of Japanese tenant farmers had already been engaged in cotton cultivation. Most of the arable and undeveloped land in the valley (Mexican side) belonged to the California-based CRLC and its white American shareholders, including Harry Chandler.[98] Indeed, Shibusawa's failed negotiations with Chandler and the CRLC in 1909 and 1915 provided a glimpse of the long-standing Japanese settler colonialist imaginations projected onto the Mexicali Valley. In 1917 Asano took the initiative in a similar but larger land acquisition deal with white American landowners of Mexicali properties. A CRLC executive later recalled that Asano's interest in the acquisition of its land was as strong as Shibusawa's had been for many years.[99]

In the spring of 1917 Asano dispatched his right-hand man, Hashimoto Umetarō, a one-time leader of Japanese ethnic community in the US Pacific Northwest, to negotiate with Chandler a lease for fifty thousand acres near Mexicali for the length of ten years. This was a deal that would be worth $3,600,000 in total value, and it would bring "four hundred to one thousand Japanese laborers," presumably from both Southern California and Japan.[100] Most likely Hashimoto was responsible for drafting this aspect of the blueprint, for he had had experience in immigrant labor contracting when he was in Seattle. To encourage Chandler's enthusiasm for this big business deal, Asano's proxy was accompanied by a member of the House of Peers and the New York branch manager of the Yokohama Specie Bank, which made this negotiation look like a state-sponsored one.[101]

Having once lived in the western United States, Hashimoto had his own agenda. His penchant for frontier life, adventure, and settler colonialism was deeply ingrained in his past trajectory as a self-styled New World pioneer. In the mid-1890s, for example, when he had learned about the discovery of gold in Alaska, Hashimoto had joined the Klondike Gold Rush, traveling to the Northern Territory with a dream of becoming a Japanese gold mining king. Although his Alaskan adventure was a disastrous failure, this enterprising leader of early Japanese America did not give in and had a try at labor contracting when emigration companies and their agents were making a bundle of money by populating the western frontier with Japanese immigrant laborers. Between 1904 and 1908 Hashimoto had taken five hundred Japanese from Seattle to the Rocky Mountains and supervised their laying of railroad tracks.[102] A decade later this colorful background induced him to envision a similar scheme of large-scale labor importation for land development and cotton cultivation in the US-Mexican borderlands.

To spearhead a new Mexicali venture, Hashimoto partnered with Gō Ryūsaburō—one of Shibusawa's protégés and a brother-in-law of the current foreign minister—who had extensive experience in the textile trade with the United States. Gō was an expansionist-minded entrepreneur in his own right, for he was involved in the establishment of the Nan'yō Society, the central organization of southward expansionists. When Hashimoto began his negotiations with Chandler and the CRLC in 1917, Gō resigned his executive position at Japan's leading brick manufacturer (Shibusawa's concern) and moved to Southern California.[103] Available sources suggest that this veteran businessman was secretly entrusted with a mission to start a model cotton farm under the triangular partnership of Shibusawa, Hashimoto/Asano, and a foreign ministry clique that stood behind them, with an eye to creating a sphere of Japanese economic influence in the northern Baja Peninsula. In Mexicali, Gō leased ten thousand acres, which instantly made him one of the largest Japanese farmers in the region at that time, and he hired an experienced Japanese immigrant farmer to oversee eighty local coethnic workers.[104] This was meant to serve as the cornerstone of a new Japanese cotton plantation when the pending negotiations materialized.

Along with Hashimoto's strenuous efforts, Asano's enthusiasm made Chandler optimistic about the "prospect [of a] big deal," leading him even to favor the idea of "sell[ing] them the whole property if things work out."[105] After initial amiable negotiations, Hashimoto was equally exuberant, writing in his June 1917 correspondence: "We believe that everything of our grand project will be smoothly carried on [sic]."[106] About two months later, however, the US State Department abruptly intervened in the business dealing and put its objection "in the form of a request to [Chandler's group] as patriotic Americans"—an argument that was hard to ignore when the United States had recently entered World War I. National security was a paramount concern of the white republic, and the idea of massive Japanese landholdings and settlements south of the California border did not sit well with US officials or the public. Chandler had to concede for the time being, yet, he did not give up on the possibility of "going back at them (Japanese) from another angle and still hope[d] to win [the deal]."[107]

The end of the war allowed Chandler and Hashimoto to revive the negotiations in December 1918. Backed by Asano's moneyed power, the Japanese side now proposed to buy up as much as 800,000 acres with $50 million instead of just leasing 50,000 acres.[108] The Japanese desire to create a huge cotton colony in the US-Mexican borderlands nonetheless met fierce resistance from within the ranks of CRLC shareholders, who were still infected by wartime patriotic fever and a racial fear of Japanese invasion.[109] Inside the company the anti-Japanese contingent mobilized a successful countermove against Chandler and his supporters by informing a War Department intelligence officer of the revival of the "repulsive" plan to construct a Japanese colony in America's backyard.[110] Along with Senator James Phelan of California, a chief voice of anti-Japanese agitation at the time, the jingoistic Hearst press was quick to pick up the leaked story with a highly sensational spin, characterizing the proposed land deal as a violation of "both Monroe Doctrine and the Lodge Resolution of 1912."[111] With the War and State Departments looking over his shoulder now, Chandler caved in to pressure by April 1919, informing Hashimoto: "Matters have taken a turn which prevent[s] me from giving further serious consideration to the business at this time."[112] After Chandler and Hashimoto/Asano withdrew, Shibusawa stepped right back in to keep communication channels open, albeit more informally, with eager CRLC shareholders/landowners. Although a company representative even visited Tokyo to speak directly with Shibusawa in 1922–1923, the Mexicali colonization scheme had been doomed for all intents and purposes since Washington's intervention.[113] While Yellow Peril fearmongering by the likes of Phelan paved the way for the US government's reaffirmation of the Lodge corollary to the Monroe Doctrine, the 1924 US Immigration Act sounded the death knell for the lingering dreams of Japanese development in northern Baja California. Combined with Washington's blocking of the land transactions between white American owners and Japanese, the total ban on immigration from Japan made it impossible to imagine any form of setter colonialism in the US-Mexican borderlands.

After the complete closure of North America, Japanese settler colonialism adapted once again by valorizing South America, which was not molested by the long reach of US imperialist diplomacy—at least not yet.[114] While Mexico dropped out of the Japanese cartography of overseas national expansion by the mid-1920s, Brazil looked even more desirable to Tokyo officials, capitalists, and the general public, as well as immigrant victims of institutionalized US racism. The next chapter examines the political, social, and discursive processes by which mass migration and agricultural colony making in "racially friendly" Brazil and selected South American countries became firmly integrated into the formal state structure and program under the enlarged authority of the ODC. Not only did this government action accelerate the union of state and private settler colonialisms, but it also consolidated the three schools of expansionist discourse under unified institutional apparatuses of the Japanese imperial state. Despite the removal of Japanese America and its vicinity from the new mapping of state-led settler colonialism, some residents of and returnees from the United States were still deeply involved in this phase of history.

4

___

US Immigration Exclusion, Japanese America, and Transmigrants on Japan's Brazilian Frontiers

For advocates and practitioners of overseas migration and Japanese settlement making, the end of World War I marked the crucial moment when they were compelled to soberly assess the role of the state in the pressing mandate of national expansion. Before 1917 the parallel trajectories of settler colonialism in Korea and Brazil were already more conducive to a proactive engagement among high-level government officials, including Prime Minister Katsura Tarō. With the resurgence of exclusionism in the United States and Japan's acquisition of Micronesia, however, Tokyo brass and the public at large felt it necessary to formalize and institutionalize the state's primary responsibility for the enterprise of migration-led colonial expansion within and without the Japanese empire. Therefore, in 1917 the state began to consolidate privately run emigration companies and colonization companies for the more rationalized, effective management of human trafficking, land acquisition, and financial and technical support for settlement and agrarian expansion abroad. It also helped give birth to a new infrastructure of colonial education for prospective emigrants. From 1917 through the 1920s, these changes made the Japanese state *the* central player in borderless settler colonialism, which lumped together Japanese-governed territories and foreign lands as the undifferentiated object of expansionist fantasies and practices under the all-encompassing language of overseas development.

This chapter traces the complex processes through which the enterprise of mass migration and settler colonialism became firmly nationalized between 1917 and 1928. Expansionistic pundits and activists connected to Japanese America, as well as many ordinary immigrants there, still made up an indispensable component of these historical processes. Although they were not in a position to formulate national policy, as inside members of the central government in Tokyo were, their transpacific influence was not difficult to detect in the ideas and visions that gave life to Japan's new policy of top-down settler colonialism. Just as former San Francisco resident Aoyagi Ikutarō was part of Prime Minister Katsura's pet project, self-proclaimed experts in US-style settler colonialism were also heavily involved in the actual implementation of Tokyo's policy mandates in the "racially friendly" frontier of South America—one that was directly contrasted with exclusionary North America where they had once or still lived. The São Paulo region and the Amazonian rainforest of Brazil occupied a central place in their imaginations and activities, and a number of US-based immigrants and former residents assisted state-led colonization projects as planners, investors, and resettlers.

UNION OF STATE AND PRIVATE SETTLER COLONIALISMS

Toward the end of World War I the state and private settler colonialisms that had tied together the agricultural development of Japanese-occupied East Asia and Japanese-friendly Latin America became even more entangled and indeed virtually indivisible. This development also facilitated the interlocking of the Nan'yō (southern frontiers) with continental and transpacific settler colonialisms, thereby making the difference between government-sponsored colonization and private expansionist initiatives more ambiguous and even inconsequential. Allied with Britain, imperial Japan acquired the new de facto territory of Micronesia from Germany during World War I, and this spoil of war rendered the Nan'yō an additional site of Japanese development, where the state was expected to take the lead in creating a source of economic profit and a civilized settlement of new immigrants from the colonial metropole. Now with the Northern Mariana and Western Caroline Islands in hand, Tokyo started to grapple with the ever-pressing question of how to turn the previously haphazard manifestations of settler colonialism in East Asia and the Americas into a more systematic enterprise of multidirectional imperial expansion under state control.[1]

Between 1917 and 1918 three-step political engineering, which Tokyo officials coordinated, contributed to the greater union of state and semiprivate settler colonialisms on both sides of the Pacific. First, the Japanese government amended the Oriental Development Company (ODC) Act to transform the company from an agent of agrarian migration and colonization to one of money supply (loans and bonds) for "private" colonial and industrial endeavors in Korea and southern Manchuria. Backed by Japanese taxpayers, the ODC's capital increase subsequently entailed the quintupling of the value of its stocks, which raised the company's value by $40 million.[2] By that time the ODC's program of "immigrant colonialism" in Korea had produced a less-than-satisfactory result, making the company function as an absentee landlord that had increasingly suffered from financial constraints.

The profits from land leases had been marginal at best, and stagnant settler migration had sent the company into the red.[3] As World War I came to an end, Tokyo officials, especially the finance minister, wanted to overhaul the ODC by refashioning it as state-controlled colonial monopoly capital—the economic engine of expansive Japan after its war victory.

With the new ODC, the Japanese government also wanted to solidify a financial base and streamline colonizing efforts relative to Latin America and the Nan'yō. In cooperation with the diplomats, the finance minister convinced private emigration companies and the Brazil Colonization Company (BCC) to merge into a single entity called the Kaigai Kōgyō Kabushiki Kaisha (KKKK; International Development Company). The ODC and Japan's top steamship companies were major stakeholders of this new firm, which was capitalized at nine million yen, since they had acquired three-quarters of the company's stock in direct response to the state's request that they invest in it. Established in late 1917, the KKKK combined the hitherto segmented tasks of emigrant recruitment, transportation, and land acquisition and management—critical components of agricultural settler colonialism—under one roof.[4] Aoyagi Ikutarō and a few other BCC executives occupied top management positions in the new semi-state-run company.

After 1918 Japan's new policy of emigration and colonialism defined the relations between the ODC and the KKKK, and hence their duties and goals, in terms of "mother and child." The former, as Finance Minister Shōda Kazue noted, would be the "nucleus of the financial institutions for emigration and colonization."[5] Controlling a 27 percent share of stock (over half a million yen), the ODC indeed treated the KKKK as its subsidiary.[6] The two companies split their jurisdictions, with the former managing Korea, Manchuria, Mongolia, Siberia, and China, and the latter in charge of Latin America, Micronesia, the Philippines, and the Malay Peninsula and Borneo.[7] Anglophone America and Oceania were already out of the picture due to local anti-Japanese exclusion and diplomatic considerations.

The ODC-KKKK alliance enabled a concerted effort in boosting overseas settler colonialism by ordinary people—whether they would move to, invest, and/or work in a part of the home empire or a "new Japan" abroad.[8] A symbol of and model for a successful settler-colonial enterprise, the Katsura Colony of Iguape, São Paulo, remained a flagship venture of the KKKK. Yet the company's projects in Latin America, as in the Nan'yō, were now deeply and formally interlocked with settler colonialism in imperial Japan's territories of Korea and southern Manchuria. In addition to the Katsura Colony, the KKKK's major investments outside the home empire encompassed a 3,600-acre coffee estate near Jaboticabal, São Paulo; a 9,700-acre cotton farm in Chancay, Peru; and a 37,350-acre abaca/oil palm plantation in Davao, Philippines. Colombia was the next in line, and in 1928 a 230-acre "colonial experimental station" in the outskirts of Cali commenced modestly, with ten families (fifty-eight settlers), albeit with an eye to making that South American country the next Brazil in the future. The KKKK's management, including Aoyagi, undertook dozens of investigative trips to potential sites of Japanese development in Latin America, Southeast Asia, and Japan's mandate of the Northern Mariana and Western Caroline Islands. Based on their findings, the company played the role of major stockholder for many other corporate agricultural enterprises in the Malay Peninsula, Borneo, the Philippines, Micronesia, Mexico, and South America. At the same time, its emigration business was responsible for the departure of over 155,000 Japanese between 1918 and 1934.[9] Coupled with the ODC's extensive coverage of the Asian continent, which encompassed Japan's occupied areas and formal colonial territories, the KKKK's entrepreneurial expansionism made major portions of the Western Hemisphere, Pacific Islands, and Southeast Asia relevant and indeed integral to Japanese imperialism in the post–World War I era.

Finance Minister Shōda Kazue was a key architect of this consolidation of the state migration regime after 1917. Having been involved in the drafting of the original ODC restructuring plan, this career bureaucrat was as enthusiastic as any other pundit about Japan's "God-given reason for the external development of [its] citizenry."[10] Yet after serving as the governor of the Bank of Korea in 1915–1916, Shōda became particularly dismayed by the weak financial base of the state colonial machine, let alone the "presence of many small (emigration) companies" that blindly "competed with each other to impair the interest of the (home) empire."[11] The merger of the KKKK with the ODC stemmed from Shōda's profound concern about the absence of colonial monopoly capital and the counterproductive nature of uncontrolled private colonial ventures.

Even though he had personally supported continental expansionism, the finance minister believed in "the state's responsibility to direct the policy of overseas development to every corner" of the world.[12] He had rejected Komura Jutarō's "complacency" in opposing transpacific migration despite his acknowledgment of possible diplomatic repercussions. "The expansion of the (Japanese) empire," Shōda thus declared publicly, should encompass "not only such new territories of ours as Taiwan, (south) Sakhalin, and Korea . . . but also Manchuria, Mongolia and China . . . as well as the Nan'yō and South America."[13] To the finance minister, any difference that might have existed among the three schools of expansionism was inconsequential, because all the locations mentioned were supposedly susceptible to the "rightful destiny of imperial subjects" to conquer and progress.[14] Coupled with his desire for the "institutionalization" of colonial monopoly capital, Shōda's omnidirectional approach to national expansion led him to engineer the alignment of the ODC with the Bank of Korea and of the KKKK with the Yokohama Specie Bank and the Bank of Taiwan, in order to facilitate the speedy and steady flow of necessary funds for settler colonialism all over the Asia-Pacific basin.[15]

It is important to note that the geopolitics of US-led anti-Japanese racism provided a crucial ideological push in the late 1910s to Japan's efforts to create a centralized, state-controlled machine of emigration and colonization under the strongly capitalized ODC. Following the end of World War I, the press-led Yellow Peril scaremongers joined forces with California exclusionist agitation in the United States, igniting a fierce political campaign against Japanese immigration during the election campaign years 1919–1920. A local racist outcry to "keep California white" correlated with the Anglo-Saxonist foreign policy of Australia and the United States to deny Japan's proposal of a racial equality clause at the Paris Peace Conference in early 1919.[16] In tandem with US politics of immigration exclusion, the white-dominated international system of the time started to circumscribe Japanese mobility in the Pacific more severely. In response, the postwar Japanese ideology of racial struggle, now imbued with an inflated sense of superiority, rationalized and buoyed the time-honored notion of racially friendly Latin America as an ideal site of overseas Japanese development. This racial lens informed the pragmatism of Tokyo officials, like Shōda, who carried out the institutional revamping of settler colonialism in the late 1910s.

While vacillating between the East Asian colonies and extraterritorial Latin America, Japan's adaptive settler colonialism still deemed Brazil to be a viable racial paradise for Japanese settlers. In its report on emigration and colonization, for example, the *Osaka Mainichi* daily drew a sharp contrast between "North America where Japanese are denigrated as Jap" and "South America where they are embraced as Japonés." Latin Americans, according to the newspaper, "showed great affection for Japanese that mirror[ed] their disdain for the overbearing white (Anglo Saxon) race." Their anti–Anglo Saxon sentiments would naturally endorse the immigration of Japanese settlers, viewing the newcomers as dutiful torchbearers bringing progress and superior civilization to their untouched frontier.[17] Likewise, the first comprehensive guide to global settler colonialism, *Nihonjin no kaigai hatten* (Overseas development of Japanese), described South America as "the New World of New Worlds" to be conquered by Japanese people.[18] Brazil topped all nations there, this 1916 treatise argued, because the country was "devoid of racial prejudice." Foreign migrants of any color in Brazil were entitled to "equal constitutional rights," including naturalization, marriage, landownership, work, and business activities.[19] Thereafter, similar views were systematically disseminated in academic discourse as well, as exemplified by a 1925 "study of emigration to Brazil" by Takaoka Kumao, a close colleague of Nitobe Inazō, who taught agricultural science and colonial studies at Hokkaido Imperial University.[20]

In line with these ideas, public representations of Latin America claimed not only the absence of racism but also the possibility of Japanese racial ascendancy. Endorsed by the state, the ODC and the KKKK were as committed as the "private" spheres to the cause of racialized discourse on transpacific expansionism. The ODC's monthly journal, which carried articles on various sites of Japanese agricultural colonization beyond East Asia, printed lengthy "deliberations on overseas (national) development." It identified South America as the most desirable destination of settler family migration—even better than the Japanese-controlled Nan'yō—because the region had the "humble Latin race."[21] After reviewing the reasons for Japan's past colonial failures and the problem of racial competition with Anglo-Saxons, the ODC's official journal reproduced the same rhetoric that US-based ideologues of the 1890s had propagated. It explained that the unfortunate Japanese encounter with US racism had spoiled the cumulative efforts at overseas development in California and Hawai'i. Then, the Japanese attempt to enter the Philippines, albeit populated by the "inferior" Malays, had likewise come to naught when the United States applied its racial exclusionism there. The North American frontiers (including Mexico) that had benefited from the pioneering work of Japanese settlers were now shutting their doors completely, as were Australia and Canada, because the Anglo-Saxon race was infected with "an arrogant superiority complex"—an "unreasonable racial prejudice" that would not go away anytime soon.[22] Without mass migration to South America, the ODC's monthly predicted, imperial Japan would inevitably suffer from "contraction," barring its meager territories in East Asia.[23] Published by the KKKK, a 1926 guidebook echoed its parent company's race-based assertions. Its extolment of Brazil for potential emigrants revolved around the twin themes of racial struggle with Anglo-Saxons and racial equality with, if not superiority to, Latin Americans, whose "mixed blood" comprised "aborigines (*dojin*) and former slaves," code words for racial inferiority.[24]

SHAPING THE NATIONAL MIND-SET FOR STATE-SPONSORED OVERSEAS DEVELOPMENT

Nevertheless, beyond the appeal of direct material or monetary gain, the encouragement of migration and overseas settlement based on the abstract notion of racial superiority required the shaping of a popular expansionist mind that would rationalize the pains of leaving the comforts of home. Such a popular mind-set would also harmonize the migrants' pursuit of personal benefits with the public extolment of their patriotic contributions to the expansive empire. As explained in chapter 3, popular expansionist journals of the early twentieth century had already attempted to do this, but with only a relatively limited reach to urban male students. Large numbers of Japanese commoners—rural farmers with a minimum education as well as young women—had been mostly left out, even though these segments of Japanese society had purportedly formed the mainstays of earlier settler colonialism in Korea and Brazil that had idealized agrarian family settlers.

Popular colonial education thus comprised a core of the state overhaul of Japan's migration regime from the late 1910s on. In his public address on the new government policy, Finance Minister Shōda indeed declared that the success of institutional reform was contingent on that of "colonial education," through which the government would instill a nationalist sense of "duty" in the mind and heart of every imperial subject.[25] The government and social elite of Japan must take the initiative in establishing special educational institutions and programs for foreign languages, practical knowledge, and skills for frontier life—a proposition that the Imperial Diet approved in principle in 1918.[26] Thereafter, Japan's home ministry operated an emigrant training school at the port of Yokohama, followed by others in Kobe and Nagasaki.

This process, too, entailed a central role being played by former and current members of Japanese America and their US-bred pedagogical philosophy and inventions. In 1892 San Francisco–based expansionists had borne the brunt of the racist press campaign, for white American agitators compared them with the Chinese, who had been excluded on grounds of their alleged uncivilized practices, economic threat, and racial inferiority. Ever since then, the self-styled Japanese frontiersmen who had chosen to remain in the American West had worked hard to vindicate their reputations and had behaved as a people who were modern, civilized, and hence acceptable to westerners. With their classist bias, however, educated leaders of Japanese America could not completely dismiss the exclusionist accusations about the "inferior" character of many of their compatriots who originated from the humble elements of rural Japan. Japanese immigrant protests against white racism were therefore always accompanied with top-down community efforts at moral reform to uplift common laborers in accordance with the values and mores of modern Japan and middle-class white America. For that reason, in 1914 immigrant leaders of San Francisco partnered with Shibusawa Eiichi and other Tokyo business elites to create a transnational network of education and moral reform directed at US-bound emigrants, including a large number of "picture brides."[27]

What motivated Shibusawa and other Japanese supporters was the prevailing idea that US immigrant intellectuals and leaders, since the days of Nagasawa Betten, had propagated regarding the presumed causes for the spread of anti-Japanese agitation in North America. With their shared belief in racial compatibility with Anglo-Saxons, the two sides desperately searched for reasons that they thought explained the "unjust" bigotry and irrational "misunderstanding" of white exclusionists about alleged Japanese unassimilability and racial peril. The explanation could not be reduced to biology or blood because that would make it impossible for immigrant leaders and their homeland allies to maintain their assertion of Japanese-white compatibility. In their eyes a major problem seemed to have been the behavior of low-class Japanese migrants, who were as yet neither properly nationalized nor sufficiently civilized to act as upright imperial subjects (and hence "American" residents). Rather than aspiring to become a settler-colonist with his own family, according to this view, a typical Japanese laborer in California lived the life of a *dekasegi* sojourner who wasted his hard-earned money on gambling and other vices. Since common migrants appeared to have made scant effort to enhance the interests of the host society, not to mention those of their home country, their presence led white Americans to misconstrue all Japanese as uncivilized, unassimilable, and perilous. In order to dispel such a "misunderstanding," the Japanese Association of America in San Francisco executed well-coordinated efforts at immigrant moral reform and an extensive publicity campaign about the assimilability of the Japanese from 1914 through the early 1920s. Known as the "campaign of education" (*keihatsu undō*) and directed at both ordinary Japanese residents and white Americans, this program of moral reform and public relations entailed close collaboration between the immigrant elite and diplomats in the US West.[28]

Back in Japan, government officials and social leaders also seized on this line of thinking. Yet whereas US-based immigrant leaders were primarily concerned with the immediate effects of racial exclusion on their livelihoods, their homeland allies anticipated the long-term benefits of migrant moral reform relative to an imperative of national expansion. These supporters of Japanese America wished to see migrant commoners—present and future—being properly educated and steered toward the life of family-based permanent settlement beyond North America. Indeed, the US-originated efforts at immigrant moral reform of the early 1910s determined the principal terms and patterns of emigrant recruitment in Japan and of overseas community building in Brazil after the latter half of the decade. For example, what Japanese leaders in California interpreted as a catalyst to white American "misunderstanding" influenced Tokyo's policy toward Okinawan emigration to Latin America. In 1919 the Japanese government's concern about "uncivilized" migrant behavior resulted in a comprehensive ban on the departure of Okinawans, whom diplomats viewed as being unable to understand the language of "mainland Japanese" and prone to run away from work and community responsibility, to wander around half naked, and to maintain bizarre customs such as tattooing on the backs of married women's hands. This ban lasted until 1926, when foreign ministry officials finally felt it possible to find reformed Okinawan youths who would be capable of acting properly as imperial subjects due to the positive influence of various educational programs under Japan's "domestic" colonial rule.[29]

From the mid-1910s, emigrant social engineering in Japan took place in the context of formal education at special training centers and schools. Under the influence of US-bred reformist ideas, the 1910s and 1920s were marked by a proliferation of such educational programs and institutions. They all sought to cultivate minds among the general public suitable for state-regulated settler colonialism. In this context, Shibusawa Eiichi was particularly instrumental. Revered as a foremost cosmopolitan philanthropist of prewar Japan, this financial mogul was deeply involved in the formal campaign of education that unfolded in Japanese America from the early 1910s. At the same time, he launched his own project of emigrant education through a brand new organization called the Japan Emigration Society (Nihon Imin Kyōkai) in Tokyo. Shibusawa and other business magnates wanted to better prepare rural migrants for their new role as representatives of modern Japan and front-line agents of national expansion and overseas development. For this purpose, the society founded the Yokohama center for emigrant training in 1916.[30] With an annual subsidy from the foreign ministry and an endowment from Shibusawa's friends and followers, the Yokohama center offered an intensive educational program for individuals bound for the United States, Brazil, Peru, the Philippines, and other countries. Over the following few years, as the restructuring of the ODC began, the government nationalized Shibusawa's endeavor to align it with the new state policy. In 1918 Japan's home ministry formally took over the Yokohama emigrant training center; it subsequently organized additional centers in Kobe and Nagasaki, from which many emigrants departed, especially for Latin America and the Nan'yō. These centers constituted an integral part of state-regulated "colonial education," as Shōda had envisaged.[31]

In terms of the curricula, the emigrant training centers embodied the elite Japanese preference for stable family life as the moral backbone of national settler colonialism—the vision popularized by educated US residents and returnees. Intended to assist in the formation of the ideal pioneer agrarian family on the frontier, instructional subjects at the Yokohama center included basic western/modern etiquette and values (six hours); practical English or Spanish (later also an option of Portuguese; six hours); living conditions in a foreign land (six hours); vital domestic skills (six hours); household management (six hours); public sanitation and feminine hygiene (three hours); and the proper/scientific method of child rearing (two hours). This thirty-five-hour program was repeated every week at no cost to emigrants. As this list suggests, attention was paid particularly to the "enlightenment" of female migrants, for they were expected to be responsible for maintaining the family life and education of the next generation of overseas Japanese.[32]

Based on this thinking, the state-run emigrant training centers made a special effort to attract women. Statistics suggest the relative success they had in influencing the wives and future mothers of Japanese frontiersmen. In 1916 Yokohama had 514 individuals bound for North America (continental United States, Hawai'i, and Canada); 410 for Latin America; and 84 for the Nan'yō. Nearly one-third of them were female "students."[33] Six years later, the combined total of emigrant students at Yokohama and Kobe was 5,357, about half of whom were now women.[34] Originally, a large number of these women were US-bound "picture brides" and other family members of bona fide US residents—a group of Japanese immigrants exempt from the Gentlemen's Agreement. US Japanese leaders who initially cooperated with the Japan Emigration Society were primarily interested in the moral uplift of these newcomers, a process that they often referred to as "Americanization."[35] Yet under the patronage of the homeland elite, and soon under the management of the state, the emigrant training centers began to cater to a larger agenda than the US immigrant pursuit of "Americanization," that is, the counterresponse to localized racial exclusion. As an integral part of the state's new policy after 1918, the schools aspired to equip common emigrants, especially women, with the kind of "modern" knowledge, "scientific" skills, and nationalist mentality that would enable them to act as self-disciplined guardians of frontier family and settlement in any outpost of expansive Japan.[36]

Aside from their historical and ideological origins, the state-run centers for colonial training revealed another link to the experience of Japanese immigrants in the United States. Commissioned by the Japan Emigration Society, the first headmaster and instructor at the Yokohama center was Nagata Shigeshi, who took charge of every aspect of the school operation in the first few years. A former California community leader, this Christian activist educator was a quintessential immigrant expansionist and self-styled pioneer farmer, who shared similar characteristics and ideas with his predecessors of the late nineteenth century. In 1914, upon his return to Tokyo, Nagata took over the operation of the Nihon Rikkōkai, Japan's most respected private emigration society, which had dispatched thousands of ambitious youth to North America from 1897 through the 1910s, and then to South America, especially Brazil, as well as Manchuria and the Nan'yō, in the 1920s and the 1930s.[37] At the Yokohama emigrant training center, he recruited another former US immigrant as an instructor and personally created the aforementioned curriculum, which subsequently became the prototype for the state-run training centers in Kobe and Nagasaki. After the Japanese home ministry took over the centers, Nagata decided to aid the state effort by organizing a Rikkō Overseas Higher School (Rikkō Kōtō Kaigai Gakkō); it served as a boarding school for future settler-colonists in Latin America.[38] Whereas the state-run training centers at Japan's major port cities offered a last-minute educational program for emigrants on their way abroad, Nagata's school aimed to imbue Japanese youth with proper knowledge, values, and mentality according to his own California-bred settler colonialism, in a more consistent and prolonged manner years before actual emigration.

Following in the footsteps of Nagata, many individuals and private institutions took up settler colonial education as a new business and a means of making a national contribution throughout the 1920s. Some of these schools paid as much attention to the making of ideal colonial homemakers as to that of frontiersmen. By organizing its women's department with a new dormitory, for example, the Kaigai Shokumin Gakkō (Overseas Colonization School) attempted to rectify "past failures of 'male-centered colonization.'" Its graduates were expected to marry overseas residents, thereby allowing otherwise shiftless bachelors to enjoy a stable family life on a new frontier, such as Brazil. Not only did this gendered emigrant training program render young women a chief object of colonial education, but it also functioned as an important device to transform *dekasegi* male migrants into real "pioneers in a [Japanese] colony" through reforming female influences.[39]

Adolescents were another holy grail of academies of settler colonialism in post–World War I Japan. Eyeing that particular age group, some existing institutions of higher education stepped in to support the national project of colonial education. Sophia University, founded by Jesuits, established a division of colonial studies specifically for aspiring migrants to Spanish- and Portuguese-speaking nations in Latin America. Takushoku (literally "Colonization") University opened a "colonial higher school" in Tokyo and a branch in Brazil. Originally this academy had come into existence as the brainchild of Prime Minister Katsura, who had wanted to produce colonial administrators and experts for Taiwan. Takushoku's new venture in Brazil effectively revealed the overlapping of foreign settler colonialism with formal state imperialism during the 1920s.[40]

Lower-level private schools also sprang up outside Tokyo; the Hiroshima Kaigai Gakkō (Hiroshima Foreign Institute) offered various courses for adolescents sixteen years old or above. The minimum educational requirement was the completion of higher elementary school (eight years), and both boys and girls were admitted. Located in Sapporo, Hokkaido, the Nihon Shokumin Gakkō (Japan Colonization School) did not even require prior education as long as the applicant had a "strong will, healthy body, and good references." These two schools sent graduates all over the world, including Asia, the Nan'yō, and South America.[41] On the state-controlled grammar school level, too, it does not seem to have been uncommon for expansionist-minded teachers to lecture in the everyday classroom on the virtue of leaving home for a foreign land as a patriotic act. In a published anthology of student essays, for example, a female fifth grader from a Hokkaido village wrote in 1928: "We must strive to move to the countries that are favorably disposed to Japan, like Brazil, Argentina and Mexico. There, we would produce cotton and rice and sell them in abundance to Japan for cheap. Japanese people must be determined to stay there permanently once they set foot in a foreign country, and we must avoid behaving badly there. . . . If we were to be stuck in this tiny Japan and were forced to prey on each other, Japan could not but perish. Once I grow up, I will go [overseas] no matter what."[42] While it is clear that student essays bear a trace of teacher's edits, this example shows that the orthodox ideas of proper settler colonialism had entered the consciousness of schoolchildren far out in Hokkaido. Just as the division between state imperialism and private settler colonialism became more and more tenuous toward the 1920s, an attempt to shape a common national mind proliferated to the effect of valorizing the goal of borderless Japanese development among all segments of society, including women and children.

1924 US IMMIGRATION ACT AND THE RISE
OF THE STATE AS THE CENTRAL AGENT
OF OVERSEAS EXPANSION

Following the consolidation of the ODC and the KKKK and the government's involvement in colonial education, the postwar years of 1919–1924 marked another watershed in the history of Japanese migration and settler colonialism. It was during these critical years that Tokyo finally incorporated migration and colonization into a core part of national policy in response to racial exclusionism in the United States. Despite the brief suspension of organized anti-Japanese agitation during World War I, California exclusionists resumed their crusade in 1919. The local Japanese Exclusion League engaged in an energetic political and press campaign against Japanese immigration, family formation (picture marriage), and land control to deter their settlement and agricultural activities in the American West. This regional movement soon influenced the US Supreme Court and Congress, inducing the former to declare the racial ineligibility of Japanese for naturalization in 1922 in *Takao Ozawa v. United States* and the latter to pass an exclusionary immigration law two years later. No more new immigrants could enter the United States from Japan after June 1924, and under the spell of shared anti-Asian racism, Canada followed suit with a similar law a few years later.[43]

Ironically, the passage of the 1924 US Immigration Act intensified the Japanese government's resolve to more fully command control of mass migration, agricultural colonization, and commercial/industrial enterprise. This turn of events prompted two interrelated developments: the rise of reactive pan-Asianism and Tokyo's decision to make "racially friendly" Brazil a primary object of a new state-led settler colonial enterprise along with Japanese-controlled Manchuria, Taiwan, and Micronesia. Reenergizing the ideology of pan-Asianism, strong anti-American sentiments swept through the island empire between the passage of the 1924 US legislation on April 12 and its enforcement on July 1.[44] While Japan was barely recovering from the devastating effects of the Great Kantō earthquake of 1923, the angry nation—from the upper to the lower echelons of society, from the educated to the working-class, and from the ultranationalist to the liberal—was engulfed in emotion-filled, race-based discourse. It specifically defined the Yamato race as the "leader of the Asiatic" in the collective struggle against the global white menace. Japanese settlement making in non-Anglophone societies was deemed one of the important means to fulfill that manifest destiny.[45] The enterprise of overseas development was no longer a simple expression of Japanese racial expansiveness. It became a prerequisite for their ability to play the incumbent role as the global master race.

The ascendancy of race in Japanese expansionist discourse became evident when diverse sectors of society responded to US white supremacy in an emotional and violent manner. In mid-1924 numerous protest meetings were held in villages, towns, and cities throughout the Japanese archipelago. Tokyo alone saw a total of 104 anti-American rallies between the middle of April and early July. Some gatherings attracted several thousand people each. On the first day of July, the city had six mass rallies with attendance of several hundred to thirty-five hundred, at which the participants observed the "Day of National Humiliation" (*kokujokubi*). With the biggest gathering being the National Conference for Anti-American Commemoration, right-wing activists and ultranationalists took the initiative in sponsoring many rallies, but a large number of ordinary Japanese also met in protest under the aegis of Christian and Buddhist organizations, student groups, and other less politically oriented entities. In Osaka, a coalition of college students, the Boy Scouts and other youth organizations, labor unions, a resident Korean association, and even a group of *sumō* wrestlers brought over two thousand people to the Congress of Far Eastern Peoples.[46] These rallies typically featured jingoistic and racist political speeches, and the conferences always concluded with anti-American/antiwhite resolutions.[47] While the domestic print media were busy reporting this nationwide spread of racial hostilities and sensational stories, statesmen and intelligentsia of Japan, including the most genuine friends of America, displayed strong indignation and protested against US racism in chorus, thus giving emergent pan-Asianism political legitimacy.[48]

Couched in highly racialized language, the major themes of discussions at the anti-American rallies and press commentaries encompassed the hypocrisy of American democracy, the domination of the world by Americans and Europeans, and the prediction of a coming "clash" between Japan and the United States/the West—the same concept that had driven the Yellow Peril scaremongers on the US side.[49] In direct response to its American counterpart, imperial Japanese racism of the mid-1920s imagined not only the collective crime of the white race against "colored" peoples all over the Asia-Pacific basin, but also the Japanese people's inseparable bond with their fellow Asians and their "noble" mission to "guide" them under Japan's "peaceful expansionism."[50] In the same vein, Japanese public discourse of the time often entertained pseudo-academic theories of racial affinity with indigenous and racially mixed peoples of not only Asia but also Latin America. As the KKKK's 1926 guide to emigration to Brazil showed, this assertion also helped rationalize the "pro-Japanese sentiments" of Latin Americans, who would automatically welcome the coming of their racial "cousins" from Japan as the role models and teachers of "development."[51]

The US Immigration Act also impressed on Japanese officials and the public more than ever the centrality of state sovereignty in the success or failure of overseas development. Since 1892 the United States had engineered political and legal measures against Japanese conquest of the western frontier, and the 1924 legislation signified a decisive end to any further attempt to erect a new Japan on North American soil in the context of global racial struggle—one that US-based Japanese expansionists had already prophesied in the early 1890s as an imperative of teleological history. As they had indeed argued, now many people of Japan also came to see that the question was not whether or not Japanese were inferior to American whites as frontier colonists. They felt it was all about the presence or absence of sovereign state control over or support for the processes of migration and settlement. Even before the first half of the 1920s, a call for proactive government policy was not difficult to find in the circle of expansionists, especially US return-ees and their allies. Yet the "national humiliation" of 1924 brought the discussion to the center stage of imperial Japan's realpolitik, where even political pragmatists and liberal internationalists were compelled to join the jingoistic advocacy for the deeper involvement of the Japanese government in the enterprise of global national/racial expansion through mass migration.[52] White American racism thus facilitated the elevation of settler colonialism to a higher priority in Japan's state policy agenda.

It is important to note, however, that the problem of race-based immigration exclusion was also deeply intertwined with an ever-intensifying Malthusian fear of overpopulation and food shortage at that juncture—the imminent threats with which Japan was being forced to grapple under the combined effects of the Russian Revolution (1917) and the ensuing communist upsurge, rice riots and postwar woes, and the devastating Great Kantō earthquake.[53] The complete closure of North America by Anglo-Saxon powers, as many pundits observed, portended the shrinking of the regions that could accommodate Japan's growing surplus population.[54] A Tokyo Imperial University professor contended that "domestic migration" to Hokkaido, Korea, and Taiwan would not be enough to alleviate the problem, thus advocating "peaceful [extraterritorial] expansion . . . without concern for reactions of Americans and Britons."[55] Commonly held by many con-temporaries of Japan, this same fear convinced less ideologized policy makers to embrace Tokyo's direct involvement in state-sponsored migration as a solution to the empire's perceived overpopulation problem.

Corresponding neatly to the rise of US Yellow Peril fearmongering and informed by domestic political concerns, the complex processes of national policy making linked to settler colonialism unfolded simultaneously in various sectors of the Japanese government in the first half of the 1920s. First, established in 1920, the social affairs bureau of Japan's home ministry spearheaded direct state involve-ment in the KKKK's migrant recruitment by providing financial subventions for both the company and individual emigrants. With a vivid memory of rice riots in 1918, many government officials—particularly home ministry brass in charge of social welfare—were alarmed by the problems of unemployment, poverty, and labor strife.[56] In this context of a fight against postwar recession and communist encroachment, the ministry's social affairs bureau coupled the policy of migration subsidies with other social relief measures, including job referral services after 1920.

During the initial few years, the home ministry provided the KKKK with a total of 100,000 yen ($50,000) annually to expand its emigrant recruitment campaign, and applicants only enjoyed an exemption from government paperwork expenses (35 yen) under this scheme. Yet after the Great Kantō earthquake, the ministry decided to offer Brazil-bound emigrants an individual payment of 200 yen to cover travel expenses as well when they signed up with the KKKK's program. To familiarize prospective emigrants with what to expect in Brazil and what the state expected of them, the nationwide network of employment referral agencies, run by the home ministry, supplied them with necessary information through pamphlets, lectures, and grassroots counseling.[57] Before emigrants left for Latin America, the training centers in Yokohama, Kobe, and Nagasaki reinscribed the idea of being/remaining a proper imperial subject in a new Japan—one who could live the moral life as a civilized frontier farmer to maintain the honor and dignity of the Japanese empire. It was to meet this very goal that the home ministry took over the Yokohama emigrant training center from the Japan Emigration Society, nationalized it, and established the additional facilities in Kobe and Nagasaki.[58]

Importantly, the Japanese foreign ministry, which had taken charge of matters relating to emigration and the KKKK, remained rather resistant to the home ministry's program, which prevented the latter's social affairs bureau from offering direct subsidies to emigrants during the first two years. In part, this was an extension of a bureaucratic turf war, but the diplomats were also worried that the rapid growth of transpacific Japanese migration, albeit to South America, might fuel anti-Japanese agitation among white American exclusionists, who had viewed the region as their "backyard" since the declaration of the Monroe Doctrine.[59] Yet the aftereffects of the 1923 earthquake tilted the balance of power in favor of the home ministry. The disaster caused more than 100,000 deaths and left 1,550,000 people homeless in Tokyo alone.[60] The entire nation was faced with the enormous challenge of rehabilitating the victims quickly despite the constraints of the postwar recession, and the expansion of the social affairs bureau's program was considered the least the government could do to help the displaced and unemployed. Thus, public opinion pushed for government-funded emigration, which one source estimated would be more economical than a domestic relief effort, even not taking into account the additional anticipated benefit of immigrant remittances.[61]

The aftermath of the 1923 earthquake also prompted serious discussion about the reconfiguration of the existing migration apparatuses in relation to the enlarged and direct roles of the government. At the same time, this discussion, which unfolded at the state-sponsored Economic Conference of the Empire (Teikoku Keizai Kaigi) in the spring of 1924, had the additional purpose of deliberating on Japan's responses to the US Immigration Act.[62] The expansion of domestic social relief efforts and the management of the impact of America's racial exclusion informed the adaptive settler colonialism of post-1924 Japan, which recast the Japanese government as the central player in the business of migration to and settler colonialism in Brazil.

After two months of deliberation in April and May, the fifteen-member conference presented a set of important proposals with regard to migration that would give birth to a new migration law, a state-sponsored colonization firm, and the ministry of colonial affairs between 1927 and 1929. Considering Japan's failure in settler colonialism within and without the empire in the prior two decades, these new measures were deemed indispensable. Adopted by Tokyo authorities, the conference report explained: "Despite billions of yen that were invested in Manchuria, Mongolia, and China (as well as Taiwan, Korea, Sakhalin and the Nan'yō), few visible signs of [Japanese] economic development and colonization are present. Migration to North America and Hawai'i has lacked good planning and coordination, thereby causing today's pathetic situation (immigration exclusion)."[63]

According to the transcripts of the conference, members also came to the conclusion that the formal territories of imperial Japan alone would not suffice to accommodate large-scale transplantation of jobless and homeless Japanese for a variety of reasons, including the presence of a large number of "natives" and the lack of available arable land for new settlers. The general failure of the ODC's earlier agricultural colonization in Korea and southern Manchuria provided a background for this pessimistic outlook. On the other hand, despite the "negatives" of foreign locations, such as the absence of direct sovereign influence, the conference agreed that Brazil was the most desirable migrant destination—an open frontier for Japanese family settlers—because the Latin American country appeared to pose the fewest problems, especially from the standpoint of race politics or the lack thereof.[64] Based on that assessment, the conference report recommended: "For the promotion and protection of migrant colonists, . . . [the Japanese government] should take the initiative in seeking undeveloped land . . ., transfer labor and capital, and establish Japanese settlement [in Brazil] on the basis of co-existence and co-prosperity [with locals]."[65]

The conference report included nine specific measures to be taken by the government. Some pertained to the "propagation of expansionistic ideology" and the "education and training of emigrants" in Japan. The home ministry was already at work on these matters, and the report gave added legitimacy to its ongoing educational program. Other measures called for the revision of migration-related legislation and the "(re)organization of administrative entities to streamline business affairs."[66] Moreover, casting its expansionist gaze on Brazil, an additional resolution demanded that a new "colonization company be established" to take charge of financing, investment (including land acquisition), and community building (i.e., the operation of schools, hospitals, and industrial/agricultural research facilities) in the Latin American country. The trauma of racial exclusion from North America moved members of the economic conference to request the government to endeavor to "deter anti-Japanese sentiment in Brazil and nurture friendship with Brazilians."[67] Submitted to the prime minister in late May 1924, this sixteen-page report cemented the position of Brazil as the centerpiece of state-sponsored settler colonialism. While the report almost immediately quelled residual opposition of diplomats to the home ministry's plan to directly fund Brazil-bound emigrants, it also paved the way for the creation of new legal and bureaucratic apparatuses, as envisioned by the government-commissioned conference.[68]

STATE-SPONSORED SETTLER COLONIALISM ON BRAZIL'S FRONTIERS AND JAPANESE AMERICA

In early 1927 the Japanese government enacted a new law regulating emigration and agricultural colonization abroad by "overseas emigration cooperatives" (*Kaigai ijū kumiai*). Known as the Overseas Emigration Cooperative Act (OECA; Kaigai ijū kumiai-hō), it allowed such a statutory corporation to act simultaneously as the initial landowner of a farm settlement in Brazil, the recruiter and dispatcher of settler-colonists from Japan as cooperative members, and the banker to provide necessary capital for the management of the overseas settlement. Under the law, Tokyo also set up an umbrella organization called the National Federation of Overseas Emigration Cooperatives (NFOEC; Kaigai ijū kumiai rengōkai), which was responsible for transferring government-allocated funds to each prefectural cooperative. What distinguished this scheme decisively from the ODC/KKKK was that the local prefectural governments took the lead in the formation of emigration cooperatives and oversaw their operation through the respective prefectural "overseas associations" (*Kaigai kyōkai*).[69] Put differently, each overseas emigration cooperative was prefecture based and tied to the prefecture-based overseas association under the aegis of the prefectural government. As established by new state legislation, the NFOEC kept all local overseas emigration cooperatives in its clutches; moreover, since 1923 the prefectural overseas associations had been organized under the Central Federation of the Overseas Associations (Kaigai kyōkai chūōkai), with the Japanese government at the helm.[70] It is also important to note that the domestic network of prefectural overseas associations encompassed the hundreds of local "prefectural association" chapters (*kenjinkai*) in Japanese migrant communities all over the Asia-Pacific basin. Not only did this overlapping web of migrant organizations (overseas emigration cooperatives and overseas associations) inside and outside Japan create a transnational safety net for individual settler-colonists, but it also served as an effective extraterritorial mechanism of state control and discipline in foreign lands where Japan's sovereign power had no reach.

In order to make the new centralized structure of migrant governance efficient and effective, Tokyo established the Ministry of Colonial Affairs (Takumushō). In September 1927, about six months after the passage of the OECA, a committee of high-level government officials adopted a formal plan for this significant change in the state bureaucratic apparatus, which would streamline "administrative functions" relative to the "enterprise of emigration and colonization" abroad and the management of "Korea, Taiwan, the Kwantung Leased Territory, and the South Sea (Nan'yō) islands."[71] Although institutional rivalries and negotiations with the foreign ministry delayed the implementation of the plan for two years, the new colonial ministry finally commenced operations in 1929. While it enjoyed supervisory power over the governors-general of Korea and Taiwan and the governors of the South Sea Mandate and Sakhalin (Karafuto) Agency except for military affairs, the new colonial ministry also placed the ODC and all its subsidiaries (including the KKKK) under its purview, taking over the business of emigrant training from the home ministry.[72] In other words, with regard to emigration and colonization, the colonial ministry established extensive jurisdiction over areas and territories both inside and outside the reach of Japan's sovereignty. The establishment of this new bureaucratic apparatus marked the completion of long and complicated political processes that not only elevated settler colonialism to the status of a major national policy but also greatly obfuscated the boundaries between the private and the state, as well as the foreign and the domestic, in the history of Japanese imperialism.

Under the aegis of the colonial ministry and the OECA, the multilayered organizational networks enabled overseas emigration cooperatives to operate more efficiently and systematically than had the ODC/KKKK alone. Anchored in a specific prefecture, each cooperative would naturally maintain strong ties to the locality where family migrants were recruited at a grassroots level, and a group of settlers from the same prefecture were then shipped out from Japan and placed in Brazil as a discrete unit. Therefore, a new Japanese farm settlement looked like a transplanted "prefecture"—more cohesive and functional than before—making it easier for settlers to work together harmoniously in the making of a new Japan on Brazilian soil. Yet in light of the lesson learned in North America, some Tokyo officials, especially diplomats, feared that excessive homogeneity and parochial exclusivity in a settler community might arouse nativist sentiments and exclusionist opposition in Brazil.[73] Others were troubled by the possibility that physical divisions among prefecture-based migrant groups might perpetuate regionalism and promote disunity and internal friction among the Japanese settlers.[74]

These conflicting concerns led the NFOEC to adopt a three-tiered policy of migration and colony making. First, in the process of building a new settlement, the NFOEC headquarters in Tokyo would coordinate the mixing of the multiple contingencies of prefecture-based migrant colonists instead of setting up a community of Japanese with a single prefectural origin. Second, in order to avoid accusations of unassimilability and racial invasion in the host society, local Brazilians, as well as Japanese immigrants who already resided in Brazil, were encouraged to move into the new settlement if they so wished. Third, a local subsidiary—later known as Sociedade Colonizadora do Brazil Limitada (Brajiru takushoku kumiai)—would be established in São Paulo to facilitate the complex process of migrant placement, local settler recruitment, and other business affairs in Brazil.[75] These measures, NFOEC officials anticipated, would facilitate the microcosmical "national" formation of a new Japan in the South American frontier with a few prefecture-based subunits of family settlers as the basic components of settlement while ensuring interracial cooperation between Japanese settlers and Brazilian natives. In order to ensure smooth working relations among emigration cooperatives and prefectural governments, Tokyo delegated the role of supervising the NFOEC's work to the home minister, who simultaneously served as its president.

For the purpose of sending one thousand Japanese households to Brazil's forest-land, the Japanese government allocated 5 million yen ($2,500,000) to the NFOEC and later doubled the amount for land purchase. Underwritten by the state, the strong financial base allowed the NFOEC to acquire over 93,300 acres in the Brazilian states of São Paulo, Paraná, and Minas Geraes by 1929.[76] These estates were made available for family settlers, who could apply for no-interest loans through overseas emigration cooperatives. For the purpose of building the infrastructures of new Japanese agricultural colonies, there were additional government subventions, which included 360,000 yen for the construction of schools, clinics, warehouses, lumber mills, ice plants, and brickyards, along with 70,000 yen for miscellaneous administrative expenses.[77] Overseas emigration cooperatives were formally set up in thirteen prefectures in the initial years of 1928 and 1929. As a key member of the NFOEC leadership and its São Paulo–based representative, Aoyagi Ikutarō, a former San Francisco resident and mastermind of the Katsura Colony, again played a central role in the initial phase of survey and negotiation with Brazilian authorities for the land acquisition. In São Paulo, Aoyagi was aided by another resettler from Japanese America.[78]

Aside from Aoyagi's team, former Californian Nagata Shigeshi was deeply involved in the process leading to this state-sponsored settler colonialism under the mechanism of overseas emigration cooperatives. Although the 1924 Economic Conference of the Empire, had envisioned a regular corporate entity in its recommendations, Tokyo adopted a prefecture-based overseas emigration cooperative approach due largely to Nagata's work. As the United States was moving toward the total exclusion of Japanese newcomers during the first half of the 1920s, the head of the Nihon Rikkōkai had shifted his gaze to Latin America, especially Brazil and Mexico. Like many pundits of the time, this Christian agriculturalist and educator resorted to race-based rhetoric and characterized Brazil as "the land of Canaan" (the promised land) for Japanese migrants.[79] According to Nagata, Latin Americans of mixed heritage shared body and mind with Japanese, and the former would always offer "fantastic respect for and treatment of" the latter. On the basis of this view, Nagata had kicked off his private crusade for the construction of a "colony of [higher] civilization" in Brazil's frontier lands, which he envisioned would consist of resettlers from the racist US West and newcomers from recession-hit Japan.[80] A number of his Rikkōkai associates and disciples in California had heeded the message and actually decided to pull up stakes in the troubled land of Anglo-Saxonist America and move to their "Canaan" after the passage of the 1924 Immigration Act.[81] This had all happened a few years prior to the establishment of the tightly structured state migration regime and machine in 1927–1928.

In order to organize a large contingent of new Japanese colonists bound for Brazil, Nagata relied on a circle of his supporters in his home prefecture of Nagano. Under the enthusiastic backing of the then prefectural governor and other local dignitaries, Nagata's tireless efforts culminated in the establishment of the Shinano (Nagano) Overseas Association for the purpose of migrant recruitment. The self-proclaimed expert on California-style settler colonialism was entrusted with the task of devising a blueprint for the entire scheme, which he drafted in 1923. In the midst of the post-earthquake economic crisis, fund-raising nevertheless proved more difficult than expected, and the prefectural overseas association also faced legal obstacles against incorporation and capitalization under the pre-OECA legal regime before 1927. A new national law would be necessary for the Shinano association to act as an emigrant recruiter, not to mention an agent of land acquisition and settlement building in a foreign country. Nagata asked his friend in the central government to craft a bill, which a Nagano-elected statesman subsequently presented at the Imperial Diet. The overseas associations of Tottori, Toyama, and Kumamoto prefectures joined the Nagano prefecture's political lobbying, and they also proved to be dependable partners in the acquisition of massive forestlands in Aliança, São Paulo, according to Nagata Shigeshi's blueprint. Enacted in early 1927, the OECA constituted a response to these complex developments that were catalyzed by the efforts of the expansionist returnee from California and his supporters. And the Aliança colony of 51,560 acres—Nagata's brainchild—became the first successful example of agricultural settler colonialism on the basis of the prefecture-based mass emigration scheme that the 1927 legislation envisioned.[82] (See map 3 in chapter 3.)

Nagata was not the only former US resident to spearhead a state program of Brazilian colonization after 1924. The transpacific network and collaboration of entrepreneurial-minded expansionists from Fukuzawa Yukichi's Keiō Academy was responsible for the entry of Japanese settler-colonists into the Amazon rainforests—the last untouched frontier of the earth as they saw it. As chapter 1 details, Fukuzawa was one of the most important ideologues of overseas migration during the 1880s. Many of his disciples took his advice and went to the United States to form the first contingent of immigrant settler entrepreneurs and farmers in early Japanese America. One of those self-styled Japanese frontiersmen was Inoue Kakugorō, who struck the first plow of settler colonialism in rural California in 1887. Others, like Mutō Sanji, stayed in the San Francisco Bay Area to acquire the secrets of American/modern business practices while toiling as student laborers in the late 1880s. After returning to Japan, Mutō became the president of the Kanebō

Cotton Mills Corporation. In addition to San Francisco, New York City was a notable hub of Fukuzawa's disciples, who took the lead in US-Japan trade, especially the importation of silk, tea, and porcelain from Japan. Morimura Yutaka set up the US branch of the Morimura Brothers Company, and after joining the firm in 1879, Murai Yasukata assumed the role of its general manager in New York and remained there until 1934. By 1907, according to one source, over one thousand Keiō alumni had immigrated to North America under the spell of their teacher's mercantilist expansionism and agrarian settler colonialism.[83]

When the adaptive gaze of Japanese settler colonialism was focused on Brazil after the closure of North America, Mutō and Murai emerged as the chief architects of frontier conquest in the Amazon basin. The former was instrumental in the establishment of the Nanbei Takushoku Kaisha (hereafter Nantaku; Sociedade Colonizadora da América do Sul or South American Colonization Company) in Tokyo and Belém (Pará, Brazil). The latter operated the Nanbei Enterprise Corporation (Nanbei Kigyō Kabushiki Kaisha) in New York. Under the new legal regime of the 1927 OECA, their endeavors united Tokyo and New York as the source of capital and corporate leadership for Japanese family migration and large-scale pioneer settlement making in the Brazilian state of Pará.

The government-private partnership in Amazonian development unfolded in response to an unexpected invitation by Pará governor Dionysio Bentes, who looked to Japanese immigrants for the opening of the uninhabited forests in his home state. Bentes's 1925 letter of invitation caught the immediate attention of the Japanese ambassador to Brazil, who had been perturbed by the spread of Yellow Peril demagoguery in São Paulo under the influence of US racist discourse.[84] Tokyo accepted the ambassador's recommendation that diverting portions of Japanese migration flow into the Amazon would help quell the fear of a Japanese takeover in São Paulo.[85] In March 1926 Japan's foreign ministry dispatched a group of field investigators to Pará. Mutō's Kanebō Corporation offered both manpower and funds for this official investigation. Headed by Fukuhara Hachirō, Mutō's right-hand man, the investigative team included three other Kanebō employees, as well as a university researcher and government agricultural engineers.[86] Even though the expedition had "no direct bearing on Kanebō's business," Mutō's pitch for the firm's "contribution to the society" managed to convince the shareholders to spare a substantial amount of money from the company's annual operational budget.[87]

Mutō was no stranger to the enterprise of migration and settler colonialism. In fact, he is credited as the first person to publish a guide to labor migration to the United States, as early as 1887. Entitled *Beikoku ijūron* (On immigration to and settlement in America), his treatise drew from his own experiences in California. As Yuji Ichioka explains, Mutō "was fascinated by the presence of Chinese immigrants," who had daringly "left their homeland" and had "compet[ed] economically with [white] Americans."[88] Only five years after the Chinese Exclusion Act of 1882, Fukuzawa's disciple, like many other US-based expansionists of the time, predicted the replacement of Chinese by Japanese, thus recommending emigrant transport as a profitable business. In addition to the economic benefit of mass migration, Mutō also believed in the advantage of foreign frontier conquest by a surplus labor population from a Malthusian standpoint of national interest. Years later, even though he admitted that US immigration exclusion had rendered his advocacy dormant, the talk of Amazonian colonization rekindled Mutō's enthusiasm for mass migration and settler colonialism. In his autobiography, Mutō compared the American West of the 1880s to "South America" of the 1920s/1930s, which he called "the only place that God has left for us to solve our country's worsening population problem."[89] Having shut down North America, Australia, and South Africa, as this ex-California resident contended, Anglo-Saxon racism had precipitated the worldwide shrinkage of frontiers for the Japanese race, which ironically valorized the standing of Brazil, especially its untouched Amazon rainforests.[90]

Mutō's recommendation of Fukuhara for the government-sponsored expedition was no coincidence, because the latter not only shared his business mentor's beliefs but had also had similar life experiences. Some fifteen years after Mutō, Fukuhara spent his formative years in the United States as a student worker in the cotton industry of the Jim Crow South. Despite the distance, his name was said to have been a familiar one among Japanese immigrant expansionists in the American West and northern Mexico at the turn of the twentieth century.[91] By the mid-1920s his embrace of settler colonialism in South America was as firm as Mutō's, and he similarly viewed the Amazon basin as "the only place that has been left open for Japanese racial development" in the white-dominated world.[92] Fukuhara's firsthand experience of US racism paradoxically made him optimistic about Japanese ascendancy on the new frontier. Just as Mutō had likened the US West to the untouched land of South America, Fukuhara characterized Brazil as "the second (southern) United States" in terms of climate, natural resources, and topography suitable for frontier development and colonial agriculture, especially plantation-style cotton production. What distinguished the two frontiers in North America and South America was the presence of different hegemonic races, that is, Anglo-Saxons versus Latinos. In the language of social Darwinism, Fukuhara depicted Anglo-Saxons positively as "progressive" and "meritocratic" despite their racist tendencies, and in contrast, he portrayed Latinos as irrational, nepotistic, and "ineffectual." Moreover, while black inferiority was taken for granted in both Americas, indigenous "Indians" of the Amazon were supposedly the "descendants of the ancient Asiatic," who would look up to Japanese newcomers as their superior brethren. As it presented abundant opportunities equivalent to those on the early US frontier and yet no formidable racial competition to future Japanese settlers, the Amazon basin would be a promised land for them.[93] Along with scientific data and agrological explanations on the topographies, soil, climate, and hygienic conditions of the region, this racialized analysis underpinned the image of Pará as a potential site of Japanese colonial development that Fukuhara delivered to Japan's leading businessmen and government officials after his expedition.

In 1928 the Nantaku was established with the enthusiastic support of Japan's industrial leaders. Capitalized with 10 million yen ($5 million), the Tokyo concern controlled the Pará government land grant of about 2,471,000 acres near Acará—about forty miles southeast of the state capital of Belém—earmarked for five thousand Japanese farm families. Financially speaking, the Nantaku maintained the appearance of a private joint-stock business under the overall command of Mutō's Kanebō Corporation, but it started out as the brainchild of the Japanese government, as shown in the original initiative of the ambassador in Brazil. Indeed, in March 1928 the first meeting of the organizing committee was held at the foreign minister's office, where Japan's top industrialists and financiers met with Prime/Foreign Minister Tanaka Giichi. In addition to Shibusawa Eiichi and Inoue Junnosuke, who was the president of the Bank of Japan, chief executives of Mitsui, Mitsubishi, and Yasuda *zaibatsu* conglomerates were among the conveners. They agreed to leave the actual task of organizing the Nantaku in the hands of Mutō and his Kanebō subordinates. Five months later, the Amazon colonization firm was formally inaugurated; while Japan's monopoly capitalists and other prominent entrepreneurs took one thousand shares each of the stock, the Kanebō Corporation and its executives controlled sixty-four thousand shares of the aggregate two hundred thousand.[94] At the behest of Mutō, Fukuhara Hachirō resigned as the head of Kanebō's Tokyo mill to take command of the Nantaku and subsequently immigrated to Belém to manage its local headquarters.

Backed by the close collaboration of the government and private business interests of Japan, the Nantaku's settler colonialism was also inseparable from the partnership of Japanese immigrant businessmen in New York City—a foothold of Fukuzawa-style entrepreneurial expansionism. Having settled down there in 1879, Murai Yasukata was one of the most revered leaders in the city's Japanese ethnic community, and he was one generation senior to Kanebō's Mutō in the clique of Keiō alumni. In 1919, at the height of anti-Japanese agitation, these two business leaders (and Fukuhara) had already met in New York to develop a shared "zeal for South America."[95] When Fukuhara's investigative team arrived in the city on its way to Brazil seven years later, Murai was ready to offer as much support as he could with his like-minded Japanese New Yorkers, who had organized an informal study group called the South America Society (Nanbei kyōkai). Based on their bitter experience of fighting white American accusations of Japanese invasion, Murai's group advised the Kanebō team that migration and colonization must take place according to the principle of population dispersal in order to avoid creating the impression of a coordinated land grab. Because the vast majority of recent

Japanese settlers had entered the state of São Paulo, they felt it desirable to designate the Amazon basin as an alternative/next site of Japanese development in Brazil. Aged seventy-two, the elderly Murai was quoted as declaring, "I consider it my last service [to the homeland] to render assistance to your Brazilian enterprise. I am determined to undergird Japan's endeavor to reclaim [the untouched land of] Brazil to the full extent of my powers."[96]

Murai's idea of patriotic "service" was twofold. First, he sought direct involvement in the organization of the Nantaku as a major investor. Murai deliberately scheduled his return visit to Japan so he could attend the first meeting of business and government representatives on the Amazon venture in March 1928. When they decided to put the task of drafting the Nantaku's articles of incorporation into Kanebō executives' hands, Murai participated in the central working group for the Nantaku project along with Mutō and Fukuhara. When the Amazon colonization company was formally incorporated, the New York immigrant business leader acquired one thousand shares of its stock—the same amount as the major *zaibatsu* conglomerates—as one of the twenty founding investors.[97]

Second, even before the establishment of the Nantaku, Murai sought to interweave his own entrepreneurial expansionism with Japan's official settler colonialism by organizing a US-based partner firm. Based on an initial capitalization of $100,000 that was collected from members of the New York–based South America Society, the Nanbei Enterprise Corporation was incorporated in the state of Delaware in March 1927 with Murai as president. He invited Fukuhara to join the company as its adviser, and the Kanebō executive obliged with his own investment. Although it consisted mostly of Japanese immigrants in New York, the Nanbei Enterprise's board of directors also included another member of Kanebō's investigative expedition, an agricultural technician who belonged to Japan's diplomatic corps. His residence in Tokyo was subsequently designated as the company's Japan office. In order to build a Japanese settlement sponsored by the Nanbei Enterprise adjacent to a future Nantaku colony, Murai asked Fukuhara to scout for a suitable tract when his team was traveling through Pará. During their land survey, Fukuhara found ideal land for the Nanbei Enterprise in Castanhal, about forty miles east of Belém, and obtained a concession of 6,845 acres there from local authorities. Until Murai dispatched a Japanese American farmer to manage the Nanbei Enterprise's new Castanhal colony, a Kanebō/Nantaku employee was temporarily placed in charge as interim overseer of its daily operations.[98] Not only did this transpacific network of capital and human movement tie together Tokyo, New York, and Belém, but it also formed the basis of corporate partnership between Japan's Nantaku and Japanese America's Nanbei Enterprise, and of their concerted colonization efforts in the Amazonian forests. (See map 3 in chapter 3.)

Thereafter, the Nanbei Enterprise primarily sent US Japanese farm families to Castanhal, which functioned as a branch settlement of the Nantaku Acará colony.

In Murai's grandiose vision, the new settlement was supposed to be a "paradise devoid of racial prejudice," where resettlers from Japanese America could contribute to Japan's new national project as diasporic imperial subjects and masters of their own destiny instead of being trapped in the life of an oppressed US minority.[99] In 1929 Murai and Fukuhara engineered the formal merger of the Nanbei Enterprise's Castanhal settlement with the Nantaku's Acará colony, signaling the union of frontiersmen from Japanese America with those from imperial Japan. In this arrangement, Castanhal was designated as the official experimental station, where experienced former US farmers could engage in and teach methods of tropical frontier farming to newcomers from Japan. The Nantaku recruited a successful Japanese immigrant rice farmer from Southeastern Texas—another Keiō alumnus and Murai's close friend—to serve as the head of the Castanhal experimental station. Over two decades earlier, Murai had invited and financed this man and his family to start a Japanese rice colony near Houston. Now, in the new site of overseas Japanese development, the former Texas rice farmer (and his Japanese American associate) worked again as an agent of Murai's long-standing dream in agricultural colonization—the kind of expansionist endeavor that the New York–based immigrant could not personally take on due to his primary involvement in international commercial trade and his urban residence.[100]

The examples of the Nantaku and Nanbei Enterprise symbolize the type of transnational collaboration between advocates of agricultural colonization who shared life experiences as self-styled frontiersmen and victims of racial discrimination in the United States. Whether they had remained in Japanese America or had returned to Japan, these individuals, such as Murai, Mutō, and Fukuhara, were committed to the goal of global Japanese expansion. As the Japanese empire incorporated settler colonialism as a core part of its agenda and national policy after the mid-1920s, a growing number of US-based Japanese immigrants also began to move back to the bosom of the home empire and its formal and de facto colonial territories. The consequence of US immigration exclusion were not limited to the rise of Brazil as a chief object of Japan's state-sponsored migration and agricultural colonization. Free from race-based discrimination, Japanese-controlled East Asia, especially Manchuria and Taiwan, increasingly drew attention from the developmentalist gaze of US-based Japanese immigrants through the latter half of the 1920s and the 1930s. Although the existing scholarship has almost completely neglected the involvement of Japanese America in the colonization of the formal territories of the Japanese empire, immigrant resettlers from the US West and Hawai'i were no less active and enthusiastic than other imperial subjects in contributing to the national mandate of overseas development. The next two chapters document their visions and activities, which entwined Japanese America and imperial Japan even more deeply and indeed rendered them indivisible in history.

PART THREE

Spearheading Japan's Imperial Settler Colonialism, 1924–1945

5

Japanese California and Its Colonial Diaspora

Translocal Manchuria Connections

California still has a vast undeveloped landmass. Yet, since small[-scale] Japanese farmers started to put down roots and conquer the (frontier) land, [white] American settlers dreaded them so much that one exclusionary law after another was passed until the final solution of 1924 took care of the land [control] problem once and for all. . . . Thousands of Japanese lost their fortune and consequently retreated (from the United States) with precipitation.[1]

Nagao Yukusuke, a post-1924 returnee from Japanese America, was the author of this narrative. He had operated the largest Japanese-owned rice farm in Northern California. Published in Japan's premier journal of international relations, the essay that Nagao penned in 1933 called for the transplantation of "large-scale American-style machine farming" to Japan's recently established puppet state "Manchukuo"—an advocacy in which he claimed he had the utmost confidence because he had "dedicated half his life to [actually practicing] it" in California.[2] Working for a state-run agricultural research institute in Manchuria, this former Japanese Californian spoke for both other transpacific remigrants and the colonial regime. Nagao's advocacy elucidated not only the partnership between the two parties in the conquest of Manchurian frontier but also the special value of the settler-colonial experience—especially the farming knowledge and technical expertise—that returnees from the American West held for the home empire during the 1930s. And as his narrative revealed, imperial Japan's acquisition of the US-originated technology of colonial development was mediated, if not made possible, by institutionalized racial discrimination against Japanese America, which precipitated the reverse migration flow of settler-farmers and agricultural experts from California to Manchuria.

Between the late 1910s and the mid-1920s, the rise of Yellow Peril demagoguery in North America prompted imperial Japan to adopt a more unified policy of emigration and settler colonialism. Having been subjected to race-based exclusion, first-generation Japanese Americans—especially those who had identified themselves as self-styled "frontiersmen"—felt that the expanding Japanese empire could offer what they did not have in the white settler republic: the ability to live and act as "pioneers of overseas racial development."[3] Whereas Japan's policy of migration and colonization increasingly obfuscated the distinction between its colonial possessions and extraterritorial lands, the minoritized status of Japanese immigrants in the United States ironically exposed the very gap between the possibility of living the life of a colonial master in the home empire and the reality of struggling as a "racial pariah" in white America. Because their home empire promised US-based settler-colonists better opportunities without the meddling of white overlords and their institutionalized racism, diasporic members of Japanese America, such as Nagao, benefited imperial Japan's settler colonialism as proven conquerors of wilderness and builders of a new civilization—something that the Asian empire desperately wanted after World War I.

This chapter traces the footsteps of colonial remigrants from the American West, especially California, who served as masterminds and teachers of agrarian colonialism in Manchuria from the early 1920s. Japan's colonization of the region is one of the most heavily studied topics in the existing scholarship. Yet its prevailing area studies slant renders the transpacific returnees utterly invisible in the historical narrative, since scholars of Japanese Manchuria have generally focused on the actions of major policy makers, bureaucrats, and ideologues or on the sufferings and/or crimes of settler-colonists from the home empire. Although they served as indispensable architects and practitioners of agrarian settler colonialism in Japan's new frontier, the remigrants from Japanese America are still stuck between the well-studied world of Japanese colonial masters and that of a racialized American minority. The in-betweenness of their identity and agency forms as important a theme of this chapter's narrative as their complicity in imperial domination.

AMERICAN RACISM AND CONTINENTAL FRONTIER CONNECTIONS

Punctuated by the periodic surges of US exclusionist agitation, the westward transpacific movement of Japanese immigrant Californians saw a recurring pattern of ebb and flow. As in the earlier watershed moment of 1892–1894, the years between 1919 and 1924 precipitated the omnidirectional exodus from Japanese America of frontier seekers who desired to escape the dominance and control of another race.[4] For those who preferred unobstructed conditions of conquest and development under the direct protection of the national flag, the Japanese territories of Manchuria, and to a lesser degree Taiwan, appeared to offer the best opportunities for the idealized life of a colonial master. This exodus included more independent farmers than other classes of Japanese immigrants, for the 1922–1923 US Supreme Court rulings (especially in *Yamashita v. Hinkle* and *Porterfield v. Webb*) in support of the denial of their tenancy and landownership in many western states provided a direct catalyst. Due to the comparable continental topography, California residents viewed Manchuria as a preferable site to move their farming operations to and make an investment in. John J. Stephan estimates that about two thousand Japanese (not counting their family members) from the United States— including Hawai'i—resettled in Manchuria alone.[5]

Past immigrant experiences—including farming methods, crop production, and living environments—constituted key factors in influencing remigrants' decision making when they moved back to the bosom of the home empire, forging specific trans*local* connections between the two Pacific empires. These factors were crucial not only because they wanted some continuity between their previous existence in North America and their new lives in Japan's colonial domains. More important, their firsthand experience in the taming of the frontier allowed former US residents to act as valued exemplars of settler colonialism for their home compatriots in building a profitable settler colony in Manchuria similar to their thriving pre-exclusion ethnic community in California. Backed by such immigrant cultural capital, a number of transpacific resettlers took on new roles as midlevel technocrats and grassroots model farmers, even though those roles often pigeonholed North American remigrants as agricultural "specialists" rather than general leaders in the management of the new settlement.[6] Their roles were by no means insignificant, however, when considering that US-originated methods of farming—unfamiliar to most people in Japan at that time—were introduced to Japan's settler colonies through them. The home empire was therefore eager to take advantage of the returnees for its own developmentalist goal. Such a relationship of mutual dependence between an empire and its "skilled" expatriates paralleled contemporaneous cases of Fascist Italy and Nazi Germany, which had their own versions of state-sponsored repatriation programs for frontier colonization. The Third Reich indeed referenced Japanese return migration from the United States in its plans to resettle German Americans—"skilled . . . workers of all kinds"—in its eastern frontiers of Wartegau and Upper Siberia.[7]

Viewed from the prevailing Japanese understanding of frontier, the translocal connections between the US West and Manchuria were almost self-evident from the time of Japan's takeover of the Kwantung Leased Territory along the South Manchuria Railway (SMR) from Russia in 1905. From the outset, that region of southern Manchuria was deemed Japan's major frontier, where an empty landmass supposedly awaited agrarian settlers with open arms. Thus, the Oriental Development Company (ODC) included the Kwantung Leased Territory in its blueprint despite its primary focus on Korea. Japanese immigrant society in the American

West had always been an eager audience for Japan's extolment of Manchuria's "frontier" qualities and potential, and some of the most revered early Japanese "pioneers" in southern Manchuria, especially around Dalian, originated from North America's Japanese settlements. Members of the Amur River (Black Dragon) Society, Takeshita Tokujirō and Miwa Sakujirō had spent eight years as self-proclaimed frontier farmers in California before settling down in the Kwantung Territory in the early twentieth century.[8] Yanagimoto Naojirō, whose Dalian farm was known to have pioneered large-scale fruit cultivation, had "learned his trade . . . from his . . . residence in California."[9] Another California farmer named Yui Kurakichi is credited as the first Japanese settler in Wafangdian, about sixty miles north of Dalian, who started to cultivate eighty-two acres in 1907 and set up the basis of a local Japanese settlement dubbed "Asahi Village" as the de facto village master.[10] Katsumata Kijūrō transplanted US methods of dairy farming, which he had learned while working as a farmhand on an American-owned ranch near San Francisco between 1894 and 1901. Later known as the "king of continental (Manchurian) dairy farming," he owned the largest dairy farm and ranch (Manshū bokujō), which controlled over 120 acres near Dalian, Anshan, and Shenyang. Katsumata also served as the president of the Manchurian subsidiary of the Meiji Dairies Corporation.[11] These individuals had formed the leadership of Manchuria's colonial agricultural industry and farm associations since the 1910s, when Japanese influence was still limited to the Kwantung Territory and SMR-controlled areas.

CHIBA TOYOJI AND THE IMPORTATION OF "CONTINENTAL FARMING"

When the American West increasingly looked like a lost paradise to many Japanese residents during the escalating exclusionist agitation from 1919 to 1924, two California agriculturalists—Chiba Toyoji and Awaya Man'ei—paved the way for the exodus of US-based Japanese farmers and agricultural experts to Manchuria. The general manager of the Japanese Agricultural Association of California in San Francisco, Chiba contributed to the shaping of the popular belief that Japanese in America would be ideal settler-colonists in Manchuria. Educated at Waseda University, he was a typical immigrant expansionist who viewed his own community in California as an integral part of borderless settler colonialism and global Japanese development. Faced with California's Alien Land Laws, which denied Asian immigrants landownership and tenancy, Chiba became increasingly pessimistic about the future of Japanese ethnic agriculture in North America as he learned the negative effects of legal discrimination firsthand from his compatriots. By 1921 he could no longer find reasons for Japanese to remain in the United States as independent farmers. Japanese America's farm leader predicted that his coethnic pioneers would "not be able to withstand the troubles caused by the strict enforcement of the [1920 alien land] law, which should eventually impel them to quit farm operations, abandon permanent residency [in America], and relinquish their vested interests there."[12]

Indignant at unjust white racism and his own political powerlessness, Chiba bade a bitter farewell to the North American frontier that he had once called his home and resolutely headed west across the Pacific to Dalian in June 1921. Speaking for many others who followed in his footsteps, he expressly wished to "live in the sphere where Japan's sovereign power extends, and work under the Japanese flag in such a way that the fruits of our labor can directly benefit our homeland."[13] Chiba later recalled that his past encounter with Matsuoka Yōsuke and Gotō Shinpei, both connected to the SMR and the Kwantung Bureau (Japan's local colonial government), had inspired him to "use the superior agricultural skills of Japanese [immigrants in California] for the promotion of Manchurian colonization."[14] Pressed again by Matsuoka, Chiba finally embarked on a new career as an SMR colonial planner and researcher in 1921.[15] Attesting to his close connection to Matsuoka, Chiba later served as a special adviser to the SMR president when the former assumed that position in the mid-1930s. It is important to note that Matsuoka himself was a student immigrant and early ethnic community leader in Portland, Oregon, prior to his return to Japan in 1902.

Chiba's assertion that Japanese farmers in the American West would make the best settler-colonists in Manchuria appeared many times in various print media outlets in Japan, Manchuria, and the United States. Throughout the 1920s and the 1930s, the narrative remained fundamentally the same, albeit with some updated information and statistics. Published in 1924, a twenty-four-page treatise articulated Chiba's beliefs most clearly and fully. The then SMR agricultural expert forcefully argued that Japanese immigrants had proven their superiority as frontier farmers in past competitions with their European and Chinese counterparts in the American West. "While having lived in an alien land with a different language and customs and having been oppressed by preceding [white] settlers," Chiba continued, "they persevered for thirty years to turn a barren desert into an irrigated green orchard, and a peaty riverbank into fertile farmland" from the scorching US-Mexican borderlands through the freezing Canadian border region. By referring to his own decision to trade a minoritized life in white California for an autonomous life in Japanese Manchuria, Chiba described the devastating effects of American racism as an ironic opportunity for imperial Japan to take advantage of the extraordinary human resources and their neglected farming expertise for the development of the Manchurian frontier—the "lifeline" (seimeisen) of the expanding empire.[16]

Chiba wrote:

Japanese farmers in America ... who seek a new destiny in Manchuria with their US-bred knowledge, capital, and experience have gradually increased in number for the past three to four years. They all share the basic propensity for self-reliance and hard work, and they all excel in the use of farm machinery. They are not many yet, but their ardent endeavors already anticipate the success of fruit growing and cotton farming in the Kwantung Leased Territory. . . . Those who contemplate remigration to Manchuria are also interested to apply [the method of] continental farming to rice cultivation, vegetable growing, and livestock farming. Of course, it is unrealistic to assume mass remigration of Japanese farmers from the United States to Manchuria, since most would stay put and persevere there. Yet, if there is a coordinated effort [by SMR, a good number of] outstanding farmers with considerable capital can be enticed to move here (to Manchuria).[17]

The "propensity for self-reliance and hard work," according to Chiba, referred to what he called the "pioneer spirit." Not only did he view it as a quintessential trait of Japanese immigrant farmers in the American West, but Chiba also celebrated the kind of rugged individualism that purportedly made them the equal of Anglo-Saxon frontiersmen. Since he constantly espoused this US-bred idea emphatically before SMR staff and local Japanese settlers, they even "nicknamed [him] Mr. Pioneer."[18] Indeed, he took every opportunity to imbue his audience with his version of the US frontier thesis in order to promote American-style agricultural development and civilization building, propelled by the self-directed effort of each individual settler. For example, when an old friend from California toured the Kwantung Territory, Chiba arranged for the man to give a series of SMR-sponsored lectures on the "history of the United States' colonization and conditions of Japanese in America," in which glorified stories of the immigrant pioneer spirit were always a key ingredient.[19] Aside from sovereign protection by their homeland, settlers' individual efforts were a major factor in colonial success. As Chiba saw it, nobody would outshine Japanese agriculturalists in America in that respect.

In addition to the US-style pioneer spirit, Chiba emphasized "knowledge, capital, and experience" as notable benefits of Japanese remigration from the American West to Manchuria. "Knowledge" and "experience" referred to accumulated expertise in "continental farm management," which North American residents had monopolized and were ready to share with their compatriots on Japan's new frontier. In Chiba's formulation, "capital" articulated a class bias toward propertied farmers and moneyed entrepreneurs. In line with the prevailing Orientalist denigration of Chinese people, Chiba contended that working-class Japanese newcomers would be no match for local Chinese due to the "considerable difference in the standard of living." Whereas Chiba discouraged the remigration of labor immigrants from North America, he anticipated for the same reason that independent Japanese settler-farmers would easily outstrip their Chinese competitors in agricultural endeavors as long as they held their own capital base. Chiba was thus selective in his advocacy of transpacific remigration. Only moneyed farmers were assumed to have the ability to put their "knowledge and experience" to productive use for the home empire.[20] Later, as Japanese residents in California contemplated the option of remigration in response to Chiba's call, this class bias came to greatly influence public discourse, and hence the residents' decision making. In 1936, for example, a San Francisco Japanese American newspaper wrote: "For a pioneer [resettler in Manchuria], a large sum of capital seems to be necessary. . . . [I]f a Japanese is to compete against cheap Chinese migrant labor, the only viable option is to engage in a large-scale [well-funded] enterprise, farming included."[21]

Almost immediately, Chiba's emphasis on the usefulness of US-style "continental farming" caught the attention of many agricultural scientists, technocrats, and significant segments of the colonial elite in Manchuria. The notion of "continental farming" entailed not only large-scale, industrialized farm operations but also the use of advanced farm equipment and gasoline- or diesel-powered machines, such as tractors. Juxtaposed with the conventional form of manpower-based small-scale farming ("island wet farming") in Japan, continental farming was synonymous with the US method of agriculture, and in the Manchurian context, the assumed translocal connections to the "American West" were amplified even more because of "similar" geographic characteristics, especially soil conditions, the vastness of the land, and climate patterns.[22] More fundamentally, what formed the quintessence of US-originated continental farming was its thoroughly scientific approach to soil and environmental conditions, crop varieties, and cultivation techniques.

Chiba's highly technical discussion on agronomy had important political implications for the kind of colonial race/ethnic relations that Japan's imperial regime and settler leaders would like to construct on its new frontier. Like many others, the former Californian regarded the majority of local Manchus as a source of cheap labor who lacked the quality or ability to appreciate scientific farming and to function as modern farmers. They would be field hands for Japanese settler-colonists, just as Chinese, Punjab, Mexican, and Filipino immigrants were deemed to be within Japanese ethnic agriculture of the American West. A minority of native Manchurian/Chinese farmers would not pose much threat, either, because they were in the position to learn a modern, efficient method of farming from experienced Japanese settlers.[23] Indeed, as Chiba asserted, "Japanese [settlers were supposed to] possess an incomparably superior talent for agricultural development," and the skill in advanced "machine farming" would enable them to shine in competition with other racial/ethnic groups.[24] There were no better facilitators than Japanese American farmers who could teach their compatriots how to practice scientific continental farming, which would ensure Japanese ascendancy in the multiracial settler colony of Manchuria and its frontier agriculture. As discussed later, this vision of hierarchical ethnic/race relations dovetailed neatly with what was to be officially propagated as the spirit of *gozoku kyōwa* (coexistence of five groups: Japanese, Han Chinese, Manchus, Koreans, and Mongolians), albeit in reality under Japanese domination.

The importation of American-style farming methods was not uncontested, however. First, adaptive settler colonialism of imperial Japan was eager to look at other potential models, albeit with less fervor, including with reference to the agricultural activities of exiled Russians (white émigrés) in northern Manchuria and the Soviet model of collective farming (Kolkhoz) in Siberia.[25] Second, and more important, was that a powerful faction of chauvinistic Japanese agricultural technocrats formed a major stumbling block against the transplanted American ("foreign") methods. Backed by some top army brass and influential statesmen, this faction comprised agronomist ideologue Katō Kanji and associates such as Nasu Shiroshi and Hashimoto Denzaemon, who taught at Tokyo Imperial University and Kyoto Imperial University, respectively.

In the existing Japanese- and English-language scholarship, these well-connected individuals are almost solely credited with being the key architects and masterminds of migration and agrarian colonization policy in Manchuria. All graduates of Tokyo Imperial University's agricultural department, the Katō group indeed effectively foisted onto the governments of Japan and Manchukuo (controlled by their clique of alumni) their version of settler colonialism, which included the exalting of ultranationalist agrarianism (*nōhon shugi*). Katō's "Japanist" rendition of settler colonialism resulted in the regime's decision to dispatch armed settlers from Japan between 1932 and 1936, and it was followed by the systematic introduction of two hundred to three hundred ordinary family farmers to replicate Japanese villages throughout the northern Manchurian frontier.[26] In this context, Katō and his associates often argued strongly *against* SMR's plan to integrate "large-scale machine farming" into the process of colonization; instead, they valorized the importance of "using immigrant man power in lieu of farm machinery" in order to promote the Japanization of Manchurian topography through mass migration and settlement.[27] Along the same lines, General Tōjō Hideki—the Kwantung Army commander of the time—squashed an attempt to bring in US-born Japanese American agriculturalists to help modernize Manchurian farming in the late 1930s.[28] Coupled with their general disdain for things "American," these "Japanist" colonial planners wished to transplant as many Japanese settlers as possible to domesticate the Manchurian landscape through their physical labor and presence. Engine-powered farm appliances would counter their design, for mechanization reduced the demand for human labor and hence for migrants and settlers from Japan.

These developments understandably put Chiba's advocacy of US-style continental farming in a vulnerable position relative to Katō's orthodox vision, which attracted considerable backing from within the militarist colonial regime of post-1928 Manchuria. And perhaps for that reason, the existing scholarship has concentrated on Katō's influence on the central policy-*making* process while failing to acknowledge the strong hold of Chiba's visions on the grassroots level of policy *implementation.*[29] Nevertheless, throughout the 1920s and 1930s the polemics over agrarian settler colonialism were actually nothing but a foregone conclusion, despite lopsided scholarly interpretations. Seeking to import knowledge and expertise in continental machine farming, the support base for Chiba and other remigrants from North America indeed persisted in a circle of some high-level officials with US connections, such as Matsuoka Yōsuke, as well as many midlevel technocrats and agronomists, who managed daily business for their superiors, distracted by other duties. In the face of dogged resistance to his "American" way, Chiba often complained about the general "narrow-mindedness" of high-level colonial bureaucrats who "detest[ed] people with foreign experience." Yet he still managed to marshal significant support from bureaucrats who did not belong to the Tokyo Imperial University clique, as well as pragmatic technocrats of the SMR and the Kwantung Army, who saw less tangible value in abstract Japanist slogans than in usable "scientific" formulas.[30] Many of these colonial technocrats and government agronomists were graduates of the Hokkaido Imperial University and other regional agricultural colleges—situated on the margins of the colonial bureaucracy.[31] Accentuated by a strong belief in the universality of scientific benefits over bureaucratic power politics, the type of utilitarianism that these Japanese technocrats exhibited cut across national boundaries, thereby making the US farming model commonly attractive on a global scale in the eyes of enlightened specialists and settler-farmers in other imperial contexts. On the Russian steppe frontier, for example, local technocrats "learned from the American network of agricultural experimental stations and more advanced agricultural machinery."[32] These were the very institutions and devices of scientific agriculture that their Japanese counterparts also wished to adapt to Manchuria's landscape for the same goal of rationalized colonization, through Chiba and other real-life experts relocating from California.

Thanks to the grassroots specialists' support, the contestation over human-based "Japanese" farming versus machine-powered "American" farming maintained a delicate balance in colonial Manchuria, shaping two distinct lines of SMR-run agricultural education and settler-colonist training. As divisions emerged over research on and the teaching of farming methods, Katō's influence tended to prevail at the SMR Gongzhuling (Kōshūryō) agricultural experimental station, and Chiba's ideas took hold more notably at the SMR Xiongyuecheng (Yūgakujō) agricultural experimental station, initially a branch station of the former.[33] When Manchukuo began to nationalize these entities and create more in the newly acquired territories of the northern Soviet border region, a few other agricultural experimental stations were organized and dedicated to research and training in "machine farming." They included the Keshan (Kokuzan) agricultural experimental station near Qiqihar and the Hulanhe (Korankō) machine farming experimental station to the north of Harbin.[34] In 1939 Japan's puppet regime adopted a three-year plan to set up a total of fifty-five "machine farms" in northern Manchuria, where tractors and other advanced farm appliances were to be tested for productivity and profitability.[35] These establishments revealed how the influence of former US agriculturalists— and transplanted American agricultural expertise through them—became quietly and steadily institutionalized in both the policy and landscape of Japanese Manchuria, albeit over the often loud protestations of Katō and other nationalist ideologues.

Published in Manchukuo's premier settler agricultural journal (see figure 4) at the height of mass immigration, this teleological cartoon of agricultural colonization reveals the Japanese thinking about the role of US-style "machine farming" as an indispensable component of "development" and "coprosperity" in the empire's new frontier. Clockwise from top right, the first two frames show the banner declaring "the reawakening of farmers" with a Japanese settler, whose attitude changes from laziness and complacency to diligence and dedication when the flag of Manchukuo is hoisted. In the third frame, the farmer is dumbfounded when he realizes that his hard work has only led to the cultivation of a small tract of land. In the fourth frame, the importance of Japanese-Manchurian cooperation is stressed as a precondition for the faster and more efficient development of farm land, which features the use of Manchurian-style farming methods and domestic animals. It still does not suffice to complete the conquest of the vast Manchurian frontier, thus necessitating the adoption of "machine agriculture"—tractors moving forward toward the Rising Sun on the horizon. This fifth stage is crucial because it paves the way for the organization of the entire agricultural industry (sixth frame) and the full mobilization of settler and local farmers (seventh frame) for colonial development. The last frame shows the final result: the "Heavenly Paradise" (Manchukuo's motto) has prevailed on Manchuria's bountiful land, where everyone, including the sun, rejoices.[36]

In order to serve as valued teachers of "continental machine farming" at the state-run machine farming experimental stations and on the ground, a number of educated immigrants and experienced farmers moved from the American West to Manchuria after the mid-1920s. A man named Ohara Keisuke relocated with his family from Oakland, California, to Xiongyuecheng to assume directorship of the SMR's agricultural training school in 1928. With degrees in agricultural science and animal husbandry from the University of California and University of Minnesota, Ohara had previously worked for the Japanese Agricultural Association of California with Chiba Toyoji while editing the agricultural section of the *Nichibei Shimbun* (Japanese American news), a major immigrant daily published in San Francisco by Abiko Kyūtarō, the father of the settler colonial ideal of *eijū dochaku*. Between 1928 and his untimely death three years later, Ohara made the Xiongyuecheng agricultural experimental station renowned as the main training ground of "American-style" farming methods for incoming settlers from Japan.[37] Another

FIGURE 4. "Manchuria at Dawn": teleology of Manchukuo's agricultural development under Japanese rule. *Source: Nōgyō no Manshū* 8, no. 11 (December 1936), 39.

former Japanese Californian joined a "model" agricultural cooperative in Dalian, which was organized jointly by the SMR and the Kwantung colonial government. As the manager of a one-hundred-acre branch farm in Jinzhou, this man made his twenty years experience in fruit growing in California available to his fellow colonists at the model farm. Not surprisingly, Chiba was a behind-the-scenes architect of this important project.[38]

Over the ensuing decade, more and more Japanese agricultural experts remigrated from the American West to Japan's new frontier to engage in research and education. Established by the Manchuria Colonization Agency (Manshū Takushoku Kōsha) in the late 1930s, an experimental "machine farm" in Ningnian (near Qiqihar) acquired a former California immigrant as its first director, who taught farmers how to cultivate wheat using the North American method of "summer fallow."[39] A US-educated agronomist, who worked as a consultant for a Mukden farm association, is credited with not only providing leaders of the Tenrikyō religious sect with an expert report on a site for their new settlement near Harbin, but also instilling in them a sense of divine/nationalist mission through a narrative that compared the Japanese Tenrikyō faithful with the American Pilgrim Fathers—a powerful metaphor of manifest destiny and successful colonization. This example resembles other attempts at Christian-based agricultural settlement making organized and/or inspired by former California residents, namely Chiba Toyoji and Nagata Shigeshi.[40]

A longtime associate of Nagata's Nihon Rikkōkai, which served as Japan's major private dispatcher of emigrant settlers and students (see chapter 4), Wakabayashi Suteichi was another US-educated agricultural expert who traded the life of a minoritized immigrant for that of a colonial technocrat. Wakabayashi, having lived in the Pacific Northwest and Hawai'i for over thirty years, remigrated with his family to Manchuria in 1939. With master's and doctoral degrees in soil science and plant nutrition from Washington State College (now Washington State University) and Rutgers University, respectively, he worked as a senior research adviser at Manchukuo's National Colonization Research Institute in Harbin. His westward trajectory was more complex than Chiba's, although the main catalyst was the same. In 1908 Wakabayashi immigrated to Tacoma, Washington, where the wide-eyed student worked as a farm laborer before graduating from a local high school, and his embrace of US-style scientific agriculture kept him going all the way to acquiring the highest academic degree and most advanced knowledge. Yet anti-Japanese racism did not spare this elite agronomist from its indiscriminate perils; dismayed, Wakabayashi seriously contemplated a move to racially friendly Brazil in the mid-1920s, although a lack of funds and the death of his first child made that untenable. As others left the Pacific Northwest, Wakabayashi became the area's only trained Japanese agronomist, on whom local immigrant farmers came to rely heavily. A nationalist committed to settler colonialism, he always wanted to promote "overseas [Japanese] development" through his agricultural expertise—whether in the American West, Brazil, or elsewhere. In 1934 Wakabayashi decided to move from the continental United States to Hawai'i, where local Japanese farmers sought out his assistance in developing skill and expertise in "scientific agriculture." By the late 1930s, escalating Yellow Peril demagoguery in the Islands finally propelled Wakabayashi to "put [his] knowledge to good use . . . in [Japanese controlled] East Asia."[41]

Even though they embraced tractors and other mechanized farm equipment, Chiba and his compatriots from the American West also emphasized flexibility and adaptability—typical immigrant traits that had made them operative in US agriculture in the first place. These traits also helped them work with "traditionalists" in the colonial regime, nativist agrarian experts such as Katō Kanji, and armchair scholar-agronomists such as Nasu Shiroshi and Hashimoto Denzaemon. From early on, Chiba cautioned "against the reasonless transplantation of a foreign farm method onto Manchuria," citing variations in climate, soil, and other conditions.[42] Given the growing scarcity of fuel, he actually began to advocate the mixing of "animal power" with "machine power" toward the mid-1930s. At a 1936 conference of agricultural experts in Manchukuo, Chiba recommended that tractors and threshers be communally used for the specific purpose of cutting short work time during initial plowing and final harvest, because northern Manchuria had a much narrower window for such activities before the long winter set in. Everyday farming operations, according to him, could be done with domestic animals during the summer months.[43] It is not clear if Chiba took into account the successful nearby Soviet enterprise of the "machine tractor station" (MTS), which entailed the same concept of communal ownership of agricultural machinery. But his proposal underscored his characteristic adaptability to local necessities, and perhaps because of that, Chiba's idea resonated with the thinking of colonial planners on the ground—even if it did not influence them directly. Supplied by the Manchuria Colonization Agency, tractors and threshers for communal use became a norm in Japanese settler colonies in northern Manchuria, including the agrarian youth training centers sponsored by diehard nationalist and anticommunist Katō Kanji after 1937.[44]

AWAYA MAN'EI, TRAILBLAZER OF CONTINENTAL FARMING IN MANCHURIA

What made Chiba's proposition so attractive to technocrats and agronomists on the ground was the glamorized story of Awaya Man'ei—an impressive example of success that Chiba always cited to shore up his advocacy for the importation of "continental farming" and its experts from Japanese America. A former resident of Clovis, California, Hiroshima-born Awaya had farmed 160 acres of vineyards with his father and brothers for over two decades. In October 1921 he abruptly pulled up stakes in central California and moved to Dalian, in response to Chiba's call. This veteran fruit grower was not only indignant at the denial of landownership under the Alien Land Law but also greatly perturbed by the dismal prospects for his US-born children in the face of institutionalized racism.[45]

In Manchuria, Awaya obtained fifty acres in a government land grant to resume the life of an independent frontier farmer without obstruction from other races.

Although he adopted certain aspects of local Chinese farming methods and supplemented with domestic animals, he proved the effectiveness of "machine farming" with his tractors and advanced equipment from California.[46] On barren land, Awaya planted a variety of fruit trees, especially apples, for which he would soon be famous. The young trees he planted started to produce profitable crops in less than three years, beating an expert's projection that it would be five years or longer before there would be a harvest. Awaya went on to expand his Dalian farm to 147 acres, where he also grew various vegetables, raised hogs, and spearheaded the commercial cultivation of American cotton varieties in Manchuria at the behest of Matsuoka Yōsuke and other SMR officials.[47] In 1934 Awaya sent for his younger brother from Fresno to join him in the establishment of another 37-acre farm estate near Port Arthur (Lushunko). Four years later, a third farm estate of 34 acres was added to his successful enterprise. Over eleven hundred tons of fruit and vegetables were shipped out from Awaya's farms to consumer markets in Manchuria, Taiwan, the Nan'yō, and South China.[48]

While helping validate Chiba's contention, Awaya's success put him on a pedestal in Manchurian agriculture. By the time the developmentalist gaze of the Japanese empire was focused firmly on newly established Manchukuo, "Manchuria [already] resound[ed] with Mr. Awaya Man'ei's fame," and he was hailed as a foremost "pioneer who has struck roots deep in [Manchurian] soil."[49] A Japanese foreign ministry publication portrayed Awaya's farm operation as a "noteworthy" model, whose example had inspired "many Japanese and Chinese imitators" to try their hands at similar methods of farming in southern Manchuria.[50] In 1936 the Kwantung Bureau selected Awaya as one of the eight "agriculturalists of distinguished merit" for his contributions "through American-style farming methods" and his "leadership in many farm organizations."[51] Four years later Tokyo formally honored Awaya's service to national expansion with a "Medal with Green Ribbon."[52]

Awaya—and the positive example of his continental farming—paved the way for the increasing presence in Manchuria of agrarian resettlers from the American West (and Hawai'i) during the late 1920s and the 1930s. Before the formation of Manchukuo, the westward transpacific mobility of Japanese immigrant farmers was not large, for many more tended to move within the Western Hemisphere, especially between the United States and Mexico/Brazil. Still, to borrow Chiba's characterization, a small number of former US-based settlers "ha[d] already made a good showing in their agricultural ventures that range[d] from over twenty acres to one hundred acres" in southern Manchuria by 1928.[53] Around the same time, another source noted that a group of Seattle Japanese "took a low-interest loan from the (Japanese) government to acquire a Kwantung property for efficacious citrus (and also likely apple) growing."[54] Personally invited by the head of the SMR agricultural bureau, another farmer named Satō Nobumoto also quit successful rice cultivation in California and moved to Manchuria with his family and associates in early 1930. While strengthening the colonial regime's belief in the usefulness of their expertise, Satō's remigration became another source of "inspiration" and "courage" for Japanese immigrant farmers who had struggled under the negative effects of the alien land laws. As a San Francisco ethnic newspaper proudly declared, it looked as though Satō was about to build a "second site of California [Japanese] rice kingdom" in Manchuria "with the [full] backing of SMR's big capital."[55]

SATŌ NOBUMOTO AND THE ESTABLISHMENT OF AN OFFICIAL "MACHINE FARM"

As California's Japanese farmers observed, Awaya's success compelled the SMR to hunt for more California farmers in pursuit of their expertise, which academic treatises and scholarly lectures could not match. The company's first choice was Satō, who visited southern Manchuria at the behest of the colonial monopoly for on-the-spot inspection and experimental cultivation for a few months in 1928 before permanently moving there a year and a half later. This widely recognized "authority on rice" had operated a thriving farm near the small town of Meridian in the northern Sacramento Valley. His method of rice growing was emblematic of the large-scale, mechanized "continental farming" that the SMR wished to transplant in accordance with Chiba's recommendations. Having immigrated to California in 1903 as a self-supporting student, Satō was a well-educated community leader in an agricultural district known for rice farming during the 1910s. A number of Japanese "rice kings," including Satō, had emerged in the context of wartime economic prosperity, and his farm operation—one of the top four in the Northern California rice-growing region—encompassed as much as 1,250 acres, where he had made extensive use of the most advanced farm appliances and tractors in addition to employing more than eighty workers.[56] The postwar bust of the rice boom caused a reduction in the acreage he cultivated for the crop, but as one of the several remaining Japanese rice growers in the region, Satō maintained 450 acres, with another 500 of barley and soybeans. Yet the 1920 Alien Land Law put most Japanese farmers in a precarious position, since their control of leased properties, including Satō's farm, became dependent on an informal verbal agreement with white landowners—an illegal but widespread arrangement that a Japanese diplomat deemed "risky." This gloomy situation understandably caused a huge drop in the number of local Japanese immigrant farmers during the mid-1920s.[57] This was when a high-level SMR representative visited the Sacramento Valley in search of a California-based rice farmer with experience in "machine farming."[58] Satō was his logical choice.

The SMR's decision to recruit the California rice farmer was intertwined with its new policy agenda. By 1929 Japanese colonial planners in Dalian, including

Chiba, had drafted a new plan for agricultural development and mass migration, which entailed a three-tiered approach of promoting "large-scale farming, medium-scale farming, and small-scale farming." The second and third forms of farming aimed to create new Japanese agricultural settlements. Recruited by an SMR-subsidized emigration company, a medium-scale settler-farmer would have twenty acres of land and a small-scale farmer, ten acres. While these measures were supposed to increase the number of new family settlers from rural Japan, the SMR's embrace of large-scale (industrial) farming aligned perfectly with Chiba's idea of continental farming, paving the way for the remigration of Satō and his four associates from California for the purpose of operating the SMR's first model "machine farm." Before his departure, Satō was specifically instructed to purchase "articles of modern farm machinery and tools from the United States" and bring them to Manchuria.[59] Starting in 1930, Satō's group carried out an SMR-backed experiment in mechanized rice farming on a 588-acre tract in Pikou, adjacent to Dalian. Three years later his experimental farm moved to a 490-acre estate in Fengcheng near the Korean border (see map 4). The SMR designated it the Feng-huangcheng Machine Farm (Hōōjō kikai nōjō), upgrading Satō's operation from a consignment to a formally sponsored enterprise under the rubric of newly founded Manchukuo's agricultural development program.[60] From 1934 through 1945, Satō's farm remained a main hub for Manchukuo's experimentation with large-scale mechanized/industrialized rice farming.

After Japan's military occupation of the entire Manchurian basin in 1932, agrarian settler colonialism became a mainstay of its economic development policy, in which the SMR and the Kwantung Army jointly recruited settler-farmers from rural Japan in accordance with the blueprint formulated by Katō Kanji and his colleagues. Despite a strong disdain for American-style agriculture in high-level colonial officialdom, Satō's imported method of rice farming still received substantial support in the context of the regime's attempt to encourage agricultural development on Japan's "new frontier" (shintenchi), especially the sparsely populated region of northern Manchuria. The SMR's 1932 policy guidelines defined rice farming as central to achieving the twin goals of Japanese mass migration and colonization. First, because a vast majority of newcomers from rural Japan were ordinary farmers, they were most acquainted with rice growing, even if the cultivation method might be different. A prospective immigrant would be less intimidated about trading the life of a Japanese villager for the life of a Manchurian settler-colonist if he knew how he would be able to make a living in the new land.[61]

Second, Manchukuo officialdom felt that rice farming must take precedence over the production of other crops in order to sustain an increasing volume of newcomers from Japan without burdening the homeland with the need to feed its colonial diaspora. Whereas the second and third phases of agricultural development in Manchuria might prioritize dry field crops, such as wheat and soybeans,

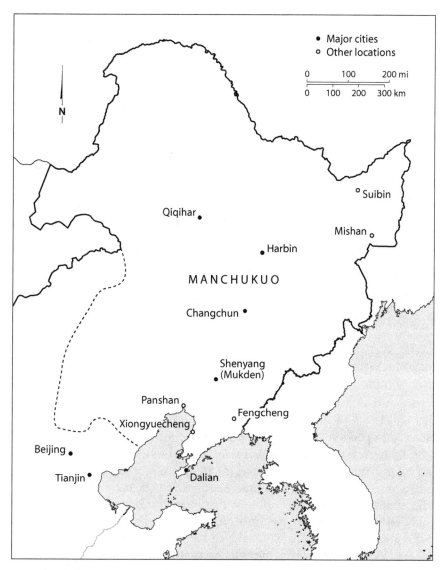

MAP 4. Map of Manchuria showing farms and settler colonies with California connections, 1930s–early 1940s. Map by Bill Nelson.

キャタピラトラクター 22型ニて五尺幅デスクハロー作業 鳳凰城

FIGURE 5. Satō Nobumoto on a Caterpillar tractor with disc harrows on his Fenghuangcheng (Hōōjō) Machine Farm. *Source:* Tetsuro Sōkyoku, "Manshū no kikai nōgyō ni tsuite" (1936).

the initial phase should concentrate largely on rice growing for these reasons, according to the SMR's colonial planners.[62] Thus, the company offered all-out support for Satō's machine farm project from 1933. To set up the basic infrastructure for his operation as soon as possible, the SMR even provided two hundred construction crews with fifteen full-time guards, despite their costing the company almost 90,000 yen ($22,500). The SMR also spent 120,000 yen purchasing land and nearly 32,000 yen for new American-made farm appliances and tractors for Satō's use. In April 1934 the fully equipped Fenghuangcheng Machine Farm commenced its first five-year experiment in mechanized rice farming.[63]

Satō successfully introduced American-style rice farming to Manchuria, as expected. With the SMR's ample financial backing, he acquired three Caterpillar tractors (see figure 5) and a large Rumley thrashing machine and other gas-powered equipment, as well as cars and trucks. Retrofitted for local use, a Fordson tractor, three John Deere bottom plows, and a reaper-binder were Satō's own from his California days. The farm was fitted out with Manchukuo's most advanced repair shop, staffed by Satō's associates from California. Initially, most of the 490-acre tract was devoted wholly to machine-based cultivation with direct sowing—a method that was common in California but entirely unfamiliar to Japanese rice growers, who usually planted seedlings from a nursery bed. Due to the efficiency of this new operation, Satō's farm required less than a dozen persons for planting. The first full year of experimentation (1936) yielded a profit of 11,200 yen. In response to the problem of overgrown weeds—a shortcoming of direct sowing— and with an abundance of cheap Chinese and Korean labor, Satō later incorporated sharecropping and the partial use of domestic animals while continuing to utilize engine-powered equipment for initial communal plowing and final threshing. By 1942 the net margin had improved further, yielding an annual gross profit of 40,000 yen. In comparison to the two other large-scale corporate rice farms in Manchukuo, Satō's enterprise was said to have achieved the best profit rate.[64]

NORTH AMERICAN RESETTLERS AND COLONIAL POLICY MAKING IN MANCHUKUO

After 1936 the Japanese colonial regime took advantage of Satō's US-bred expertise for a different purpose as well. In Japan's puppet state of Manchukuo, that year marked the beginning of the twenty-year plan to transplant one million Japanese agrarian households (or five million immigrant settlers) to its frontier regions, especially the northern borderlands along the "Manchurian-Mongol lifeline."[65] North Manchuria encompassed a much larger uninhabited landmass than the Kwantung Territory to the south. Due to a dry "continental" climate and extreme temperatures there, traditional wheat/barley cultivation and Mongolian-style ranching were the mainstays of the local agricultural economy. With the military acquisition of this massive wilderness lying along the border with the Soviet Union, SMR colonial planners—now a core part of Manchukuo's state apparatus— were pressed with the urgent need to populate the region with Japanese settler-farmers to increase food production and consolidate borderland defense.[66] Thus, mass migration to and systematic colonization in northern Manchuria became a top priority for Japan's state policy, overshadowing the existing settler-colonist programs in Brazil, which had adopted a restrictive immigration policy against Japanese in line with US-led "hemispheric Orientalism."[67]

Against this background emerged the extolment of the American West as a preferred template for the development of northern Manchuria during the latter half of the 1930s. In this context, the idea of continental machine farming reinforced the interests of the SMR's colonial planners and Japanese technocrats within the puppet Manchukuo government. Shortly after he took up the position of SMR president, Matsuoka Yōsuke publicly declared his wish "to turn northern Manchuria into our California."[68] The former Oregon resident offered the same argument that he had presented to Chiba Toyoji back in 1920. "Why should the Japanese farmer remain in the United States where he is not wanted?," asked Matsuoka rhetorically. "Let him come to Manchukuo. Here he will find opportunity and a hearty welcome." North Manchuria was particularly suitable for experienced farmers from the American West, and the SMR president "hope[d] to induce some of the best [Japanese] farmers in the United States to make it home."[69] Coming from "one of [their] own" (a former U.S. resident), Matsuoka's appeal convinced more US residents to entertain the idea of moving to Manchuria after the mid-1930s.[70]

Matsuoka's advocacy also valorized the value of Satō's expertise, to the point that the latter was formally invited to take part in the formulation of major state policy regarding settler colonialism in northern Manchuria in the critical years 1936–1937. As Tokyo was moving to adopt the new state mandate of mass migration to Manchuria during the spring of 1936, a series of important meetings convened in Manchukuo's capital. In March, leading agriculturalists organized a roundtable discussion on a "policy of agrarian development" with technocrats and middle managers of the SMR, the Manchukuo government, and the Kwantung Army. Key attendees on the practitioner side were Chiba Toyoji, Awaya Man'ei, and Satō Nobumoto, along with three other farm representatives. This means that one-half of the expert agriculturalists were former US residents, who carried the banner of continental farming. As the organizer put it, these individuals were supposed to represent "the most outstanding farmers who ha[d] established [a] solid reputation as the pioneers of Japanese agriculture in Manchuria."[71]

While Awaya and Chiba discussed more generic matters relating to the agrarian training of settler youth and an ideal development model for northern Manchuria, Satō explained the advantages of machine farming, based solely on his own experience at Fenghuangcheng. Those advantages included the ability to reclaim a large field for cultivation in a short time frame; to cut labor costs to compete with local Chinese farmers and workers, who could supposedly subsist in less "civilized" conditions than modern Japanese; and to facilitate communal farm development and operations through the sharing of tractors.[72] The chairperson lent his support to Satō's contention by declaring it was "extremely desirable to promote machine farming" and "necessary to endeavor to make it happen."[73]

Inspired by this roundtable, the Bureau of [Manchuria] Railways (Tetsuro Sōkyoku) sponsored another roundtable specifically on mechanized farming in May 1936. A new division of the SMR, the bureau was responsible for maintaining existing railroad tracks and laying new ones in the recently occupied northern provinces of Manchukuo. Officials knew that an increase in arable land and the resultant influx of settler-farmers would greatly benefit business while contributing to the national goal of frontier development. In order to achieve these results, they had been at work on drafting a plan for the North Manchuria Colonization Company since the fall of 1935. In this context, the bureau sought to elicit candid opinions and solicit advice from "leading authorities in machine farming of Manchuria, especially those who accumulated experiences in a foreign country (America)."[74] At the bureau's roundtable, Satō was featured as a keynote speaker, whose substantive observations and invaluable insights were shared at length with reference to his own machine farm experimentation. Almost 40 percent of the sixty-eight-page report on the May 1936 roundtable was dedicated to Satō's presentation and a lively question-and-answer session that followed it.[75]

A few other resettlers from North America were in attendance at the roundtable to pose expert questions and provide commentaries.[76] Chiba represented the SMR as a senior agricultural adviser, as did Uchino Raisuke, a former resident of Washington and Alberta, where he had once owned a fifty-acre farm until white racism ruined his settler colonialism in the Western Hemisphere. Later in the 1930s, Uchino worked for the renowned SMR Research Bureau (Mantetsu Chōsabu), whose expert recommendations on the North American summer-fallow method of wheat cultivation were adopted in some parts of northern Manchuria, including the Ningnian Machine Farm.[77] A twenty-year resident of Northern California and a pioneer rice farmer there, Nagao Yukusuke belonged to the North Manchuria Economic Institute (Hokuman Keizai Kenkyūsho), a subsidiary of the SMR Research Bureau. Having immigrated to the United States after attending an imperial university, he had run the state's biggest rice farm in Chico, California, with twenty-five hundred acres under his control during the latter half of the 1910s. Satō was a partner in this venture.[78] Known as a "walking encyclopedia on rice," Nagao embraced mechanized farming as much as Satō did, but the former opted to leave exclusionist North America for Japanese-dominated Manchuria a few years earlier than the latter. In the capacity of an SMR-affiliated researcher, Nagao published a number of reports and articles—including one discussed at the beginning of this chapter—that lauded the virtues of machine farming during the 1930s and early 1940s. The former California agriculturalist also engaged in research on charcoal-powered tractors, an important project that aspired to sustain the use of farm machinery in the context of a severe gasoline shortage.[79]

With these resettlers from North America taking center stage, the roundtable effectively showcased the impressive array of knowledge, experience, and insight that only they could offer for Japan's developmentalist agenda. In his presentation, Satō cited his Fenghuangcheng experience to stress that the "most effective and economical use [of mechanized farm instruments in Manchuria] turned out to be to plow, harrow, and flatten with rollers—that is, activities relating to tillage."[80] Processes of sowing and threshing could also be rationalized with the shift from a traditional human-based operation to a machine-based one.[81] Nagao and Uchino added their technical comments about the advantages of tractors.[82] In relation to different climate and crop patterns outside southern Manchuria, Satō conceded that his experience in rice farming might not be directly applicable to the northern frontier regions. Nonetheless, he maintained his belief in the pivotal role that

American-style mechanized farming should play there, predicting that the cultivation of "dry field crops" (wheat/barley varieties) would bring about "increased productivity" with "more income" as the result.[83] At the end of the roundtable, Chiba had the honor of wrapping up the discussion, reiterating the points made by Satō, Nagao, Uchino, and himself. While acknowledging the need for localized adaptation, he, too, underscored the benefits of mechanized farming. Chiba proclaimed that the introduction of machine-based tillage and harvesting would enable a single immigrant household to command as much as 120 to 200 acres when combined with the use of draft animals.[84]

As the Bureau of Railways picked the brains of former North American farmers, the Kwantung Army concurrently contemplated ways by which to encourage mass immigration through the bureau's colonization company scheme from the standpoint of border defense. While being involved in the two roundtables as an observer in the spring of 1936, military officialdom came up with a proposal to probe possibilities for setting up an experimental "machine farm" in the district of Suibin along the Soviet border—a strategically important but insufficiently populated region (see map 4). Sandwiched between the Amur River and the Songhua River, Suibin formed a large delta where there had once been a frustrated effort at mechanized farming by a group of US investors before the rise of the communist regime nearby.[85] The military's obvious choice of experts for this land survey expedition were Satō Nobumoto and other former US residents. Under the cosponsorship of the Bureau of Railways and its parent company, the SMR, the Kwantung Army assembled a special investigative team of twelve members shortly after the May 1936 roundtable. While the military brass "specifically requested Satō's participation," Nagao, Uchino, and another US returnee named Watanabe Kinzō also joined the team, taking charge of core aspects of research "regarding [the establishment of] a machine farm, gasoline-powered cultivation, flour milling, . . . [and] land improvement" in the frontier land of Suibin.[86] The transplantation of American-style farming and the contributions of transpacific remigrants were now deemed integral to the national security agenda of imperial Japan.

Recruited personally by SMR president Matsuoka Yōsuke, Watanabe was added to the group because he had extensive experience reclaiming swampland in California's San Joaquin River delta in the first quarter of the twentieth century. This former US resident of thirty years had served as a chief manager of the Golden State's largest potato farm on behalf of Ushijima Kinji, then widely known as "Potato King George Shima." For assessing the feasibility of the Suibin delta land for reclamation and agriculture, Watanabe was unarguably the most ideal authority.[87] A revered community leader in Japanese America, Watanabe had also been well connected to Japan's elite intellectual and social circles since the early twentieth century.[88] Through marriage, he was related to Ukita Kazutami, a prominent political scientist and trusted adviser to former premier Ōkuma Shigenobu. In

1925 Ukita and Watanabe jointly published a book that called for peaceful US-Japanese relations while strongly castigating America for its immigration exclusion. Despite his criticism of US racism, Watanabe's writing celebrated the Anglo-Saxon conquest of the western frontier as an example to emulate, and he had already advocated similar Japanese efforts in Northeast Asia, especially Manchuria. His interest in the frontier of the Asian continent, and its American-style development, can hence be traced to the mid-1920s, specifically to the consequences of US immigration exclusion.[89] Reminiscent of Chiba's wishes to enhance Japan's national interests through his work as a resettler, Watanabe similarly professed his vision of a patriotic duty to "make a greater contribution to Manchurian colonization than what Ushijima and [he] had done to California agriculture." It was his deep sense of nationalist mission that convinced sixty-nine-year-old Watanabe to respond enthusiastically to Matsuoka's request that he come out of retirement and serve as an SMR special adviser in 1936.[90]

Satō, Nagao, Uchino, and Watanabe embarked on a one-month investigative tour under the full military guard of the Kwantung Army in the early summer of 1936. This official Manchukuo venture resembled a reunion of older settler colonialists (all of them over age fifty by then), whose initial dream of frontier conquest in the New World had been dashed by American exclusion. Yet the former victims of white racism now literally enjoyed "work[ing] under the Japanese flag in such a way that the fruits of [their] labor [could] directly benefit [their] homeland," as Chiba had put it earlier. After the tour, based on their draft plan and recommendations for the use of "American-made tractors, equipment, and tools," the SMR formally adopted the Suibin machine farm project in February 1937—presumably with the full support of the military.[91]

Despite the important place that American-style farming continued to occupy in Japan's colonial enterprise, this episode marked the virtual end of its representation in public and policy-related discourse of the empire. For this reason, there is little mention of continental/machine farming in existing scholarly narratives. Instead, historical studies generally delineate a simple transition from "conventional (Manchurian) farming" (*zairai nōhō*) to a "Hokkaido (improved) farm method" (*Hokkaido nōhō* or *kairyō nōhō*; also dubbed "plow farming") during the period 1938–1941.[92] Discussion of the spread of American-style continental farming, spearheaded by US returnees such as Chiba, Awaya, and Satō with state support, is almost nowhere to be found. Building on a linear story line of Japanization devoid of transpacific American influence, some historians have debated whether or not the Hokkaido-bred farming ways actually took hold in Manchuria by replacing the traditional (if not "inferior") Manchurian ways.[93] In view of Manchukuo's official policy, it is true that the Hokkaido farm method was formally adopted in 1941 as an integral part of the state colonization scheme, and that some agricultural stations began research and experimentation by recruiting model farmers from Hokkaido, Japan's northernmost prefecture. After 1940, several contingents of settler-colonists were also dispatched from rural Hokkaido to northern Manchuria.[94]

What is missing from the scholarly literature is how this new method did *not* depart fundamentally from what former California residents had practiced and advocated in Manchuria since the mid-1920s. Hokkaido-style "plow farming" referred to the use of domestic horses in lieu of tractors to pull plows, harrows, and cultivators on large tracts of farmland. Also, according to contemporary observers, practitioners of plow farming still wanted such equipment to be US made, especially John Deere products.[95] Indeed, any contemporaries familiar with a history of Hokkaido's plow farming would be well aware of its significant US origin. In the 1870s, American agricultural advisers Horace Capron and William Penn Brooks had introduced the combined use of horses and mechanical farm appliances to Hokkaido, a method that was later supplemented but never replaced by Denmark's more agroecologically conscious manner of livestock farming.[96] Seen from this historical background, Chiba's continental farming and the official Hokkaido method shared ample confluences in regard to the ways and means of cultivation. It is for this reason that Nagao Yukusuke could so easily embrace the Hokkaido method after 1940 and asserted that settler-farmers should look to the original "Capron plan," while criticizing the half-baked "domestication" that he claimed had caused Hokkaido agriculture to stagnate in more recent years.[97] The official adoption of the Hokkaido method neither contradicted the preexisting practice of American-style farming nor meant the vanishing of engine-powered farm vehicles in Manchuria. One expert observer, for example, contended that an ideal form of farming in colonial Manchuria should consist of a combination of "indigenous," "American," and "Hokkaido" methods, in the ratio of 4:3:3, respectively. A professor at Hokkaido Imperial University and a leading expert in Hokkaido farming methods, Watanabe Kan, also conceded: "The conquest of the [Asian] continent requires machine power. . . . [T]rucks and tractors are of the essence."[98]

Indeed, even though German-made and home-manufactured vehicles were increasingly in use in the early 1940s, gasoline-powered tractors actually remained a quintessential symbol of frontier conquest, modern colonial agriculture, and a new civilization in Japanese Manchuria until the demise of the empire. Printed in the May 13, 1942, issue of *Shashin shūhō* (pictorial weekly), a government propaganda magazine sponsored by the Cabinet Information Bureau, an SMR pictorial advertisement (see figure 6) exemplifies the centrality of machine farming in Manchurian colonization throughout the war years. This image was intended to not only commemorate the ten-year anniversary of the establishment of Manchukuo but also celebrate its achievements "for frontier development and increased food production." Note that the SMR company logo is superimposed on the front of the

建國十周年
興亞の據大満洲

滿鐵鐵道總局

FIGURE 6. McCormick-Deering tractors in Japan's wartime frontier: official representation of Manchukuo's progress and accomplishments during the US-Japan war. *Source: Shashin shūhō* 220 (May 13, 1942).

tractor, but the original emblem of McCormick-Deering is still visible above it, illuminating Manchurian colonial agriculture's ties to America despite the ongoing war against that country.[99]

Why, then, did the term "continental (American)" farming largely disappear from the official and scholarly nomenclature of Manchurian colonial agriculture, especially after the Suibin investigative expedition of 1936? The reason is that public mention of US influence—or for that matter any reference to an American background of a farming method—had become increasingly difficult, if not untenable, in the Japanese empire by that time. The alternative language of "Hokkaido/plow farming" offered rational-minded technocrats and agronomists a convenient euphemism for what became deemed of "enemy" origin by ultranationalists and militarist clique, that is, "American-style" mechanized farming, in the political climate of post-1937 Japan.[100] Primary sources on the official Hokkaido method follow this pattern of an absent presence, wherein uninformed readers—historians included—can hardly recognize the influence of remigrants from the United States, who opted to blend in with the masses of Japanese settler-farmers without illuminating their American background/identity. But because of their lived expertise and colonial cultural capital based on it, they could still manage to carry on with their prescribed roles as exemplary farmers, agricultural advisers, and colonial planners in Japanese Manchuria despite an intensified anti-American climate. Nagao and Uchino continued to conduct major research projects, sponsored by the SMR and its subsidiaries, on machine farming and the advantages of "western" (*yōshiki*) farming methods. In the twilight of their professional careers, these two individuals—both presumably in their late fifties—compiled a number of research treatises and policy papers. Chiba also actively participated in an official research group regarding the "improved farm method" in the capacity of a special adviser to the SMR president. Satō's farm, too, continued to receive keen attention from SMR researchers and other observers during the Pacific War.[101] And the mark of their US-originated settler farming had been firmly inscribed on the frontier land. As much as the communal use of tractors continued to be widely practiced in combination with horses, official support for machine farms and related research projects remained steadfast in Manchukuo until 1945 despite the vilification of everything American in the realm of wartime public discourse.[102]

WATANABE KINZŌ, AN ARCHITECT OF MAJOR COLONIAL RECLAMATION PROJECTS

Watanabe Kinzō did not suffer as much public obscurity in spite of his American background after 1936. Because of his invaluable experience and expertise in reclamation and land improvement, the veteran delta farmer was entrusted with a new mission greater than the Suibin venture. Matsuoka Yōsuke asked his longtime friend and now personal adviser to assess the feasibility of swampland development throughout Manchukuo. Following the conclusion of the Suibin tour, Watanabe parted from other North American resettlers and proceeded to conduct a four-month-long, extensive land survey that he claimed covered almost "two-fifths of Manchuria," including a couple of major wetland regions in northern Manchuria and one in the southwest. He spent another four months in 1937 drafting his recommendations and conferring with the authorities. Out of this survey emerged two pointed proposals, the policy initiatives that the Manchukuo regime subsequently incorporated into its official colonization enterprises.[103]

One proposal was to insulate the wet landmass around the Soviet border region of Mishan from the often overflowing Muling River, and another called for massive reclamation in the Panshan region of the Liao River delta to the south (see map 4). Watanabe recommended the deep dredging of streams and sloughs as well as the building of levees and reservoirs with advanced heavy equipment (all American inventions), such as "excavators, draglines, and dredgers," to dry up 122,500 acres and 73,520 acres of marshy land, respectively. In his justification for the proposals, the agriculturalist habitually referred to his California delta experience and positively compared the topography of the Manchurian frontier with that of the American West, as if to guarantee surefire success. For example, Watanabe stated in a public presentation: "With the help of science, machinery, and human perseverance, American pioneer migrants have transformed a place (wasteland) resembling present-day Mishan . . . into a center of world civilization." In order to facilitate the US-style conquest of frontier land, the former Japanese Californian even offered to assemble his friends and associates who had once worked on the San Joaquin delta farm.[104]

Combined with enticing historical anecdotes of marvelous frontier conquests in the New World, Watanabe's recommendations generated considerable support from Manchukuo officialdom for the Mishan and Panshan reclamation projects. On the one hand, after the middle of 1937 Watanabe's imprint on northern Manchurian swampland appeared in the form of a state-sponsored land improvement effort for 80,870 acres lying waste west of the Mishan railroad station. On the other hand, in the lower Liao River delta, an official land improvement program commenced in November 1939 that aimed to develop 75,970 acres of rice paddies and dry farms within the next five years.[105] The Liao River delta program formed part and parcel of larger colonial infrastructure building, which Aaron Stephen Moore examines, but his book mainly looks into the role of state civil engineers and "technology bureaucrats" without acknowledging expert input from outside that circle, especially from agronomists and migration specialists. Yet the "Liao River Improvement Project" was fraught with tensions between Moore's study subjects and a coalition of "reform bureaucrats" and technocratic proponents of mass immigration and agricultural settlement, including Watanabe's supporters.[106] While state civil engineers were mostly concerned with the construction of reservoirs, dams, and dikes from a technical and scientific standpoint, Watanabe's supporters were intrigued by his articulation of the tangible benefit of such newly built infrastructure, specifically for the goal of promoting agricultural settler colonialism. This explains why some of Manchukuo's most influential policy-minded techno-bureaucrats, such as Naoki Rintarō, also came around and actually embraced Watanabe's proposals.[107]

Thus, Watanabe's proposal had direct ramifications for Japanese immigration and settlement in the swamplands of Manchuria. In the north, a number of migrant-settlers started to enter the Mishan region in the early summer of 1937, when the SMR commenced a formal land survey, presumably in response to Watanabe's proposal. The government of Hiroshima prefecture was asked to organize the first contingent of three hundred pioneer colonists. Dubbed the "Hiroshima village," their settlement took on systematic land development while putting the virgin territory to the plow from late 1937 on.[108] This method of organizing a settlement ("migrant village") as a prefecture-based unit resonated with Nagata Shigeshi's Aliança scheme, which Tokyo had incorporated into its Brazilian colonization program after 1927, as explained in chapter 4. During the initial few years, following in the footsteps of the Hiroshima settlers, other groups of Japanese immigrants generally settled down in the relatively dry areas of Mishan. Yet in 1940 those from Nagano were assigned to a twenty-five-hundred-acre tract—of which almost one-third was a deserted marsh—in the immediate north of the wettest area. Their initial task was to set up infrastructure, such as a new road across muddy fields, while the authorities were busy erecting levees along the adjacent Muling River per Watanabe's plan.[109] Japanese settlers in the area had access to diesel-engine tractors for the leveling and plowing of reclaimed fields, because immigrant manpower alone did not suffice.[110] In Panshan in the Liao River delta, mass immigration and settlement began in 1942 after the first phase of reclamation created forty-nine thousand arable acres. In the spring an aggregate 549 households, or 1,991 migrants from rural Japan, settled on this site of Japanese development, as Watanabe had envisaged in his California-inspired proposal.[111]

When juxtaposing Watanabe's idyllic blueprint with the settlers' actual experiences, one realizes the more profound consequences of his US-bred settler colonialism. Embedded in his technical recommendations was a highly ideologized vision of ethnic/race relations that reinforced an official narrative of "coexistence" and "coprosperity" under Japanese dominance. In other words, Watanabe's discussion of technical matters was coupled with the idea of Japanese manifest destiny, that is, Japanese settlers as teachers of modern farming and civilized life to Chinese and Koreans. Always colored by positive renditions of California examples, his narrative of tutelary colonialism resembled—or drew from—a white American discourse on benevolent assimilation, as well as Watanabe's own racial experience in the San Joaquin River delta. While disparaging local Chinese residents of Panshan as "primitive" and "destitute" over and over, for example, Watanabe asserted that a "modern method of draining and flood control" and Japanese immigration would be indispensable for uplifting "the prehistoric state of [local Chinese] living" to a "level of modern civilization similar to rural California [of the present day]."[112] Just as Satō Torajirō had already exhibited (see chapter 2), Watanabe's paternalistic arrogance entailed a disavowal of outright exclusion, one that drew from his personal experience as a former California resident. He argued: "Even if Chinese have been already [in and around the reclaimed area], there would be no reason to exclude them. Japanese should act as the second [group of] pioneers to lend Chinese (the first but inferior group) a hand in the construction of a new civilization. . . . If Japanese kindly assist Chinese, the latter . . . would not oppose the former. Let Chinese people admire and be grateful for the paradise of the kingly way that Japan would offer them."[113]

In Watanabe's call for benevolence to "uncivilized natives," he articulated a disdain for the racial exclusionism that white American settlers had displayed and practiced, stressing that it should be viewed as an example *not* to follow, even though he embraced other aspects of American-style frontier conquest and development. His past struggle with American racism led him to think that Japanese, as a civilized master race, should refrain from making the same mistakes that white Americans had made, compelling him to adopt the language of coexistence when discussing colonial race/ethnic relations on Japan's frontier. In Manchuria, as in other parts of the Japanese empire, this curious line of thought and the paternalistic assimilationism that stemmed from it were not uncommon among other colonial resettlers from the United States, such as Chiba Toyoji. In addition to many ideas and techniques of frontier development, this rhetoric of inclusive settler racism formed another significant imprint of inter-imperial resemblance that US-based immigrants left on Japanese thinking on colonial race/ethnic relations, if not on its official assimilation policy. And equally important was that this rhetoric was seamlessly blended with Japan's pan-Asianist propaganda, as exemplified by Watanabe's invocation of Manchukuo's national motto: "the paradise of the kingly way" (ōdō rakudo).

A self-congratulatory, covertly racist celebration of Japanese settler colonialism by Watanabe mirrored anything but the reality of oppressive ethnic relations in colonial Manchuria. When one group after another of Japanese settlers entered the marshy lands of Mishan after 1937, for instance, Chinese and Korean residents already living there were usually removed—sometimes not even given a small amount of monetary compensation or sent to a less desirable alternative site. Whereas the existing farms and rice paddies after the native displacement enabled newcomers from Japan to sustain themselves in the initial phase of settlement making, thousands of migrant Chinese workers (usually referred to as "coolies") were put to work in horrendous conditions for the purpose of building levees and flood control channels to make additional room for new Japanese settlers. One Nagano colonist recalled: "When the construction of levees along the Muling River was carried out, . . . almost all workers were coolies from Shandong. They were housed in shabby huts made from straw mats. [Japanese supervisors] drove them like beasts, whipped them [to discipline/punish] even when they had to go to relieve themselves somewhere [for a short time], and let many die of malnutrition."[114] Just as white American talk of "equality" and "democracy" did not mean much to the minoritized Japanese immigrants who subsequently gave up on the United States after the early 1920s, imperial Japan's slogan of ethnic cooperation and coprosperity illuminated a fundamental contradiction in transpacific settler colonialism. The utterances of Watanabe and many other resettlers symbolized how victims of race-based exclusion so easily and willingly turned into enforcers of another kind of racial oppression when they had the power and ideological rationale to do so after moving from North America to Manchuria or elsewhere in the Japanese empire. American racism, as experienced and rendered by transpacific remigrants, provided an ironic support for imperial Japan's settler colonialism by which to disguise itself as a quest for antiracism, thereby sustaining the official mottoes of benevolence and mutual benefit, as well as a Japanese brand of exceptionalism based on them.

Accompanied by paternalistic assimilationism rooted in their minority experience, the activities of architects and teachers of agricultural settler colonialism from the United States exemplified how deeply and intricately intertwined Japanese America and the Japanese empire were through the effects of white American racism during the 1930s. This chapter has explained the ways in which imperial Japan accommodated and took advantage of immigrant settler-colonist visions and practices, when many US-based compatriots vacillated between the reality of being the persecuted racial minority in the white men's empire and the promise of an autonomous life in the home empire based on their racial and national background. Chiba Toyoji, Awaya Man'ei, Satō Nobumoto, Nagao Yukusuke, and Watanabe Kinzō, to name a few, remigrated from North America to offer their US-bred knowledge to their home empire, whether of their own volition or upon request. In the process, they also obtained what they thought they had lost on the white men's frontier: the status and ability to live as independent frontiersmen and a superior race. In the bosom of the home empire, they could reinvent themselves as colonial overlords—self-styled protectors and guides of Han Chinese, Manchus, and Koreans—instead of being demoted by white Americans to the same standing as despised Orientals. From across the Pacific, these "pioneers of overseas racial development" interjected their US-bred knowledge, expertise, and hard-earned money to bolster the backbone of Japan's colonial economy and the paternalistic racism that sustained asymmetrical colonial social relations on its new frontier of Manchuria and beyond.

6

Japanese Hawai'i and Its Tropical Nexus

Translocal Remigration to Colonial Taiwan and the Nan'yō

During the 1920s and the 1930s some Japanese residents in Hawai'i were also caught up in colonialist fantasies as resettlers and investors, similar to their compatriots in the continental United States. Chiba Toyoji's extolment of continental farming, as well as the lure of Japan's new frontier for minoritized residents in the American West, hinged largely on the presumption that comparable ecological conditions in the two locations would make US-based immigrants ideal teachers and exemplary practitioners of agrarian settler colonialism in Manchuria. In a similar vein, both Hawai'i's Japanese and their homeland compatriots directed special attention to Taiwan (and the Nan'yō), drawing a translocal parallel between America's colonial tropics and its Japanese counterparts. While suggesting that Manchuria could be a land of opportunity for Hawai'i residents, for example, a 1936 publication unequivocally advocated for their relocation "in the direction of the South Seas":[1]

If Manchuria forms the lifeline of our national defense, the South Seas should be deemed the lifeline of food production [for the Japanese homeland]. Our compatriots shall take an active role in this endeavor. Those in Hawai'i have experience in a similar tropical environment, rendering [the area] the most suitable site of resettlement for them. . . . Hawai'i is as small as [Japan's] Shikoku Island, and since it is already placed under the tight clutches of the United States, especially its Navy, there seems to be little chance for dramatic acceleration of Japanese economic development. . . . It is high time that a second Hawai'i is sought out [within Japan's sphere of influence].[2]

Like their counterparts in the American West, Japanese residents in Hawai'i tended to hold disproportionately positive views of Japan's colonial tropics, largely due to the disadvantageous effects of their subordinate status in the US territory. Many felt that the cultivation of pineapple, and to a lesser degree coffee, offered a promising future for remigrants and investors from Hawai'i.[3] In Taiwan, for example, these commercial crops—which were already familiar to Hawai'i's Japanese— had escaped the monopolized control of major business conglomerates from the colonial metropole until the late 1920s. In contrast, sugar production—the most important part of Taiwan's colonial agriculture next to rice cultivation—had been firmly dominated by moneyed interests connected to a few *zaibatsu* families, thus making it less desirable for new ventures or investment in the eyes of Hawai'i's Japanese residents. Notable exceptions were dozens of returnee experts in sugarcane milling and cultivation, who found employment at Taiwan's sugar companies due to their prior experience in Hawai'i's advanced industry. Amid the US anti-Japanese agitation in 1906–1907, for example, Taipei's colonial regime acted on behalf of the islands' nascent sugar companies to recruit experienced Hawai'i residents who had been either visiting or returned to their home prefectures, including Hiroshima and Kumamoto. While promising "considerable remunerations" to successful applicants, the governor-general's office served as a remigrant recruitment center for the goal of jump-starting the pivotal new industry by bringing invaluable technological knowledge and skills to private colonial enterprises.[4] Like their counterparts at the South Manchuria Railway and its research institutes, these individuals followed the basic pattern of becoming an indispensable cog in Taiwan's monopolized sugar machine.[5] Aside from these experts, two other kinds of remigrants were drawn from America's insular colony to Japan's southern frontier, where they transplanted their hard-to-get knowledge, experience, and money relating to coffee and, especially, pineapple growing and canning.

COLONIAL INVESTORS AND EXPERT COFFEE
GROWERS IN THE JAPANESE TROPICS

Following US immigration exclusion in the mid-1920s, one small group of Hawai'i's Japanese immigrants served as the basis of independent colonial investment in Japan's South Pacific Mandate and colonial Taiwan by starting Kona-style coffee cultivation. Established in 1926 and 1931, respectively, the Nan'yō Coffee Company of Saipan and the Sumida Coffee Farm of Wuhe (forty miles south of Hualien City) were primarily supported by Hawai'i's immigrant capital rather than the Japanese state or monopoly capital, such as from the South Manchuria Railway. Nevertheless, these genuine immigrant enterprises received strong backing from the colonial regime, because their proprietors and investors from Hawai'i could also offer the kind of valuable cultural capital that very few individuals in Japan had at that time: that is, expertise in coffee cultivation. As Japanese historian Mariko Iijima explains, the transfer of Hawaiian-style coffee production to Saipan and Taiwan helped tie the colonial tropics of the two Pacific empires through the agency of a Japanese immigrant merchant and his associates from Kona after the mid-1920s.[6]

Sumida Tajirō was one of the most successful Japanese entrepreneurs in prewar Hawai'i, and he was responsible for organizing a transpacific pathway of immigrant capital and coffee-related expertise from Kona to Saipan and Hualien after 1926. Having immigrated to what was about to become a US tropical colony as a self-supporting student in 1898, Sumida was not a typical Hawai'i Japanese who toiled in sugarcane fields; rather, he resembled the entrepreneurial expansionists of earlier decades who had swarmed to San Francisco and Honolulu. In 1918, entrusting the management of his Honolulu-based businesses (including the largest ethnic bank) to his brother, Sumida established the headquarters of T. Sumida & Company (Sumida Bussan Kaisha) in Osaka, with branches in Tokyo, Kobe, and Honolulu. This new transpacific trading and colonization enterprise engaged in the "import and export of domestic and foreign merchandise and brokerage" and the "cultivation of coffee, and [other forms of] agriculture."[7]

In 1926 Sumida joined forces with over two dozen Kona coffee farmers and prominent Honolulu merchants to organize the Nan'yō Coffee Company (Nan'yō Kōhī Kabushiki Kaisha) to launch Hawaiian-style coffee production in Saipan, the main island of the Northern Marianas under Japanese control. The initial idea came from a longtime Kona resident, who had paid two visits to that island between 1922 and 1925 to assess the feasibility of transplanting the prized farming expertise that Hawai'i's Japanese immigrants could offer to the far-flung corners of their homeland's overseas development. Similarities of climate and topographic features between the Big Islands of Hawai'i and the Nan'yō seemed to promise success in commercial coffee production should the expertise of Kona's veteran Japanese growers be transferred across the two Pacific empires. The company was capitalized at half a million yen ($250,000), an impressive sum at that time for a Japanese immigrant enterprise independent of Japan's moneyed interests.

According to a 1930 company profile, Nan'yō Coffee had forty-four Japanese stockholders, including nineteen investors from Kona as well as another four from Honolulu and elsewhere in Hawai'i. Several other investors were also former Hawai'i residents, and Sumida involved his wife and three US-born Nisei sons as shareholders. The core group of founder-investors, who also served as company executives, consisted of four prominent Kona coffee growers, along with Sumida and a Honolulu immigrant, and these six Hawai'i Japanese controlled the majority of the aggregate ten thousand shares of the company. Three of the four principal Kona investors relocated to Saipan to pioneer systematic coffee growing within the Japanese empire.[8] As a Honolulu ethnic newspaper described their "diaspora" as the transplanting of a "Kona [coffee] village in the island of Saipan," it is not far-fetched to argue that the company's new coffee estate constituted an extension of Hawai'i's Japanese coffee farming and economy to Japan's southern frontier, as well as a spillover of their borderless settler colonialism.[9] By 1936 the land under Nan'yō Coffee's cultivation had increased to 736 acres. The company also acquired an additional 490 acres on the neighboring island of Rota for future expansion. Managed by resettlers from Kona, Nan'yō Coffee had its own mill fitted out with the "latest equipment" from Hawai'i, and the final product was distributed in Japan's domestic market through Sumida's wholesale channels.[10]

Taiwan was the next object of this expansionistic entrepreneurial gaze. In early 1929, Nan'yō Coffee's executives met in Osaka and resolved to dispatch Sumida and a Kona remigrant on a one-month investigative tour to the island, where they sought out a suitable site for a new coffee farm.[11] They decided on the undeveloped sloped river terrace of Wuhe, surrounded by pockets of indigenous settlements, in the southernmost edge of Hualien Province (see map 5). Instead of diluting Nan'yō Coffee's limited resources by splitting off part of what had been established in Saipan, Sumida set up a separate firm—a direct subsidiary of T. Sumida & Company—for his new Taiwan venture, with an initial capital of 380,000 yen.[12] In late 1930 the island's first large-scale cultivation of coffee commenced with the planting of seedlings imported from Saipan and Kona. US-made Fordson tractors were brought over from Hawai'i to assist the process of land clearing and development. The governor-general of Taiwan lent full support to Sumida's enterprise by granting the use of 971 acres of public land with a future purchase option—an option that was granted in 1940 along with 50 additional acres.[13] This example of utilizing Kona's Japanese coffee experts inspired other colonial capitalists to follow suit by attempting to recruit or collaborate with them for new plantations in Taitung, Chiayi, and Pingtung during the latter half of the 1930s.[14]

In the context of postexclusion transpacific mobility between the US and Japanese colonial tropics, however, coffee's place was limited mostly to the Kona-Saipan-Hualien triangle interlinked by Sumida and his Kona associates. The genesis of Taiwan's modern pineapple industry, on the other hand, owed much to the larger migration pathway that emerged between the colonial tropics of the two Pacific empires, as well as to the expertise remigrants from Japanese Hawai'i brought to Japan's colonial tropics.

HAWAI'I'S JAPANESE AND THE RISE OF THE EXPORT-ORIENTED PINEAPPLE INDUSTRY IN TAIWAN

For a greater number of Japanese in Hawai'i, pineapple—a "trophy of empire" as Gary Okihiro calls it—particularly appeared to offer opportunities for acquiring or maintaining the lifestyle and identity of independent "frontier" settlers in the aftermath of US racial exclusion.[15] The colonial regime's policy of prioritizing pineapple cultivation reinforced the perception that experienced Japanese growers and workers in Hawai'i could readily attain personal fulfillment and make patriotic contributions at the same time.[16] In the context of Japan's attempt to make its trop-ical territories economically profitable, the Hawaiian-style industrialized produc-tion of pineapples and canned commodities formed an important part of Taiwan's agricultural development policy after the early 1920s. Combined with escalating anti-Japanese racism stateside, this policy carried out by Japan's colonial regime provided another context for the mobility and investment of self-selected groups of Japanese immigrant "pioneers" from Hawai'i's ethnic community.

In colonial Taiwan, formal efforts to develop settler agriculture started in 1899 with the attempt to establish an "immigrant village" in Hualien, a coastal valley region of east-central Taiwan that previously had only been dotted with small set-tlements of indigenous peoples. Intended as a site for sugarcane and camphor lau-rel plantations to be managed by Japanese immigrants, this first settler-colonist project took the form of a private business endeavor commissioned by the gover-nor-general of Taiwan. After neutralizing indigenous resistance and co-opting local residents, more than 480 Japanese moved into the region in 1906, forming the backbone of Taiwan's first Japanese agricultural colony, known as Kada Village (see map 5). Three years later the colonial regime adopted a comprehensive "immi-gration" policy to populate Taiwan's eastern frontier with agrarian settlers from rural Japan under direct government sponsorship, which paved the way for the formation of three Japanese farm "villages" in Hualien between 1910 and 1914.[17] The first village was erected after dozens of local aboriginal inhabitants were forci-bly removed and relocated elsewhere after a failed revolt. Replacing indigenous residents with immigrant newcomers according to the pervasive "logic of elimina-tion," it marked the beginning of Japanese settler colonialism in the empire's first overseas frontier, which faithfully followed western settler-society precedents of land grabbing and native removal, including what had been done in Hawai'i.[18]

Indeed, Hawai'i served as a key reference point and a template when Japan's colonial brass contemplated the manner in which Taiwan might build agro-indus-trial infrastructures and form Japan's first tropical settler society. The Dutch colony of Java and British Malaya were also often on their radar, but the similar geo-graphical conditions of Hawai'i and Taiwan (island environments and close latitudes) rendered the US tropical colony a direct object of comparison to its Japanese counterpart and a chief example for the latter to emulate. The history of Japanese immigration to the islands also solidified the Hawai'i-Taiwan nexus in the imaginations of many officials, ideologues, entrepreneurs, and settlers. The cir-cumstances in which Taiwan's sugar industry came into being provide a prime example, since that industry had a strong imprint of Hawai'i's Japanese experience from the beginning. Established in 1900 with a capital infusion from the *zaibatsu* Mitsui, the Taiwan Seitō (Sugar Production) Company involved the same core group of individuals who had orchestrated a state-backed scheme to transport more than twenty-nine thousand Japanese plantation workers to Hawai'i between

1885 and 1894. One of these elite Japanese moved to Honolulu with the first batch of these government-sponsored immigrants; not only was he the first Japanese to graduate from Oʻahu College (Punahou School), but he also became widely recognized in Japan's elite circles as a rare "expert" on the sugar business—an expertise that few Japanese shared when the Asian empire acquired its first overseas colony of Taiwan in 1895. Soon this man joined forces with the same Mitsui executives who had worked in the government-sponsored immigration scheme and served as a founding board member of the newly established Taiwan Seitō. Under his influence, this monopoly enterprise built a number of modern sugar mills, modeled after those in Hawaiʻi (with imported equipment), while recruiting dozens of the islands' experienced Japanese immigrants as sugarcane mill engineers and farming experts.[19] Having been brought under the control of the United States and Japan, respectively, around the same time, these two island colonies in the tropical Pacific emerged under similar circumstances and with some of the same people intimately involved in the establishment of the sugar and other settler agricultural industries as well as migrant communities.

From around the turn of the twentieth century, policy makers and agronomists of colonial Taiwan selected pineapple as another targeted commodity—one that also had strong connections to Hawaiʻi's ethnic Japanese farmers. Since before the coming of Japanese colonizers, Taiwanese farmers had grown native variants of the crop for local consumption, but these were considered unsuitable for food processing and export-grade canning. Given the contemporary rise of the pineapple canning business in Southeast Asia and Hawaiʻi, the Japanese colonial regime was keen on experimenting with "foreign" varieties of pineapple from those places instead. The significant presence and involvement of Japanese immigrants in Hawaiʻi's pineapple industry put the US tropical colony ahead of Southeast Asia in terms of colonial Taiwan's attempts to import industrial and farming expertise and appropriate crop varieties for the development of a canning business. Pineapple thus attracted two types of remigrants from Hawaiʻi: experienced growers of the Hawaiian variety "Smooth Cayenne" and those with experience in the canning process. Their involvement in Taiwan's pineapple industry—which would become its third most important agro-industrial sector next to rice and sugar by the late 1920s—dovetailed with the governor-general's policy to create an export-oriented economy to contribute to the empire's economic independence, if not dominance, in the Asia-Pacific basin.[20] During the first two decades of the twentieth century, the pioneering roles of these Japanese Hawaiian "experts" anticipated what could be termed the full-scale "Hawaiianization" of Taiwan's pineapple industry by many more transpacific remigrants in the 1920s and the 1930s.

Japan's insular colony underwent the first phase of Hawaiianization in the area of mechanized canning when Okamura Shōtarō constructed a small cannery in Fengshan (near Kaohsiung) in 1902 with the financial backing of the colonial regime, even though this phase revealed a mixture of Hawaiian and Southeast Asian influences. Revered now as the founder of Taiwan's pineapple canning business, he is said to have briefly worked in a pineapple cannery and packing plant in O'ahu. On his fifteen-acre Kaohsiung farm, Okamura tried his hand at growing imported Hawaiian Smooth Cayenne plants for his nascent canning business, although this first experiment did not produce a favorable enough result to replace the "inferior" native varieties of pineapple. Still, by 1907 Okamura's cannery managed to produce 330,000 cans of pineapple by using the native crop variety despite its being less suitable for canning. While operating Taiwan's first pineapple cannery, the transpacific resettler also managed to entice the governor-general to fund an official "research" trip to investigate the state of the thriving pineapple export industry in Singapore (British Malaya) and Java (Dutch East Indies)—top exporters of canned pineapples at that time.[21] Following in Okamura's footsteps, other Japanese with a background in pineapple farming and/or canning remigrated from Hawai'i to Taiwan with "trade secrets" that the colonial regime desperately wanted. In the 1920s, for example, one such immigrant, Nagai Toshio, was recruited to manage a highly capitalized canning factory in Kaohsiung, which was equipped with the most advanced machinery from the United States. This long-term Hawai'i resident was said to have had more than a dozen years' experience in pineapple cannery work, along with a ten-year stint as a pineapple farmer in O'ahu.[22]

Under the influence of these experienced industry leaders with Hawaiian backgrounds, there emerged a commonly held belief that the prosperity of the pineapple canning business would be untenable without conversion to the Hawaiian variety of the crop, Smooth Cayenne. Filled with solid dietary fiber and with a higher sugar and acid content, its larger body was deemed more suitable for canning and product marketing than the native or Southeast Asian pineapple varieties. The first *successful* attempt to grow the Smooth Cayenne variety in Taiwan involved Ōtsuki Kōnosuke, an influential early leader of Hawai'i's Japanese community and a celebrated "hero" of frontier conquest in eastern Taiwan (see the introduction). Around 1911 this transpacific/trans-imperial pioneer had experimented with the propagation of fifty imported plants near Hualien, impressing the real potential of Smooth Cayenne cultivation upon state agricultural engineers and local growers. A few years later, however, there was an attempt by a Japanese settler with Singapore connections to counter the increasing popularity of Smooth Cayenne by introducing a Southeast Asian variety of "Sarawak" pineapple plants into Taiwan.[23] This situation induced the central agricultural research center of the colonial regime to carry out a comprehensive study on the suitability of various foreign pineapple varieties, resulting finally in the formal adoption of Smooth Cayenne in 1924.[24]

The triumph of Smooth Cayenne, and Ōtsuki's role in demonstrating its potential for successful commercial cultivation, elucidates how the Hawaiianization of

Taiwan's pineapple industry, if not its inception, was inseparable from the arrival of former Hawai'i residents such as Ōtsuki. Before finding himself in colonial Taiwan, Ōtsuki was a leading figure in a group of Hawai'i-based immigrant expansionists who had opposed the US-backed overthrow of the Hawaiian Kingdom in 1893–1894. An advocate of Japan's manifest destiny in the Pacific basin, Ōtsuki had been active in the circle of self-styled builders of a second Japan in Hawai'i. After working as an instructor of practical farming at Tokyo Imperial University, he became a leader of the first contingent of government-sponsored Japanese immigrants bound for Hawaiian sugar plantations in 1885. Until his bittersweet departure from what he—and many others—came to view as the white man's frontier, Ōtsuki had tried his hand at various enterprises of agrarian settler colonialism in the mid-Pacific Islands, including the first ever Japanese immigrant endeavor to set up a coffee and sugar cane plantation near Hilo, albeit in vain. During the boom years of labor migrant trafficking in the early 1900s, Ōtsuki also ran an emigration company that aimed to populate Hawai'i with a large number of new settlers from his home prefecture, to offset the political and economic ascendancy of white *haole* elite following US annexation. This venture came to a sudden halt when exclusionist agitation resulted in the end of Japanese labor migration under the Gentlemen's Agreement. Ōtsuki then assisted Tokyo capitalists in drafting plans for a new sugar plantation in Taiwan between 1905 and 1907, because his twenty years' experience in Hawai'i's sugar industry made him stand out as a foremost expert on the endeavor. Thus, after the repeated failures of private settler colonialism in the US tropical colony, it did not take Ōtsuki long to decide to leave Hawai'i for good and join Taiwan's first rural settler community when he moved to Kada Village in Hualien in response to a formal invitation to serve as a chief farm manager.[25] Eastern Taiwan was now his new frontier, and Smooth Cayenne was one of his gifts to the home empire. Along with the story of Okamura, Ōtsuki's trajectory reveals the distinctly Hawaiian origin of Taiwan's pineapple industry— both farming and canning—as well as the mediating role of America's white supremacy and its settler discourse, which motivated some immigrants, including Ōtsuki, to seek resettlement on Japan's colonial frontier.

After the passage of the 1924 US Immigration Act, a new pathway of human mobility took shape between Hawai'i and Taiwan, similar to the transpacific reverse migration between the American West and Manchuria. This flow of veteran settler-colonists—albeit smaller than its California-Manchuria counterpart—entailed the inter-imperial transfer of hard-to-find immigrant expertise in large-scale pineapple farming and industrialized canning. A number of Japanese plantation workers and tenant farmers in Hawai'i returned to the bosom of their racial homeland and its sovereign protection, swapping the life of an American minority for that of a Japanese colonial master. In the wake of US immigration exclusion, the governor-general of Taiwan implemented a new policy to grant Japanese (re)settlers inexpensive government land, which had been de facto communal property of native inhabitants. In 1930, for example, a Japanese immigrant near Honolulu applied for the sale of "open land" for the building of a pineapple plantation and cattle ranch. This man had organized an O'ahu-based group of "thirteen to fourteen partners with $500 investment from each," and a few of the members were ready to move from Hawai'i to Taiwan as soon as the application was approved.[26] In the following year, over a dozen Japanese pineapple growers on Maui and their families were reported to have organized a colonization scheme in which they obtained twenty-five hundred acres of government "homestead" in the far-flung barren land of eastern Taiwan. These veterans of pineapple cultivation from Hawai'i intended to join forces with additional immigrant families from mainland Japan for the advancement of genuine Japanese settler agriculture in their new Taitung frontier. Interviewed by a local newspaper, the leaders specifically cited the inability to acquire land in white-dominated Maui and bleak prospects for the future as primary reasons for their interest in eastern Taiwan.[27] Although available sources do not show what became of these enterprises, they suggest the appeal of large-scale pineapple farming for some of Hawai'i's Japanese residents based on the availability of "open land" usurped from local people in Japan's tropical colony.

OKAZAKI NIHEI, COLONIAL MONOPOLY CAPITAL, AND THE HAWAIIANIZATION OF TAIWAN'S PINEAPPLE INDUSTRY

In 1925 the arrival of a longtime O'ahu resident named Okazaki Nihei signaled the beginning of a new era in the history of Taiwan's pineapple industry, wherein a state-endorsed effort at industrial development consciously appropriated the immigrant desire to seek an independent life and freedom from white racism. One year after the total exclusion of the Japanese race from the United States, Okazaki gave up on Hawai'i and took an offer from Japan's capitalists to help build and manage the day-to-day operations of the first Hawaiian-style pineapple farm-cannery complex in the Laopi (Laobei) district of rural Pingtung Province (see map 5). When he gave a speech before top colonial officials in Taipei in 1925, Okazaki declared that "colonization" had been his "pursuit" and that he and his family were now willing to "die for the cause of [laying the ground for the] pineapple industry" in Taiwan.[28] Local settler newspapers also lauded his move to Taiwan, representing Okazaki as a "leading expert in Hawai'i's pineapple industry who has lived there for [almost] twenty years."[29]

Indeed, after two years of preparation, Okazaki's new venture facilitated the spread of plantation-style operations in the Kaohsiung-Pingtung region. Land cultivated for "foreign" pineapple varieties (mostly Smooth Cayenne) also jumped from 11.7 to 24.7 percent in just one year, between 1929 and 1930, although the first half of the ensuing decade saw some stagnation in growth due to overproduction, plant diseases, and the worldwide Depression.[30] Before World War II, the first mechanized modern cannery to which Okazaki was connected—and the three newer facilities that followed it—"packed only the foreign [pineapple] varieties" that were harvested on company-owned plantations in order to produce top-grade canned products for export. At the same time, many preexisting "small, old-fashioned canneries with little machinery" continued to procure native pineapple varieties from independent growers (mainly Taiwanese), mostly for local consumption, until they went out of business under industry-wide consolidation in the mid-1930s.[31]

Behind the rise of the mechanized canning business that relied on Smooth Cayenne lay a new economic policy of Taiwan's colonial regime and associated investment from Japan's industrialists, especially Takasaki Tatsunosuke of Tōyō Can Manufacturing Company (TCMC; Tōyō Seikan Kabushiki Kaisha), which was Japan's leading tin can manufacturer. Okazaki's remigration from Hawai'i dovetailed with the regime's attempt to "modernize" Taiwan's pineapple industry so that it could compete with its Hawaiian (American) and Singaporean (British) counterparts—the top two exporters of canned pineapples—on the world market. The new agro-industrial policy encompassed the priority sale of state-owned lands for pineapple plantations, free distribution of Smooth Cayenne saplings from a newly established government agricultural center near Kaohsiung (not far from Okazaki's farm in Laopi), and state subventions (one-third of the cost) for the purchase of the latest canning equipment—often from the United States. Hawai'i remained a central reference point—and was indeed always hailed as a preferred model—in this colonial policy mandate.[32] These measures particularly benefited—and thus were fervently supported by—the Osaka-based TCMC, which had just built Taiwan's first can manufacturing factory in 1922. With the backing of these government measures, Takasaki wanted to set up a large-scale pineapple plantation and introduce rationalized cultivation and canning processes. A firm believer in modern scientific farming, Okazaki held views similar to his sponsor Takasaki's, and he wanted to act as the initiator of "progress in scientific and systematic [farming] methods . . . for the pineapple industry" in Japan's southern frontier.[33] The triangular partnership among former Hawai'i residents, Japanese metropole capitalists, and the colonial regime constituted the backbone of Taiwan's challenge to its US and British rivals in the global pineapple trade.[34]

In this context, Okazaki assumed a specific identity—and was expected to act—as the teacher for Taiwan's pineapple growers and cannery operators through his trailblazing act of establishing the first mechanized modern plantation. Having arrived in Honolulu in 1907 and graduated from McKinley High School, he had firmly embraced the settler-colonist idea of "overseas development" and consciously aspired to emulate America's legendary Puritan pioneers to promote

Japan's settler colonialism and national expansion.[35] Not content with working as a sugarcane field hand under the thumb of *haole* plantation owners, Okazaki looked to pineapple farming as an avenue to carve out a niche for economic independence and racial prosperity in white-dominated Hawai'i. Only a decade after James Dole had organized the island's first pineapple plantation-cannery complex, Okazaki's choice of the crop not only demonstrated his penchant for romantic, if naïve, expansionism mixed with strong racial nationalism, it also followed the general pattern of appropriating white American colonial practice and scientific agriculture by self-styled Japanese immigrant frontiersmen. In order to deepen his grasp of the most advanced farm methods, Okazaki completed a special certificate program on pineapples at the University of Hawai'i.[36]

In 1909 Okazaki formed a partnership with a few like-minded immigrants to create their own farm in Wahiawā, the hub of O'ahu's pineapple industry. This enterprise failed, however, due to financial problems and interference from white competitors, yet Okazaki did not give up on his desire to build a self-sufficient settlement of Japanese pioneer farmers through pineapple production. Moving to the northern part of O'ahu, he picked Pupukea as the next site for his vision, and pineapple cultivation there proved to be very promising in its first year. While organizing a Honolulu-based joint stock company for this Japanese-owned plantation in 1914, Okazaki and his partners also strove to build a canning facility of their own. These ambitious ventures nonetheless met a disappointing end, again at the hands of obstructive *haole* competitors, who successfully drove Japanese growers out by orchestrating a boycott against their harvest in cooperation with white-owned canneries. For the next several years Okazaki worked as a farm foreman for a local pineapple plantation in Pupukea. This period of hibernation allowed him to lay the groundwork for bigger enterprises.[37]

In the early 1920s Okazaki moved back to Honolulu to manage an all-Japanese land firm and its brand new pineapple plantation in the Manoa Valley. At the same time, he diligently attended classes on agricultural science related to pineapple farming and techniques of canning and production management at the nearby University of Hawai'i. In defiance of Hawai'i's *haole* agribusiness interests, Okazaki also took an offer from a British concern to participate in its project to build a pineapple plantation in Fiji. Although these endeavors, too, collapsed in the end, Okazaki had become widely known as one of Hawai'i's foremost Japanese authorities on the pineapple. Indeed, when Nitobe Inazō stopped in Honolulu on his way to the continental United States, the then professor of colonial policy studies at Tokyo Imperial University personally conferred with Okazaki about Hawai'i's pineapple industry. Impressed by the depth of Okazaki's knowledge, Nitobe told the Hawai'i resident about opportunities in Taiwan, where he had once served as the chief agricultural engineer and helped another Hawai'i remigrant, Okamura Shōtarō, start a pineapple canning venture two decades earlier. Thereafter, with an eye to assisting the development of modern pineapple farming on Japan's tropical frontier, Okazaki periodically shipped stumps, tops (crowns), and suckers of Smooth Cayenne for experimental vegetative propagation at Taiwan's state-run agricultural center.[38]

Encouraged originally by Nitobe, Okazaki's interest in Taiwan intensified when Takasaki Tatsunosuke visited Honolulu to inspect Hawai'i's pineapple canning industry in 1924. With the help of Japanese industrialists, Takasaki had played a central role in the establishment of the TCMC in 1917 and was closely linked to manufacturers of canned fish products, Japan's top export food commodity. But his involvement in the canning business was not the only point of intersection with Okazaki. Takasaki's past trajectory also entailed many years of US immigrant experience along the California-Mexico borderlands. A graduate of the Tokyo Institute of Fishery, he had initially worked as an engineer in sardine canning. In 1912, when the International Fish Company of Los Angeles (owned by a Mexican businessman named Aurelio Sandoval) had invited him to set up a cannery in Magdalena Bay, Baja California, Takasaki had moved to Southern California to become a part of early Japanese America.[39] Between 1912 and 1915, he had lived the life of a transborder Japanese immigrant. While going back and forth between Los Angeles/San Diego and Magdalena Bay, Takasaki was instrumental in solidifying the Japanese presence in the fishing industry of the US-Mexican borderlands through his fish canning work.[40] Takasaki's American experience also provided the basis for his decision to organize a modern tin can factory in Japan based on American machinery and technology when he returned home to Osaka in 1915 at the behest of like-minded industrialists there.

It was also during that period that Takasaki had entertained the idea of combining can manufacturing with the harvest of content materials in order to dominate the business process and maximize profitability. As the governor-general of Taiwan adopted a pro-"modernization" policy, Takasaki put that idea into practice by founding the island's first and only tin can factory and a large pineapple plantation in the Kaohsiung area in 1922 and 1925, respectively. That crop was a natural choice for Takasaki, because he had had a chance to observe James Dole's pineapple canning facility in Honolulu during his transpacific journey to Los Angeles a decade or so earlier. A vivid memory of Hawai'i's magnificent modern cannery had been deeply engraved on the mind of this canning engineer turned entrepreneur since then.[41] Takasaki's observations of the two tropical islands also convinced him that Hawai'i and Taiwan were "relative(s)."[42] Furthermore, after the Great Kantō earthquake in 1923, Japan's newly adopted customs duties on luxury items reduced the import of canned pineapple from Hawai'i and elsewhere dramatically, thereby boosting a demand for the Taiwan-made product in Japan's metropole market. To Takasaki, transplanting Hawaiian-style pineapple cultivation and canning to Taiwan mirrored a personal ambition as much as a logical business decision backed by the colonial regime's policy mandate at that juncture.[43] And with similar visions and immigrant experience, Okazaki was an ideal partner for Takasaki's new enterprise.

In 1924 the trajectories of these two individuals crossed during Takasaki's investigative trip to Hawai'i. In order to prepare for the Taiwan project, the can manufacturer sought the Honolulu resident's expertise and hired him as an adviser and guide to Hawai'i's plantation industry. After his first-hand observation, Takasaki invited Okazaki to Taiwan to assess the suitability of large-scale Smooth Cayenne cultivation and mechanized canning there. Because the governor-general's office supported Takasaki's endeavor in the context of its new promodernization (or Hawaiianization) policy, Okazaki was joined by a colonial technocrat who specialized in pineapple affairs on this inspection tour. His three-month sojourn subsequently generated a positive report, which likened southern Taiwan's soil and climate to those in its Hawaiian counterpart. Produced by Hawai'i's foremost Japanese expert on the pineapple, the assessment was precisely what Takasaki had awaited since the building of his tin can factory in Kaohsiung in 1922. Okazaki specifically selected the hillside of northeastern Pingtung near the town of Laopi, a large tract of land reminiscent of Dole's pineapple fields in Wahiawā, O'ahu, which was uninhabited but adjacent to Paiwan aboriginal villages.[44]

Subsidized by the TCMC, Taiwan Pineapple Cultivation Company (TPCC; Taiwan Hōri Saibai Kaisha) was established in 1925 with an initial capital of 300,000 yen ($150,000; later increased to 1 million yen or $500,000). In the countryside of Pingtung, the company ran a plantation-style pineapple estate, which was accessible from Takasaki's tin can factory and later its affiliated canneries in the greater Kaohsiung region. Although its rural Laopi land was initially almost completely untouched, the 3,185-acre property was intended to become the biggest pineapple farm in Japan's tropical colony. Not only was Okazaki asked to serve as the inaugural general manager of the Laopi plantation, but he was also the TPCC's third largest stockholder, not to mention the principal stockholder as a Taiwan resident investor.[45] When the Japanese settler newspaper reported the establishment of the company and its plantation in 1925, the transpacific remigrant was habitually billed as the "utmost authority of pineapple enterprise," whose comparisons of the Laopi venture to the early days of Hawai'i's industry predicted, albeit cautiously, a hopeful future for Taiwan's counterpart in a global export market.[46]

On the TPCC pineapple fields he reigned over, Okazaki apparently assembled a team of former Hawai'i residents as his full-time aides. In early 1929 a Japanese visitor noted that "everything [was] done in a Hawaiian way because leading staff [had] gained [their knowledge and skills] from years of experience in Hawai'i."[47] During an investigative tour of 1931–1932, a second-generation Japanese American agronomist from Honolulu also noted: "Most of the (pineapple) plantation managers [in southern Taiwan] were once in Hawaii and they are following the methods which they learned [t]here."[48] His statement suggested that Okazaki's arrival had enticed other Hawai'i residents to seek employment as pineapple experts elsewhere in Taiwan, as a few more plantation-style farms were established after the late 1920s. Indeed, Nakao Magoichi, Okazaki's old friend, separately moved from Hawai'i to Kaohsiung to assume a managerial position at a pineapple plantation in Fengshan, another subsidiary of the TCMC conglomerate, headed by none other than Takasaki's business associate, a former Southern California resident.[49]

Not only did Okazaki help bring human resources from across the Pacific, but he and other Hawai'i residents also helped introduce the increasingly harder-to-get Smooth Cayenne saplings and the latest US farm machinery to Taiwan's pineapple fields. Just when Taipei's new policy mandate called for the importation of pineapple saplings from abroad, Hawai'i's pineapple monopoly began to restrict the export of Smooth Cayenne around 1924. Yet Japanese residents in the US tropical colony played an indispensable role in circumventing this new obstacle to the transfer of precious industrial technology. After visiting O'ahu and traveling throughout the island while being guided by Okazaki (before his move to Japan's colonial tropics), Taiwan's top agricultural technocrat boasted that he could successfully arrange for the shipment of one hundred thousand saplings from Honolulu to Kaohsiung in 1925: "In Hawai'i, taking improved (Smooth Cayenne) breeds [out of the territory] has become more and more difficult, but I could obtain [saplings] easily because there [we]re so many Japanese farmers in Hawai'i [who were willing to help]." He also commented on the difficulty of accessing "industrial secrets." In the end, however, he noted that he "somehow" got ahold of necessary information and some samples, thus implying that he had received the assistance of local residents (and Okazaki).[50] Another agricultural scientist, an employee of Taiwan's Mitsubishi subsidiary, also dismissed the alleged "difficulty of purchasing saplings" in Hawai'i, citing the "special effort" of a Japanese American who purportedly claimed that "supplying the best saplings inexpensively [wa]s his contribution to the motherland's new industry."[51]

Just like their California counterparts in Manchuria, Okazaki and his Hawai'i associates spearheaded the use of mechanized farm equipment and canning machinery on the pineapple fields of southern Taiwan. Based on his previous experience, Okazaki put two Fordson tractors and a 150-horsepower steam plow in service for initial plowing and harrowing of virgin soil, much to the surprise of local observers, who had never seen such a spectacle of modernity. The gasoline-powered tractors were among the first to be introduced to Taiwan, for most existing machines on the island were still antiquated steam tractors used on sugarcane fields. In addition to Hawaiian-style mechanized agricultural operation, a half million Smooth Cayenne saplings were also procured from Hawai'i through Okazaki's connections and were planted on the TPCC's newly developed farmland under his supervision. In order to promote the industry's conversion to Smooth Cayenne, the company and Takasaki's can manufacturing firm actively distributed tens of thousands of imported slips and suckers to other pineapple growers, farm organizations and firms, and agricultural experimental stations throughout the island.[52]

In early 1930 another guest of Okazaki from Japan marveled at the "massive scale and systematic manner" of farming at the new Laopi plantation: "The planting of pineapple crowns has thus far taken place only on 450 acres, but wilderness is being steadily conquered and giving way to rows of pineapples. Tractor plows are always on the move. . . . Over 2,680,000 plants of the Smooth Cayenne variety [from Hawai'i] occupy the cultivated field, and . . . by 1935, the annual yield should reach 10,000,000 plants, which is worth 400,000 boxes of canned pineapples. Mr. Okazaki . . . has carried through with his beliefs [in a Hawai'i-bred farming method], and his experience, skills, and enthusiasm should deserve much admiration."[53] (See figures 7 and 8.) While his wife depicted the mechanized farm operation as a "continental (American) style," Okazaki himself proudly compared his scientific "conquest of nature" in Taiwan to the development of Hawai'i's "barren lands" by white American "pioneers" like James Dole.[54] And this civilizationist analogy was not lost on the colonial brass. Because of the plantation's reputation as a driving force of modern Taiwan's export industry, it was no surprise that the governor-general took the trouble to pay a personal visit to Okazaki's residence and plantation in the far-flung countryside of Pingtung.[55]

In addition to the establishment of a plantation-style pineapple farm in rural Taiwan, Okazaki was also entrusted with the role of helping introduce a highly mechanized way of canning there in accordance with his Hawaiian experience and expertise. In 1926, as the first modest harvest of Smooth Cayenne crops was being made on the Laopi farm, the transpacific remigrant oversaw the experimental production of canned pineapples and their quality improvement at an existing factory near Kaohsiung. Preparations for a brand-new "Hawaiian-style" cannery were already under way, and in 1927 Okazaki was dispatched to Honolulu to negotiate the purchase of the most advanced machinery, including the Ginaca automated peeling and slicing machines, one of the revolutionary changes that Dole's pineapple empire brought to the industry. A group company of the TPCC, this new cannery was open for business in central Kaohsiung (not far from Takasaki's can manufacturing factory) in June 1928 (see figures 9 and 10).[56] The spectacle of mechanized assembly lines, which only partially required the basic work of low-wage female staff, led a newspaper reporter to marvel that "compared to existing methods of canning, the splendid power and effectiveness of machinery [wa]s all evident, because there [wa]s no waste" in terms of time and material.[57] In order to encourage other canners and investors to follow the example of modernization, the governor-general's office designated this project the first recipient of official

FIGURE 7. Japanese manager and Taiwanese workers on a Laopi pineapple farm, ca. early 1930s. *Source: Nettai Engei* 6, no. 3 (September 1936).

FIGURE 8. Harvesting and transporting pineapples on a Laopi pineapple farm, ca. early 1930s. *Source: Nettai Engei* 6, no. 3 (September 1936).

FIGURE 9. First Hawaiian-style pineapple cannery in colonial Taiwan, Kaohsiung, early 1930s. *Source: Nettai Engei* 6, no. 3 (September 1936).

FIGURE 10. Ginaca automated peeling and slicing machine, Kaohsiung, ca. early 1930s. *Source: Nettai Engei* 6, no. 3 (September 1936).

subventions for the acquisition of mechanized cannery equipment and devices; the program lasted through the mid-1930s.[58] In order to streamline the manufacture and transport of canned pineapple for export, the TPCC also took advantage of the 33 percent subsidy for machine imports in 1932 by building its own cannery with brand-new equipment from Hawai'i near a railroad station about five miles southwest of the Laopi estate.[59]

Similar to a prevailing practice of labor management in Hawai'i's colonial agriculture, Okazaki utilized an ethnically mixed workforce for land clearing and cultivation. The ethnic division of labor had traditionally ensured the effective control and low cost of field-workers in Hawai'i's sugarcane and pineapple plantations. The transpacific remigrant faithfully re-created this practice by setting an almost equal number of local Taiwanese and aborigines to work in Laopi. To Okazaki, the cheapness of indigenous labor had indeed constituted a major reason for his positive assessment of southern Taiwan when he had undertaken the TCMC-funded investigative tour. The Laopi estate bordered a concentration of Paiwan aboriginal tribes, from which Okazaki procured some fifty to one hundred people especially for the demanding task of clearing tropical jungles, which tractors and other mechanical equipment could not handle (see figure 11). These Paiwan wage workers were placed at the bottom of the economic hierarchy and treated as cheap and expendable labor. Around 1929–1930, as Okazaki explained at the time, a group of aborigines usually "descended" from a nearby hillside village to work for one week before another group replaced them—a routine that was repeated throughout the year. In line with the prevailing prejudices of Japanese settlers, Okazaki did not feel these aboriginal field hands required more than temporary shacks for the duration of employment, and their wages were kept lower than those paid to Taiwanese workers because they had their own residences and maintained a semitraditional lifestyle up in the mountains. The company did not even have to pay for their food, since the workers brought their own provisions. In highly racist terms, a visitor from Tokyo described how the Laopi farm operation reified what was deemed the proper order of Japan's settler colony and ethnic power relations there. Ten Japanese managers and supervisors, including Okazaki, reigned over the "bestial" aborigines, as the observer condescendingly characterized them, and the workers behaved like "tamed lions" under the benevolent supervision of Okazaki and other Japanese, allegedly attending to their task faithfully from six o'clock in the morning till six thirty in the evening (see figure 12).[60]

It is important to note that this Hawaiian-style labor management dovetailed neatly with the colonial regime's effort to "civilize" Taiwan's aborigines, that is, to make them productive and functional in the overall economy of Japan's settler empire. As a part of its civilizationist enterprise of "pacification" and uplift, Taipei strove to get the aboriginal tribes to abandon the lifestyle of hunter-gatherers, instead embracing the commercial economy through officially established "trading

FIGURE 11. Paiwan workers on a Laopi pineapple plantation, ca. 1927. *Source:* Ono Fumihide, *Taiwan tōgyō to Tōgyō kaisha* (Tokyo: Tōyō Keizai Shuppanbu, 1930).

FIGURE 12. Commercially produced picture postcard displaying Paiwan "natives" on a Laopi pineapple plantation, ca. 1929. *Source:* Author's personal collection.

posts," settling down in the lower lands, and engaging in wage labor and agricultural pursuits (especially rice farming).[61] In this context, Okazaki's methods of exploiting indigenous labor drew the keen attention of local authorities in Kaohsiung, prompting high-ranking officials of the police and aborigine control section to visit the Laopi plantation in 1926. Impressed by the possibilities of pineapple work for serving as a main source of "industrial employment" for "the uncivilized," the local authorities soon incorporated the cultivation of Smooth Cayenne into the core of the "program to promote aboriginal economic development" in the region.[62]

In the name of making the aborigines functional in the market economy, remigrants from Hawai'i justified the low wages paid to and exploitation of the indigenous workforce with the commonly held idea of their inferiority, which would require tutelary colonialism by Japanese settler-masters. These ideas resembled what had surrounded Hawaii's Japanese residents (and other racialized minorities) in the discursive space of paternalistic American assimilationism. For example, Okazaki's associate on the Laopi plantation, another resettler from O'ahu, disparaged the "natives" (*dojin*) as "ineffectual," but his paternalist thinking also led him to predict that they would "improve" after gaining experience as they had been working "obediently" (under Japanese guidance). With a mixture of racist contempt and benevolence, Nakao Magoichi also had this to say about the aboriginal workers whom he probably managed on a nearby farm: "[They] are generally very simple-minded, and if guided properly, they would be a docile bunch. . . . In terms of labor, they are largely inept at skilled work, so we put them to work for miscellaneous reclamation and land clearing." Therefore, the more complicated task of planting pineapple suckers seems to have been handled mainly by Taiwanese male workers after tractors leveled and plowed the cleared field, while local female workers and even children engaged in weeding and various similar tasks.[63] For the same reason, aboriginal workers were the first to be let go when financial conditions were not good, even though Okazaki and his associates claimed that the reason was in fact their being ignorant of how the economy worked and hence not amenable to (even) lower wages.[64] Okazaki's ethnicity-divided labor management, and the plantation-style farming based on it in rural Pingtung, contrasted with other well-capitalized corporate operations that followed it in Japan's tropical colony, since the latecomers tended to adopt a Taiwanese tenancy-based production method without incorporating indigenous labor.[65] With this salient feature, it is not unreasonable to describe the TPCC's Laopi farm as the outright symbol of a transplanted Hawai'i in colonial Taiwan's modern pineapple industry.

Indeed, Hawaiianization appears to have been a common phenomenon in other agricultural sectors where there was direct involvement of former Hawai'i residents. While only scarce sources are available with regard to the labor conditions on Okazaki's pineapple plantation, there are substantial materials on Sumida

Tajirō's coffee plantation in southern Hualien—another pointed example of this aspect of Hawaiianization, albeit in the production of a different tropical crop. There, the regimented system of ethnicity-divided labor management prevailed, as the former Honolulu merchant consciously selected a frontier surrounded by aboriginal settlements just as did Okazaki. Sumida's labor management method in eastern Taiwan bore an uncanny likeness to the manner in which Hawai'i's sugar industry not only depended on multiple groups of plantation workers but also pitted them against one another. Perhaps his knowledge of Hawai'i's sugar industry allowed Sumida to transplant a proven method of plantation labor management directly from his old stomping grounds. Based on an ethnic division of labor, that method featured a differentiated wage scale and middleman labor contracting to make the plantation operation cost effective and profitable.[66]

According to a 1941 study, Sumida's coffee plantation was vertically organized in a highly systematic fashion, and the work positions, roles, and wage schedules were allocated to different groups according to a prevailing ideology of ethnic/race hierarchy. At his Hualien estate, twelve Japanese settlers occupied managerial positions, including the estate general manager, the accounting director, the secretary, and the chief farm technician—likely from Hawai'i. The 971 acres were divided into four sections, and each had a Japanese farm manager and a field supervisor. Another settler took charge of the estate's day-to-day coffee mill operation, while there was also a full-time Japanese truck driver.[67] In addition to these colonial settlers, who dominated the managerial roles, six Taiwanese worked as full-time aides to Japanese field supervisors, and two were regular skilled laborers, probably at the mill. The plantation also employed fourteen aborigines—most likely local Ami people—as full-time field hands. The wage schedule for the resident workforce showed different scales according to gender, age, and ethnicity/race. Adult Taiwanese men received 125 to 145 sen daily, while women and children (adolescents) grossed only 90 sen and 30–70 sen, respectively. Even worse, aboriginal workers qualified for 10 sen less than their Taiwanese counterparts across the board.[68] Citing the statements of Japanese supervisors, the 1941 study explained the underlining assumptions of ethnic/race differences that sustained this practice on Taiwan's coffee land—and in the pineapple fields, as mentioned. The study noted: "Compared to aborigines, Taiwanese workers were less submissive and hence harder to manage. Thus, it sometimes required a stern attitude to keep them in line and productive. Aboriginal workers, on the other hand, are generally so submissive that they obediently follow orders without becoming lazy. Yet, their intelligence and skills are not up to the level of Taiwanese, and hence it is necessary for [Japanese] supervisors to be patient and benevolent."[69]

A method of ethnic middleman labor contracting was another practice that followed the Hawaiian plantation model. Forming segmented labor markets based on ethnicity, the steady supplies of coffee pickers and field hands were secured through the intermediary role of Chinese "coolie masters," who assembled gangs of Cantonese and Fujianese immigrant workers separately. Japanese managers at Sumida's coffee plantation only had to deal with these labor contractors, who received commissions and a lump sum of money for hiring workers for specified jobs. All necessary farm tools and ethnically segregated "coolie shacks" were provided for the contractors as well. Usually of Cantonese and Fujianese origin, these "coolie masters" then carried out their contractual obligations by bringing workers of the same ethnicities from northwestern Taiwan and overseeing their day-to-day work in the fields under the watchful eye of resident Japanese supervisors and their Taiwanese assistants.[70] Thus, a three-tiered ethnic/race hierarchy formed the core of labor management and labor relations, with Japanese settlers at the top, Taiwanese residents (Hakka Chinese included) in the middle, and aboriginal dwellers and Chinese immigrants at the bottom. Within the bottom tier there existed asymmetrical differences between full-time indigenous employees of the company and itinerant "coolie" workers controlled by coethnic labor contractors. This form of Hawaiianization made farm operation highly rationalized, efficient, and economical for Japanese settler-farmers on coffee or pineapple land.

Despite its myriad advantages, Okazaki's attempt at Hawaiianization did not go completely uncontested in Taiwan's pineapple industry. Every now and then, both observers from Japan and local experts, including old-time farmers and rival cannery owners, questioned his Hawai'i-centered approach—with a hint of nationalist irritation and turf-war sentiment. While being intrigued by the way Okazaki ran his plantation, a Japanese visitor could not but "wonder if his mode of operation was not too much of a direct translation (blind imitation)."[71] A canned pineapple wholesaler from Tokyo questioned the wisdom of large growers and canneries (presumably connected to Takasaki and Okazaki), who were "completely slanted toward the Hawaiian way." He acknowledged that Smooth Cayenne would be more agreeable to foreign consumers. Given the dominance of Hawaiian-made canned pineapple in the global marketplace, Americans and Europeans would likely prefer the Hawaiian variety to its native Taiwanese counterpart. Still, the wholesaler could not help asking rhetorically if the unconditional valorization of Smooth Cayenne might inflict a "disadvantage" on the trade, since Japanese consumers should be deemed just as important.[72] Coming from a domestic wholesaler, this criticism likely stemmed from business concerns about the export-centered government policy as much as from pervasive antiforeign and anti-US sentiments.

Other detractors of Hawaiianization, especially those local growers and cannery owners who felt forced to adapt to or compete with the "foreign" way, were much less circumspect in their criticism. At the industry's first-ever forum, held in Kaohsiung in January 1929, for example, a veteran leader in the pineapple canning business was apparently quite perturbed by the discussion, which "focused principally on the Hawaiian (Smooth Cayenne) variety," for "the local variety should require different consideration vis-à-vis the imported one."[73] He publicly took strong exception to a reference to Hawai'i—its canning methods or crop variety— when Okazaki's fellow resettler attempted to offer an explanation about the new method of cultivation and mechanized canning. This unusually open display of opposition, which a published report would not normally have recorded, reflected a deep-seated rivalry between the old-time, small-scale producers who had been accustomed to the canning of native varieties, and the newcomers from Hawai'i, who were backed by large moneyed interests from the colonial metropole. The critic indeed was the owner of one of the conventional canneries near Kaohsiung, which had suddenly found itself faced by the threat of those modern facilities established by Takasaki's syndicate.[74] A part of the same good-old-boy network, the son of another veteran cannery owner similarly took pains to express a negative impression of Smooth Cayenne at a public lecture during the same forum. Because this locally educated man held the position of a government agricultural engineer in Taiwan, his "academic" talks helped augment doubts about the Hawaiian variety and the imported cultivation methods associated with it when he posed a rhetorical question about whether "it would be advisable to operate a farm with Smooth Cayenne only."[75]

It was not mere coincidence that these attacks were mounted in 1929. That year saw the first spread of plant diseases caused by mealy bugs and fusarium wilt among the foreign pineapple varieties, especially Smooth Cayenne. While this situation resulted in the suspension of new plant importations for a few years, it gave the critics ammunition to discredit the imported Hawaiian method and crop as unfit for Taiwan. It proved to be a temporary problem, however, for government research came up with some effective solutions, including the discovery of a suitable environment for Smooth Cayenne cultivation in central Taiwan. Combined with the (re-)planting of Smooth Cayenne in southern Taiwan (especially at Pingtung and Tainan), the entry of the Hawaiian variety into the Yuanlin/Doulin/Chiayi regions led to steady growth in the procurement of Smooth Cayenne by newly established modern canneries during the latter half of the 1930s—so much so that almost two-thirds of Taiwan-made canned pineapples contained the Hawaiian variety by the next decade (see map 5).[76]

The temporary setback, as well as the many voices of criticism from industry insiders, did not deter Okazaki and other remigrants from preaching the advantages of Smooth Cayenne or the Hawaiian method of canning. In January 1931 managers and employees of the three major firms that comprised Takasaki's Taiwan syndicate organized an exclusive "social club," which was actually dedicated to the study and promotion of Smooth Cayenne cultivation and canning. While describing "Taiwan's Hawaiian pineapple variety" as a "baby that just uttered his first cry," Takasaki declared that the club members were "entrusted with the great

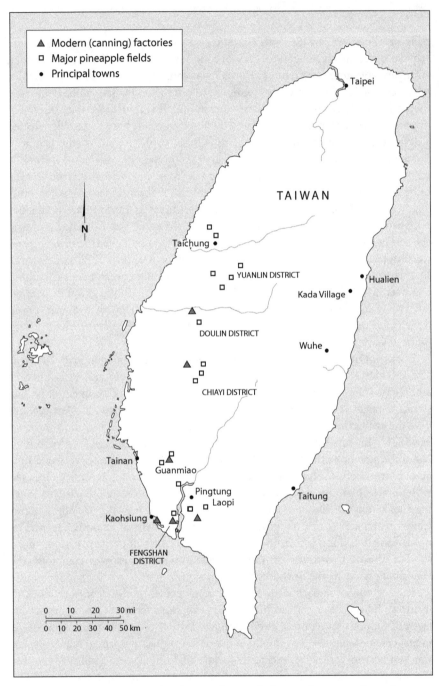

Legend:
- ▲ Modern (canning) factories
- ▢ Major pineapple fields
- • Principal towns

N

TAIWAN

Taipei

Taichung •

☐ YUANLIN DISTRICT

Hualien •

Kada Village •

▲

DOULIN DISTRICT

Wuhe •

▲ ☐

CHIAYI DISTRICT

Tainan •
▲
Guanmiao ☐ ▲

Pingtung •
Laopi

Taitung •

Kaohsiung • ▲ ▲

FENGSHAN
DISTRICT

0   10   20   30 mi

0   10 20 30 40 50 km

MAP 5. Map of Taiwan showing distribution of pineapple farms and canneries focused on Hawaiian-origin Smooth Cayenne, early 1930s. Map by Bill Nelson.

mission of raising that baby splendidly." As a core founder, Okazaki had the honor of making the inaugural speech, telling his colleagues to carry on with the mission "in defense of Smooth Cayenne when it [was] under attack by [those who held onto] the native varieties."[77] Their optimism was not unrelated to the continuous support that government technocrats and agricultural scientists showed for Hawai'i's precedent during these few years of tribulation. Indeed, established by the governor-general in 1925 and 1929, the two official pineapple seedling and experimental stations were staffed by horticulturists who had firsthand research experience in Hawai'i.[78] Just like Chiba Toyoji in Manchuria, Okazaki and other resettlers from Hawai'i found many allies among pragmatic colonial technocrats.

The colonial authorities' interest in Smooth Cayenne and Hawai'i's industrial model gave Okazaki an opportunity to take two commissioned "investigative trips" to the Nan'yō and Southeast Asia. In early 1929 his first trip—funded by the TPCC—took him to Japan's mandate of Micronesia as well as the pineapple-growing regions of British Malaya, Dutch Indonesia, and South China. During the latter portion of the trip, Okazaki observed the rival Sarawak variety and different production models. His visit to the Japanese-controlled island of Palau exceeded simple inspection, because he orchestrated the further transfer of his Hawai'i-bred expertise to that part of Japan's southern frontier.[79] Accompanied by a chief agricultural scientist of colonial Taiwan and a TPCC executive, Okazaki managed to convince the local Japanese technocrats to adopt Smooth Cayenne to promote scientific pineapple farming in Palau's first Japanese settler "village." A modest cannery was subsequently established in 1932, making the settlement a well-recognized hub of the brand-new local agricultural industry in the Nan'yō. There is no doubt that the senior state agricultural scientist who traveled with Okazaki played a crucial intermediary role in the whole process of this transfer of the crop and farming/canning expertise; this colonial official went on to assume the position of chief agronomist in the entire Nan'yō a few years later.[80] Through Okazaki and his supporters of Taiwan's colonial regime, like this official, Hawaiianization spread throughout other parts of Japan's colonial tropics during the 1930s.

The core component of Okazaki's commissioned research came into play in the summer of 1930, when he traveled intensively throughout the southern Philippines for two months with state sponsorship. Appointed as a special government expert-investigator, Okazaki conducted an on-the-spot field survey to study the state of imported Smooth Cayenne cultivation and canning in the nearby US colony—a matter of concern for Taipei's Japanese authorities at that time.[81] Having just received a large investment from Hawai'i's agribusiness concerns, the Philippines appeared to have risen as a formidable competitor to Taiwan's pineapple industry. In December 1930 Okazaki's report was published by the governor-general's office. Since many officials had a keen interest in the potential rivalry with the US-controlled Philippines in the Asia-Pacific agricultural commodity market, Okazaki's report was reprinted for wider circulation by the South Seas Society (Nan'yō kyōkai), a semiofficial, politico-academic organization that had served as the central voice for Japanese penetration into the South Seas and Southeast Asia since 1915.[82] In the context of Taiwan's role as "a regional [research] center for [Japan's] southern expansion," as historian Seiji Shirane calls it, Okazaki's work constituted an important aspect of the empire's "area studies of South China and Southeast Asia."[83]

Okazaki's treatise on "the pineapple industry in the Philippine Islands" mostly encompassed technical and academic discussions of soil and weather conditions there, but he did not neglect to present a very positive depiction of plantation and canning operations relating to the Smooth Cayenne variety in the Philippines. As he noted (perhaps for his own benefit), all the executives of the new US colonial monopoly were experienced *haole* pineapple experts from Hawai'i. With the effect of highlighting Okazaki's own expertise and close relations to America's top industrial leaders, his published report included snapshots of these white men with the author himself, surrounded by rows and rows of Smooth Cayenne plants on a massive plantation. The concluding section of the report provided Okazaki's expert recommendations for the future of Taiwan's pineapple industry. He strongly emphasized the advantages of Smooth Cayenne despite, or because of, ongoing plant disease problems and pushback from critics back home. Without any reference to their counteradvocacy for returning to the native or Sarawak varieties, Okazaki's report assumed the central position of the imported Hawaiian crop in Taiwan's future and offered a threefold recommendation to the government and his industry colleagues. First, there should be a concerted state-industry effort at experimenting with and selecting higher-grade Smooth Cayenne seedlings. His second proposal called for a search for better-suited sites for Smooth Cayenne cultivation than traditional areas of native pineapple farming. Finally, Okazaki stressed, the industry must simultaneously strive for the improvement of standardization of canned pineapple products, especially with an eye to meeting market demands in Europe and North America, not just in Japan's small domestic market. According to Okazaki, the use of modern "sanitary cans" (with no solder), which only Takasaki's company manufactured at that time, would be absolutely indispensable for successful distribution of canned pineapple products in the western consumer market.[84]

In the context of Okazaki's fight for the Hawaiianization of Taiwan's pineapple industry, these recommendations were fundamentally self-serving. Yet they also constituted what many colonial officials and capitalists wanted to hear when they were at work on the construction of an export-oriented colonial economy. Okazaki was by no means the first person to propagate these ideas, nor was he responsible for the adoption of the policies based on these ideas. But it was crucial that his recommendations entered public discourse via a state-sanctioned report at this critical juncture, when doubts about Hawaiianization were emerging. To the extent that the key points of Okazaki's contention were incorporated into the formal policy agenda of the colonial regime and the industry during the 1930s, it is indeed reasonable to argue that his expert assessment had a significant influence on government horticulturalists and technocrats, as well as large-scale investors and industrialists from Japan.

As mentioned, Okazaki's first recommendation was faithfully carried out later by the two state-owned pineapple seedling stations to redeem the position of Smooth Cayenne in the pineapple canning business. And his second contention led to the "discovery" of ideal regions for the Hawaiian variety in central Taiwan. Furthermore, under the aegis of the governor-general, the industry also successfully undertook consolidation and modernization of pineapple canneries and farms in the mid-1930s—an endeavor that was dominated by Takasaki's firm and its associated canneries and plantations. As a result, Taiwan Consolidated Pineapple Company (Taiwan Gōdō Hōri Kabushiki Kaisha) and Taiwan Pineapple Colonization Company (Taiwan Hōri Takushoku Kabushiki Kaisha) were established in 1935 for the monopolization of cannery ownership and farm operations, respectively. This state-capitalist effort at consolidation reduced the number of canneries from seventy-eight to twenty-nine by the summer of 1936, putting older less- or nonmechanized facilities out of business. Takasaki's modern factories reigned as the largest and most advanced facilities among the survivors. Moreover, his tin-can manufacturing monopoly benefited from its role as the exclusive supplier of sanitary cans for export-grade products. Under the dominance of TCMC-affiliated interests, Taiwan's new pineapple monopoly controlled over 33,500 acres, where the cultivation of Smooth Cayenne quickly increased toward the early 1940s.[85] While Taiwan's total output of canned pineapple products grew by 34 percent from 1934 through 1939, foreign exports increased threefold during the same five-year period.[86]

Since his move from Hawai'i, Okazaki—and his fellow remigrants—had functioned as an indispensable component in the industrial development program of Takasaki's syndicate and colonial Taiwan. His Hawai'i-bred expertise gave him a unique task that exceeded the simple role of a cog in the colonial capitalist machinery. Around the time of his state-commissioned Philippine trip, Okazaki formally resigned as a TPCC executive and left its Laopi plantation, although he continued to be connected to Takasaki's pineapple farm-cannery complex. His new role was to set up a fully mechanized cannery in the Guanmiao district of Tainan for the processing of Smooth Cayenne with imported equipment from Hawai'i (see map 5). On paper, this new enterprise listed Okazaki as the "individual proprietor," but portions of its initial and operational capital must have come from not only Takasaki's group but also the colonial government. In the 1929–1930 fiscal year, the latter had started a three-year program of subsidizing the procurement of advanced canning equipment, but both state subventions and permission for a new cannery were given to only one establishment annually. Formally incorporated in April 1932, Okazaki's new venture had to be the one authorized establishment that year.[87] The choice was not surprising at that juncture, because the local authorities of Tainan were calling for the construction of a new mechanized pineapple cannery specifically in the Guanmiao district in order to expand the acreage of pineapple cultivation there. Indeed, as the local press reported in 1926, it appears that Okazaki's visit to Guanmiao during his 1924 investigative tour had inspired the area's Taiwanese growers to try their hand at Smooth Cayenne in the first place.[88]

For this new project, Okazaki partnered with another former Hawai'i resident, Nakao Magoichi, in 1931–1932, making it a virtual "Hawaiian resettler" operation. After several years' absence, Okazaki and Nakao returned to Honolulu to negotiate the purchase of a cannery facility in Waiau (now Pearl City) at the cost of 500,000 yen ($125,000), for the purpose of relocating canning machinery to Okazaki's Guanmiao facility. The Waiau factory, which was located near Okazaki's former Hawaiian residence, had been for sale since the Great Depression made it a part of a US-government-led liquidation program. To Okazaki and Nakao, the acquisition of this cannery looked like a vindication of their unfulfilled and undying dream—a dream that had once been dashed by O'ahu's white agribusiness. Okazaki had tried to establish a pineapple cannery of his own in Pupukea during the mid-1910s, and Nakao had seen his small cannery near Kaneohe fold quickly in the early 1920s. Now, free from the clutches or obstructions of *haole* overlords, Okazaki and Nakao were finally able to be masters of their own destiny on Japan's tropical frontier. They had the Waiau facility disassembled, transported all equipment and machinery parts to Taiwan, and reconstructed them in a retrofitted cannery in rural Tainan.[89] Subsequently, while Nakao returned to his former job as the manager of the 1,062-acre pineapple plantation near Fongshan owned by Takasaki's group, the Okazakis moved to Guanmiao—presumably with a few other Hawai'i-returnee associates and their families. They were among 64 Japanese settlers in a community of 12,938 Taiwanese residents.[90]

Under Okazaki's sole management, Taiwan Fruit Canning Company (Taiwan Kajitsu Kanzume Kaisha) ran automated canning lines in its factory, but it was a smaller operation than other highly capitalized factories. In the context of the Takasaki syndicate's effort to control the industry, however, this facility was more important than its modest size would seem to suggest. Compared with the neighboring pineapple-growing regions of Kaohsiung and Taichung, Tainan Province had received less attention from growers and canners, especially big moneyed interests. The first major cannery was founded by Mitsubishi-affiliated capitalists in 1930, and one year later, Takasaki's group hastily set up a competing factory. These modern canneries were situated in the northern end of Tainan Province, and their locations (Douliu and Chiayi) were actually much closer to Taichung City. Until Okazaki's move to Guanmiao, there was no modern canning facility in the central and south-ern regions of Tainan—a reason for the limited cultivation of Smooth Cayenne there despite the availability of unused prime land.[91] Okazaki's cannery represented the first entry into the region of Japan's colonial agro-industrial capital in general, and of Takasaki's group in particular, which had found itself in intensified competi-tion with the established *zaibatsu* interests elsewhere in Taiwan.

As expected, Okazaki's concern proceeded to acquire over five hundred acres on the outskirts of Guanmiao for a new pineapple farm.[92] Over sixty years later, a Taiwanese elder leader of the small farm town—now known as the pineapple king-dom of Taiwan—recalled that this eccentric Japanese from Hawai'i was responsi-ble for "planting the seed" of the local industry with the gift of Smooth Cayenne.[93] But at the same time, as in Laopi, Okazaki maintained the familiar practice of pay-ing much lower wages to Taiwanese employees at his new cannery and farm—so much so that the locally hired cannery manager and canning expert—arguably one of the most educated Taiwanese individuals in Guanmiao—protested colonial discrimination and demanded fair treatment and equal pay to local staff workers, in vain, then quit Okazaki's cannery in disgust.[94]

Effected in 1935, the industry-wide consolidation of pineapple canneries and farms was a mixed bag for Okazaki and his own colonial enterprise. On the one hand, it enabled the ascent of Hawaiian-style farming and canning in Taiwan's pineapple business under the control of his allies and capitalist backers, including Takasaki. On the other hand, it deprived Okazaki of the free hand he had enjoyed in managing his own Guanmiao cannery and farm in accordance with his own visions and desires. Moreover, the terms of consolidation entailed a manner of calculating the amount of monetary compensation that tended to depreciate the value of canning facilities, especially for individual proprietors. Perhaps for these reasons, Okazaki initially resisted the merger of his property with a few other small-scale cannery owners, although he later reversed his position and joined the new monopoly.[95] Appointed as the head of Taiwan Consolidated Pineapple Com-pany's "No. 77" factory in Guanmiao, Okazaki continued to take charge of his own creation until 1938, but even after that remained involved in the management of the pineapple monopoly as a private stockholder.[96]

DARK LEGACIES OF HAWAIIANIZATION AND TRANSBORDER JAPANESE SETTLER COLONIALISM

Notwithstanding the successful rationalization of industrial pineapple farming and the façade of civilization building in colonial Taiwan, Hawaiianization pri-marily served the material interests and psychological fulfillment of settlers—from both imperial Japan and Japanese Hawai'i. Published in 1936, a strong leftist criticism of cannery consolidation by a local Taiwanese intellectual offered insight into the negative impact of the collaborative effects of Takasaki and Okazaki—especially the spread of Smooth Cayenne for export purposes—on Taiwanese entrepreneurs and farmers. Most of the small-scale cannery owners were "native" proprietors who were faced with the dreadful choice of participating in the consolidation scheme for an "unfair" amount of monetary compensation or refusing to do so for no compensation at all. Neither option spared the life of their cannery operations, and hence their posts as managers, in the end, for their outdated, poorly mechanized facilities were bound to be phased out, if not outright abolished, under the monopoly's modernization plan. Okazaki's modest factory was an exception, because it was equipped with imported machinery from Hawai'i. Most victims of consolidation were therefore Taiwanese canners. Furthermore, because the vast majority of independent Taiwanese growers had been engaged in the cultivation of native pineapple varieties, the ascendancy of Smooth Cayenne in a new export-centered industry led to their economic downfall and, even worse, their displacement. It is for this reason that Taiwanese commentators specifically criticized Takasaki's capitalist syndicate, denouncing its hideous "plot" to "gobble up small-to-medium sized factories run by Taiwanese people and bring the whole pineapple canning industry under their thumb."[97]

Okazaki and other remigrants from Hawai'i were indispensable to the success of that "plot," whether or not they were cognizant of that fact. Their departure from the US empire constituted a part of their "pursuit" of "colonization" without the obstruction of white men, as Okazaki once declared before Japanese colonial officialdom. Yet their pursuit of racism-free settler colonialism made the former Hawai'i residents chief facilitators of local Taiwanese displacement in pineapple farming and canning. This formed an ironic legacy of their "antiracist" response to America's anti-Japanese exclusion—a response that transformed a racialized minority into oppressors of Japan's own minoritized subjects. But it is also useful to conclude this story of settler racism's enduring life with a brief postscript on Taiwanese displacement. After the consolidation in 1935, some of the Taiwanese cannery owners and growers sought a new opportunity outside their beloved island—a new frontier for this minoritized group of imperial subjects—on one of the nearby Yaeyama Islands, the southwestern archipelago of Okinawa Prefecture. As early founders of its pineapple industry, these displaced Taiwanese took Smooth Cayenne with them and ironically lived as settler-colonists on Ishigaki Island, just as racially persecuted Japanese immigrants from Hawai'i did in their new frontiers of Taiwan. Not only did ethnic clashes ensue with residents of Ishigaki, but these Taiwanese—better educated and self-conscious about coming from more "civilized" Taiwan—were also often inclined to act as model imperial subjects and civilization builders vis-à-vis the local islanders, although their standing as colonized ethnic non-Japanese always put them at a disadvantage. Adopted and transmitted across imperial and national borders by these minoritized migrants, settler colonialism had the capacity to adapt to different environments, whether colonial Taiwan or Ishigaki Island. Having been brought over from Hawai'i, Smooth Cayenne remained indispensable as the symbolic technology of that adaptive settler colonialism in both trans-imperial and intra-imperial contexts.[98]

Chapters 5 and 6 have explained why and how some Japanese residents of the US West and Hawai'i renewed their ties and commitment to their home empire's settler colonialism after the mid-1920s. They have also detailed the ways in which the colonial regime and metropole co-opted and took advantage of immigrant visions and practices, when many US-based compatriots vacillated between the reality of being a persecuted racial minority and the promise of a new life as colonial masters because of their racial and national heritage. The transpacific mobility of their bodies, knowledge, ideas, and money resulted from the concurrent unfolding of US racial exclusion and Japan's geopolitical ascent, since the local and international developments made Japan's colonial territories exceptionally attractive and welcoming to many minoritized US residents. The stories of experienced California farmers in Manchuria, and those of Hawai'i-based investors and resettlers in Taiwan and Saipan, all shed light on the hitherto unknown translocal colonial migration circuits and the homeland-immigrant nexus that rendered the formal empire and its extraterritorial immigrant society indispensable partners in the common goal of overseas Japanese development. The examples of Chiba Toyoji, Satō Nobumoto, Watanabe Kinzō, and Okazaki Nihei also reveal that their utility to the Japanese empire was rather limited in scope, because they almost always assumed the role of teachers and conveyors of California- or Hawaiian-style agrarian settler colonialism. The authorities welcomed these remigrants into the empire's bosom with a view to introducing the specific farming methods or crops that the regional colonial economies needed. Yet since their expertise drew exclusively from their hands-on experience as immigrant residents in America's continental or tropical frontiers, it constituted monopolized cultural capital that no one else could match. Despite their narrowly prescribed roles and positions, these remigrants from Japanese America shored up the backbone of imperial Japan's colonial agricultural industries and the structure of interethnic/racial oppression with their knowledge and experience in a significant but disturbing way.

PART FOUR

History and Futurity in Japan's Imperial Settler Colonialism, 1932–1945

7

Japanese Pioneers in America and the Making of Expansionist Orthodoxy in Imperial Japan

During the 1930s Japanese America was more than a supplier of human, material, and financial resources for Japan's settler-colonist enterprises. Japan's public representation of the "pioneers of overseas development" on the American frontier also functioned as an effective ideological device to shape the national minds in line with new colonial policy after 1931. In particular, Japanese intelligentsia and officialdom found Japanese America a useful partner in cultural politics through which to present family migration to and agrarian settler colonialism in Manchuria as the nation's manifest destiny. This cultural politics was concerned first and foremost with the deep-rooted popular prejudice against the emigrant/immigrant (*imin*) that deemed him or her the "abandoned" (*kimin*)—a low-class and good-for-nothing person—because that image was considered a major factor in discouraging the masses to pull up stakes and emigrate from home. In Japan's public discourse, Japanese America had epitomized the negative meanings associated with being the emigrant/immigrant. Not only did its history mark the beginning of mass mobility of ordinary "peasants" from the boondocks, many Japanese thought, but it was also marred by American discourse on Japanese unassimilability, a rhetorical basis of racial exclusion. By following the example of the "campaign of education" in Japanese America, Tokyo officials and social elites, such as Shibusawa Eiichi, had attempted to civilize those rural masses through reformist educational efforts, press propaganda, and other forms of social engineering since the 1910s. What was inseparable from this top-down process of imperial subject formation was a settler-colonist idea of *ishokumin*, in which differences between working-class sojourning (*imin*) and colonization (*shokumin*) were obscured and literally conflated under an overarching discourse on overseas development and its derivative practices of place-specific expansionism. Imperial Japan took further steps during the 1930s to fill every remaining gap between what *imin* and *shokumin* signified in its attempts to mobilize the entire nation for the new goal of populating Manchuria with ordinary emigrants as self-motivated frontiersmen and their dedicated wives. The contrived representations of Japanese America and its history formed the core of the new cultural politics in service of state-sponsored settler colonialism in East Asia.

This collaborative work by the state and its intelligentsia sought to harmonize the disparate experiences of immigrants abroad and colonizers within the home empire in popular culture, mass consciousness, and public history. In this aspect of borderless Japanese colonialism, Japanese America was placed en masse on the center stage of systematic historical mythologizing and (mis)represented as the first group of imperial Japan's expansionist pioneers in emergent national orthodoxy. Japanese residents in the United States joyfully embraced that contrived role, too, because it conformed well to their own group identity and history, forged in their ethnic community since the late 1920s. This chapter delves into the complex processes of transpacific history making that brought Japanese America and imperial Japan together in constructing a unified narrative of Japanese colonial diaspora and its worldwide development during the 1930s. While it managed to enshrine all American residents as model colonialist men and women who were purportedly unrelated to the despised horde of *imin/kimin*, this ideological project generated a singular history of national/racial expansion with Japanese America as its origin. Involving a wide array of intellectuals and cultural workers, this history making employed all sorts of means and venues, ranging from academic studies to motion pictures, and from public ceremonies to exhibitions, in the critical decade preceding the Pacific War.

ISSEI HISTORY MAKING

Not until the 1930s did imperial Japan begin to think it needed a synthesized narrative of national expansion. But when it did so in conjunction with the new policy mandate of mass emigration and colonization in Manchuria, the Japanese government brass and domestic intelligentsia found a ready-made narrative to draw from in the writings of their compatriots across the Pacific. Indeed, expansionistic history making was a reciprocal process, and dramatic (or traumatic) changes in Japanese immigrant society in the United States helped spur that process first among educated residents there. In the early 1920s, when discriminatory American laws took their agricultural and immigration rights away on the basis of their status as "aliens ineligible for citizenship," Japanese immigrants were collectively faced with a prodigious crisis that appeared to threaten the survival of their ethnic economy and community. Institutionalized racism against the first generation (Issei) of

Japanese America, many felt, expedited the coming of a second-generation (Nisei) era, wherein the Nisei's "superior" racial traits, coupled with their birthright of US citizenship, would soon enable them to defeat white racism and further enlarge America's "new Japan." In this context, some immigrant intellectuals took on the teleological project of summing up the passing first-generation era for future resurrection, chronicling their records of collective struggle and racial persecution as a contrived story of overseas Japanese development: the nation's progress on American soil that was temporarily arrested by white racism. Significantly, in that narrative Issei writers not only juxtaposed their trajectory with the disparate footsteps of Japanese emigrants and colonialists elsewhere, but they also asserted their doubly pioneering roles in the expansion of Japan's national influence in the United States, as well as in an American epic of frontier conquest.[1] In this sense, their history making constituted a transimperial discursive effort to assert their Japanese and American identities simultaneously within the respective expansionist national histories and settler colonialisms.

Incorporating elements of Japan's peaceful expansionism and US frontier discourse, Japanese immigrant history was thus fundamentally transnational, directed to audiences in both countries. Avoiding choosing one over the other, Issei writers endeavored to carve out a legitimate place in the histories of their native and adopted empires, and the emergent narrative of progress usually combined a two-pronged argument, although it might well have appeared contradictory to the nationalized eyes of each domestic public. On the one hand, a typical example read: "We have been here for some sixty years. Ever since the beginning of modern Japan, no other group of Japanese has spent as long as sixty years in a foreign land. We are indeed the first ones. Our history is not quite the same as our homeland's, but it is still part of it. Our history constitutes the first page of the history of Japanese expansion."[2] On the other, another example read: "We, the Japanese in America, all crossed the Pacific [and] entered the half-untouched wilderness of North America with such heroic determination. Unfamiliar with the language and customs, we still managed to build today's foundations with many tears and much sweat. . . . We all have done our best for our own lives and this society (the United States). . . . No one can deny that we have performed distinguished service for the advancement of North America."[3] Predicated upon the theme of double national contributions, this historical mythologizing still formed a poignant aspect of Issei's minority politics against race-based exclusion in the US domestic context; hence, to the first generation of Japanese Americans, the latter rhetoric supporting inclusion in America's frontier history was paramount—a point to which imperial Japan was oblivious.

In this immigrant-produced history, the narrative of the Issei "pioneers" revolved around their remarkable ascent in American agriculture and their struggle against western racism, which drew a parallel with Japan's rise and contestation with the "racist" Euro-American powers in international politics. Immigrant intellectuals adopted this rhetorical strategy to argue for socioeconomic parity with white Americans and cultural compatibilities between the two races *because of their recent exclusion*. In order for the Japanese in America to (re)elevate their status in American society, a redefinition of racial meaning was necessary, and their homeland offered perfect material support for this. In seeking acceptance into white America on an equal basis, Issei writers deliberately likened their preexclusion achievements as American frontiersmen to the current rise of the Japanese empire as a world power. Not only had the Issei tamed much forsaken western land, the immigrant historians reasoned, they had "always kept their farms green and supplied produce of higher quality" owing to their "superiority in [farming] skills" and outstanding racial character—which also made it possible for Japan to compete so effectively with the West.[4] Such historical inventions were also predicated on the view that their community was a partner with Japan in a struggle against white racism, local and global, and this contention was canonized in *Zaibei Nihonjinshi*, the massive 1,300-page *History of Japanese in America*. Compiled collaboratively by immigrant intellectuals and community leaders throughout California, the 1940 publication argued that the Issei had preceded all other groups of Japanese, including those in the homeland, in confronting the challenges posed by Anglo-Saxons. At the same time, these pioneers had also singlehandedly spearheaded Japan's external growth as an expansive race/nation when the homeland had exhibited no commitment to that destiny.[5]

Integral to these formulations and narrative schema was the simplification of the Japanese immigrant identity, whereby the contrasting images of settler-colonizers and *dekasegi* migrant laborers were reconciled in favor of the former. The majority of Japanese in America initially came to work on Hawaiian sugar plantations and western farmlands between 1885 and 1924, whereas smaller numbers of educated individuals and student immigrants indeed arrived in search of a "new Japan" on American soil, as chapter 1 detailed. Although some returned to the home empire or dispersed elsewhere after the outbreaks of anti-Japanese agitation, other immigrant intelligentsia remained on their original frontier of the US West. That the numerical minority could dominate the process of ethnic identity formation in particular, and of history making in general, had to do with the access they enjoyed to community leadership, financial resources, and the ethnic print media. With the backing of propertied farming and business classes, Issei writers projected an undifferentiated image of patriotic settler-colonists upon their group identity while rejecting any connection to the archetypical *imin*, an uncivilized laboring horde that was much despised in prewar Japan and white America. On the one hand, these self-proclaimed Japanese "frontiersmen" demanded inclusion in America through calculated historical constructions that countered the white exclusionist accusations of Japanese unassimilability and servitude. On the other, they also hoped to attire themselves in more honorable clothing with the goal of debunking the prevalent Japanese stereotype that American residents were a worthless lot of shiftless field hands.[6]

In order to fabricate these classist notions of national legitimacy, *Zaibei Nihonjinshi* characterized the Issei first and foremost as "imperial subjects . . . with the determination to enrich the country and strengthen the military." Indignant at the domineering attitudes of Russia and other European powers following the Sino-Japanese War of 1894–1895, this canonical Issei history argued that thousands of "young Japanese pushed their way to the gold-filled United States, where they could tap into the wealth of no parallel in the world" for the benefit of the resource-deprived homeland.[7] According to the immigrant orthodoxy, then, no *dekasegi* laborers had come to the United States. The Japanese in America were all patriotic trailblazers in pursuit, not of trivial personal gains, but of national interests, and "only with such a sense of mission could we build today's Japanese community and have attained the present level of development" in America's frontier land.[8] This invented identity of Issei settler-colonists served a pivotal agenda for imperial Japan during the 1930s, inflating the value of permanent colonial settlement over a more common historical practice of temporary work abroad. Brushing aside earlier connotations of shiftlessness and selfishness, immigrant history redefined the word *imin* to bring it in line with the notion of *takushi*, or "colonial fighter"—the official designation Tokyo gave to agricultural settlers in Manchuria after 1932. Ironically, as Japan's colonial minister explained at the Imperial Diet, it was the term that the government had adopted in order to distinguish clearly between the despised transpacific *dekasegi* emigrant of yesteryear and the Manchuria-bound family settler of the 1930s. What Japanese in America attempted to do was to reverse the official meaning by reidentifying themselves as prototypical *takushi*, the model for Manchuria-bound frontiersmen.[9]

Buoyed by the discourse on overseas development, history making allowed Japanese residents in the United States to claim legitimacy—at least rhetorically—in terms of Japan's imperialistic imagination, even though their purpose was to win respect from their homeland, not necessarily to collaborate in state-sponsored expansionist aggression in Asia. Since peaceful expansionism had permeated both Japanese America and imperial Japan, the particular historical visions Issei writers presented did not ring hollow in the ears of the Japanese public. Not until the mid-1930s, however, did Japan proactively seek to co-opt Issei experiences and confer on US residents a recognizable place in the annals of national expansion. Prior to that decade, Japan had no consistent position on overseas development despite its decisions to formulate state policy around Brazilian colonization, and various factions of elites had continued to advance different types of expansionism. Yet the military seizure of Manchuria in 1931 prompted Tokyo to consolidate its resources to develop the so-called Mongol-Manchurian lifeline for the Japanese empire.

Adopted in 1936, the government's twenty-year plan to send one million Japanese farm families (or five million emigrants) to the region marked the formal adoption of Manchurian agricultural development as a national mandate of the highest importance.[10] With the new state-led settler-colonial enterprise, the prior experiences of Japanese abroad suddenly became a matter of concern for policy and opinion makers in Japan. In order to convince the conservative farming population to give up the comfort of their native villages for new opportunities on the Manchurian frontier, imperial Japan needed a synthesis of national emigration history, which would demonstrate that building a new Japan was not only a historical destiny for the nation but also as honorable an act for an imperial subject as dying for the emperor in war. It was in this context that Issei history finally attracted close attention from Japan's intellectuals, its domestic print media, and the state itself.

ORTHODOXY MAKING IN IMPERIAL JAPAN

In his *Hōjin kaigai hattenshi* (History of overseas Japanese development; originally published in 1936), Iriye Toraji first systematically appropriated the Issei's historical narrative solely for the benefit of imperial Japan's new policy mandate. He did so by purging another key theme of the American pioneer story and hence subverting the original dual-national orientation of immigrant history making. A foreign ministry employee, Iriye was an ardent advocate of peaceful expansionism and hoped to compile a comprehensive record of Japanese emigration and overseas colonization since the Meiji Restoration. Drawing on diplomatic papers, emigration company documents, and a wide range of secondary sources, his 1,100-page volume presented the subject as a serious academic study. While it might have turned away the ordinary reading public, Iriye's scholastic narrative had a tremendous impact on the shaping of historical knowledge of emigration in Japan. Reprinted in 1938 and again in 1942, the book became canonized as an official publication of the Society for the Study of the Emigration Problem, an affiliate to the foreign ministry, which looked to "disseminate information on the conditions of overseas Japanese development" in conjunction with the official Manchurian enterprise.[11] As such, Iriye's massive monograph not only established the manner in which the historical epic of national expansion was subsequently interpreted and narrated in imperial Japan, but also defined the meaning of the Issei past for an educated audience of the empire.

Divided into two parts, the volume grouped divergent flows of emigration into a single trajectory of overseas Japanese development; it detailed the varied but unified experiences of residents in Hawai'i, the United States, Micronesia and other Pacific Islands, Southeast Asia, Mexico, Canada, Peru, Australia, the Philippines, Brazil, and Manchuria in chronological order between 1868 and 1936. Iriye explained how Japan had reached the point at which the Japanese government, after many years of neglect and failure, had finally come to its senses to embrace Manchurian colonization as a full-fledged national project. Filled with stories of "tribulation," including the Issei's struggles in the United States, Iriye's narrative suggested by contrast a better future for emigrants to Manchuria in the post-1936 era. His optimism, accentuated by gloomy anecdotes of the past, hinged on one crucial difference between the trailblazers of overseas development and the current "colonial fighters." Unlike the Issei, the residents in Manchuria could expect full support from Japan's colonial ministry and live comfortably under the protection of its mighty imperial forces and the puppet regime. Learning from their mistakes, Iriye surmised, the Japanese of the 1930s were fully cognizant of their expansionist heritage, as well as of their colonial destiny, which now looked brighter than ever.[12]

Overall, Iriye faithfully adopted key aspects of the Issei's historical constructions, that is, their purported patriotism and status as pioneers of modern Japanese expansionism. Nevertheless, in his book the position that the Japanese in America occupied was very specific: they were victims of Anglo-Saxon racism and an inept government at home. Fifteen of its fifty-five chapters detailed the doings of Japanese residents in Hawai'i and the continental United States, and their fight against white oppression was a particular focus of the volume, which suggested to readers that the lives of Japanese in America revolved mostly around interracial struggle.[13] Incorporating similar stories of racial injustice and exclusionary politics in Australia and Canada, Iriye expressly elucidated the heroism of Japanese residents in the United States, who stood up single-handedly to Anglo-Saxon racism despite receiving no support from the homeland. While reiterating the Issei's arguments for the most part, the author also inserted a new interpretation that American racism derived from the whites' "fear of Japanese superiority." By resorting to discriminatory legislation, Iriye wrote, white Americans ironically "have confessed their defeat" as a race. Although the Issei's development in America had fallen victim to institutionalized practices of exclusion, they still proved themselves to be "victors of racial competition, because, after all, white Americans could not compete with them fair and square."[14]

The moral of Issei history—as rendered by Iriye—was clear. Now, with the awakening of the home government and the full support of imperial armed forces, emigrant-colonizers bound for Manchuria would be able to exploit their racial superiority to the fullest. Iriye saw in the Issei's past a historical crystal ball that revealed Japan's bright colonial future. But at the same time, the incorporation of Japanese in America into the chronicle of national expansion relegated them to a ruptured past, against which the redeemed present was appreciated as something qualitatively different. Indeed, this is why Iriye's metanarrative concluded the discussion of the Issei's experience with the subheading "Gravestone of the Victors"—as if they had altogether disappeared from history by the mid-1920s after the unfortunate conclusion of interracial struggle in exclusionist America.[15] In the end, the record of Japanese in America rhetorically justified why Tokyo needed to proactively intervene and take the lead in the project of overseas development elsewhere, while concomitantly underscoring the immutability of Japanese racial superiority, which the passage of time or difference in historical circumstances could not efface. This pattern of incorporation characterized the Issei's standing in other expansionist narratives that emerged in imperial Japan in the ensuing years.[16]

OKEI: AT THE CROSSROADS OF AGRICULTURAL EMIGRATION AND MANCHURIAN COLONIZATION

In tandem with Iriye's orthodoxy making, Okei—purportedly Japan's first immigrant woman—was put on a historical pedestal during the mid-1930s. Just as Issei history became significant as a monument to illuminate the triumph of Japanese blood in the interracial struggle, her legend lived on as a threshold of national expansion through a modest tombstone in a desolate field in Gold Hill, California. A seventeen-year-old nanny, Okei was among a small group of Japanese immigrants, led by a German merchant named John Henry Schnell, who crossed the Pacific in 1869 to grow tea and silkworms in a "new Japan" on the American frontier. This endeavor failed within a year due to financial problems, which led to a quick dispersal of its members. While the Schnells and some immigrants returned to Japan, others stayed near the remnants of the California colony. Okei lived with a sympathetic white family, but she contracted malaria and died at the age of nineteen. A few decades later, another colony member built a modest grave in her memory. No Issei cared for it until the end of the 1920s, when her tombstone suddenly became memorialized in the Japanese immigrant community.[17]

No sooner had Issei ethnic history laid claim to Okei as its starting point than their native land declared its proprietary rights to the female legend. The synchronous process of history making surrounding her legend exemplified how the ethnic and national histories informed each other. In the United States, immigrant writers used Okei to transcend the recorded presence of Japanese prostitutes, which they saw as a dishonorable past. By defining her as "the pioneer Issei woman" who supposedly died a virgin, the immigrant master narrative separated Okei from the "women of disgraceful profession" who had congregated in Chinatowns, mining towns, and railroad construction sites in the American West during the 1880s and the 1890s. Instead, Okei—pure and dedicated—was rendered the authentic precursor of contemporary Issei women, many of whom came as "picture brides" to build immigrant households in California's new Japan between 1908 and 1920 in accordance with Abiko Kyūtaro's ideal of *eijū dochaku* (putting down roots and settling permanently), as discussed in chapter 3.[18] This cleansing of historical female identity went hand in hand with the invention of Issei patriotism that obfuscated the migratory labor heritage of most Japanese immigrant men. Combined, Issei history making discursively transformed the Japanese in the United States into worthy members of the expansive nation of Japan, as well as moral American frontiersmen and -women.

Whereas Japanese America authenticated its dual national heritage through the deification of Okei, imperial Japan found her story desirable for different reasons. Bits and pieces of her story had been introduced to Japan since the 1920s, but the novelist and literary scholar Kimura Takeshi played a central role in hijacking the Okei legend and putting it to use on behalf of the program of Japanese colonial expansionism. In January 1932 the writer first published a report of his visit to Gold Hill in a popular Tokyo magazine. While interviewing area residents about the female pioneer, Kimura was also quoted as stating that "the bravery of the beautiful Japanese Girl, Okei, first woman of her race to venture to California in 1870 [sic]" inspired him so much that he was determined to seek more information about her for a new book project.[19] Three years later the author published a novel in which Okei was metamorphosed into a "forerunner," not simply of Japanese emigration to the United States, but of "Japanese imperialism."[20]

Entitled *Meiji kensetsu* (Building Meiji [Japan]), the 1935 publication offered a mixture of historical fabrication and ideological indoctrination under the façade of romance and adventure. Set in Tokyo, Aizu, and Yokohama, during the civil war of 1868 and its aftermath, the story revolved around three protagonists: Fukuzawa Yukichi, Shijimi Heikurō, and Okei. In the first scene Fukuzawa, Japan's foremost westernizer, appeared as the founder of Keiō Academy, where he was educating future leaders of Meiji Japan, including Shijimi, a fictional character. While Fukuzawa epitomized the shift from feudalism to modernity, his nineteen-year-old disciple was depicted as a genius in English studies and a devoted nationalist—a quintessential leader of the first generation of modern Japan. In May 1868 the imperial forces clashed with pro-Tokugawa fighters inside Tokyo, which resulted in a significant victory for the new government. In the midst of warfare and turmoil, Fukuzawa continued to teach normal courses, admonishing his agitated students to concentrate on "learning for a new Japan."[21] Yet Shijimi sneaked out to volunteer for the imperial forces, because he believed destroying Tokugawa feudalism was necessary in order to "unify the nation as one" and "build a new Japan based on it."[22]

The second scene took place in Aizu, where the imperial forces had their final confrontation with retreating feudal factions in the summer of 1868. Shijimi was injured in this battle, but a local merchant took him in, leaving him in the care of a maid named Okei. Temporarily blinded by shell fragments, Shijimi was not able to see Okei, but he developed strong feelings for her. Okei turned out to be an assassin from the pro-Tokugawa Aizu domain, but she, too, yielded to her feelings toward the young enemy.[23] Their romance was nonetheless short-lived, for Okei disappeared when Shijimi had his eyesight restored. After unsuccessfully searching for Okei in the town of Aizu Wakamatsu, Shijimi found himself in the port of Yokohama, where the dejected man subsequently eked out a living as a translator for foreign merchants. One evening Shijimi saved a young woman, the live-in nanny for a couple called the Schnells, from local gangsters. At first Shijimi did not recognize her, but he soon realized it was Okei when he was invited to visit the Schnell residence. The young woman confided to him that she was about to leave for California with the other emigrants. On the following day, despite their wish to stay together, the two reluctantly parted, Okei leaving for America and Shimeji for Tokyo. Okei tragically died a few years later across the Pacific, while Shijimi resumed his studies and in 1873 devoted himself to organizing the Meirokusha, Japan's first society of westernized scholars, including Fukuzawa, which disseminated Enlightenment ideas in the nascent modern nation-state. As the editor of *Meiroku zasshi*, the society's organ, Shijimi spearheaded the creation of a forum for free and civilized public discussions—an institution that had not existed in the feudal era. The novel concludes with Fukuzawa commenting that whereas the sword that Shijimi carried into the Aizu battle left no mark on history, his pen was affecting the world more significantly than was the Meiji government.[24]

Key ideological messages regarding "imperialism" can be found in the novel in a conversation between Shijimi and Okei in Yokohama. First, Kimura tacitly affirmed Japan's current policy in Manchuria through the words of the female Japanese trailblazer in America. Shijimi marveled when Okei told him that she was on her way to the United States to "establish a Japanese village" on its frontier. "'This young woman is heading for America!,'" he muttered. "'Even I, a student of western studies, have never dared to think of such a thing.'"[25] However, he cautioned Okei about the seemingly unrealistic nature of her undertaking, pointing out that no remnants of Japanese settlements were now detectable in Southeast Asia, where many emigrants were said to have moved before the seclusion policy of the Tokugawa regime. Okei's reply flabbergasted Shijimi: "'That's because our ancestors did not take hoes with them.'" Some, according to her, "'took swords and conquered foreign places,'" and others "'took abacuses in pursuit of profits only.'"[26] Okei continued: "'No way could they sink roots by such means. With hoes, they should have cultivated the land, developed rice fields, and grown vegetables—in other words—they should have engaged in agriculture. Then, I think the Japanese villages in Southeast Asia could have remained prosperous even today. . . . And farming takes more than male labor. Perhaps, warfare and commerce would only need men, but farming requires women to raise families. A Japanese settlement would thrive only if men farm to sink roots in the land and women produce descendants for them.'"[27]

In light of Japan's Manchurian policy, under way at the time Kimura authored this treatise, Okei's idea of family-based agricultural colonization had many ramifications. From the example of Okei, readers were led to believe that the expansion of modern Japan had since the very beginning taken the current form sanctioned by the militarist government. Fukuzawa's dismissal of the "sword" as an agent of change also bears a close parallel to Okei's preference for a "hoe" over a sword as a means for nonviolent overseas development, the time-honored ideological underpinning of Japanese settler-colonialist thought. Through this agrarianist focus, Kimura's narrative implicitly likened peaceful expansionism in America, exemplified by the first Wakamatsu colony, to the state-sponsored colonialist enterprise in Manchuria of the 1930s. The theme of the Issei's agricultural success, which occupied a central place in their ethnic history, dovetailed neatly with this process, shaping and reinforcing a popular belief in the inseparable ties between land and race, between farming and national expansion.[28] Previously, as historian Louise Young argues, "almost no one [in the elite circles had] considered Japanese agricultural migration an indispensable pillar of empire."[29] Yet the appropriation and distortion of the Japanese immigrant legend enabled Kimura and other ideologues to invent an agrarian tradition in Japanese imperialism and to assert the authenticity of the family farm settlement over other ways of colonization by evoking the example of the Issei experience in America.

By linking the American agricultural development of yesteryear to the Manchurian colonial enterprise of today, Okei's inclination for domesticity played an especially important role. Before Tokyo adopted the 1936 guidelines for Manchurian colonization, Japan mainly shipped men of reserve military status as armed emigrant-settlers due to the general disorder in newly occupied territories. Still, in order to encourage family-based colonization, government and military authorities tackled the question of coupling these men with so-called continental brides (*tairiku no hanayome*). After the departure of the first thirty such women for Manchuria in 1934, there was a steady influx of emigrant wives in order for them to "raise families" and "produce descendants" in Japanese agricultural settlements there. Imperial colonialism of the 1930s valorized the role of women precisely for the reasons Kimura outlined in terms of Okei's gendered utterances. In tandem with his novel, indeed, various outlets of the mass media—news reports, fiction, movies, and popular songs—glorified "continental brides" in a similar manner during the latter half of the decade.[30] Together they shaped a public opinion that normalized female emigration despite the contrary historical realities of masculinized working-class Japanese diasporas.

While effacing the gender bias in emigration history, Kimura's *Building Meiji [Japan]* underscored the patriotic nature of Okei's emigration-led colonization and hence of all Issei trailblazers and Manchurian emigrants as her followers. In the novel, the author emphasized Shijimi's dedication to Meiji Japan time and time again, and the young nationalist's approval of Okei testified to how much her dream of building a new Japan in America was to be revered as an act of patriotism as well. That neither protagonist attempted to abort the colonialist endeavor for their romantic interests and personal happiness made clear what should be a priority to citizen-subjects of the expanding empire.[31] Along the same line, the title of the novel inflated the meaning of emigration to America in the past and of that to Manchuria in the present. Whereas Shijimi helped to establish the modern press and a space for public discourse in the new civil society of Meiji, Okei laid the foundation for overseas Japanese development. They were both "builders" of modern Japan, but in the context of ongoing Manchurian colonization, Okei's deed was more relevant—and hence more important—to the contemporary agenda of the empire than Shijimi's contribution to the early stage of domestic modernization.

Insofar as Kimura's fiction targeted a popular audience who would not read Iriye's academic history, the co-optation of Okei in that genre had particular influence over the consciousness of the masses. The novel was issued by Kaizōsha, a major publishing house in prewar Japan, as a part of its Restoration Epic Novel Series. Because Okei's story was juxtaposed with eleven well-known sagas of the Meiji Restoration in the series, Kimura's presentation of Okei likely appeared factual and hence irrefutable. Indeed, the fifty-five-page appendix in the book contained clippings of historical newspaper articles and a report of the author's visit to the remains of the Wakamatsu Colony in 1931, which enhanced that impression.[32]

The messages that the Okei legend generated underwent another ideological transformation with the production of a popular movie based on Kimura's novel in July 1940. The film version of the novel promoted the confusion of fact and fiction with even more fabrications, ones that were no longer recognizable as such. A major production of Tōhō Cinema featuring top celebrities of the time, *Arashi ni saku hana* (Flower in the storm) made notable changes to the identities of Okei and Shijimi.[33] In the film, the former was of a prominent Aizu agriculturalist-samurai family, not of more humble origins as commonly assumed. In place of her aging father and soldier brother, Okei guided agitated peasant-servants in the defense of her family farms—and agriculture, which she called "the foundation of [the] nation"—from the devastation of war. After her family members were killed and her servants dispersed, Okei and Shijimi encountered and parted in the same way as Kimura's novel described, but one notable difference in the film was that the dejected man subsequently joined a gang of smugglers in Yokohama. In addition, instead of her being a mere nanny, the movie made Okei a central figure of the Wakamatsu colony expedition, who was instrumental in reassembling her former servants and steering those hesitant peasant-emigrants toward the cause of overseas agricultural colonization. Right before her departure for America, Okei and Shijimi met again, and she persuaded him to leave the criminal organization, urging him to "dedicate [himself] to the country." As Okei and her fellow agricultural colonizers sailed off at the crack of dawn in search of a new Japan across the Pacific, Shijimi embarked on a new life as a determined nationalist for modern Japan, a country that had just awakened to the limitless possibilities of progress and expansion. Amid images of beaming morning light and overflowing hopes, the film ended with no suggestion of Okei's early death or of her colony's swift demise. Rather, only a bright future appeared to await both protagonists, whose lives seemed to be—albeit "separated tragically by fate"—still connected by and entangled in a larger destiny of the expansive nation and its borderless empire.[34]

Considering that most ordinary Japanese were unfamiliar with Issei history other than having a vague notion of their agricultural successes, the 1940 film resulted in more profound inventions than simple manipulations of the characters. It detemporalized and universalized the historical experience of Japanese in America by melting it into the ongoing enterprise of Manchurian colonization. Although they both defined Okei as the origin of Japanese America, neither Iriye's academic narrative nor Kimura's fictive account denied a temporal distance between the Wakamatsu colonization and the mainstay of Japanese experience in the United States, because readers would know that Okei had died and her colony had gone under decades before the emigration of the current Issei residents. The film did away with that distance by not showing the aftermath of her departure. By not including her death and her colony's failure, the film immortalized Okei and the Wakamatsu colony, and through the absence of vital historical information it hinted at a direct causal linkage between her and Japanese development in the United States and other new Japans, including Manchukuo. In *Arashi ni saku hana*, the past was not simply a historical crystal ball for a different present; in it, what was unfolding in Manchuria directly mirrored what had happened in America.

The nationwide screening of the Okei film marked an important moment, in which significant aspects of Issei history making overlapped with orthodox renditions of national expansion. Eliding the distinctions between *shokumin* (settler-colonizer) and *imin* (labor-migrant), the film purged heterodox historical facts and presences until all that remained was an essentialized and homogenous image of overseas residents in line with the glorified figures of "colonial fighters" and "continental brides." Therefore, Okei's dramatized stories specifically helped organize popular knowledge around her dual identity as the thresholds of Japanese America and of Manchurian settler colonization—the knowledge that enabled the masses to grasp the current imperative of Japanese imperialism relative to the Issei past, and vice versa. Ironically, or perhaps inevitably, the defeat of the Japanese empire quickly buried in oblivion the theory of overseas development, and the Issei's pivotal place in expansionist national history that the theory had carved out, after 1945. As a postwar narrative of their Nisei children as loyal Americans developed in popular and academic discourses of both countries, Japanese immigrants became simply Japanese "Americans," a group of people whom few historians of modern Japan have considered to be thematically relevant. Symbolically, too, Okei has since become virtually the sole property of Japanese American history, for her grave is now designated as part of an official California state historic landmark—one that commemorates the beginning of an immigrant success story, or what Nisei leaders proudly call an "American saga." Okei is no longer a symbol of "Japanese imperialism," as Kimura had argued in 1935 and as her contrived image in the 1940 film had presented her to the empire.[35]

1940 TOKYO CONFERENCE OF OVERSEAS JAPANESE

In the history of Japanese imperial expansion, 1940 was a crucial year for another reason. Extolling the exploits of all Issei, such as Okei in the film, the 1940 Tokyo Conference of Overseas Japanese (Kaigai Dōhō Tokyo Taikai) was a completely ideological project that fused Iriye's scholarly construction and Kimura's popular inculcation into unprecedented national pageantry. Jointly sponsored by the Japanese ministries of foreign and colonial affairs, this conference placed the subject of overseas development at the center of a historic yearlong commemoration that celebrated the 2,600th anniversary of the mythical first emperor Jinmu's accession to the throne.[36] Culminating in a grand finale that featured Emperor Hirohito, the Conference of Overseas Japanese took place between November 4 and November 8 and attempted to assemble all segments of Japanese society—elites and commoners, domestic and overseas—in glamorization of Japan's expansionist past, present, and future.

The Japanese government based this national mobilization on the ties of blood among overseas racial comrades (*kaigai dōhō*), which cut across differences in class, gender, ideology, geography, and even citizenship background. In the context of inter-imperial interchange, Tokyo apparently took inspiration from Hitler's rallying of worldwide Volksdeutsche and the Germanization of the Reichsgau Wartheland and beyond, which entailed the creation of settlement networks of ethnic Germans linked up to the "Fatherland." According to American intelligence reports, Heinrich Georg Stahmer, Hitler's emissary to Japan on a mission to finalize the Tripartite Pact, purportedly "suggested to the Japanese Government the establishment of [an] overseas Japanese central society" in conjunction with the November conference. It is also notable that Fascist Italy had already carried out a similar project since 1939 to forge tighter connections between the home empire and its racial compatriots abroad.[37]

Aside from the comparable programs of constructing a borderless empire based on the ties of blood, what directly motivated imperial Japan to assemble its racial comrades abroad regardless of their legal status was a new national doctrine of *hakkō ichiu* (unifying every corner of the world under one roof). In July 1940, Prime Minister Konoe Fumimaro announced a new set of guidelines to consolidate resources—human and material—for ongoing war efforts in China. This totalitarian reform featured Emperor Jinmu's purported motto in founding the nation, which now connoted the creation of a supraregional "New Order" in the

Asia-Pacific under Japanese leadership. From the early 1940s on, the *hakkō ichiu* doctrine became the ideological foundation of imperial colonialism, which found Iriye Toraji's synthesis, and the Issei's past in particular, useful in mobilizing all overseas Japanese settlements under the yoke of the home empire. The Tokyo conference was an official attempt to enlist the history of emigration, as well as emigrants themselves, in the service of Japanese imperialism. An internal government document, which detailed the unpublicized but central goals of the 1940 event, prioritized "uniting and solidifying the bonds between the homeland and the organizations of overseas Japanese" for the general purposes of *hakkō ichiu*.[38] Thus, a mass rally at the five-day event resulted in the formation of the Central Federation for Overseas Japanese (Kaigai Dōhō Chūōkai) in Tokyo as the nucleus of the "expanding Yamato people" worldwide. In this sense, this conference signaled the state's effort to produce a diasporic imperial Japanese race that was no longer attached to a particular location, culture, or citizenship status. Based on the ties of blood alone, Tokyo strove to construct a borderless settler empire that entailed a network of overseas immigrants and their descendants.

The coming together of overseas racial comrades gave the Japanese public an opportunity to learn about the "heroic" struggles of emigrants firsthand, as well as to understand from their deeds the national mission to extend Japanese influence to "every corner of the world." The government invited nearly fifteen hundred delegates from Japanese settlements in China and Manchukuo, Southeast Asia and the Nan'yō, and the Americas. Among all the regional groups, the North American contingent was the most prominent, represented by 794 delegates, followed by those from the Nan'yō (314), East Asia (198), and Latin America (193).[39] To "requite our compatriots throughout the world for their longstanding contributions to overseas development," Prime Minister Konoe, Foreign Minister Matsuoka Yōsuke, Army Minister Tōjō Hideki, Prince Higashikuni, and other dignitaries were present at the opening session (see figure 13).[40] In their speeches, which Japan's censored press reported in detail, these state leaders honored the participants in keeping with the conference manifesto, which read:

> For the past seventy years, the number of overseas compatriots has reached over one million and several hundred thousand, and they have extended the national influence to every corner of the world. They left for distant foreign lands, struggled against all kinds of adversities, and yet established today's sound social standing in their respective societies. Not only have they worked hard to enlarge their enterprises for future generations, but they have also promoted the development of industries and cultures in the host countries with proud Japanese traits. In this they have embodied the spirit of *hakkō ichiu*.[41]

Tied to the current policy mandate, the central themes of Issei experience—tribulations, triumphs, and racial superiority—were notable in this manifesto, and

FIGURE 13. Opening ceremony of the Conference of Overseas Japanese, November 1940.
Source: Author's personal collection.

as mentioned, these were what Iriye had woven into his synthetic History of overseas Japanese development. By turning Iriye's narrative into state orthodoxy, the 1940 event made the history of Japanese America formally a national past. Just as Okei was made a symbol of modern-day colonial expansionism in the 1940 motion picture, that nationalized past also became equated with the imperialist present in public, because the former reified "the spirit of *hakkō ichiu*" that defined the latter.

Indeed, the spectacular pageantry inundated the audience's sense of historical changes and differences. The dialectics of historicizing and dehistoricizing especially cluttered the minds of Japanese people with teleological symbolism, resulting in an even greater confluence of emigration with colonization in their consciousness. Full of suggestive visual representations, the first day of the conference was most significant in its ideological effects. On November 4 a grand celebration march kicked off the five-day program. Accompanied by musical bands and thousands of domestic participants, overseas invitees paraded through central Tokyo between Hibi Park and the Imperial Palace. Following the Rising Sun flag came the first overseas residents, two elderly Issei from Northern California (see figure 14).[42] Conference officials picked them to head the procession because their frail but

FIGURE 14. The front of the grand celebration march on emigration history, November 1940. *Source*: Kaigai Dōhō Chūōkai, *Kaigai Dōhō Tokyo Taikai gahō* (Tokyo: Kaigai Dōhō Chūōkai, 1940).

dignified bodies symbolized the official starting point of Japan's seventy years of external growth that was still progressing under the banner of *hakkō ichiu*. The parade was a concrete expression of that history, which united the disparate paths of emigration and colonization into a monolithic, unilinear trajectory. After the two Issei came the entire Hawaiian delegation, then those from the continental United States, Canada, the Nan'yō, and Latin America, and finally delegates from China and Manchukuo—the order clearly marking the undifferentiated chronology of Japanese emigration history. The end of the parade consisted of some three thousand domestic high school and college students who aspired to join the ranks of their overseas compatriots as colonial fighters and continental brides.[43] After the procession reached the Imperial Palace, a metaphor of Japanese return from faraway lands to the heart and soul of the "expansive nation," one of the elder Issei led three cheers of hurrah for the emperor.[44] The participants' "enthusiastic banzai" was then met with the prime minister's affirmation of the consolidated expansionist past and present. "Your presence here," remarked Konoe, "is a reminder of the history of Japanese colonization [abroad], the opening pages of which have been written in your blood and that of your forerunners."[45]

Demonstrating the history Iriye had crafted in words with actual agents of overseas development, the 1940 commemoration formed a "mnemonic site," which engaged, and enmeshed, both its participants and observers in the emerging state orthodoxy. As historian Takashi Fujitani explains, *mnemonic site* refers to "non-verbal official signs and the dominant meanings, customs, and practices associated with them," which unfold in national ceremonies and rituals.[46] In order for Iriye's expansionist narrative to acquire public consent and to turn it into a national consensus, such a site was indispensable. Choreographed by the state, the personified representations of the expansionist past and present communicated to the Japanese of every class and every age these official messages: that emigration and colonization were identical and indivisible, and that the Japanese in America were exemplars of the empire's "peaceful fighters in the frontlines of [overseas development]."[47]

The Japanese government placed Issei participants at the helm to consolidate these orthodox meanings. At the opening ceremony, an immigrant newspaper publisher from San Francisco responded to the dignitaries' speeches on behalf of those from abroad. He pledged that each and every one of them would begin anew, taking to heart the glory of being an imperial subject, and "advance with the spirit of *hakkō ichiu* in a respective site of overseas Japanese expansion." The closing ceremony on November 8 reinforced the notions of their unequivocal patriotism and their relevance to the empire. For this event, conference officials brought the two North American pioneers to center stage again, uniting them with Japan's foremost nationalist-expansionist, Tōyama Mitsuru, who had led the ultra-Right Kokuryūkai (Amur River Society) movement since the turn of the twentieth century. The revered national hero voluntarily approached the two Issei to shake their hands, an action that moved the audience of nearly two thousand to a standing ovation. This emotional demonstration was followed by another oath of commitment to the national cause, wherein a female representative from Hawai'i repeated the Issei newspaperman's earlier comments.[48]

In terms of their ideological effects, the second and fourth days were equally significant, albeit through historicizing rather than dehistoricizing. By adopting Iriye's narrative scheme, the conference established a nuanced gradation of the meaning that each regional group held in view of Japan's present policy mandate. At the discussion sessions on November 5 and 7, officials steered the Issei toward "talking specifically about the several decades of their tribulations," the aftermath of racial exclusion, and the resultant challenges they faced in the United States. In order to avoid the possibility of Issei's interjecting heterodox ideas into state-led orthodoxy making and the empire's policy mandate, the authorities dissuaded the North American participants from taking up current affairs in Asia as a subject of deliberation at their group session; instead, foreign ministry officials simply briefed the Issei on "Japan's recent conditions and international politics."[49] This focus on a localized past revealed a stark contrast to what transpired in the Nan'yō and East Asian sessions. There, the discussions revolved around future courses for their respective "developments," because both contingents resided on the new frontiers upon which the fate and progress of the Japanese empire depended. While the Nan'yō group exchanged thoughts and opinions that "might serve as a compass for Japan's policy of southward expansion," the delegates from Manchuria confidently declared "the centrality in the coming era of their status among overseas compatriots." And at the evening public lecture on November 5, this temporally organized order of priorities was still manifest. Juxtaposed against the presentations of ongoing overseas development, the Issei's anecdotes were meant to serve as a source of inspiration for the expansive nation, yet there was an unambiguous reminder that the Japanese in America were not in a position to actively partake in the current phase of empire building in East Asia and the Nan'yō.[50]

Fundamentally, the 1940 conference was a project of what Michele Foucault describes as "total history," which drew "all [past] phenomena around a single center," mainly that of the Manchurian colonization enterprise. With the help of the state's ideological apparatuses, this total history not only disavowed discontinuities and ruptures among Japanese experiences abroad but also denied the audience disparate interpretations of overseas "development." The principles of continuity and unity shaped the grammar of popular historical consciousness relative to the question of national expansion, which subsequently determined the possibilities of knowing for a domestic public.[51] The manner and circumstances in which Issei participants performed their parts deterred contemporary observers from appreciating their real standing as a persecuted minority in white America. And perhaps more critical, the pageant made it impossible for the Japanese public to delve into the Issei's reasons for history making, since they looked perfectly congruent in their beliefs with those of Japanese officials, who merely glorified "the superior quality of the Japanese as a race" without regard to their social standing in the United States, as well as the real meaning of their development there.[52] Divorcing the story of immigrant tribulations and triumphs from its constitutive context of American race relations, Japanese intelligentsia, popular culture, and the state jointly co-opted Issei history in service of the new policies of agricultural colonization in Manchuria and national mobilization. This is not to say that common people suddenly forgot what were now deemed heterodox ideas about overseas Japanese, especially those in America. Anti-*imin* biases, whereby Issei were despised categorically as low class *dekasegi* workers, remained firm. Still, orthodoxy appeared to have taken root in Japanese society in 1940, if only temporarily, as many Issei participants fondly recalled a dramatic shift in Japanese attitudes from derision to respect after the conference.[53]

For the most part, many Japanese in America were willing accomplices, pleased with the formal acknowledgment of their historical role and the homeland's acceptance of US residents as worthy members. As auspicious as it was, that official recognition nevertheless accounted for only a partial fulfillment of the Issei's goal. Having lived in the interstices of both countries, they wished to reconcile their in-betweenness by claiming an integral place in each nation and its history simultaneously. Thus, while vouching for their Japanese patriotism, Issei writers and leaders always stressed how much they had contributed to American society in what historian Gary Gerstle calls "the political language of Americanism."[54] And in order to convince white America to admit them as equals despite their "Oriental" ancestry, Issei opted to emphasize their outstanding racial character through the example of imperial Japan's rise as a world power. This politics of dualism, which set Issei apart from their compatriots at home, turned out to be no match for a totalizing imperial nationalism and its insistence on a monolithic Japanese identity that was written into new orthodoxy and its total history. The compromised designation of the Issei as "soldiers of *hakkō ichiu*" at the expense of their other, American identity revealed the fundamental vulnerability of their diasporic imagination to the nationalist binarism that disallowed cosmopolitan ambiguities and ambivalences.[55] But it was also true that without such eclectic immigrant transnationalism, Japan would have found it much harder to co-opt the experience of American residents and all the convenient ideas it offered.

Indeed, the Japanese press made certain that the dedication of overseas patriots was transparent, undiluted, and most important, singular. Newspapers throughout the empire meticulously reproduced the doings of rapturous Issei and other participants at the conference, embellishing the reports with tales of their struggles and other historical facts appropriate solely for the agendas of imperial Japan. Their stories were accompanied with exaggerated headlines such as "Overflowing Patriotism!" and "The Spirit of National Foundation Kept Alive in a Distant Foreign Land."[56] Tokyoites who witnessed the parade, according to the press, held the marchers in high esteem. As a reporter of the *Tokyo Nichinichi Shinbun* noted, the two Issei elders at the head of the procession made a particularly strong impression (see figure 14): "Among the proud participants . . . are Mr. Tsukamoto [Matsunosuke of San Francisco] who is as thin as a heron and Mr. Minami [Kunitarō of Oakland] who barely walks forward one step at a time with the help of an assistant. Wearing morning coats, both men slowly proceed in tears, perhaps recalling the tribulations that they have withstood for half a century [in America] and rejoicing at the honor of taking part in this national celebration. This sight cannot but touch our hearts deeply."[57]

Aided by powerful graphic imagery that "touch[ed their] hearts," hegemonic renditions of expansionist history encroached on the minds of the Japanese masses, helping to homogenize their way of seeing their overseas compatriots, especially the Issei pioneers from the United States. As effective as it may have been, however, Tokyo officials knew only too well that the 1940 conference alone would not suffice to make the people suddenly enthusiastic about a policy of mass emigration to Manchuria, the ultimate purpose of the event. Whereas the spectacular pageantry moved, exhilarated, and engulfed the audience in a flood of emotion, other means of ideological mobilization took a subdued approach that was repetitive and reinforcing. At the beginning of 1940 and during the conference, the Japanese government generated additional mnemonic sites that packaged Issei history more comprehensively in national history—projects aided by other unofficial endeavors, including the showing of the Okei film.

Organized by the Cabinet Information Bureau, a grandiose exhibition named "Our New Frontiers" was held in January 1940, when the 2600th anniversary celebration commenced. Although it offered a relatively minor place for the Japanese in America, this exhibition contextualized the Issei record within Japan's history of twenty-six hundred years, thereby making it neatly dovetail with major historic episodes and legendary figures of overseas development through the entire span of the nation's existence. Among the topical features that purportedly mirrored the Issei experience were the so-called advance of the Yamato state into Korea (AD 200–600), the penetration of Japanese commerce into Southeast Asia (1400–1600), and various displays on Japan's modern colonization endeavors. Utilizing photos, documents, dioramas, and mannequins of emigrants and colonialists, the exhibition attracted over one million visitors, including Prince Chichibu, Hirohito's younger brother.[58]

At the conclusion of the 2600th-year festivities, a second exhibition showcased emergent expansionist orthodoxy in tandem with the overseas Japanese conference. At a Nihonbashi department store, the Grand Exhibition of Overseas Japanese Development presented "the microcosm of our modern-day national expansion" in order to "cherish the memory of the pioneers with a view to promoting further overseas development."[59] Sent directly from abroad, the displayed artifacts consisted of local agricultural specialties; large panoramic photos of Japanese farms, businesses, and community activities; materials related to regional pioneers; and published immigrant histories. Just as in the grand celebration march, the exhibition placed a particular focus on the achievements of Japanese in America. A large farm tractor with a life-sized mannequin of an Issei agriculturalist sat in the hallway leading to the North American section (see figure 15), which arrested visitor attention with the central theme on a large sign: "It is the Japanese who have built the foundation of development and prosperity on the [US] Pacific Coast!"[60] While singing the praises of colonial success and racial superiority through a variety of artifacts, the exhibition also highlighted the undiluted patriotism of overseas Japanese through a display of thousands of their *imon bukuro*, or care packages for imperial soldiers. These symbols were conspicuously placed at the main show windows along a trolley route and throughout the exhibit halls inside the department store. More than 690,000 people visited this mnemonic site during the first two weeks of November 1940.[61]

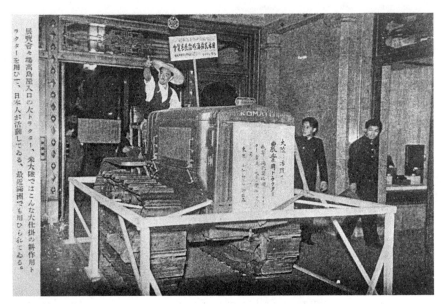

FIGURE 15. Display of Japanese immigrant agriculturalist in California as model settler-colonist, November 1940. *Source:* Kaigai Dōhō Chūōkai, *Kaigai Dōhō Tokyo Taikai gahō* (Tokyo: Kaigai Dōhō Chūōkai, 1940).

Other manifestations of the total ideological project included the fixation of the meanings engendered by the state-sponsored pageantry and exhibitions in accordance with what historian Kenneth Ruoff calls "the cult of the pioneer."[62] In an effort to elevate the social status of emigrants and promote the popular appreciation of emigrating in line with the emergent master narrative, the government honored 628 overseas residents, including 91 leading Japanese from North America, with a commemorative sake cup and a letter of commendation signed by the foreign minister. On November 10, the climax of the yearlong national commemoration, five leading Issei men were awarded the Sixth Order of the Sacred Treasure and the Medal of Honor with Green Ribbon, as were five other emigrants from elsewhere. Just like distinguished scholars, meritorious statesmen, devoted bureaucrats, and self-sacrificing military men, the Issei gained officially sanctioned "distinction" to enter the ranks of national heroes.[63] For these Issei, the price of that recognition, and of their pivotal place in imperialist orthodoxy, was not inconsequential, because US authorities kept a close eye on their activities in Japan. After Japan's attack on Pearl Harbor, they would pay the price of prolonged confinement in US Justice Department detention camps as "*dangerous* enemy aliens."

As much as Tokyo officials strove to craft a variety of symbolisms and meanings around the aged bodies of US Issei pioneers solely for the benefit of the empire's new expansionist agenda, they were also intent on taking advantage of the second-generation youth of Japanese ancestry (Nisei) for the goal of *hakkō ichiu*. Japan's lack of legal ownership of the foreign-born Japanese, especially Japanese American citizens, nonetheless made it difficult for the state to mobilize the Nisei freely. The question of sovereign control and legal belonging emerged as a major stumbling block, creating different strains of thought about proper relations between Nisei and their ancestral land. But as chapter 8 details, Tokyo still fundamentally believed in and presumed the primacy of blood ties over legal citizenship status. While treading a thin line, the organizing committee for the 1940 conference of overseas Japanese planned to put together a separate worldwide congress of Nisei, at which representatives would be encouraged to engage in "free discussion" about their role as successors of overseas racial development, albeit with the committee's "authorization," "supervision," and "assistance." Leading Japanese American representatives of the Tokyo region registered objections to such an event, which might present itself as a Nisei-initiated one, "in consideration of complicated international situations." Instead, the US-born Nisei requested that the committee hold a simple invitation-only banquet for them. The Japanese side obliged, sponsoring a Nisei rally (*Dai-Nisei konshinkai*) for 550 youths of Japanese ancestry who currently resided in Japan's capital region. Reflecting the demography of foreign-born Japanese in Japan at that time, the vast majority of attendees were North American Nisei (Hawai'i included). Yet the organizing committee also made a special effort to bring in second-generation participants originating from South America and other regions, so that the event could be billed as a variant but constituent element of the ongoing *pan-Japanese* conference. About fifty Japanese dignitaries joined them as guests of honor at the Nisei rally.[64]

The gathering took place at a large banquet hall in central Tokyo on November 5, the second night of the five-day conference. During a western-style multicourse dinner, Nisei attendees were entertained by traditional Japanese dance and songs as well as classical western music, but the most important program—integral to the overall ideological project—came last: a speech presented by Nagata Hidejirō, a member of the House of Peers and a former colonial minister. His message crystallized Tokyo officials' view of Nisei and the basic rationale behind their efforts to mobilize young foreign citizens of Japanese ancestry. In his speech, Nagata emphasized the "superior racial quality" of the Japanese people—the intrinsic trait that continued to exist in the blood of foreign-born Japanese regardless of their upbringing or legal status. Nisei attendees were reminded that they, too, had inherited that immutable racial blood, which was qualitatively different from the mutable cultural and political characters of each country. In conclusion, Nagata "appealed to the Nisei to realize this fact and take home to their respective countries the knowledge of new Japan."[65] In the context of the times, the political message of his racial speech was not difficult to discern: the Nisei's blood ties to the ancestral land should always remain the most fundamental part of their identity and behavior, which would lead them to act as Japan's defenders, if not apologists, in their home country when necessary. Legal belonging and acculturation were only secondary to their continuous membership in the diasporic Yamato race. Along the same line of racial thinking, a Japanese convener of the Nisei rally reiterated Nagata's point in more politically timely expressions. In his welcome address, this man stated: "Nisei are a shining example of our racial blood and spirit in a foreign land. . . . The Yamato spirit must form a [leading] strain of the national character that comprises [the backbone of] every country in North America, South America, and other areas of the world [through your presence]. It is in this way that our national ideal of *hakkō ichiu* can spread and reign all over the world."[66]

The racialist discourse at the Nisei rally, especially the belief in the primacy of blood ties, anticipated the manner in which an institutional mechanism was constructed to mobilize foreign-born youths of Japanese ancestry. Shortly after the founding of the Central Federation for Overseas Japanese, its Young People's Bureau (Kaigai Dōhō Chūōkai Seinenbu) was formed in April 1941, and despite its appearance of being a "voluntary "organization," Tokyo officials almost coerced resident Nisei leaders into "resolv[ing] to organize the bureau" as if it were their own initiative.[67] Subsequently, the Young People's Bureau came under the direct jurisdiction of Japan's foreign ministry.

This marked a significant moment, when the Japanese state successfully effaced the different ways in which Japaneseness was being defined and practiced within and without the empire. Foreign-born Japanese, especially those in the United States and Canada, had tended to maintain and insist on separate ethnicized identities as Japanese Americans/Canadians in relation to Japanese nationals or other overseas-born Japanese under Japan's sovereign control. In this instance of intraracial differentiation, US- or Canadian-born Nisei had navigated the fault lines of citizenship, culture, and race by emphasizing the importance of legal belonging and acculturation over blood ties. While still preserving a sense of connection to imperial Japan and homeland Japanese, this form of identity politics had also enabled Japanese American/Canadian residents in Japan to form their own community and ethnicity as foreign citizens of Japanese ancestry without being absorbed into the masses of imperial subjects when many youths crossed the Pacific for education and employment during the 1930s.[68] The Young People's Bureau almost completely wiped out the intraracial difference between "Japanese American citizens" and other second-generation people born outside the Japanese archipelago in the all-encompassing language of "overseas-born compatriots" (*Kaigai shussei dōhō*), who supposedly comprised the borderless racial empire.

The nationalization of US-born Nisei nonetheless did not take place in a matter of months between November 1940 and April 1941. The Young People's Bureau only signified the culmination of what had been transpiring over the previous decade regarding the question of how to educate and nationalize US-born Nisei students in the Japanese school system when a larger number of those youths had suddenly flocked to their ancestral land. The next chapter examines how state officials and educators managed to come up with pedagogical blueprints and institutional mechanisms for the education of the next generation of Japan's settler-colonists. In anticipation of similar future needs in other parts of the borderless Japanese empire, they experimented with new teaching principles and instructional methods on US-born Nisei students, purportedly the first group of overseas-born compatriots in modern times.

8

The Call of Blood

*Japanese American Citizens and the Education
of the Empire's Future "Frontier Fighters"*

*Born in North America, brought up in North America, and speaking English,
the second-generation Japanese (Nisei) are Americanized souls whose
thoughts cannot be understood and who live as in a different world, but in
their veins courses the blood of the Japanese race of Asia. When the mask is
torn away and the sleeper awakens, on that day the Yamato Spirit will blossom forth. Ah, this solemn, utter truth!*[1]

This statement, penned by Natori Jun'ichi, who was considered a foremost expert
in the education of foreign-born Japanese, captures an essential aspect of Japanese
thinking regarding what was increasingly being deemed a national problem during much of the 1930s. Replace "North America" with any other location in the
world to get the basic ideological underpinnings of foreign-born Japanese education during this decade. A belief in blood ties was so strong that many Japanese
educators presumed racial heritage would always supersede the contradicting
national characters and other cultural attributes that a foreign-born Japanese
would have acquired from being raised and educated elsewhere. According to the
emergent educational ideology, learning Japanese language and culture in the
ancestral land would ensure that the "Yamato Spirit" (or "Japanese spirit") would
be (re)awakened in a foreign-born Japanese, replacing his seemingly alien "mask"
with a genuine Japanese one.

This chapter looks at the intersections between the education of US-born Japanese Nisei in their ancestral land and that of sons and daughters of Japanese
settler-colonists in the Asia-Pacific region, including Manchuria, the Nan'yo, and
other parts of the expanding Japanese empire. The homeland education of American Nisei offers an ideal lens through which to not only deterritorialize studies of
Japanese imperialism but also illuminate a critical nexus between the history of
the Japanese immigrant (Issei) community in the United States and that of Japan's

formal colonies. As the previous chapters show, former and current members of Japanese America often played an indispensable role as self-proclaimed experts in agrarian colonization and pioneers of national expansion in facilitating the (con) fusion of those histories. Japan's imperial regime and public eagerly accepted their views, opinions, and recommendations, as they saw fit, in the context of building and governing a borderless colonial empire. During the 1930s the problem of how to preserve "second Japans" in the coming era of the local-born generation formed another crucial area in which imperial Japan turned to Japanese America for strategies and solutions for anticipated challenges.

The homeland education of American-born Nisei served as a model case and the first viable experiment attempting to reproduce the next generation of Japanese settler-colonists. Both social ideologues and government officials embraced this vision and legitimized it as if it were crucial to the survival of the home empire. Because they could claim authoritative knowledge about the "second-generation problem," educators and intellectuals with prior American experience—including former Issei leaders—were instrumental in conflating the education of Nisei US citizens and that of children of imperial colonizers under the Japanese flag. These self-proclaimed experts presented the homeland education of Japanese Americans as a means of "spreading the national glory abroad," a prevailing pedagogical orientation that one Nisei expatriate in Tokyo bitterly criticized. Indeed, some resident Japanese American leaders in Tokyo protested "this type of thinking," because they felt it represented "nationalistic ideology" that would compromise their American identity and citizenship in favor of blood ties.[2] Despite Nisei's defiance or confusion, Japanese educators still postulated and insisted on a causal relationship between the successful Japanization of foreign-born compatriots and Japan's continuous ascent as a global colonial power, arguing that the former was a precondition for the latter. The Nisei's homeland education would ensure the preservation of racial bonds and the national spirit in overseas Japanese settlements upon their return from their ancestral land, because this education was meant to transform these future leaders of Japan's frontier development. Through the pro-homeland activities of foreign-born compatriots with a strong sense of national mission, many educators anticipated, the Japanese empire would solidify its extraterritorial influence over the countries of the second generation's birth even after the passing of the pioneer immigrant generation.

NISEI EDUCATION IN JAPAN AND NATIONALIZING THE FOREIGN-BORN RACIAL COMPATRIOTS

The phenomenon of American Nisei's going to Japan to study, or *bokoku ryūgaku*, became notable in the early 1930s. As Goro Murata, a Los Angeles–born Nisei journalist in Tokyo, observed, "Their migration to Japan did not become conspicuous until after the Manchurian Incident of 1931 when the rise of Japan first impressed the nisei in America." Since then, according to Murata, "there had been a continuous stream of these youngsters, both men and women, coming to Japan to study."[3] These American-born students were of mostly high school to college age, and they congregated mainly in Tokyo, where by the mid-1930s their numbers reached as many as four thousand.[4] While hundreds of these ethnic Americans attended institutions of secondary and higher education, many others learned basic Japanese language and culture at special schools for the foreign born in the capital city. Economic and ideological factors precipitated the educational sojourn of these Nisei adolescents. First, the decline of the Japanese currency relative to the US dollar made it possible for immigrant parents to afford supporting their Nisei children's education in Japan. In December 1931, Japan's decision to take the country off the gold standard accelerated the plunging of the yen-dollar exchange rate by 50 percent. Ideologically, the concept of the Nisei as a "bridge of understanding" between the United States and Japan led many Issei parents to believe in the need for Nisei heritage learning, since they felt agents of international friendship, cultural exchange, and commercial development must possess adequate knowledge of and appreciation for both countries between which they would mediate. A product of immigrant transnationalism, the bridge concept made Nisei study abroad a conspicuous social practice of the 1930s—one that allowed the home empire to hold the American born captive for its pedagogical experiment.[5] In the eyes of many educators and social leaders in Japan, the Nisei's sudden arrival only seemed to foreshadow the coming from elsewhere of other foreign-born Japanese, whose numbers had been rising rapidly in tandem with the increased migration and settlement of imperial subjects throughout the Asia-Pacific since the previous decade.

Just as a growing number of American Nisei flocked to their ancestral land for heritage education, some among the Japanese social elite and intelligentsia were busy formulating an educational philosophy and pedagogy suitable for them. In their eyes, Japanese American students represented the first group of foreign-born racial compatriots following the emergence of modern Japan as an expansive empire. The 1930s began with the extension of Japan's formal territorial boundaries to all of Manchuria, since the establishment in 1932 of its puppet Manchukuo provided a massive de facto new colony. Combined with the systematic emigration of Japanese family settlers to Brazil since 1928, the state-sponsored agricultural development of the Manchurian frontier engulfed the whole nation, creating a massive outward movement of Japanese farm families to northeast Asia. This emigration flow was augmented even more by Tokyo's policy mandate in 1936 to ship one million Japanese families (or five million agricultural colonists) to Manchukuo over the following two decades. As the population of Japanese agricultural settlers there jumped from 108,532 to 376,036 between 1929 and 1936, the other sites of Japanese "development" likewise saw a remarkable, if less impressive, increase in the number of emigrant-settlers in the same period. In Brazil and the Nan'yo (especially Micronesia), for example, the local Japanese populations rose from 103,166 to 193,057 and from 16,021 to 55,948, respectively.[6]

These settlements were still first generation and immigrant centered, but because most colonists moved there in family units, Japanese officials and expansionist ideologues were already concerned with the anticipated growth of unconventional imperial subjects, that is, "foreign-born compatriots" (*kaigai shussei dōhō*). The crux of their interest was the question of how to keep the next generation of settler-colonists sufficiently "Japanese" in their disposition and consciousness—enough that the empire could continue to rely on them for the maintenance and elevation of Japan's national power and prestige abroad. American Nisei seekers of heritage education arrived in their ancestral land just when it was mired in these concerns. In the eyes of many Japanese, however, the wide-eyed youngsters from across the Pacific looked like pitifully "Americanized souls," with "materialistic" beliefs and "hedonistic" tendencies—utter contradictions to what imperial subjects were supposed to be.[7] Homeland pundits, such as Natori Jun'ichi, were still convinced that the proper education could rehabilitate and eventually "awaken" their "Yamato spirit," which supposedly remained dormant in their racial blood, when a proper stimulus was applied through a systematic Japanizing education. Educators and intellectuals took it upon themselves to formulate an instructional philosophy and devise the best pedagogy to achieve that goal, and an active debate ensued throughout the 1930s. Central players in this debate were former residents of the United States, who offered their "expert" advice on the educational challenges of American-born Japanese.

A young sociologist named Ōtsuka Yoshimi, who had trained at the University of Oregon, was especially instrumental in the early phase of pedagogical and policy formulation relative to Americanized souls and other foreign-born compatriots who would follow them. Published in early 1933, his academic monograph defined the basic goal of heritage education for Nisei from the standpoint of the empire's ongoing settler-colonist enterprise, especially the agricultural development of Manchuria. Drawing on his field research among Japanese immigrant communities in Oregon and California, this self-styled expert on the second-generation problem presented an academic case study of the subject and characterized it as "the best reference" for the future of Japanese expansionism.[8] In the introduction to his 319-page book, Ōtsuka contended: "As the expansive power of the Japanese nation has made an explosive move in the direction to South America, Mongolia, and Manchuria, we must now reflect on our past failures and successes [in colonial endeavors]. . . . If one deems "Japanese in America" merely an isolated example of Japanese emigration that would be irrelevant [to the current colonial project and destiny of the empire], and if he argues that there would be no use studying their experience because no emigrant has been admitted into the United States [since 1924], he is greatly mistaken."[9]

As is obvious, this line of argument resembled the ideology that shored up the 1940 Tokyo Conference of Overseas Japanese, at which immigrants in America—and by extension their US-born children—were presented as the purveyors of Japan's manifest destiny of *hakkō ichiu* in the Asia-Pacific. Whereas the 1940 expansionist pageantry reduced US immigrant pioneers to an integral part of modern Japanese colonialism, Ōtsuka's rhetoric subsumed American-born Nisei under the general rubric of "overseas Japanese children" (*zaigai shitei*), albeit specifically as the *first* cohort. This familiar narrative of historical confusion and homogenization rendered American citizens of Japanese ancestry fundamentally no different from other foreign-born Japanese, including sons and daughters of colonial masters in Manchuria and the empire's formal territories. Indeed, to Ōtsuka and many pundits who followed him, the goal of American-born Nisei's education was always subordinate to the mandate of ongoing global Japanese expansion, a perspective that juxtaposed US immigrant settlements on "the eastern front of Japanese [overseas] development" with the Manchurian colony at its "western edge."[10] Yet insofar as Japanese residents in America were entrusted with the role of being the *"pioneers of overseas development"* because they had emigrated before all other compatriots in modern national history, US Nisei seekers of heritage learning also became the first case study of the broader problem of foreign-born Japanese education. In this sense, American Nisei in Japan appeared to be the most promising pedagogical guinea pigs for investigating the challenges the expanding empire would have to confront when second-generation youngsters from other locations would begin rushing over to their ancestral land for education.

Underlying this valorization of Nisei's Japanese identity was the familiar theme of privileging blood ties among the compatriots of all places, generations, cultural upbringing, and citizenship. Unlike immigrant parents in the United States and liberal ideologues of Japan, Ōtsuka refused to support the primacy of Nisei's legally constituted American identity. According to him, nobody could *academically* determine whether Nisei were American or Japanese, but he also added, "even if one insists that he is American, the chance is that he would be dismissed as Japanese [in the United States]" due to white racism.[11] Despite his cursory acknowledgment of Nisei's US citizenship, Ōtsuka thereby declared the purpose of educating Japanese American youth as "activating the effective workings of the inner strength that embodies (their) qualification as [members of] the Yamato race."[12] Bearing an uncanny resemblance to the US mind-set that would send the Nisei to the internment camps during World War II, this "blood-will-tell" racialist thinking rendered the basic orientation of Nisei education in Japan as an attempt, as Ōtsuka termed it, at "Japanization" (*nihonka kyōiku*). And such an endeavor would require more

than half-baked language instruction at community-run schools in overseas settlements on the weekends and after public school hours—a common practice in
prewar Japanese America. "American Nisei who are Japanese [by blood]," he thus
stressed, "are destined to come to Japan for education."[13]

Given the enormous implications of the education of American-born pupils for
the future of the empire and race, Ōtsuka inevitably concluded that it should fall
within the realm of governmental responsibility. He elaborated on this theme in
his discussion of Nisei education in Japan as follows: "With an eye to promoting
emigration and colonization as well as overseas Japanese development, it is of
the utmost importance to get the state involved in the education of overseas
Japanese children."[14] Published under the aegis of the newly established, state-
backed Institute for the Education of Overseas Japanese (Kaigai Kyōiku Kyōkai;
hereafter IEOJ), Ōtsuka's 1933 publication—under the guise of objective scholarly
exposition—allowed expansionist statesmen and intellectuals of Japan to play an
active role in the construction of an educational ideology in support of Nisei's
"Japanization." His book indeed begins with celebratory remarks and enthusiastic
endorsements by the colonial minister and an elected member of parliament, who
not only collaborated in the organization of IEOJ but also advocated for state
patronage of its school's operations on the floor of the Imperial Diet and in public
discourse.[15]

In Ōtsuka's formulation, the responsibility of the home state for all overseas
children regardless of their citizenship status was inseparable from another principle of Nisei education in Japan. That is to say, his call for the nationalization of
Japanese Americans and other foreign-born Japanese under state auspices hinged
on the belief in their racial and cultural superiority—an idea that was shared
widely by other proponents of Nisei education in Japan.[16] Again and again, Ōtsuka
drew from the lessons of the Japanese immigrant experience in America—their
"mistakes" in particular—to argue for the critical importance of preserving the
exceptional national character and culture in Nisei. According to his rendition of
racial struggle in America:

> Those groups [of European extraction] have always forced their ways on lesser races
> with different customs and mores by treating them as savages. Such an act has pro-
> vided for the ascendancy of [European settlers]. The Japanese race, on the contrary,
> has been rather timid and accommodating to others' wishes and ways. . . . They have
> given up their own (culture and racial strength), since they were wrongly moved by
> [white exclusionist] accusations of unassimilability. . . . They have never thought
> about making others comply; rather, they have always propelled themselves to be
> influenced for the sake of being accepted [in white America].[17]

Ōtsuka wanted all immigrant compatriots and their local-born children to remain
Japanese in every sense possible and "influence others" with their exceptional culture.

He continued: "We, the Japanese, must reflect seriously on this problem; we must regain our confidence in Japanese culture. Compared with the cultures of others, indeed, there is no dispute about the superiority of ours. Then, we must realize that it is our mission to . . . civilize others."[18] Citing another expert's statement, Ōtsuka suggested that the tragic ramifications for the slight on Japanese culture and racial strength in the upbringing of Nisei would presage "their eventual downfall to the sorry lot of American Indians" under white racial dominance.[19] That would also mean the demise of a second Japan in North America, an example that should not exist in the annals of expansionistic racial/national history.

In the years following the publication of Ōtsuka's canonical work, other pundits actively theorized about the supposed correlation between nationalization of foreign-born Japanese and success in colonial endeavors. Many of these ideologues had profiles similar to Ōtsuka's, in which their previous immigrant experience living in the United States not only granted them a contrived public persona as "experts" but also greatly influenced their viewpoints on the education of foreign-born compatriots. Takahashi Taiji was a case in point. Having attended the sociology graduate program at the University of Oregon, he most likely interacted with Ōtsuka when both men resided in the Pacific Northwest as immigrant students. Between 1930 and 1932, Takahashi also worked as the principal of the Portland Japanese Language School, thus becoming directly involved in Nisei education there. After returning to Japan, in 1935 Takahashi joined the faculty of Mizuho Academy (Mizuho Gakuen), a special school for foreign-born Japanese set up by IEOJ, where he was charged with the task of putting together its general curriculum.[20] In an academic journal for professional teachers, Takahashi published a piece that discussed the imperative of educating overseas Japanese pupils in the bosom of their ancestral home from the viewpoint of racial survival and competition:

> Those (foreign-born Japanese) who do not know either the language of their fathers or the culture of their mothers, that is, those who lack the spirit of "samurai," would be no different from being "blacks with slightly paler skin." Look at those culturally deprived blacks, who have been completely acculturated into [white] America! They know no fatherland, no home language, and no ancestral culture. They are utterly useless to America. . . . It is obvious that assimilation will not automatically lead to racial development. . . . Who would want to denigrate the proud Japanese race to the level of [American] Indians or blacks? What would prevent it from happening is the [Japanese] mentality (spirit) that can only be imbued by Japanizing education.[21]

This heart-wrenching thought—the possibility of losing Japaneseness and becoming like inferior "natives"—cut across the fault line between the formal colonies of imperial Japan and other overseas settlements, since Takahashi and many other experts felt that not only the Americas but also colonial Korea and Manchukuo suffered from an acute shortage of qualified "Japanese teachers who should carry out the education of the next generation of imperial subjects."[22] For the same reason, the Ministry of Colonial Affairs was compelled at this juncture to dispatch state-certified teachers all over the world (except North America, due to diplomatic concerns) in collaboration with the Ministry of Education.[23] At the same time, the likes of Ōtsuka and Takahashi asserted that a concerted public effort was necessary to bring foreign-born children—especially future community leaders—to their ancestral land to properly transform them into Japanese subjects. Considering the general deficiencies in staffing and resources in Japanese settlements abroad, it was not surprising that other educators also came to agree that homeland education was not an option but a necessity for selected overseas pupils.[24] For them, study in Japan was an effective means of instilling national knowledge and Japanese consciousness in those Americanized souls and in their younger "siblings" elsewhere.

Paired with the belief in racial superiority, the mythical notion of the "Japanese spirit" (*Nippon seishin*)—which Ōtsuka often referred to simply as the "Japanese character"—was another pivotal concept in the emergent ideology of Japan's colonialist education. Whereas the Nisei's background allegedly predicted their superiority as settler-colonists, blood itself did not suffice to actualize Japanese ascendancy; it must be shored up by their self-awareness as diasporic members of the Japanese nation, race, and empire. Therefore, when commenting on pedagogy, Takahashi succinctly explained: "The essence of Nisei education is . . . to instill the Japanese spirit."[25] With an eye to letting "the Yamato Spirit . . . blossom forth" in "Americanized souls," Natori Jun'ichi also embraced the same pedagogical principle as Takahashi. As the wellspring of inner strength that defined the worth of a Japanese person, Natori explained, the "*Nippon seishin* characterize[d] utmost loyalty, that is, the spirit of altruistic sacrifice and dedication . . . to the emperor."[26] In concrete terms, it encompassed national morality, martial virtue, racial pride, and patriotism. To acquire these qualities, Natori and other educators emphasized, these foreign-born children needed to gain a holistic understanding of the Japanese language, culture, national history, and society. Following his return to Japan in 1934 after a six-year residence in the United States, Natori actually tried his hand at teaching Nisei and other foreign-born compatriots about the essential elements of the Japanese spirit at Waseda International Institute, which he managed under the aegis of the prestigious Waseda University.[27]

In order to better understand the larger politico-ideological context in which the new expansionist pedagogy took shape, it is important to look into the shifting meaning of "study abroad" (*ryūgaku*) in imperial Japan at that juncture. Japanese educators' embrace of the national spirit mirrored the prevailing belief that Japan had already departed from its status as a student of western modernity and had successfully established itself as a teacher of a higher civilization to the world. This transformation unfolded in conjunction with a radical change in the Japanese perspective on the relative value of knowledge, western versus Japanese.[28] Since the Meiji Restoration, Japan had been an eager student of Euro-American civilization in its quest for modernization and national ascent, and the transmission of knowledge had predominantly taken place unidirectionally from the western powers to the nascent Asian empire. While Caucasian teachers and technical advisers who worked in Japan formed a major pathway of imported western knowledge, government-sponsored domestic students (*kokuhi ryūgakusei*) served as another vital source of information from Europe and the United States before the late 1920s. Traditionally, therefore, "study abroad" referred to the outward travel of elite domestic students for the study of things western rather than foreign students—whether of Japanese or non-Japanese extraction—coming in search of Japanese knowledge. Cases of Chinese students who attended universities in late Meiji Japan (such as the novelist Lu Xun) were more the exception than the rule.

In the early 1930s the direction of the flow of "study-abroad" students began to change in accordance with the reversal of the value placed on western and Japanese civilizations. As many contemporary Japanese saw it, the ongoing phenomenon of American Nisei's studying in Japan presaged the shifting of gravity in global power relations. The "rise" of the Japanese empire as a foremost global colonial power after the Manchurian Incident of 1931 was not simply a result of its military prowess and political success. It accounted for the growing ascendancy of Japanese civilization, in which the material and scientific strength of the Occident was fused with the spiritual superiority of the Orient that imperial Japan purportedly embodied. Japan would no longer be a sender of international knowledge seekers; it would be a destination since the Asian empire could now offer a truly universal civilization that cut across the alleged East-West divide. Following these views, Tokyo adopted new policies in the early 1930s under which it reduced the annual total of students officially dispatched to the West from 150 to fewer than 60 and cut the terms of state-funded study abroad by half from 1930 onward. Three years later, the Japanese government announced its plan to phase out the government-sponsored outbound study-abroad program in the near future.[29]

Driven by the new outlook and policy on the international exchange of knowledge, Tokyo officialdom developed a state-sponsored "study-in-Japan" program for peoples of the Asia-Pacific regions over which imperial Japan wished to exert influence. Starting in 1932, Tokyo began to bring to Japan more and more students from Manchukuo and other spheres of Japanese influence, on a full scholarship. By 1936 the number of Manchurian students in Tokyo had reached fifteen hundred. One year later, the first fully funded student of Chamorro origin arrived in Tokyo from the Nan'yo.[30] Meanwhile, established in 1935, the state-backed International Student Institute (Kokusai Gakuyūkai) annually invited dozens of elite students and young scholars from outside of the Japanese empire and its de facto territories.[31] In the context of Japan's cultural propaganda, these foreigners were supposed to help transmit "Japanese knowledge" to the areas under western colonial influence as well as the independent nation-states after returning from their schooling, thereby extending and increasing the empire's global prominence. Intertwined with the state enterprise of mass migration and settler colonialism after 1932, this form of public diplomacy made up an important part of what historian Akira Iriye calls global "cultural internationalism" of the decade—imperialist "soft power" politics that also involved other empires, such as Nazi Germany and Great Britain.[32]

Hence, the policy mandate of nationalizing the next generation of overseas Japanese colonists, which Ōtsuka and other educators put together for the government, stemmed partly from Japan's new imperialistic public diplomacy, which envisaged its cultural hegemony over the Asia-Pacific and beyond through study-abroad ventures. For this reason, the institutionalization of special schools for American Nisei and other overseas-born pupils occurred in tandem with the establishment of the state-run International Student Institute. Indeed, some of the major academies, namely IEOJ's Mizuho Academy, commenced operations in the same year as the International Student Institute. Other, smaller entities, such as the Imperial Way Institute of the North American Martial Virtue Society (Hokubei Butokukai Kōdō Gakuin), joined them in the first few years after 1935. With American Nisei students as the chief object of pedagogical experimentation, these schools shared similar visions of national expansion and racial superiority initially articulated by Ōtsuka Yoshimi. The varied educational programs of these schools, albeit working independently, together constituted a mosaic of nationalizing forces that engulfed all foreign-born individuals in order to ensure the reproduction of the future purveyors of Japanese settler colonialism within and outside the home empire.[33] The rest of this chapter explores the two examples of state-backed Japanizing education that were made available to Nisei study-abroad students in Tokyo in the latter half of the 1930s.

SECOND-GENERATION EDUCATION AS A DIRECT STATE ENTERPRISE

Founded by IEOJ in 1935, Mizuho Academy (hereafter Mizuho) carried out government-backed experimentation in the education of foreign-born Japanese. The parent organization of Mizuho had strong ties to Ōtsuka's assertions, as its leadership not only wholeheartedly embraced his ideas but also sponsored the publication of his 1933 study. In fact, it is not an exaggeration to state that Ōtsuka and IEOJ collaborated closely with one another from the beginning.[34] When policy formulations were at work within the Japanese government for IEOJ's establishment between late 1931 and early 1933, the self-proclaimed expert in Nisei education served as an indispensable academic source for statesmen and officials, business leaders, and expansionist ideologues, who joined forces to set up a central national institution of "Japanization" in line with his contentions. To mark the finale of the preparatory stage in tandem with the publication of Ōtsuka's book, this collaborative endeavor led to an ad hoc committee meeting hosted by the Japanese prime minister on March 22, 1933. Representing the premier and the colonial minister in attendance, Foreign Minister Uchida Yasuya rationalized Tokyo's formal sponsorship for IEOJ's establishment, arguing that "if Japan is to neglect the education of overseas pupils . . ., we will leave their character flaws unrectified and let our overseas development fall short of real success in the end."[35] The special education that the new institute would offer, according to Uchida, would "make [foreign-born children] conversant with the Japanese spirit, Japan's [national] might, and the essence of the Japanese race . . . before returning to the endeavors of their forefathers (in overseas development)."[36]

In November 1933 IEOJ formally commenced full-scale operations, with an annual subvention of 50,000 yen (or $12,500) from the Japanese government, as well as donations from Japan's business conglomerates. The institute had its head office inside the Ministry of Colonial Affairs, while the Ministries of Foreign Affairs and Education also served as its cosponsors. Viscount Ishii Kikujirō, a member of the Privy Council, presided over the IEOJ's board of directors, which consisted mostly of members of the Houses of Peers and Representatives.[37] A virtual arm of the government, the IEOJ was an embodiment of Ōtsuka's statist vision for foreign-born Japanese education—the vision that subsequently characterized the basic curriculum of its boarding school, the Mizuho Academy.[38]

On behalf of IEOJ, Satō Tadashi, a board member who was a parliamentarian, expounded on the meaning of educating foreign-born compatriots under its wing. "Wherever a Japanese person might live and whatever citizenship he might hold," argued Satō, "he is first and foremost a member of the Japanese race, and he stands at the forefront of its [global] expansion."[39] IEOJ, as Satō put it, aimed to make "the third column of emigrants (settler colonists)" out of the Japanized Nisei, who would re-emigrate to their birthplace to strive to be the "vanguard of [Japanese] racial development."[40] Not only would they be dependable partners of the first column (immigrants), but they would also be leaders of the second column (local born with no homeland education) in overseas settler colonialism. Printed in forewords to Ōtsuka's book, these assertions were later incorporated into the institute's mission statement. Established in the outskirts of Tokyo, Mizuho Academy was meant to serve as a preparatory school for "the third column" of Japanese settler-colonists from North America and elsewhere so that they could pursue secondary and higher education in their ancestral land.

For the purpose of facilitating the smooth integration of overseas pupils into regular Japanese intermediary schools and universities, Tokyo officialdom removed various legal and bureaucratic barriers from the highly exclusive educational system of Japan's colonial metropole. Prior to the early 1930s, no legal mechanism existed in Japan to admit students with foreign citizenship to domestic primary and secondary schools. Nor did Japanese schools recognize the completion of foreign public schools as a qualification for admission even if students possessed Japanese citizenship. For IEOJ or any other agency to promote the serious homeland education of foreign-born Japanese, these obstacles had to be dealt with, or students would not be able to gain a sufficient amount of national knowledge and a proper grasp of the Japanese spirit. Therefore, in March 1934 the Ministry of Education issued special instructions to treat students of Japanese ancestry, regardless of their citizenship, as "domestic students" when they applied for admission into public schools. The ministry also pledged to offer "any and every necessary assistance to attempts in private sectors" to organize special educational programs for the incoming Nisei.[41]

In 1935 Mizuho Academy welcomed its first cohort of students. Even though it had a library and five two-story dormitories sufficient to house 150 coed students, the school initially started out with a modest group of 12 foreign-born Japanese. But student enrollment grew steadily, to 41 in 1938 and 91 in 1940. Because it was not concerned with the citizenship status of pupils, Mizuho accepted youngsters from all over the Pacific basin as long as they traced their blood lineage to Japan. According to the geographic breakdown of the school's admission quota, Hawai'i and North America received 50 slots; South America 10; the Japanese mandate of Micronesia 15; the rest of the Nan'yo (including Southeast Asia) 45; and India, Malay, and other overseas locations combined 30. In the mid-1930s, China and Manchuria were yet to be included in the projected total of 150 students at Mizuho.[42] Initially, North American Nisei actually constituted a decisive majority of the student body, but those from other regions gradually increased in number toward the end of the decade. By 1940, out of 84 students, 19 hailed from Hawai'i and 37 from the continental United States; the rest were born in Mexico, Brazil, the Philippines, Guam, Singapore, and Java (Indonesia). This diverse group of students spoke six different languages. Their ages ranged from thirteen to twenty-six, but the majority were recent graduates of foreign high schools.[43] According to the official blueprint, Mizuho was supposed to be the first small step toward a much larger colonial educational enterprise, which would "encompass a kindergarten up to a university as well as a cultural research institute," specializing in the education and Japanization of the second generation.[44]

Most students, having traveled to Japan alone, lived on Mizuho's campus for one to three years to complete the three-tiered program. It comprised the "common department" and two levels of the "higher department."[45] The basic weekly curriculum at Mizuho entailed one hour each of "Japanese civics," an "outline of the conditions of Japan," and Chinese classics; two hours each of the national and cultural history of Japan, traditional martial arts, mathematics, and geography;

four hours each of physical exercise (including martial arts) and translations (English, Spanish, or Portuguese); and nine hours of Japanese language.[46] For female students, there were also a few hours of gendered instruction on domestic skills and traditional arts, such as Japanese dressmaking, tea ceremony, and flower arrangement.[47] Notwithstanding the diverse subjects of instruction, in reality the academy emphasized the Nisei's basic acquisition of Japanese. With students' being unable to understand the language, teachers indeed had a hard time explaining "the essential aspects of Japanese culture" or "the cause of our overseas development," with which Mizuho claimed it intended to inculcate Nisei.[48] Nevertheless, after completing the program many students moved on to regular Japanese higher schools and universities.

Although the preponderance of language instruction suggests the very practical orientation of Mizuho's education, the focus on martial arts—as well as civics and history classes—symbolized the valorization of the Japanese spirit in the school curriculum and pedagogy that resonated with the rising militarism of the time. Architects of Mizuho's nationalizing education, such as Takahashi Taiji, believed that *kendō* (Japanese swordsmanship) enabled male students to assimilate "the way of the warrior" (*bushidō*) through physical and mental exercise. *Kyūdō*, or Japanese archery, availed female students of gendered "training in the Japanese spirit, which made Nisei practitioners look just like reliable, valiant Japanese women in the defense of the home front."[49] Mizuho's school catalog boasted that the formal courses on, and the extracurricular activities in, these martial arts had successfully "stirred up the [Japanese] blood of Nisei."[50] By the same token, the teaching of traditional domestic arts was intended to implant and nurture in female students the unique cultural lens through which to "see the world in the Japanese way."[51] Mizuho's teachers highlighted the nationalizing effects of their pedagogy rather than students' intellectual development per se, celebrating such gains as "a major part of the goal of their study in Japan."[52] Colonel Soneda Kenji, an IEOJ board member and frequent lecturer at Mizuho, even insisted that Nisei students "should be taught to pray for (Shinto) gods, peace and prosperity of the nation, and . . . continued luck in the fortunes of war for [Japanese] soldiers on the [China] front." According to him, the daily practice of "worshipping the imperial palace" was also indispensable for the Nisei's "learning of the Japanese Way."[53] In Soneda's rendition, Nisei education at Mizuho should not simply be an attempt at nationalizing them; it was almost synonymous with their "imperialization," that is, making a full-fledged imperial subject out of a foreign-born youngster, including a Nisei US citizen. This assimilationist endeavor involving foreignized Japanese bore a striking resemblance to the simultaneous process that other unconventional members of the empire had undergone, that is, the well-studied example of Japan's attempt to imperialize colonized Koreans and Taiwanese (*kōminka*) through state-sanctioned education.

MILITARIST ATTEMPTS TO IMPERIALIZE
FOREIGN-BORN JAPANESE

Established in November 1937, the Imperial Way Institute (Hokubei Butokukai Kōdō Gakuin) embraced the goal of imperialization from the outset. Affiliated with an influential *kendō* organization of Japanese America called the North American Martial Virtue Society (Hokubei Butokukai; hereafter NAMVS), this modest boarding school fully conformed with the imperialist ideology of the time. Its pedagogy specifically valorized the role of *kendō* and its martial virtue in helping instill the national spirit in American Nisei. Whereas Mizuho Academy received full-scale support from the main body of Tokyo officialdom, the Imperial Way Institute enjoyed the patronage of the military branch of the government, as well as political groups associated with it. Smaller official financial subventions notwithstanding, the school crystallized the vision of Japan's military clique and the powerful ultra-right factions, which came to overshadow Japan's conventional political establishment toward the late 1930s. The school formed the Japan wing of a transpacific educational enterprise organized by Nakamura Tōkichi of California, a *kendō* master with close ties to leaders of the Black Dragon Society (Kokuryūkai: Amur River Society), colonial administrators in Korea, and military brass in Tokyo.[54] Since 1930 Nakamura had successfully built up a network of forty-one martial arts schools under NAMVS' umbrella—with over ten thousand Nisei members—throughout the American West, before this transnational endeavor.

Nakamura's school operations in Japanese America catered to the sense of urgency among Issei parents to provide their Nisei children with a Japanese-style moral education.[55] Informed simultaneously by immigrant nationalism and a pluralistic notion of American identity, first-generation immigrant parents wanted their US-born children to appreciate their cultural heritage and racial background positively while living as good American citizens. Because most Issei parents took it for granted that they were supposed to raise their Nisei sons and daughters as Americans despite their insistence on heritage learning, Nakamura was always careful not to contravene the wishes of his tuition-paying patrons even when he himself was principally concerned with transforming Americanized souls into self-conscious members of the homeland empire. Hence, instead of discussing *kendō*'s educational effects in terms of Japan's national interests in his public lectures, he usually portrayed the martial art as the most efficacious means to develop Nisei's moral character and enhance self-discipline, which immigrant parents deemed useful to make their children outstanding ethnic Americans. His shrewd pragmatism enabled Nakamura to downplay his conflicting agenda to his immigrant patrons while operating in the United States.[56] Yet at heart, Nakamura wanted to teach Nisei the primacy of uncompromising loyalty to the imperial throne and their ancestral land. And it seems that in informal conversations and during actual training, the *kendō* master did not hesitate to divulge his true vision and share it with his students and close associates. For example, one of Nakamura's Nisei protégés recalled him once berating her, demanding to know if she were seriously "willing to sacrifice the [interest of the] homeland for that empty thing (her U.S. citizenship)" when she insisted on her allegiance to her birth country.[57] Sensing his political intentions, the foreign ministry had a very negative opinion of Nakamura's US endeavors, because diplomats regarded him as an "agitator" who was supposedly manipulating "dumb immigrants" (and their impressionable children). From a diplomatic standpoint, Nakamura's "sensationalized utterances" could also disrupt US-Japanese bilateral relations, which were already strained since the Manchurian Incident of 1931.[58]

Nakamura's imperialist agenda was embodied in his personal trajectory, which sought to link up colonial Korea and Japanese America. Crisscrossing Japan's formal territories and a US immigrant settlement, his career as a colonial educator encompassed efforts to assimilate colonized Koreans in the 1920s and the NAMVS enterprise to imperialize Nisei during the 1930s. Prior to his relocation to California from Korea, Nakamura was deeply involved in the campaign to pacify Korean youths through Japanese martial arts under the aegis of the governor-general. He made a transpacific trip in 1929, initially intending to collect funds from US Japanese residents for his Korean venture. The *kendō* master, however, decided to switch his focus to educating Nisei in the American West after witnessing the sad state of "moral denigration" and the proliferation of excessive "materialism" among American-born Japanese. Nakamura was seriously perturbed by what he viewed as the perilous effects of "Americanization," and he was compelled to ponder the enormous task that these lost souls were supposed to shoulder for continuous racial development in white-dominated America. In harmony with Ōtsuka's pessimistic view of the assimilated Nisei, Nakamura believed that education based on the extolment of the national spirit was absolutely indispensable for transforming American-born youths into truly Japanese persons. Only then could they work with their racial compatriots elsewhere as credible agents of global Japanese expansion.[59]

Established in a Tokyo suburb, the Imperial Way Institute symbolized Nakamura's dream of offering selected Nisei a full-fledged Japanizing education without regard for conflicting expectations of Issei parents.[60] By 1937 Nakamura felt his American endeavor had generated sufficient interest in the serious learning of the Japanese spirit in significant cohorts of Nisei *kendō* enthusiasts, who would happily entertain the option of extended study abroad in their racial homeland. The time was ripe for moving the core of his educational endeavor from the American West to the home empire, where he would organize a special school for thorough imperialization of nationalist-minded Nisei. The *kendō* master first looked to obtain accreditation from the Japanese government for his institute as a formal higher school (equivalent to US high school and junior college). But following advice from his Tokyo supporters, Nakamura opted to start small, as a private boarding school equipped with *kendō* training facilities. Until a formal educational wing was set up, qualified Nisei students would attend regular Japanese schools elsewhere during the daytime, and those with an insufficient command of the language would receive individualized tutorials on the institute's premises. Morning and evening hours were devoted to vigorous martial arts practice under Nakamura and his associates. Between 1938 and 1940, the student body grew steadily, to more than seventy pupils at the peak.[61]

In order to marshal material and political backing for the Imperial Way Institute, Nakamura capitalized on his Korean connections, which included former and current colonial administrators, leaders of the imperial armed forces stationed there, and core members of the Black Dragon Society. These included such powerful connections as Army general and educational minister Araki Sadao; Admiral Katō Kanji; Black Dragon Society founder Tōyama Mitsuru; and Maruyama Tsuruo, former security head of colonial Korea and the chief of the National Police Agency of Japan. With Tōyama as honorary adviser, Nakamura requested that Maruyama assume the presidency of the institute. Together they managed to quickly rake in nearly 100,000 yen (about $25,000) from Japan's major corporations, which enabled Nakamura to acquire a nine-acre tract for future expansion. Many Issei patrons of NAMVS also pitched in with a large sum of donations from the United States, as they were led to believe Nakamura would simply assist Nisei in the study of culture and language in Tokyo.[62] But the Imperial Way Institute was not meant to serve the heritage learning of ethnic Americans. Illuminating his indiscriminate treatment of all foreign-born Japanese as imperial subjects, Nakamura made no distinction between US Nisei citizens and Japanese nationals. His institute indeed accepted a number of adolescents from Manchuria and Korea to live and study with those from the United States.[63] One year later, to mark the first anniversary of his institute, Nakamura publicly unveiled before Tokyo newspaper reporters a plan to built additional dormitories for Japanese pupils born in Manchuria and China, for "the control of the Asian continent requires [their mastering of] the Japanese spirit."[64]

Nakamura invited Ashizawa Hirozumi, an Issei language-school teacher and his close associate in California, to manage day-to-day teaching and school operations at the Imperial Way Institute. While the *kendō* master was busy marshaling political and financial support from right-wing demagogues and militarists in Japan, Ashizawa appears to have taken charge of pedagogical matters as the full-time director of instruction beginning in 1938. His writings provide a good glimpse into the school's operations and the key ideas that characterized its political orientation. Entitled *Nippon seishin to Jinbutsu yōsei* (Japanese spirit and character building), Ashizawa's book detailed his experience as an Issei teacher in an ethnic-language school in Auburn, California, during the 1920s; his realization of *kendō*'s power to transform American-born children after meeting Nakamura; and the expansionist educational philosophy that the two men had developed for Nisei— one that Japanese parents and educators of Manchuria, for example, "should refer to as a model," according to Ashizawa.[65]

The architect of the institute's academic program deemed it imperative for American Nisei to learn to "embrace the essence of the Imperial Rescript on Education" for the goal of "internalizing the strength of the Japanese race," that is, "the Japanese spirit."[66] While ostensibly acknowledging that US citizenship carried some degree of significance for Nisei, Ashizawa dwelled on the contingency of their allegiance to the birth country vis-à-vis the primacy of indivisible blood ties to their ancestral home. Not only would the learning of the Imperial Rescript expedite the Nisei's "internalizing" of the Japanese spirit, Ashizawa reasoned, it would also precondition their absolute dedication to the interests of their fatherland. The conventional pedagogy of language instruction, which tended to focus on the mechanics of writing and reading, did not suffice to dispel the erroneous understanding of the Japanese spirit as the epitome of Japan's aggression and duplicity—the view that was being rammed into the Nisei's heads by white American demagogues and Chinese propaganda. Because *kendō* supposedly embodied the moral foundation of the Imperial Rescript and the true essence of Japan's traditional ethics, including the pursuit of justice, loyalty, and filial piety, Nisei's immersion in the martial art would result in their recovering racial pride and national consciousness. At the Imperial Way Institute, Ashizawa devoted much of his *kendō* training and in-class lectures to the explanation of these precepts.[67]

In the political context of the late 1930s, this abstract pedagogical discussion boiled down to a very specific scenario. First, because the Imperial Rescript on Education directed "our subjects" to "offer yourselves courageously to the State" and to "guard . . . Our Imperial Throne," what Ashizawa and Nakamura called "spiritual education" would likely propel Nisei to revere the emperor no less than their own parents. Indeed, although Ashizawa's writing did not make an explicit connection, filial piety and reverence for race (with the emperor as the symbol) formed the foundational subjects in the institute's curriculum centered on the teaching of the Japanese spirit. Thus, Ashizawa instructed Nisei students to "pray in the direction of their [Issei] parents five thousand miles east of Japan" every morning and night, just as they revered the imperial throne.[68] Indeed, in addition to the extolment of filial piety, one of the anecdotes that Ashizawa recounted in his book as an example of the benefit of *kendō*-based education involved the dramatic metamorphosis of his Nisei pupils into virtual imperial subjects, who purportedly "became overwhelmed with irresistible joy to weep" when they caught a glimpse of the Japanese naval training squadron at San Francisco harbor. Another favorite episode was the story of a California Nisei girl who was said to have guarded a picture of the emperor at the risk of her own life when a local Japanese-language school was engulfed in flames. According to Ashizawa, these "rehabilitated" racial compatriots "needed no verbal cues" any longer; they were instinctively "moved by the call of the blood" to act according to the "Japanese" way.[69]

These were the kinds of foreign-born Japanese that the Imperial Way Institute also endeavored to produce systematically in the bosom of their racial home through its kendō-based education. Perhaps an example of a Nakamura publicity stunt, a Tokyo newspaper printed a contrived report of Nisei students who allegedly professed their desire to "return to the United States to stand on the frontlines of [our] struggle for racial self-determination" and "recount to our compatriots in America . . . spectacles of Japan's war efforts" for frontier development and peace in Manchuria and China.[70] When the statist vision of foreign-born Japanese education dominated Japan's discursive space following Ōtsuka's publication, it was extremely difficult for the Nisei seekers of heritage education to evade the clutches of imperialization. Contrary to the predictions, however, the call of blood caused more confusion than homogenization in their minds, as the students struggled as much as they could to safeguard their eclectic identity as Japanese Americans and maintain a sense of connection to their (other) home across the Pacific.[71]

As shown in this and previous chapters, the 1930s saw the elevation of Japanese America in Japan's state policy and public discourse, for its long-standing linkage to settler colonialism came to appear more and more relevant to the empire's destiny, which now banked on the success of mass migration to and family settlement in Manchuria. Just as the press, movie industry, and state collaboratively constructed a teleological "total history" of Japanese migration and overseas development, a wide array of social elites, statesmen, and educators, including many former Issei US residents, joined forces to put together a pedagogical philosophy and educational infrastructure through which to imperialize children of overseas Japanese residents. In this simultaneous unfolding, the two generations of Japanese America always occupied a central place—as the origin of the empire's progressive expansionist history, on the one hand, and as the first cohort of foreignized Japanese to be rehabilitated, on the other. Whereas the immigrant generation symbolized expansive Japan's past struggle and quest for its manifest destiny, the young Japanese American citizens personified the anticipated challenge for the nation and race to overcome in order to shine as a truly global empire in the coming era. Even long after US immigration exclusion went into effect, Japanese America remained a central historical reference—a yardstick of imperial Japan's colonial success or failure in the past, present, and future.

Yet it soon became all too evident, in the aftermath of Japan's attack on Pearl Harbor in 1941, that such a future was simply untenable. The empire's dogged efforts to imperialize American Nisei and other foreignized youngsters did not weather the Pacific War, which terminated the influx of new students from the Western Hemisphere and many other foreign regions. In June 1942 the Imperial Way Institute merged with the Central Association for Overseas Japanese after its remaining Nisei pupils had graduated from or left the school for war-related work. Repurposed as a "central training camp for overseas compatriots," the boarding school started to accept domestic Japanese "males with strong body and resolute will" who were "committed to the construction of Great East Asia" and willing to work as "directive leaders" of new Japanese settlements in military-occupied regions.[72] Mizuho Academy continued to operate, albeit increasingly with non-American Nisei until early 1945, but it experienced rapidly shrinking student enrollment. The eventual collapse of these state-backed Nisei education schemes during the Pacific War only foreshadowed the vanishing altogether of Japan's borderless colonial empire, whose future supposedly hinged on the reproduction of the next generation of settler-colonists at these and other similar schools.

In the final analysis, imperial Japan's desire to domesticate American citizens of Japanese ancestry also anticipated white America's decision to disown them as part of a racial enemy during the wartime mass incarceration. In the context of perennial inter-imperial intimacy, the contrasting actions of the two imperialist regimes paradoxically revealed a logical culmination of the "blood-will-tell" settler racism that they both had practiced. That intimacy explained other manifestations of parallel imperialism and racism in the United States and Japan during and even after the Pacific War, as documented in some studies.[73] Adaptive Japanese settler colonialism indeed survived the demise of Japan's borderless empire and its expansionist pedagogy and became neatly subsumed under US Cold War imperialism. And its "afterlife" still featured the brokering role of Japanese America, which not only assisted in training new colonists from Japan during the 1950s but also served as an indispensable partner in the postwar rearticulation of Japanese-style frontier conquest in South America through mass migration and agricultural settlement.[74]

Epilogue

The Afterlife of Japanese Settler Colonialism

This book has narrated the hitherto unknown history of Japanese America's role in the unfolding of Japan's settler colonialism within and without its formal empire before the Pacific War. In order to document the complex nature of these historical processes, this study has employed an inter-imperial framework that focused on US imperialism and its attempts to create a white-dominated North America and Pacific, and adaptive Japanese settler colonialism, which sought its own frontiers and a race-based, borderless empire. Not only has that framework critically examined colonial collusions between Japanese America and imperial Japan, but it has also illuminated points of divergence for Japanese between being a racial minority in a white settler society and being colonial overlords in their own racial empire. Immigrant residents and remigrants from the United States lived and traveled across these two contrasting spaces in the vast Pacific basin, equipped with their firsthand knowledge and US-bred expertise as frontier conquerors and civilization builders through agricultural colonization.

This book has delved into a constellation of ideas, practices, and decisions that were usually couched in the language of "overseas Japanese development." Acting on this elusive but enchanting concept, some members of Japanese America opted to move from the Anglo-Saxon controlled frontier to their monopolized sites of "racial development" under the rising sun flag; others acted as colonial investors and ideologues for imperial Japan while remaining in the United States. Despite many variations in individual stories and circumstances, there were certain common patterns and trajectories, which revolved around the central role of American frontier discourse. Integral to the discourse on overseas development, the idea of US-style frontier conquest was rendered, adapted, and transplanted by first-generation residents of and remigrants from Japanese America in Japan's colonial territories and areas of the Asia-Pacific basin under its influence, as well as various parts of Latin America. Indeed, as this book has narrated, Japanese settler colonialism continuously held the US historical precedent of agrarian settlement and frontier colonization as a principal point of reference. It portrayed the act of emigrating to and building a "new Japan" on foreign soil as nonviolent, progressive, and beneficial to the spread of modern civilization and the well-being of local inhabitants. Japanese settler colonialism was represented as one variety of "peaceful (national) expansion," which actually constituted an important half of Japanese imperialism and remained compatible with the aggressive territorial aggrandizement carried out simultaneously by state military force.

The problem of race, specifically that of racial struggle with white settlers and their hegemonic state, formed another important aspect of the manner in which Japanese America helped shape and facilitate Japanese settler colonialism, particularly its adaptability. National debates on Japan's expansionist destiny almost always entailed serious consideration of whether another colonial "master race"— especially Anglo-Saxons—was present in a site being considered for mass Japanese immigration and settlement. Many people had believed that the first such sites— the American West and Hawai'i—were lost due to exclusionist politics of white settlers backed by their racial supremacist republic(s) ever since returnees from San Francisco and Honolulu had disseminated that notion in Japan's public discourse during the early 1890s. Whereas Japan's formal colonial territories came to look like ideal "racism-free" frontiers to many Japanese settlers, including those remigrants from North America, such locations as Brazil and northern Mexico also drew keen attention. According to the social Darwinist view of the time, not only was there no rival race in those nations, but local inhabitants also were purportedly racially inferior to Japanese immigrant settlers. At the same time, the perils of racial exclusion, experienced and narrated by returnees from the United States, colored the ways in which imperial Japanese thought about their proper attitude toward their own colonized "natives." As exemplified in colonial Korea, assimilationist thinking was often propagated by former US residents, who embraced paternalistic benevolence toward "weaker" racial/ethnic groups while dismissing outright racial oppression as incompatible with Japan's standing as a truly superior, civilized race/nation, at least on the level of rhetoric.

Thus, with American frontier discourse and its quintessential New World frontier as central reference points, Japanese settler colonialism constantly mutated and adapted to different political economies and race/social relations inside or outside the formal empire. Its flexibility allowed for the coexistence of three schools of national expansionism, which advocated waves of mass emigration and colonization eastward, northward, or southward from the Japanese archipelago. And that flexibility also contributed to the blurring of multiple epistemological boundaries between being immigrants (*imin*) and being colonizers (*shokumin*), between out-of-sovereign foreign land and formal colonial territories, and between private colonial and state-sponsored enterprises. This supple orientation of settler colonialism rendered Japanese imperialism itself highly adaptive and transborder, making it possible to disguise itself at times as a form of "peaceful" penetration of superior civilization without the support of sovereign military force or political aggression. In other words, just as its American and European counterparts did, Japan's adaptive imperialism always carried two dimensions that might have looked rhetorically contradictory: military-led violent colonization and emigration-led unbelligerent colonization. The former has been well-studied in the existing literature on Japanese imperialism, but the latter has largely escaped serious scholarly analysis. By examining transpacific and borderless settler colonialism, this book has attempted to document that forgotten side of Japanese imperialism that extended outside the bounds of its sovereign and military power. This neglected transpacific imperial history is inseparable from the now fragmented and divergent narratives of foreignized/ethnicized Japanese immigrants (such as Japanese Americans or Japanese Brazilians) who have been placed beyond the pale of spatially defined Japanese studies.

An untold story of the Japanese American experience constitutes an equally important dimension of this book's narrative. A challenge to the domestic if not nationalist focus in the historiography, this book has revealed the transimperial context of Japanese American history in relation to the persistent mobility of US residents—their bodies, ideas, experiences, expertise, and money—across the Pacific in search of their own frontiers that still looked like California or Hawai'i. This story of remigration, resettlement, and colonial investment was punctuated by the surges of US exclusionist politics, which made members of Japanese America not only a US racial minority struggling against discrimination but also transborder frontier trotters pursuing the life of a colonial master. This book therefore has presented a global history of Japanese Americans beyond the narrow confines of US ethnic studies, which is usually driven by domestic civil rights agendas and the national teleology of becoming Americans. The question that this book's introduction posed about the elusive identities of Ōtsuki Kōnosuke and Yokokawa Shōzō may still require of readers as convoluted an answer as before they reached this point. But it should now be possible for them to disentangle domestic, transnational and translocal dimensions of these migrant-settlers' experiences in Japanese American history while linking the latter to their integral roles in the history of imperial Japan.

The adaptability of Japanese imperialism, especially its settler colonialism, anticipated the enduring legacy of prewar collusions between Japanese America and imperial Japan. Elements of the Japanese discourse on overseas development were able to survive the destruction of the formal colonial empire and the supposed demise of state imperialism in 1945. In the familiar language of peaceful expansion, progress, and civilization, prewar architects of agricultural colonization in Manchuria revived a postwar variety of settler colonialism shortly after the US military occupation.[1] Subsumed under Cold War US public diplomacy of the 1950s, the Japanese farm training program and the short-term agricultural worker program emerged as new ways of promoting Japan's national expansion through emigration and agricultural colonization in the New World frontiers. The American West and Brazil had occupied central places in Japanese settler colonialism since the late nineteenth century, and these quintessential frontiers yet again became the training ground for and the ultimate destination of postwar family settlers from Japan, respectively, for "the development of co-prosperous civilization . . . through the [peaceful] advance of Japanese agricultural techniques, not for an imperialistic colonial policy goal."[2]

Established in January 1952—months before the end of the postwar military occupation—the Association for International Collaboration of Farmers (AICF; Kokusai Nōyūkai) began an agriculturally oriented education abroad program in California for selected Japanese rural youths with the support of the US federal and California state governments. Intended to produce the next generation of pro-American grassroots leaders who would champion US "agricultural techniques [and] encourage democracy in [post-occupation] Japan," this program involved Nasu Shiroshi and Ishiguro Tadaatsu as core organizers.[3] During the 1930s these men had worked as key architects and masterminds of migration and colonization policies in Japan's puppet state, Manchukuo. A former professor of agricultural studies at Tokyo Imperial University, Nasu was once an academic expert for scientific agricultural colonization on imperial Japan's new frontier. As the vice minister of agriculture and forestry, Ishiguro was then a driving force to push through the policy blueprints that Nasu and his colleagues formulated within the military-dominated bureaucracy of the 1930s.[4] With a former US resident as his close partner, Ishiguro also had been personally involved in state-sponsored settler colonialism in Brazil before his work in Manchukuo. Therefore, Nasu and Ishiguro were deeply committed to the cause of Japan's global expansion when the empire was aggressively conquering its new frontiers before the Pacific War. Their embrace of California as the training ground for postwar Japanese settler colonialism may appear contradictory when considering their earlier critical stance toward Chiba Toyoji's advocacy of American-style "machine farming." But it actually exemplified a salient feature of their imperialism's adaptability. It explains the type of brazen opportunism that enabled many prewar Japanese elites to weather the turmoil of defeat by refashioning themselves as supporters of US-led "democratization" and the making of a nonmilitarist, peace-loving Japan—a new national identity that could still accommodate the long-standing idea of "peaceful (national) expansion." Like these architects of agricultural colonization in imperial Japan's former frontier, other founding members of the AICF were "surviving trailblazers of Manchurian colonization."[5]

To Nasu, Ishiguro, and their former colleagues in Manchuria, the agricultural education abroad program in California was an extension of their original colonialist "ideal."[6] The only difference was that this ideal was now being practiced under the aegis of Pax Americana, not under the ostensible banner of Japan's state imperialism. Yet Nasu still professed that he expected Japanese youths to assist agricultural and social "development" in China and Southeast Asia as well as Brazil after mastering American-style farming methods.[7] In his view, Japanese remained to be "leaders of the Asiatics," albeit now as America's junior partner in the region.[8] Backed by this vision, two dozen youths from rural Japan traveled to California as the very first group of postwar Japanese "emigrants" under the aegis of AICF in July 1952.

Another brainchild of Nasu and Ishiguro, the short-term Japanese agricultural worker program stemmed partially from the AICF's agricultural education abroad scheme.[9] While the latter only sent a few members of the rural elite, the former shipped thousands of ordinary rural Japanese for three years of farmwork in California. Although it was officially designated as a guest worker program, Nasu and Ishiguro viewed it as an expanded educational program to get young Japanese ready for future settlement in Brazil and other Latin American countries as frontier farmers. Japanese government officials—especially those in the agricultural ministry who had prewar ties to Manchurian colonization and/or used to work under Ishiguro—enthusiastically supported this view, depicting it as part of a free Japan's nonviolent contribution to progress and civilization in the postwar world. Moreover, in order to produce "peaceful emigrants that other countries can welcome" after the conclusion of a peace treaty, the Japanese foreign ministry had already set up an affiliated research bureau, which had commenced preparation for mass emigration to preexisting Japanese agricultural settlements in Brazil and Paraguay as early as April 1951.[10] As Brazil and some other countries in South America accepted new immigrants from Japan after late 1952, the California-based guest worker program indeed explicitly aspired to function as a training ground for many Latin America–bound emigrants under the control of Nasu and Ishiguro. Between 1956 and 1965, these men made it a priority to recruit farm labor applicants who clearly intended to "emigrate" to South America as "agricultural settlers" after returning from their work in California.[11] This brand of Japan's peaceful expansionism was placed firmly under the larger global program of US Cold War cultural diplomacy, and it was specifically designed to aid the US capitalist modernizationist effort in its hemispheric backyard in the general context of the fight against Communist encroachment and its collectivist developmentalism. This formed another prominent example of inter-imperial accommodations in postwar US-Japanese relations.

As in the prewar years, Japanese America was an eager partner in the establishment and operation of this two-step settler-colonist scheme disguised as a simple guest worker program. Based on his earlier AICF work, Nasu had cultivated a close partnership with some of the most influential Japanese American farmers in the Golden State. One was Kōda Keisaburō, the renowned "rice king" of California, who had directly supported imperial Japan's effort to start large-scale rice farming in China's Yellow River delta during the early 1940s.[12] Other Japanese American supporters of Nasu's project included Minami Yaemon and Etō Tameji; the former was known as California's "lettuce king," and the latter was a leading pea grower in the state.[13] In postwar Japanese America, these elderly immigrant farmers were revered community leaders, and they were more than happy to and actually did sponsor a large number of Japanese farmhands dispatched by Nasu's organization.[14]

Just as Nasu, Ishiguro, and their allies in postwar Japan and Japanese America desired, a not insignificant number of Japanese youths pursued a postwar variety of settler colonialism in South America after their on-the-job "training" for large-scale scientific farming in California. According to a 1961 report on returnees from the Golden State, a total of 135 people either had already emigrated or would be emigrating to Brazil, Paraguay, Argentina, and Venezuela with their families as agricultural colonists. After their work in California, these immigrant resettlers took part in the formation of transplanted Japanese farm villages in the frontier lands of South America. They constituted 11.6 percent of the aggregate 1,156 returnees from California as of 1961. Three years later, in another survey as many as ninety-seven Japanese guest workers expressed their desire to move to Japanese settlements in South America after completing their three-year contract in the Golden State.[15]

The complex mobility of these Japanese guest workers, and the colonialist visions that supported their decisions to migrate from North America to South America via Japan, elucidated the remnants of imperial Japan's settler colonialism—one that had adapted to new geopolitical realities of US imperial ascendancy. While that settler colonialism was revived by the likes of Nasu and Ishiguro, who survived the empire's demise, it was also nurtured by members of Japanese America who maintained a contrived self-identity as the pioneers of overseas national/racial development. Most other flag carriers of peaceful expansion, such as Takekawa Tōtarō, Satō Torajirō, Chiba Toyoji, and Okazaki Nihei, had died by the 1950s, just as Japan's state imperialism was no longer in the public eye. Yet many of the ideas and aspirations that they had embraced and practiced persisted in postwar manifestations of Japanese settler colonialism in South America. And the United States still figured largely as a source of inspiration, a central reference point, and an actual training ground for frontier conquest and racial supremacy in that settler colonialism—a postwar version of settler colonialism that portrayed itself as a symbol of peace-loving

Japan's contribution to the "development" of the "free" world under US military hegemony. This book has offered empirical explanations and theoretical paradigms for understanding the complex transpacific and transimperial histories of the entangled settler colonialism of Japanese America, imperial Japan, and the United States before 1945.

GLOSSARY OF JAPANESE NAMES: REMIGRANTS FROM THE CONTINENTAL UNITED STATES AND HAWAIʻI

Aoyagi Ikutarō 青柳郁太郎 (1867–1944)

Arai Tatsuya 荒井達弥 (1864–1922)

Ashizawa Hirozumi 芦沢碩純 (1895–?)

Awaya Man'ei 粟屋万衛 (1885–?)

Chiba Toyoji 千葉豊治 (1881–1944)

Fukuhara Hachirō 福原八郎 (1874–1943)

Hashimoto Umetarō 橋本梅太郎 (1871–1938)

Hinata Terutake 日向輝武 (1870–1918)

Inoue Keijirō 井上敬次郎 (1861–1947)

Ishibashi Usaburō 石橋禹三郎 (1869–1898)

Itō Yonejirō 伊東米次郎[米治郎] (1861–1942)

Masuda Kōichirō 増田幸一郎 (?–?)

Murai Yasukata 村井保固 (1854–1936)

Mutō Sanji 武藤山治 (1867–1934)

Nagao Yukusuke 長尾行介 (?–?)

Nagasawa Setsu [Betten] 長澤説 [別天] (1868–1899)

Nagata Shigeshi 永田稠 (1881–1973)

Nakamura Tōkichi 中村藤吉 (1887–1971)

Nakao Magoichi 中尾孫市 (1881–?)

Natori Jun'ichi 名取順一 (1901–1985)

Ohara Keisuke 小原啓介 (1885–1931)

Okazaki Nihei 岡崎仁平 (1883–1950)

Ōtsuka Yoshimi 大塚好 (1899–?)

Ōtsuki Kōnosuke 大槻幸之助 (1852–1931)

Saibara Seitō 西原清東 (1861–1939)

Satō Nobumoto 佐藤信元 (1887–?)

Satō Torajirō 佐藤虎次郎 (1864–1928)

Sugawara Tsutau 菅原伝 (1863–1937)

Sumida Tajirō 住田多次郎 (1882–1950)

Takahashi Taiji 高橋堆治 (1900–?)

Takekawa Tōtarō 竹川藤太郎 (1868–1911)

Uchino Raisuke 内野来助 (1879–?)

Wakabayashi Suteichi 若林捨一 (1890–1943)

Watanabe Kanjūrō 渡邊勘十郎 (1864–1926)

Watanabe Kinzō 渡邊金三 (1870–?)

Yokokawa Shōzō 横川省三 (1865–1904)

NOTES

INTRODUCTION

1. This memorial is now registered as a historical heritage site by Taiwan's Hualien County Cultural Affairs Bureau; see www.hccc.gov.tw/zh-tw/CulturalHeritage/Detail/137 (accessed 22 February 2019). On this instance of settler colonialism, consult Yamaguchi Masaji, *Higashi Taiwan kaihatsushi* (Taipei: Chūnichi Sankei Shijin, 1999), 165–172, 215–217; and Liao Gaoren, *Yue du Riben guan ying yi min cun* (Hualien: Fenglin Township Office, 2014), 76–85.

2. See Matsushima Shūē, *Resshi Yokokawa Shōzō* (Morioka: Resshi Yokokawa Shōzō Dōzō Kensetsukai, 1928); and Mantetsu Kōhōka, ed., *Yokokawa Shōzō bakuhakō* (Dalian: Manshū Nichinichi Shinbun, 1941).

3. On the early history of Japanese settler colonialism in Taiwan, see Akagi Takeichi, *Taiwan ni okeru Bokokujin nōgyō shokumin* (Taipei: Taiwan Sōtokufu Shokusan-kyoku, 1929), 2–36; Kurihara Jun, "Taiwan Sōtokufu ni yoru kan'ei imin jigyō ni tsuite," in *Chūgoku minshū e no shiza*, ed. Kanagawa Daigaku Chūgokugo Gakka (Tokyo: Tōhō Shoten, 1998), 161–184; and Aratake Tatsurō, "Nihon tōchi jidai Taiwan tōbu e no imin to sōshutsuchi," *Tokushima Daigaku Sōgō Kagakubu ningen shakai bunka kenkyū* 14 (2007), 91–104.

4. Matsukuma Toshiko, *Fumetsu no isan* (Tokyo: Tōgasha, 1987), 61–62, 90–91, 97–98; and Kawazoe Zen'ichi, *Imin hyakunen no nenrin* (Honolulu: Imin Hyakunen no Nenrin Kankōkai, 1968), 95–97.

5. Matsushima, *Resshi Yokokawa Shōzō*, 83–89; and Mantetsu Kōhōka, *Yokokawa Shōzō bakuhakō*, 32–35.

6. See Patrick Wolfe, "Settler Colonialism and the Elimination of the Native," *Journal of Genocide Research* 8, no. 4 (December 2006), 387–388.

7. The following work provides an insightful discussion of *imin* and *shokumin*. See Shiode Hiroyuki, *Ekkyōsha no seijishi* (Nagoya: Nagoya Daigaku Shuppankai, 2015), 1–23.

8. Patrick Wolfe, *Settler Colonialism and the Transformation of Anthropology* (London: Cassell, 1999), 163; Lorenzo Veracini, *Settler Colonialism: A Theoretical Overview* (Basingstoke: Palgrave Macmillan U.K., 2010), 8; and Caroline Elkins and Susan Pedersen, "Introduction, Settler Colonialism: A Concept and Its Uses," in *Settler Colonialism in the Twentieth Century*, ed. Caroline Elkins and Susan Pedersen (New York: Routledge, 2005), 2–3.

9. For example, whereas California had ruling white settlers and minoritized Mexicans, Chinese, and Native Americans at the time of Japanese mass immigration, Taiwan was populated with Hakka Chinese and aboriginals, as well as Han Chinese, including recent immigrants from Fujian and Guangdong, under Japanese colonial rule. On the binary colonial race relations in Hokkaido, see Katsuya Hirano, "Thanatopolitics in the Making of Japan's Hokkaido: Settler Colonialism and Primitive Accumulation," *Critical Historical Studies* 2, no. 2 (Fall 2015), 191–218, esp. 196–197. Hirano examines how the "politics of death" served as the main modus operandi of settler colonialism in Hokkaido, whose "masterless land" was rather sparsely populated with Ainu people before the coming of armed Japanese settlers. However, most other sites of Japanese immigration and community building did not fit that description.

10. Hyung Gu Lynn, "Malthusian Dreams, Colonial Imaginary: The Oriental Development Company and Japanese Emigration to Korea," in Elkins and Pedersen, *Settler Colonialism in the Twentieth Century*, 32.

11. The following studies look into the entanglements of imperial Japan and Japanese America, although many do not explicitly discuss settler colonialism. See Emily Anderson, *Christianity and Imperialism in Modern Japan: Empire for God* (London: Bloomsbury Publishing, 2014), 95–121, 217–237; Kenneth J. Ruoff, *Imperial Japan at Its Zenith: The Wartime Celebration of the Empire's 2,600th Anniversary* (Ithaca, NY: Cornell University Press, 2010), 148–179; Sayuri Guthrie-Shimizu, *Transpacific Field of Dreams: How Baseball Linked the United States and Japan in Peace and War* (Chapel Hill: University of North Carolina Press, 2012); Sidney Xu Lu, "Colonizing Hokkaido and the Origin of Japanese Trans-Pacific Expansion, 1869–1894," *Japanese Studies* 36, no. 2 (2016), 251–274; Sidney Xu Lu, *The Making of Japanese Settler Colonialism: Malthusianism and Trans-Pacific Migration, 1868–1961* (New York: Cambridge University Press, 2019); Jun Uchida, "From Island Nation to Oceanic Empire: A Vision of Japanese Expansion from the Periphery," *Journal of Japanese Studies* 42, no. 1 (2016), 57–90; Martin Dusinberre, *Hard Times in the Hometown: A History of Community Survival in Modern Japan* (Honolulu: University of Hawai'i Press, 2012), esp. 83–116; John J. Stephan, *Hawaii under the Rising Sun: Japan's Plans for Conquest after Pearl Harbor* (Honolulu: University of Hawaii Press, 1984); Yuji Ichioka, *The Issei: The World of the First Generation Japanese Immigrants, 1885–1924* (New York: Free Press, 1988); Eiichiro Azuma, *Between Two Empires: Race, History, and Transnationalism in Japanese America* (New York: Oxford University Press, 2005); and Takashi Fujitani, *Race for Empire: Koreans as Japanese and Japanese as Americans during World War II* (Berkeley: University of California Press, 2011). For older, less-sophisticated treatment of the subject, see Hilary Conroy, *The Japanese Frontier in Hawaii, 1868–1898* (Berkeley: University of California Press, 1953); and Alan Takeo Moriyama, *Imingaisha: Japanese Emigration Companies and Hawaii, 1894–1908* (Honolulu: University of Hawaii Press, 1985).

12. A notable exception is an edited volume by Caroline Elkins and Susan Pedersen, which interrogates the operation of settler colonialism in Europe, East Asia, Africa, and the

Middle East. See Elkins and Pedersen, eds., *Settler Colonialism in the Twentieth Century* (New York: Routledge, 2005). The vast majority of English-language case studies are still Anglocentric, with a focus on North America/Hawai'i, Oceania, and South Africa, though some works extend the scope of research to other parts of Africa and Israel/Palestine. For example, see Z. Laidlaw and Alan Lester, eds., *Indigenous Communities and Settler Colonialism: Land Holding, Loss and Survival in an Interconnected World* (Basingstoke: Palgrave Macmillan U.K., 2015); Annie E. Coombes, ed., *Rethinking Settler Colonialism: History and Memory in Australia, Canada, Aotearoa New Zealand and South Africa* (Manchester, UK: Manchester University Press, 2006); and Patrick Wolfe, *Traces of History: Elementary Structures of Race* (London: Verso, 2016). Theorization of settler colonialism has followed suit with a heavily Anglocentric slant. For representative works, see Wolfe, *Settler Colonialism and the Transformation of Anthropology*, esp. 1–9, 163; Veracini, *Settler Colonialism*; and Lorenzo Veracini, "'Settler Colonialism': Career of a Concept," *Journal of Imperial and Commonwealth History* 41, no. 2 (2013), 313–333, esp. 324–325.

13. On Asian settler colonialism in Hawai'i, see Candice Fujikane and Jonathan Y. Okamura, eds., *Asian Settler Colonialism: From Local Governance to the Habits of Everyday Life in Hawai'i* (Honolulu: University of Hawai'i Press, 2008).

14. See Jun Uchida, *Brokers of Empire: Japanese Settler Colonialism in Korea, 1876–1945* (Cambridge, MA: Harvard University Asia Center, 2011); Emer O'Dwyer, *Significant Soil: Settler Colonialism and Japan's Urban Empire in Manchuria* (Cambridge, MA; Harvard University Press, 2015); Anderson, *Christianity and Imperialism in Modern Japan*, esp. 217–237; Lu, "Colonizing Hokkaido and the Origin of Japanese Trans-Pacific Expansion"; Lu, *The Making of Japanese Settler Colonialism*; and Hirano, "Thanatopolitics in the Making of Japan's Hokkaido." For older works on migration and colonialism, see Mark R. Peattie, *Nan'yo: The Rise and Fall of the Japanese in Micronesia, 1885–1945* (Honolulu: University of Hawai'i Press, 1988); Louise Young, *Japan's Total Empire: Manchuria and the Culture of Wartime Imperialism* (Berkeley: University of California Press, 1998); and Sandra Wilson, "The 'New Paradise': Japanese Emigration to Manchuria in the 1930s and 1940s," *International History Review* 17, no. 2 (May 1995), 249–286. Although Anderson and Wilson explicitly look at rural dimensions of settler colonialism, most other studies tend to focus on urban/professional/commercial migrants and settlers.

15. The notable exceptions are Anderson, *Christianity and Imperialism in Modern Japan*; Lu, "Colonizing Hokkaido and the Origin of Japanese Trans-Pacific Expansion"; and Lu, *The Making of Japanese Settler Colonialism*.

16. On the compartmentalization of migration studies and colonial studies between US ethnic studies and Asian area studies, see Eiichiro Azuma, "Pioneers of Overseas Japanese Development: Japanese American History and the Making of Expansionist Orthodoxy in Imperial Japan," *Journal of Asian Studies* 67, no. 4 (November 2008), 1187–1191. On the Asian Americanist rationale for maintaining the disciplinary divides in light of persistent academic Orientalism, see Shirley Hune, "Asian American Studies and Asian Studies: Boundaries and Borderlands of Ethnic Studies and Area Studies," in *Color-Line to Borderlands: The Matrix of American Ethnic Studies*, ed. Johnnella E. Butler (Seattle: University of Washington Press, 2001), 227–239.

17. On how US history and Asian history spatially organized and dichotomized the domains of academic research into the northeastern and northwestern Pacific, see Eiichiro Azuma, "Is There the Pacific?," *Amerasia Journal* 42, no. 3 (2016), 7–11.

18. On the concept of inter-imperial relations, see Augusto Espiritu, "Inter-Imperial Relations, the Pacific, and Asian American History," *Pacific Historical Review* 83, no. 2 (May 2014), 238–254; and Azuma, *Between Two Empires*, esp. 5–7.

19. Anne Laura Stoler, "Tense and Tender Ties: The Politics of Comparison in North American History and (Post) Colonial Studies," in *Haunted by Empire: Geographies of Intimacy in North American History*, ed. Anne Laura Stoler (Durham, NC: Duke University Press, 2006), 55.

20. The bustling field of "Atlantic history" has produced many such studies, especially around themes such as slavery, migration, and settler colonialism. In the Pacific context, Paul A. Kramer offers perhaps the best historical case study of "compounded colonialisms" between Britain and the United States around the turn of the twentieth century. See Kramer, "Empires, Exceptions, and Anglo-Saxons: Race and Rule between the British and American Empires, 1880–1910," *Journal of American History* 88, no. 1 (March 2002), 1315–1353; and Kramer, *The Blood of Government: Race, Empire, the United States, and the Philippines* (Chapel Hill: University of North Carolina Press, 2006).

21. Robert Thomas Tierney, *Tropics of Savagery: The Culture of Japanese Empire in Comparative Frame* (Berkeley: University of California Press, 2010), 14–22. The quote is from page 18. Earlier works on Japanese imperialism emphasized its "imitation" of Western precedents and examples, often suggesting its "inferior" nature or "deviations." See, for example, Peter Duus, *The Abacus and the Sword: The Japanese Penetration of Korea, 1895–1910* (Berkeley: University of California Press, 1995), 1–23. Many other studies are more subtle in disseminating a view similar to Duus's, but they also generally underscore the imitated and/or incomplete nature of Japanese imperial practices. For examples of old and new works that still reveal a Eurocentric bias, see Ramon H. Myer and Mark R. Peattie, eds., *The Japanese Colonial Empire, 1895–1945* (Princeton, NJ: Princeton University Press, 1984); and S.C.M. Paine, *The Japanese Empire: Grand Strategy from the Meiji Restoration to the Pacific War* (Cambridge, UK: Cambridge University Press, 2017). Most of the recent works on Japanese imperialism avoid the trappings of a Eurocentric framing, and the following books particularly offer a powerful challenge to it: Uchida, *Brokers of Empire*, 1–27; Anderson, *Christianity and Imperialism in Modern Japan*, 6–15; Tierney, *Tropics of Savagery*, 1–34; and Paul D. Barclay, *Outcasts of Empire: Japan's Rule on Taiwan's "Savage Border," 1874–1945* (Berkeley: University of California Press, 2018), 11–15.

22. Mark. I. Choate, *Emigrant Nation: The Making of Italy Abroad* (Cambridge, MA: Harvard University Press, 2008), 167–168, 180, 222–223. The quotes are from pages 167–168 and 180. A recent work by James Q. Whitman examines the American influence on the racist legal regime of Nazi Germany. An exchange and mutual learning of settler colonial knowledge and agricultural techniques appear to have existed between the United States (North America) and imperial/Soviet Russia as well. See James Q. Whitman, *Hitler's American Model: The United States and the Making of Nazi Race Law* (Princeton, NJ: Princeton University Press, 2017); and David Moon, "In the Russians' Steppes: The Introduction of Russian Wheat on the Great Plains of the United States of America," *Journal of Global History* 3, no. 2 (July 2008), 203–225. Many thanks to Peter I. Holquist for alerting me to these Russian connections.

23. Tierney, *Tropics of Savagery*, 18.

24. Prewar Japanese learned different things from different imperial archetypes and precedents. When it comes to the question of national expansion and progress through migration, settlement, and agrarian colonization, the United States stood as *the* main reference point and inspiration in Japanese imperialist discourse.

25. On the critique of these categories as givens, see Ann Laura Stoler, "Rethinking Colonial Categories: European Communities and the Boundaries of Rule," *Comparative Studies in Society and History* 31, no. 1 (January 1989), 134–161.

26. On the colonized Egyptian of the late nineteenth century who "could aspire to be a colonizer" to his former Sudanese subject within the "fluid relationship" that British colonialism established in the post-Ottoman era, see Eve M. Troutt Powell, *A Different Shade of Colonialism: Egypt, Great Britain, and the Mastery of the Sudan* (Berkeley: University of California Press, 2003), 8, 14. On African Americans' migration and (re)settlement in Liberia and their "civilizing" role there, see Claude Andrew Clegg III, *The Price of Liberty: African Americans and the Making of Liberia* (Chapel Hill: University of North Carolina Press, 2004); Kenneth C. Barnes, *Journey of Hope: The Back-to-Africa Movement in Arkansas in the late 1800s* (Chapel Hill: University of North Carolina Press, 2004); and Amos J. Beyan, *African American Settlements in West Africa: John Brown Russwurm and the American Civilizing Efforts* (New York: Palgrave, 2005).

27. See Ann Laura Stoler, *Race and the Education of Desire: Foucault's History of Sexuality and the Colonial Order of Things* (Durham, NC: Duke University Press, 1995), 16, 53, 97, 99–100; and Kramer, "Empires, Exceptions, and Anglo-Saxons," 1319.

28. Uchida, *Brokers of Empire*, 12–15.

29. On the special preference top colonial officials in Taiwan exhibited for British administrative methods, see Adam Clulow, "British Influence on the Formation of Colonial Policy in Taiwan: The Impact of Montague Kirkwood's 1898 Report" (unpublished paper provided by author, n.d.); Edward I. Chen, "Goto Shimpei, Japan's Colonial Administrator in Taiwan: A Critical Reexamination," *American Asian Review* 13, no. 1 (Spring 1995), 29–59; Yoichi Kibata, "British and Japanese Colonial Rule in Comparison," *Proceedings of the Department of Foreign Languages and Literature, University of Tokyo*, 42, no. 3 (1995), 56–74; and Lung-chih Chang, "From Island Frontier to Imperial Colony: Qing and Japanese Sovereignty Debates and Territorial Projects in Taiwan, 1874–1906" (PhD diss., Harvard University, 2003), 168–176, 181–182. On Gotō's "followership," see also Barclay, *Outcasts of Empire*, 25–26.

30. Choate, *Emigrant Nation*, 169–180. The quotes are from pages 172 and 180.

31. David Moon, *The Plough That Broke the Steppes: Agriculture and Environment on Russia's Grasslands, 1700–1914* (Oxford: Oxford University Press, 2013), 285.

32. See David M. Wrobel, *Global West, American Frontier: Travel, Empire, and Exceptionalism from Manifest Destiny to the Great Depression* (Albuquerque: University of New Mexico Press, 2013), 3–5.

33. Fukuzawa Yukichi, "Sekai kuni zukushi" (1869), in *Fukuzawa Yukichi zenshū*, ed. Keiō Gijuku (Tokyo: Iwanami Shoten, 1959), 2:636–637. He visited the United States in 1860 as a member of the Tokugawa Shogunate's first diplomatic mission.

34. Fukuzawa, "Sekai kuni zukushi," 636.

35. Fukuzawa, "Sekai kuni zukushi," 637.

36. Fumiko Fujita, *American Pioneers and the Japanese Frontier: American Experts in Nineteenth-Century Japan* (Westport, CT: Greenwood Press, 1994), 7–8, 15–41; Hirano, "Thanatopolitics in the Making of Japan's Hokkaido," 200–203; Lu, "Colonizing Hokkaido and the Origin of Japanese Trans-Pacific Expansion," 258–261; and Lu, *The Making of Japanese Settler Colonialism*, ch. 1.

37. See Hirano, "Thanatopolitics in the Making of Japan's Hokkaido," 202. The subsequent acquisition of Taiwan, the Kwantung Leased Territory (southern Manchuria), southern Sakhalin, Korea, Micronesia (the Nan'yō), and Japan's puppet regime "Manchukuo" resulted in state-led developmentalist policies and programs that were not dissimilar to the Hokkaido precedent—which featured mass migration, family settlement, and agricultural colonization—albeit with a different degree of success.

38. Anders Stephanson, *Manifest Destiny: American Expansion and the Empire of Right* (New York: Hill and Wang, 1996), 66–112.

39. See Genkakusei [pseud.], "Tōyō ni okeru bōchōteki kokumin to shukushō kokumin," *Nihonjin* 30 (5 November 1896), 38–39; Nagasawa Betten, "Yankii" (1893), in *Seikyōsha Bungakushū*, ed. Matsumoto Sannosuke (Tokyo: Chikuma Shobō, 1980), 316–342; and Takayama Rintarō, "Shokuminteki kokumin to shiteno Nihonjin," *Taiyō* 5, no. 6 (20 March 1899), 48–55.

40. See Akira Iriye, *Pacific Estrangement: Japanese and American Expansion, 1897–1911* (Cambridge, MA: Harvard University Press, 1972), 131.

41. Elkins and Pedersen, "Introduction, Settler Colonialism," 2. Imperial Russians also claimed a supposedly benevolent, gentle, and nonracist character for their settler colonialism and assimilationism. See Willard Sunderland, *Taming the Wild Field: Colonization and Empire on the Russian Steppe* (Ithaca, NY: Cornell University Press, 2004), esp. 55–95.

42. See Roger Daniels, *The Politics of Prejudice: The Anti-Japanese Movement in California and the Struggle for Japanese Exclusion* (Berkeley: University of California Press, 1999).

43. On the intersections of these tridirectional migration patterns and the advocacy for them, see Lu, "Colonizing Hokkaido and the Origin of Japanese Trans-Pacific Expansion," 260–267; and Uchida, "From Island Nation to Oceanic Empire," 58, 69–77, 81. On migration histories of southward and continental expansionisms, see Peattie, *Nan'yo*; and Young, *Japan's Total Empire*.

44. This lack of attention to the complex nexus between race and ethnicity (or their nuanced differences) is not uncommon even in recent works on colonial relations between Japanese and their East Asian subjects. Scholars have tended to focus on political, economic, legal, and social aspects of historical formation in the Japanese empire, and when they discuss matters relating to race/ethnicity, they usually wrap their narratives around the more encompassing analytics of "culture," often at the cost of specificities of Japan's colonial race politics or its entanglement with other imperial racisms. This is prevalent in the studies of colonial assimilation in Korea, even among some of the most sophisticated works to date. For example, Todd A. Henry's study of colonial Seoul occasionally discusses "racist" Japanese practices in their assimilation programs, but he does so without addressing how those practices were related to "ethnic" differences that he also implies throughout the book. Mark E. Caprio devotes little to no attention to the question of race/ethnicity, simply reducing it to "cultural" aspects of Japan's assimilation policies. See Todd A. Henry, *Assimilating*

Seoul: Japanese Rule and the Politics of Public Space in Colonial Korea, 1910–1945 (Berkeley: University of California Press, 2014), esp. 39, 147, 153–154; and Mark E. Caprio, *Japanese Assimilation Policies in Colonial Korea, 1910–1945* (Seattle: University of Washington Press, 2009). Although it may reflect a view of the translator more than that of the author, Eiji Oguma's translated work on heterogeneity in the Japanese nation and empire tends to illuminate "ethnicity" (*minzoku*) more than "race" even when he often discusses ideas of blood ties and lineages. In the Japanese version of this book, Oguma does not (have to) delve into the problem of race versus ethnicity in relation to the all-encompassing term *minzoku*. See Eiji Oguma, *A Genealogy of Japanese Self-Images*, trans. David Askew (Melbourne, Australia: Trans Pacific Press, 2003). On minority experiences in Japan as "race" issues, see Michael Weiner, ed., *Japan's Minorities: The Illusion of Homogeneity* (New York: Routledge, 1997); and Michael Weiner, *Race and Migration in Imperial Japan* (New York: Routledge, 1994), esp. 7–37.

45. Paying attention to the dynamic relations or "intersectionality" of race and ethnicity (instead of seeing them as separate or detached analytics) is theoretically useful and productive, especially when one considers the slippery Japanese words/concepts of *jinshu* and *minzoku*, which are often mechanically translated as "race" and "ethnicity"/"culture"/"nation," respectively. Whereas prewar Japanese generally employed the term *jinshu* specifically when they referred to a (pseudo)biological definition of group difference, they used *minzoku* very flexibly and loosely. Depending on the context, it could mean "nation," "ethnicity," or even "race," as the phrase *Yamato minzoku* sometimes is translated as the "Yamato race." In this book I translate *minzoku* as race (or racialized ethnicity/nation) when a primary source stresses the difference in lineages, bloodlines, or physiological features; in other contexts, I may translate the term as ethnicity or nation. On a useful discussion of this matter, see Michael Weiner, "Discourses of Race, Nation, and Empire in Pre-1945 Japan," *Ethnic and Racial Studies* 18, no. 3 (July 1995), 433–456; and Tessa Morris-Suzuki, *Re-Inventing Japan: Nation, Culture, Identity* (New York: Routledge, 1998), 5–8, 79–108.

46. Azuma, *Between Two Empires*, ch. 2.

47. On pan-Asianism, see Eri Hotta, *Pan-Asianism and Japan's War, 1931–1945* (New York: Palgrave Macmillan, 2007); Uchida, "From Island Nation to Oceanic Empire," 69–77; Prasenjit Duara, "Between Empire and Nation: Settler Colonialism in Manchukuo," in Elkins and Pedersen, *Settler Colonialism in the Twentieth Century*, 59–78; and Cemil Aydin, *The Politics of Anti-Westernism in Asia: Visions of World Order in Pan-Islamic and Pan-Asian Thought* (New York: Columbia University Press, 2007), 39–189.

48. On this articulation of assimilation policy in imperial Japan, see Hirano, "Thanatopolitics in the Making of Japan's Hokkaido," 210–215, 218; and Barclay, *Outcasts of Empire*, 30–31, 136–155. While Hirano discusses Japan's "liberal humanist" racism and its "assimilationist [and yet simultaneously] eliminationist politics" against the indigenous Ainu people, Barclay examines colonial Taiwan's "polite racism" and its disciplinary measures, including "compulsory assimilation programs." See also Leo T.S. Ching, *Becoming Japanese: Colonial Taiwan and the Politics of Identity Formation* (Berkeley: University of California Press, 2001), esp. 89–131.

49. On this "hemispheric Orientalism," see Erika Lee, "The 'Yellow Peril' and Asian Exclusion in the Americas," *Pacific Historical Review* 76, no. 4 (November 2007), 537–562.

50. Marilyn Lake and Henry Reynolds, *Drawing the Global Colour Line: White Men's Countries and the International Challenge of Racial Equality* (Cambridge, UK: Cambridge University Press, 2008); David C. Atkinson, *The Burden of White Supremacy: Containing Asian Migration in the British Empire and the United States* (Chapel Hill: University of North Carolina Press, 2016); Kornel Chang, *Pacific Connections: The Making of U.S.-Canadian Borderlands* (Berkeley: University of California Press, 2012); Gerald Horne, *Race War! White Supremacy and the Japanese Attack on the British Empire* (New York: New York University Press, 2005); and Naoko Shimazu, *Japan, Race and Equality: The Racial Equality Proposal of 1919* (London: Routledge, 1998), 13–37, 68–88, 137–163, esp. 30–31, 115–119.

1. IMMIGRANT FRONTIERSMEN IN AMERICA AND THE ORIGINS OF JAPANESE SETTLER COLONIALISM

1. Ishida Kumajirō, *Kitare Nihonjin* (Tokyo: Kaishindō, 1887), 5.

2. Ishida, *Kitare Nihonjin*, 5–6.

3. On Japan's state-sponsored Hokkaido colonization as an origin of transpacific Japanese migration and expansion, see Sidney Xu Lu, "Colonizing Hokkaido and the Origin of Japanese Trans-Pacific Expansion, 1869–1894," *Japanese Studies* 36, no. 2 (2016), 251–274.

4. In her study of Ōmi merchants and their ideological supporter Sugiura Shigetake (Jūgō) in the late nineteenth century, Jun Uchida describes southward expansionism as a vision and an attempt to construct a "maritime empire." See Jun Uchida, "From Island Nation to Oceanic Empire: A Vision of Japanese Expansion from the Periphery," *Journal of Japanese Studies* 42, no. 1 (2016), 57–90. On southward expansionism, see Mark R. Peattie, *Nan'yo: The Rise and Fall of the Japanese in Micronesia, 1885–1945* (Honolulu: University of Hawai'i Press, 1988), 15–20.

5. See especially Jun Uchida, *Brokers of Empire: Japanese Settler Colonialism in Korea, 1876–1945* (Cambridge, MA: Harvard University Press, 2011); Emer O'Dwyer, *Significant Soil: Settler Colonialism and Japan's Urban Empire in Manchuria* (Cambridge, MA: Harvard University Press, 2015); and Louise Young, *Japan's Total Empire: Manchuria and the Culture of Wartime Imperialism* (Berkeley: University of California Press, 1999). The following works are also useful: Peter Duus, *The Abacus and the Sword: The Japanese Penetration of Korea, 1895–1910* (Berkeley: University of California Press, 1995); and Peattie, *Nan'yo*.

6. English-language scholarship on Japanese imperialism (or colonialism) tends to focus on specific regions of the formal Japanese empire and its de facto territories. Korea and Manchuria have by far attracted the greatest amount of scholarly attention. Corresponding with preponderant interest in the colonial era among modern Korean historians, studies of Korea under imperial Japan are too numerous to list, but only a few works—referenced in note 5—deal seriously with Japanese immigration and settler colonialism, the questions that have been obscured under an emphasis on popular culture and (forced) Korean migration to the colonial metropolis and beyond. Louise Young, also mentioned in note 5, sheds light on the role of Japanese immigration and agricultural colonization in 1930s Manchuria. English-language studies of (settler) colonialism in Taiwan, the Nan'yō, and Sakhalin are not as readily available. For a few noteworthy works, consult Paul D. Barclay, *Outcasts of Empire: Japan's Rule on Taiwan's "Savage Border," 1874–1945* (Berkeley:

University of California Press, 2018); Leo T. S. Ching, "*Becoming Japanese*": *Colonial Taiwan and the Politics of Identity Formation* (Berkeley: University of California Press, 2001); Peattie, *Nan'yo*; and Tessa Morris-Suzuki, "Northern Lights: The Making and Unmaking of Karafuto Identity," *Journal of Asian Studies* 60, no. 3 (August 2001), 645–671. None of these works looks into the intersections of transpacific expansion with the state-guided manifestations of Japanese imperialism and colonial expansion. Recently, Emily Anderson and Sidney Xu Lu have explicitly examined such linkages. See Emily Anderson, *Christianity and Imperialism in Modern Japan: Empire for God* (London: Bloomsbury Publishing, 2014); and Sidney Xu Lu, *The Making of Japanese Settler Colonialism: Malthusianism and Trans-Pacific Migration, 1868–1961* (New York: Cambridge University Press, 2019).

7. See Matthew Frye Jacobson, *Barbarian Virtues: The United States Encounters Foreign Peoples at Home and Abroad, 1876–1917* (New York: Hill and Wong, 2001), 15–57.

8. Coined by Kenneth Pyle, the phrase "new generation of Meiji Japan" refers to Japanese youth who spent their formative school years during the 1870s and early 1880s under the influence of wholesale westernization. Thoroughly modernized in consciousness and thinking, many individuals of this generation simultaneously developed skepticism of, if not outright hostility toward, the slighting of national tradition and identity compounded by their teachers' generation. From among these youths emerged Japan's first modern "nationalists," who were often dubbed "Japanists" (*Nihon shugisha*), including Japan's early expansionists. See Kenneth B. Pyle, *The New Generation in Meiji Japan: Problems in Cultural Identity, 1885–1895* (Stanford, CA: Stanford University Press, 1969).

9. Michael Weiner writes that "the heterogeneity of [the] ideological terrain . . . made possible the construction of a Japanese nation and national identity," while Peter Duus more specifically points out the importance of this heterogeneity in the formation of Japanese colonialism. In his words, "[t]o understand any particular case of imperialist expansion, we must disaggregate the imperialist coalition. . . . Meiji imperialism, and more specifically expansion into Korea, was the product of a complex coalition uniting the Meiji leaders, backed and prodded by a chorus of domestic politicians, journalists, businessmen, and military leaders, with a subimperialist Japanese community in Korea." Duus's contention—one that Jun Uchida pushed even further—is very important, because this book also stresses the involvement and often leading role of US-based Japanese immigrant expansionists in developing ideology. See Michael Weiner, "Discourses of Race, Nation, Empire in Pre-1945 Japan," *Ethnic and Racial Studies* 18, no. 3 (July 1995), 454; and Duus, *Abacus and the Sword*, 23. See also Uchida, *Brokers of Empire*; and Carol Gluck, *Japan's Modern Myths: Ideology in the Late Meiji Period* (Princeton, NJ: Princeton University Press, 1985), 248.

10. On Fukuzawa's thought and role in early Meiji Japan, see Carmen Blacker, *The Japanese Enlightenment: A Study of the Writings of Fukuzawa Yukichi* (Cambridge, UK: Cambridge University Press, 1964); and Albert Craig, "Fukuzawa Yukichi: The Political Foundations of Meiji Nationalism," in *Political Development in Modern Japan*, ed. Robert E. Ward (Princeton, NJ: Princeton University Press, 1973), 99–148.

11. Fukuzawa Yukichi, "Aete kokyō o sare," 30 May 1884, in *Fukuzawa Yukichi zenshū* (hereafter *FYZ*) (Tokyo: Iwanami Shoten, 1932), 9:525–528; and Fukuzawa, "Kin'i nanzo kanarazushimo kokyō ni kazaran," 19 November 1885, in *FYZ*, 10:469.

12. Fukuzawa, *Seiyō tabi annai*, 1867, in *FYZ*, 2:146. He was an official translator to the samurai delegates who traveled to Washington, DC via San Francisco.

13. A number of Fukuzawa's commentaries on emigration appeared in bulk again after the Sino-Japanese War. These writings emphasized mass migration and a teleological notion of national destiny, which dovetailed with the mainstream discourse of the time. Fukuzawa's earlier "utilitarian" view of the benefits of emigration was still detectable, however, for he even encouraged prostitutes to seek "opportunities" abroad for a better income. Fukuzawa also argued that their presence would help stabilize a typically male-dominated overseas settlement in the initial stage of colonialism. See Fukuzawa, "Jinmin no ijū to shōfu no dekasegi," in *FYZ*, 15:362–364.

14. On trade, see Fukuzawa, "Kuni o fukyō suru wa bōeki o seidai ni suruni ari," 16 January 1884, in *FYZ*, 9:351–353; and Fukuzawa, "Fukoku-saku," 1 April 1885, in *FYZ*, 10:248–250.

15. Fukuzawa, "Ijūron no ben," 12 April 1884, in *FYZ*, 9:459–460.

16. Fukuzawa, "Aete kokyō o sare," 526.

17. See Fukuzawa, "Beikoku wa shishi no seisho nari," 25 March 1884, in *FYZ*, 9:442–444; Fukuzawa, "Zashite kyūsuru nakare," 5 April 1884, in *FYZ*, 19:683–684; and Fukuzawa, "Fuki kōmyō wa oyayuzuri no kuni ni kagirazu," 1 July 1884, in *FYZ*, 9:545–546. On the impact of Fukuzawa's mercantilist ideas on Japanese immigration to the United States, see Yuji Ichioka, *The Issei: The World of the First Generation Japanese Immigrants, 1885–1924* (New York: Free Press, 1988), 11.

18. Lu, "Colonizing Hokkaido and the Origin of Japanese Trans-Pacific Expansion," 252–253, 262–264.

19. Fukuzawa, "Beikoku wa shishi no seisho nari," 444.

20. Fukuzawa, "Fuki kōmyō wa oyayuzuri no kuni ni kagirazu," 546.

21. Fukuzawa, "Zashite kyūsuru nakare," 683.

22. On the Gapsin coup, see Mark E. Caprio, *Japanese Assimilation Policies in Colonial Korea, 1910–1945* (Seattle: University of Washington Press, 2009), 14.

23. Fukuzawa (unsigned), "Datsu-A ron," 16 March 1885, in *FYZ*, 10:238–240.

24. On this see also Lu, "Colonizing Hokkaido and the Origin of Japanese Trans-Pacific Expansion," 264.

25. Fukuzawa, "Naichi ni gakkō wo setsuritsu suruto gaikoku ni ijū suruo tasukuruto sono ri furi ikan," 11 January 1886, in *FYZ* 11:182–183; Ishikawa Kanmei, *Fukuzawa Yukichi den* (Tokyo: Iwanami Shoten, 1932), 2:211–214; and Irie Toraji, *Hōjin kaigai hattenshi* (Tokyo: Imin Mondai Kenkyūkai, 1938), 1:289–291.

26. Washizu Shakuma, "Rekishi inmetsu no tan," *Nichibei Shimbun*, 24 and 25 June 1922. By the end of 1886, at least twenty-five Keiō alumni were living the life of immigrant merchants (or would-be merchants) in San Francisco. See Arai Katsuhiro and Tamura Norio, "Jiyū minkenki ni okeru Sōkō wangan chiku no katsudō," *Tokyo Keizai Daigaku jinbun shizen kagaku ronshū* 65 (December 1983), 118.

27. Kojō Yutaka, *Inoue Kakugorō-kun ryakuden* (Tokyo: Inoue Kakugorō-kun kōrō hyōshōkai, 1919), 50–52.

28. Ishikawa, *Fukuzawa Yukichi den*, 2:210–211; Kojō, *Inoue Kakugorō-kun ryakuden*, 52–53; and Irie, *Hōjin kaigai hattenshi*, 1:290–291. See also Lu, "Colonizing Hokkaido and the Origin of Japanese Trans-Pacific Expansion," 264.

29. On the roles of Seikyōsha members—especially Sugiura Shigetake—in forging expansionist ideas, see Uchida, "From Island Nation to Oceanic Empire," 59–64; and Lu, "Colonizing Hokkaido and the Origin of Japanese Trans-Pacific Expansion," 266.

30. See Pyle, *The New Generation in Meiji Japan*, 99–102; and Nakanome Tōru, *Seikyōsha no kenkyū* (Kyoto: Shibunkaku Shuppan, 1993), 101–145.

31. See Satō Yoshimaru, *Meiji Nashonarizumu no kenkyū: Seikyōsha no seiritsu to sono shūhen* (Tokyo: Fuyō Shobō Shuppan, 1998), 11–38.

32. For example, see Genkakusei [pseud.], "Tōyō ni okeru bōchōteki kokumin to shukushō kokumin," *Nihonjin* 30 (5 November 1896), 38–39.

33. See Nakanome, *Seikyōsha no kenkyū*, 207–211; and Kirk W. Larsen, *Tradition, Treaties, and Trade: Qing Imperialism and Chosŏn Korea, 1850–1910* (Cambridge, MA: Harvard University Press, 2011), 43–196.

34. On the Liberal Party and its role in the Freedom and Popular Rights movement, see Roger Bowen, *Rebellion and Democracy in Meiji Japan* (Berkeley: University of California Press, 1980).

35. See Zaibei Nihonjinkai, *Zaibei Nihonjinshi* (San Francisco: Zaibei Nihonjinkai, 1940), 727; Ichioka, *The Issei*, 19–28; and Eiichiro Azuma, *Between Two Empires: Race, History, and Transnationalism in Japanese America* (New York: Oxford University Press, 2005), 35–36.

36. See Shōji Ichirō, ed., *Sugawara Tsutau sensei no shōgai to sono ikō* (Sendai: Sugawara Tsutau-ō Kenpi Kyōankai, 1938), 29–43; Ebihara Hachirō, *Kaigai hōji shinbun zasshi-shi* (Tokyo: Gakuji Shoin, 1936), 110–111, 132–143; Arai and Tamura, "Jiyū minkenki ni okeru Sōkō wangan chiku no katsudō," 100–116; and Ichioka, *The Issei*, 14–16.

37. Shōji, *Sugawara Tsutau sensei no shōgai to sono ikō*, 38, 48–51.

38. Ariyama Teruo, "Zasshi 'Ensei' no genron katsudō," in *Beikoku shoki no Nihongo shinbun*, ed. Tamura Norio and Shiramizu Shigehiko (Tokyo: Keisō Shobō, 1986), 260–263, 274–275.

39. On the experiences of these student immigrants, see Ichioka, *The Issei*, 16–28.

40. Beikoku Sōkō Dai-Nihonjinkai, *Dai-Nihonjinkai nen hōkoku* (1887), 1–8, 15, in Zaibei Honpōjin no jōkyō narabi toraisha torishimari kankei 1, Diplomatic Archives of the Ministry of Foreign Affairs (hereafter DA-MOFA), Tokyo.

41. Like *Aikoku*, this mimeographed monthly contained contributions by San Francisco's Japanese expansionists. Essay themes typically ranged from reports on geopolitics (especially East Asian affairs and activities of European imperial powers) to commentaries on local race relations and politics, and from literary works to news on Japanese ethnic communities in the American West and Hawai'i.

42. See Ebihara, *Kaigai hōji shinbun zasshi-shi*, 119–127; Ichioka, *The Issei*, 15–16, 20, 49–51; and Irie, *Hōjin kaigai hattenshi*, 1:285–288.

43. For an example of a mixture of various expansionist schools, see "Kaikoku shinron 2," *Aikoku* 29 (14 May 1892); and "Inoue-shi jitsureki-dan" (1921), 28, in item 156, Inoue Keijirō Papers, Modern Japanese Political History Materials Room, National Diet Library (hereafter MJPH-NDL).

44. "Jisei no ichidankai," *Aikoku* 36 (1 July 1892).

45. Toryū ishi, "Kaigai jigyō ni tsuite no kōsatsu," *Ensei* 7 (1 January 1892).

46. "Shinnen ni saishite Ensei no shōkai o chinsu," *Ensei* 23 (1 January 1893).

47. Zaibei Nihonjinkai, *Zaibei Nihonjinshi*, 39; and Washizu Shakuma, "Wagahai no Beikoku seikatsu," *Nichibei Shimbun*, 3 and 4 December 1924. Following their return to Japan a few years later, Itō and Hirota ascended to important positions in the Japanese corporate world. The former headed the Nippon Yūsen Kaisha (NYK) Shipping Company, while the latter managed the Takashima Mining Company. Among those who remained in the United States was Takezaki Saikichi. He later served as the president of the Japanese Association of Sacramento.

48. On the Kochi Colonization Society, see *Kōchi Shokumin Kyōkai hōkoku* 1 (October 1893), esp. 9–12.

49. Takeuchi Kōjirō, *Beikoku Seihokubu Nihon iminshi* (Seattle: Taihoku Nippōsha, 1929), 36–37, 768–769; Fujioka Shirō, *Ayumi no ato* (Los Angeles: Ayumi no Ato Kankō Kōenkai, 1957), 319–322; Irie, *Hōjin kaigai hattenshi*, 1:292–293; and Katō Jūshirō, *Zaibei Dōhō hattenshi* (Tokyo: Hakubunkan, 1908), 141–142. Arai had a very colorful life. Before moving to the United States in 1884, he was involved in a scheme to supply laborers to a Canadian railroad company, which the Meiji government did not permit due to the informal ban on Japanese emigration at that time. In 1887, when the political controversy over treaty revision swept Tokyo, he crossed the Pacific back to Japan to join in antigovernment agitation. Satisfied by the development that led to the convocation of the first Imperial Diet in 1890, Arai remigrated to Tacoma, Washington, to prepare for his colonization project. As explained in chapter 2, the Guatemala emigration scheme, in which he collaborated with Itō and Hirota, was expected to provide a financial base and political connection for entering into parliamentary politics again in Japan. His later involvement in Korean affairs stemmed from the same political and colonial ambitions that had made him crisscross the Pacific. After returning to the United States, Arai played a leading role in organizing the local Japanese Association before his death in 1923. Arai's son, Clarence, later became a lawyer and one of the first mainland US Nisei to launch an unsuccessful bid for a seat in the Washington State legislature in 1934. Arai is now remembered as a Japanese American pioneer in the Pacific Northwest, but his settler-colonial past has been buried in oblivion.

50. On Hoshi's conflation of transpacific settler colonialism and state-led imperialism, see "Watanabe Kanjūrō-kun danwa 4," 271–272, in Hoshi Tōru denki kōhon 14 (1915), Hoshi Tōru kankei monjo, MJPH-NDL; and "Hoshi Tōru-shi no seiji iken," *Tokyo Asahi Shinbun*, 21 October 1890. On a similar colonization venture by California-based immigrant expansionists, see "Kōkoku," *Aikoku* 25 (15 April 1892).

51. "Mōko jinshu jiken enzetsu," *Chōya Shinbun*, 5 November 1889; and "Mōkojin jiken no enzetsu," *Chōya Shinbun*, 22 October 1889. Furukawa Iwao filed a lawsuit. He had applied for admission into the University of California's Law School, but his application was denied due to his "Mongolian" race status. Upon returning to Japan for a series of public lectures, Furukawa published a book entitled *Mōko jiken* (Mongolian case) in 1890 to garner support for his intended lawsuit against racist student exclusion/segregation policies in California. In the book, he explained the brief history of Chinese immigration and anti-Chinese agitation, compared the Chinese immigrant life with its Japanese counterpart, and called for resolute legal action to demand public acknowledgment that the Japanese were a progressive race not to be confused with the uncivilized "Mongolian" race, exemplified by segregated Chinese. He argued that such a court declaration would facilitate the expansion of

Japanese influence ("civilization") on the US frontier. See Furukawa Iwao, *Mōko jiken* (Tokyo: Mōko Jiken Nihon Dōshikai, 1890), esp. 82–84.

52. See Nagasawa Betten (Setsu), "Nihonjin mondai," *Ajia* 42 (6 June 1892), 9–11; "Mata Nihonjin mondai," *Ajia* 50 (1 August 1892), 15–16; and "Beikoku ni okeru Nihonjin," *Tō-hō* 20 (10 September 1892), 30.

53. "Zaibei Nihon minzokuron 2," *Aikoku* 27 (29 April 1892).

54. "Nihonjin kōgeki hajimaru," *Aikoku* 29 (14 May 1892).

55. "Mata Nihonjin mondai" and "Nihonjin shūgaku kyozetsu," *Tō-hō* 40 (10 July 1893), 33–34.

56. The firsthand racial experience of US residents, as I detailed in my first book, set them apart from the people of Japan in the long run as long as they opted to remain on American soil as minoritized "Orientals." While most early expansionists returned to Japan to pursue the life of a colonial master rather than that of a racial minority, those who stayed were compelled to seek interracial conciliation with and acceptance by white exclusionists in order to survive. The people of Japan, including many returnees, became growingly indignant at white racism and global hegemony, providing a background for pan-Asianist ideologies of the 1930s and the early 1940s in Japan. See Azuma, *Between Two Empires*, esp. chaps. 2–3.

57. Shōji, *Sugawara Tsutau sensei no shōgai to sono ikō*, 46.

58. Yamazaki Bungo, "Zai-Beikoku waga dōhō yūshi no jinshi ni nozomu," *Ensei* 4 (15 August 1891), 2.

59. "Kōkai, imin," *Ensei* 13 (1 July 1892), 2–3.

60. "Kōkai, imin," 2–3.

61. See Abe Toryū, "Peruyu (Peleliu), Hawai to Nihonkoku," *Ensei* 26 (1 May 1893), 4–5; Aoki Hirotarō, "Hawai ni okeru Nihonjin no shinsō," *Ensei* 30 (20 July 1893), 4–5; and "Jisei no dai ichi dankai," *Aikoku* 36 (1 July 1892).

62. Abe, "Peruyu (Peleliu), Hawai to Nihonkoku," 3–5. The quotes are from page 3.

63. Nagasawa Betten, "Yankii" (1893), in *Seikyōsha bungakushū*, ed. Matsumoto Sannosuke (Tokyo: Chikuma Shobō, 1980), 311–342. Nagasawa's original 1893 book was reprinted in the above collection of Seikyōsha writers.

64. Nagasawa Setsu, "Daishōtotsu," *Nihonjin* 7 (18 January 1894), 16.

65. On American racial Anglo-Saxonism, see Reginald Horsman, *Race and Manifest Destiny* (Cambridge, MA: Harvard University Press, 1981), 272–297. Gary Gerstle and Paul Kramer variously call the same phenomenon "racial nationalism" and "racial exceptionalism," respectively. See Gary Gerstle, "Theodore Roosevelt and the Divided Character of American Nationalism," *Journal of American History* 86, no. 3 (December 1999), 1280–1307; and Paul A. Kramer, "Empires, Exceptions, and Anglo-Saxons: Race and Rule between the British and American Empires, 1880–1910," *Journal of American History* 88, no. 1 (March 2002), 1315–1353.

66. Nagasawa, "Daishōtotsu," 11–13.

67. Nagasawa, "Yankii," 316–318, 335–342.

68. Nagasawa, "Yankii," 338.

69. Nagasawa, "Yankii," 337, 340–341.

70. Nagasawa, "Yankii," 341.

71. Nagasawa, "Yankii," 339.

72. The Bayonet Constitution of 1887 enabled white Americans in Hawai'i to consolidate their economic and political control of the kingdom. On the one hand, it deprived the monarch of the power to appoint a cabinet and the absolute veto of the legislation. Voting rights were extended to noncitizen white residents, while Asians and those who did not meet literacy and property requirements were disenfranchised. These new rules subordinated the native Hawaiian political elite to the dictates of propertied white denizens, of whom a majority were US citizens. See Tom Coffman, *Nation Within: The History of the American Occupation of Hawai'i* (Kihei, HI: Koa Books, 2009), 69–134.

73. Nagasawa, "Yankii," 339–340. See also Nagasawa Setsu, "Daini no Seikanron," *Ajia* 2, no. 6 (1 July 1893), 12–13. The issue of Japanese suffrage in Hawai'i first drew attention when the Bayonet Constitution of 1887 disenfranchised Japanese. Wary of discriminatory treatment of its subjects, the Japanese government filed a formal protest, but in vain. After the controversy over Japanese suffrage in the islands captured the attention of Meiji intellectuals again in 1893, Seikyōsha's journal *Ajia* published a series of Hawai'i-related articles throughout the year. Most likely penned by Nagasawa, the articles lambasted Tokyo's "gutless" response. Other nationalist journals expressed similar views, underlining the prevalence of expansionist interest in Hawai'i among Japanese intellectuals and political activists of diverse affiliations at that time.

74. Nagasawa, "Yankii," 339.

75. Toyama Yoshifumi, *Nippon to Hawai* (Tokyo: Hakubunkan, 1893), 14–15.

76. Toyama, *Nippon to Hawai*, 22–30.

77. See Coffman, *Nation Within*, 149–166.

78. Matsumoto Sannosuke, ed., *Seikyōsha bungakushū* (Tokyo: Chikuma Shobō, 1980), 352, 459.

79. Toyama, *Nippon to Hawai*, 1–2, 93.

80. Irie, *Hōjin kaigai hattenshi*, 1:87–89. See also the formal manifesto and commentaries in the Liberal Party bulletin. These were authored by Sugawara Tsutau and issued in the name of the Patriotic League. "Aikoku dōmei-in ikensho," *Tō-hō* 34 (10 April 1893), 30–32, esp. 31; see Sugawara, "Hawai mondai," *Tō-hō* 38 (10 June 1893), 8–16; Sugawara, "Hawai-ron," *Tō-hō* 40 (10 July 1893), 9–15; Sugawara, "Hawai-ron," *Tō-hō* 41 (25 July 1893), 14–17; and Sugawara, "Hawai-ron," *Tō-hō* 42 (10 August 1893), 8–11.

81. See W. E. B. Du Bois, *The Souls of Black Folk: Essay and Sketches* (Chicago: A. C. McClurg, 1903), ch. 2. That chapter starts with this famous statement: "The problem of the twentieth century is the problem of the color-line,—the relation of the darker to the lighter races of men in Asia and Africa, in America and the islands of the sea."

82. Sugawara, "Hawai-ron," *Tō-hō* 40, 14.

83. The quote is from Sugawara, "Hawai-ron," *Tō-hō* 42, 8–9. See also Sugawara, "Hawai-ron," *Tō-hō* 41, 14–17. Sugawara characterized Hawai'i as a "little Japan."

84. On June 6, 1893, Sugawara gave a two-hour lecture on the "Hawaiian problem" at the Liberal Party Hall in Tokyo before hundreds of like-minded expansionists, including the party brass. The lecture was printed in full in the official bulletin. See Sugawara, "Hawai mondai." Sugawara also sent a letter of general appeal outside the circle of his partisan friends. Fukuzawa's *Jiji Shinpō* printed Sugawara's manifesto. See *Jiji Shinpō*, 8 March 1893.

Periodic reports on Sugawara's activities also appeared in the same newspaper during that year.

85. Ebihara, *Kaigai hōji shinbun zasshi-shi*, 131; and Arai and Tamura, "Jiyū minkenki ni okeru Sōkō wangan chiku no katsudō," 132.

86. Toyama, *Nippon to Hawai*, 2; Shōji, *Sugawara Tsutau sensei no shōgai to sono ikō*, 50–51; and "Aikoku dōmei kurabu," *Tō-hō* 30 (10 February 1893), 27.

87. Ebihara, *Kaigai hōji shinbun zasshi-shi*, 135; "Buchō rijikai," *Tō-hō* 38 (10 June 1893), 21–22; and "Hawai danpan," *Tō-hō* 39 (25 June 1893), 34.

88. Toyama, *Nippon to Hawai*, 93. See also Gaimushō, *Nihon Gaikō bunsho* (Tokyo: Gaimushō, 1952), 26:779–782; and United Japanese Society of Hawaii, ed., *Hawai Nihonjin iminshi* (Honolulu: United Japanese Society of Hawaii, 1964), 143–144.

89. Gaimushō, *Nihon Gaikō bunsho*, 26:754–759, 780–782, 784–785, 787–788. Three petitions came from Honolulu, while the fourth originated from Hilo. Two petitions indicated the direct involvement of Sugawara's group. On an analysis of the responses of the Japanese government and Hawai'i's immigrant leaders, see also Shiode Hiroyuki, *Ekkyōsha no seijishi* (Nagoya: Nagoya Daigaku Shuppan, 2015), 119–129.

90. Gaimushō, *Nihon Gaikō bunsho*, 26:754–756.

91. Gaimushō, *Nihon Gaikō bunsho*, 26:784–785. The quote is from page 785.

92. Gaimushō, *Nihon Gaikō bunsho*, 26:768–769.

93. Coffman, *Nation Within*, 149–166, 206. The quote is from page 206.

94. According to official Japanese statistics, the number of US-bound emigrants who later handed back their passports to the government after their return increased significantly between 1892 and 1893, from 243 to 356. In 1894, 35 more emigrants than in the previous year came back from the United States. See Naikaku Tōkei-kyoku, ed., *Nihon Teikoku tōkei nenkan* (Tokyo: Nihon Tōkei Kyōkai, 1896), 15:76–77.

95. See Ichioka, *The Issei*, 256–257n29); and Ariyama, "Zasshi 'Ensei' no genron katsudō," 278n44. By 1897 the Expedition Society was disbanded, and many members went back to Japan or moved elsewhere. Those who remained in the American West adjusted their goals and expectations to the new "racial" situation, concentrating on entrepreneurial success in pursuit of overseas development. See Azuma, *Between Two Empires*, chaps. 2–3.

2. VANGUARD OF AN EXPANSIVE JAPAN: KNOWLEDGE PRODUCERS, FRONTIER TROTTERS, AND SETTLEMENT BUILDERS FROM ACROSS THE PACIFIC

1. See Roger Daniels, *The Politics of Prejudice: The Anti-Japanese Movement in California and the Struggle for Japanese Exclusion* (Berkeley: University of California Press, 1999), 16–105.

2. Marilyn Lake and Henry Reynolds, *Drawing the Global Colour Line: White Men's Countries and the International Challenge of Racial Equality* (Cambridge, UK: Cambridge University Press, 2008); Gerald Horne, *The White Pacific: U.S. Imperialism and Black Slavery in the South Seas after the Civil War* (Honolulu: University of Hawai'i Press, 2007); Kornel Chang, *Pacific Connections: The Making of the U.S.-Canadian Borderlands* (Berkeley: University of California Press, 2012); and David C. Atkinson, *The Burden of White Supremacy:*

Containing Asian Migration in the British Empire and the United States (Chapel Hill: University of North Carolina Press, 2016).

3. Within ten months of its founding, the society's membership increased from 469 to over 600, including those in Hawai'i, the United States, and all over Japan. By March 1897 the number had reached 967. On its early history, mission statement, and membership rosters, see *Shokumin Kyōkai hōkoku* 1 (15 April 1893), 102–118; "Enomoto kaichō no enzetsu," *Shokumin Kyōkai hōkoku* 8 (18 December 1893), 53; *Shokumin Kyōkai hōkoku* 46 (9 March 1897), 39–53 (membership roster); and "Watanabe Kanjūrō-kun danwa 4," 281, in Hoshi Tōru denki kōhon 14 (1915), Hoshi Tōru kankei monjo, Modern Japanese Political History Materials Room, National Diet Library (hereafter MJPH-NDL), Tokyo. Membership statistics were tallied by the author. Some leaders of the Japanese Patriotic League and Expedition Society joined the society after returning to Japan, including Sugawara Tsutau, Watanabe Kanjūrō, Aoyagi Ikutarō, and Takekawa Tōtarō. See *Shokumin Kyōkai hōkoku* 8 (18 December 1893), 53–54.

4. Carol Gluck, *Japan's Modern Myths: Ideology in the Late Meiji Period* (Princeton, NJ: Princeton University Press, 1987), 10–11.

5. Kokuryūkai, ed., *Tōa senkaku shishi kiden: Jōkan* (Tokyo: Kokuryūkai Shuppanbu, 1933), 417–418; Nakanome Tōru, *Seikyōsha no kenkyū* (Kyoto: Shibunkaku Shuppan, 1993), 207–211; Joël Joos, "The Genyosha (1881) and Premodern Roots of Japanese Expansionism," and Sven Saaler, "The Kokuryukai, 1901–1920," in *Pan-Asianism: A Documentary History*, ed. Sven Saaler and Christopher W.A. Szpilman (Lanham, MD: Rowman & Littlefield, 2011), 1:61–64, 121–132, respectively.

6. Jun Uchida, "From Island Nation to Oceanic Empire: A Vision of Japanese Expansion from the Periphery," *Journal of Japanese Studies* 42, no. 1 (Winter 2016), 58, 69–77, 81. The quotes are from pages 58 and 81.

7. See, for example, the list of board members and officials in *Shokumin Kyōkai hōkoku* 69 (16 August 1899), 4; *Shokumin Kyōkai hōkoku* 10 (17 February 1894), 75–81 (membership rosters); and *Shokumin Kyōkai hōkoku* 46 (9 March 1897), 39–53.

8. As Japan's public discourse turned increasingly warlike toward Russia, reports and commentaries on the Malay Peninsula, Taiwan, Korea, Manchuria, and Far East Siberia increased in number in *Shokumin Kyōkai hōkoku*, eventually rivaling those on the Latin American frontiers by the end of the 1890s.

9. On the types of early Japanese migrants to Korea and China, see Kimura Kenji, *Zaichō Nihonjin no shakaishi* (Tokyo: Miraisha, 1989), 10–24; Jun Uchida, *Brokers of Empire: Japanese Settler Colonialism in Korea, 1876–1945* (Cambridge, MA: Harvard University Press, 2011), 36–58; and Kodama Masaaki, *Nihon iminshi kenkyū josetsu* (Hiroshima: Keisuisha, 1992), 480–482. On similar geographic and class origins of emigrants bound for Korea and Hawai'i, see Martin Dusinberre, *Hard Times in the Hometown: A History of Community Survival in Modern Japan* (Honolulu: University of Hawai'i Press, 2012), 86–98. For Japanese passport statistics, see "Kaigai ryoken uketori jin'in," in *Nihon Teikoku tōkei nenkan*, vols. 14–20, ed. Naikaku Tōkei-kyoku (Tokyo: Nihon Tōkei Kyōkai, 1895–1901).

10. "Enomoto Kaichō no enzetsu," *Shokumin Kyōkai hōkoku* 1 (15 April 1893), 7.

11. "Enomoto Kaichō no enzetsu," 9.

12. On Enomoto's advocacy of large-scale emigration and overseas colonization, albeit not yet specifically to Mexico, see "Iminka secchi iken," *Yūbin Hōchi*, 5 August 1891.

13. See Tsunoyama Yukihiro, *Enomoto Takeaki to Mekishiko shokumin ijū* (Tokyo: Dōbunkan Shuppan, 1986), 93–99, 124–125. The first investigative team consisted of prominent Colonization Society members, including Tsuneya Seifuku and Enomoto Ryūkichi, Takeaki's nephew. Partially funded by the foreign minister and Enomoto's private money, they produced two sets of official reports to the Japanese government while publishing a number of articles in various journals as well as the society's organ. The acting Japanese consul in Mexico City undertook the second investigative trip, and Nemoto Shō conducted the third. All these "expeditions" transpired between 1892 and 1894. See Tsunoyama, *Enomoto Takeaki to Mekishiko shokumin ijū*, 93–112, 124–125.

14. "Shokuminchi ni taisuru Honkai no iken," *Ensei* 5 (1 September 1891), 2.

15. Takekawa Tōtarō, "Dai ni san ryū no jinbutsu o motte Bokkoku o tandai tarashimeyo," *Ensei* 27 (15 May 1893), 4. See also Takekawa, "Mōshinsha to kōkatsukan to imyōdōtai," *Ensei* 14 (15 July 1892), 8–11. The latter article was reprinted in the monthly journal of Seikyōsha in Tokyo; see Takekawa, "Mōshinsha to kōkatsukan to imyōdōtai," *Ajia* 50 (1 August 1892), 2–4.

16. Takekawa, "Dai ni san ryū no jinbutsu o motte Bokkoku o tandai tarashimeyo," 5.

17. Takezawa Taichi, Fukuda Kenshirō, and Nakamura Masamichi, *Mekishiko tanken jikki* (Tokyo: Hakubunkan, 1893), 9. Nakamura was a member of the Japanese Patriotic League of San Francisco. Hoshi Tōru provided a preface to the volume. For examples of published journal reports on Peru, see Aoyagi Ikutarō, "Nan'yū kikō," *Shokumin Kyōkai hōkoku* 19 (November 1894), 1–46; and Aoyagi Ikutarō, "Nanbei shakai no kansatsu oyobi kibō," *Shokumin Kyōkai hōkoku* 20 (20 December 1894), 57–62.

18. See "Zaibei Nihonjin to tankentai," *Ensei* 25 (15 April 1893), 1–3, 17–18; "Nikaragua yori no shokan," *Ensei* 30 (20 July 1893), 5–6; "Imin no kyūmu Tankenka no ketsubō," *Ensei* 32 (14 October 1893), 4–6; and Matsumoto Sannosuke, ed., *Seikyōsha bungakushū* (Tokyo: Chikuma Shobo, 1980), 352. See also Ariyama Teruo, "Zasshi 'Ensei' no genron katsudō," in *Beikoku shoki no Nihongo shinbun*, ed. Tamura Norio and Shiramizu Shigehiko (Tokyo: Keisō Shobō, 1986), 266, 276.

19. "Bokkoku tankenka shoshi no kikoku o okuru" and "Bokkoku tankenka no kibei," *Ensei* 20 (15 November 1892), 3–4, 12–13. See also Tsunoyama, *Enomoto Takeaki to Mekishiko shokumin ijū*, 93–98.

20. "Kaigai tanken danwakai," *Kaihō* 30 (10 February 1893), 21; Tsuneya Seifuku, "Mekishiko tankendan," *Kaihō* 31 (25 February 1893), 17–24; and Takano Shūshō, "Mekishiko tankendan," *Kaihō* 34 (10 April 1893), 12–21.

21. "Kaihō," *Shokumin Kyōkai hōkoku* 8 (18 December 1893), 54–55.

22. Tsunoyama, *Enomoto Takeaki to Mekishiko shokumin ijū*, 161–162. See also "Kaihō," 55.

23. Tsunoyama, *Enomoto Takeaki to Mekishiko shokumin ijū*, 179–182.

24. See "Enomoto kaichō no enzetsu," 54–55; and "Zappō," *Kōchi Shokumin Kyōkai hōkoku* 2 (February 1894), 24. See also Tsunoyama, *Enomoto Takeaki to Mekishiko shokumin ijū*, 170.

25. Daniel M. Masterson, *The Japanese in Latin America* (Urbana: University of Illinois Press, 2004), 27–28; and Jerry García, *Looking Like the Enemy: Japanese Mexicans, the Mexican State, and U.S. Hegemony 1897–1945* (Tucson: University of Arizona Press, 2014), 24–26.

26. See Tsunoyama, *Enomoto Takeaki to Mekishiko shokumin ijū*, 198–219.

27. Tōtenkō-sei [pseud.], "Yūsen shachō Itō Yonejirō kun," *Shokumin* 3, no. 10 (October 1924), 112; Itō Yonejirō, "Chūbei Guatemara kyōwakoku tankenroku," *Shokumin Kyōkai hōkoku* 21 (19 January 1895), 1–26; Itō Yonejirō, "Guatemara jikkenroku," *Shokumin Kyōkai hōkoku* 22 (20 February 1895), 1–16; Takeuchi Kōjirō, *Beikoku Seihokubu Nihon iminshi* (Seattle, WA: Taihoku Nippōsha, 1929), 769–770; Fujioka Shirō, *Ayumi no ato* (Los Angeles: Ayumi no Ato Kankō Kōenkai, 1957), 321–322; and Katō Jūshirō, *Zaibei dōhō hattenshi* (Tokyo: Hakubunkan, 1908), 142–143.

28. See Itō, "Chūbei Guatemara kyōwakoku tankenroku"; and Itō, "Guatemara jikkenroku." Other former US residents who contributed their reports on the New World frontiers to the bulletin included Sugawara Tsutau and Hinata Terutake (the US West), Watanabe Kanjūrō (British Columbia), Takekawa Tōtarō (gold mining in North America), and Aoyagi Ikutarō (Peru).

29. Itō, "Guatemara jikkenroku," 8, 11–13. The quotes are from page 8. At another meeting, Arai and one Japanese diplomat expounded on Guatemala along the same lines as Itō's argument. See "Kaihō," *Shokumin Kyōkai hōkoku* 20 (20 December 1894), 107.

30. See Yamada Michio, *Fune ni miru Nihon iminshi* (Tokyo: Chūō Kōronsha, 1998). The rise of Japanese steamship companies was inseparable from the growth of transpacific migration. Shortly after the Japanese government decided to send manual laborers to Hawaiian sugar plantations in 1885, the Nippon Yūsen Kaisha (NYK) was established with the full backing of the government to help ship many migrants to the islands in the subsequent years. Eleven years later, NYK became responsible for the first regular steamship service between Yokohama (later extended to Hong Kong) and Seattle, when the number of Japanese migrants to the US Pacific Coast suddenly surged after the conclusion of the military clash with China. In 1898 another Japanese shipping concern named the Oriental Steamship Company (Tōyō Kisen) started its regular service between Hong Kong and San Francisco; that service was taken over by NYK in 1926. After the beginning of Peru-bound migration, in 1905 the Oriental Steamship Company extended its service to the Pacific Coast of South America via Los Angeles, which subsequently carried many migrants to Mexico and Peru. With Brazil as a major migrant destination after the US-Japan Gentlemen's Agreement of 1908, the Osaka Merchant Shipping Company (Osaka Shōsen) and NYK also established regular service from Yokohama to São Paulo and other Brazilian ports through the Indian Ocean and the South Atlantic in 1916 and 1917, respectively.

31. See "Kaigai ryoken uketori jin'in," in *Nihon Teikoku tōkei nenkan*, vols. 14–21, ed. Naikaku Tōkei-kyoku (Tokyo: Nihon Tōkei Kyōkai, 1895–1902), various pages. All tallies were made by the author. I did not include the 1903 figures, because the source appears to give the wrong number for Hawai'i-bound emigrants.

32. See "Ishibashi-shi no shokan," *Ensei* 1 (1 July 1891), 12–13. Although the short biographies of Ishibashi claim that he fought in Chile with a volunteer militia group from the United States for seven months, his own letter presents a different story, which I narrate in the main text. See Hanawa Kunzō, "Ishibashi Usaburō-shōden," in Hanawa Kunzō, *Ura Keiichi* (Tokyo: Junpū Shoin, 1924), 5–7; and Kokuryūkai, ed., *Tōa senkaku shishi kiden: Gekan* (Tokyo: Kokuryūkai Shuppanbu, 1936), 47.

33. Kokuryūkai, *Tōa senkaku shishi kiden: Gekan*, 47–48. The quotes are from page 48.

34. Cemil Aydin, *The Politics of Anti-Westernism in Asia: Visions of World Order in Pan-Islamic and Pan-Asian Thought* (New York: Columbia University Press, 2007), 56–58. See also Kokuryūkai, *Tōa senkaku shishi kiden: Jōkan*, 118–121, 414–416, 569–738.

35. Kokuryūkai, *Tōa senkaku shishi kiden: Gekan*, 47, 321; Hanawa, "Ishibashi Usaburō-shōden," 7; and Irie Toraji, *Hōjin kaigai hattenshi* (Tokyo: Ide Shoten, 1942), 1:214–215.

36. Kokuryūkai, *Tōa senkaku shishi kiden: Gekan*, 30–31, 48, 684–685; Hanawa, "Ishibashi Usaburō-shōden," 8–12; Irie, *Hōjin kaigai hattenshi*, 1:215–231; and Yoshikawa Toshiharu, "'Ajia shugi'-sha no Tai shinshutsu," *Tōnan Ajia kenkyū* 16, no. 1 (January 1987), 86–88.

37. On America's racialized concern over Japanese control of the region, see Walter LaFeber, *The Clash: A History of U.S.-Japan Relations* (New York: W. W. Norton, 1997), 79–89.

38. Ariiso Itsurō [pseud. Yokoyama Gennosuke], *Kaigai katsudō no Nihonjin* (Tokyo: Shōkadō, 1906), 217–221; and Uoura-sei [pseud. Yokoyama Gennosuke], "Zaigai katsudō no Nihon danji," *Shōgyōkai* 4, no. 4 (October 1905), 173–174.

39. E. W. Birch, "Governor's Office, Sandakan 29.4.1903," in Onimaru Kitagawa-ke shiryō (08952), Saga Prefectural Library, Japan.

40. Koichiro Masuda, "Description of British North Borneo," *Shōgyōkai* 7, no. 1 (January 1907), 7.

41. Koichiro Masuda, "Description of Borneo Woods," *Shōgyōkai* 7, no. 2 (February 1907), 17.

42. Yokoyama Gennosuke, "Nan'yō ni okeru Nihonjin no shinjigyō," *Shōgyōkai* 6, no. 2 (1 August 1906), 96–98; Nakahara Zentoku, *Eiryō Kita Boruneo no jitsujō* (Tokyo: Nan'yō Tsushinsha, 1938), 9, 21; and Shizugashima Sumito, "Soto Nan'yō shisatsu no issetsu," *Nan'yō guntō* 5, no. 6 (June 1939), 46.

43. "To Mr. Ishimaru Katsuichi," ca. January 1909, in Onimaru Kitagawa-ke shiryō (08952); and Someya Nariaki, "Eiryō Kita Boruneo-shū imin jōkyō," in *Imin chōsa hōkoku*, ed. Gaimushō Tsūshō-kyoku (Tokyo: Gaimushō, 1910), 5:1–2. The quotes are from the first source.

44. Yokoyama Gennosuke, "Masuda Kōichirō-kun Boruneo Kigyōkai o setsuritsusu," *Shōkō Sekai Taiheiyō* 8, no. 3 (1 February 1909), 102–104; and "Kaigai-ki: Boruneo," *Shōkō Sekai Taiheiyō* 8, no. 4 (1909), 111. Masuda's colonization project had the backing of a major expansionist commercial monthly of the time, entitled *Shōkō Sekai Taiheiyō* (Pacific as [Japan's] commercial and industrial world). Published by a powerful publishing house named Hakubunkan, the magazine both printed reports on Masuda's endeavors and offered a forum for questions and answers relative to British North Borneo.

45. See Fujii Minoru to Ishii Kikujirō, 29 June 1916, in Nan'yō ni okeru Hōjin kigyō kankei zakken, and Sakata Jūjirō to Honolulu Consul Moroi, 16 June 1916, in Mensakuchi oyobi menka saibaigyō torishirabe zakken, Diplomatic Archives of the Ministry of Foreign Affairs (hereafter DA-MOFA), Tokyo; and Tōma Heiichirō, *Zaikai ippyakunin* (Tokyo: Chūō Hyōronsha, 1912), 76. On paper, the key figure in this endeavor appeared to be a person by the name of Andō Yasutarō, Inoue's old colleague in Tokyo city government. By 1916 Ando had left city government, while Inoue stayed on as a high-ranking public servant. For this reason, Inoue usually kept a low profile without using his own name on public records relating to Borneo and other overseas ventures. Likewise, because he was not in Japan to

process paperwork for it, Masuda's name did not surface on public records as often as Andō's and Inoue's did. Yet a careful analysis of available sources points to the central roles of Inoue (on the Japan side) and Masuda (on the Borneo side).

46. Masuda, "Description of British North Borneo," 8.

47. See [Inoue Keijirō], "Inoue Keijirō-shi danwa yōshi 5," *Chiyū zasshi* 3, no. 11 (November 1937), 26–28; "Marai gomu kaisha setsuritsu," *Hōchi Shinbun*, 27 August 1912.

48. [Inoue], "Inoue Keijirō-shi danwa yōshi 5," 27; Fujii to Ishii, 29 June 1916, and Fujii to Ishii, 27 July 1916, in Nan'yō ni okeru Hōjin kigyō kankei zakken; Sakata to Moroi, 16 June 1916; and Mochizuki Masahiko, "Sandakan to Nihonjin: Kado Norimaru, Yasutani Kiyoji o megutte," *JAMS News* 25 (10 February 2003), 31–32. Kado Norimaru was Masuda's business associate in Sandakan, and Yasutani Kiyoji, Kado's brother-in-law, ran a two-hundred-acre farm there.

49. Fujii to Ishii, 27 July 1916.

50. [Inoue], "Inoue Keijirō-shi danwa yōshi 5," 27; and Takumushō, *Nan'yō saibai jigyō yōran* (Tokyo: Takumushō Takumu-kyoku, 1929), 86. The quote is from the first source.

51. Ariiso, *Kaigai katsudō no Nihonjin*, 216–217; Tazawa Shingo, *Nangoku mitamama no ki* (Tokyo: Bunmeidō Shoten, 1922), 34; and Uoura-sei, "Zaigai katsudō no Nihon danji," 171–172.

52. See Someya, "Eiryō Kita Boruneo-shū imin jōkyō," 20; and Nakahara, *Eiryō Kita Boruneo no jitsujō*, 11, 16–18.

53. Fujiwara Seika, "Mokuyōjima no kingu to tonawaretaru Satō Torajirō," *Kaigai no Nippon* 1, no. 4 (April 1911), 129–130; Arai Katsuhiro, "Amerika de hakkō sareta shinbun 'Dai Nippon' kō," *Tanaka Shōzō to sono jidai* 3 (1982), 120–122; Iikura Shōhei and Hasegawa Kōzō, eds., *Minakata Kumagusu Doki Hōryu ōfuku shokan* (Tokyo: Yasaka Shobō, 1990), 17; and Kira Yoshie, "Satō Torajirō, Sono sūkina isshō," *Kaikō no hiroba* 37 (29 April 1992), 6.

54. Yūkōku-sei [pseud.], "Dai Nippon hakkō no shui," *Dai Nippon* 1 (1 February 1889); Arai Katsuhiro, "Minakata Kumagusu no Zaibei jidai," in *Minakata Kumagusu hyakuwa*, ed. Iikura Shōhei and Hasegawa Kōzō (Tokyo: Yasaka Shobō, 1991), 36–38; Fujiwara, "Mokuyōjima no kingu to tonawaretaru Satō Torajirō," 131; and Tōtenkō-sei, "Yūsen shachō Itō Yonejirō kun," 114. The quotes are from the first source.

55. Fujiwara, "Mokuyōjima no kingu to tonawaretaru Satō Torajirō," 131–132; Kasai Kiyoshi, *Minakata Kumagusu gaiden* (Tokyo: Yoshikawa Kōbunkan, 1986), 94–95; Wakayama-ken, ed., *Wakayama-ken iminshi* (Wakayama: Wakayama-ken, 1957), 192, 580–582; and Irie, *Hōjin kaigai hattenshi*, 1:403. According to the last source, in 1897 about 80 percent of the Japanese population of Thursday Island was of Wakayama origin.

56. Wakayama-ken, *Wakayama-ken iminshi*, 580; and Fujiwara, "Mokuyōjima no kingu to tonawaretaru Satō Torajirō," 132.

57. Wakayama-ken, *Wakayama-ken iminshi*, 603.

58. Lake and Reynolds, *Drawing the Global Colour Line*; and Chang, *Pacific Connections*.

59. Satō Torajirō, "Gōshū tsūshin," *Shokumin Kyōkai hōkoku* 74 (16 January 1900), 16–18; Satō, "Shika seika," *Shokumin Kyōkai hōkoku* 76 (21 March 1900), 3–12; and Satō, "Gaijin ni tochi shoyū o yurusubekarazu," *Shokumin Kyōkai hōkoku* 84 (10 December 1900), 14–21, esp. 19–21. The quote is from the first source, page 18.

60. Satō, "Gaijin ni tochi shoyū o yurusubekarazu," 18; and Fujiwara, "Mokuyōjima no kingu to tonawaretaru Satō Torajirō," 132.

61. Dōshi Kenkyūkai, *Taigai seisaku* (Tokyo: Dōshi Kenkyūkai, 1901), 18, 29, 33, and Satō Torajirō, *Taiheiyō-saku* (n.p.: n.p., 1901), 3–4, in Meiji Publications Collection, Waseda University Library, Tokyo, Japan; and "Satō Torajirō no Taigai-saku enzetsu" (4 March [1901]), in Kimitsu zakken, vol. 2, DA-MOFA.

62. Dōshi Kenkyūkai, *Taigai seisaku*, 18. See also Satō, *Taiheiyō-saku*, 3–4; and "Satō Torajirō no Taigai-saku enzetsu."

63. Dokusei Ishi [pseud.], "Teikoku shugi 4," *Kokumin Shinbun*, 9 November 1901.

64. Dōshi Kenkyūkai, *Taigai seisaku*, 30; Satō Torajirō, *Shin Seikei* (Tokyo: Dai Kokuminsha, 1903), 173–176, 182; and *Tokyo Asahi Shinbun*, 7 and 30 August 1903.

65. *Yomiuri Shinbun*, 2 September 1903.

66. See Tokutomi Sohō, *Taishō seinen to Teikoku no zento* (Tokyo: Min'yūsha, 1916), 400–404. Like Satō, Tokutomi was perturbed by anti-Japanese agitation in California, among other places, when he advocated his rendition of pan-Asianism.

67. Dōshi Kenkyūkai, *Taigai seisaku*, 29–31; and Satō, *Taiheiyō-saku*, 3.

68. Satō Torajirō, *Shina keihatsuron* (Yokohama: Yokohama Shinpōsha, 1903), 2–3, in Meiji Publications Collection, Waseda University Library.

69. Eri Hotta, *Pan-Asianism and Japan's War, 1931–1945* (New York: Palgrave Macmillan, 2007), 19–52, esp. 43–44; and Uchida, "From Island Nation to Oceanic Empire," 69–77.

70. Satō, *Taiheiyō-saku*, 6; and Dōshi Kenkyūkai, *Taigai seisaku*, 33. On a thorough discussion of his blueprint for "edifying the Chinese," see Satō, *Shina keihatsuron*.

71. Satō, *Taiheiyō-saku*, 7–9. The quote is from page 9.

72. On the concepts of inclusionary "polite" racism and exclusionary "vulgar" racism, see Takashi Fujitani, *Race for Empire: Koreans as Japanese and Japanese as Americans during World War II* (Berkeley: University of California Press, 2011), 25. Paul A. Kramer's discussion of US colonialism in the Philippines as "inclusionary" and US domestic racism as "exclusionary" also illuminates the duality of imperialism, in which inclusion and exclusion were mutually reinforcing rather than being incompatible or opposite. See Paul A. Kramer, *The Blood of Government: Race, Empire, the United States, and the Philippines* (Chapel Hill: University of North Carolina Press, 2006), 159–220, 347–422.

73. Fujimoto Jitsuya, *Hara Sankei-ō den* (Kyoto: Shibunkaku Shuppan, 2003), 109–112; and Morimoto Sō, *Hara Tomitarō* (Tokyo: Jiji Shuppansha, 1964), 174–175.

74. "Satō fukukaichō no seikyo o itamu," *Dōmin* 49 (1 October 1928), 1; and Kira, "Satō Torajirō, Sono sūki na isshō," 7.

75. Uchida Jun, "Shokuminchi-ki Chōsen ni okeru dōka seisaku to Zaichō Nihonjin," *Chōsenshi Kenkyūkai ronbunshū* 41 (October 2003), 174, 179–181. The quote is from page 174.

76. Uchida, "Shokuminchi-ki Chōsen ni okeru dōka seisaku to Zaichō Nihonjin," 182.

77. Uchida, "Shokuminchi-ki Chōsen ni okeru dōka seisaku to Zaichō Nihonjin," 182–186; and "Kyūji," *Dōmin* 49 (1 October 1928), 4–5.

78. Uchida, "Shokuminchi-ki Chōsen ni okeru dōka seisaku to Zaichō Nihonjin," 178.

79. Uchida, "Shokuminchi-ki Chōsen ni okeru dōka seisaku to Zaichō Nihonjin," 181; and "Kyūji," 5. In his eulogy, the Dōminkai president characterized Satō as the "founder of founders."

80. See Kobe Shiyakusho Shakaika, "Zaishin hantō minzoku no genjyō" (February 1927), in *Zainichi Chōsenjin kankei shiryō shūsei*, ed. Pak Kyon-sik (Tokyo: San'ichi Shobō, 1975), 1:582–590. The quotes are from pages 583, 585, 586, and 590.

81. See Prasenjit Duara, "Between Empire and Nation: Settler Colonialism in Man-chukuo," in *Settler Colonialism in the Twentieth Century*, ed. Caroline Elkins and Susan Pedersen (New York: Routledge, 2005), 63.

82. Patrick Wolfe, "Settler Colonialism and the Elimination of the Native," *Journal of Genocide Research* 8, no. 4 (December 2006), 387–388, 402–403; and Patrick Wolfe, *Settler Colonialism and the Transformation of Anthropology* (London: Cassell, 1999), 163. The quotes are from pages 402 and 403 of the first source.

83. On similar manifestations of "Hokkaido's liberal humanist racism" in Japan's indig-enous policy, see Katsuya Hirano, "Thanatopolitics in the Making of Japan's Hokkaido: Set-tler Colonialism and Primitive Accumulation," *Critical Historical Studies* 2, no. 2 (2015), 210–218.

84. See *Dōmin* 49 (1 October 1928), 9.

85. Washizu Shakuma, "Wagahai no Beikoku seikatsu," no. 50 and no. 66, *Nichibei Shimbun*, 31 August and 16 September 1924.

86. Tōa Dōbunkai, ed., *Tai-shi kaikoroku* (Tokyo: Tōa Dōbunkai, 1936), 995; Kokuryūkai, *Tōa senkaku shishi kiden: Gekan*, 301–302; and *Shokumin Kyōkai hōkoku* 69 (16 August 1899), 4.

87. Nakamura Tadayuki, "'Jūkei Nippō' no sōshisha Takekawa Tōtarō," no. 1, *Tenri Daigaku gakuhō* 14, no. 3 (March 1963), 18–20; Kokuryūkai, *Tōa senkaku shishi kiden: Gekan*, 301–302; and Katō Masahiko, *Maboroshi no "Jūkei Nippō"* (Kofu: Yamanashi Furusato Bunko, 1995), 24–25. On Konoe's pan-Asianism, see Aydin, *The Politics of Anti-Westernism in Asia*, 54–56.

88. Nakamura, "'Jūkei Nippō' no sōshisha Takekawa Tōtarō," no. 1, 18–20; Kokuryūkai, *Tōa senkaku shishi kiden: Gekan*, 301–302; and Katō, *Maboroshi no "Jūkei Nippō"*, 24–25. Uncovering the forgotten history of the *Chongqing Ribao* as a background for local Chinese resistance to the Qing rule, the third source was simultaneously translated and published in Chinese language. See Katō Masahiko, *Meng duan ba shu: Zhuchuan Tengtailang he ta de "Chongqing Ribao"*, trans. Xiang Shu Zhen, Luo Jun, and Luo Jiang Long (Chengdu: Sichuan Renmin Chubanshe, 1995).

89. Nakamura, "'Jūkei Nippō' no sōshisha Takekawa Tōtarō," no. 1, 19.

90. "Hakkan no ji," *Shanghai Nippō*, 26 December 1903, quoted in Nakamura, "'Jūkei Nippō' no sōshisha Takekawa Tōtarō," no. 1, 21–22.

91. "Hakkan no ji," *Shanghai Nippō*, 26 December 1903.

92. Nakamura, "'Jūkei Nippō' no sōshisha Takekawa Tōtarō," no. 1, 26.

93. Nakamura Tadayuki, "'Jūkei Nippō' no sōshisha Takekawa Tōtarō," no. 2, *Tenri Daigaku gakuhō* 15, no. 1 (July 1963), 65–70.

94. The communist Chinese government and its nationalist orthodoxy recognized Bian Xiao-wu as a revolutionary hero, (mis)representing Takekawa's newspaper as Bian's creation. See, for example, the following Chinese government websites: http://dangshi.people.com.cn /GB/15922510.html; and http://qingming.chinamartyrs.gov.cn/info/1020 (both accessed 22 February 2019).

95. Nakamura, "'Jūkei Nippō' no sōshisha Takekawa Tōtarō," no. 1, 71–73; and Katō, *Maboroshi no "Jūkei Nippō"*, 204–215, 223, 250–253. The school also set up a branch in Chengdu.

96. Nakamura, "'*Jūkei Nippō*' no sōshisha Takekawa Tōtarō," no. 2, 59–60. The *Chong-qing Ribao* ceased to exist in 1908 after the arrest and execution of Bian Xiao-wu by the Qing government. Dejected, Takekawa also returned home to Japan, where he died of illness in Tokyo in 1911. His school in Chongqing, however, survived, and so did his match factory until 1917.

97. "Watanabe Kanjūrō-kun danwa 4," 271–273, 276–280, in Hoshi Tōru denki kōhon 14 (1915), Hoshi Tōru kankei monjo, MJPH-NDL; and Ariizumi Sadao, *Hoshi Tōru* (Tokyo: Asahi Shinbunsha, 1983), 220.

98. Yuji Ichioka, *The Issei: The World of the First Generation Japanese Immigrants, 1885–1924* (New York: Free Press, 1988), 14–16, 40–46; and Robert Bowen, *Rebellion and Democracy in Meiji Japan* (Berkeley: University of California Press, 1980), 8–66.

99. See Itō, "Guatemara jikkenroku," 12–16; and Nagasawa Betten, "Yankii" (1893), in *Seikyōsha bungakushū*, ed. Matsumoto Sannosuke (Tokyo: Chikuma Shobō, 1980), 316, 335, 337–341.

100. See the society's "prospectus for [its] establishment," in "Shokumin Kyōkai set-suritsu shuisho," *Shokumin Kyōkai hōkoku* 1 (15 April 1893), 105–107.

101. See Sidney Xu Lu, "Colonizing Hokkaido and the Origin of Japanese Trans-Pacific Expansion, 1869–1894," *Japanese Studies* 36, no. 2 (2016), 255–256; Sidney Xu Lu, *The Making of Japanese Settler Colonialism: Malthusianism and Trans-Pacific Migration, 1868–1961* (New York: Cambridge University Press, 2019); Yoshida Hideo, *Nihon jinkōron no shiteki kenkyū* (Tokyo: Kawade Shobō, 1944), 21–33, 152–158; and, for example, Fukuzawa Yukichi, "Soto o sakini subeshi," in *Fukuzawa Yukichi zenshū* (Tokyo: Iwanami Shoten, 1932), 11:538–541. Lu's book specifically discusses the role of Malthusian population discourse in Japanese settler colonialism.

102. On these changes in late Meiji Japan, see Gluck, *Japan's Modern Myths*, 26–35; and Andrew D. Gordon, *Labor and Imperial Democracy in Prewar Japan* (Berkeley: University of California Press, 1992), 11–120.

103. On how the recruitment and migration processes unfolded under emigration companies relative to Hawai'i and the continental United States, see Alan Takeo Moriyama, *Imingaisha: Japanese Emigration Companies and Hawaii* (Honolulu: University of Hawaii Press, 1985); and Ichioka, *The Issei*, 47–51, 57–64.

104. Kodama, *Nihon iminshi kenkyū josetsu*, 261; and Kurabe Kiyotaka, *Tōge no bunkashi* (Tokyo: PMC Shuppan, 1989), 77.

105. See Toyohara Matao, *Sakuma Teiichi-den* (Tokyo: Shūeisha Teikeikai, 1904), 81–83; and Ariiso Itsurō, "Iminkai no katsudōsha 1," *Shōgyōkai* 3, no. 6 (1 May 1905), 30–37.

106. Kodama, *Nihon Iminshi kenkyū josetsu*, 261; and Moriyama, *Imingaisha*, 49–54.

107. The quote is from Okumura Naohiko, "Nihon Meiji Imin Gaisha ni tsuite," *Kirisutokyō shakai mondai kenkyū* 34 (March 1986), 71. See also Moriyama, *Imingaisha*, 33–37. The Emigrant Protection Act was officially enacted as the national law in 1896 and amended a few times until 1910.

108. On California examples, see Eiichiro Azuma, *Between Two Empires: Race, History, and Transnationalism in Japanese America* (New York: Oxford University Press, 2005), 17–18, 35–60, 98–105.

109. Irie, *Hōjin kaigai hattenshi*, 1:120–138, 393–415.

110. Kodama, *Nihon iminshi kenkyū josetsu*, 261.

111. Kodama, *Nihon iminshi kenkyū josetsu*, 413–432; and Ichioka, *The Issei*, 50–51.

112. Maeda Renzan, *Hoshi Tōru-den* (Tokyo: Takayama Shoten, 1948), 275–276; and Inoue Keijirō, "Haran chōjō no nanajūnen 8," *Higo* 19, no. 2 (January 1939), 36.

113. "Inoue Keijirō-shi danwa yōkō 4," *Chiyū zasshi* 3, no. 10 (October 1937), 29.

114. Kodama, *Nihon iminshi kenkyū josetsu*, 216.

115. Ariiso, "Iminkai no katsudōsha 1," 31–33; and Kurabe, *Tōge no bunkashi*, 85–86.

116. United Japanese Society of Hawaii, ed., *Hawai Nihonjin iminshi* (Honolulu: United Japanese Society of Hawaii, 1964), 160–164; Kurabe, *Tōge no bunkashi*, 78–85; Maeda, *Hoshi Tōru-den*, 324–326; Ariiso, "Iminkai no katsudōsha 2," *Shōgyōkai* 3, no. 7 (1 June 1 1905), 30–31; and "Inoue Keijirō-shi danwa yōkō 4," 31.

117. Inoue, "Haran chōjō no nanajūnen 6," *Higo* 18, no. 11 (November 1938), 40–41; Inoue, "Haran chōjō no nanajūnen 7," *Higo* 18, no. 12 (December 1938), 52–53; Inoue, "Haran chōjō no nanajūnen 9," *Higo* 19, no. 2 (February 1939), 44; and Mantetsu Kōhōka, ed., *Yokokawa Shōzō bakuhakō* (Dalian: Manshū Nichinichi Shinbun, 1941), 34–36.

118. Inoue Keijirō, "Mekishiko-dan 4," *Keizai Jihō* 26 (1903), 10. See also Inoue Keijirō, "Mekishiko zakki," *Chigaku zasshi* 15, no. 6 (June 1903), 492–493.

119. Inoue, "Mekishiko-dan 3," *Keizai Jihō* 25 (1903), 12–14. The quotes are from page 14.

120. "Inoue Keijirō-shi danwa yōkō 4," 31.

121. Nichiboku Kyōkai, ed., *Nichiboku kōryūshi* (Tokyo: Nichiboku Kyōkai, 1990), 246.

122. Ichioka, *The Issei*, 51–52.

123. Gaimusho Ryōji Ijūbu, *Waga kokumin no Kaigai hatten: Shiryō-hen* (Tokyo: Gaimushō, 1971), 144–145.

124. "Kaigai ryoken uketori jin'in," in Naikaku Tōkei-kyoku, ed., *Nihon Teikoku tōkei nenkan*, vols. 19–21 (Tokyo: Nihon Tōkei Kyōkai, 1899–1901).

125. "Kaigai ryoken uketori jin'in."

126. Ariiso Itsurō, "Waga imin gaisha 1," *Shōkō Sekai Taiheiyō* 5, no. 20 (1 October 1906), 73–76; Yokoyama Gennosuke, *Meiji fugōshi* (Tokyo: Shakai Shisōsha, [1904] 1989), 173–178; Kurabe, *Tōge no bunkashi*, 77–78, 85–86. The Tairiku Shokumin's headquarters was set up in the same building as Hoshi Tōru's law office. The Tōyō Emigration Company, formerly the Nihon Kissa, later tried to get a share of the Mexican market dominated by the Kumamoto Imin and the Tairiku Shokumin, but its Mexico endeavor was short lived. After the Gentlemen's Agreement shut the Mexican market and the two companies folded, the Tōyō successfully controlled a large portion of Japanese labor emigration to the new market of Brazil from 1908 though 1917.

127. Nichiboku Kyōkai, *Nichiboku kōryūshi*, 248–251, 253–258.

128. Murakami Taizō, "Bokkoku imin-dan," *Amerika* 12, no. 6 (June 1908), 59.

3. TRANSPACIFIC MIGRANTS AND THE BLURRING BOUNDARIES OF STATE AND PRIVATE SETTLER COLONIALISM

1. Ōkawahira Takamitsu, *Nihon iminron* (Tokyo: Bunbudō, 1905), 266–267, 274.

2. Nitobe Inazō, Jo [foreword] to Ōkawahira, *Nihon iminron*, 1–2, 4–5.

3. See Kornel Chang, *Pacific Connections: The Making of U.S.-Canadian Borderlands* (Berkeley: University of California Press, 2012), 89–116.

4. "Nōkōshō Kōtō Kaigi giji sokkiroku: Dai-sankai (1898)," Tokyo, 1899, 673, 675–676, 678 (microfilm), National Diet Library (hereafter NDL), Tokyo. Chaired by Shibusawa Eiichi, the higher commission on agriculture and industry had a number of specialist groups. This subcommission included some individuals, such as Inoue Kakugorō, Takahashi Korekiyo (a future finance minister), and Taguchi Ukichi, who had overseas experience. As chapter 1 shows, Inoue unsuccessfully tried his hand at settler colonialism in California in the 1880s, and Takahashi was also a onetime California resident, who became involved in a scheme to start a silver mining venture in Peru. Taguchi played an important role in the early phase of Japanese commerce in German-controlled Micronesia. They strongly advocated the protection of overseas Japanese by the home state.

5. Gaimushō, ed., *Gaimushō no hyakunen* (Tokyo: Hara Shobō, 1969), 1:579.

6. Shumpei Okamoto, "Meiji Imperialism: Pacific Emigration or Continental Expansionism," in *Japan Examined: Perspectives on Modern Japanese History*, ed. Harry Wray and Hilary Conroy (Honolulu: University of Hawaii Press, 1983), 143.

7. See, for example, Jun Uchida, *Brokers of Empire: Japanese Settler Colonialism in Korea, 1976–1945* (Cambridge, MA: Harvard University Asia Center, 2011), 58–59; and Kurose Yūji, *Tōyō Takushoku Kaisha* (Tokyo: Nihon Keizai Hyōronsha, 2003), 15.

8. Okamoto, "Meiji Imperialism," 144.

9. Makino Nobuaki, "Ōshū shokoku ni okeru Shokumin no keikō o ronjite Wagakuni kongo no Shokumin seisaku ni oyobu" (1910), in folder C139-189, Makino Nobuaki monjo, Modern Japanese Political History Materials Room, National Diet Library (hereafter MJPH-NDL), Tokyo. This commentary was printed in *Taiyō* 16, no. 15 (10 November 1910), 11–18.

10. Earl H. Kinmonth, *The Self-Made Man in Meiji Japanese Thought: From Samurai to Salary Man* (Berkeley: University of California Press, 1981), 158–160, 262–271; and Mitziko Sawada, *Tokyo Life, New York Dreams: Urban Japanese Visions of America, 1890–1924* (Berkeley: University of California Press, 1996), 87–115.

11. See Kinmonth, *The Self-Made Man in Meiji Japanese Thought*; and "Kyōkoku no sandai yōso: Shokumin bungaku no hitsuyō," *Kaigai no Nippon* 1, no. 1 (1 January 1911), 3.

12. Ōkuma Shigenobu, "Shokumin shisō o ippenseyo," *Kaigai no Nippon* 1, no. 1 (1 January 1911), 5.

13. "Sairyō no iminchi wa doko," *Kaigai no Nippon* 1, no. 2 (1 February 1911), 30–48.

14. Hinata Terutake, "Mankan shūchū shugi no akueikyō," *Kaigai no Nippon* 1, no. 2 (1 February 1911), 41–42. The quotes are from page 42.

15. See special issue on the expansion of the Japanese race/nation, *Taiyō* 16, no. 15 (1 November 1910), esp. 2–97, 106–113, 158–160, 170–194.

16. On this concept (*heiwateki bōchō*), see Akira Iriye, *Pacific Estrangement: Japanese and American Expansion, 1897–1911* (Cambridge, MA: Harvard University Press, 1972), 131.

17. Ōkuma Shigenobu, "Nihon minzoku no bōchō ni tsuite," *Taiyō* 16, no. 15 (1 November 1910), 9. On US liberal developmentalism, see Emily S. Rosenberg, *Spreading the American Dream: American Economic and Cultural Expansion, 1890–1945* (New York: Hill and Wang, 1982), 7–13.

18. Ōkuma, "Nihon minzoku no bōchō ni tsuite," 9, 11.

19. Ōkuma Shigenobu, "Yamato minzoku bōchō to shokumin jigyō," *Shokumin Sekai* 1, no. 1 (May 1908), 3.

20. See Iriye, *Pacific Estrangement*, 131.

21. Ukita Kazutami, "Nanbei no shōrai to kongo no imin seisaku," *Taiyō* 16, no. 6 (1 May 1910), 3.

22. See *Taiyō* 14, no. 3 (15 February 1908) and *Taiyō*, 14, no. 9 (15 June 1908), 177–200, respectively.

23. Jeffrey Lesser, *Negotiating National Identity: Immigrants, Minorities, and the Struggle for Ethnicity in Brazil* (Durham, N.C.: Duke University Press, 1999), 86–87 and 38; see also Ana Paulina Lee, *Mandarin Brazil: Race, Representation, and Memory* (Stanford, CA: Stanford University Press, 2018), chaps. 2, 4–5.

24. Inoue Katsuo, "Satō Shōsuke 'Shokuminron' kōgi nōto," *Hokudai Bungakubu kiyō* 46, no. 3 (March 1998), 1–2. On colonial policy studies under Nitobe's successor Yanaihara Tadao, see Shiode Hiroyuki, *Ekkyōsha no seijishi* (Nagoya: Nagoya Daigaku Shuppan, 2015), 156–170.

25. Nitobe Inazō, *Beikoku kenkoku shiyō* (Tokyo: Yūhikaku, 1919), 25–26.

26. Yanaihara Tadao, ed., *Nitobe hakase shokumin seisaku kōgi oyobi ronbunshū* (Tokyo: Iwanami Shoten, 1943), 64–73. The quotes are from pages 65–66. This book contains Nitobe's lecture notes, taken by his former students at Tokyo Imperial University, including the editor who succeeded to the professorship in colonial policy studies.

27. Yanaihara, *Nitobe hakase shokumin seisaku kōgi oyobi ronbunshū*, 9–10.

28. Yanaihara, *Nitobe hakase shokumin seisaku kōgi oyobi ronbunshū*, 68–69.

29. "Imin hogohō chū kaisei hōritsuan iinkai gijiroku: Dai yonkai" (18 March 1907), 15–16, in "Shūgiin iinkai gijiroku, v. 21," Tokyo, Shūgiin, 1907; and "Imin hogohō chū kaisei hōritsuan iinkai gijiroku: Dai nikai" (15 March 1907), 5, in "Shūgiin iinkai gijiroku, v. 21," Tokyo, Shūgiin, 1907, NDL. See especially article 5 of the 1907 law. The Diet committee that deliberated on the 1907 law included former US residents and emigration company executives, such as Hinata Terutake, Yamaguchi Yuya, and Matsumoto Kimihei.

30. "Imin hogohō chū kaisei hōritsuan iinkai gijiroku: Dai yonkai," 15, 18. Dissatisfied with the official's lukewarm response, Hinata, Yamaguchi, Matsumoto, and three other Diet members engineered the passage of a parliamentary resolution for the formation of a new "colonization bureau" within the government. This move amplified political pressure on the cabinet to come up with a definitive blueprint for Korea and Manchuria. See "Shokuminchō setsuritsu ni kansuru kengian iinkai gijiroku: Dai nikai" (25 March 1907), in "Shūgiin iinkai gijiroku, v. 21," Tokyo, Shūgiin, 1907.

31. Tōyō Takushoku Kabushiki Kaisha, *Tōyō Takushoku Kabushiki Kaisha sanjūnen-shi* (Tokyo: Tōyō Takushoku Kabushiki Kaisha, 1939), 1–9. See also Hyung Gu Lynn, "Malthusian Dreams, Colonial Imaginary: The Oriental Development Company and Japanese Emigration to Korea," in *Settler Colonialism in the Twentieth Century*, ed. Caroline Elkins and Susan Pedersen (New York: Routledge, 2005), 29–31.

32. Kurose, *Tōyō Takushoku Kaisha*, 15–38. All conversions to acreage are mine.

33. Usagawa Kazumasa, "Chōsen ni okeru takushoku jigyō," *Kaigai no Nippon* 1, no. 1 (January 1911), 12.

34. Tōyō Takushoku Kabushiki Kaisha, *Kaisei Chōsen ijū tebikisho* (Seoul: Tōyō Takushoku Kabushiki Kaisha, 1915), 2–3.

35. It is important to note that Abiko and other immigrant leaders understood that "assimilation" with white America, or "Americanization," was perfectly compatible with being a good imperial subject, insofar as becoming "Americanized" was deemed another means of becoming civilized and modern. See Eiichiro Azuma, *Between Two Empires: Race, History, and Transnationalism in Japanese America* (New York: Oxford University Press, 2005), 35–60.

36. Yuji Ichioka, *The Issei: The World of the First Generation Japanese Immigrants, 1885–1924* (New York: Free Press, 1988), 146–150; and Azuma, *Between Two Empires*, 24, 40–41. Abiko usually used the term in reverse order as *dochaku eijū*.

37. Ichioka, *The Issei*, 174.

38. Ichioka, *The Issei*, 146–148.

39. "Beikoku ni okeru yuiitsu no Nihonjin shokuminchi," *Taiyō* 14, no. 1 (1 January 1908), no pagination.

40. See Rafu Shimpō, ed., *Rafu nenkan* (Los Angeles: Rafu Shimpōsha, 1907), 1:54–55; Eiichiro Azuma, "A History of Oregon's Issei, 1880–1952," *Oregon Historical Quarterly* 94, no. 4 (1993–1994), 329–331; "Shin Nihon-mura kensetsu keikaku," *Amerika* 12, no. 6 (June 1908), 59–60; Okazaki Tsunekichi, "Shin Nihon-mura no kensetsu ni tsuite," *Nōgyō zasshi* 31, no. 12 (April 1906), 177–179; and Nagatani Buemon, "Kanada Aruberuta-shū no Nihonmura kensetsu," *Shokumin Sekai* 1, no. 2 (June 1908), 9–12. Ōtsuki Kōnosuke, former Hawai'i-based expansionist, was instrumental in the short-lived Alberta venture before remigrating to Taiwan's eastern frontier.

41. See, for example, Noda Otosaburō, "Zaibei Nihonjin no jigyō," *Amerika* 11, no. 12 (December 1907), 57–60; Tsuboya Mizuya, "Hokubei ni okeru Nihon shokuminchi no kensetsu," *Taiyō* 14, no. 3 (15 February 1908), 193–197; and Fūraibō [pseud.], "Yamato shokuminchi o shōkai su," *Shōkō Sekai Taiheiyō* 7, no. 20 (15 September 1908), 101–103. On Abiko's trip to Japan, see *Tokyo Asahi Shinbun*, 14 and 28 November 1908.

42. See, for example, "Imin hogohō chū kaisei hōritsuan iinkai gijiroku: Dai yonkai," 4–5.

43. See Aratake Tatsurō, "Nihon tōchi jidai Taiwan tōbu eno imin to sōshutsuchi," *Tokushima Daigaku Sōgō Kagakubu ningen shakai bunka kenkyū* 14 (2007), 92–94.

44. Uchida, *Brokers of Empire*, 62, 66. The quote is from page 62.

45. Uchida, *Brokers of Empire*, 66.

46. Kimura Kenji, "Tōtaku imin no sōshutsu katei," *Keizaishi kenkyū* 6 (March 2002), 125–131; and Martin Dusinberre, *Hard Times in the Hometown: A History of Community Survival in Modern Japan* (Honolulu: University of Hawai'i Press, 2012), 83–116. On a similar situation in a neighboring prefecture, see Hannah Shepherd, "Fukuoka's Meiji Migrants and the Making of an Imperial Region," *Japan Forum* 30, no. 4 (2018), 490–492.

47. Uchida, *Brokers of Empire*, 60; Kurose, *Tōyō Takushoku Kaisha*, 42–44; and Lynn, "Malthusian Dreams, Colonial Imaginary," 31–34.

48. Kurose, *Tōyō Takushoku Kaisha*, 18; and Katsura Tarō, "Shukuji," *Kaigai no Nippon* 1, no. 1 (1 January 1911), 5. The quotes are from the second source.

49. Asada Kōson, "Rikugun taishō kōshaku Katsura Tarō-kun," *Taiyō* 15, no. 9 (July 1909), 25.

50. Nagata Shigeshi, *Burajiru ni okeru Nihonjin hattenshi* (Tokyo: Burajiru ni okeru Nihonjin Hattenshi Kankōkai, 1953), 8–9; *Jiji Shimpō*, 24 May 1912; Fujita Toshirō, "Sanpauro-shū Iguape chihō junkai hōkokusho" (ca. March 1912), 63, in Burajiru Sanpauro-shū Iguape-gun Nihonjin shokuminchi kaisetsu ikken, vol. 1, Diplomatic Archives of the Ministry of Foreign Affairs (hereafter DA-MOFA), Tokyo; and Burajiru Takushoku Kabushiki Kaisha (hereafter BTKK), "Jigyō yotei setsumeisho" (1915), 1–2, folder 96-7, Hashida Masao kenkei shiryō, MJPH-NDL. Conversions to acreage are mine.

51. Nagata, *Burajiru ni okeru Nihonjin hattenshi*, 2–3; and "Iguape shokuminchi enkaku," in Kaigai Kōgyō Kabushiki Kaisha (hereafter KKKK), *Burajiru-koku Iguape shokuminchi sōritsu nijusshūnen kinen shashinchō* (1933), no pagination, Nikkei imin kankei shiryō, MJPH-NDL. On the involvement of syndicate members in the ODC, see Tōyō Takushoku Kabushiki Kaisha, *Tōyō Takushoku Kabushiki Kaisha sanjūnen-shi*, 2–3.

52. "Nanbei ni okeru Nihonjin hatten no shin undō," *Jitsugyō no Nihon* 16, no. 7 (1 April 1913), 10–11; Nagata, *Burajiru ni okeru Nihonjin hattenshi*, 3, 6; and Nihon Imin Gojūnensai Iinkai, ed., *Bukko senkusha retsuden* (São Paulo, Brazil: Nihon Imin Gojūnensai Iinkai, 1958), 3–4.

53. Irie Toraji, *Kaigai dōhō hattenshi* (Tokyo: Ide Shoten, 1942), 1:208; *Shokumin Kyōkai hōkoku* no. 33 (28 January 1896), 77.

54. Nagata, *Burajiru ni okeru Nihonjin hattenshi*, 3–4.

55. Nagata, *Burajiru ni okeru Nihonjin hattenshi*, 4–5. In the *Jiji Shimpō*, Aoyagi published a series of twenty-four essays detailing his observations and experiences in Brazil. See Aoyagi Ikutarō, "Burajiru ryokō" 1–24, *Jiji Shimpō*, 23 July–29 August 1912.

56. Nagata, *Burajiru ni okeru Nihonjin hattenshi*, 6–8; and *Jiji Shimpō*, 24 May 1912.

57. Miyashita Takuma, "Burajiru kaitaku to Katsura-kō" 4, *Kaigai* 13, no. 71 (January 1933), 83–85; and Shibusawa Seien Kinen Zaidan, ed., *Shibusawa Eiichi denki shiryōshū* (hereafter *SEDS*) (Tokyo: Shibusawa Eiichi Denki Shiryōshū Kankōkai, 1964), 55:565–566.

58. On Shibusawa's interest in land development in Korea, see Uchida, *Brokers of Empire*, 40.

59. *SEDS* 55:568–572.

60. See "Kabunushi meibo" (10 March 1913), 1–2, in Burajiru Sanpauro-shū Iguape-gun Nihonjin shokuminchi kaisetsu ikken, vol. 1.

61. BTKK, "Dai-nikai hōkokusho" (1914), 2, 4, in folder 96-6, Hashida Masao kankei shiryō, MJPH-NDL.

62. BTKK, "Shokuminchi jijō" (November 1915), 3; and BTKK, "Dai-sankai hōkokusho" (1915), 4–5, both in folder 96-6, Hashida Masao kankei shiryō, MJPH-NDL.

63. KKKK, "Kaigai Kōgyō Kabushiki Kaisha shōshi" (August 1935), 34–36, NDL.

64. [Hara Umesaburō], *Nanbei Burajiru no ikkaku ni sobietatsu Nihonjin shokuminchi dai-ichigō, Iguape Shokuminchi* (Tokyo: Nōgyō Takushoku Kyōkai, 1966), 33.

65. See Eiichiro Azuma, "Community Formation across the National Border: The Japanese of the U.S.-Mexican Californias," *Review: Literature and Arts of the Americas* 39, no. 1 (2006), 36–39.

66. Yuji Ichioka's seminal work set the tone for later studies' monolithic characterization of Abiko; see Ichioka, *The Issei*, 149–150, 154.

67. Azuma, *Between Two Empires*, 36–58, 91–98.

68. "Beikoku ni okeru yuiitsu no Nihonjin shokuminchi," no pagination.

69. "Need Larger Navy," *Washington Post*, 4 April 1912; "Warning to Japan on Magdalena Bay," *New York Times*, 5 April 1912; S. Doc. No. 62-640 (1 May 1912), 4; and Nagai Matsuzō to David Starr Jordan, 9 April 1912, in Bokkoku Taiheiyō engan ni oite Honpōjin gyogyōken shutoku ikken (hereafter BTH), DA-MOFA.

70. William L. Holland to John D. Pope, 3 May 1913, in folder "Leasing Land to Japanese," box 1, Enrique Cortes Papers, Colorado River Land Company Collection (hereafter CRLCC), Sherman Library and Gardens, Corona Del Mar, California.

71. Noda Otosaburō, "Bokkoku ryokōdan," *Hokubei Nōhō* 3 (March 1912), 10.

72. Noda, "Bokkoku ryokōdan," 6–7. See also Eugene Keith Chamberlin, "The Japanese Scare at Magdalena Bay," *Pacific Historical Review* 24 (November 1955), 351. The Chamberlin article, which did not consult Japanese immigrant sources, misrepresents Abiko and Noda as having no intention to "establish there a Japanese colony on a large scale."

73. Nagai Matsuzō to Uchida Yasuya, 14 March 1912, in BTH, DA-MOFA.

74. Azuma, *Between Two Empires*, 52–53.

75. E. E. Easton to Henry Z. Osborne, 26 November 1909, in folder 35, box: "Anderson's Portfolios," Colorado River Land Company Papers, CRLCC. In 1909 Chandler met personally with Shibusawa in Los Angeles when the latter led the first commercial commission, consisting of many major business figures in Japan.

76. "An outline of book on *L.A. Times* and development of So. Calif.," no date, in folder "Sale of Lands of CRLC to Japanese, 1915, 1923," box 1, Enrique Cortes Papers, CRLCC.

77. S. Doc. No. 62-640, at 4 (1912).

78. *San Francisco Examiner*, 31 January 1912; "Japanese Deal with Mexico Is Blocked," *Portland Telegram*, 31 January 1912; and "Japan and Mexico," *New York Times*, 4 April 1912. The quotes are from the last source.

79. David H. Grover, "Maneuvering for Magdalena Bay: International Intrigue at a Baja California Anchorage," *Southern California Quarterly* 83 (2001), 265, 268.

80. "Fear Grip of Japan," *Washington Post*, 3 April 1912; H.R. Res. 522, 62nd Cong. (3 May 1912); S. Doc. No. 62-640, at 1.

81. Tom Coffman, *Nation Within: The Story of America's Annexation of the Nation of Hawai'i* (Kaneohe, HI: Koa Books, 1998), 220–221.

82. 48 Cong. Rec. 10,045 (1912).

83. Walter LaFeber, "The Evolution of the Monroe Doctrine from Monroe to Reagan," in *Redefining the Past: Essays in Diplomatic History in Honor of William Appleman Williams*, ed. Lloyd C. Gardner (Corvallis: Oregon State University Press, 1986), 139–140; Grover, "Maneuvering for Magdalena Bay," 267–277; and Jerry García, *Looking Like the Enemy: Japanese Mexicans, the Mexican State, and U.S. Hegemony 1897–1945* (Tucson: University of Arizona Press, 2014), 48–55.

84. "Japan's Premier Tells the *Times* There Is No Magdalena Bay Incident," *New York Times*, 6 April 1912; S. Rep. No. 62-996 (31 July 1912); Chinda Sutemi to Uchida Yasuya, 3 and 14 April 1912, in BTH, DA-MOFA.

85. "An outline of book on *L.A. Times* and development of So. Calif."

86. See Roger Daniels, *The Politics of Prejudice: Anti-Japanese Movement in California and the Struggle for Japanese Exclusion* (Berkeley: University of California Press, 1962), 46–64.

87. See Hasegawa Shin'ichirō, *Bokkoku ichiran* (Tokyo: Nihonsha, 1917), 1–39, 261–282.

88. Kamiya Tadao, "Nanbei sonota ni okeru Nihon imin no jōtai," *Taiyō* 16, no. 15 (10 November 1910), 62–63.

89. "Nichi-Boku Colony: Nichiboku shokuminchi" (May 1914), 11, in the author's personal collection.

90. "Nichi-Boku Colony," 14–15, and maps. The quotes are from a colony subdivision map (no pagination). See also "Nichi-Boku Sangyō Kabushiki Kaisha jigyō setsumei" (1918); and Takekawa Minetarō to Adachi Mineichirō, 1 October 1915, both in Honpō kaisha kankei zakken: Nichi-Boku Sangyō Kabushiki Kaisha (hereafter HNB), DA-MOFA.

91. "Tochi baibai keiyakusha," in HNB, DA-MOFA. The tally is by the author.

92. "Nichi-Boku Sangyō Kabushi Kaisha kabunushi roku," in HNB, DA-MOFA; and Ōkagawa Kō, "'Kyogyōka' ni yoru giji benchā tōshi fando to risuku kanri," *Shiga Daigaku Keizai Gakubu kenkyū nenpō* 14 (2007), 14–15.

93. Yamamoto Teijirō to Tanaka Tōkichi, "Nichi-Boku shokuminchi shisatsu hōkokusho," 4 November 1920; and Ōyama Ujirō to Hanihara Masanao, 16 February 1921, both in HNB, DA-MOFA.

94. See, for example, a company advertisement for investment published in *Tokyo Nichinichi Shinbun*, 13 July 1920. Its Tokyo office was headed by the former chargé d'affaires of Japan to Mexico.

95. Ōyama Ujirō to Nakamura Takashi, 7 December 1917; Ōyama to Uchida Yasuya, 2 December 1920; and "Nichi-Boku Sangyō Kabushiki Kaisha Mekishiko nōjō ijūsha annai," ca. 1920, all in HNB, DA-MOFA.

96. KKKK, *Kaigai Kōgyō Kaisha shōshi* (August 1935), 19, NDL. On the legal trouble in which NIBC was engulfed, see *Osaka Asahi Shinbun*, 15 June 1921.

97. See Nichiboku Kyōkai, ed., *Nichiboku kōryūshi* (Tokyo: PMC Shuppan, 1990), 422–423; Nihonjin Mekishiko Ijūshi Hensan Iinkai, ed., *Nihonjin Mekishiko ijūshi* (Mexico City: Nichiboku Kyōkai 1971), 163–164, 235, 239–241, 326–328; and Murai Ken'ichi, *Paionia retsuden* (1975), 63–64, 66–67, 101–102, 107, Nikkei imin kankei shiryō, MJPH-NDL.

98. On CRLC, see Dorothy Pierson Kerig, "Yankee Enclave: The Colorado River Land Company and Mexican Agrarian Reform in Baja California, 1902–1944" (PhD diss., University of California, Irvine, 1988), 16–179, esp. 169–170.

99. See page 2 of a ten-page report with no date in folder "118-a, Colonization, Allison Matters ½," box "Q," CRLCC.

100. [Harry Chandler] to M. Sugawara, U. Hashimoto, and K. Imanishi, 12 June 1917; and Chandler to T. E. Gibbon, 19 June 1917, both in folder "1917," box 7, MHS Letters, CRLCC. The quote is from the second source. The tally is by the author.

101. [Chandler] to Sugawara, Hashimoto, and Imanishi, 12 June 1917; and "Seek Cotton Lands on the Colorado," *Los Angeles Times*, 14 June 1917.

102. Ōta Kōji, ed., *Hashimoto Umetarō* (Tokyo: Hashimoto Umetarō-kun Denki Hensankai, 1939), 63–94, esp. 78–83, 91–94.

103. Gakubuchi-sei [pseud.], "Gō Ryūsaburō-shi," *Jitsugyō no Nihon* 10, no. 26 (15 December 1907), 64–67; Matsushita Denkichi, ed., *Jinteki Jigyō taikei* (Tokyo: Chūgai Sangyō Chōsakai, 1942), 2:178; and Higashi Kōji, *Bei-Boku jūō* (Tokyo: Seikyōsha, 1920), 365. Gō remained in Southern California as a leader of the ethnic community and ran a trading

firm until 1935, when he moved to Thailand to set up a Tokyo-backed cotton plantation. See Yatabe to Hirota, 20 August 1935, in Honpō kigyōka no sōmen kōjō oyobi mengyō saien keiei ni kansuru ken; and "Shōmeisho," 27 April 1939, in Kakkoku ni okeru Nōsanbutsu kankei zakken: Men oyobi menka no bu vol. 18, DA-MOFA.

104. Ōta, *Hashimoto Umetarō*, 138–139; Higashi, *Bei-Boku jūō*, 365–368; page 3 of a ten-page report with no date, in folder "118-a, Colonization, Allison Matters ½," box "Q," CRLCC; and Gaimushō Tsūshō-kyoku, ed., "Kaigai Nihon jitsugyōsha no chōsha" (December 1918), 231, DA-MOFA.

105. Chandler to M. H. Sherman, telegram, 28 April 1917; and Chandler to [Sherman], 19 April 1917, both in folder "1917," box 7, MHS Letters, CRLCC.

106. Hashimoto and Sugawara to Chandler, 15 June 1917, in folder "1917," box 7, MHS Letters, CRLCC.

107. Chandler to Sherman, 9 August 1917, in folder "1917," box 7, MHS Letters, CRLCC. Hashimoto's published biography contradicts what primary sources reveal. According to the book, Hashimoto allegedly spearheaded the land deal of his own volition without Asano's prior knowledge. Asano, as it narrates, convinced Hashimoto to cancel the deal after it was successfully concluded—advice that Hashimoto accepted reluctantly. Most likely this distorted narrative reflects an effort to absolve Asano from the rather embarrassing demise of the land deal caused by Yellow Peril demagogues. See Ōta, *Hashimoto Umetarō*, 138–139.

108. Hashimoto to Chandler, telegram, 4 January 1919, in folder "Japanese to Buy Land, 1918–1919," box 1, Enrique Cortes Papers, CRLCC.

109. O. F. Brant to Chandler, 6 January 1919, and 17 January 1919, in folder "Japanese to Buy Land, 1918–1919," box 1, Enrique Cortes Papers, CRLCC.

110. C. A. Wardlaw to Frederick Simpich, 1 March 1919; and Brant to Chandler, 17 January 1919, both in folder "Japanese to Buy Land, 1918–1919," box 1, Enrique Cortes Papers, CRLCC.

111. "Landowners Called upon to Give Full Explanation," *Los Angeles Examiner*, 22 March 1919.

112. [Chandler] to Hashimoto, draft letter, no date; and Chandler to Brant, 21 January 1919, both in folder "Japanese to Buy Land, 1918–1919," box 1, Enrique Cortes Papers, CRLCC.

113. See *SEDS*, 55:604–629.

114. On the influences and roles of US-bred racial scaremongering in those nations in the 1930s, see Lesser, *Negotiating National Identity*, 93–94, 116–132, esp. 116; and Erika Lee, "The 'Yellow Peril' in the United States and Peru," in *Transnational Crossroads: Remapping the Americas and the Pacific*, ed. Camilla Fojas and Rudy P. Guevera Jr. (Lincoln: University of Nebraska Press, 2012), 315–358.

4. US IMMIGRATION EXCLUSION, JAPANESE AMERICA, AND TRANSMIGRANTS ON JAPAN'S BRAZILIAN FRONTIERS

1. Kurose Yūji, *Tōyō Takushoku Kaisha* (Tokyo: Nihon Keizai Hyōronsha, 2003), 106–113.

2. Tōyō Takushoku Kabushiki Kaisha (hereafter TTKK), *Tōyō Takushoku Kabushiki Kaisha nijūnenshi* (Tokyo: TTKK, 1928), 3–4.

3. Kurose, *Tōyō Takushoku Kaisha*, 44–89, esp. 44–45, 82.

4. Kaigai Kōgyō Kabushiki Kaisha (hereafter KKKK), "Kaigai Kōgyō Kabushiki Kaisha shōshi" (1935), 1–6, National Diet Library (hereafter NDL), Tokyo. See also Sakaguchi Mitsuhiro, "Darega imin o okuridashitanoka," in *Nihonjin no kokusai idō to Taiheiyō sekai*, ed. Yoneyama Hiroshi and Kawahara Norifumi (Kyoto: Bunrikaku, 2015), 55–59.

5. KKKK, "Kaigai Kōgyō Kabushiki Kaisha shōshi," 8.

6. TTKK, *Tōyō Takushoku Kabushiki Kaisha sanjūnen-shi* (Tokyo: TTKK, 1939), 106.

7. During the 1930s the ODC extended its jurisdiction from East Asia and parts of Southeast Asia to Brazil and Thailand in order to supplement the KKKK, particularly in the area of capital supply. As of 1938, of the ODC's fifty-two subsidized colonization enterprises, six pertained to the Nan'yō, and two to Brazil. See TTKK, *Tōyō Takushoku Kabushiki Kaisha sanjūnen-shi*, 73–74, 98–107.

8. Kurose, *Tōyō Takushoku Kaisha*, 210–214, 246–275.

9. See KKKK, "Kaigai Kōgyō Kabushiki Kaisha shōshi," chart 1 ("Shagyō ichiranhyō") and table 3 ("Imin toriatsukai ichiran"), as well as pages 13–20; and KKKK, "Kaigai Kōgyō Kabushiki Kaisha gensei yōran" (September 1935), 1, 13–14, 28–34, Library of Economics, University of Tokyo (hereafter LE-UT).

10. KKKK, "Kaigai hatten ni kansuru Shōda ōkura daijin kōen" (1918), 13, NDL. See also Kurose, *Tōyō Takushoku Kaisha*, 110–111.

11. KKKK, "Kaigai hatten ni kansuru Shōda ōkura daijin kōen," 26–27.

12. KKKK, "Kaigai hatten ni kansuru Shōda ōkura daijin kōen," 12.

13. KKKK, "Kaigai hatten ni kansuru Shōda ōkura daijin kōen," 17, and 14–15.

14. KKKK, "Kaigai hatten ni kansuru Shōda ōkura daijin kōen," 17.

15. KKKK, "Kaigai hatten ni kansuru Shōda ōkura daijin kōen," 19; and KKKK, "Kaigai Kōgyō Kabushiki Kaisha shōshi," 9.

16. On the geopolitics of anti-Japanese racism in the late 1910s, see Naoko Shimazu, *Japan, Race and Equality: The Racial Equality Proposal of 1919* (London: Routledge, 1998), 13–37, 68–88, 137–163, esp. 30–31, 115–119; and Marilyn Lake and Henry Reynolds, *Drawing the Global Colour Line: White Men's Countries and the International Challenge of Racial Equality* (Cambridge, UK: Cambridge University Press, 2008), esp. 263–334.

17. "Shokumin kōenkai," *Osaka Mainichi*, 9 July 1918.

18. Dai-Nippon Bunmei Kyōkai, *Nihonjin no kaigai hatten* (Tokyo: Dai-Nippon Bunmei Kyōkai, 1916), 370.

19. Dai-Nippon Bunmei Kyōkai, *Nihonjin no kaigai hatten*, 397–398.

20. Takaoka Kumao, *Burajiru imin kenkyū* (Tokyo: Jitsubunkan, 1925), esp. 56–57, 78–94.

21. "Kaigai hatten ni kansuru kōsatsu," *Tōtaku geppō* no. 7 (February 1921), 12.

22. "Kaigai hatten ni kansuru kōsatsu," 10–13. The quotes are from pages 12–13.

23. "Kaigai hatten ni kansuru kōsatsu," 22.

24. KKKK, "Nanbei Burajirukoku to Nihon ishokumin" (July 1926), 3–4, 12, LE-UT.

25. KKKK, "Kaigai hatten ni kansuru Shōda ōkura daijin kōen," 32.

26. KKKK, "Kaigai hatten ni kansuru Shōda ōkura daijin kōen," 32–42. See also KKKK, "Kaigai Kōgyō Kabushiki Kaisha shōshi," 9.

27. Shibusawa Seien Kinen Zaidan, ed., *Shibusawa Eiichi denki shiryōshū* (hereafter SEDS) (Tokyo: Shibusawa Eiichi Denki Shiryōshū Kankōkai, 1959), 25:477–78; Zaibei

Nihonjinkai, *Zaibei Nihonjinkai hōkokusho* vol. 1 (San Francisco: Zaibei Nihonjinkai, 1909), 5, vol. 6 (1914), 13–14, vol. 8 (1916), 7–8, 22–24, and vol. 9 (1917), 15–16; and Zaibei Nihonjinkai, "Zaibei Nihonjinkai ikensho," ca. December 1915, in Taibei keihatsu undō ni kansuruken vol. 7, Diplomatic Archives of the Ministry of Foreign Affairs (hereafter DA-MOFA), Tokyo. See also Eiichiro Azuma, *Between Two Empires: Race, History, and Transnationalism in Japanese America* (New York: Oxford University Press, 2005), 53–54.

28. See Yuji Ichioka, *The Issei: The World of the First Generation Japanese Immigrants, 1885–1924* (New York: Free Press, 1988), 146–148, 186–196; and Azuma, *Between Two Empires*, 47–58, esp. 51–53.

29. See Akamatsu Hiroyuki to Shidehara Kijūrō, 7 June 1926; and Kamei Mitsumasa to Shidehara, 1 July 1926, in Honpō imin kankei zakken: Bessatsu Hakkoku no bu, DA-MOFA.

30. Nihon Imin Kyōkai, *Nihon Imin Kyōkai Yokohama Kōshūjo gairan* (Tokyo: Nihon Imin Kyōkai, 1916); Nihon Imin Kyōkai, *Saikin ishokumin kenkyū* (Tokyo: Nihon Imin Kyōkai, 1917), 120–21; "Nihon Imin Kyōkai Yokohama Kōshūjo setsuritsu," *Nihon Imin Kyōkai hōkoku* no. 8 (15 April 1916), 32–33; and Kurachi Tetsukichi to Nakamura Taka, 25 January 1917, in Honpō imin kankei zakken (hereafter HIKZ) vol. 9, DA-MOFA.

31. Shidehara Kijūrō to Kobashi Ichita, 21 July 1919; Watanabe Katsusaburō to Uchida Yasuya, 6 October 1920; and Hyogo prefectural governor to foreign ministry, 3 December 1920, all in Kaigai Tokō Imin Kensajo oyobi Kōshūjo kankei zakken (hereafter KTIK); and Tominaga Kō to Shidehara, 24 July 1924, in Bessatsu chihōchō: Imin Kōshūjo sonota hogo shisetsu ni kansuru ken (hereafter BCIK), DA-MOFA.

32. Nihon Imin Kyōkai, "Nihon Imin Kyōkai Yokohama Kōshūjo gairan" (1916), 1–7, HIKZ vol. 9, DA-MOFA.

33. Kurachi to Nakamura, 25 January 1917, HIKZ vol. 9. The tally is by the author.

34. See the statistical charts in Hyogo prefectural governor to foreign ministry, 19 June 1923, in BCIK, DA-MOFA. The tally is by the author. Until 1920, these female emigrants included a large number of US-bound "picture brides" and other female family members of bona fide Japanese residents in the United States.

35. See Azuma, *Between Two Empires*, 52–58. In the eyes of many Japanese—both in the United States and Japan—immigrant moral reform was synonymous with the interchangeable concepts of "civilization," "modernization," "westernization," and in the specific context of assimilating to US society, "Americanization."

36. On the state acquisition of emigrant training centers, see Shidehara to Kobashi, 21 July 1919; Watanabe to Uchida, 6 October 1920; and Hyogo prefectural governor to foreign ministry, 3 December 1920, all in KTIK, DA-MOFA.

37. Nihon Rikkōkai, ed., *Nihon Rikkōkai hyakunen no kiseki* (Tokyo: Nihon Rikkōkai, 1997), 95, 102–104; Nagata Shigeshi, *Rikkōkai nanajūnenshi* (Tokyo: Nihon Rikkōkai, 1966), 39–42; and "Nihon Imin Kyōkai Kōshūjo (handwritten)" (ca. 1918), in HIKZ vol. 9, DA-MOFA. The foreign ministry source identifies Nagata as a "chief advocate of [the school's] establishment." On the curriculum and pedagogy that he had developed at the Yokohama emigrant training center, see Nagata Shigeshi, *Shin tokōhō* (Tokyo: Nihon Rikkōkai, 1916).

38. Nagata, *Rikkōkai nanajūnenshi*, 114–118; and Nihon Rikkōkai, *Nihon Rikkōkai hyakunen no kiseki*, 160.

39. See Imai Shūichi, "Kaigai Shokumin Gakkō Joshibu no setsuritsu ni saishite," *Shokumin* 7, no. 8 (August 1928), 103–104.

40. "Kaigai hatten kankei dantai ichiran," *Shokumin* 12, no. 4 (April 1933), 152; Takumushō Takumu-kyoku, *Ishokumin oyobi kaigai takushoku jigyō* (March 1931), 50; and Den Hajime, "Takushoku Daigaku hōmonki," *Shokumin* 10, no. 5 (May 1931), 137–139.

41. "Kaigai hatten kankei dantai ichiran," 155–156. The quote is from page 155.

42. "Kaigai hatten no kibō," *Shokumin* 7, no. 3 (March 1928), 63.

43. See Roger Daniels, *The Politics of Prejudice: The Anti-Japanese Movement in California and the Struggle for Japanese Exclusion* (Berkeley: University of California Press, 1999), 79–105.

44. See Izumi Hirobe, *Japanese Pride, American Prejudice: Modifying the Exclusion Clause of the 1924 Immigration Act* (Stanford, CA: Stanford University Press, 2001), 21–51; and Nancy Stalker, "Suicide, Boycotts and Embracing Tagore: The Japanese Popular Response to the 1924 US Immigration Exclusion Law," *Japanese Studies* 26, no. 2 (2006), 153–170.

45. See, for example, Yoneda Minoru, "Kongo no imin mondai," *Gaikō Jihō* 471 (15 July 1924), 1–13; Hioki Susumu, "Nihon jinkō shobun mondai to gaikō seisaku," *Gaikō Jihō* 474 (1 September 1924), 20–32; and Imai Jirō, "Beikoku wa taihai seri," *Gaikō Jihō* 469 (15 June 1924), 35–36. The *Gaiko Jiho* (*Revue diplomatique*) featured dozens of essays, commentaries, and editorials throughout 1924 in response to the US Immigration Act.

46. "Taibei mondai ni kansuru shūkai (Tokyo)," Ōta Masahiro to Gaimushō, 12 July 1924, in Beikoku ni okeru Hainichi mondai zakken: Naigai hantai undō jōkyō chōsa (hereafter BHNH), DA-MOFA; "Taibei mondai ni kansuru taishū undō ni kansuru ken (Osaka)," Nakagawa Nozomi to Shidehara Kijūrō, 1 July 1924, in Beikoku ni okeru Hainichi mondai zakken: Beikoku iminhō ni taisuru haibei jōhō (hereafter BHBI), vol. 4, DA-MOFA.

47. "Taibei mondai shimin taikai jii undō torishimari keikaku," 27 April 1924, in BHBI, vol. 1.

48. On the press coverage, see Stalker, "Suicide, Boycotts and Embracing Tagore," 156–158. As historian Izumi Hirobe reveals, liberal "pro-American" intellectuals expressed a mixture of profound shock and ire toward US racism, which "diminished the influence of Japanese internationalists" in Japan's domestic politics and its relations to the U.S. See Hirobe, *Japanese Pride, American Prejudice*, 29–30.

49. See handwritten transcripts of speeches given at anti-American rallies in Yokohama. Kanagawa-ken, "Shūkai jōkyō hōkoku," 4, 7 July 1924, in BHNH, DA-MOFA. On examples of published essays, see *Gaikō Jihō* 467 (15 May 1924) and 468 (1 June 1924). Many book-length publications on similar themes came out during the mid-1920s. See, for example, Kokumin Taibeikai, ed., *Tai-Beikokusaku rōnshū* (Tokyo: Yomiuri Shinbunsha, 1924); and Higuchi Reiyō, *Nihon kiki beika kitaru* (Tokyo: Nihon Shoin, 1924). On the US side, comparable ideas of global race war existed, as famously articulated in Lothrop Stoddard, *The Rising Tide of Color Against White World-Supremacy* (New York: Charles Scribner's Sons, 1921).

50. Eri Hotta, *Pan-Asianism and Japan's War 1931–1945* (New York: Palgrave Macmillan, 2007), 45–52. On how these ideas paved the way for the ideology of the Greater East Asian Co-Prosperity Sphere in the early 1940s, see Miwa Kimitada, "Tokutomi Sohō no rekishizō

to Nichibei Sensō no genriteki kaishi," in *Seiyō no shōgeki to Nihon*, ed. Haga Tōru et al. (Tokyo: Tokyo Daigaku Shuppankai, 1973), 183–210; and Stalker, "Suicide, Boycotts and Embracing Tagore," 164–167.

51. See Yoshiyama Kitoku, *Chūmokusubeki Mekishiko* (San Francisco: Nichiboku Kenkyūsha, 1928), 98–103, 126–129; Fukunaka Mataji, *Inka teikoku to Nihonjin* (Tokyo: Tōzanbō, 1940), 11–24; and KKKK, *Nanbei Burajiru-koku to Nihon ishokumin* (Tokyo: KKKK, 1926), 11.

52. Yamamoto Kumatarō, "Imin seisaku no igi," *Gaikō Jihō* 535 (15 March 1927), 66–68; and Kamikawa Hikomatsu, "Shidehara gaishō no shōkyokuteki imin seisaku o haisu," *Gaikō Jihō* 527 (15 November 1926), 9.

53. On the impact of Malthusian thinking on emigration to Brazil during this period, see Sidney Xu Lu, *The Making of Japanese Settler Colonialism: Malthusianism and Trans-Pacific Migration, 1868–1961* (New York: Cambridge University Press, 2019), ch. 6.

54. See Hioki, "Nihon jinkō shobun mondai to gaikō seisaku," 24–25, 31–32; Kamikawa, "Shidehara gaishō no shōkyokuteki imin seisaku o haisu," 2–9; and Imai, "Beikoku wa taihai seri," 35.

55. Kamikawa, "Shidehara gaishō no shōkyokuteki imin seisaku o haisu," 2–4. The quote is from page 4.

56. On Japan's domestic social politics during this period, see Sheldon M. Garon, *State and Labor in Modern Japan* (Berkeley: University of California Press, 1987), 39–119; and Andrew D. Gordon, *Labor and Imperial Democracy in Prewar Japan* (Berkeley: University of California Press, 1991), 60–133.

57. Iikubo Hideki, "1920-nendai ni okeru Naimushō Shakai-kyoku no Kaigai imin shōreisaku," *Rekishi to Keizai* 181 (October 2003), 42–46.

58. See Shidehara to Kobashi, 21 July 1919; Watanabe to Uchida, 6 October 1920; and Hyogo prefectural governor to foreign ministry, 3 December 1920, all in KTIK, DA-MOFA. The Yokohama emigrant training center began to receive subventions from the Kanagawa prefecture in 1918.

59. Iikubo, "1920-nendai ni okeru Naimushō Shakai-kyoku no Kaigai imin shōreisaku," 46.

60. Shakai-kyoku, "Shinsai chōsa hōkoku" (10 December 1923), 56, NDL.

61. Kaigai Kyōkai Chūōkai, "Shinsai zengosaku to kaigai hatten" (30 September 1923), 9–10, NDL.

62. Haraguchi Kunihiro, "1924-nen no imin mondai," in *Nichibei kiki no kigen to hain-ichi iminhō*, ed. Miwa Kimitada (Tokyo: Ronsōsha, 1997), 3–43; and *Yomiuri Shinbun*, 23 April 1924. See especially the motion made by Kagawa Toyohiko at the conference.

63. [Teikoku Keizai Kaigi], "Teikoku Keizai Kaigi ni okeru ishokumin no hogo shōrei hōsaku ni kansuru shijun narabi tōshin" (1924), 4, Parliamentary Documents and Official Publications Room, National Diet Library, (hereafter PDOP-NDL), Tokyo. The proposal also called for the promotion of migration to and agricultural settlement in Hokkaido. See also Iikubo, "1920-nendai ni okeru Naimushō Shakai-kyoku no Kaigai imin shōreisaku," 47; and Haraguchi, "1924-nen no imin mondai," 9–21.

64. See Ishizuka Eizō's opening statement in "Teikoku Keizai Kaigi Shakaibu Takush-okubu Rengōbukai giji sokkiroku (Dai nikai)," 26 May 1924, in Teikoku Keizai Kaigi shorui: 55 Teikoku Keizai Kaigi sokkiroku (14), Shakai Takushoku Rengōbu vol. 1., National Archives of Japan (hereafter NAJ), Tokyo.

65. [Teikoku Keizai Kaigi], "Teikoku Keizai Kaigi ni okeru ishokumin no hogo shōrei hōsaku ni kansuru shijun narabi tōshin," 4, 10, PDOP-NDL.

66. [Teikoku Keizai Kaigi], "Teikoku Keizai Kaigi ni okeru ishokumin no hogo shōrei hōsaku ni kansuru shijun narabi tōshin," 10–12. The quotes are from pages 11 and 12.

67. [Teikoku Keizai Kaigi], "Teikoku Keizai Kaigi ni okeru ishokumin no hogo shōrei hōsaku ni kansuru shijun narabi tōshin," 13–16; and the statements by the conference chair and Ishizuka Eizō in "Teikoku Keizai Kaigi Shakaibu Takushokubu Rengōbukai giji sokkiroku (Dai nikai)," NAJ. The quote is from page 16 of the first source.

68. Iikubo, "1920-nendai ni okeru Naimushō Shakai-kyoku no Kaigai imin shōreisaku," 38, 43, 47–48.

69. See Aoyagi Ikutarō, *Burajiru ni okeru Nihonjin hattenshi* (Tokyo: Burajiru ni okeru Nihonjin Hattenshi Kankō Iinkai, 1942), 2:98–115; Kimura Kai, *Kyōsei no daichi Ariansa* (Tokyo: Dōjidaisha, 2013), 160–208; and Sakaguchi, "Darega imin o okuridashitanoka," 59–64.

70. Kaigai Kyōkai Chūōkai, *Kaigai Kyōkai Chūōkai yōran* (Tokyo: Kaigai Kyōkai Chūōkai, 1923), 4–5, 8–12; and Nagata, *Rikkōkai nanajūnenshi*, 73–77.

71. "Takumushō secchi ni kansuru ken," 7 September 1927, in Takumushō secchi kankei ikken vol. 1, DA-MOFA. On the colonial ministry, see Iikubo, "1920-nendai ni okeru Naimushō Shakai-kyoku no Kaigai imin shōreisaku," 112–113.

72. Takumushō Kanbō bunshoka, *Takumushō shomu teiyō* (1932), 1–3, 61–66, NDL. Meanwhile, the foreign ministry maintained its normal consular duties in foreign locales. The notable exception in this new arrangement was Anglophone North America (the United States and Canada), which the colonial ministry excluded from its jurisdiction altogether due to fear of US exclusionist agitation. See Gaimushō, ed., *Nihon Gaikō monjo: Showa-ki I, Dai ni-bu* (Tokyo: Gaimushō, 1991), 4:274, 280, 283–286.

73. Akamatsu Hiroyuki to Tanaka Giichi, 22 July 1927, in "Kaigai Ijū Kumiai Rengōkai ijūchi konyū ni kansuru keika gaiyō" (July 1927–February 1928), Kensei Shiryōshitsu shūshū monjo (#1389-13), Modern Japanese Political History Materials Room, National Diet Library (hereafter MJPH-NDL), Tokyo,; and "Kaigai Ijū Kumiai Rengōkai-shi 2" (May 1930), 35, in Ōno Ryokuichirō kankei monjo 758, MJPH-NDL.

74. "Kaigai Ijū Kumiai Rengōkai-shi 2," 30, 34–35.

75. "Kaigai Ijū Kumiai Rengōkai-shi 2," 36–41; and Akamatsu to Tanaka, 15 January 1928, in "Kaigai Ijū Kumiai Rengōkai ijūchi konyū ni kansuru keika gaiyō," MJPH-NDL

76. "Kaigai Ijū Kumiai Rengōkai-shi 2," 61; and Takumushō Takumu-kyoku, "Kaigai Ijū Kumiai Rengōkai gaiyō" (ca. 1930), no pagination, in Shōwa zaiseishi shiryō 5:134, Zaimushō, NAJ.

77. Takumushō Takumu-kyoku, "Kaigai Ijū Kumiai Rengōkai gaiyō," (ca. 1930), no pagination.

78. "Kaigai Ijū Kumiai Rengōkai-shi 2," 29–30; Akamatsu to Tanaka, 15 January 1928, no pagination, MJPH-NDL; and Aoyagi Ikutarō, "Ijū kumiai no shokuminchi o katte kaette," *Shokumin 7*, no. 11 (November 1928), 33–36. Aoyagi's associate was Wako Shungorō. Having relocated from the United States after the passage of California's Alien Land Law of 1913, he served as the founding editor of the first Japanese newspaper in Brazil, worked under Aoyagi as a supervisor of new settlers from Japan at the Katsura Colony, and cooperated with

Nagata Shigeshi as his right-hand man in the establishment of the Aliança colony in Saõ Paulo before his involvement in the NFOEC's venture. Wako noted that combined with American racism, the news from Japan about Aoyagi's Katsura colony project inspired him to move from the US West to the Brazilian frontier. See Wako Shungorō, *Ruten no ato* (Tokyo: self-pub., 1941); and Kimura, *Kyōsei no daichi Ariansa*, 46–80, 114–122, 136–138, 188–210.

79. Nagata Shigeshi, "Zaibei Nihonjin ni atau sho," *Rikkō Sekai* (1 June 1924), 17.

80. Nagata, "Zaibei Nihonjin ni atau sho," 17, 19. Because Nagata did not live in Brazil, Wako Shungorō did much of the groundwork for the building of a new agricultural colony in Aliança, including land surveys and negotiations with Brazilian authorities for land acquisition. Nagata handled political and business dealings with Japanese authorities. See Kimura, *Kyōsei no daichi Ariansa*, 114–138; and Nagata Shigeshi, *Kaigai risshiden* (Tokyo: Nihon Rikkōkai, 1926), 144–155.

81. On reemigration of California Japanese to Brazil under Nagata's influence, see Azuma, *Between Two Empires*, 81; and Nihon Rikkōkai, *Nihon Rikkōkai hyakunen no kiseki*, 152. From the beginning, Nagata set aside a tract for North American remigrants in his Aliança colony.

82. Shinano Kaigai Kyōkai, *Nanbei Burajiru 'Ariansa' ijūchi no kensetsu* (Nagano: Shinano Kaigai Kyōkai, 1927), 1–6, 40–105; Nihon Rikkōkai, *Nihon Rikkōkai hyakunen no kiseki*, 136–139; [Nagata Shigeshi], "Nanbei ijūchi kensetsu shian," *Rikkō Sekai* (1 June 1924), 1–7; Irie Toraji, *Kaigai dōhō hattenshi* (Tokyo: Ide Shoten, 1942), 2:381–386; Nagata, *Rikkōkai nanajūnenshi*, 76–77; and Nagata Shigeshi, *Ryōbei saijun* (Tokyo: Nihon Rikkōkai, 1926), 351–356. On Nagano emigration to Brazil under the yoke of "Malthusian expansionism," see Lu, *The Making of Japanese Settler Colonialism*, ch. 7.

83. Azuma, *Between Two Empires*, 22. On Mutō, see also Ichioka, *The Issei*, 12; and Yamamoto Chōji, "Mutō Sanji to Nanbei Takushoku Kabushiki Kaisha no setsuritsu," in *Jitsugyōka to Burajiru ijū*, ed. Shibusawa Eiichi Kinen Zaidan Kenkyūbu (Tokyo: Fuji Shuppan, 2012), 80–83.

84. Jeffrey Lesser, *Negotiating National Identity: Immigrants, Minorities, and the Struggle for Ethnicity in Brazil* (Durham, N.C.: Duke University Press, 1999), 93–94, 116–132, esp. 116.

85. Aoyagi, *Burajiri ni okeru Nihonjin hattenshi*, 160–163.

86. Aoyagi, *Burajiri ni okeru Nihonjin hattenshi*, 163–165; and Yamamoto, "Mutō Sanji to Nanbei Takushoku Kabushiki Kaisha no setsuritsu," 87.

87. Mutō Sanji, *Watashi no minoue banashi* (Osaka: Kokumin Kaikan, 1959), 344–345.

88. Ichioka, *The Issei*, 12.

89. Mutō, *Watashi no minoue banashi*, 58–59, 345–347. The quote is from page 59. See also Yamamoto, "Mutō Sanji to Nanbei Takushoku Kabushiki Kaisha no setsuritsu," 81–83.

90. Mutō's view was described by Fukuhara. See Fukuhara Hachirō, "Saikin no Amazon jijō" (1933), in *Amazon ni sosoida Senjin no jōnetsu*, ed. Nōgyō Takushoku Kyōkai (Tokyo: Nōgyō Takushoku Kyōkai, 1966), 15–16.

91. Nagami Shichirō, "Amazon kaitaku no kyojin: Fukuhara Hachirō-shi no hansei," *Shokumin* 11, no. 11 (November 1932), 128–130. Fukuhara worked and studied in the United States between 1899 and 1903. Having lived in Georgia and North Carolina, he had bitter, firsthand experience of white supremacy. With his belief in the overseas development

ideal, he was also well connected to the circles of immigrant expansionists in the American West.

92. Fukuhara, "Saikin no Amazon jijō," 24.

93. Fukuhara Hachirō, *Burajiru jijō* (Tokyo: Jitsugyō Dōshikai Chōsabu, 1927), 53–56 and 29–34; Fukuhara, "Hakkoku keizai jijō," in *Takushoku kōshūkai kōenshū*, ed. Miyagi-ken (Sendai: Miyagi-ken, 1934), 86, 112; and Fukuhara, "Saikin no Amazon jijō," 104–107.

94. *SEDS*, 55:641–650; Aoyagi, *Burajiri ni okeru Nihonjin hattenshi*, 167–170; and Yamamoto, "Mutō Sanji to Nanbei Takushoku Kabushiki Kaisha no setsuritsu," 88–95.

95. Nagami, "Amazon kaitaku no kyojin," 131; and Yamamoto, "Mutō Sanji to Nanbei Takushoku Kabushiki Kaisha no setsuritsu," 86–87.

96. Fukuhara, *Burajiru jijō*, 10–12, the quote is from page 12; Fukuhara, "Dai-Amazon no shinpi to kakuretaru fugen o tazunete," *Shokumin* 6, no. 4 (April 1927), 34; and Fukuhara, "Dai-Amazon tankenki 1," *Shokumin* 6, no. 6 (June 1927), 57. On Murai and other New York Japanese entrepreneurs, see Daniel H. Inouye, *Distant Islands: The Japanese American Community in New York City, 1876–1930s* (Louisville: University Press of Colorado, 2018), 25–32, 35–36.

97. *SEDS*, 55:645; Aoyagi, *Burajiri ni okeru Nihonjin hattenshi*, 167–168; and Yamamoto, "Mutō Sanji to Nanbei Takushoku Kabushiki Kaisha no setsuritsu," 94.

98. "Nanbei Kigyō Kabushiki Kaisha," *Nyūyōku Shinpō*, 8 June 1927; *Kobe Shinbun*, 26 June 1927; XYZ-sei [pseud.], "Sōsetsu saretaru Nanbei Kigyō Kabushiki Kaisha," *Shokumin* 6, no. 11 (November 1927), 43–46; Tsuji Kōtarō, *Burajiru no dōhō o tazunete* (Kobe: Nichi-Haku Kyōkai, 1930), 245–248; and Han-Amazonia Nichi-Haku Kyōkai Kasutanyāru-shibu, ed., *Kasutanyāru Hōjin gojūnen no ayumi* (Castanhal, Pará: Han-Amazonia Nichi-Haku Kyōkai Kasutanyāru-shibu, 1975), 17–18. A Japanese immigrant family named Ōnishi initially relocated from Texas's rice-growing region in response to Murai's call. Other Japanese Texas rice farmers resettled there to join with the Ōnishis, including Saibara Seitō, a prominent scholar and statesman of Meiji Japan who had moved to Texas in 1903 to build a three-hundred-acre rice colony in the outskirts of Houston. Between 1929 and 1932 Saibara served as the manager of the Castanhal estate for the New York–Japanese owned colonization company. In the mid-1930s Saibara was also involved in US-style rice farming experimentation in colonial Taiwan with the support of the island's largest sugar company. On Ōnishi, Saibara, and other Japanese settler-farmers in Southeastern Texas, see Mamiya Kunio, *Saibara Seitō kenkyū* (Kōchi: Kōchi Shimin Toshokan, 1994), esp. 367–369, 372–376; Lu, *The Making of Japanese Settler Colonialism*, ch. 4; and Thomas K. Wells, *The Japanese Texans* (San Antonio: University of Texas Institute of Texan Cultures, 1997), 39–100.

99. "Nanbei Kigyō Kabushiki Kaisha no maki," *Shokumin* 10, no. 9 (September 1931), 67; and Han-Amazonia Nichi-Haku Kyōkai Kasutanyāru-shibu, *Kasutanyāru Hōjin gojūnen no ayumi*, 18.

100. Han-Amazonia Nichi-Haku Kyōkai Kasutanyāru-shibu, *Kasutanyāru Hōjin gojūnen no ayumi*, 19–20; and Han-Amazonia Nichi-Haku Kyōkai, ed., *Amazon, Nihonjin ni yoru rokujūnen no ijūshi* (Belém: Han-Amazonia Nichi-Haku Kyōkai, 1994), 17, 24–25, 59. Even after the merger with the Nantaku colony, the New York Japanese concern maintained separate tracts of farmland for other resettlers from the United States in the vicinity of the agricultural experimental station until at least 1935.

5. JAPANESE CALIFORNIA AND ITS COLONIAL DIASPORA: TRANSLOCAL MANCHURIA CONNECTIONS

1. Nagao Yukusuke, "Manshū jihen no kōkyūsei to Hōjin imin no hōshin," *Gaikō Jihō* 67, no. 5 (May 1933), 175.

2. Nagao, "Manshū jihen no kōkyūsei to Hōjin imin no hōshin," 180.

3. Eiichiro Azuma, *Between Two Empires: Race, History, and Transnationalism in Japanese America* (New York: Oxford University Press, 2005), 89–119.

4. In the latter half of the 1920s a few pockets of new Japanese settlements emerged in northern Baja California, whose farming and fishing endeavors were deeply entangled with the Los Angeles Japanese immigrant economy. In addition to these border-crossing resettlers, some other US residents joined Japan's new settler-colonist ventures in Brazil, including the Aliança colony, which set aside a special tract for North American resettlers. On these examples of Japanese remigration within the Western Hemisphere, see Eiichiro Azuma, "Community Formation across the National Border: The Japanese of the U.S.-Mexican Californias," *Review: Literature and Arts of the Americas* 39, no. 1 (May 2006), 37–38; Azuma, *Between Two Empires*, 81; and Nihon Rikkōkai, ed., *Nihon Rikkōkai hyakunen no kiseki* (Tokyo: Nihon Rikkōkai, 1997), 152.

5. John J. Stephan, "Hijacked by Utopia: American Nikkei in Manchuria," *Amerasia Journal* 23, no. 3 (1997), 3. Korea did not attract a significant number of remigrants from North America because of the dearth of available farmland for newcomers and the past failure of agricultural settler colonialism there. See Jun Uchida, *Brokers of Empire: Japanese Settler Colonialism in Korea, 1876–1945* (Cambridge, MA: Harvard University Asia Center, 2011), 59–60.

6. Janis Mimura studies the inner workings of Manchukuo's complex bureaucracy, in which "the dual processes of specialization and integration" unfolded. She specifically examines the roles played by colonial "techno-bureaucrats" who were engaged in the integration of various governmental tasks as "managers and administrators" using their "technical grasps and organizational skills." Yet as this chapter shows, on the question of agricultural colonization, these technocrats still relied on the expertise of former US residents. This book thus looks at the missing link in Mimura's study, in which techno-bureaucrats are presented as singlehandedly taking charge of "translat[ing] planning into policy" and "managing technical projects" in Manchukuo. Underscoring this problem, Mimura's discussion of colonial agriculture (as opposed to industrial development) is minimal even though the former was deemed to require as much "science" and "rationalization" as the latter. See Janis Mimura, *Planning for Empire: Reform Bureaucrats and the Japanese Wartime State* (Ithaca, NY: Cornell University Press, 2011), esp. 12–13.

7. On the repatriation and resettlement of overseas Italians and Germans, including US citizens, see Matteo Pretelli, "Mussolini's Mobilities: Transnational Movements between Fascist Italy and Italian Communities Abroad," *Journal of Migration History* 1, no. 1 (2015), 106–118, esp. 116–117; Michael Burleigh, *Germany Turns Eastwards: A Study of Ostforschung in the Third Reich* (Cambridge, UK: Cambridge University Press, 1988), 161–186; and Arthur L. Smith Jr., *The Deutschtum of Nazi Germany and the United States* (Hague: Martinus Nijhoff, 1965), 2–25, 117–151, esp. 143–144.

8. Kokuryūkai, ed., *Tōa senkaku shishi retsuden: Gekan* (Tokyo: Kokuryūkai, 1936), 307–308.

9. Okita Shūji, ed., *Kinenshi* (Dalian: Ryōtō Shinpōsha, 1924), no pagination.

10. Tōyō Keizai Gakkai, ed., *Shin Nihon jinbutsu taikei: Gekan* (Tokyo: Tōyō Keizai Gakkai, 1936), 247–248.

11. Okita, *Kinenshi*; Tōyō Keizai Gakkai, *Shin Nihon jinbutsu taikei: Gekan*, 168–169; Murakami Osamu, *Tairiku no gyūnyū-ō* (Beijing: Nihon Kirisuto Kyōdan Pekin Tōka Kyōkai, 1944); and Nakanishi Rihachi, ed., *Manshū shinshi-roku* (Tokyo: Manmō Shiryō Kyōkai, 1937), 1:337–338.

12. Chiba Toyoji, *Beikoku Kashū hainichi jijō* (San Francisco: Nichibei Kankei Chōsakai, 1921), 52.

13. Chiba Toyoji, "Chiba Toyoji ikō" (1944), 2: 616, in folder 100, box 197, Miscellaneous Manuscripts Collection, Department of Special Collections, UCLA. On Chiba's biography, see Itō Takuji, *Tenkai no kisoku* (Furukawa: Ōsaki Taimususha, 1987).

14. Chiba, "Chiba Toyoji ikō" (1944), 2: 592.

15. Tetsuro Sōkyoku, "Manshū no kikai nōgyō ni tsuite" (March 1936), 1, National Diet Library (hereafter NDL), Tokyo.

16. Chiba Toyoji, "Kantōshū-nai ni okeru Hōjin nōjō no sōsetsu" (ca. 1924), 3–4, Library of the Research Centre for Information and Statistics of Social Science, Institute of Economic Research, Hitotsubashi University (hereafter IER-HU), Tokyo. See also Chiba Toyoji, "Manmō kaihatsu-saku no kōshin 2," *Shokumin* 4, no. 2 (February 1925), 22–23; Chiba Toyoji, "Manshū nōgyō kaihatsu no byōho toshite no soshakuchi ni okeru Hōjin nōjō sōsetsu," in *Manmō nōkai no gyokkō*, ed. Manshū Nōji Kyōkai (Dalian: Manshū Nōji Kyōkai, 1928), 70–71; and Chiba Toyoji, *Manshū nōgyō no tokushitsu to Nichiman nōgyō hikaku kenkyū* (Dalian: Minami Manshū Tetsudō Kabushiki Kaisha, 1927), 83–84. When Manchuria's colonial regime decided to bring tens of thousands of new agricultural settlers from Japan beginning in 1932, Chiba fervently supported that plan by citing an example of farming success by Japanese in the American West and their superiority to their Chinese rivals. See Chiba Toyoji, *Manshū ishokumin-ron* (Dalian: Manshū Bunka Kyōkai, 1932), 16–19. On Chiba's ideas and their relevance to Japanese policy in Manchuria, see Kimura Kenji, "Senzenki no Kaigai yūhi to shisōteki keifu," *Keizaigaku* 53, no. 4 (March 1992), 29–40; and Hasegawa Yūichi, "Hainichi imin-hō to Manshū, Burajiru," in *Nichibei kiki no kigen to Hainichi imin-hō*, ed. Miwa Kimitada (Tokyo: Ronsōsha, 1997), 43–61.

17. Chiba, "Kantōshū-nai ni okeru Hōjin nōjō no sōsetsu," 4–5, IER-HU.

18. Chiba Toyoji, "Kaitaku seishin o mote," *Rikkō Sekai* 329 (May 1932), 12.

19. Nakamura Junzō, *Hoshi ni utsuru Senmanshi* (Tokyo: self-pub., 1935), 36–37.

20. Chiba, "Kantōshū-nai ni okeru Hōjin nōjō no sōsetsu," 3–5, 17; and Chiba, *Manshū nōgyō no tokushitsu to Nichiman nōgyō hikaku kenkyū*, 3–4, 80–85.

21. *Shin Sekai*, 12 July 1936 (English section).

22. See Hasegawa, "Hainichi imin-hō to Manshū, Burajiru," 60–62; Chiba, *Manshū nōgyō no tokushitsu to Nichiman nōgyō hikaku kenkyū*, 29–30; and Stephan, "Hijacked by Utopia," 2.

23. Chiba, "Kantōshū-nai ni okeru Hōjin nōjō no sōsetsu," 17–20; Chiba, *Manshū nōgyō no tokushitsu to Nichiman nōgyō hikaku kenkyū*, 1–5, 64–65, 90–93; and Chiba, "Kaitaku seishin o mote," 11.

24. Chiba Toyoji, "Manshū no nōgyō kaihatsu," *Nōgyō no Manshū* 8, no. 2 (February 1936), 3.

25. The SMR's research bureaus compiled a number of reports, some of which were classified, on the Soviet agricultural policies and Kolkhoz as well as farm settlements of exiled Russians in Heilongjiang and Hulinbuir. The former, known as "Romanofuka (Romanovka) Village," became something of a cultural icon in Manchukuo in the early 1940s, leading to the production of a film and novels that hailed them as pioneer settlers in a multiethnic Manchurian frontier. On Kolkhoz, see Matsumura Shirō, "Sorenpō nōgyō seisaku ni tsuite" (1937), Library of Economics, University of Tokyo; and Hokuman Keizai Chōsasho, ed., *Hokuman no nōgyō* (Harbin: Hokuman Keizai Chōsasho, 1936).

26. Louise Young, *Japan's Total Empire: Manchuria and the Culture of Wartime Imperialism* (Berkeley: University of California Press, 1998), 318–322, 326–327, 333, 385–392; and Sandra Wilson, "The 'New Paradise': Japanese Emigration to Manchuria in the 1930s and 1940s," *International History Review* 17, no. 2 (May 1995), 261–264.

27. See *Manshū Nippō*, 4 December 1934; and Fujiwara Tatsushi, *Torakutā no sekaishi* (Tokyo: Chūō Kōronsha, 2017), 210–211.

28. Takasaki Tatsunosuke-shū Kankō Iinkai, ed., *Takasaki Tatsunosuke-shū: Jō* (Tokyo: Takasaki Tatsunosuke-shū Kankō Iinkai, 1965), 136–137.

29. This slant in the historiography, it seems, stems from two sources. One is the general tendency of historians to look at recognizable political and ideological figures directly connected to high-level officialdom and central decision-making apparatuses rather than grassroots, if not minor, officials and practitioners. More important, Katō Kanji, along with Hashimoto and Nasu, managed to control the flow and availability of historical data after World War II. While much primary source material was lost during the demise of Manchukuo and settler-colonists, the Kato gang survived the war's end and emerged in the postwar years to narrate what had transpired and what they had done in a self-serving/self-congratulatory manner. It is for this reason that the most authoritative account of Manchurian colonization history was put together under their supervision in 1966. See Manshū Kaitakushi Kankōkai, ed., *Manshū kaitakushi* (Tokyo: Manshū Kaitakushi Kankōkai, 1966).

30. "Chiba Toyoji-shi ni Manshū ijū mondai o kiku," *Rikkō Sekai* 330 (June 1932), 44; and Tetsuro Sōkyoku, "Manshū no kikai nōgyō ni tsuite," 2. Also, on Nagao Yukusuke's criticism of "Ph.Ds., . . . technical experts, and ministers who obstruct[ed] the endeavors of practitioners [of machine farming]," see Nagao, "Manshū jihen no kōkyūsei to Hōjin imin no hōshin," 181.

31. On government agronomists in Manchuria, see Yamamoto Haruhiko, *Manshū no nōgyō shiken kenkyūshi* (Tokyo: Nōgyō Tōkei Shuppan, 2013), 107–130, esp. 126–127. "Dozens" of former US residents also worked for the SMS and colonial bureaucracy. See Sōga Yasutarō, *Nira no nioi* (Honolulu: Nippu Jijisha, 1925), 110; and Stephan, "Hijacked by Utopia," 15.

32. David Moon, *The Plough That Broke the Steppes: Agriculture and Environment on Russia's Grasslands, 1700–1914* (Oxford: Oxford University Press, 2013), 285–286.

33. Itō, *Tenkai no kisoku*, 373–376; and "Chiba Toyoji-shi ni Manshū ijū mondai o kiku," 44. On agricultural experimental stations in colonial Manchuria, see Yamamoto, *Manshū no nōgyō shiken kenkyūshi*, 31–53. In the late 1920s, the director of the agricultural training school at Gongzhuling was Sō Mitsuhiko, Katō Kanji's close associate.

34. See Murakoshi Nobuo, "Kokuritsu Kokuzan Nōji Shikenjō gaiyō" (1936), 10–13, Old Colonial Collections: Manchuria, Faculty of Agriculture Library, Kyoto University

(hereafter OCC-KU); and "Manshū ijūchi no kaikon o kikaika," *Nōgyō no Manshū* 9, no. 7 (July 1937), 23–24.

35. "Kikai nōjō o secchi," *Nōgyō no Manshū* 10, no. 10 (October 1938), 41; and Manshū Kaitakushi Kankōkai, *Manshū kaitakushi*, 19–20.

36. See Saeki-sei [pseud.], "Reimei no Manshū," *Nōgyō no Manshū* 8, no. 11 (December 1936), 39.

37. Manshū Kaitakushi Kankōkai, *Manshū kaitakushi*, 19–20; *Nichibei Shimbun*, 21 March 1932; Chiba, "Manshū nōgyō kaihatsu no byōho toshite no soshakuchi ni okeru Hōjin nōjō sōsetsu," 74–75; "Chiba Toyoji-shi ni Manshū ijū mondai o kiku," 44; and Ohara Kei, "Marīzu ga tazuneta Yokohama no engeika Akasaburō," *Chigasaki shizen no Shinbun* 269 (15 October 2005), 8. See also Itō, *Tenkai no kisoku*, 374.

38. Chiba, *Manshū nōgyō no tokushitsu to Nichiman nōgyo hikaku kenkyū*, 32–33, 84, 86–87; Chiba, "Kantōshū-nai ni okeru Hōjin nōjō no sōsetsu," 14, IER-HU; and Itō, *Tenkai no kisoku*, 396, 443.

39. Manshū Kokuritsu Kaitaku Kenkyūsho, *Hokuman kaitakuchi nōgu shisatsu hōkoku* (Changchun: Manshū Kokuritsu Kaitaku Kenkyūsho, 1940), 6. See also *Hawai Hōchi*, 4 February 1939.

40. See Nara-ken Takuyūkai, ed., *Nara-ken Manshū kaitakushi* (Nara: Nara-ken Takuyūkai, 1996), 190, 221; and Akagi Yuzuru, *Yamato minzoku no seikyō* (Harbin: Seo Ryūtarō, 1933), esp. 17–19. On the influences of Chiba and Nagata, see Emily Anderson, *Christianity and Imperialism in Modern Japan: Empire for God* (London: Bloomsbury Publishing, 2014), 222–229; Nihon Rikkōkai, *Nihon Rikkōkai hyakunen no kiseki*, 234–241; and Sidney Xu Lu, *The Making of Japanese Settler Colonialism: Malthusianism and Trans-Pacific Migration, 1868–1961* (New York: Cambridge University Press, 2019), ch. 7.

41. *Rikkō Sekai* 138 (October 1915), 6; 188 (June 1920), 4; 200 (June 1921), 6; 237 (September 1924), 18–19; 254 (February 1926), 21–22; and 465 (December 1943), 6; *Rikkō-mō* 1 (December 1930), 3; *Nippu Jiji*, 27 April 1933 and 24 January 1940; Wakabayashi Suteichi, "Beikoku nōgyō no hiai to Zairyu dōhō," *Tairiku kaitaku* 2 (March 1942), 55, 57; and *Tairiku kaitaku* 7 (November 1943), 151. Between 1920 and 1923, Wakabayashi studied at the New Jersey Agricultural Experimental Station for his doctorate. He was then affiliated with the state agricultural experimental stations in Washington and Hawai'i, though his main work appeared to be linked closely to the local Japanese ethnic farm industries. In 1943 Wakabayashi died of an endemic disease, which he contracted while conducting field research in a swampland of northern Manchuria. A friend of Wakabayashi, another US-trained agronomist named Itano Arao, also went to Manchukuo in 1939 to serve as an adviser to its Continental Science Institute (Tairiku Kagakuin). After a brief internment in postcolonial China, Itano was recruited to teach at a university in Shanyang and served as an adviser to a project to increase the production of soy beans under the communist regime. See Yamamoto, *Manshū no nōgyō shiken kenkyūshi*, 171–175; and "watashi wa kaeranai," *Sanyō Shinbun*, 15 April 1953.

42. Minami Manshū Tetsudō Kabushiki Kaisha (hereafter SMR), ed., *Manshū no kishō to kansōchi nōgyō* (Dalian: SMR, 1925), 36.

43. Tetsuro Sōkyoku, "Manshū no kikai nōgyō ni tsuite," 62.

44. See, for example, Manshū Kaitakushi Kankōkai, *Manshū kaitakushi*, 346–347; SMR, *Manshū wa imin no rakudo* (Dalian: SMR, 1937), 9; and Manshū Takushoku Kōsha, "Mantaku" (1943), NDL.

45. Nagata Shigeshi, *Manshū imin yazen monogatari* (Tokyo: Nihon Rikkōkai, 1942), 137–138; *Rikkō Sekai* 345 (September 1933), 59; Awaya Man'ei, "Beikoku ni okeru nōgyō jijō," *Nōgyō no Manshū* 5, no. 6 (June 1933), 33; *Shin Sekai*, 1 February 1932 and 19 May 1934; and *Rafu Shimpō*, 29 August 1933.

46. *Osaka Asahi Shinbun*, 16 January 1932 and 19 March 1934.

47. Gaimushō Tsūshō-kyoku, ed., *Jinko mondai o kichō to shita Manmō takushoku-saku no kenkyū* (Tokyo: Gaimushō Tsūshō-kyoku, 1927), 208–209; Nakanishi Rihachi, ed., *Shin Nihon jinbutsu taikei* (Tokyo: Tōhō Keizai Gakkai, 1936), 2:372–373; Chiba, "Kantōshū-nai ni okeru Hōjin nōjō no sōsetsu," 2–3; Chiba, *Manshū nōgyō no tokushitsu to Nichiman nōgyō hikaku kenkyū*, 33, 104–106; and "Nōgyō kaiko zadankai," *Nōgyō no Manshū* 8, no. 11 (December 1936), 21–22.

48. Nakanishi, *Shin Nihon jinbutsu taikei*, 2:373; Manmō Shiryō Kyōkai, ed. *Manshū shinshi-roku* (Tokyo: Manmō Shiryō Kyōkai, 1937), 1:97–98; and Manmō Shiryō Kyōkai, ed., *Manshū shinshi-roku* (Tokyo: Manmō Shiryō Kyōkai, 1940), 2:452.

49. *Kashū Mainichi*, 19 January 1933; and *Osaka Asahi Shinbun*, 16 January 1932.

50. Gaimushō Tsūshō-kyoku, *Jinko mondai o kichō to shita Manmō takushoku-saku no kenkyū*, 208–211. The quotes are from pages 208 and 211.

51. "Nōgyō kōrōsha shōkai," *Nōgyō no Manshū* 8, no. 10 (November 1936), 29.

52. Yamashita Sōen, *Hōshūku kigen Nisen roppyakunen to Kaigai dōhō* (Tokyo: Hōshūku Kigen Nisen Roppyakunen to Kaigai Dōhō Kankōkai, 1941), 131.

53. Chiba, "Manshū nōgyō kaihatsu no byōho toshite no soshakuchi ni okeru Hōjin nōjō sōsetsu," 71.

54. Hayashi Tomihei, *Nihon ni kaettekara nani o suru?* (Tokyo: Kaigai Tsūshinsha, 1927), 147.

55. "Satō Nobumoto-shi no Nanman iki" and "California Farmers Are Succeeding in Manchuria," *Nichibei Shimbun*, 6 February 1930 and 23 July 1930, respectively.

56. *Shin Sekai*, 23 May 1928; Gaimushō Tsūshō-kyoku, ed., "Zaigai Honpō jitsugyōsha shirabe" (December 1919), 375–376, NDL (the tally of 1919 statistics is by the author); Nichibei Shimbunsha, ed., *Zaibei Nihonjin jinmei jiten* (San Francisco: Nichibei Shimbunsha, 1922), 325; and Zaibei Nihonjinkai, ed., *Zaibei Nihonjinshi* (San Francisco: Zaibei Nihonjinkai, 1940), 233.

57. Gaimushō Tsūshō-kyoku, ed., "Zaigai Honpō jitsugyōsha shirabe" (December 1921), 461, NDL; and Taketomi Toyohiko to Shidehara Kijūrō, "Honpōjin nōkōsha ni kansuru chōsa hōkokusho," 27 December 1926, no pagination, in Honpōjin no Kaigai nōgyō kankei zakken, Diplomatic Archives of the Ministry of Foreign Affairs (hereafter DA-MOFA), Tokyo.

58. Shindō Kan, "Manshū miyage," *Nippon to Amerika* 6, no. 9 (September 1937), 24–25.

59. "Mantetsu ga sekkyokuteki ni nōgyō keiei o shōrei," *Chūgai Shōgyo Shinpō*, 22 February 1929; "Japan Plans U.S. Methods in 'Manchu,'" *Nichibei Shimbun*, 20 March 1929; "Plan Rice Raising in Manchuria," *Rafu Shimpō*, 2 December 1929; and Tetsuro Sōkyoku, "Manshū no kikai nōgyō ni tsuite," 2, 6.

60. Nichiman Nōsei Kenkyūkai Shinkyō Jimusho, ed., *Nanman ni okeru Suiden kikai nōgyō no ichijirei* (Changchun: Nichiman Nōsei Kenkyūkai Shinkyō Jimusho, 1943), 1; Minami Manshū Tetsudō Kabushiki Kaisha Chihōbu, ed., *Chihō keiei kōgai* (Dalian: SMR, 1935), 221; and Shindō, "Manshū miyage," 25.

61. Mantetsu Keizai Chōsakai Dai-nibu, "Nihonjin imin taisakuan" (June 1932), no pagination, NDL.

62. Mantetsu Keizai Chōsakai Dai-nibu, "Nihonjin imin taisakuan." See also Satō's statement in Tetsuro Sōkyoku, "Manshū no kikai nōgyō ni tsuite," 6–7.

63. Kantōchō Keimu-kyoku, "Junpō" 12 (21 April 1934), 1, in Kantōchō hōkokusho zassan, DA-MOFA; and Satō Nobumoto, "Manshū ni okeru kikai nōgyō" (30 November 1934), no pagination, in Nihon Rikkōkai Emigration Archives, Tokyo.

64. Tetsuro Sōkyoku, "Manshū no kikai nōgyō ni tsuite," 7–11, 22; Satō, "Manshū ni okeru kikai nōgyō"; Manshū Nippō, 22 April 1934; Shindō, "Manshū miyage," 25; Nichiman Nōsei Kenkyūkai Shinkyō Jimusho, Nanman ni okeru Suiden kikai nōgyō no ichijirei, 7, 12–14, 16–17; Yoshioka Kin'ichi, Nichiman nōgyō kikaika no mondai (Tokyo: Nihon Yūchiku Kikai Nōgyō Kyōkai, 1943), 17; and Yokoyama Toshio, Manshū suitōsaku no kenkyū (Tokyo: Kawade Shobō, 1945), 315–318, 327.

65. See Young, Japan's Total Empire, 352–362.

66. Minami Manshū Tetsudō Kabushiki Kaisha Keizai Chōsakai (hereafter SMR-ERI), ed., "Manshū nōgyō imin hōsaku: Hokuman Nōchi Kaitaku Kaisha setsuritsu hōsaku" (March 1937), 1, NDL; Hokuman Keizai Chōsasho, ed., Hokuman to Hokkaido nōhō (Dalian: SMR, 1941), 4–5; and Minami Manshū Tetsudō Kabushiki Kaisha Harubin Jimusho, ed., Kita Manshū gaikan (Dalian: Manshū Bunka Kyōkai, 1934), 360–362.

67. See Jeffrey Lesser, Negotiating National Identity: Immigrants, Minorities, and the Struggle for Ethnicity in Brazil (Durham, N.C.: Duke University Press, 1999), 116–120; and Erika Lee, "The 'Yellow Peril' and Asian Exclusion in the Americas," Pacific Historical Review 76, no. 4 (November 2007), 537–562.

68. See Matsuoka's statement cited in Nagata Shigeshi, "Hokuman o Kashū ni," Rikkō Sekai 381 (September 1936), 2.

69. "Matsuoka Invites Japanese Farmers in America to Find Opportunities in Manchou," Shin Sekai, 4 November 1936. The same subject was formally deliberated at a budgetary committee meeting of the Imperial Diet in February 1939. See "Dai-nanajūyonkai Teikoku Gikai: Shūgiin, Yosan Iinkai Dai-ichi Bunkakai-giroku, Dai-yonkai" (7 February 1939), 3–4, NDL.

70. On reports of Japanese residents moving from California/Hawai'i to Manchuria, see Shin Sekai, 6 October 1939; Nippu Jiji, 18 January 1940; and Nichibei Shimbun, 25 December 1940.

71. Tanabe Toshiyuki, "Manshū nōgyō kaihatsusaku zadankai no ken," 13 February 1936, in Mantetsu Keizai Chōsakai shiryō, ed. Kobayashi Hideo (Tokyo: Kashiwa Shobō, 1998), 6:246–248; and "Manshū nōgyō kaihatsusaku zadankai," Nōgyō no Manshū 8, no. 3 (March 1936), 2. The quote is from the latter source.

72. See "Manshū nōgyō kaihatsusaku zadankai," Nōgyō no Manshū 8, no. 4 (April 1936), 22–24, 27, 29–30.

73. "Manshū nōgyō kaihatsusaku zadankai," 30.

74. Tetsuro Sōkyoku, "Manshū no kikai nōgyō ni tsuite," 1 and 2–3.

75. Tetsuro, "Manshū no kikai nōgyō ni tsuite," 6–31.

76. Tetsuro, "Manshū no kikai nōgyō ni tsuite," "reigen" and 1–2.

77. See Uchino Raisuke, "Kanada to Manshū nōgyō hikaku," ca. late 1930s, 74–76, OCC-KU. See also Uchino, "Manshū no nōgyō wa korede yuke," Kaigai 12, no. 7 (July 1932), 16–17;

Uchino, "Manshū no nōkō doryoku to nōba no kairyō," *Gendai Nōgyō* 5, no. 11 (November 1939), 15–16; and "Nōmin taishū Manmō hatten zadankai," *Kaigai* 11, no. 3 (March 1932), 41–43. Compared with Satō and others, Uchino was less enthusiastic about the advantage of tractors, as he viewed their use as a transition to the widespread use of domestic animals in the context of worsening fuel shortages.

78. Gaimushō Tsūshō-kyoku, "Zaigai Honpō jitsugyōsha shirabe" (December 1919), 406; Fujioka Shirō, *Ayumi no ato* (Los Angeles: Ayumi no Ato Kankō Kōenkai, 1957), 439–443; and Murai Kō, *Zaibei Nihonjin sangyō sōran* (Los Angeles: Beikoku Sangyō Nippōsha, 1940), 463–465.

79. See *Shin Sekai*, 27 August 1927; *Nichibei Shimbun*, 1 August 1928; and Tetsuro Sōkyoku, "Manshū no kikai nōgyō ni tsuite," 5, 66–67. On Nagao's research treatises, see, for example, [Nagao Yukusuke], "Hokuman ni okeru kikai nōgyō" (20 December 1937), NDL; and Hokuman Keizai Kenkyūsho, ed., *Manshū zairai nōhō hihan* (Dalian: SMR, 1942).

80. Tetsuro Sōkyoku, "Manshū no kikai nōgyō ni tsuite," 12.

81. Tetsuro Sōkyoku, "Manshū no kikai nōgyō ni tsuite," 13–14.

82. Tetsuro Sōkyoku, "Manshū no kikai nōgyō ni tsuite," 32–34, 51–52.

83. Tetsuro Sōkyoku, "Manshū no kikai nōgyō ni tsuite," 6–7.

84. Tetsuro Sōkyoku, "Manshū no kikai nōgyō ni tsuite," 62.

85. See a timeline of events in SMR-ERI, "Manshū nōgyō imin hōsaku," 3–4 and 690–692.

86. "Keichō jūyō shori jikō 331.2: Suihin-ken kikai nōjō tekichi chōsa no ken," 13 June 1936, no pagination, in *Mantetsu Keizai Chōsakai shiryō*, ed. Kobayashi Hideo (Tokyo: Kashiwa Shobō, 1998), 4:309–315, esp. 310, 315; and "Suihin-ken kikai nōjō keikaku-an" (August 1936), 480–481, and "Sankō-shō Suihin-ken nōgyō chōsa hōkoku" (August 1936), 621–622, in SMR-ERI, "Manshū nōgyō imin hōsaku."

87. On Watanabe, see *Rafu Shimpō*, 31 May 1939; Kashiwamura Keikoku, *Hokubei tōsa taikan* (Tokyo: Ryūbundō, 1911), apps. 10–12; and Kanai Shigeo and Itō Banshō, *Hokubei no Nihonjin* (San Francisco: Kanai Tsūyaku Jimusho, 1909), 149–151. Having immigrated in 1890, Watanabe stayed in California for a quarter century before spending "five to six years in Mexico" as a transborder resettler in the late 1910s. Like Chiba, he returned to Japan in the early 1920s. See Watanabe Kinzō, *Nichibei mondai no shinsō* (Tokyo: Kirisutokyō Fujin Kyōfūkai, 1924), 1.

88. Watanabe spent over ten months in 1908–1909 as the Tokyo representative of the Japanese Association of America, the leading immigrant organization that was formed in partnership with Japanese diplomats in 1908. Shibusawa Eiichi offered his personal office as a base for Watanabe's activities in Tokyo. See Zaibei Nihonjinkai, *Zaibei Nihonjinshi*, 91; and Azuma, *Between Two Empires*, 43–44, 52–53.

89. On this, see Ukita Kazutami and Watanabe Kinzō, *Nichibei hisen-ron* (Tokyo: Jitsugyō no Nihonsha, 1925).

90. [Watanabe Kinzō], *Dai-Kōga chisui jigyō ni tsuite* (Tokyo: Dai-Ajia Kensetsusha, 1938), 3–4.

91. SMR-ERI, "Manshū nōgyō imin hōsaku," 4. Attesting to the value of their rare expertise, the team also lent support to another major research project on "farm machinery for large-scale agriculture," which entailed the cataloging and testing of mechanized tools and engine-powered equipment used throughout Manchuria. See Mantetsu Sangyōbu, ed., *Dainō-shiki nōgyo kikai chōsa* (Dalian: SMR, 1937), jo.

92. In Japanese-language scholarship, representative works are Tama Shinnosuke, "Manshū kaitaku to Hokkaido nōhō," *Hokkaido Daigaku nōkei ronsō* 41 (February 1985), 1–22; and Takashima Hiroshi, "Manshū imin to Hokkaido," *Kushiro Kōritsu Daigaku chiiki kenkyū* 12 (December 2003), 5–7. For English-language writing about the subject, see Shinnosuke Tama, "Hokkaido Farming Methods in Manchukuo in 1940s," *Tokushima Daigaku chiiki kagaku kenkyū* 2 (2012), 30–41. Louise Young has adopted the orthodox rendition in her study. See Young, *Japan's Total Empire*, 403.

93. On this historiography, see Shirokizawa Asahiro, "'Manshū kaitaku' ni okeru Hokkaido nōgyō no yakuwari," *Sapporo Daigaku sōgō kenkyū* 2 (March 2011), 189.

94. Matsuno Den, *Manshū to Hokkaido nōhō* (Sapporo: Hokkaido Nōkai, 1943), 1–32; and Manshū Kaitakushi Kankōkai, *Manshū kaitakushi*, 351–356.

95. Hokuman Keizai Chōsasho, ed., *Hokuman to Hokkaido nōhō* (Dalian: SMR, 1941), 30–31; and Hokuman Keizai Chōsasho, *Zaiman Hōjin no einōhō ni tsuite* (Dalian: SMR, 1940), 53–54.

96. Asaoka Yukihiro, "Nōminteki gijutsu no hatten to nōgyō kyōiku no kadai," *Shakai kyōiku kenkyū* 7 (September 1986), 61–64. Asaoka defines the Hokkaido method as "cultivation by animal and harvest by human hand," which he argues should not be seen as a direct consequence of what Capron brought from America in the 1870s. In Manchuria, however, harvest was not done exclusively by human hands, and insofar as the use of the plow, harrow, and cultivator was still integral to Asaoka's definition, there was no substantive difference between the manner of farming between Hokkaido and Manchuria. For primary sources that discuss an American origin of the Hokkaido farming method contrary to Asaoka's contention, see Hokuman Keizai Chōsasho, ed., *Hokuman to Hokkaido nōhō*, 8; and Hokkaido Nōkai, ed., *Hokuman no einō* (Sapporo: Hokkaido Nōkai, 1938), 80–81.

97. Nagao Yukusuke, "Zaiman Hōjin nōkōsha ni yōkyū seraruru seikatsu yōshiki no henkō" 4, *Nōgyō no Manshū* 13, no. 8 (August 1941), 22–24, esp. 24.

98. See Hokuman Keizai Chōsasho, *Zaiman Hōjin no einōhō ni tsuite*, 11; and Watanabe, "Manshū kaitaku to Hokkaido nōgyō," in *Manshū nōgyō ni kansuru shiryō*, ed. Hokkaido Nōkai (Sapporo: Hokkaido Nōkai, 1941), 10, 12.

99. See the back cover image of *Shashin shūhō* 220 (13 May 1942). One of the Japanese captions reads as follows: "Iron Ox Corps of the North (Northern Manchuria) that is working hard for frontier development and increased food production in collaboration with Iron Ox Corps of the South." In the language of prewar Japan, "Iron Ox Corps" (Tetsugyū butai) refers to a tank battalion in the imperial army, underscoring the importance of mechanized farming in Manchuria (like military operations elsewhere). In this contrived propaganda photo, the tractor driver also wears what appears to be military garb.

100. Matsuno Den, a professor at Harbin Agricultural College, was a self-proclaimed "introducer" of the Hokkaido farming methods to Manchuria, who often disparaged American-style farming as inimical to Japan's efforts at colonization. See Matsuno, *Manshū to Hokkaido nōhō*, 7; and Matsuno, *Manshū kaitaku to Hokkaido nōgyō* (Tokyo: Seikatsusha, 1942), 17, 20.

101. Note that the word "American" was sometimes replaced with "western" after 1941. On the post-1940 activities of these former US residents, see Hokuman Keizai Kenkyūsho, *Manshū Zairai nōhō hihan*; Uchino, "Kanada to Manshū nōgyō hikaku"; Hokuman Keizai

Chōsasho, ed., *Kairyō nōhō no jisseki hōkoku* (Dalian: SMR, 1942); Nichiman Nōsei Kenkyūkai Shinkyō Jimusho, *Nanman ni okeru suiden kikai nōgyō no ichijirei*; and Yokoyama Toshio, "Nanman ni okeru suitō no seisan jijō" 1–2, *Nōgyō no Manshū* 14, nos. 11–12 (November–December 1942), esp. 25, 27 and 23, 28, respectively.

102. On the widespread use of US-originated farm machinery even during the Pacific War, see Yoshioka, *Nichiman nōgyō kikaika no mondai*, 1–2, 15–17, 24–27, esp. 15.

103. Watanabe Kinzō, "Manshū shicchi tōsa no kekka to sono kaitakuan" (March 1937), 3–20, in Honpō tainai keihatsu kankei zakken: Nihon Gaikō Kyōkai kōenshū, vol. 1, DA-MOFA; and Watanabe, *Tōhōku Manshū oyobi Minami Manshū no shicchi tōsa no kekka to sono kaitaku ni tsuite* (Tokyo: Meirinkai, 1937), 1–4.

104. Watanabe, "Manshū shicchi tōsa no kekka to sono kaitakuan," 21–23, 29–34, 40–43; Watanabe, *Tōhōku Manshū oyobi Minami Manshū no shicchi tōsa no kekka to sono kaitaku ni tsuite*, 3, 18–27, 31, 36; and [Watanabe], *Dai-Kōga chisui jigyō ni tsuite*, 4–5. The quote is from page 42 of the first source. Conversions to acreage are mine.

105. Watanabe, *Tōhōku Manshū oyobi Minami Manshū no shicchi tōsa no kekka to sono kaitaku ni tsuite*, 4–5; Watanabe, "Manshū shicchi tōsa no kekka to sono kaitakuan," 42–43; Hokkaido Kaihatsu-kyoku, ed., *Manshū ni okeru Okazaki Bunkichi hakase* (Sapporo: Hokkaido Kaihatsu-kyoku, 1990), 90; and Watanabe Mitsugu, "Bansan no suiden kaitaku jigyō o miru," *Kaitaku, Tōa ippanshi* 6, no. 9 (September 1942), 121–122. Conversions to acreage are mine.

106. See Aaron Stephen Moore, *Constructing East Asia: Technology, Ideology, and Empire in Japan's Wartime Era 1931–1945* (Stanford, CA: Stanford University Press, 2013), 108–115.

107. [Watanabe], *Dai-Kōga chisui jigyō ni tsuite*, 4. Naoki Rintarō was Manchukuo's chief civil engineer, and another influential supporter of Watanabe was Kubo Makoto, the chief director of Fushun Colliery, Manchuria's largest coal mine. On Naoki, see Moore, *Constructing East Asia*, 66–67, 107. In 1938 Watanabe traveled to the recently occupied areas along the Yellow River delta to develop policy recommendations on wetland management and agriculture. As a special adviser to the SMR president, Watanabe's access to Japan's political heavyweights helped his Yellow River reclamation proposal obtain widespread interest and endorsement from powerful statesmen, as well as colonial planners of occupied North China. Watanabe's call for Yellow River reclamation was twice submitted to the Japanese government through the hands of political insiders, including former premier Ōkuma Shigenobu. Most likely recruited by the authorities, Taro J. Watanabe, Kinzō's Nisei son, subsequently moved to Japanese-ruled North China to set up an American-style cotton plantation. A trained agricultural engineer with a graduate degree from Texas A&M University, this Japanese American transferred his hard-to-get expertise to the new "frontier" of the expanding Japanese empire. Indeed, Taro was not unfamiliar to Japan's colonial technocrats, because he had once served as the guide and adviser for an SMR engineer who had visited the US West and the Mississippi River delta on an official mission. For Watanabe's Yellow River reports, see [Watanabe], *Dai-Kōga chisui jigyō ni tsuite*; Watanabe Kinzō, *Dai-Kōga chisuiron* (Tokyo: Nihon Gaikō Kyōkai, 1938); Watanabe, "Dai-Kōga chisuiron," *Gaikō Jihō* 812 (October 1938), 60–136; [Watanabe], "Dai-Kōga chisui mondai," *Bunmei Kyōkai nyūsu* 164 (June 1940), 1–53; "Kōga chisui mondai no gutaiteki shinten" and "Kōga chisui ni

kansuru seigan," *Bunmei Kyōkai nyūsu* 173 (March 1940), 42–52; and Watanabe, "Kōga chisui keikaku suishin no kengen," *Kaikō* 135 (April 1941), 35–56. On Taro J. Watanabe's resettlement in occupied China, see *Rafu Shimpō*, 31 May 1939; and *Shin Sekai*, 1 June 1939, 18 March 1940, and 16 December 1940.

108. Watanabe, "Manshū shicchi tōsa no kekka to sono kaitakuan," 42–43; and Hiroshima-ken, ed., *Hiroshima-ken ijūshi: Shiryō-hen* (Hiroshima: Hiroshima-ken, 1991), 732–738, esp. 736, 738.

109. Nagano-ken Kaitaku Jikōkai, ed., *Nagano-ken Manshū kaitakushi: Kakudan-hen* (Nagano: Nagano-ken Kaitaku Jikōkai, 1984), 350–351; see also 750–751.

110. Nagano-ken Kaitaku Jikōkai, *Nagano-ken Manshū kaitakushi: Kakudan-hen*, 130–131, 750–751; and Hiroshima-ken, *Hiroshima-ken ijūshi*, 737, 739.

111. Watanabe, "Bansan no suiden kaitaku jigyō o miru," 122, 126–127. See also Manshū Kaitakushi Kankōkai, *Manshū kaitakushi*, 699–700; and Moore, *Constructing East Asia*, 115–117.

112. Watanabe, "Manshū shicchi tōsa no kekka to sono kaitakuan," 21–23, 29–30.

113. Watanabe, "Manshū shicchi tōsa no kekka to sono kaitakuan," 44–46.

114. Nagano-ken Kaitaku Jikōkai, *Nagano-ken Manshū kaitakushi*, 352.

6. JAPANESE HAWAI'I AND ITS TROPICAL NEXUS: TRANSLOCAL REMIGRATION TO COLONIAL TAIWAN AND THE NAN'YŌ

1. Fujii Shūgorō, "Hawai no genzai oyobi shōrai ni tsuite," in *Nippu Jihō*, ed. Fujii Shūgorō(Osaka: Bijutsu Nippōsha, 1936), 5.

2. Fujii, "Hawai no genzai oyobi shōrai ni tsuite," 5.

3. Murasame Yoshimi, "Hawai-shū no yukue," in *Nippu Jihō*, 60.

4. *Taiwan Nichinichi Shinpō*, 30 June 1907. See also Ōzono Ichizō, *Taiwan rimenshi* (Taipei: Nihon Shokiminchi Hihansha, 1936), 354–355.

5. See Kawazoe Zen'ichi, *Imin hyakunen no nenrin* (Honolulu: Imin Hyakunen no Nenrin Kankōkai, 1968), 220; and Taiwan Seitō Kabushiki Kaisha, ed., *Taiwan Seitō Kabushiki Kaisha shashi* (Tokyo: Taiwan Seitō Kabushiki Kaisha, 1939), 153–154. Kawazoe reports that the Taiwan Sugar Company had more than thirty employees from Japanese Hawai'i, many of whom were steam plow specialists and sugar mill machinists.

6. Mariko Iijima, "Coffee Production in the Asia-Pacific Region: The Establishment of a Japanese Diasporic Network in the Early 20th Century," *Journal of International Economic Studies* 32 (2018), 75–88. See also Iijima Mariko, "Senzen Nihonjin kōhī saibaisha no gurōbaru hisutorī," *Imin kenkyū nenpō* 7 (2011), 1–24.

7. Yamashita Sōen, *Hōshuku Kigen Nisen Roppyakunen to Kaigai dōhō* (Tokyo: Hōshuku Kigen Nisen Roppyakunen to Kaigai Dōhō Kankōkai, 1941), 124–125; Sogawa Masao, *Hawai Nihonjin meikan* (Honolulu: Hawai Nihonjin Meikan Kankōkai, 1927), 387; "Mirai no kōhī-ō o motte ninzuru Sumida Tajirō-kun," in *Nippu Jihō*, 63–64; Kawazoe Zen'ichi, *Ishokuju no Hana hiraku* (Honolulu: Ishokuju no Hana Hiraku Kankōkai, 1960), 251–252; *Osaka Asahi Shinbun*, 24 September 1930; and "Sumida Bussan Kabushiki Kaisha teikan" (n.d.), 1–2, in Eigyō Hōkokusho Collection (hereafter EHC), Library of Economics, University of Tokyo.

8. "Nan'yō Kōhī Kabushiki Kaisha teikan" (ca. 1926), 7–8, and "Nan'yō Kōhī Kabushiki Kaisha kabunushi meibohyō" (30 April 1930), in EHC; Asami [Shōichi], "Shihonkin gōjūmanen no Nanyō Kōhī Kaisha," *Nippu Jiji*, 4 May 1926; Mihira Masaharu, *Nan'yō Guntō ijū annai* (Tokyo: Dai-Nippon Kaigai Seinenkai, 1938), 24; Kōhī Kaikan Bunkabu, ed., *Nihon kōhīshi* (Tokyo: Kōhī Kaikan Bunkabu, 1959), 29–30; Ōgimi Tomonori, *Waga tōchi Nan'yō Guntō annai* (Tokyo: Nantōsha, 1930), 54; and Ōgimi Tomonori, *Waga tōchichi Nan'yō Guntō annai* (Tokyo: Kaigai Kenkyūsha, 1934), 156. See also Iijima, "Coffee Production in the Asia-Pacific Region."

9. "Saipan-tō no Kona kōhī jōdeki," *Nippu Jiji*, 3 April 1929.

10. Nan'yō Kōhī Kabushiki Kaisha, "Dai-rokki gyōmu hōkokusho" (May 1932), in EHC; Uehara Tetsusaburō, *Shokuminchi to shite mitaru Nan'yō Guntō no kenkyū* (Palau: Nan'yō Bunka Kenkyūsho, 1940), 12; Ōgimi, *Waga tōchi Nan'yō Guntō annai*, 54; and Handa Susumu, "Kokusan kōhī no ganso oboegaki 13," *Beifu Jihō* 195 (June 1968), 3, in the Hawaiian Collection, Hamilton Library (hereafter HCUH), University of Hawai'i at Manoa. The tally and conversion are by the author.

11. Nan'yō Kōhī Kabushiki Kaisha, "Dai-sanki gyōmu hōkokusho" (30 April 1929), in EHC.

12. "Karenkō-chō ka de kōhī no saibai jigyō," *Taiwan Nichinichi Shinpō*, 18 December 1930.

13. Munakata Kan, "Taiwan ni okeru Kōhīen keiei ni tsuite" (graduation thesis, Taihoku Imperial University Agricultural Branch, 1941), 32–33, 35, 59, in the Taiwan Agricultural History Collection (hereafter TAHC), National Chung Hsing University Library, Taichung; "Taiwan ni kōhī saibai," *Jiji Shinpō*, 13 December 1930; Karenkō-chō, ed., *Karenkō no sangyō* (Hualien: Karenkō-chō, 1935), 15, and Mori Yukitoshi, *Higashi Taiwan tenbō* (Taitung: Higashi Taiwan Gyōseikai, 1933), photo caption, both in the Taiwan History Collection (hereafter THC), National Taiwan University Library, Taipei; Zen Nihon Kōhī Shōkō Kumiai Rengōkai, ed., *Nihon kōhīshi: Jōkan* (Tokyo: Zen Nihon Kōhī Shōkō Kumiai Rengōkai, 1980), 185; *Nippu Jiji*, 9 April 1940; and "Sumida-shi ni haraisage," *Shōgyō Jihō* 12, no. 4 (April 1940), 20, in HCUH. The tally and conversion are by the author. See also Iijima, "Coffee Production in the Asia-Pacific Region."

14. See *Nippu Jiji*, 16 October 1936; and *Taiwan Nichinichi Shinpō*, 13 May 1933.

15. Gary Y. Okihiro, *Pineapple Culture: A History of the Tropical and Temperate Zones* (Berkeley: University of California Press, 2009), 173 and 73–92.

16. Murasame, "Hawai-shū no yukue," 60.

17. On Kada Village, see Hōgikai, ed., *Kada Kanesaburō-ō shōden* (Tokyo: Hōgikai, 1923), 63–84; Yamaguchi Masaji, *Higashi Taiwan kaihatsushi* (Taipei: Chunichi Sankei Shishin, 1999), 76–121, 158–197; and Liao Gaoren, *Yue du Riben guan ying yi min cun* (Hualien: Fengling Township Office, 2014), 71–176. On the early history of Japanese settler colonialism in Taiwan, see Akagi Takeichi, *Taiwan ni okeru Bokokujin nōgyō shokumin* (Tapei: Taiwan Sōtōkufu Shokusan-kyoku, 1929), 2–36; Kurihara Jun, "Taiwan Sōtōkufu ni yoru kan'ei imin jigyō ni tsuite," in *Chūgoku minshū e no shiza*, ed. Kanagawa Daigaku Chūgokugo Gakka (Tokyo: Tōhō Shoten, 1998), 161–184; and Aratake Tatsurō, "Nihon tōchi jidai Taiwan tōbu e no imin to sōshutsuchi," *Tokushima Daigaku Sōgō Kagakubu ningen shakai bunka kenkyū* 14 (2007), 91–104. The first three Japanese settlements were Yoshino (Jiye), Toyoda

(Fengtian), and Hayashida (Lintian) Villages. Until the early 1930s, eastern Taiwan mostly attracted the attention of state and private settler colonialism, which increased the number of Japanese farm settlements to nine in Hualien and Taitung Provinces. In concurrence with state-led promotion of mass migration to Manchuria in 1932, other parts of Taiwan started to receive a greater number of new agricultural settlers from Japan despite the already greater presence of Taiwanese farmers and residents.

18. On the settler-colonist "logic of elimination," see Patrick Wolfe, "Settler Colonialism and the Elimination of the Native," *Journal of Genocide Research* 8, no. 4 (December 2006), 387–388.

19. This man was Takechi Tadamichi, who was related to Robert Walker Irwin—the Kingdom of Hawai'i's minister to Japan during the 1880s—by a close relative who was married to the white American businessman. Irvin and Japan's foreign minister Inoue Kaoru were close associates and partnered in the conclusion of the emigration treaty between the two countries—the legal machination that sustained the government-sponsored emigration scheme. Both Takechi and Irvin became top executives of Taiwan's first major sugar company, the former becoming its president later. On Takechi (and Irwin), see Jitsugyō no Nihonsha, ed., *Zaikai kyotō-den* (Tokyo: Jitsugyō no Nihonsha, 1930), 252–262; "Takechi Tadamichi-shi," *Nippon to Amerika* 8, no. 9 (September 1938), 32–33; Kōno Shinji, *Nihon tōgyō hattatsushi: Jinbutsuhen* (Kobe: Nihon Tōgyō Hattatsushi Hensansho, 1931), 156–160, 180–202; Chen Mingyan and Yang Jinhua, *Taiwan jindai tangye xianquzhe* (Taipei: Taiwan Wuzhi Jinian Jijinhui, 2005), esp. 46–55, 171, 196, 202–203, 226; and Kawazoe, *Imin hyakunen no nenrin*, 220.

20. Chen Tsu-yu, "Nihon tōchiki ni okeru Taiwan yushutsu sangyō no hatten to hensen (jō)," *Ritsumeikan Keizaigaku* 60, no. 5 (January 2012), 29–31; Ōkurashō Kanri-kyoku, *Nihon-jin no Kaigai katsudō ni kansuru rekishiteki chōsa 6: Taiwan-hen 1* (Tokyo Yumani Shobō, 2000), 75–76; and Sekizawa Toshihiro, "Shokuminchi-ki Taiwan ni okeru Nikkei pain kanzume kōjō no keiei," *Keiei shigaku* 46, no. 1 (June 2011), 32–33. Rice and sugar production constituted the two most important agricultural sectors, but neither was export oriented.

21. See *Taiwan Nichinichi Shinpō*, 17 September 1902 (Chinese section); "Taiwan no Hōri kanzume seizōgyō," *Taiwan Jihō* 95 (20 August 1906), 9–21; "Hōzanchō shozai kanyūchi o Okamura Shōtarō ni kashisage no ken," vol. 852 (1903), in Taiwan Sōtōkufu Collection (hereafter TSC), Institute of Taiwan History, Academia Sinica, Taipei; Itō Kozō, "Taiwan ni okeru kanzume jigyō ni tsuite" (graduation thesis, Taihoku Imperial University Agricultural Branch, 1929), 33, in TAHC; Sakurai Yoshijirō, "Hōri saibai ni kansuru ni san no mondai ni tsuite," *Taiwan Nōjihō* 270 (June 1929), 2; Iwamoto Masaichi, "Taiwan painappuru jigyō tōsei ni kansuru shiken" (1936), 2, National Diet Library (hereafter NDL), Tokyo; and Kao Shu-yuan, *Jing ji zheng ce yu chan ye fa zhan: Yi Ri zhi shi qi Taiwan feng li guan tou ye wei li* (Ban Qiao shi, Taipei: Dao xiang, 2007), 14–15. The tally is by the author. On Okamura's experience in Hawai'i, see Itō's 1929 thesis. He most likely worked at the island's first cannery in Ewa. During the 1920s and 1930s, Sakurai Yoshijirō behaved as if he were an expert on the history of the pineapple industry in Taiwan and extensively wrote on the "pioneering" role of Okamura. Yet he always left out references to Okamura's background in Hawai'i or his ties to Smooth Cayenne—an omission that was often inherited by and reflected in other primary and secondary sources. Sakurai's narrative also tended to down-

play the centrality of Smooth Cayenne or the Hawaiian influence on the rise of Taiwan's pineapple canning business, probably because his father was connected to rival factions. See Sakurai Yoshijirō, "Taiwan no painappuru kanzume jigyō no sōgyō," *Nettai Engei* 6, no. 3 (September 1936), 212–220. An earlier primary source misidentifies Okamura's Hawai'i experience as if it took place in Hong Kong, where there was no modern pineapple cannery. See *Taiwan Nichinichi Shinpō*, 21 October 1925.

22. Itō, "Taiwan ni okeru kanzume jigyō ni tsuite," 213 and 126. By the early 1930s Nagai had moved on to an executive position at a nearby cannery, whose owner had visited Hawai'i in 1924 to obtain Smooth Cayenne crops and learn how to grow them. See Taiwan Jitsugyō Kōshinsho, ed., *Taiwan Ginkō kaisharoku* (Taipei: Taiwan Jitsugyō Kōshinsho, 1932), 115; and *Hawai Hōchi*, 16 September 1924.

23. See Yamada Kinji, "Hontō no pain jigyō to Nonomura-ō," *Taiwan Jihō* 214 (September 1937), 105–107; and K. Sakimura, "On the Pineapple Industry in Formosa," *Pineapple Quarterly* 5, no. 1 (March 1935), 30–32, in HCUH.

24. Kayashima Hideki, "Hontō ni okeru Hōri saibai narabi ni kakō ni tsuite" (graduation thesis, Taihoku Imperial University Agricultural Branch, 1926), 22–23, in TAHC.

25. See Ōkubo Kiyoshi, *Hawai-shima Nihonjin iminshi* (Hilo: Hilo Times, 1971), 171; Honji Kyōsaburō, "Ōtsuki Kōnosuke-kun kigyōdan," *Shokumin Kyōkai hōkoku* 17 (20 September 1894), 61–68; Ariiso Itsurō [pseud.], "Waga imin gaisha 5," *Shōkō Sekai Taiheiyō* 5, no. 25 (15 December 1906), 41–42; Kawazoe, *Imin hyakunen no nenrin*, 95–97; Nakagome Masumi, *Hawai o kizuita Nihonjin* (Tokyo: Gentōsha, 2016), 72–85; and Matsukuma Toshiko, *Fumetsu no isan* (Tokyo: Tōgasha, 1987), 54–67, 90–91, 97–98, 110–111, 115, 143.

26. Shibata Ichitarō to Shidehara Kijūrō, 25 November 1930, in Honpō ni okeru tochi baibai kankei zakken, Diplomatic Archives of the Ministry of Foreign Affairs (hereafter DA-MOFA), Tokyo.

27. "Taiwan no haraisagechi shisatsuno tame shuppatsu," *Nippu Jiji*, 2 March 1931. On their preliminary inspection tour and interview, see *Taiwan Nichinichi Shinpō*, 17 April 1930.

28. Okazaki Nihei, "Hawai no hōri jigyō ni tsuite," *Taiwan Jihō* 70 (August 1925), 30.

29. See "Hōri no ken'isha Okazaki-shi raitai," *Taiwan Nichinichi Shinpō*, 2 May 1925; and "Hawai no shoki ni nita Taiwan no hōri sangyō," *Taiwan Nichinichi Shinpō*, 22 July 1925.

30. See Ōta Takeshi, ed., *Taiwan taikan* (Tainan: Tainan Shinpōsha, 1935), 144; and Taiwan Keizai Kenkyūsho, ed., *Hōri gōdō no shinsō* (Taipei: Taiwan Keizai Kenkyūsho, 1936), 8–10, in Asanuma Inajirō monjo, Modern Japanese Political History Materials Room, NDL. The tally is by the author. The latter source notes that most producers of the native pineapple varieties were Taiwanese farmers.

31. Sakimura, "On the Pineapple Industry in Formosa," 32.

32. Katō Ken'ichi, "Hōri no kōshu yōshiki ni tsuite," *Taiwan Nojihō* 27, no. 6 (June 1931), 28–29; Taiwan Sōtōkufu Shokusan-kyoku, *Taiwan no Hōri sangyō* (Taipei: Taiwan Sōtōkufu Shokusan-kyoku Tokusan-ka, 1934), 40; and Chen, "Nihon tōchiki ni okeru Taiwan yushutsu sangyō no hatten to hensen (jō)," 30. See also *Taiwan Nichinichi Shinpō*, 3 July 1923.

33. Okazaki, "Hawai no hōri jigyō ni tsuite," 31.

34. "Sekaiteki shōhin toshite no Taiwan hōri kanzumegyō no chii," *Kanzume Jihō* 6, no. 3 (March 1927), 11–14; Takasaki Tatsunosuke, "Taiwan hōri kanzumegyō seisaku," *Kanzume Jihō* 4, no. 2 (February 1925), 4–11; and Ōta, *Taiwan taikan*, 143.

35. Fukushima Hawai-kai, ed., *Ko Okazaki Nihei-ō tsuitō kinenshi* (Fukushima: Fukushima Hawai-kai, 1952), 84–85.

36. See Okazaki Nihei, "Rirekisho" (ca. 1930), in Kanbō Hishoka: Han ninkan ika shintai gengi (July–September 1930), in TSC.

37. Fukushima Hawai-kai, *Ko Okazaki Nihei-ō tsuitō kinenshi*, 2–4, 17–30, 47–49, 82–86; Takahashi Kanji, *Fukushima iminshi* (Fukushima: Fukushima Hawai-kai, 1958), 11–12; and Kawazoe, *Ishokuju no Hana hiraku*, 303–304.

38. Fukushima Hawai-kai, *Ko Okazaki Nihei-ō tsuitō kinenshi*, 82–86; Takahashi, *Fukushima iminshi*, 11–12; Katō, "Hōri no kōshu yōshiki ni tsuite," 28; Kawazoe, *Ishokuju no Hana hiraku*, 303–304; Okazaki, "Rirekisho"; Okazaki, "Hawai no hōri jigyō ni tsuite," 27–28; and "Hōrika kōshū," *Hawai Hōchi*, 16 February 1923.

39. Takasaki Tatsunosuke-shū Kankō Iinkai, ed., *Takasaki Tatsunosuke-shū: Jō* (Tokyo: Tōyō Seikan Kabushiki Kaisha, 1965), 94–98.

40. Takasaki Tatsunosuke-shū Kankō Iinkai, *Takasaki Tatsunosuke-shū: Jō*, 69–108; and Andrew F. Smith, *American Tuna: The Rise and Fall of an Improbable Food* (Berkeley: University of California Press, 2012), 60–63, 69. Takasaki's academic mentor and business partner, Kondō Masaji (Atsuhiro), later built a thriving transborder fishing enterprise tying together San Diego and the Baja California coast after taking over Sandoval's enterprise. See Zaibei Nihonjinkai, *Zaibei Nihonjinshi* (San Francisco: Zaibei Nihonjinkai, 1940), 307; and Nichiboku Kyōkai, ed., *Nichiboku kōryūshi* (Tokyo: PMC Shuppan, 1990), 429–433.

41. Takasaki Tatsunosuke-shū Kankō Iinkai, *Takasaki Tatsunosuke-shū: Jō*, 63–65; Takasaki, "Taiwan hōri kanzumegyō seisaku," 4; and Taiwan Ginkō Chōsa-ka, "Hōri kanzume kōgyō chōsa no ken," no. 161, 3 January 1934, no pagination, in Fenri guantou xiangwan diaocha 1 (Hōri kanzume sōkan chōsa 1), in TSC.

42. See Takasaki Tatsunosuke, "Shōwa Shichinen tobeiki" 1, *Kanzume Jihō* 11, no. 10 (October 1932), 42.

43. Sakata Kunisuke, ed., *Dai nikai Hontō keizai jijō chōsa hōkoku* (Taipei: Nanshi Nan'yō Keizai Kenkyūkai, 1932), 110; and Taiwan Sōtōkufu Shokusan-kyoku, ed., *Taiwan no Hōri sangyō* (Taipei: Taiwan Sōtōkufu Shokusan-kyoku Tokusan-ka, 1930), 2. Based on his connections to the steel industry through tin can manufacturing, Takasaki later moved to Manchuria to become involved in the management of Manchou Heavy Industries Development Company (Manshū Jūkōgyō Kaihatsu), the largest industrial conglomerate in Japan's puppet regime of Manchukuo.

44. Takasaki Tatsunosuke, *Hawai ni okeru Hōri kanzume jigyō* (Tokyo: Kanzume Fukyū Kyōkai, 1924), 1; Takasaki, "Taiwan hōri kanzumegyō seisaku," 4; *Nippu Jiji*, 23 August 1924; Taiwan *Nichinichi Shinpō*, 19 September 1924 and 30 August 1925; Okazaki Nihei, "Hōri ni tsuite," *Kanzume Jihō* 5, no. 7 (July 1925), 2–4; Takahashi, *Fukushima iminshi*, 12; Taiwan Seikan Kabushiki Kaisha, "Taiwan hōri-gyō seisaku" (1925), 3–4, 12–16, Library of Agriculture, Forestry and Fisheries Research Council, Tsukuba; and Tōyō Seikan Kabushiki Kaisha, *Tōyō Seikan gojūnen no ayumi* (Tokyo: Tōyō Seikan Kabushiki Kaisha, 1967), 45.

45. Takemoto Iichirō, ed., *Shōwa jūnen Taiwan kaisha nenkan* (Taipei: Taiwan Keizai Kenkyūsho, 1934), 391; and Taiwan Hōri Saibai Kabushiki Kaisha, "Dai-hakkai eigyō hōkokusho," ca. 1929, no pagination, in Hōri jigyō chōsa no ken 2, in TSC.

46. See, for example, *Taiwan Nichinichi Shinpō*, 2 May, 22 July, and 30 August 1925.

47. Kengaku Eijirō [pseud.], "Hōri kanzume hanbai gyōsha no Taiwan yūki," *Kanzume Jihō* 8, no. 4 (April 1929), 69. Izumi Kyūsaburō, one of Okazaki's close associates, was a leading pineapple grower at Wahiawā—the site of Dole's main plantation—before the mid-1920s. See *Nippu Jiji*, 3 March 1939.

48. Sakimura, "On the Pineapple Industry in Formosa," 35.

49. Nakao first immigrated to Alameda, California, in 1895, where he studied English for three years before moving to Hawai'i. For a few years he ran a general merchandise store, but the O'ahu sugar strike of 1909 resulted in the closing of his business. His first involvement in the pineapple industry was working as a manager of a Japanese-owned plantation in Wahiawā in the early 1910s. By 1915 Nakao had become a landowning pineapple farmer near Kaneohe, and he set up his own modest cannery there in 1919. See Hata Yoshimatsu, ed., *Fukuoka kenjin Hawai zairyū kinen shashinchō* (Honolulu: Hata Jimusho, 1924), 65. Between his move to Taiwan in the mid-1920s and his retirement in the late 1930s, Nakao remained with Takasaki's pineapple concerns, which also ran a Hawaiian style modern cannery in Kaohsiung. That cannery and its pineapple farm were managed by Hoshino Naotarō, another former US resident who had worked with Takasaki in the fish canning business in the US-Mexican borderlands during the 1910s. See Kōnan Shinbunsha, ed., *Taiwan jinshiroku* (Taipei: Kōnan Shinbunsha,1943), 358.

50. *Taiwan Nichinichi Shinpō*, 13 and 20 December 1925.

51. *Taiwan Nichinichi Shinpō*, 28 October 1925. Mitsubishi later established a large pineapple cannery and farm near Douliu in central-western Taiwan. It seems that the continuous support of this Japanese American was crucial in the initial preparation phase of the firm's establishment.

52. Akagi, *Taiwan ni okeru Bokokujin nōgyō shokumin*, 172–184; "Kōbō no Taiwan hōri kanzumegyō," *Jigyō no Nihon* 8, no. 3 (March 1929), 46–47; Fujiwara Tatsushi, *Torakutā no sekaishi* (Tokyo: Chūō Kōronsha, 2017), 184–185; Taiwan Seikan Kabushiki Kaisha, "Taiwan hōri-gyō seisaku," 27–30; and Sakimura, "On the Pineapple Industry in Formosa," 31.

53. Ono Fumihide, *Taiwan tōgyō to Tōgyō kaisha* (Tokyo: Tōyō Keizai Shuppanbu, 1930), 234–235.

54. Fukushima Hawai-kai, *Ko Okazaki Nihei-ō tsuitō kinenshi*, 59; and Okazaki Nihei, *Hiripin guntō ni okeru Hōri jigyō* (Taipei: Taiwan Sōtokufu, 1930), 21, 26.

55. Fukushima Hawai-kai, *Ko Okazaki Nihei-ō tsuitō kinenshi*, 59.

56. Operated by Naigai Foods (Naigai Shokuhin), a sister company of the TCMC group, this cannery was equipped with the automated canning devices that Okazaki Nihei personally procured in Hawai'i. Invented in Hawai'i in 1911, the Ginaca automated peeling and slicing machine revolutionized the process of commercial pineapple canning. Not only did it allow James Dole to cut down on labor costs, but it also made production much faster and more efficient. Okazaki Nihei was instrumental in the acquisition of this machine by Takasaki Tatsunosuke's pineapple syndicate in Taiwan.

57. *Taiwan Nichinichi Shinpō*, 30 September 1925, 13 December 1926, 9 November 1927, and 28 June 1928. The quotes are from the last source.

58. Taiwan Sōtokufu, ed., *Taiwan Sōtokufu jimu seiseki teiyō* (Shōwa yonen-do bun), vol. 35-1 (Taipei: Taiwan Sōtokufu, 1938), 506–507, in THC.

59. See *Taiwan Nichinichi Shinpō*, 18 January 1932; Naihoshō Yakuba, ed., "Shōwa Jūichinen-do Chōshūgun Naiho shōsei ichiran" (1936), 9–10, in Taiwan Studies Center, National Taiwan Library, New Taipei City; and Saitō Kazue, "Hōri kanzume no seizō hōhō," *Nettai Engei* 6, no. 3 (September 1936), 302–304.

60. "Hawai no shoki ni nita Taiwan no hōri sangyō"; Shimoda Masami, *Nantō keizaiki* (Tokyo: Osaka Yagō Shoten, 1929), 204–206; Sawamoto Kōnan, *Taiwan o bekken shite* (Tokyo: Aoyama Shoin, 1930), 36–37; Itagaki Hōki, *Taiwan kenbutsu* (Tokyo: Itagaki Rikiko, 1931), 84–85; and "Kōbō no Taiwan hōri kanzumegyō," 46–47. Entitled "Pineapple," the commercially distributed postcard (see figure 12) features variously dressed Paiwan people surrounded by full-grown Smooth Cayenne plants on Okazaki's Laopi farm. Clearly contrived, the picture is intended to showcase Japanese colonialism's achievements (large-scale pineapple farming) in rural Pingtung and the ongoing mission to civilize Taiwanese aborigines there. These workers most likely hailed from nearby Jiayi Village.

61. See Paul D. Barclay, *Outcasts of Empire: Japan's Rule on Taiwan's "Savage Border," 1874–1945* (Berkeley: University of California Press, 2018), 176–181; and Chen Xiuchun, *Riju shiqi Taiwan shandi shuitian zuo de zhankai* (Ban Qiao shi, Taipei: Dao xiang, 1998), 11–55.

62. *Taiwan Nichinichi Shinpō*, 3 September 1926 and 12 October 1927; and Fujisaki Sainosuke, *Taiwan no banzoku* (Tokyo: Kokushi Kankōkai, 1931), 884.

63. *Nippu Jiji*, 6 May 1929 and 2 March 1939; Shiten-ka, "Hōri chōsho," ca. 1929, no pagination, in TSC; and Yeh Chuin-cheng, "Pingtung Neipu bei jing yan shan ju luo kai fa" (master's thesis, National University of Tainan, 2007), 77. The quotes are from the first two sources. On Japanese perceptions and representations of Taiwan's indigenous peoples, see Barclay, *Outcasts of Empire*, esp., 190–249.

64. *Taiwan Nichinichi Shinpō*, 1 November 1931.

65. Ono, *Taiwan tōgyō to Tōgyō kaisha*, 237.

66. See "Taiwan ni kōhī saibai"; Munakata, "Taiwan ni okeru Kōhīen keiei ni tsuite," 18–20, 29–30, 63, 67; "Saishoku-shiki kōhīen keiei kōzō," in *Taiwan Keizai Nenpō*, ed. Taiwan Keizai Nenpō Kankōkai (Tokyo: Kokusai Nihon Kyōkai, 1942), 418–419; and Satō Jikō, "Taiwan ni okeru kōhī saibai no genjyō to shōrai," *Taiwan kin'yū keizai geppō* 103 (May 1929), 16, in THC. In his influential 1968 study on colonial land ownership, Asada Kyōji, a prominent Japanese historian, discusses Sumida's coffee farm operation as an example of imperial Japan's industrial capital that engaged in "forced labor" of indigenous people with the help of "police authorities." As primary sources show, Asada's Marxist analysis, which mirrors his politicized presumptions more than anything, is flawed. In fact, he only cites limited statistical data. See Asada Kyōji, *Nihon teikoku shugi to kyū shokuminchi jinushisei* (Tokyo: Ochanomizu Shobō, 1968), 57. On labor management and Japanese labor responses at Hawaiʻi's sugar plantations, see Moon-Kie Jung, *Reworking Race: The Making of Hawaii's Interracial Labor Movement* (New York: Columbia University Press, 2006), 55–105.

67. Munakata, "Taiwan ni okeru Kōhīen keiei ni tsuite," 61–63, 68; and "Saishoku-shiki kōhīen keiei kōzō," 418.

68. Munakata, "Taiwan ni okeru Kōhīen keiei ni tsuite," 68; and "Saishoku-shiki kōhīen keiei kōzō," 423. One hundred *sen* equalled one yen.

69. Munakata, "Taiwan ni okeru Kōhīen keiei ni tsuite," 64.

70. Munakata, "Taiwan ni okeru Kōhīen keiei ni tsuite," 59, 65, 67–68; and "Saishoku-shiki kōhīen keiei kōzō," 422.

71. Ono, *Taiwan tōgyō to Tōgyō kaisha*, 234.

72. Kengaku, "Hōri kanzume hanbai gyōsha no Taiwan yūki," 69.

73. "Hōri Kanzume Kaikan Kenkyūkai," *Kanzume Jihō* 8, no. 2 (February 1929), 5.

74. Hōri Kanzume Kaikan Kenkyūkai," 5; and Ono, *Taiwan tōgyō to Tōgyō kaisha*, 239–240.

75. See Sakurai Yōshijirō, "Hōri saibai ni kansuru ni san no mondai ni tsuite," *Kanzume Jihō* 8, no. 1 (January 1929), 10–25. The quote is from page 13. On Sakurai's lopsided historical narrative, see also note 21.

76. Sakimura, "On the Pineapple Industry in Formosa," 31, 39; Watanabe Shōichi, *Pain dokuhon* (Taipei: Taiwan Engei Kyōkai, 1939), 68–71; Watanabe Shōichi, "Taiwan ni okeru pain saibai no enkaku genkyō oyobi shōrai," in *Taiwan keizai sōsho*, ed. Taiwan Keizai Kenkyūshō (Taipei: Taiwan Keizai Kenkyūshō, 1942), 10:32–33; Yutoku Masao, "Taiwan hōri sangyō no keizaiteki kenkyū" (graduation thesis, Taihoku Imperial University, March 1940), 19–22, in TAHC; and Kao, *Jing ji zheng ce yu chan ye fa zhan*, 226.

77. Kanae Kurabu, *Kanae* (Kaohsiung: Kanae Kurabu, 1931), 1:3 and 82, in THC.

78. Watanabe, "Taiwan ni okeru pain saibai no enkaku genkyō oyobi shōrai," 31; K. Sakimura and John Stanley, "Pineapples in Formosa," *Pineapple Quarterly* 1, no. 2 (June 1931), 104, in HCUH; and *Nippu Jiji*, 8 October 1936. Government agricultural scientist Ogasawara Kinsuke was appointed the first chief of these seedling stations because of his previous research experience in Hawai'i. Another government horticulturalist, Watanabe Shōichi, spent several months in Hawai'i during the mid-1930s, forging a close working relationship with local Japanese immigrant farmers as his guides. Perhaps for this reason, Watanabe held former Hawai'i residents, including Okazaki and Nakao, in high regard, often citing their contributions as "Smooth Cayenne pioneers" in Taiwan. See the first source in this note. Due to his expertise in that crop variety, the Guomintang government kept Watanabe as a special adviser to postwar Taiwan's pineapple industry even after he was repatriated to Japan.

79. Fukushima Hawai-kai, ed., *Ko Okazaki Nihei-ō tsuitō kinenshi*, 60, 87–89; and "Kōbō no Taiwan hōri kanzumegyō," 47.

80. *Nippu Jiji*, 6 May 1929; Kofukada Sadao, "Parao no nōsangyō," *Pashifikku uei*, no. 120 (2002), 20–21; Noguchi Masaaki, "Asahi-mura Shokuminchi," *Nan'yō Guntō* 5, no. 10 (October 1939), 73–82; and Maruyama Yoshiji, *Nan'yō Guntō* (Tokyo: Ōtō Shobō, 1942), 207–211. Ogasawara Kinsuke, Okazaki's close ally in the government expert circle of colonial Taiwan, was said to be instrumental in the subsequent systematic introduction of Smooth Cayenne into Palau. The official had cultivated a close personal relationship with Okazaki since they had visited each other in Hawai'i and Taiwan, respectively, in 1924. In the same year, he spearheaded the importation of one hundred thousand Smooth Cayenne saplings from Hawai'i on behalf of the colonial government. From 1929, Ogasawara served as the head of the government sapling station near Kaohsiung, and a few years after the trip he was transferred to the Nan'yō's colonial government to serve as the head of its agricultural research center in Palau. Ogasawara was a staunch supporter of Smooth Cayenne and Hawai'i-style pineapple farming inside government circles.

81. "Jirei-an," 24 July 1930, and Ishikawa Shigeo to Ishizuka Eizō, "Jimu shokutaku no ken," 24 July 1930, both in Kanbō Hishoka: Han-ninkan ika shintai gengi (July–September 1930), in TSC.

82. Fukushima Hawai-kai, *Ko Okazaki Nihei-ō tsuitō kinenshi*, 88; Takahashi, *Fukushima iminshi*, 12; and Okazaki Nihei, *Hiripin guntō ni okeru Hōri jigyō* (Taipei: Nan'yō Kyōkai Taiwan Shibu, 1930).

83. Seiji Shirane, "Mediated Empire: Colonial Taiwan in Japan's Imperial Expansion in South China and Southeast Asia, 1895–1945" (PhD diss., Princeton University, 2014), 2, 22, and 108–154.

84. Okazaki, *Hiripin guntō ni okeru Hōri jigyō*, 20–26.

85. Kao, *Jing ji zheng ce yu chan ye fa zhan*, 143–171,182–188, esp. 185; Kitamura Yoshie, "Painappuru kanzume kara miru Tai-Ryū-Nichi kankeishi," special issue of *Kyōkai kenkyū* [no vol. number](2013), 135; Yutoku, "Taiwan hōri sangyō no keizaiteki kenkyū," 31–33, 42–43 (the tally is by the author); Negishi Benji, *Nanpō nōgyō mondai* (Tokyo: Nihon Hyōronsha, 1942), 179–180, 191–193, 202–204, 211–214; Kōmoto Masanobu, "Taiwan hōri kanzume jigyō no hattatsu," *Nettai Engei* 6, no. 3 (September 1936), 228–233, in THC; and Taiwan Keizai Kenkyūsho, *Hōri gōdō no shinsō*, 20–33, 45–47, 53–58.

86. Watanabe, "Taiwan ni okeru pain saibai no enkaku genkyo oyobi shōrai," 28; and Kao, *Jing ji zheng ce yu chan ye fa zhan*, 268. The tally is by the author.

87. See Yutoku, "Taiwan hōri sangyō no keizaiteki kenkyū", 28, 29; Taiwan Sōtōkufu Shokusan-kyoku, ed., *Taiwan no Hōri sangyō* (Taipei: Taiwan Sōtōkufu Shokusan-kyoku, 1932), 22, 40–41; and *Taiwan Nichinichi Shinpō*, 19 May 1932 (Chinese section). Okazaki took over a small canning facility owned by a local Taiwanese entrepreneur in Guanmiao and retrofitted and expanded it with imported equipment from Hawai'i. Some sources thus indicate June 1928 as the time of establishment—the month in which the original owner built his old-fashioned factory.

88. *Taiwan Nichinichi Shinpō*, 2 August and 15 November 1926; *Tainan Shinpō*, 21 May 1932; Lee Hsien-Ching, "Guanmiao diqu kaifude lishi bianqian" (master's thesis, National University of Tainan, 2009), 115–116; and Hsu Tiwen, "Feng li ye bian zhi yi shi," https://kmweb.coa.gov.tw/ct.asp?xItem=1624340&ctNode=919&mp=1&kpi=0&rowId=3&hashid= (accessed 10 March 2019). In a Facebook post dated 19 July 2017 (Internet link no longer available; printout in the author's possession), Ms. Hsu specifically mentioned that Okazaki was responsible for introducing Smooth Cayenne to Guanmiao (courtesy of Ms. Hsu Tiwen). Okazaki's investigative tours of 1924–1925 also fostered positive views on Smooth Cayenne cultivation in particular, and on Hawai'i-style pineapple farming in general, among settler leaders, entrepreneurs, and policy makers in eastern Taiwan. On the discussion of the merit of pineapple farming after Okazaki's visit to Hualien, see Seikashi [pseud.], "Yubō naru Hōri jigyō," in *Higashi Taiwan no genjō*, ed. Higashi Taiwan Kenkyūkai (Taipei: Higashi Taiwan Kenkyūkai, 1925), 40; and Hoshino Naotarō, "Taiwan Hōrigyō seisaku ni tsuite," in *Tōbu no tsuchi ni shitashime*, ed. Higashi Taiwan Kenkyūkai (Taipei: Higashi Taiwan Kenkyūkai, 1925), 23–48. In 1926 Okazaki and another TPCC executive also visited Taitung to promote and inspect Smooth Cayenne cultivation there. See *Taiwan Nichinichi Shinpō*, 18 May 1926.

89. Fukushima Hawai-kai, *Ko Okazaki Nihei-ō tsuitō kinenshi*, 88–89; Takahashi, *Fukushima iminshi*, 12; and Hata, *Fukuoka kenjin Hawai zairyū kinen shashinchō*, 65. The second source notes that the cannery was worth 900,000 yen (or $225,000). Since the first source seems to be the basis for the latter's narrative, I have decided to cite the figure it offers. It appears that the Waiau cannery used to belong to the white-owned Pearl City Fruits Com-

pany, and Okazaki had served as a labor contractor for Japanese cannery workers at this factory from 1917 to 1921. See labor recruitment advertisements in *Nippu Jiji*, 21 June 1917 and 2 June 1921; and Richard A. Hawkins, *A Pacific Industry: The History of Pineapple Canning in Hawaii* (London: I. B. Tauris, 2011), 135–136.

90. See statistics in Kanbyō-shō (Guanmiao) Yakuba, "Shōsei ichiran" (April 1934), no pagination, in THC.

91. See Taiwan Sōtōkufu Shokusan-kyoku, ed., *Shōwa shichinen Kōjō meibo* (Taipei: Taiwan Sōtōkufu Shokusan-kyoku, 1934), 113–114; and Taiwan Sōtōkufu Shokusan-kyoku, ed., *Kōjō meibo* (Taipei: Taiwan Sōtōkufu Shokusan-kyoku, 1936), 127.

92. Kamata Isao, "Taiwan ni okeru hōri sangyō ni tsuite" (graduation thesis, Taihoku Imperial University Agricultural Branch, 1939), 36, 60–61, in TAHC; and Wang Youde (Oh Tomotoku), "Taiwan ni okeru hōrien keiei ni tsuite" (graduation thesis, Taihoku Imperial University Agricultural Branch, 1940), 52–53, in TAHC. On Okazaki's five-hundred-acre farm, about ninety acres were under cultivation exclusively for Smooth Cayenne in 1937, while the rest still awaited the clearing of forests, leveling, and plowing. Okazaki resorted to the native tenant system, perhaps because he was unable to oversee canning and farming operations simultaneously. Aboriginal labor was not as easy to procure as in Laopi, either.

93. Taiwan sheng wen xian wei yuan hui, ed., *Tainan xian xiang tu shi liao* (Nantou-shi: Taiwan sheng wen xian wei yuan hui, 1999), 802.

94. Interviews with Fang Jianxing, Guanmiao, 1 November 2016 and 11 October 2018. The first interview was conducted by Hsu Tiwei and second by the author. The author wishes to acknowledge the assistance and courtesy of Ms. Hsu Tiwei, who shared her earlier interview with Mr. Fang and arranged another on behalf of the author. Along with Ms. Hsu, Ms. Kuo Tingyu kindly offered simultaneous translation in Mandarin Chinese and Taiwanese during the author's interview with Mr. Fang on his late father.

95. *Taiwan Nichinichi Shinpō*, 23 March 1934; Yutoku, "Taiwan hōri sangyō no keizaiteki kenkyū," 31–32; Kōmoto, "Taiwan hōri kanzume jigyō no hattatsu," 229; and Taiwan Keizai Kenkyūsho, *Hōri gōdō no shinsō*, 24–31.

96. See Fukushima Hawai-kai, *Ko Okazaki Nihei-ō tsuitō kinenshi*, 90; and Taiwan Sōtōkufu Shokusan-kyoku, ed., *Kōjō meibo* (Taipei: Taiwan Sōtōkufu Shokusan-kyoku, 1937), 125. On Okazaki's investment in the company stock, see Taiwan Gōdō Hōri Kabushiki Kaisha, "Dai-rokkai eigyō hōkokusho" (July–December 1937), 14–15; and Taiwan Gōdō Hōri Kabushiki Kaisha, "Dai-jūgokai eigyō hōkokusho" (January–June 1942), 14, 17, in EHC.

97. Taiwan Keizai Kenkyūsho, *Hōri gōdō no shinsō*, 8, 45, 62. The quote is from page 45.

98. See Lin Fa (Hayashi Tatsuo), *Okinawa pain sangyōshi* (Ishigakishi: Okinawa Pain Sangyōshi Kankōkai, 1984), 7–35; Kitamura, "Painappuru kanzume kara miru Tai-Ryū-Nichi kankeishi," 135–139; and Noiri Naomi, "Painappuru to Kaitaku imin," *Shisō* no. 1119 (July 2017), 77–81, esp. 78–80.

7. JAPANESE PIONEERS IN AMERICA AND THE MAKING OF EXPANSIONIST ORTHODOXY IN IMPERIAL JAPAN

1. Eiichiro Azuma, "The Politics of Transnational History Making: Japanese Immigrants on the Western 'Frontier,' 1927–1941," *Journal of American History* 89, no. 4 (March 2003), 1401–1413.

2. *Rafu Shimpō*, 16 October 1935.

3. Nakagawa Mushō, *Zaibei tōshiroku* (Los Angeles: Rafu Shimpōsha, 1932), 2.

4. Zaibei Nihonjinkai, *Zaibei Nihonjinshi* (San Francisco: Zaibei Nihonjinkai, 1940), 157.

5. Zaibei Nihonjinkai, *Zaibei Nihonjinshi*, 1–4; and Azuma, "The Politics of Transnational History Making," 1412–1413.

6. Azuma, "The Politics of Transnational History Making," 1408–1409, 1412–1417.

7. Zaibei Nihonjinkai, *Zaibei Nihonjinshi*, 77.

8. Zaibei Nihonjinkai, *Zaibei Nihonjinshi*.

9. The colonial minister stated that his office had employed the term *takushi* because Japanese settlers in Manchuria should not be confused with earlier *imin*—shiftless *dekasegi* emigrants—to the Americas. He noted the difficulty the government had faced in recruiting new emigrants to Manchuria because many people refused to join the ranks of low-class *dekasegi* laborers. The colonial ministry also had to respond to repeated complaints from the residents in Manchuria, who disliked being called *imin*. See Teikoku Gikai, *Shūgiin iinkaigiroku, Shōwa-hen* (1939), 100:338–339.

10. Louise Young, *Japan's Total Empire: Manchukuo and the Culture of Wartime Imperialism* (Berkeley: University of California Press, 1998), 307. As explained in previous chapters, the Japanese government had backed settler-colonist endeavors in Korea and Brazil, but through subsidized companies or organizations such as the Oriental Development Company.

11. Iriye Toraji, *Hōjin kaigai hattenshi*, vols. 1–2 (Tokyo: Ida Shoten, 1942); and Imin Mondai Kenkyūkai, *Imin Mondai Kenkyūkai to sono jigyō* (Tokyo: Imin Mondai Kenkyūkai, 1938), 1–2, in folder 12, box 363, Japanese American Research Project Collection, University of California, Los Angeles.

12. Iriye, *Hōjin kaigai hattenshi*, vols. 1–2.

13. See, for example, Iriye, *Hōjin kaigai hattenshi*, 1:75–82, 304–317, 450–457, 496–511 and 2:162–178, 257–274, 313–332, 512–516, 522.

14. Iriye, *Hōjin kaigai hattenshi*, 2:326–327.

15. Iriye, *Hōjin kaigai hattenshi*, 2:326–327.

16. On examples of this genre mimicking Iriye's pioneering work, see Makishima Tokuhisa, *Nihon imin gaishi* (Tokyo: Kaigai Kōgyō, 1937); Kikuchi Kan, *Kaigai ni yūhishita hitobito* (Tokyo: Shinchōsha, 1940); and Shibata Ken'ichi, *Nihon minzoku kaigai hattenshi* (Tokyo: Kōa Nihonsha, 1941).

17. Zaibei Nihonjinkai, *Zaibei Nihonjinshi*, 19–29; and Kawamura Masahei, *Hainichi sensen o toppashitsutsu* (Isleton, CA: self-pub., 1930), 11–20, 161–182.

18. Azuma, "The Politics of Transnational History Making," 1418.

19. Kimura Takeshi, "Los Angeles chihō ni 'Okei' no iseki o saguru," *Sandē Mainichi* 11, no. 2 (3 January 1932), 33; and "Japanese Girl Pioneer to be Immortalized," *Sacramento Bee*, 27 May 1931.

20. In the introduction to his 1935 publication, Kimura made this point clear. See Kimura Takeshi, *Meiji kensetsu* (Tokyo: Kaizōsha, 1935), 1.

21. Kimura, *Meiji kensetsu*, 72.

22. Kimura, *Meiji kensetsu*, 61–62.

23. Kimura, *Meiji kensetsu*, 158. Kimura altered the class origin of Okei from a commoner to the daughter of a samurai, which the 1940 film inherited.

24. Kimura, *Meiji kensetsu*, 346–347.

25. Kimura, *Meiji kensetsu*, 213.

26. Kimura, *Meiji kensetsu*, 220–223.

27. Kimura, *Meiji kensetsu*, 223–224.

28. According to many Issei who visited Japan in the 1930s, people tended to assume that they were connected to agriculture simply because they lived in America. One immigrant writer who was interviewed by a Tokyo newspaper noted his embarrassment when he subsequently found that it had identified him as an "agricultural tycoon" from California. Though he protested the error, the newspaperman told him that no one would read the article unless it was about a successful Issei farmer. That stereotype was most likely a by-product of the Issei's own history making. See Yusa Hanboku [pseud.], *Hanboku zenshū* (Santa Maria, CA: self-pub., 1940), 522.

29. Young, *Japan's Total Empire*, 310 and 307–321. On the agricultural aspect of Manchurian colonization and the ideologizing of its importance, see also Sandra Wilson, "The 'New Paradise': Japanese Emigration to Manchuria in the 1930s and 1940s," *International History Review* 17, no. 2 (1995), 249–286; and Louise Young, "Colonizing Manchuria: The Making of an Imperial Myth," in *Mirror of Modernity: Invented Traditions of Modern Japan*, ed. Stephen Vlastos (Berkeley: University of California Press, 1998), 95–109.

30. See Jin'no Morimasa, *Manshū ni okurareta onnatachi* (Tokyo: Nashi no Ki-sha, 1992); and Aiba Kazuhiko et al., *Manshū "Tairiku no hanayome wa dou tsukuraretaka* (Tokyo: Akashi Shoten, 1996). A movie and a popular song were titled *Tairiku no hanayome* (Continental bride). These and other similar propagandist materials were cranked out around 1939, when the state drove forward the official plan of recruiting one million continental brides for the Manchuria lifeline.

31. The movie advertisements in *Shūkan Asahi* 37, no. 29 (30 June 1940), 26; and *Kinema Junpō* 719, 720, (21 June and 1 July 1940) emphasized the fateful struggle of their "love" and "ideals" in this "elegy that unfolded behind the opening of Meiji Japan." In the end, national interest took precedence over individual happiness as a matter of course—a circumstance that the audience was led to take for granted however "tragic" it was. The film is available at the Library of Congress, Washington, DC.

32. See Kimura, *Meiji kensetsu*, 351–407.

33. A rising star of Tōhō Motion Pictures, Yamada Isuzu played the role of Okei, while Kurokawa Yatarō took the role of Shijimi. A top samurai movie actor, Ōkōchi Denjirō, was Fukuzawa in the film.

34. *Shūkan Asahi* 37, no. 29 (30 June 1940), 26.

35. On an example of the postwar nationalized narrative, see John Van Sant, *Pacific Pioneers: Japanese Journeys to America and Hawaii, 1850–80* (Urbana: University of Illinois Press, 2000), 129. While most postwar Japanese obliterated Okei from their memory, the city of Aizu Wakamastu reclaimed its native daughter by erecting a replica of her California tombstone in 1957. Local schoolchildren and residents collected donations for this project, hailing her simply as an inspiration for the people of Aizu.

36. The Japanese government spent five years preparing for this event. There were also many other national, prefectural, and municipal gatherings and celebrations, as well as exhibitions, book projects, and sports events, including an "East Asian athletic games." In

addition, the 1940 Olympics and an international exposition were scheduled to take place in Tokyo, but the war in Europe resulted in their cancellation. See Naikaku Jōhōbu, *Kigen Nisen Roppyakunen Shukuten kiroku* vols. 1–13 (ca. 1942), National Archives of Japan (hereafter NAJ), Tokyo. On the historical importance of these events, see Kenneth J. Ruoff, *Imperial Japan at Its Zenith: The Wartime Celebration of the Empire's 2,600th Anniversary* (New York: Columbia University Press, 2010).

37. On Nazi Germany's mobilization of *Auslandsdeutsche* (overseas Germans), see Michael Burleigh, *Germany Turns Eastwards: A Study of* Ostforschung *in the Third Reich* (Cambridge, UK: Cambridge University Press, 1988), 161–186; Mark Mazower, *Hitler's Empire: How the Nazis Ruled Europe* (New York: Penguin Press, 2008), 80–102; and Arthur L. Smith, *The* Deutschtum *of Nazi Germany and the United States* (Hague: Martinus Nijhoff, 1965), 2–25, 117–151. On US intelligence reports on how Japanese officials might have been inspired by the Third Reich's program, see F. G. Tillman, "Overseas Japanese Central Society," 15 December 1940, 4, Federal Bureau of Investigation (FBI), Honolulu, in box 554, Military Intelligence Division Correspondence 1917–1941, Records of the War Department General Staff, Record Group (RG) 165, National Archives and Records Administration (NARA) II, College Park, MD. On Italy's program, see "Italy Wants Ten Million Citizens to Return Home," *Chicago Tribune*, 9 January 1939. For comparison with Germany and Italy, see Ruoff, *Imperial Japan at Its Zenith*, 178–179.

38. "Jōshinsho," in Kakushu chōsakai iinkai monjo (microfilm #143), 498–509, esp. 499, NAJ. Initially there was no orchestrated effort on the part of the Japanese government to absorb overseas residents into the new political structure of the empire. In February 1940 the Overseas Japanese Newspaper Association, which included former immigrant journalists and newspapermen connected to Japanese settlements abroad, initiated a project to assemble overseas Japanese in Tokyo for a mass rally. While the organization enlisted support from social and political leaders for the plan by March, the colonial and foreign ministries separately began to plan a meeting of immigrant leaders from various Japanese settlements, because the officials felt it worthwhile to "exchange viewpoints and have [them] understand the (new) reality of the homeland." As the foreign minister noted in an internal memo, their conference was to be completely different from the one planned by the newspapermen, since the ministry only intended to invite twenty-seven representatives from the Americas and the Nan'yō. In short, the initial official plan was to hold a discussion session of selected elites from outside Asia, with no element of public pageantry. Then in late April Konoe Fumimaro agreed to serve as the head of the special committee organized by the newspapermen, who adopted his doctrine of *hakkō ichiu* as the basic guideline for their rally. As Konoe captured political power in the next few months, government officials decided to merge their planned meeting into the rally, making it a national event of unprecedented scale and a project of expansionist orthodoxy making. On this development, see Arita Hachirō, "Kaigai zairyū hōjin daihyōsha Honpō shōshū ni kansuru ken," 8 April 1940, in Zaigai Nihonjin kankei zakken: Kaigai Dōhō Chūōkai kankei, Diplomatic Archives of the Ministry of Foreign Affairs (hereafter DA-MOFA), Tokyo; and Naikaku Jōhōbu, *Kigen Nisen Roppyakunen Shukuten kiroku* 1:202, NAJ.

39. Kaigai Dōhō Chūōkai, *Kigen Nisen Roppyakunen Hōshuku Kaigai Dōho Tokyo Taikai hōkokusho* (Tokyo: Kaigai Dōhō Chūōkai, 1941), 80–96 (hereafter *Hōkokusho*). On the activ-

ities of the Hawaiian delegation, see John J. Stephan, *Hawaii under the Rising Sun: Japan's Plans for Conquest after Pearl Harbor* (Honolulu: University of Hawaii Press, 1984), 48–53.

40. Kaigai Dōhō Chūōkai, *Hōkokusho*, 4–8; and Hōshuku Kaigai Dōhō Tokyo Taikai Honbu, *Hōshuku Kaigai Dōhō Tokyo Taikai yōkō* (Tokyo: Hōshuku Kaigai Dōhō Tokyo Taikai Honbu, 1940), 2 (hereafter *Taikai yōkō*). The quote is from the latter source. As seen in figure 13, with Prince Higashikuni (behind the center podium) as the official convener, this conference featured virtually all top government officials of the time in honor of overseas ethnic comrades, emigrants, and colonialists alike. On the right-hand side, Prime Minister Konoe stands closest to Higashikuni; Army Minister General Tōjō and Foreign Minister Matsuoka are in the fourth and the eighth places, respectively. They cheer in union with representatives of overseas settlements (left side) for the past and future success of national expansion. The giant maps show the distribution of Japanese residents in various areas of the borderless empire's "overseas development," including the United States.

41. Hōshuku Kaigai Dōhō Tokyo Taikai Honbu, *Taikai yōkō*, 1–2.

42. Tsukamoto Matsunosuke, the "oldest" surviving emigrant (eighty-four years old), who was an original member of Fukuzawa Yukichi's settler colonist expedition in 1887 (see chapter 1), leads the procession, followed by Minami Kunitarō, the emigrant who spent the longest time overseas (fifty-six years in the United States).

43. Kaigai Dōhō Chūōkai, *Hōkokusho*, 2–3.

44. *Tokyo Nichinichi Shinbun*, 5 November 1940; *Yomiuri Shinbun*, 5 November 1940; and *Miyako Shinbun*, 5 November 1940.

45. *Trans-Pacific*, 7 November 1940.

46. Takashi Fujitani, *Splendid Monarchy: Power and Pageantry in Modern Japan* (Berkeley: University of California Press, 1996), 11.

47. Kaigai Dōhō Chūōkai, *Hōkokusho*, 6.

48. Kaigai Dōhō Chūōkai, *Hōkokusho*, 23–26; *Shin Sekai*, 9 November 1940; *Nichibei Shimbun*, 9 November 1940; and *Kashū Mainichi*, 8 November 1940. The conference ended with three cheers of *banzai* led by a Seattle immigrant leader.

49. "Zaigai Hōjin Daihyōsha Hokubei Bukai kaisai ni kansuru ken," 23 October 1940, in Zaigai Nihonjin kankei zakken: Kaigai Dōhō Chūōkai kankei, DA-MOFA. On examples of "heterodox ideas" and points of "contention" that North American participants sometimes brought to the conference, see Ruoff, *Imperial Japan at Its Zenith*, 162–164.

50. Kaigai Dōhō Chūōkai, *Hōkokusho*, 17–18; and Takumushō and Gaimushō, ed., *Kigen Nisen Roppyakunen Hōshuku Dai-ikkai Zaigai Dōhō Daihyōsha Kaigi* (1940), 36–37, National Diet Library, Tokyo.

51. Michel Foucault, *The Archaeology of Knowledge*, trans. A.M. Sheridan Smith (London: Tavistock, 1972), 9–10; and Michel Foucault, *The Order of Things: An Archaeology of the Human Sciences* (London: Tavistock, 1980), 168.

52. *Trans-Pacific*, 7 November 1940.

53. See Hatakeyama Kikuji, "Minasama tadaima," *Shin Sekai*, 7–8 December 1940; *Nichibei Shimbun*, 15 December 1940; and "Kaigai jijō o kikukai," *Kaigai no Nippon* 15, no. 2 (February 1941), 29.

54. Gary Gerstle, *Working-Class Americanism: The Politics of Labor in a Textile City, 1914–1960* (Princeton, NJ: Princeton University Press, 2002), 8–13.

55. See, for example, *Hōchi Shinbun*, 5 November 1940.

56. *Hōchi Shinbun*, 5 November 1940; and *Tokyo Nichinichi Shinbun*, 5 November 1940.

57. *Tokyo Nichinichi Shinbun*, 5 November 1940.

58. "Nihon minzoku no Kaigai hatten: 'Warera no Shintenchi' keikakuan" (1940), no pagination, in Kakushu chōsakai iinkai monjo, 309–314, NAJ; Naikaku Jōhōbu, *Kigen Nisen Roppyakunen Shukuten kiroku* vol. 11, 429–459, NAJ; and Isetan, *Warera no shintenchi* (Tokyo: Warera no Shintenchi, 1940), no pagination.

59. Kaigai Dōhō Chūōkai, *Hōkokusho*, 54–71. The quote is from page 54.

60. Kaigai Dōhō Chūōkai, *Kaigai Dōhō Tokyo Taikai gahō* (Tokyo: Kaigai Dōhō Chūōkai, 1940), no pagination. The display of the life-sized mannequin of a first-generation Japanese American on a farm tractor illuminates an "advanced" and "modern" characteristic of Japanese immigrant farming in California, an example for ongoing Manchurian colonization. In figure 15, the caption on the right side says, "The Japanese excel in agricultural endeavors in the continental United States by utilizing such a huge tractor. In recent years, a similar machine is being used in Manchuria." The quote is from the same source.

61. Kaigai Dōhō Chūōkai, *Hōkokusho*, 54–59, 74–76.

62. See Ruoff, *Imperial Japan at Its Zenith*, 154. He defines "the cult of the pioneer" as one "employed at the time to encourage emigration by agriculturalists to Manchuria."

63. See *Tokyo Nichinichi Shinbun*, 11 November 1940; *Shin Aichi*, 11 November 1940; *Rafu Shimpō*, 12 November 1940; and *Nichibei Shimbun*, 12 and 15 November 1940.

64. "600 Attend Nisei Rally," *Nippon to Amerika* 10, no. 12 (December 1940), 5, 7 (English section); "2600th Anniversary Fete," *Nippon to Amerika* 10, no. 11 (November 1940), 7 (English section); and Kaigai Dōhō Chūōkai, *Hōkokusho*, 40. On this rally, see also Ruoff, *Imperial Japan at Its Zenith*, 163–164.

65. Kaigai Dōhō Chūōkai, *Hōkokusho*, 42–44; "600 Attend Nisei Rally," 5, 7, 15; and Yamashita Sōen, *Hōshuku Kigen Nisen Roppyakunen to Kaigai dōhō* (Tokyo: Hōshuku Kigen Nisen Roppyakunen to Kaigai Dōhō Kankōkai, 1941), 63–64. The quote is from page 15 of the second source.

66. Yamashita, *Hōshuku Kigen Nisen Roppyakunen to Kaigai dōhō*, 66; and Ruoff, *Imperial Japan at Its Zenith*, 164.

67. "Hawai Nisei Kurabu daihyō gomei no raichōki," *Nippon to Amerika* 11, no. 5 (May 1941), 24; and "Nisei Highlights," *Nippon to Amerika* 11, no. 5 (May 1941), 7-8 (English section). The quote is from the first source.

68. See Eiichiro Azuma, *Between Two Empires: Race, History, and Transnationalism in Japanese America* (New York: Oxford University Press, 2005), 111–159.

8. THE CALL OF BLOOD: JAPANESE AMERICAN CITIZENS AND THE EDUCATION OF THE EMPIRE'S FUTURE "FRONTIER FIGHTERS"

1. Translated and cited in S. [Jun'ichi] Natori, "The Ideal of the Second-Generation Japanese and the Japanese Spirit," 5, in Yokohama Consul, "American Citizens of Japanese Race Residing in Japan," 25 March 1940, Records of the US Department of State Relating to the Internal Affairs of Japan, 1940–1944, State Department Central Decimal File, Record Group 59, US National Archives II, College Park, MD.

2. *Rafu Shimpō*, 29 December 1940; and Eiichiro Azuma, *Between Two Empires: Race, History, and Transnationalism in Japanese America* (New York: Oxford University Press, 2005), 150–151. All quotes are from the first source.

3. Goro Murata, "Nisei in Nippon," *Kashū Mainichi*, 31 March 1940.

4. A reliable source estimated that there were about thirty-seven hundred Nisei students in Japanese secondary and higher education in 1936. Some seventeen hundred of them came to Japan alone in pursuit of education, and the rest lived with their extended families or relatives in Japan. The number most likely continued to increase through the late 1930s. See Yamashita Sōen, *Nichibei o tsunagu mono* (Tokyo: Bunseisha, 1938), 177–178, 319–332.

5. See Eiichiro Azuma, "'The Pacific Era Has Arrived': Transnational Education among Japanese Americans, 1932–1941," *History of Education Quarterly* 43, no. 1 (Spring 2003), 39–73; and Azuma, *Between Two Empires*, 135–159.

6. Gaimushō Ryōji Ijūbu, ed., *Waga kokumin no Kaigai hatten: Shiryōhen* (Tokyo: Gaimushō, 1971), 166–169.

7. On the vilification of things American in Japan's militarist regime, see Miriam Silverberg, "Constructing the Japanese Ethnography of Modernity," *Journal of Asian Studies* 51, no. 1 (February 1992), 49–50.

8. Ōtsuka Yoshimi, Jijo [Introduction] to *Ishokumin to Kyōiku mondai* (Tokyo: Tōkō Shoin, 1933), 6.

9. Ōtsuka, *Ishokumin to Kyōiku mondai*, 5–6.

10. Ōtsuka, *Ishokumin to Kyōiku mondai*, 247–248; see also 207, 307–308.

11. Ōtsuka, *Ishokumin to Kyōiku mondai*, 207. US immigrants and some liberal educators of Japan insisted on the distinction between racial ancestry and legal belonging when devising an education program for Nisei. Essentially, they envisioned what can be termed "heritage education" in a multicultural society. The study of things Japanese by Nisei, whether in the United States or in Japan, was not supposed to make them completely "Japanese" in disposition and identity. Ōtsuka and many other Japanese educators held a different perspective due to their tendency to privilege race. On the conflicting ideals and practices of heritage learning in imperial Japan, see Azuma, "'The Pacific Era Has Arrived,'" 41–64.

12. Ōtsuka, *Ishokumin to Kyōiku mondai*, 209.

13. Ōtsuka, *Ishokumin to Kyōiku mondai*, 305.

14. Ōtsuka, *Ishokumin to Kyōiku mondai*, 307–309. The quote is from page 309. Advancing Ōtsuka's contention, other ideologues even demanded that the government also take charge of educating all foreign-born Japanese outside Japan. See, for example, Ōshima Masatoku, "Kokusaku to shite no Kaigai kyōiku mondai," *Sangyō to Kyōiku* 2, no. 12 (December 1935), 14–16; and Takahashi Taiji, "Zaigai 'Dai-Nisei' no kyōiku o ikani suruka," *Jidō* 4, no. 1 (January 1936), 326–327.

15. Compare Ōtsuka, *Ishokumin to Kyōiku mondai*, 307–308, 310, with the forewords by Colonial Minister Nagai Ryūtarō and Satō Tadashi in the same book.

16. Ōtsuka, *Ishokumin to Kyōiku mondai*, 303–305. For similar arguments, see Sano Yasutarō, "Kaigai ni okeru Kokugo kyōiku," *Iwanami kōza, kokugo kyōiku* (Tokyo: Iwanami Shoten, 1936), 17–18; and Kaneda Chikaji, "Zaigai Hōjin Nisei kyōiku mondai o ronzu," *Takushoku Shōreikan kihō* 1, no. 4 (February 1940), 25–27.

17. Ōtsuka, "Jijo," in *Ishokumin to Kyōiku mondai*, 3–4.

18. Ōtsuka, *Ishokumin to Kyōiku mondai*, 4.

19. Ōtsuka, *Ishokumin to Kyōiku mondai*, 153–154. Ōtsuka dressed his cryptic writing in scholarly clothes, often citing other "experts"—even opposing views—to make his argument look more objective and acceptable.

20. Takahashi was a longtime grammar school teacher before pursuing a degree in social psychology at Waseda University, Ōtsuka's alma mater. In 1930 he traveled to Oregon for graduate education. After his work as the chief instructor at the state-backed Mizuho Academy, Takahashi shifted his career focus to the area of labor management in Japan's corporate world, while continuing his research and writing in educational psychology.

21. Takahashi, "Zaigai 'Dai-Nisei' no kyōiku o ikani suruka," 322. For a similar argument, see Yamada Tatsumi, *Kaigai Dai-Nisei mondai* (Tokyo: Kibundō, 1936), 41.

22. *Yomiuri Shinbun*, 18 July 1938, 2 (evening ed.).

23. See Watanabe Sōsuke, "Kyōin no kaigai haken," in *Zaigai shitei kyōiku no kenkyū*, ed. Kojima Masaru (Tokyo: Tamagawa Daigaku Shuppanbu, 2003), 337–347.

24. See, for example, Matsumoto Toraichi, "Dai-Nisei no Nihonteki kyōiku," *Aiji* 8, no. 5 (May 1939), 47–49, esp. 49.

25. Takahashi, "Zaigai 'Dai-Nisei' no kyōiku o ikani suruka," 323.

26. Natori Jun'ichi, *Nikkei Dai-Nisei no shisō to Nippon seishin* (Tokyo: Tanchōsha, 1939), 3–4.

27. On Natori and Waseda International Institute, see Azuma, "'The Pacific Era Has Arrived,'" 64–69; and Eiichiro Azuma, "The Perils of Heritage Learning in Their Ancestral Land: Educating Japanese American Nisei as 'Foreign-Born Compatriots' of the Empire," in *Japaneseness across the Pacific and Beyond*, ed. Tomoko Ozawa (Tokyo: Sairyūsha, 2019), 43–48.

28. See Tetsuo Najita and Harry Harootunian, "Japanese Revolt against the West," in *The Cambridge History of Japan*, Vol. 6, *The Twentieth Century*, ed. Peter Duus (Cambridge, UK: Cambridge University Press, 1988), 711–774.

29. For examples of such views, see Ōtsuka, *Ishokumin to Kyōiku mondai*, 304–305. On Tokyo's outbound study-abroad policy, see *Yomiuri Shinbun*, 5 February 1930 and 10 October 1933.

30. *Yomiuri Shinbun*, 14 April 1932, 22 November 1932, 20 January 1934, and 10 October 1937; and Nagata Shigeshi, "Rikkō Ryūgakusei Gakuryō no kaisetsu ni tsuite," *Rikkō Sekai* 375 (March 1936), 6.

31. See papers in Honpō ni okeru kyōkai oyobi bunka dantai kankei zakken: Kokusai Gakuyūkai kankei, Diplomatic Archives of the Ministry of Foreign Affairs (hereafter DA-MOFA), Tokyo. Its student rosters included those from Southeast Asia, South Asia, and the Americas, including the United States.

32. Akira Iriye, *Cultural Internationalism and World Order* (Baltimore, MD: Johns Hopkins University Press, 1997), 51–130, esp. 119–125. Iriye tends to emphasize international "cooperation" and cultural "exchange" in his analysis of "internationalism," but I argue that nationalism-driven propagandist agendas always lay beneath, if not characterized, such activities. Nationalism was thus not simply an antithesis of internationalism, or vice versa. For an example of a narrative of cosmopolitan internationalism's "defeat" by nationalism in

prewar US-Japan relations, see Michael R. Auslin, *Pacific Cosmopolitans: A Cultural History of U.S.-Japan Relations* (Cambridge, MA: Harvard University Press, 2011).

33. On some of these special schools for American Nisei with which this chapter does not deal, see Azuma, "'The Pacific Era Has Arrived,'" 49–69; and Azuma, "The Perils of Heritage Learning in Their Ancestral Land," 40–53.

34. In the initial preparatory phase, Ōtsuka served as the interim director of IEOJ, but he resigned by 1934. Following the publication of his book and another academic article on Nisei education, Ōtsuka's career revolved principally around corporate labor management. On the latter, see Ōtsuka, "Ishokumin kyōiku no tenbō," *Kyōiku* 2, no. 8 (August 1934), 54–64. On Ōtsuka's activities as a chief public advocate of IEOJ, see "Ishokumin kyōiku zadankai" and "Ishokumin kyōiku mondai no ichi kōsatsu," *Shokumin* 12, no. 6 (June 1933), 38–53 and 54–56; and Ōtsuka, "Ishokumin kankei kikan renraku no igi," *Shokumin* 12, no. 7 (July 1933), 4–9.

35. "Uchida Gaimu daijin aisatsu" (22 March 1933), in Hirota Kōki, "Zaigai Hōjin shitei no kyōiku ni kansuruken," 2 February 1934, in Kaigai Kyōiku Kyōkai ikken, DA-MOFA.

36. "Uchida Gaimu daijin aisatsu."

37. See IEOJ, *Kaigai Kyōiku Kyōkai yōran* (Tokyo: IEOJ, 1937), 1–3; IEOJ, *An Outline of the Kaigai Kyoiku Kyokai* (Tokyo: IEOJ, 1937), 1–2, 12; *Nichibei Shimbun*, 3 December 1932 and 25 July 1933; and Hirota, "Zaigai Hōjin shitei no kyōiku ni kansuru ken."

38. On the official pledge of government support for Mizuho Academy, see "[Foreign Minister] Hirota Asks Aid for Nisei School," *Rafu Shimpō*, 25 February 1934.

39. See Satō's forewords in Ōtsuka, *Ishokumin to Kyōiku mondai*. In order to acquire firsthand knowledge of the Nisei problem, Satō visited Japanese communities in Hawai'i and California in 1933. See *Nichibei Shimbun*, 25 July 1933. He then shifted his attention to foreign-born Japanese outside North America, compiling perhaps the first serious treatise on the topic after Ōtsuka's. In Satō's edited anthology, supporters of IEOJ provided commentaries on the matter in terms almost identical to Ōtsuka's arguments. See Satō Tadashi, ed., *Kaigai Dai-Nisei kyōiku no taiken o kataru* (Tokyo: IEOJ, 1933).

40. Cited from Satō's forewords in Ōtsuka, *Ishokumin to Kyōiku mondai*.

41. "Dai Nisei no kyōiku o dōsuruka," *Shin kyōiku kenkyū* 4, no. 9 (September 1934), 49; and "Gaikokujin jidō no shōgakko nyūgaku toriatsukaikata," 18 July 1935, 130; "Nikkei Beijin chūgakkō, kōtō jogakkō-tō nyūgaku toriatsukaikata," 19 February 1935, 463; and "Migi futsū gakumu-kyoku kaitō," 26 February 1935, 6, all three in Gakusei seito sōki, Education Ministry (Monbushō) Papers, National Archives of Japan. The quote is from a ministry official's testimony.

42. IEOJ, *Kaigai Kyōiku Kyōkai yōran* (1937), 4–7; IEOJ, *Kaigai Kyōiku Kyōkai yōran* (Tokyo: IEOJ, 1940), 6, 18–20, 33; *Rafu Shimpō*, 20 February 1934; and Satō Tadashi to Kosaka Masayasu, 7 November 1933, 155–156, in Shōwa hachi-nen Kyōiku hōjin vol. 183 (317. A6.07: "Kaigai Kyōiku Kyōkai"), Tokyo Metropolitan Archives, Japan. Statistics are taken from the last source.

43. IEOJ, *Kaigai Kyōiku Kyōkai yōran* (1940), 34–40; and Matsuoka Mataichi, "Dai-Nisei no kyōiku kikan 'Mizuho Gakuen' no zenbō," *Umi o koete* 3, no. 11 (November 1940), 53.

44. Matsuoka, "Dai-Nisei no kyōiku kikan 'Mizuho Gakuen' no zenbō," 53.

45. IEOJ, *An Outline of the Kaigai Kyoiku Kyokai*, 6; and IEOJ, *Kaigai Kyōiku Kyōkai yōran* (1940), 21.

46. IEOJ, *Kaigai Kyōiku Kyōkai yōran* (1940), 5, 16–27; IEOJ, *An Outline of the Kaigai Kyoiku Kyokai*, 7–9; IEOJ, *Kaigai Kyōiku Kyōkai yōran* (1937), 9; and "Kaigai Kyōiku Kyōkai," *Umi o koete* 2, no. 5 (May 1939), 49.

47. IEOJ, *Kaigai Kyōiku Kyōkai yōran* (1940), 22–23; and "Kaigai Kyōiku Kyōkai," 49.

48. The quotes are from IEOJ, *Kaigai Kyōiku Kyōkai yōran* (1940), 20. On Mizuho's language instruction, see Matsuoka Mataichi, "Bokoku ni okeru Dai-Nisei kyōiku ni tsuite," *Kairen kaihō* 10, no. 3 (March 1941), 27.

49. IEOJ, *Kaigai Kyōiku Kyōkai yōran* (1940), 22.

50. IEOJ, *Kaigai Kyōiku Kyōkai yōran* (1940), 22. The high value that Mizuho placed on martial arts is manifest in its decision to erect training facilities for *kendō*, *jūdō*, and *kyūdō* as a special project to commemorate the 2,600th anniversary of Japan's national foundation. See Matsuoka, "Dai-Nisei no kyōiku kikan 'Mizuho Gakuen' no zenbō," 52–53.

51. IEOJ, *Kaigai Kyōiku Kyōkai yōran* (1940), 23.

52. IEOJ, *Kaigai Kyōiku Kyōkai yōran* (1940), 23.

53. Soneda Kenji, "Dai Nisei kyōiku no taikcn o kataru," *Nippon to Amerika* 7, no. 2 (February 1938), 42. On his "pedagogical principle," see also Yamashita, *Nichibei o tsunagu mono*, 352–353.

54. Existing official sources, including Japanese diplomatic papers, do not offer evidence for a transfer of funds from the Japanese government to the Imperial Way Institute. However, Nakamura's son recalls that his father received "subventions from the state." See Nakamura Fujio's essay in *Kendō jidai* 433 (September 2008), 34. Most likely, such support came from the military branch of the government, whether formally or informally. In particular, Army General Araki Sadao and Navy Captain Kurosaki Rinzō are acknowledged as being Nakamura's chief patrons.

55. On the Japanese immigrant views of Nisei's moral education, see Azuma, *Between Two Empires*, 122–134.

56. Rarely did Nakamura communicate his true thinking to Issei parents and Nisei *kendō* enthusiasts, probably due to a fear of losing their support, since his clients were primarily interested in simple moral inculcation and heritage learning. Evidence nonetheless suggests that the *kendō* master was especially dismayed by Japanese Americans' insistence on their undivided allegiance to the United States. On this, see Eiichiro Azuma, "Interstitial Lives: Race, Community, and History among Japanese Immigrants caught between Japan and the United States, 1885–1941" (PhD diss., University of California at Los Angeles, 2000), 265–268, 487–488. On diplomats' views of Nakamura, see Okamoto Issaku to Satō Naotake, 1 April 1937; and Hori Kōichi to Satō Naotake, 19 April 1937, in Zaigai Honpōjin hogo narabi torishimari kankei zakken: Beikoku no bu, DA-MOFA.

57. See Higuchi Yoshiko, *Fuji no takane o orogamimatsuru* (Monterey, CA: self-pub., 1935), 30–31; and "Amerika umare no Nihonjin," *Kingu* 9, no. 10 (October 1933), 154–175.

58. See Okamoto to Satō; and Hori to Satō.

59. On Nakamura's life trajectory before and after NAMVS, see Momii Ikken, *Hokubei kendō taikan* (San Francisco: Hokubei Butokukai, 1939), 600–615; and Maruyama Tsuruo, *Nanajūnen tokoro dokoro* (Tokyo: Nanajūnen Tokoro Dokoro Kankōkai, 1955), 324–333. On positive effects of *kendō* on Nisei's character building, see Nakamura Tōkichi, "Nisei no kyōyō to Nippon budō," *Nichibei Shimbun*, 24 October–1 November 1935; Momii, *Hokubei kendō taikan*, 636–637; and Ashizawa Hirozumi, *Nippon seishin to Jinbutsu yōsei* (Tokyo: Hokubei

Butokukai Kōdō Gakuin Shuppanbu, 1938), 425–432. As these sources were to be read by his Issei supporters, they offered a subdued version of Nakamura's view, which was actually more in line with Tōyama Mitsuru's ultranationalism and General Araki's statist militarism.

60. See the statement of purpose for the Imperial Way Institute by Nakamura, cited in Momii, *Hokubei kendō taikan*, 636.

61. Maruyama, *Nanajūnen tokoro dokoro*, 330–332.

62. Maruyama, *Nanajūnen tokoro dokoro*, 330–331; and Momii, *Hokubei kendō taikan*, 635, 638. Maruyama erroneously states that the idea of the Imperial Way Institute was initially conceived by parents of Nisei *kendō* practitioners. In fact, as Momii notes, it was the *kendō* master who disclosed his plan in the form of a "surprise announcement" in the summer of 1937.

63. Momii, *Hokubei kendō taikan*, 638.

64. *Miyako Shinbun*, 21 November 1938.

65. The quote is from Ashizawa, *Nippon seishin to Jinbutsu yōsei*, 435. On his background, see "jo," 1–3, and "jijo," 1–2, in the same source.

66. Ashizawa, *Nippon seishin to Jinbutsu yōsei*, 417–418, and 426. The quote is from page 417.

67. Ashizawa, *Nippon seishin to Jinbutsu yōsei*, 417–418, 426–430; and *Yamanashi Nichinichi Shinbun*, 18 January 1936.

68. Ashizawa, *Nippon seishin to Jinbutsu yōsei*, 418, 421, 444–447. The quote is from page 444.

69. Ashizawa, *Nippon seishin to Jinbutsu yōsei*, 454–457. The quote is from page 455.

70. On the public praise of Nakamura's program along this line, see *Miyako Shinbun*, 21 November 1938.

71. On the dilemmas of their transnational heritage learning, see Azuma, *Between Two Empires*, 150–151, 156–158.

72. Kaigai Dōhō Chūōkai, "Kaigai Dōhō Chūō Renseisho yōran" (1943), in the author's personal files.

73. See Takashi Fujitani, *Race for Empire: Koreans as Japanese and Japanese as Americans during World War II* (Berkeley: University of California Press, 2011); and Yukiko Koshiro, *Trans-Pacific Racisms and the U.S. Occupation of Japan* (New York: Columbia University Press, 1999).

74. On postwar Japanese migration to and settler colonialism in South America, see Sidney Xu Lu, *The Making of Japanese Settler Colonialism: Malthusianism and Trans-Pacific Migration, 1868–1961* (New York: Cambridge University Press, 2019), ch. 8.

EPILOGUE: THE AFTERLIFE OF JAPANESE SETTLER COLONIALISM

1. On collusions between postwar Japanese and American racism in emigration/immigration policies, see Yukiko Koshiro, *Trans-Pacific Racisms and the U.S. Occupation of Japan* (New York: Columbia University Press, 1999), 123–158.

2. Sugino Tadao, *Kaigai takushoku hishi* (Tokyo: Bunkyō Shoin, 1959), 124–125.

3. See Kokusai Nōgyōsha Kōryū Kyōkai, ed., *Nōgyō seinen kaigai haken jigyō gojūnenshi* (Tokyo: Kokusai Nōgyōsha Kōryū Kyōkai, 2002), 4–13; Nihon Nōgyō Kenkyūjo, ed., *Ishiguro Tadaatsu-den* (Tokyo: Iwanami Shoten, 1969), 442–446; and Michael Conlon, "A Brief

History of the Japan Agricultural Exchange Council," *GAIN Report* JA0501 (1 February 2010), no pagination. The quote is from the last source. See also Mary Ting Yi Lui, "Nōson seinen no Kariforunia hōmon," trans. Tsuchiya Yuka and Nakamura Nobuyuki, in *Senryō suru me, Senryō suru koe*, ed. Tsuchiya and Yoshimi Shunya (Tokyo: Tokyo Daigaku Shuppankai, 2012), 157–181.

4. Asada Kyōji, "Takumushō no Manshū nōgyō imin keikaku," *Komazawa Daigaku Keizai Gakubu kenkyū kiyō* 32 (1974), 90; and Nasu Shiroshi, *Nasu Shiroshi-sensei* (Tokyo: Nōson Kōsei Kyōkai, 1985), 90–96.

5. Yoshizaki Chiaki, *Kokusai Nōyūkai ni tsuite* (Tokyo: Kokusai Nōyūkai, 1987), 3–4.

6. Yoshizaki, *Kokusai Nōyūkai ni tsuite*, 8; Sugino, *Kaigai takushoku hishi*, 124–125; and Yoshizaki Chiaki, "Kokusai Nōyūkai ga umareru made," *Kokusai nōson* 1 (September 1952), 6–7.

7. Nasu Shiroshi, "Kokusai Nōyūkai no risō," *Kokusai nōson* 1 (September 1952), 4; and Nasu, *Nasu Shiroshi-sensei*, 99.

8. See Nasu Shiroshi, "Kisetsuteki idō nōgyō rōmusha o Beikoku e sōshutsu suru anken," ca. 5 March 1955, in Nōgyō rōmusha habei kankei: Habei jisshi made no keii, vol. 1, Diplomatic Archives of the Ministry of Foreign Affairs (hereafter DA-MOFA), Tokyo.

9. On the Japanese guest worker program, see Eiichiro Azuma, "Japanese Agricultural Labor Program: Temporary Worker Immigration, U.S.-Japan Cultural Diplomacy, and Ethnic Community Making among Japanese Americans," in *A Nation of Immigrants Reconsidered: US Society in an Age of Restriction, 1924–1965*, ed. Maddalena Marinari, Madeline Hsu, and Maria Cristina Garcia (Urbana: University of Illinois Press, 2019), 161–190.

10. Kaigai Tokō Mondai Chōsakai, "Kaigai Tokō Mondai Chōsakai no gaiyō" 1 September 1951, 1–8, in Japan International Cooperation Agency Library (hereafter JICA), Yokohama. The quote is from page 7. On the conflicting interests of Japan's diplomats and agricultural bureaucrats, see Itō Atsushi, "Nōgyō rōmusha habei jigyō no seiritsu," *Nōgyō keizai kenkyū* 83, no. 4 (2012), 221–233.

11. Kokusai Nōgyōsha Kōryū Kyōkai, ed., *Nōgyo seinen kaigai haken jigyō gojyūnenshi*, 68, 72.

12. *Nichibei Shimbun*, 22 January 1941.

13. Kokusai Nōgyōsha Kōryū Kyōkai, ed., *Nōgyo seinen kaigai haken jigyō gojyūnenshi*, 13; and Sugino, *Kaigai takushoku hishi*, 102–113.

14. Nasu, "Kisetsuteki idō nōgyō rōmusha o Beikoku e sōshutsu suru anken." On the important roles played by other Japanese Americans, including Nisei leaders and farmers, see Azuma, "Japanese Agricultural Labor Program," esp. 162–170, 176–177.

15. Council for Supplementary Agricultural Workers, "Activities of the Returned Japanese Supplementary Agricultural Workers," 1 June 1961, 3, JICA; and Nihon Kokusai Nōson Seinen Renmei, "Burokku kaigi shiryō," July 1964, 6, in Nōgyō rōmusha habei kankei: Nōgyō Rōmusha Habei Kyōgikai, DA-MOFA.

INDEX

Abiko Kyūtarō, 105–7, 115–16, 118–19, 162, 224
adolescents, recruitment for settler colonialism,
   134–35. *See also* education
agriculture: Abiko Kyūtarō, Yamato Colony
   project and, 105–6; American frontier myth,
   13–22, 19*map*; in British North Borneo,
   66–69, 67*fig*; coffee growers, 184–86, 203;
   continental (American) farming practices,
   156–65, 163*fig*, 175–78, 177*fig*, 196–97; cotton
   farming, 68–69, 87, 116, 121, 122, 123, 127, 135,
   146, 158, 166; farm uprisings in Japan (1885),
   81–82; Hokkaido method, 175–78, 177*fig*; Japan's imperialism and, 2–3; Katsura Colony,
   109–14, 113*map*; in Korea, 72–73, 104–8; land,
   immigrant land rights, 6, 18, 95, 119, 165, 167;
   lessons from California migrants, 153, 155–56;
   in Manchuria, 153, 155–56, 165–67, 171–78,
   222; in Mexico, 60–61; post-1950 Japanese
   emigration to US, 264–65; Satō Nobumoto
   and machine farming, 166–71, 169*map*,
   170*fig*; in Taiwan, overview of, 183–84; in
   Taiwan, sugar production, 187–88; in Taiwan
   pineapple industry, Hawaianization of,
   191–213, 198*fig*, 199*fig*, 201*fig*, 206*map*; in
   Taiwan pineapple industry, rise of, 186–91; in
   Thailand, 65–66; in US-Mexico borderlands,
   114–24; Watanabe Kinzō and reclamation
   projects, 178–82. *See also* rice production;
   settler colonialism; sugar production
Aguinaldo, Emilio, 66

Aikoku, 41, 45
Akira Iriye, 251
Alianca, Sao Paulo, Brazil, 113*map*, 144, 180,
   307n78, 307n80, 309n4
Alien Land Law (1913), California, 95, 119, 156,
   157, 165, 167
Alliance against Russia (Tai-Ro Dōshikai), 73
American frontier myth, 13–22, 19*map*, 31, 105–7,
   262–63
American Land and Produce Company (ALPC),
   115–16
"American racial Anglo-Saxonism," 47
Amur River/Black Dragon Society
   (Kokuryūkai), 56, 65, 156, 234, 255, 257
Andō Yasutarō, 289–90n45
Anglophone colonial history: American frontier
   myth, 13–22, 19*map*; inter-imperial frame-
   work, overview of, 9–13; land, control of, 6;
   settler/migrant racism, 17–22, 19*map*; U.S.
   imperialism in Asia and the Pacific, 54–55.
   See also United States
Aoyagi Ikutarō, 110–11, 126, 127, 143
Arai Tatsuya, 43, 61–62, 282n49
Arashi ni saku hana (Flower in the storm),
   228–29
Asahi Shōkai (Rising Sun Mercantile Company),
   68
Asahi Village, 156
Asano Sōichirō, 121, 122, 123
Ashizawa Hirozumi, 257–59

Founded in 1893,
UNIVERSITY OF CALIFORNIA PRESS
publishes bold, progressive books and journals
on topics in the arts, humanities, social sciences,
and natural sciences—with a focus on social
justice issues—that inspire thought and action
among readers worldwide.

The UC PRESS FOUNDATION
raises funds to uphold the press's vital role
as an independent, nonprofit publisher, and
receives philanthropic support from a wide
range of individuals and institutions—and from
committed readers like you. To learn more, visit
ucpress.edu/supportus.